AMERICA BEFORE

The Key to Earth's Lost Civilization

GRAHAM HANCOCK

CORONET

First published in Great Britain in 2019 by Coronet
An Imprint of Hodder & Stoughton
An Hachette UK company

1

A CIP catalogue record for this title is available from the British Library

Hardback ISBN 9781473660571
Trade Paperback ISBN 9781473660595
eBook ISBN 9781473660564

Typeset in AGaramond Pro

Printed in the United States of America by LSC Communications

Hodder & Stoughton policy is to use papers that are natural, renewable
and recyclable products and made from wood grown in sustainable forests.
The logging and manufacturing processes are expected to conform to the
environmental regulations of the country of origin.

Hodder & Stoughton Ltd
Carmelite House
50 Victoria Embankment
London EC4Y 0DZ

www.hodder.co.uk

For Santha,

through many lives, past, present, and future, my soul mate always.

Looking forward to more amazing adventures!

AMERICA BEFORE

ALSO BY GRAHAM HANCOCK

Magicians of the Gods: The Forgotten Wisdom of Earth's Lost Civilization

War God: Nights of the Witch

Entangled: The Eater of Souls

Supernatural: Meeting with the Ancient Teachers of Mankind

Talisman: Sacred Cities, Secret Faith

Underworld: The Mysterious Origins of Civilization

Heaven's Mirror: Quest for the Lost Civilization

The Mars Mystery: A Tale of the End of Two Worlds

The Message of the Sphinx: A Quest for the Hidden Legacy of Mankind

Fingerprints of the Gods: The Evidence of Earth's Lost Civilization

The Sign and the Seal: The Quest for the Lost Ark of the Covenant

CONTENTS

ACKNOWLEDGMENTS   ix
INTRODUCTION   xiii

PART I

MANITOU: THE MYSTERY OF SERPENT MOUND

1. An Enchanted Realm   3
2. A Journey in Time   13
3. The Dragon and the Sun   31

PART II

NEW WORLD? THE MYSTERY OF THE FIRST AMERICANS

4. A Past Not So Much Hidden As Denied   47
5. Message from a Mastodon   59
6. Millennia Unaccounted For   71

PART III

GENES: THE MYSTERY IN DNA

7. Siberia   83
8. Hall of Records   98
9. The Strange and Mysterious Genetic Heritage of   111
   Native Americans
10. A Signal from the Dreamtime?   123

PART IV

MEMES: THE AMAZON MYSTERY

11. Ghost Cities of the Amazon   137
12. The Ancients Behind the Veil   150
13. Black Earth   160
14. Gardening Eden   170

15. Sacred Geometry 178

16. The Amazon's Own Stonehenge 201

17. The Vine of the Dead 215

PART V

STUFF JUST KEEPS ON GETTING OLDER: THE MYSTERY OF THE PRIMEVAL MOUNDS

18. Sun 233

19. Moon 246

20. The Poverty Point Time Machine 262

21. Glimpses Behind the Veil 277

PART VI

EQUIPPED FOR JOURNEYING: THE MYSTERY OF DEATH

22. Quietus? 297

23. The Portal and the Path 309

24. Astronomy and Geometry in the Afterlife 346

PART VII

APOCALYPSE THEN: THE MYSTERY OF THE CATACLYSM

25. Eloise 373

26. Fire and Ice 387

27. Cape Fear 409

PART VIII

SURVIVE! THE MYSTERY OF THE INVISIBLE MAN

28. Hunter-Gatherers and the Lost Civilization 431

29. Unknown Unknowns 442

30. The Key to Earth's Lost Civilization 465

APPENDIX 1. MELAZONIA, AKA AMANESIA 491

APPENDIX 2. ANCIENT MAPS OF THE ICE AGE 503

APPENDIX 3. FIRST THERE WAS A FOREST, THEN THERE 511
WAS NO FOREST, THEN THERE WAS . . .

NOTES 517

INDEX 581

ACKNOWLEDGMENTS

I MAY, THROUGH OVERSIGHT, FAIL TO acknowledge properly here some of the many wonderful people who have helped me in the efforts that led to this book. If so, I hope I can be forgiven. The years grow long and memory short!

It is my wife, soul mate, and fellow adventurer, photographer Santha Faiia, to whom I owe the greatest debt. During the making of this book I suffered two terrifying episodes of seizures and loss of consciousness, as a result of which it is no longer responsible, or legal, for me to drive. So for all our thousands of miles of road trips through some of the most spectacular landscapes in California, Arizona, New Mexico, Colorado, South Dakota, Wyoming, New Hampshire, Massachusetts, upstate New York, North and South Carolina, Louisiana, Mississippi, Arkansas, Alabama, Tennessee, Missouri, Illinois, and Ohio I was in the passenger seat and Santha was behind the wheel. I therefore want to thank my extraordinary wife for her grit in the face of adversity, for her inspiring presence, for her creative talent in always taking the right photograph at the right moment, and for her immense capacity for love. I would have stalled and come to a grinding halt long ago if not for you, Santha. Thank you. Thank you for EVERYTHING.

Aside from its photographic content, this book contains large numbers of designed images illustrating some of the more complex aspects of the argument. An art director was needed, and my son Luke took on this responsibility, working around the clock to prepare the graphics and illustrations that accompany the text. Gratitude and respect for an excellent job well done.

My research assistant, Holly Lasko Skinner, worked with me on gathering documentation and tracking down hard-to-find facts from the early days of this project. She brilliantly sought out, churned through, and made sense of bewildering masses of data, carefully checked all sources, and constantly alerted me to new scientific developments. Thank you, Holly.

Ross Hamilton, an inspiring teacher of the ancient mysteries, opened my eyes to the enigma of Ohio's Serpent Mound and helped me grasp the implications of its numinous connection to the summer solstice sunset.

William Romain, in my opinion the most important archaeologist presently studying the earthwork-building cultures of the Mississippi Valley, kindly took time to exchange views with me and granted me permission to reproduce a number of his excellent photographs and diagrams illustrating the archaeoastronomical implications of his research.

Gary David, whose work on the archaeoastronomy of the Southwest is of the first importance, generously shared his extensive knowledge and insights with me on a journey through Arizona and New Mexico.

I'm grateful to Randall Carlson, a true comrade in arms, and to Bradley Young and Camron Wiltshire, who all contributed to this project in different and important ways.

Special thanks to the scientists of the Comet Research Group whose groundbreaking Younger Dryas Impact Hypothesis provides the most complete explanation for the mysterious end of the last Ice Age and casts world prehistory in an entirely new light. Allen West, Al Goodyear, Chris Moore, and George Howard were particularly generous with their time.

I'm grateful to Tom Deméré, chief paleontologist at the San Diego Natural History Museum, for meeting with me and taking me behind the scenes to the archives to share the full implications of the discoveries at the Cerutti

Mastodon Site. Indicative of a human presence in North America at least 130,000 years ago, this is a find that rewrites prehistory.

Eske Willerslev of the University of Copenhagen, a world expert in the study of ancient DNA, patiently answered my questions and shared his thoughts on the anomalous Australasian genetic signal found among certain isolated peoples of the Amazon rainforest.

Meanwhile archaeological research of immense importance is under way across the Amazon, revealing the existence of stone circles and of hundreds of immense geometrical earthworks. In this context I'd like to thank Mariana Petry Cabral of the Universidade Federal de Minas Gerais, Sanna Saunaluoma, and Martti Pärssinen of the University of Helsinki, and Christopher Sean Davis of the University of Illinois, for the positive spirit with which they greeted my request to reproduce photographs and maps illustrating their findings.

For their thoroughly professional and friendly support with every aspect of our research visit to Denisova Cave in Siberia, huge thanks to Sergey Kurgin, who organized the trip and did all the driving, and to Olga Votrina, our excellent interpreter. Thanks and appreciation also to the Siberian Branch of the Institute of Archaeology and Ethnography, Russian Academy of Sciences for their kind cooperation and for their permission to reproduce photographs of artifacts from Denisova Cave.

My editors, Peter Wolverton of St. Martin's Press in the United States and Mark Booth of Coronet in the United Kingdom, and my literary agent, Sonia Land, of Sheil Land Associates, have been superb allies and friends, giving me the benefit of their excellent advice and top-class professional expertise at every turn.

Any merits in *America Before* owe much to those named here, and to the many scientists and vocational researchers around the world whose discoveries are reviewed in the pages that follow. I have been diligent in my attempts to represent their work correctly, but if there are any errors or misinterpretations, then the responsibility is entirely my own.

Last but by no means least, I am blessed to be surrounded by a beautiful rainbow family without frontiers. Santha and Luke are mentioned here already, and now is the moment to put on record my love and appreciation for our other five grown-up children—Sean, Shanti, Leila, Ravi, and Gabrielle. I'm British, born in Scotland to an English father and a Scottish mother. I spent 4 years of my childhood in the Indian state of Tamil Nadu. Santha is of Tamil origin but was born and brought up in Malaysia. Sean and Leila are both half Somali and half British by birth. Shanti and Ravi are both half Tamil Malaysian and half Italian American by birth. Luke and Gabrielle are both British by birth. Leila's husband, Jason, is Greek; Ravi's wife, Lydia, is American; Luke's wife, Ayako, is Japanese; and they have gifted us with three magical grandchildren, Nyla, Leo, and Henry, who brighten our lives with their innocence, infant wisdom, and laughter.

INTRODUCTION

I HAVE IN MY SHELVES A renowned and much respected book titled *History Begins at Sumer*.[1] The reference, of course, is to the famous high civilization of the Sumerians that began to take shape in Mesopotamia—roughly modern Iraq between the Tigris and Euphrates rivers—around 6,000 years ago. Several centuries later, ancient Egypt, the very epitome of an elegant and sophisticated civilization of antiquity, became a unified state. Before bursting into full bloom, however, both Egypt and Sumer had long and mysterious prehistoric backgrounds in which many of the formative ideas of their historic periods were already present.

After the Sumerians and Egyptians followed an unbroken succession of Akkadians, Babylonians, Persians, Greeks, and Romans, and there were, moreover, the incredible achievements of ancient India and ancient China. It therefore became second nature for us to think of civilization as an "Old World" invention and not to associate it with the "New World" at all.

Besides, it was standard teaching in the nineteenth and twentieth centuries that the Americas—North, Central, and South—were among the last great landmasses on earth to be inhabited by humans, that these humans were nomadic hunter-gatherers, that most of them subsequently remained hunter-gatherers, and that nothing much of great cultural significance began to happen there until relatively recently.

This teaching is deeply in error and as we near the end of the second decade of the twenty-first century, scholars are unanimous not only that it must be thrown out but also that an entirely new paradigm of the prehistory of the Americas is called for. Such momentous shifts in science don't occur without good reason and the reason in this case, very simply, is that a mass of compelling new evidence has come to light that completely contradicts and refutes the previous paradigm.

Everyone has and does their own "thing," and my own thing, over more than quarter of a century of travels and research, has been a quest for a lost civilization of remote prehistory—an advanced civilization utterly destroyed at the end of the Ice Age and somewhat akin to fabled Atlantis.

Plato, in the oldest-surviving written source of the Atlantis tradition, describes it as an island "larger than Libya and Asia put together"[2] situated far to the west of Europe across the Atlantic Ocean.[3] Hitherto I'd resisted that obvious clue which I knew had already been pursued with unconvincing results by a number of researchers during the past century.[4] As the solid evidence that archaeologists had gotten America's Ice Age prehistory badly wrong began to accumulate in folders on my desktop, however, and with new research reports continuing to pour in, I couldn't help but reflect on the significance of the location favored by Plato. I had considered other possibilities, as readers of my previous books know, but I had to admit that an immense island lying far to the west of Europe across the Atlantic Ocean does sound a lot like America.

I therefore decided to reopen this cold case. I would begin by gathering together the most important strands of the new evidence from the Americas. I would set these strands in order. And then I would investigate them thoroughly to see if there might be a big picture hidden among the details scattered across thousands of scientific papers in fields varying from archaeology to genetics, astronomy to climatology, agronomy to ethnology, and geology to paleontology.

It was already clear that the prehistory of the Americas was going to have to be rewritten; even the mainstream scientists were in general agreement on that. But could there be more?

This book tells the story of what I found.

PART I

MANITOU

⟨ ⟩ ● ⟨ ⟩

The Mystery of Serpent Mound

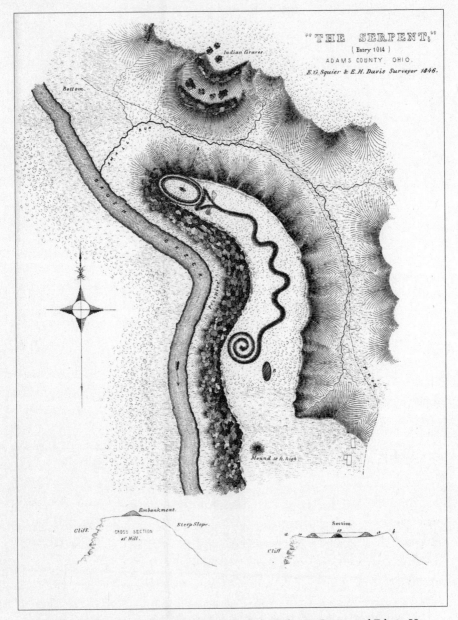

The first survey map of Serpent Mound, made by Ephraim Squier and Edwin H.
Davis in 1846 and published by the Smithsonian Institution in 1848, described
the mound as "the most extraordinary earthwork thus far discovered in the West."

AN ENCHANTED REALM

ARCHAEOLOGY TEACHES US THAT THE vast, inviting, resource-rich continents of North and South America were among the very last places on earth to have been inhabited by human beings. Only a handful of remote islands were settled later.

This is the orthodoxy, but it is crumbling under an onslaught of compelling new evidence revealed by new technologies, notably the effective sequencing of ancient DNA. The result is that many of the most fundamental "facts" of American archaeology, many of the "ground truths" upon which the theories and the careers of its great men and women were built in the nineteenth and twentieth centuries, now stand exposed as fallacies.

Far from being very recent, it is beginning to look as though the human presence in the Americas may be very old—perhaps more than 100,000 years older than has hitherto been believed.

This greatly extended time frame, taking us back deep into the Ice Age, has profound implications for how we view, interpret, and date all the monuments of the Americas built before the time of Columbus. The possibility that they might have an unrecognized prehistoric backstory can no longer be discounted. Moreover, the New World was physically, genetically, and culturally separated from the Old around 12,000 years ago when rising sea levels submerged the land bridge that formerly connected Siberia to Alaska.[1] This separation remained total until just 500 years ago when genetic and cultural exchanges restarted during the European conquest. It follows, therefore, that any deep connections between the Americas and the Old World that are not the result of recent European influence and that cannot be attributed to coincidence must be more than 12,000 years old.

It was with all this in mind, on June 17, 2017, that I made my first visit to Serpent Mound, a national historic landmark in southern Ohio described as "the finest surviving example of a prehistoric animal effigy mound in North America, and perhaps the world."[2]

It's in Adams County, about 75 miles east of Cincinnati and 7 miles north of the town of Peebles by way of SR-41N and OH-73W. With its rolling hills and green meadows, this is a predominantly rural, substantially forested part of the state, running northward from the Ohio River. On that vibrant summer day every tree was in full, luxuriant leaf, every flower was in bloom, the fields glowed, and the winding lanes seemed part of a bucolic dream.

In some remote epoch, however, this entire idyllic area suffered a devastating cataclysm, the most striking remnant of which has all the features of a classic impact crater 14 kilometers in diameter with a pronounced central uplift, sunken inner ring-graben, transition zone, and outer rim.[3] Millions of years of erosion have softened its contours but Google Earth or an overflight reveal its obvious crater-like appearance. Most geologists agree that it is the result of some kind of explosive event but the nature of the explosion for a long while remained unsettled and there were heated arguments between those who favored volcanism and those who favored an impact by an asteroid or comet.[4] Because Serpent Mound is the best-known feature within it, and because of the uncertainty caused by the dispute, the crater was therefore officially known for many years as the "Serpent Mound Cryptoexplosion Structure."[5] Only since the late 1990s has mounting evidence led to today's widespread consensus that it was, as many had long suspected, formed by a hypervelocity cosmic impact.[6]

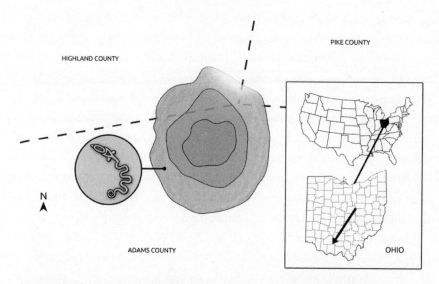

HIGHLAND COUNTY

PIKE COUNTY

N

ADAMS COUNTY

OHIO

Variously referred to as the "Serpent Mound Crypto-Explosive Structure" and as the "Serpent Mound Disturbance," most scientists now agree that the bizarre geological feature within which the mound was built is an ancient impact crater with a diameter of around 14 kilometers.

As to timing, the impact was "later than Early Mississippian, because rocks of this age [about 345 million years old] were involved in the disturbance, and earlier than the Illinoian glaciation (125,000 years ago), because these sediments are undisturbed in the northern part of the structure."[7]

That's a pretty wide window! Nonetheless, most of the experts seem confident that the crater's age must be in the hundreds of millions, not just hundreds of thousands, of years.[8] And while it's thought unlikely that the Native Americans who built Serpent Mound could have known anything about cosmic impacts, many scholars speculate that as keen observers of nature they would certainly have noticed the curious, jumbled, cataclysmic, ringlike structure of the area and been impressed by it.[9]

"They had to know there was a significance to that spot," says Ohio geologist Mark Baranoski. "They placed a deep reverence in old Mother Earth. It's almost mystical that they built a spiritual site."[10] Similarly, geoscientist Raymond Anderson of the University of Iowa describes Serpent Mound crater as "one of the most mysterious places in North America. The Native Americans found something mystical there. And they were right."[11]

Dating back to the time of the impact, an intense magnetic anomaly[12] centered on the site causes compasses to give wildly inaccurate readings. There are also gravity anomalies caused by the impact and there are multiple underground caverns, streams, and sinkholes that, in the view of Ohio archaeologist William Romain, would have been seen by the ancients as entrances to the underworld: "Among many peoples, unusual or transitional areas such as this are often considered sacred. Indeed such places are often considered supernatural gateways, or portals, between the celestial Upperworld and the Underworld. . . . One can only conclude that the Serpent Mound builders were aware of at least some of the more unusual characteristics of the area and that they located the effigy in this anomalous area for a very specific reason."[13]

As we drove the last few miles along OH-73W, I could reflect that we were entering the lair of the Serpent—a sacred domain where the forces of earth and sky had once collided with sufficient energy, according to the calculations of state geologist Michael Hansen, "To disturb more than 7 cubic miles of rock and uplift the central portion of the circular feature at least 1,000 feet above its normal position."[14]

One might expect the great effigy mound to be located on the high point of that central uplift, but instead it uncoils and undulates along a sinuous ridge in the southwestern quadrant of the crater near the edge of the ring-graben. At the northern end of the ridge, where it takes a turn to the northwest, lies the serpent's head.

I'd seen it all in plan and maps many times before, but now, for the first time, I was about to see the real thing. I was traveling with my wife, photographer Santha Faiia, and with local geometrician and archaeoastronomer Ross Hamilton, who has devoted much of his life to the study of Serpent Mound and whose book on the monument is a thought-provoking reference on the subject.[15]

Not only here but elsewhere in the world I have noticed that very special ancient places such as Serpent Mound seem able to invoke mechanisms to protect themselves from human folly. Among these mechanisms, from time to time, a passionate and devoted individual will be prompted by a particular site to go forth as its advocate—Maria Reiche at the Nazca Lines, for example, or Klaus Schmidt at Göbekli Tepe—and ensure not only its preservation but also the dissemination of key knowledge about it.

For the past decades, with absolute commitment, lean and gray-bearded and ascetic as a Buddhist monk, Ross Hamilton has been that individual for Serpent Mound.

GROUND AND SKY

WE TURN OFF 73W JUST before Brush Creek and enter a manicured park, maintained by the Ohio History Connection. Leaving our vehicle, we follow the footpath through scattered stands of trees, pass the visitor center, and come after a few moments to a grass-covered embankment about three feet high.

"The tail of the Serpent," Ross says.

I frown. It's a bit of an anticlimax! I don't immediately see the mystic spiral I've been expecting from the plans I've studied. But modern steps surmount the outer curve and from this vantage point the inner coils of the earthwork become visible.[16]

The effect remains underwhelming, largely because the present management of the site has allowed a thick clump of trees to block the view that would otherwise open up to the north across the full length of the Serpent's body from its tail to its head.

To see the immense effigy as a whole, therefore, rather than in isolated parts, we need to observe it from the sky. Fortunately, Santha has come prepared for this with a recently acquired MavicPro drone equipped with a high-resolution camera. She fires up the little quadcopter right away and suddenly we're looking down through the monitor from an altitude of 400 feet with the Serpent beneath us, unfolding outward from that coiled tail.

The site is almost deserted but there are a few people in the shot and they give me a sense of its scale. I know it already from my background research, but to see it with my own eyes is quite another matter. This undulating Serpent, with its gaping jaws, is 1,348 feet long.[17] The earthwork mound that forms its body averages around 4 feet in height and tapers from a width of about 24 feet to about 22 feet through its seven principal meanders before narrowing farther into the spiral of the tail.[18] People beside it appear as midgets or elves in the shadow of a dragon and for the first time, with a shiver down my spine, I become aware—not in

From an altitude of 400 feet, the full form of the great Manitou of Serpent Mound becomes visible. PHOTO: SANTHA FAIIA.

my intellect, but in my heart, in my spirit—that a mighty and uncanny power slumbers here.

Ross seems to read my mind. "Some call it a Manitou," he says. "But I'd go further. I'd say our Serpent is *Gitché Manitou*—the Great Spirit and ancestral guardian of the ancient people."

For those reared in the materialist-reductionist mind-set of Western science, the Native American notion of Manitou seems slippery and elusive. Though it may be materialized it cannot be reduced to matter. Nor can it be weighed, measured, or counted. It is an unquantifiable, formless but *sentient* force, "supernatural, omnipresent and omniscient,"[19] in one sense a spiritual entity in its own right, in another the mysterious, unseen power that animates all life and that can manifest both in natural phenomena and in man-made objects and structures that have been created with correct intent. "The profoundness of a spiritual presence of Manitou, and through it recognition of the supernatural," comments one authority, "was and is a tangible entity seen and felt by hundreds of generations of the Indian people of North America. . . . In essence, Native people perceived a spiritual landscape imprinted on the physical landscape as both one and the same. This 'duality' of the natural world still inspires the Native population to revere as sacred certain places and rocks deemed to possess 'Manitou.'"[20]

THE SERPENT AND THE EGG

WE BRING THE DRONE DOWN to earth for a battery change then send it back into the sky.

From an altitude of 400 feet it's notable how the sinuous natural ridge on which Serpent Mound was built has distinct "head" and "tail" ends and how the head of the Serpent is placed at the "head" end of the ridge, while the undulating body, all the way back to the tail, follows the contours of the ridge exactly.

Encouraged by the modern management of the site,[21] however, the luxuriant tree cover that prohibits observation along the main north–south axis also crowds the east and west sides of the body, seeming to hem in the great Manitou. A tangled mass of greenery chokes the steep western slope of the bluff down to Brush Creek, and I note how the tree growth is particularly tall and dense to the northwest, around the Serpent's head, as though intentionally allowed to flourish there to blind it.

I ask Santha to point the camera at the head—which is not a work of artistic realism but is instead a triangular geometric construct extending forward from the Serpent's neck and formed of the two gaping "jaws" with a curved earthwork running between them.

Partly within those gaping jaws sits a substantial and clearly defined ellipse. It's a feature that Ephraim Squier and Edwin Davis, the earliest scientific surveyors of the mound, were intrigued by. Writing in 1848, in the very first official publication released by the then newly established Smithsonian Institution, they observed that this curious structure was

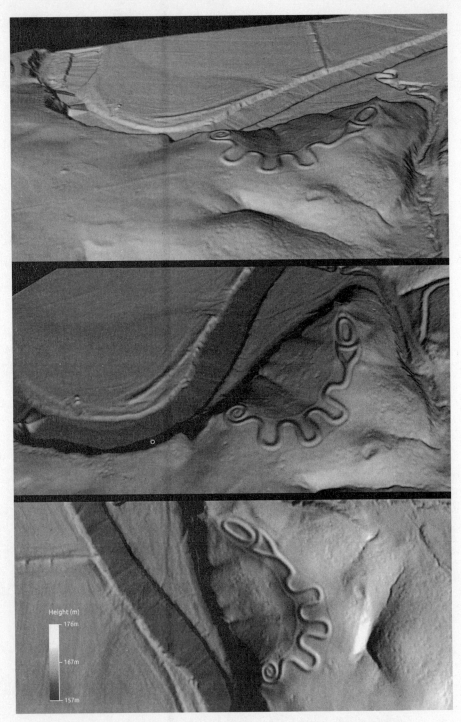

Height (m)

176m

167m

157m

By stripping out all trees, vegetation, and other surface features, Lidar offers
views of the Serpent Mound Manitou and the sinuous natural ridge on which it
stands that cannot otherwise be seen today. LIDAR GRAPHICS BY JEFFREY WILSON.

formed by an embankment of earth, without any perceptible opening, four feet in height, and . . . perfectly regular in outline, its transverse and conjugate diameters being one hundred and sixty and eighty feet respectively. The ground within the oval is slightly elevated: a small circular elevation of large stones, much burned, once existed at its centre; but they have been thrown down and scattered by some ignorant visitor, under the prevailing impression probably that gold was hidden beneath them. The point of the hill within which this egg-shaped figure rests, seems to have been artificially cut to conform to its outline, leaving a smooth platform.[22]

Squier and Davis go on to remind us that "the serpent, separate or in combination with the circle, egg, or globe, has been a predominant symbol among many primitive nations."[23] They draw our attention in particular to the southwest of England, where Stonehenge stands, and to the nearby great henge, stone circles, and serpentine causeways of Avebury, but nonetheless decline the twin challenges of tracing "the analogies which the Ohio structure exhibits to the serpent temples of England" and of pointing out "the extent to which the symbol was applied in America."[24] Almost wistfully, however, they describe such an investigation as "fraught with the greatest interest both in respect of the light which it reflects upon the primitive superstitions of remotely separated people, and especially upon the origin of the American race."[25]

Scholars in the nineteenth century, and indeed well into the early twentieth century, routinely applied words like "primitive" and "savage" to the works of our ancestors. At Serpent Mound, however, as Ross Hamilton points out, these so-called superstitious primitives were demonstrably the masters of some very exacting scientific techniques. He gives me a penetrating look. "Just consider the precision with which they found true north and balanced the whole effigy around that north–south line. It was a long while before modern surveyors could match it. In fact everyone got it wrong until 1987, when William Romain carried out the first proper survey of the mound and gave us a map with correct cardinal directions."

Connecting the hinge of the effigy's jaws to the tip of the inner spiral of its tail, Serpent Mound's meridian axis combines aesthetic refinement with astronomical and geodetic precision of a high order. Moreover, although they

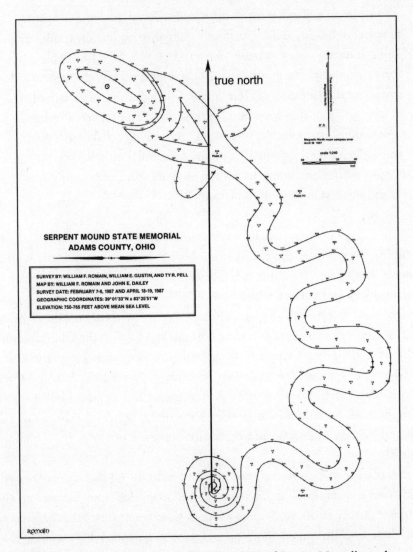

true north

SERPENT MOUND STATE MEMORIAL
ADAMS COUNTY, OHIO

SURVEY BY: WILLIAM F. ROMAIN, WILLIAM E. GUSTIN, AND TY R. PELL
MAP BY: WILLIAM F. ROMAIN AND JOHN E. DAILEY
SURVEY DATE: FEBRUARY 7-8, 1987 AND APRIL 18-19, 1987
GEOGRAPHIC COORDINATES: 39°01'33"N x 83°25'51"W
ELEVATION: 750-765 FEET ABOVE MEAN SEA LEVEL

William Romain's 1987 map revealed the precision of Serpent Mound's north–
south axis.

themselves took the matter no further, Squier and Davis were right to draw
comparisons with Stonehenge and Avebury, for these great English earthworks, as we shall see in the next chapter, both bear the imprint of the same
"artistic science."

2

A JOURNEY IN TIME

JOIN ME IN A TIME machine. I've set it to take us back to the peak of the last Ice Age 21,000 years ago and to bring us, on a midsummer's day, to the amazing, mysterious, and atmospheric location where the Great Serpent Mound National Historic Landmark can now be found.

Of course there was no "National Historic Landmark," no such entity as the United States of America, and no Adams County in the very different world of 21,000 years ago. At that time, from roughly the Ohio and the Missouri Rivers northward, a wide horizontal strip of the United States, and all of Canada as far as the Arctic Ocean, lay beneath a giant shroud of ice.

At no point, however, even at the last glacial maximum 21,000 years ago, did the ice ever advance quite far enough to the south to bury the sinuous natural ridge on which Serpent Mound stands today.

We'll get to the question of *when* the great effigy itself was first heaped up in the form of a serpent. But for now let's step out of our time machine onto that serpentine ridge and breathe the crisp fresh air under the blue midsummer skies of an unpolluted world.

We might see some of the great beasts of the North American Ice Age—the famed "megafauna," such as mammoths, mastodons, giant sloths, short-faced bears, and saber-toothed tigers. They thrived at the last glacial maximum and would continue to do so for several more millennia until they were all swept from the earth between roughly 12,800 and 11,600 years ago in what is known as the "Late Pleistocene Extinction Event."[1] The creatures I've named were by no means its only casualties. All together thirty-five genera of North American megafauna (with each genus consisting of several species) were wiped out during this enigmatic cataclysm that brought the Ice Age to an end.[2] But all that was still far in the future 21,000 years ago, and we're not at Serpent Mound for the megafauna. Instead I want you to shade your eyes and look to the horizon, approximately a dozen miles to your north. There, armored in brilliant, scintillating, dazzling reflections, a spectacle awaits you the like of which exists nowhere in the world today outside of Antarctica. That sight, a sheer, looming, continuous cliff of ice rising more than a mile high and extending across almost the entire width of North America from the east coast to the west coast, marks the southernmost extent of the ice cap in these parts. Elsewhere it stretched out its lobes and tongues a few tens of miles farther south, but here, just short of the outer rim of Serpent Mound crater, the advance was decisively stopped.

If humans had been present in Adams County 21,000 years ago to witness the phenomenon, what would they have made of it? Would they have thought this sudden halt of the march of the ice cliffs was random? Just one of those things that happen?

Or might it have seemed that some great Manitou protected this land?

Let's get back in our time machine.

I'm going to set it to stay in the same location but to jump 8,000 years forward to a midsummer's day 13,000 years ago, just a couple of hundred years before the onset of the Late Pleistocene Extinction Event.

The first thing you'll notice as we step out onto the ridge is that the world is warmer—indeed it has been warming steadily since about 18,000 years ago and particularly dramatically since 14,500 years ago. In consequence, although it is still a giant force of nature, the ice cap has receded about 600 miles to the latitude of Lake Superior, and those looming ice cliffs that formed a massive artificial horizon just 12 miles north of Serpent Mound are completely gone. Minus the roads and telecommunications cables, therefore, the view that confronts us at midsummer 13,000 years ago is pretty much the same as the view at midsummer today where the natural horizon encircling the effigy is formed by broken and eroded ranges of low hills—themselves the remnants of the ancient hypervelocity cosmic impact that created this unique landscape.

So, a timeline for time travelers:

> 300 million years ago, or thereabouts, a giant cataclysm forms the Serpent Mound crater.

> 21,000 years ago, the North American ice cap reaches the southernmost point of its advance, stopping just a few miles north of the eroded crater rim.

> By 13,000 years ago the ice cliffs are gone and Serpent Mound's natural horizon has been restored.

On June 17, 2017, I made my first research visit to Serpent Mound, reported in chapter 1, and on June 20, midsummer's eve, Santha, Ross Hamilton, and I returned to the site to fly the drone again and to observe sunset over the effigy from the viewpoint of the gods.

A MATTER OF PERSPECTIVE

MIDSUMMER—THE SUMMER SOLSTICE—IS the longest day of the year (presently June 20/21 in the Northern Hemisphere), when the sun rises at the farthest point north of east and sets at the farthest point north of west on its annual journey. It is also a particularly significant day at Serpent Mound—for it is on the summer solstice that the open jaws of the Serpent most directly confront the setting point of the sun, as though about to engulf it.

This is because the northern end of the ridge, which Squier and Davis

SUMMER SOLSTICE SUNSET

Serpent Mound alignment to the summer solstice sunset.

believed had been terraformed ("artificially cut" as we saw in the last chapter), terminates in a pronounced turn to the west that defines the orientation of the Serpent's head. It seems implausible, whoever they may have been and whenever they first conceived of the mound (open questions, as we shall see), that the ancient builders were unaware that this natural westward curve aligned the leading edge of the ridge with the point of sunset on the summer solstice.

I believe they were acutely aware of it.

Indeed, the presence of the Serpent here, and the orientation of its head, bear all the hallmarks of great minds at work, manifesting a carefully thought-out design not meant to stand alone but rather to enhance and elucidate the solstice alignment—the sacred communion of earth and sky—that nature had already put in place.

From the perspective of twenty-first-century science, the fact that the end of a natural ridge is oriented toward the summer solstice sunset is a matter of chance. It would be foolish to invest it with any significance—let alone with so much significance that it could motivate a huge construction project and bring it to triumphant completion.

We should keep in mind, however, that matters seemed very different to the ancients, who perceived the earth and sky as living spirits in communion with one another.

In our century, when technology is king and the majority of the human race live and die in cities, we cut down rainforests, pollute and defile the earth, and shun and scrape the sky. Serried blades of immense buildings dice our view of the horizon into jagged, glittering, meaningless origami, while light pollution is so intense that we cannot see the stars. Ironically, however, any number of astronomy programs will bring those stars flickering into virtual reality on our computer screens. Ironically, too, ours is a culture that has advanced the scientific study of the cosmos to an exceptionally high degree.

It seems we want to see everything, but only at a distance, through a technological filter.

Little wonder, therefore, that, for so many of us, the sky has entirely lost the numinous aura that once clung about it, and has been reduced to a vague, out-of-focus, largely irrelevant, not even beautiful background to the much more important material business of our daily lives. Reared in a culture that focuses all its energies on the production and consumption of commercial goods and services, it just looks to us like bad business to commit huge resources, intelligence, and energy to building great monuments aligned—for example—to the rising or setting points of the sun on the equinoxes or on the summer or winter solstices.

Yet for thousands upon thousands of years this is exactly what happened all around the world.

WHERE HEAVEN AND EARTH MEET

GO TO THE CITY OF Luxor in Upper Egypt, place yourself at the western entrance of the great Temple of Karnak in the predawn on December 20/21 (the winter solstice and shortest day of the year in the Northern Hemisphere), and wait patiently until the sun appears. When it does you will see that its first rays shine directly down the kilometer-long axis of the temple that is oriented south of east at precisely the correct angle to target the rising point of the sun on that special day.

Or go to Stonehenge in the predawn on June 20/21, the summer solstice, enter the great stone circle, and face north of east along its axis toward a rough, unquarried megalith—the Heel Stone—standing prominently outside the circle. As light floods the sky you will see how carefully and purposefully the Heel Stone seems to have been placed, almost like the front sight on the barrel of a rifle, to target the rising sun on that special day.

Or go to Angkor Wat in Cambodia and position yourself dead center at the western end of the entrance causeway of the great temple complex in the predawn on March 20/21, the spring equinox, or on September 20/21, the autumn equinox, when night and day are of equal length and the sun rises perfectly due east. On either of these two special occasions you will discover that the causeway and temple are so precisely oriented that the sun, as it rises, perches for a moment atop Angkor's central tower and lights up the entire majestic complex like a fairy-tale kingdom.

All these places are man-made sanctuaries that speak to the union of heaven and earth at key moments of the year. They might rightly be described as hierophanies because their fundamental purpose is to reveal and manifest the sacred connection between macrocosm and microcosm, sky and ground, "above" and "below."

Scattered around this majestic garden planet we call Earth, however, are other, even more powerful hierophanies, put in place not by human beings but by nature, where ground and sky whisper to one another with exceptional intimacy. Wise ancients, who knew the garden long before us, sought out such spots, which they held to be sacred, and when they found them they would sometimes modify them to honor and enhance the communion witnessed there.

Research published in 2018, though subject to further confirmation, suggests that Stonehenge may be one of them. Archaeologists have long believed that its taller, heftier pillars—the big limestone "sarsens"—did not occur locally on Salisbury Plain where Stonehenge stands but had to be dragged 18 miles from the Marlborough Downs.[3] The enduring mystery, therefore, was, why anyone would go through all that trouble and effort moving megaliths weighing up to 50 tons to Salisbury Plain when Stonehenge could simply have been erected on the Marlborough Downs instead?

The new research offers a rather surprising answer. It seems that two of the sarsens—Stone 16 in the southwestern quadrant of the great circle, and the

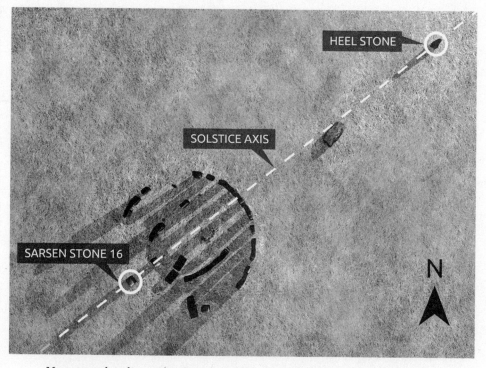

New research indicates that Stone 16 and the Heel Stone were present on Salisbury Plain, aligned by nature to the solstices, before Stonehenge was built. IMAGE: DERIVATIVE OF "STONEHENGE" BY RUSLANS3D, CC BY 4.0.

Heel Stone outside the circle to its northeast—were NOT after all brought here from the Marlborough Downs but have stood naturally on Salisbury Plain for millions of years.[4] What's magical about them, however, is their alignment. An observer behind Stone 16 looking **northeast** toward the Heel Stone at dawn on the summer solstice will see the sun **rise** behind it. Then 6 months later, at the winter solstice, an observer behind the Heel Stone looking **southwest** at Stone 16 will see the sun **set** behind it.

Archaeologist Mike Pitts, who led the research, suggests that the way the alignment of these two sarsens signaled midwinter and midsummer would not have gone unnoticed by the ancient Britons, who would have accorded special significance to the site long before they planned the geometry of Stonehenge and raised up the whole spectacular complex of megaliths around the preexisting axis. Indeed, if Pitts is right, it is **because** of this natural solstice axis that Stonehenge was built here in the first place.[5]

Another example of humans sacralizing a place where earth speaks to sky is the Great Sphinx of Giza in Egypt, which is thought to have begun life as a "yardang"—a ridge of bedrock shaped by millennia of desert winds into a completely natural form somewhat resembling a lion.[6] Many such outcrops, described by European explorers of the eighteenth and nineteenth centuries as "sphinxlike" and as resembling "lions," exist in Egypt's Western Desert.[7] But what was special about this one was its situation overlooking the Nile Valley and the curious fact that nature had oriented it, with considerable precision, to due east and thus to the rising point of the sun on the equinoxes. As suggested at Stonehenge, it looks like this celestial alignment is what attracted human beings to it in the first place, motivating them to transform it into a giant monolithic work of sculpture, first enhancing its naturally leonine form and much later, in the time of the pharaohs, recarving its (by then heavily eroded) leonine head into a human likeness.

Go to Giza at dawn on the winter solstice and you will see the sun rising far to the south of east, and thus far to the right of the gaze of the Sphinx. Go there at dawn on the summer solstice and you will see the sun rising far to the north of east, and thus far to the left of the gaze of the Sphinx. But go there at dawn on either the spring or the autumn equinox and you will witness the sacred communion of heaven and earth, with the gaze of the Sphinx perfectly aligned to the disk of the sun as it rises.

Such enchanted but fleeting conjunctions of earth and sky are not confined to the Old World.

In the New World, Native Americans likewise built immense structures to honor and channel precisely the same moments and energies and sought out certain striking topographical features—regarded as sacred—through which the celestial and terrestrial spirits were already bound in intimacy. Thus, just as Egypt has its Great Sphinx, natural but modified and enhanced by humans to bind sky and ground at sunrise on the equinoxes, and just as the natural solstitial axis of Stonehenge has been modified and enhanced by humans with numinous and beautiful effect, so North America has its Great Serpent Mound, a natural ridge, modified and enhanced by humans to join heaven and earth at sunset on the summer solstice.

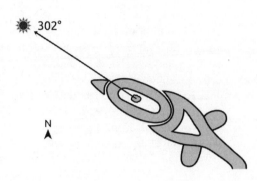

In their 1987 paper the Hardmans proposed a viewpoint near the center of the oval formation in front of the Serpent's head where an altar of large stones was reported to have remained in place until it was destroyed in the nineteenth century. From this viewpoint they settled on an alignment at azimuth 302 degrees targeting sunset on the summer solstice.

HERE COMES THE SUN

SERPENT MOUND'S STRIKING CONNECTION TO the summer solstice went unnoticed, unobserved, and unstudied by anyone in our era until 1987. That was the year in which the fall issue of the *Ohio Archaeologist* published a landmark paper by Clarke and Marjorie Hardman titled "The Great Serpent and the Sun."

In this paper, the ridge behind which the sun sets on June 20/21 as viewed from Serpent Mound was daringly renamed "Solstice Ridge" by the authors, and the orientation of the open jaws of the Serpent to the setting point of the sun on the summer solstice was recognized and made explicit for the first time.[8]

What has been seen cannot be unseen, even in an age so radically disconnected from the cosmos as our own. Thanks to the Hardmans, therefore, no one who takes a serious look at Serpent Mound can now fail to observe the way the Serpent's jaws line up to the setting summer solstice sun. Because those jaws gape wide, however, it's an alignment that would have been as general and obvious 13,000 years ago as it is today. The Hardmans therefore sought to refine it. As shown in the diagram above, they selected as their viewpoint the reported location, near the center of the oval formation in front of the Serpent's head, of the former "elevation of large stones" described by Squier and Davis as destroyed when they visited the site in the mid-nineteenth century.[9] The Hardmans argued that an observer who positioned himself in

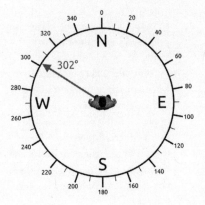

The "azimuth" of an object is its distance from true north in degrees counting clockwise. North is nominated as 0 degrees, so azimuth 90 degrees is due east, azimuth 180 degrees is due south, and azimuth 270 degrees is due west. An azimuth of 302 degrees will therefore be 32 degrees north of west.

this location on the evening of the summer solstice would see the sun set at an azimuth of 302 degrees behind a specific feature on "Solstice Ridge"—a feature something like the front sight on a rifle that they nominated "Solstice Knob."[10]

ROASTING THE HARDMANS

IT'S OFTEN THE CASE IN archaeological scholarship, and actually good science, that whenever an adventurous and unusual new thesis is published attempts will be made to falsify it. It was therefore only to be expected, as I turned to the winter 1987 issue of *Ohio Archaeologist,* that I would find a refutation of the Hardmans' work. Titled "Serpent Mound Revisited," the paper was written by William F. Romain, a very interesting and important researcher in this field.

On the assumption that Serpent Mound had been built around 2,000 years ago (the consensus archaeological opinion in the 1980s) Romain pointed out that the Hardmans proposed alignment had failed to take into account a well-established archaeoastronomical phenomenon, namely that the sun's rising and setting points along the horizon do not remain fixed but slowly change down the ages.[11]

This happens because sunrise and sunset positions are constrained not only by the latitude from which they are observed, but also by the tilt of the earth's axis in relation to the plane of its orbit. Presently the angle of the tilt stands at around 23° 44'.[12] This angle, however, is not fixed but slowly increases and decreases in a 41,000-year "obliquity cycle" between a minimum of 22.1° and a maximum of 24.5°.[13] The resulting changes to sunrise and sunset positions along the horizon over long periods are "sizable," according to leading archaeoastronomer Anthony F. Aveni,[14] whose calculations Romain used in his 1987 paper to highlight what he believed was the fatal flaw in the Hardmans' case. They had accepted the epoch of 2,000 years ago for the construction of Serpent Mound, but their proposed sunset azimuth of 302° made no sense. Viewed from Serpent Mound 2,000 years ago, as Romain correctly pointed out, "the summer solstice sun would have set at an azimuth of about 300.4 degrees. . . . In other words, the summer solstice sun would have set roughly 1.6 degrees, the equivalent of 3 sun diameters, south of Solstice Knob."[15] If Serpent Mound really was that far out of alignment 2,000 years ago when it was supposed to have been built, then only four logical conclusions presented themselves: (1) its builders were very poor astronomers; (2) they hadn't intended to orient the monument to the summer solstice sunset at all; (3) the Hardmans were right in their general thesis but had gotten the proposed observation point and sight line wrong; or (4) The alignment had not been made 2,000 years ago but at a completely different time.

In another paper, published in *Ohio Archaeologist* a year later, Robert Fletcher and Terry Cameron picked up where Romain had left off in a renewed roasting of the Hardmans. Noting that the summer solstice sun as viewed from Serpent Mound currently sets at azimuth 300° 05', and noting the effects of the obliquity cycle, they treat with sarcasm the Hardmans' claim that the Serpent's primary orientation was to azimuth 302°: "If a horizon marker at 302 degrees was used at one time to mark the summer solstice sunset position, the Serpent, by implication, must have been constructed around 11,000 BC. There may be some who would have problems with that date."[16]

It's the last line that reveals the scorn.

You bet there would have been "some" in 1988 who would have had problems with that date! Indeed, not just some but all archaeologists would have regarded it as the province of the lunatic fringe to suggest that Serpent Mound might in any way go back as far as 11,000 BC, that is, to around 13,000 years ago.

In the 1980s, as we'll see in part 2, there was a general acceptance that

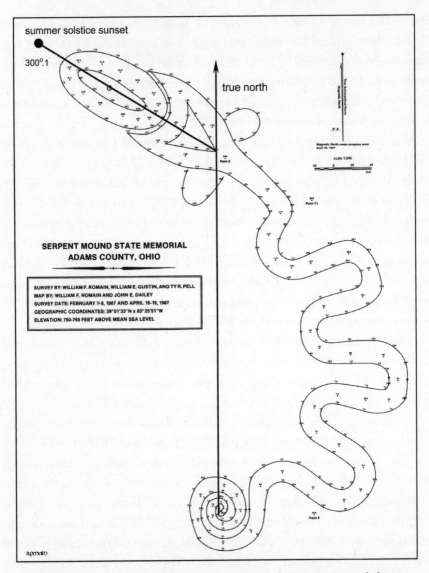

SERPENT MOUND STATE MEMORIAL
ADAMS COUNTY, OHIO

SURVEY BY: WILLIAM F. ROMAIN, WILLIAM E. GUSTIN, AND TY R. PELL
MAP BY: WILLIAM F. ROMAIN AND JOHN E. DAILEY
SURVEY DATE: FEBRUARY 7-8, 1987 AND APRIL 18-19, 1987
GEOGRAPHIC COORDINATES: 39°01'33"N x 83°25'51"W
ELEVATION: 750-765 FEET ABOVE MEAN SEA LEVEL

William Romain's summer solstice sunset alignment for Serpent Mound along azimuth 300.1 degrees. This alignment would have targeted the summer solstice sunset 2,000 years ago and differs by 1.9 degrees from the alignment proposed by the Hardmans.

humans might have first arrived in the Americas by 12,000 or even 13,000 years ago. But those earliest migrants were deemed by archaeologists to have been scattered hunter-gatherer groups, living from hand to mouth and lacking the vision, sophistication, and level of organization required to create a monument on the scale of Serpent Mound.

The real implication of the Hardmans' "error"—the clue they'd inadvertently stumbled upon, of possibly much more ancient origins for the site—was therefore never followed up because the prevailing theory of the peopling of the Americas would not admit it as evidence.

Meanwhile, as the years passed, William Romain changed his mind. In 1987 he had written in his critique of the Hardmans that the orientation of Serpent Mound could be "better explained by a set of facts having nothing to do with the summer solstice."[17] By the year 2000, however, he was ready to accept as "unequivocal" an alignment from the head of the Serpent "through the oval embankment to the summer solstice sunset,"[18] and showed in a map how this could be done to target azimuth 300.4 degrees, later revised to azimuth 300.1 degrees (personal communication October 31, 2018), where the summer solstice sun would have set 2,000 years ago.[19] He also reiterated the definitive north–south line he'd identified in 1987 running through the monument from the inner spiral of its tail to the hinge of its jaws.[20]

BUT IS THE SERPENT REALLY 2,000 YEARS OLD?

BACK IN THE 1980s, WHEN Romain first laid into the Hardmans, the one thing both sides agreed on was that Serpent Mound was about 2,000 years old and was one of the later works of "the Adena," a Native American culture thought to have flourished between approximately 800 BC and AD 100.[21] Though no carbon dating had been done, this was the consensus view of almost all experts at the time, and Romain and the Hardmans not only accepted it without question but also used it as the basis for their own calculations of alignments.

Imagine their surprise, therefore, when Robert Fletcher of the University of Pittsburgh (one of the early critics of the Hardmans), William Pickard of Ohio State University, and Bradley T. Lepper of the Ohio Historical Society carried out the first carbon-dating of Serpent Mound and found it to be much **younger** than everyone had supposed—not 2,000 years old or more, but 1,000 years old or less.[22] To be precise, they concluded that the most likely date for its construction was 920 years (plus or minus 70 years) before the present,[23] and that it must therefore be the work of the so-called Fort Ancient culture thought to have flourished at around that time.[24]

Published in spring 1996 in a respected peer-reviewed journal, this notion of a much younger Serpent Mound went on to enjoy a level of widespread acceptance among American archaeologists that would certainly not have been accorded to it if the redating had gone in the other direction. Moreover, after being quickly and uncritically adopted into doctrine,[25] it was then disseminated to the public for most of the next 20 years as unquestioned historical fact.[26]

As part of this process, an Orwellian scene took place at Serpent Mound in 2003 when the official Ohio historical marker that had previously attributed the monument to the Adena culture was "unhappened" and replaced by another in which visitors were informed that the earthwork had been built "around 1000 A.D. by the Fort Ancient culture."[27]

Let's take a look at the evidence on which Fletcher, Pickard, and Lepper based the 1996 claim that so effectively redefined Serpent Mound.

Part of it has to do with an *absence* of evidence of typical Adena cultural artifacts—indeed an absence of any artifacts—in those parts of the Serpent excavated prior to the 1990s.[28] As Fletcher & Co. rightly point out, it was only because a number of "definite Adena burial mounds" had been found nearby that Serpent Mound had been attributed to the Adena in the first place—an attribution that was therefore "somewhat tenuous."[29]

As to the positive evidence for their claim, Fletcher & Co. give special prominence to stone flakes and tools uncovered by their excavations at Serpent Mound, including "a classic Fort Ancient Madison point."[30] They also recovered twenty-nine pottery shards "assignable to some period between A.D. 350 and 950."[31] Finally—and clearly the clincher as far as they're concerned—they list the radiocarbon dates for three samples of charcoal retrieved during their excavations.

One, with a date of 2920 plus or minus 65 years before the present, they immediately dismiss because it came from a level "far below the estimated original surface upon which Serpent Mound was built."[32]

But the other two they like. Both were recovered from the "intact sediment used to create the effigy," and both returned the same calibrated radio-carbon date of AD 1070.[33]

These two identical dates, Fletcher, Pickard, and Lepper conclude, "Represent valid chronological evidence for the construction of Serpent Mound sometime during the Late Prehistoric or Early Fort Ancient periods."[34]

Lepper even speculates (he does admit it's speculation)[35] that the Serpent was made in response to the passage of Halley's Comet in 1066—recorded elsewhere as far afield as Europe and China: "It was a spectacular, fiery display. And it seems to me it's more than possible that the Native Americans may have viewed Halley's comet as a serpent snaking across the sky. It's possible they looked up at it and recorded it as an omen and built the serpent."[36]

And that's it! With a wave of the archaeologist's magic wand, a fairy-tale castle of speculation is conjured into being on the foundations of just two tiny fragments of charcoal. In the process, while being rendered less old, less venerable, and less mysterious, the sublime artistry, astronomy, geometry, and imagination expressed in Serpent Mound are snatched from one culture and handed to another by the so-called experts of a third!

SKIN CHANGER

NORTH AMERICAN ARCHAEOLOGY HAS A long track record of wanting Native American sites to be young, as we'll see in part 2. In the case of Serpent Mound, however, there were some archaeologists, notable among them William Romain, who were never happy with the "somewhat tenuous" nature of the evidence on which Fletcher, Pickard, and Lepper had built their castle in the sky. As Romain tactfully put it in 2011, "Since the charcoal that was dated did not come from a foundation feature or event, the A.D. 1070 date may not reflect when the effigy was actually constructed."[37]

Soon afterward Romain followed up his hunch by joining forces with a multidisciplinary team of fellow researchers "to re-evaluate when and how Serpent Mound was built."[38] It was a thorough, professional, long-term project deploying the latest technologies and involving fresh excavations, core sampling, and multiple radiocarbon dates. The results, published in the *Journal of*

Archaeological Science in October 2014, thoroughly ripped the rug out from under the comfortable consensus of the previous 18 years that the Serpent was around 900 or 1,000 years old and was the work of the Fort Ancient culture.

"We believe that taken as a whole," Romain and his colleagues reported, "our data strongly support that Serpent Mound was first constructed ~2300 years ago, rather than ~1400 years later. Our results indicate the presence of a pre-construction paleosol beneath Serpent Mound, and that charcoal from different locales along its surface dates consistently to ~300 BC. The youngest calibrated age within the 95% probability range is 116 BC and we obtained no dates associated with the later Fort Ancient occupation of the site."[39]

Charitably, however, there was no crowing in triumph, no pouring of scorn on Fletcher, Lepper, and Pickard. Instead Romain's team saw the real answer in a compromise:

> The evidence compiled by Fletcher et al. concerning the reliability of their C-14 ages is generally convincing and supports the charcoal as authentically related to a Fort Ancient (re)construction episode 900 years ago, which leaves the contradiction between the two initial construction chronologies unresolved. To settle this contradiction, we propose that Serpent Mound was constructed and then later modified during two distinct episodes: an Adena construction ~2300 years ago during which the mound was first built, followed ~1400 years later by an episode of Fort Ancient renovation or repair.[40]

Because their work was well done, their evidence solid, and their arguments compelling, but also because their "redating" was more of a return to the pre-1996 consensus than anything dangerously new or radical, the model proposed by Romain and his colleagues has subsequently displaced Fletcher et al. Serpent Mound has been returned to the Adena and, despite some unpersuasive protests from Bradley Lepper[41] and incomplete information foisted on the public at the site itself, few today would seriously attempt to argue that it is less than 2,300 years old.

The lingering question, though, is, could it be older?

Perhaps very much older?

After all, is it not the defining quality of the serpent that from time to time

This noticeboard, which remained in place at the site in 2018, underinforms the public by making Serpent Mound more than 1,000 years younger than the most accurate carbon dates suggest. PHOTO: ROSS HAMILTON.

it sheds its skin? And is it not precisely on account of this that it served for many ancient cultures as a symbol of reincarnation?[42] It is therefore reasonable to ask how often Serpent Mound has shed its skin and renewed itself.

The 1996 and the 2014 studies, taken together, provide solid evidence of a change of skin around 900 years ago—a "renovation" project. However, largely because of the "pre-construction paleosol" (soil stratum laid down in an earlier age) forming the foundation of the mound,[43] it is taken for granted that the earlier episode at 2,300 years ago was the **birth** of the project. Setting aside the one anomalous charcoal fragment, dated to 2,920 years ago in the 1996 study, and the two fragments testifying to the Fort Ancient renovation, all the datable materials from the 2014 study, which clustered around 300 BC as we've seen, were found **above** this bed of ancient soil. "The sub-mound paleosol was buried," the archaeologists therefore conclude, "and Serpent Mound construction began . . . 2300 years ago during the Early Woodland (Adena) Period."[44]

It seems like a reasonable argument but it leaves another possibility unconsidered—namely that 2,300 years ago Serpent Mound was **already** an enormously ancient structure, perhaps very much eroded and damaged, and that it was cleared down to the level of the paleosol and remade by the Adena culture at this time.

In that case the archaeologists behind the 2014 study would not have documented the birth of the Serpent but its **rebirth**—or reincarnation.

Why not?

The 2014 study did not gather the necessary data to confirm whether the mound was in continuous use from the Adena period 2,300 years ago until the Fort Ancient renovations 1,400 years later: "However, a possible erased coil near the head of the serpent indicates that other alterations, potentially several hundred years earlier than the Fort Ancient repairs, may also have occurred. This suggests a deeper, richer, and far more complex history for Serpent Mound than previously known."[45]

Again—why should this deeper, richer, far more complex history be limited to the relatively recent past? Since Romain and his coauthors are prepared to consider the possibility that Serpent Mound "was regularly used, repaired, and possibly reconfigured by local groups for more than 2000 years,"[46] then why not for longer?

Even Fletcher & Co. admit that their anomalous 2,920-year-old piece of charcoal, and nearby Adena burial mounds, are evidence of "the use of the area during the Early Woodland Period."[47] But why should such use have been "ephemeral," as they assert?[48] Why shouldn't those Early Woodland peoples also, like later cultures, have been present to tend to, maintain, restore, and sometimes reorient and reconstruct the great Manitou?

If so, and if others who came before them had done the same work in their time, inheriting that sacred responsibility from even earlier cultures and participating down the millennia in an irregular process of restoration and refurbishment, then the possibility cannot be ruled out that the first incarnation of the effigy might indeed have been in the Ice Age 13,000 years ago. Were that to be confirmed, everything we've been taught about the state of early Native American civilizations and the global timeline of prehistory would have to be rethought.

3

THE DRAGON AND THE SUN

IN 2017 THE CLOSEST SUNSET to the precise astronomical moment of the summer solstice occurs on the evening of June 20—which is why Santha, Ross Hamilton, and I are back at Serpent Mound on that day rather than on the 21st, when the solstice is more often celebrated. Angles, calculations, and astronomical software are all very well, but nothing beats direct, on-the-spot observation. Our project on the 20th, therefore, having familiarized ourselves with the site and its surroundings on our first visit on the 17th, is for Santha to fly the drone 400 feet above the great effigy, and photograph it at sunset from a point overlooking both its head and the horizon, commanding its field of view, so that we can see for ourselves what its alignment is really all about.

It's around 3 pm and the sky is cloudless, giving us hope of a clear horizon this evening. With more than enough time to spare on what, after all, is the longest day of the year, Ross beckons for us to follow him on a steep, wind-ing path that leads down from behind the coiled tail of the Serpent through

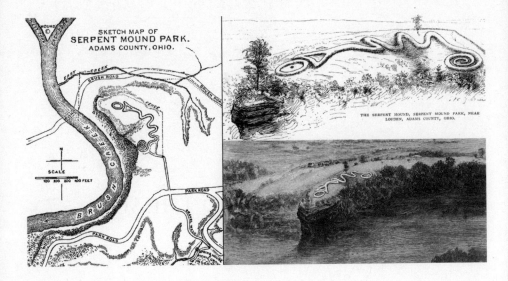

dense woods to the base of the ridge on which the great effigy stands. It's such a calm, clear, peaceful afternoon, filled with the sweet notes of birdsong and so poignant a dance of light and shadow between the leaves and the sun that the three of us fall silent, descending slowly and steadily, just breathing it all in. The path levels out along the bank of Brush Creek and we follow it toward the northwest. The creek is on our left and the ridge looms 100 feet above us on our right. Its slope is not entirely overgrown. In places it is sheer, almost a cliff, on which the trees and bushes can get no purchase and the bare limestone bedrock is exposed.

As we walk Ross goes over the implications of his own investigations into the true age of Serpent Mound. I refer the reader to his masterwork, *The Mystery of the Serpent Mound,* for full details.[1] In brief, though, his view as to when exactly the effigy was first constructed is not derived from any of the radiocarbon assays, or from calculations to do with the azimuth of the summer solstice sunset. Instead he focuses on the *form* of the serpent, which he perceives as a terrestrial image of the constellation Draco.

I have my own history with Draco, as those who have followed my work over the years will know. In my 1998 book *Heaven's Mirror,* for example, I present evidence that this enormous constellation, widely depicted as a serpent by many ancient cultures,[2] served as the celestial blueprint according to which the temples of Angkor in Cambodia were laid out on the ground—

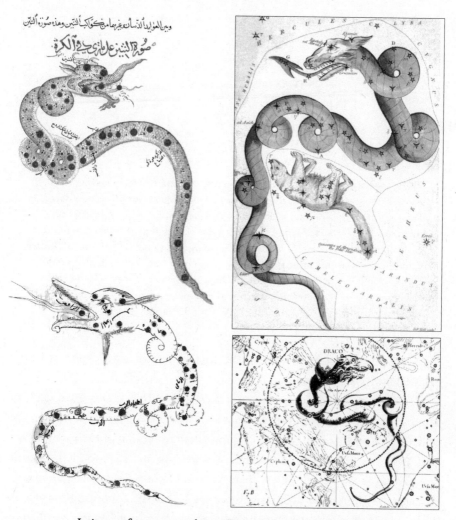

In images from many cultures, Draco is depicted as a serpent.

with each temple "below" matching a star "above." The essence of my case is that the notion of "as above so below" expressed in the architecture of Angkor is part of an ancient globally distributed doctrine—or "system"—that set out quite deliberately to create monuments on the ground, all around the world, to mimic the patterns of certain significant constellations in the sky. Moreover, since the positions of all stars as viewed from earth change slowly but continuously due to the phenomenon called "precession," it is possible to use particular configurations of astronomically aligned monuments to deduce the

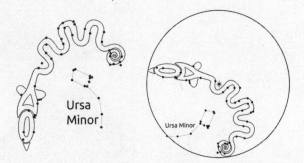

The constellation of Draco overlaid on Serpent Mound. The neighboring
constellation is Ursa Minor, the Little Bear, which houses our present pole star,
Polaris. LEFT: The accuracy of Romain's 1987 survey is demonstrated by the
many-starred asterism of Draconis. Each point of light is given equal size in order
to demonstrate the accuracy of the original designer's vision (Hamilton 1997, after
Cambridge and Romain). RIGHT: The ancient north star Thuban, which preceded
the present pole star Polaris (the dot touching the outside of the circle), is used as
the center of this geometry. Both ends of the Serpent are equal in distance from
the center point, Thuban (Hamilton 1997, after Romain).

dates that they represent—that is, the dates when the stars were last in the
celestial locations depicted by the monuments on the ground.

This process of constant change unfolds, of course, over a great cycle of
25,920 years and has nothing to do with the motions of the stars, or with the
obliquity cycle. Its cause is another quite different motion of the earth driven
by the contradictory pull of the gravity of the sun and the moon. The result
is a slow circular wobble of the planet's axis of rotation, at the rate of one
degree every 72 years, much resembling the wobble of a spinning top that is
no longer upright. The earth is the viewing platform from which we observe
the stars, so these changes in orientation cause changes in the positions of all
stars as viewed from earth.

To envisage the process, picture the earth's axis passing through the geographical south and north poles and thence extended into the heavens. The
south and north pole stars in any epoch are the stars at which the two "tips"
of this extended axis point most directly.

Serpent Mound is in the Northern Hemisphere and the north celestial
pole is presently occupied by our "pole star" Polaris (*Alpha Ursae Minoris*,
in the constellation of the Little Bear). The effect of precession, however, is
to cause the tip of the axis to inscribe an immense circle in the heavens over

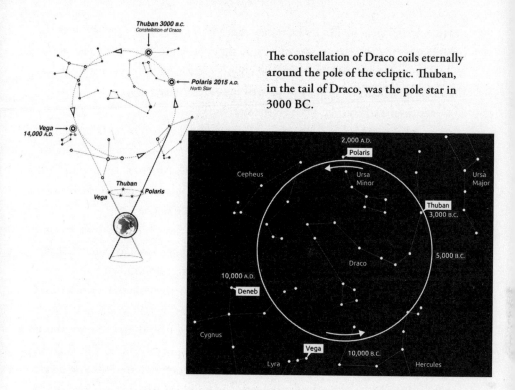

The constellation of Draco coils eternally around the pole of the ecliptic. Thuban, in the tail of Draco, was the pole star in 3000 BC.

the cycle of 25,920 years. Thus around 3000 BC, just before the start of the Pyramid Age in Egypt, the pole star was Thuban (*Alpha Draconis*) in the constellation Draco.[3] At the time of the Greeks it was *Beta Ursae Minoris*. In AD 14000 it will be Vega.[4] Sometimes in this long cyclical journey the extended north pole of the earth will point at empty space and then there will be no useful "pole star."

As one of the notable circumpolar constellations, and also one of the most widely recognized, and one of the oldest for which written records have survived,[5] what makes Draco particularly significant and remarkable was summed up in 1791 in two lines from a poem by Charles Darwin's grandfather, the physician and natural philosopher Erasmus Darwin:

With vast convolutions Draco holds
Th' ecliptic axis in his scaly folds.[6]

This "ecliptic axis"—astronomers today call it the "pole of the ecliptic"—is the still, fixed point in the celestial vault around which the vast circle of the north celestial pole makes its endlessly repeated 25,920-year journey. It is the one place in the sky that **never** moves or changes while everything else about it dances and shifts, and once you recognize it for what it is—nothing less than the very heart of heaven—it's striking how the serpentine constellation of Draco seems to coil protectively around it.

If at Angkor that constellation was honored in the form of temples laid out in its image on the ground, then I could see no reason in principle why a similar project should not have been mounted in North America. In one case the medium was stone, with temples targeting the equinox sunrise. In the other it was a great earthwork targeting the summer solstice sunset.

In both cases the result was a symbolically powerful union of ground and sky—a union, according to Ross Hamilton, that was made manifest not 1,000 years ago, nor even 2,300 years ago, but around 4,800 to 5,000 years ago. That was the time when Thuban in Draco was the pole star. And at that same remote date, almost 1,000 miles to the south in Louisiana, a site now known as Watson Brake was built. I will have a great deal more to say about Watson Brake in part 5. As we shall see, it is indisputably 5,000 years old in its present form, and it is Ross's argument that the same mysterious and as yet unidentified group of Native American geometers and astronomers who made Watson Brake also made the great Manitou at Serpent Mound.

As usual in these matters, however, there's complexity and nuance behind the headlines. So, yes, Ross **is** of the view that a major project was undertaken at Serpent Mound around 5,000 years ago. But as we talk now he clarifies what, for him, is obviously an extremely important point: "I always make an effort NOT to give people the impression that 5,000 years ago is when the first mound structure was built on this spot," he says emphatically:

> I believe it was a sacred place, with a structure upon it, its connection to the solstice recognised long before, but that it was remade, renovated, and renewed around 5,000 years ago, reinforcing the worn-down traces of older foundations unrealised by conventional dating methods.
>
> So there was something here already, a legacy from much earlier times, but 5,000 years ago or thereabouts a very well-developed version of the current serpentine effigy was created as an active,

fully functioning Manitou. In accord with Native American legend and mythology it would have been outfitted with the necessary accoutrements to facilitate earth–sky interaction phenomena, quite similar to the way some feel the Great Pyramid and its two sibling pyramids once operated.

The Cherokee say there was once a powerful crystal mounted at the head of the serpent—a crystal mentioned in Mooney's nineteenth-century collection of Cherokee "myths. . . ." That crystal put out a brilliant light that "sullied the meridian beams of the sun." As the story goes, the crystal was stolen and afterward the people fell into darkness. They revisited the former residences of their godly forebears whom they held in highest regard, and gradually took away relics of the remaining parts of the Serpent as well, leaving only dirt. Then they started taking the dirt also until the culture that archaeologists call the Adena decided to stop the practice and refurbish all the old sites with fresh earth and stone to ensure they would survive and that the people would have a living testament to the former glories of their ancestors. This reclaiming of the old holy sites began roughly around 2,500 to 2,300 years ago (in other words 2,500 years after the creation of the Manitou), and continued until about AD 500 when everyone mysteriously vanished or went their separate ways to look for other places in the Mississippi Valley to refurbish. The ancient country of Manitouba was vast, and so there were plenty of other sites to fix up and rededicate. Hence an explosion of remarkably adept architectural masterpieces all throughout much of the Great South and of the Mississippi as we approach the historic period—returning full circle to Ohio. In this model, the same wave of inspiration refurbished the Manitou twice, the refurbishments 1,400 years apart, making it the oldest and youngest, the alpha and omega, of the Ohio Valley antiquities.

I'm doing the mental arithmetic. "So the 'Fort Ancient' work at Serpent Mound 1,000 years ago was the second of these restoration projects?"

"That's right," Ross replies, "as hopefully everyone, even the archaeologists involved in wrongly attributing the Mound solely to the Fort Ancient culture back in 1996, are now beginning to realize."

THE MANITOU AND THE MEGALITH

DEEP IN CONVERSATION, WE'VE WALKED along the bank of Brush Creek at the base of Serpent Mound ridge to its northwestern end where it comes to a point naturally targeting the summer solstice sunset. Trees and bushes cover everything here except the snout of the ridge itself, which thrusts a gnarled and weathered limestone cliff forward through the green veil, revealing an overhang and hints of caves.

Ross stops and holds up a hand. "Do you see it?" he says.

I look around. I'm bad at tests! Then my eyes fall on a chunky, moss-covered limestone megalith leaning into the bank among the undergrowth.

ABOVE RIGHT: Unenhanced image (PHOTO: SANTHA FAIIA) of the Serpent's head simulacrum in the cliff directly beneath the head of Serpent Mound. ABOVE LEFT: An enhanced image helps to explain why many travelers, and the ancients before them, could imagine this natural rocky outcrop as the head of a serpent. BELOW: Juxtaposition of Serpent Mound and the ridge on which it stands with its natural "serpent-like head."

It's not finely quarried but its relatively straight sides and corners, and the curved section cut out at one end, make it likely that humans have worked on it. It's over 9 feet in length, about 2 feet wide and something more than a foot thick, almost big enough to stand in at Avebury or Stonehenge as a replacement for one of the smaller megaliths there.

"Do you mean this megalith?" I ask.

"We'll come to that," says Ross, "but look past the megalith. Look above it."

"I see a cliff."

"But do you see the **face** in the cliff?"

The moment Ross says the word "face" everything swings into focus for me. It's not a human face but a serpent's face. That overhang is an upper jaw, there's the line of a mouth below it. Above the corner of the mouth to the right, much darker than the rest of the face, a distinct eye seems to gaze down at us.

In later research I'll find that many visitors have noticed the resemblance of this completely natural outcrop to the head of a serpent. In 1919, for example, Charles Willoughby of Harvard University's Peabody Museum visited Serpent Mound and concluded:

> The site chosen for this great effigy was probably determined largely by superstitions which may have been connected with the headland upon which it was built. This headland, rising to a height of about 100 feet, gradually narrows and terminates in a cliff, bearing a certain resemblance to the head of a reptile. . . . The contour of the head, the muzzle, the eye and mouth are clearly indicated. The Indians may also have seen in the promontory extending backward from the head along the shore of Bush creek, the body of the serpent deity. Natural formations, peculiarly shaped stones, concretions, and other objects resembling human or animal forms or any of their parts were generally supposed to possess supernatural powers, and in this instance, with a little imagination, one can easily approach the Indian's point of view.[7]

Earlier, in 1886, archaeologist W. H. Holmes came away from Serpent Mound with a similar impression. "Having the idea of a great serpent in the mind," he wrote in *Science,* one is at once struck with the remarkable contour of the bluff, and especially of the exposure of rock, which readily assumes the appearance of a colossal reptile lifting its front from the bed of the stream. The head is the point of rock, the dark lip-like edge is the muzzle, the light coloured underside is the white neck, the caves are the eyes, and the projecting masses to the right are the protruding coils of the body. The varying effects of light must greatly increase the vividness of the impressions, and nothing would be more natural than that the Sylvan prophet . . . should recognize this likeness and should at once regard the promontory as a great Manitou. His people would be led to regard it as such and the celebration of feasts upon the point would readily follow.

With a mound-building people, this would result in the erection of suitable enclosures and in the elaboration of the form of the reptile, that it might be the more real. The natural and the artificial features must all have related to one and the same conception. The point of naked rock was probably at first and always recognised as the head of both the natural and the modified body. It was to the Indian the real head of the great serpent Manitou.[8]

We're still standing by the megalith that first caught my attention. "What about this?" I ask. "Is this part of the Serpent Mound story or just a random chunk of rock?"

Ross shrugs. "Nobody knows for sure." He pauses before adding, "I've got my own theory though."

"Which is?"

"I think it's one of the large stones that Squier and Davis reported had stood in the oval earthwork in front of the Serpent's head in the nineteenth century."

"The ones they said had been scattered by some treasure hunter?"

"That's right," Ross replies. "And if I recall correctly, they also said those stones had been arranged in a circle before they were thrown down."

I know what Ross is reminding me of here is a connection he's written about between the geometry of Stonehenge and the geometry of Serpent Mound, which he regards as "two elements comprising a larger picture pointing to a highly evolved school of astro-architecture, the origin of which is not known."[9]

Graham Hancock (left) with Ross Hamilton (right) at Serpent Mound megalith. PHOTO: SANTHA FAIIA.

Therefore, while he does not dispute that Serpent Mound was the work of Native American geometers and astronomers, he believes that they were members of a much older school and implementing a much older design which likewise—at many different times and in many different media—was brought into commission in many other parts of the world as well.

This fundamental, endlessly reiterated, endlessly reincarnated design, he says, "seems to have no home base—no specific country or culture responsible for its phenomenon."[10]

This, however, is precisely what we would expect if it's "home base" were a lost civilization destroyed so completely, and so deeply buried in time, that it has been reduced to the stuff of myths and legends.

WHAT THE SERPENT SEES

IN THE HOUR BEFORE SUNSET, as a refreshing chill enters the air, we're back at the upper level of Serpent Mound with all batteries charged and the drone ready to fly.

The sun, which rose north of east this morning, seems already drawn down low on its arc toward its setting point on the northwestern horizon, and again we notice the effective "blinding" of the serpent by the dense trees allowed to flourish along its line of sight as a matter of deliberate policy by the Ohio History Connection. It's obvious, if we did not have the drone, that we would get at best only faint impressions and hints of the alignment if a few scattered sunbeams somehow found their way through the thicket.

"This isn't how it's supposed to be!" I say to Ross. "It feels almost like sacrilege."

"But the good news is people are waking up again, here and everywhere else. Regardless of what the Ohio History Connection wants or does, or what the archaeologists tell us we should believe, we're at one of those junctures in the cycle where the Manitou is reactivated as a source of knowledge and wisdom."

With a soft buzz of its rotors, Santha's little drone climbs into the sky and we cluster around the monitor to share the aerial view. It's 7:55 pm and from an altitude of 400 feet uncluttered by trees, we can see that the sun still has some distance to travel before it conjuncts the range of hills forming the local horizon to the northwest. The warm, mellow light of the end of a summer's day interspersed with patterns of cool, deep shade dapples the immense earthwork along its entire length and despite the trees closing in around its head it seems truly master of its enchanted kingdom.

Santha has the drone hovering in place near the back of the Serpent's neck overlooking its open jaws, the great oval, the trees, and the horizon far beyond. It's the perfect shot but by 8:12 pm, the glare is so intense that it's difficult to be certain exactly where the sun now sits in relation to the horizon. There's a great scooped out hollow of silver light there and the sun's disk is somewhere in the middle of it. A shift in position of the drone, however, confirms that sunset is still some time off.

At 8:13 pm, we bring the device down for a battery change and relaunch it, but just 11 minutes later, at 8:24, the control panel lights up with a low-battery warning. The ponderous roll of the earth toward the east, the majestic descent of the sun toward the west, seem to have synced into a kind of slow-motion dream sequence and, with no alternative, hoping we have not miscalculated the timing of the universe, we bring the drone back to earth.

There's something seriously wrong with it. Not the battery problem—that was easily solved—but something in the communications between the control unit and the little quadcopter. In the 28 minutes it takes to fix it we can feel the light leaching out of the sky. The evening air grows cool and the shadows cast by the trees lengthen. The sun's still in the heavens—somewhere!—but whether it has dropped behind the hills yet or whether we'll still have a chance to witness that moment is completely unclear when the drone finally starts to obey orders again and we're able to relaunch it at 8:52 pm.

Santha rockets it straight up to 400 feet, to the vantage point she'd found before, and we all give a cheer as we see in the monitor, as though by some miracle, that the sun is indeed still with us and poised exactly on the rim of the hills that the Hardmans dubbed "Solstice Ridge."

The next 3 minutes are magical as the great luminary, source of all life on earth, begins its final descent into night. It's a transformation and a transition rather than an abrupt change of state.

The glare that dazzled the camera earlier is much reduced now, and little by little the sky fills with the most seductive soft glow and the sun's disk seems to excavate a niche in the horizon, where, as readers can confirm from the photographs, its setting is indeed in very fine alignment with the open jaws of the Serpent.

There it reclines, seemingly still, shedding its brilliance and beneficence across this golden land of bounteous fields and forests, as though in deep communion with the earth. I'm reminded of a passage from the *Ancient Egyptian Book of the Dead,* a hymn addressed to Ra the Sun God:

Men praise thee in thy name "Ra" and they swear by thee, for thou art lord over them. Thou hearest with thine ears and thou seest with thine eyes. Millions of years have gone over the world; I cannot tell the number of those through which thou hast passed. . . . Thou dost pass over and dost travel through untold spaces requiring millions and hundreds of thousands of years to pass over; thou passest through them in peace and thou steerest thy way across the watery abyss to the place which thou lovest; this thou doest in one little moment of time, and then thou dost sink down and dost make an end of the hours.[11]

Over Serpent Mound the drama continues to unfold, this love affair of planet and star, ground and sky, above and below, this beautiful and moving alignment sustained for a long, lingering interval as the sun continues its descent.

Half its disk has disappeared from view now, then three quarters, then just a glimmering, radiant shimmering sliver somehow enduring on the horizon, and then at last it's gone entirely but for a warm, all-embracing afterblush that blossoms in the gloaming.

OLD CERTAINTIES

IF SERPENT MOUND HAD BEEN kept clear of trees by the successive cultures that venerated and repeatedly restored the great effigy, then the alignment within the wide spread of the Serpent's jaws would always have been a striking feature here from the time of the retreat of the ice sheets more than 13,000 years ago. Because of the shifting tilt of the earth's axis, however, the exact point on the horizon where the summer solstice sun would set would shift several degrees north and south of its present position over the 41,000-year obliquity cycle.

We've already seen how the Hardmans were taken to task in the 1980s for mistakenly proposing a summer solstice sunset alignment at an azimuth as viewed from Serpent Mound that—according to the calculations of their critics Fletcher and Cameron—coincided with a date of 11,000 BC. Archaeologists at the time considered that date far too early for any civilization capable of creating a structure of the scale and complexity of Serpent Mound to have evolved in North America and accordingly no further investigation of this rather intriguing anomaly was ever undertaken.

The 1980s are long gone, however, and in the twenty-first century, as we'll see in part 2, new evidence has emerged that calls all the old certainties into question.

PART II

NEW WORLD?

⟨ ⟩⟩ ● ⟨⟨ ⟩

The Mystery of the First Americans

4

A PAST NOT SO MUCH
HIDDEN AS DENIED

ALTHOUGH HE HIMSELF IS NOT an archaeologist, Tom Deméré, curator of paleontology at the San Diego Natural History Museum in California, does have occasion to work with archaeologists. I was therefore not surprised when his response to my request to interview him and have him show me certain stones and bones in the museum's archives was declined. My initial approach was on September 18, 2017, and the polite refusal came on September 20, not from Dr. Deméré himself but from Rebecca Handelsman, the museum's communications director. "While we're unable to accommodate your request for a meeting," she wrote, "I'd like to share with you our online press kit which has a wealth of information about the project and the discovery."[1]

Though they have their place, press kits are low on my list of priorities when I'm researching books, and because of the very special nature of what Rebecca called "the project and the discovery," I was not going to be so easily fobbed off. Demèré had been closely involved from the outset with the excavation of a controversial site near San Diego and had published a paper in 2017 claiming that humans had been present there as early as 130,000 years ago.[2] The paper was a prominent one, since it appeared in the prestigious scientific journal *Nature,* and almost immediately aroused the fury of archaeologists committed to a much later date for the peopling of the Americas.

Among them was Professor Donald Grayson of the University of Washington.[3] "I have read that paper," he sniped, "and I was astonished by it. I was astonished not because it is so good, but because it is so bad."[4]

In a response that was typical of many, David J. Meltzer, professor of prehistory at Southern Methodist University in Dallas, Texas, also dismissed the paper. "If you are going to push human antiquity in the New World back more than 100,000 years in one fell swoop," he said, "you'll have to do so with a far better archaeological case than this one. I'm not buying what's being sold."[5]

Gary Haynes, professor emeritus of anthropology at the University of Nevada, went so far as to accuse *Nature* of "an editorial lapse in judgment" for publishing the paper at all.[6]

Jon M. Erlandson, director of the University of Oregon's Museum of Natural and Cultural History, said "the site is not credible."[7]

Earlier, foreseeing such reactions, George Jefferson, former associate curator of the Page Museum in Los Angeles, had warned Demèré that the archaeological community, invested in long-established notions of the recent peopling of the Americas, wasn't even close to being ready for a claim of antiquity as remote as 130,000 years. "Keep it under wraps," he advised. "No one will believe you."[8]

But Demèré was sure of the evidence and decided to go ahead. The *Nature* paper, published in April 2017, was the result and quickly caught my attention.

DON'T SAY A WORD ABOUT LOST CIVILIZATIONS

COULD DEMÈRÉ'S CLAIM BE TRUE? Rather than having been in America for 30,000 years or less, as archaeologists have recently been dragged kicking and screaming to accept, could our ancestors have populated the continent 130,000 years ago or more?

If the facts checked out (and, I had to keep reminding myself, despite the hostile reactions of some academics, that *Nature* would not have published the paper without having it thoroughly peer-reviewed first), then they raised serious question marks over how complete our understanding of prehistory really is.

In particular, and to get right to the point, what could those very early Americans and their descendants have been *doing* during all the tens of thousands of years that archaeologists insisted they weren't present at all? My whole focus, since long before the publication of *Fingerprints of the Gods* in 1995, has been a quest for a high civilization of remote antiquity, a civilization that can rightly be described as "lost" because the very fact that it existed at all has been overlooked by archaeologists. I couldn't help but wonder, therefore, whether some traces of it might be found in those 100,000 lost years of the Americas.

So I persisted with Deméré, writing to him several times through the formidable Rebecca Handelsman, setting out the reasons why I wanted to interview him and providing more background on my own work. "Is it possible," I asked, "that missing pages in the story of the origins of civilization might await discovery in North America—the very last place, until now, that archaeologists have thought to look?"[9]

Pointing out that other, now-extinct human species had been present in the world 130,000 years ago and had interbred with anatomically modern humans, I also asked which *species* of human he thought might have been involved at his site. "Were they anatomically modern? Were they Neanderthals? Were they Denisovans? Or were they one of the several other species of *Homo* that will likely be identified by further research in the coming years?"[10]

For days I heard no more and then, on October 2, 2017, Rebecca wrote again to report that Dr. Deméré had agreed to a "brief meeting" with me, that he was willing to discuss his site and the evidence for an early human presence that it yielded, but that he would not "speculate on what species it may have been or on broader topics/hypotheses re ancient civilizations."[11]

I accepted these constraints and the interview was arranged for the next day, Tuesday, October 3. Whatever I got out of him it would surely add something to the museum's press kit and, besides, Deméré's reticence made perfect sense to me. The last thing he wanted while his own work was under attack was to be associated with what archaeologists call "crackpot theories" about a lost civilization promulgated by a "pseudoscientist" like myself. If I were in his shoes, frankly, I would have been cautious, too. Indeed, I was quite surprised that he'd agreed to talk to me at all.

FORGOTTEN AMERICA

AT THE OUTSET OF THE twentieth century many scholars took the view that the Americas had been devoid of any human presence *until less than 4,000 years ago.*[12]

To put that in perspective, by 4,000 years ago the civilization of Egypt was already ancient, Minoan Crete flourished, and Stonehenge and other great megalithic sites had been built across Europe. Likewise, by 4,000 years ago, our ancestors had been in Australia for about 65,000 years and had found their way to the farthest reaches of Asia at almost equally remote dates.[13]

So why should the Americas have escaped this global migration, and this seemingly unstoppable march toward high civilization, until so late?

The answer, perhaps, is that the most influential figure in disseminating and enforcing the view that the New World had only recently been populated by humans was a frowning and fearsome anthropologist named Aleš Hrdlička who, in 1903, was selected to head the newly created Division of Physical Anthropology at the Smithsonian Institution's National Museum of Natural History in Washington, DC. There he would remain until his death in 1943, deploying his intimidating authority as "the most eminent physical anthropologist of his time," "the gatekeeper of humankind's recent origins in the New World" to quash any and every attempt to suggest great human antiquity in the Americas.[14] Frank H. H. Roberts, a colleague of Hrdlička's at the Smithsonian, would later admit of this period, "Questions of early man in America became virtually taboo, and no anthropologist desirous of a successful career would tempt the fate of ostracism by intimating that he had discovered indications of respectable antiquity for the Indian."[15]

But eminence can only suppress facts for so long, and throughout the

1920s and 1930s compelling evidence began to emerge that people had reached the Americas thousands of years earlier than Hrdlička supposed. Of particular importance in this gradual undermining of the great man's authority was a site called Blackwater Draw near the town of Clovis, New Mexico, where bones of extinct Ice Age mammals were found in 1929 and assumed, rightly, to be very old. The Smithsonian sent a representative, Charles Gilmore, to take a look at the site but—perhaps unsurprisingly under Hrdlička's malign shadow—he concluded that no further investigation was justified.[16]

Anthropologist Edgar B. Howard of the University of Pennsylvania disagreed.[17] He began excavations at Blackwater Draw in 1933, quickly finding quantities of beautifully crafted stone projectiles with distinctive "fluted" points—so-called on account of a characteristic vertical "flute" or channel cut into the base. The points were found in direct association with (and in a few cases even buried between the ribs of) extinct Ice Age fauna such as Columbian mammoth, camel, horse, bison, saber-toothed cat, and dire wolf.[18] In 1935, on the basis of these finds, Howard published a book in which he concluded that it was possible that humans had been in North America for tens of thousands of years.[19] Further seasons of meticulous fieldwork followed before he presented his findings, to widespread approbation and acceptance, at a prestigious international forum on Early Man and the Origins of the Human Race held in Philadelphia on March 18–20, 1937.[20]

Hrdlička was there. He gloweringly ignored the implications of the discoveries at Blackwater Draw and instead used his time onstage to reaffirm his long-held position that, for American Indians, "So far as skeletal remains are concerned, there is at this moment no evidence that would justify the assumption of great, i.e. geological, antiquity."[21]

But the clock was ticking. Before and after 1943, the year in which both Howard and Hrdlička died, further discoveries of fluted points of the Blackwater Draw type—increasingly referred to as "Clovis points" after the nearby town of that name—continued to be made. This ever-accumulating mass of new evidence left no room for doubt and even the most stubborn conservatives (Hrdlička excepted) were eventually forced to agree that the Clovis culture had hunted animals that became extinct at the end of the last Ice Age and that humans must therefore have been in the Americas for at least 12,000 years.

This gave a huge boost to research, leading in the decades ahead to the discovery of around 1,500 further Clovis sites, and more than 10,000 Clovis

An array of Clovis points with a Clovis blade second from left. PHOTOS: SANTHA
FAIIA AND, FAR RIGHT, NATURAL HISTORY MUSEUM OF UTAH.

points, at locations scattered all across North America.[22] As the net widened,
however, a number of anomalies of the culture began to be identified. A confusing outcome of this is that there are now two schools of thought around
its proposed antiquity and duration. The so-called long interval school dates
the first appearance of Clovis in North America to 13,400 years ago and
its mysterious extinction and disappearance from the archaeological record
to around 12,800 years ago—a period of 600 years.[23] The "short interval"
school also accepts 12,800 years ago for the end date of Clovis but sets the
start date at 13,000 years ago—therefore allowing it an existence of just 200
years.[24] Both schools agree that this unique and distinctive culture must have
originated *somewhere else* because, from the first evidence for its presence, it
is already sophisticated and fully formed, deploying advanced weapons and
hunting tactics.[25] Particularly puzzling, since it is the archaeological consensus that the human migration into the Americas was launched from northeast
Asia, is the fact that no traces of the *early* days of Clovis, of the previous
evolution and development of its characteristic tools, weapons, and lifeways,
have been found anywhere in Asia.[26] All we can say for sure is that once it had
made its presence felt in North America the Clovis culture spread very widely
across a huge swath of the continent,[27] with sites as far apart as Alaska, northern Mexico, New Mexico, South Carolina, Florida, Montana, Pennsylvania,

and Washington state.[28] Such an expansion would have been extremely rapid were it to have occurred in 600 years and seems almost miraculously fast if it was in fact accomplished in 200 years.[29]

THE LAND BRIDGE AND THE
ICE-FREE CORRIDOR

DURING THE 1940s AND 1950s, as the fame of Clovis continued to grow, no evidence was forthcoming—or, to state the matter more exactly, none that was generally accepted, approved, and confirmed by the archaeological community—of any kind of human presence in the Americas older than the earliest Clovis dates of around 13,400 years ago.

As regards the matter of general acceptance, despite a few dissenting voices[30] a consensus soon began to emerge that no older cultures would *ever* be found—and what is now known as the "Clovis First" paradigm was conceived. We might say, however, that it was not officially "born" until September 1964. That was when archaeologist C. Vance Haynes, today Regents Professor Emeritus of Anthropology at the University of Arizona and a senior member of the National Academy of Sciences, published a landmark paper in the journal *Science*. Snappily titled "Fluted Projectile Points: Their Age and Dispersion,"[31] the paper presented, and persuasively supported, a number of key assertions.

First, Haynes pointed out that, because of lowered sea level during the Ice Age, much of the area occupied today by the Bering Sea was above water, and where the Bering Strait now is, a tundra-covered landscape connected eastern Siberia and western Alaska. Although not a particularly easy environment, it would, Haynes argued, "have presented no obstacle" to nomadic hunters who were already masters of the Siberian tundra and who would certainly have followed the herds of bison, deer, and mammoth that roamed across it.[32]

Once over the land bridge, however, it was Haynes's case that the migrant hunters could not have ventured very far before confronting the daunting barrier of the Cordilleran and Laurentide Ice Sheets, which were at the time merged into a single impassable mountainous mass covering most of the northern half of North America.

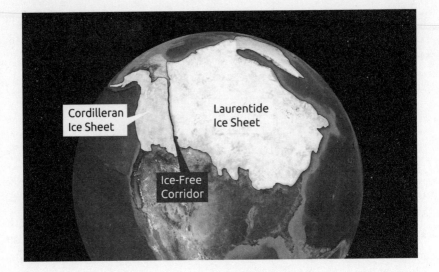

They therefore had no access to the lands that lay beyond. As a result, prevailing in the ice-free southern half of North America during this phase of the last Ice Age were "conditions as favorable to the existence of herbivorous megafauna, which man could hunt, as conditions during the time of the Clovis occupation, yet there is not the slightest evidence of man's presence."[33]

Things changed around 14,100 years ago, Haynes claimed, when a generalized warming of global climate caused an ice-free corridor to open up between the Laurentide and the Cordilleran ice caps, allowing entry for the first time in many millennia to the rich, unglaciated plains, teeming with game, that lay to the south.[34]

Some 700 years later, around 13,400 years ago, the stratigraphic record of those plains starts to include Clovis artifacts. Their "abrupt appearance," Haynes argued, supports the view "that Clovis progenitors passed through Canada" and that "from the seemingly rapid and wide dispersal of Clovis points . . . it appears these people may have brought the technique of fluting with them."[35]

As noted earlier, no Clovis points have ever been found in Asia,[36] but when Haynes published his landmark paper in *Science* in 1964 he reported correctly that four had been found "on the surface" in Alaska and another in the Canadian Yukon, all undated,[37] with the oldest dated points south of the former ice margin going back no further than 13,400 years. To Haynes this looked like the last link "in a logical sequence of events, and the pieces begin to fall into place. If Clovis progenitors traversed a corridor through Canada . . . and dispersed through the United States south of the . . . ice border in the ensuing 700 years, then they were probably in Alaska some 500 years earlier. . . . The Alaskan fluted points . . . *could* represent this occupation and *could,* therefore, be ancestral to Clovis points and blades."[38]

The paper was welcomed by archaeologists,[39] most of whom were already convinced that Clovis was "First," and virtually overnight what had been at best a persuasive and seemingly well-constructed theory morphed into the new ruling orthodoxy. Worse, it soon became every bit as rigid and intolerant as the orthodoxy of Hrdlička's time and it would retain ultimate authority over archaeological careers and research priorities for decades to come with a grip every bit as firm as Hrdlička's iron fist.

In a familiar refrain, those who disagreed with "Clovis First," or were fool-hardy enough to report possible pre-Clovis sites, did so "at significant risk to their careers."[40] Indeed by 2012 the bullying behavior of the Clovis First lobby had grown so unpleasant that it attracted the attention of the editor of *Nature,* who opined: "The debate over the first Americans has been one of the most acrimonious—and unfruitful—in all of science. . . . One researcher, new to the field after years of working on other contentious topics, told *Nature* that he had never before witnessed the level of aggression that swirled around the issue of who reached America first."[41]

CHALLENGING CLOVIS FIRST

TOM DILLEHAY, PROFESSOR OF ANTHROPOLOGY at Vanderbilt University in Tennessee, began excavations at Monte Verde in southern Chile in 1977 and found evidence that humans had been present there as far back as 18,500 years ago.[42] The progress of science eventually vindicated him, as we shall see, but before it did so Dillehay had to endure sustained and often deeply unpleasant personal attacks from Clovis Firsters for more than 20 years.

He was attacked because there are no Clovis artifacts at Monte Verde, it is 5,000 years older than the oldest securely dated Clovis sites, and it is located more than 8,000 miles south of the Bering Strait.

The reader will not have forgotten that the strait was dry during the lowered sea level of the last Ice Age—a tundra-covered land bridge across which the Clovis people were believed to have migrated on foot from northeast Siberia and thence into the Americas through the ice-free corridor between the Cordilleran and Laurentide Ice Sheets. The credibility of Clovis First depends crucially on the supposed close chronological link between the opening up of that ice-free corridor around 14,100 years ago and the first appearance of Clovis artifacts south of the ice margin around 13,400 years ago. By putting humans in the Americas more than 4,000 years *before* the opening of the ice-free corridor, Monte Verde showed that "link" to be illusory. Moreover, by putting them not in North America but in South America, with no means of transport available to them other than boats of some sort, it questioned fundamental assumptions about the technical and organizational capacities of our ancestors, hitherto judged to be too low to allow such adventures at such a remote period.

Tom Dillehay's most dogged and determined critic, perhaps predictably, has been C. Vance Haynes, whose 1964 paper launched the Clovis First theory and who by 1988 had used his influence, and his outreach in the scientific journals, to dismiss every case thus far made for supposedly pre-Clovis sites in the Americas.[43]

Except Monte Verde. Even for Haynes, this Chilean site was proving to be an exceptionally tough nut to crack. Realizing that the implications for American archaeology of Tom Dillehay being right were immense, Haynes wrote to David Meltzer at SMU to suggest that "a panel of objective conservatives should be formed and funded by NSF [National Science Foundation] to visit the site, examine it, take samples, etc. If a positive consensus results we can then accept the interpretation and formulate new hypotheses for the peopling of the New World. If not, Monte Verde will have to be relegated to the bin of possible pre-Clovis sites awaiting further data."[44]

James M. Adovasio, a world expert in perishable artifacts and former director of the Mercyhurst Archaeological Institute at Mercyhurst University in Erie, Pennsylvania, was closely involved in the events that followed. He tells us that he would be remiss if he "did not point out that by the oxymoron 'objective conservatives,' Haynes meant himself and the Clovis First disciples."[45]

In the end, however, after 7 years of haggling, a balanced group was put together, "not configured as a panel of pre-Clovis skeptics or, conversely, pre-Clovis enthusiasts," says Adovasio: "rather, it was, as designed, a mixed bag reflecting a range of views."[46]

The site visit took place over 3 days in January 1997, and far from relegating Monte Verde to the "bin," all members of the group eventually signed on to an official report confirming that it was indeed an archaeological site and that Dillehay's dates were correct. The report was published in October 1997 in *American Antiquity* and left no room for any conclusion other than that Monte Verde predated Clovis; it even considered the "extremely intriguing" possibility that the human presence there might go back as far 33,000 years.[47]

In his important book *The First Americans*, Adovasio, who was present at the proceedings throughout, provides a blow-by-blow account of how the panel arrived at its conclusions, and of the follow-up.[48] It seems that Haynes was not happy, despite being a signatory to the report, and even as it appeared in print he began to voice doubts over it to colleagues, questioning again the antiquity of Monte Verde and "suggesting a wondrous new array of hypothetical events that could have contaminated the site in some previously unperceived way."[49]

Haynes and Adovasio had crossed swords before—over Meadowcroft, a site in Pennsylvania that Adovasio had excavated in the 1970s that revealed eleven well-defined stratigraphic units with evidence of human occupation "spanning at least 16,000 years and perhaps 19,000 years."[50] Inevitably, because it threatened Clovis First, this attracted the hostility of Haynes, who, in the years that followed, sought to quibble away almost every aspect of Adovasio's evidence: "In scientific paper after scientific paper, Haynes . . . asked for yet another date, yet another study, raising yet other picayune and fanciful questions about Meadowcroft, most of which had been answered long before he asked them—not just in the original excavation procedures but in report after report."[51]

Again, as was the case with Monte Verde, the constant quibbling and demands for ever more evidence, when the evidence in place was already more than adequate, was demoralizing and had the effect of slowing down the research effort but ultimately did not prevent formal recognition of Meadowcroft Rockshelter as a National Historic Landmark with an age of more than 16,000 years.[52]

Likewise, in the 1990s, Canadian archaeologist Jacques Cinq-Mars excavated Bluefish Caves in the Yukon and found evidence of human activity there dating back more than 24,000 years—older than Meadowcroft and much older than Clovis. The price he paid was high. His competence and his sanity were questioned and when he attempted to present his findings at conferences he was ignored or insulted.[53] One colleague stated matters bluntly: "When Jacques proposed [that Bluefish Caves were] 24,000 [years old], it was not accepted."[54]

As a result of such attitudes, funding drained away and Cinq-Mars had to stop his work, only to be proved correct, many years later, by a new scientific study of the evidence from the caves published in January 2017.[55]

That study, one of several that confirmed the existence of pre-Clovis sites of increasingly ancient dates,[56] was titled *Earliest Human Presence in North America*.

Only 4 months later, on April 27, 2017, Tom Demére's paper announcing the discovery of "a 130,000-year-old archaeological site in southern California, USA," appeared in *Nature*.[57]

That's about ten times older than Clovis, eight times older than Meadowcroft, and more than five times as old as Bluefish Caves.

The resulting furor was, in retrospect, inevitable.

5

MESSAGE FROM A MASTODON

THE SAN DIEGO NATURAL HISTORY Museum, affectionately known to locals as "The Nat," is situated in the lush gardens of Balboa Park, which served as the venue for the 1915 Panama-California Exposition. Originally called "City Park," it was renamed for the exposition in honor of Spanish-born Vasco Nuñez de Balboa (1475–1519), who conducted a murderous exploratory raid across Panama and became the first European to see the Pacific Ocean.[1]

Balboa Park was repurposed after the closure of the exposition and now hosts seventeen museums and cultural institutions, among which The Nat stands out for its excellent collections and for its research expertise. As Santha and I strolled toward it on a bright Southern California morning, we couldn't help but reflect on the irony. In a museum in a park named after an arriviste European adventurer, we were about to be shown evidence that might speak to the truly vast antiquity of Native Americans in the lands that Europeans had stolen from them with fire and sword.

Rebecca Handelsman had asked us to meet her at The Nat's south entrance but we were early so we spent some time in the north atrium first, which is dominated by a looming skeleton cast of an Allosaur, a predatory dinosaur a bit like its more famous younger cousin Tyrannosaurus rex.

Scientists now agree that *T. rex* and the entire nonavian Dinosauria clade became extinct virtually overnight after a large asteroid or comet—more likely the latter[2]—hit the Gulf of Mexico around 65 million years ago. There is also no doubt that it was this sudden and cataclysmic eradication of dinosaurs from the planet that opened the way for the rapid, uncontested expansion into new niches of the hitherto-insignificant mammalian line. We humans today are among the descendants of those early mammals.

It's thought-provoking, isn't it, that cosmic impacts, whether by asteroids or by comets, can sometimes be of such magnitude that they drastically redirect the evolutionary path of life on earth. It has happened more than once, as we shall see. However, a cataclysm was **not** to blame 130,000 years ago when a lone mastodon, perhaps old or sick, died on a floodplain in Southern California and was subsequently scavenged, with the carcass then quite rapidly covered by, and entombed in, a deposit of silty, sandy, fine-grained sediment.[3] There it remained undisturbed until November 1992, when the California Department of Transportation undertook highway construction on State Route 54 where San Diego borders National City.[4] It was routine practice for paleontologists from The Nat to monitor road-grading in Southern California in case any important fossil material was exposed, and Richard Cerutti, the monitor on duty at SR 54, spotted the fossilized bones and the tusk of what he at first thought was a mammoth.[5] He halted construction in the immediate vicinity until a proper excavation could be undertaken, and called in his boss, Dr. Tom Deméré, to lead it.[6]

Working together with a team of other researchers from The Nat, Cerutti and Deméré very quickly established that the fossilized remains, including many bones, both tusks, and several of the animal's teeth, belonged to a mastodon.[7] Like the mammoths, to which they were closely related, mastodons were swept from the face of the earth in the sudden and mysterious extinction of America's Ice Age megafauna that took place around 12,800 years ago[8]—

the same epoch exactly that saw the equally abrupt and equally mysterious disappearance of the Clovis culture.

From quite early on both Cerutti—after whom the site is now named—and Deméré were intrigued by what the excavation revealed: "Many of the bones were strangely fractured—or missing entirely. And there were several large stones, found in the same sediment layer as the bones and teeth, that appeared out of place. It looked like an archaeological site—like the preserved evidence of human activity."[9]

As well as the hefty rocks, unusual in fine-grained sediment, smaller pieces of sharply broken stone were found peppered throughout the Cerutti Mastodon Site: "This is not typically something you would see as a result of normal geological processes. The combination of stones . . . together with broken bones was interesting and instigated speculation regarding the possibility of human activity at the site."[10]

At first intriguing, the implications of the data grew worrying when it began to become obvious that the site was *extremely* ancient, lying embedded in sediments "that had been deposited much earlier, during a period long before humans were thought to have arrived on the continent."[11] In the early 1990s, radiometric techniques capable of peering much further back into the past than the standard 50,000-year limit for carbon dating[12] were already available. Unfortunately, however, they had not yet attained sufficient accuracy to give scientists a high level of confidence in the age range suspected for the Cerutti Mastodon Site.[13]

The end result, after key finds were moved to The Nat where they were housed in the archives, was that the site was reburied and abandoned. Despite its anomalous character and suspected importance, it was just too explosive to put before the scrutiny of hostile archaeologists while the dates remained uncertain. "If you claim something is that old you get blasted," Cerutti said, referring to the Clovis First lobby, "which is why some archaeologists stopped working on sites like this. They didn't want to get blasted."[14]

It wasn't that the Cerutti Mastodon Site was completely forgotten in the 25 years after the excavation stopped. It's on record that Tom Deméré invited several other researchers to study the collection of key finds kept at The Nat, but none did so.[15]

Robson Bonnichsen, founder of the Center for the Study of the First

Americans, warned him that "research that contributes to First American Studies is a game of hardball."[16]

Months ran into years with no journal article on the site even drafted, let alone published, nor any further investigation undertaken. Cerutti, reportedly, was so disappointed that he stopped going anywhere near State Route 54.[17] The whole exciting matter seemed to have fallen into stagnation.

It was not until 2014, more than two decades after the mastodon's discovery, that the tide decisively turned.[18] Built on improved understanding of processes that incorporate natural uranium and its decay products in fossil bone, a newly enhanced technique, known as 230 Th/U radiometric dating, was now available that could settle the age of the Cerutti deposit once and for all. Demeré therefore sent several of the mastodon bones to the US Geological Survey in Colorado, where geologist Jim Paces, using the updated and refined technique, established beyond reasonable doubt that the bones were buried 130,000 years ago.[19]

Now things began to move much more swiftly and it was time to reexamine the strange fractures on some of the bones that had been noticed back in 1992 and also to take a much closer look at the "out of place" stones and rocks found in the same sediment layer. To this end the large and eclectic team of investigators who would eventually coauthor the landmark 2017 paper in *Nature* had already begun to form. Tom Demeré and Richard Cerutti were at the heart of it but other members included Dr. Steve Holen, curator of archaeology at the Denver Museum of Nature and Science, a specialist in the ancient uses of bone, Professor Daniel Fisher of the Department of Earth and Environmental Sciences, University of Michigan, Dr. Richard Fullagar of the Centre for Archaeological Science, University of Wollongong, and Dr. James Paces, Research Geologist at the US Geological Survey.[20]

It was a formidable team, their work was meticulous, and publication of the paper in *Nature* meant that archaeologists, just then cautiously emerging from the shadow of the Clovis First paradigm and adjusting themselves with difficulty to ages in the few tens of thousands of years for sites like Monte Verde, Meadowcroft, and Bluefish Caves, were now obliged to contemplate a site dating back to the Eemian, the last interglacial period that extended from roughly 140,000 years ago down to about 120,000 years ago when the Pleistocene ice sheets began to expand again.[21]

At that point in 2017 it was still believed—though new evidence would soon substantially change the picture[22]—that anatomically modern humans had not even left their African homeland 140,000 years ago.

So how could they possibly have gotten to America before they'd even set out on the epic migrations by which they populated the world?

Having researched the Clovis First wars, and indeed the whole story of prehistoric archaeology in the United States from the late nineteenth century onward, I was just beginning to realize how staggering the implications of all this really were.

TOM DEMÉRÉ'S BONES AND STONES

THE NAT'S MAIN ATRIUM, WHERE the allosaur lurks, is accessed through the museum's north entrance, so just before 11 am Santha and I walked around the west side of the four-story building and presented ourselves at the south entrance. Beyond it was a second atrium, where we were encouraged to see that much of the space was devoted to a well-attended exhibition honoring the Cerutti Mastodon Site.

Out of the crowd, Rebecca Handelsman appeared. Tom Deméré would join us in a moment, she said. While we waited, she walked us over to a display case containing a mock-up of the sediment matrix from the site into which, point down and visible through the glass side of the case, was set a mastodon tusk. It was a little shorter than my arm, but it was obviously not complete as the upper part had been crudely broken off.

"This is the tusk that first attracted Richard Cerutti's attention," Rebecca explained, and before I could ask she added, "Its upper part was clipped off by the backhoe before he could stop the construction work."

"Is the way it's displayed here the way it was found?" I asked.

"Exactly that way." She paused and waved. "Look, here's Tom. He can tell you all about it."

Weaving through the crowd was a man of pleasant aspect, spare and lean after a lifetime of fieldwork, wearing blue jeans and a brick-red shirt. From my background reading I knew he was 69 years old, though he appeared younger, and as we shook hands I saw he had penetrating gray eyes and an easy smile. Despite the risk to his reputation of even talking to a "pseudoscientist" like me, he seemed relaxed and friendly.

I launched straight in on the subject of the tusk. "What's so special about it?" I asked Tom.

"The way it was set into the ground so it would have stood upright. The other one lay in a natural horizontal position beside it but this one was found like you see it in the display. Vertical. And that, to us, immediately looked like an anomaly."

"Why?"

"One suggestion is that it was perhaps left there as a marker to come back to the site on a floodplain where everything is low relief. . . . I mean, who knows? I don't know what sort of noncultural process would put a tusk vertical. I just don't understand it."

"So what you're saying is that this looks like the result of human behavior? That it's evidence of a deliberate, intelligent act?"

"It seems like that to me, and to many others—though I have to say our critics aren't persuaded!"

I take this as my cue to ask Tom if he and his team had been surprised by the level of skeptical response to the *Nature* paper.

"I expected we'd have pushback," he replied. "I just hoped it would have been more objective."

"I suppose that in any profession and any career people get very emotionally involved . . ."

"Apparently! I'm not used to it from a paleontological standpoint. I mean, there's passion in paleontology, too, but I'm not used to this sort of thing."

I restrain myself from stating my view that "this sort of thing"—namely sniping, quibbling, misrepresentation, straw-man arguments, and vituperative ad hominem attacks leveled against anyone suggesting deep antiquity for the First Americans—is perfectly normal among archaeologists, and Santha and I gratefully accept Tom's offer to talk us through the exhibits.

The anomalous tusk is just a small part of the story, he says. The stronger evidence comes from the mastodon's fossilized bones, and from the rocks and stones of various sizes found distributed around the site.[23]

In humans the femur is the long bone of the thigh. At its upper end it has a ball-like protrusion, the femur head, that articulates with a socket in the pelvis and thus—wondrous nature!—enables us to walk. Though they stood on four legs it was no different for mastodons. Their femora were their upper hind limbs and, just like our femora, were surmounted by ball-like heads set into their pelvic sockets.

Tom draws our attention to the hefty, almost hemispherical detached heads of the mastodon's two femora, one with the rounded end down, the other with the rounded end up, sitting side by side in a display case. "This is how they were found when we excavated them," he says. And he points out a rock next to them that he calls an "anvil stone," adding that there wasn't much left of the femora themselves.

The significance of this is not immediately obvious to me so I ask Tom to elaborate.

"We suggest that this was a work station,[24] that both femora were hammered and broken here on the anvil stone and that the heads were detached and just set off to the side. It feels purposeful, like the tusk. It feels like humans were breaking these bones and it's not only what's *here* that's important but also what's not here. I mean, originally the femora from which these heads came were three feet in length and massively thick, yet we have just a few pieces of them . . ."

"So that would suggest, what, that the other pieces were taken away?"

"Yes. I mean, if it was equipment damage, you'd think you'd have the whole femur, right? So the fact that we have missing bits suggests to us that they were taken away, which fits this idea of human processing and transportation."

In the next display case are the few large fragments of femur that were found at the site and multiple smaller flakes of bone that were found lying around them.

"We interpret these as cone flakes," Tom explains. "So when a bone is struck by a stone hammer you have damage on the impact side but also you have these flakes come out on the other side. At the point of impact you have a small hole and the exit point of that impact is a larger hole, and so these are flakes that are created by impacts."

"I suppose one question would be—they took away bits of the femora, so why didn't they take the tusks? Because the tusks, presumably, would have offered them useful materials, too?"

"But they're also heavy," Tom points out. "Whereas bones are relatively transportable. We have a pattern and the pattern begs for an explanation and what we feel fits that pattern is human transportation."

"Did you find anything that was obviously a tool?"

"No." Tom appears untroubled by what some critics regard as a fatal argument against his case.

I seek clarification. "So if we're saying that humans did this, then we're saying that they just took advantage of natural rocks and they used those as hammers and anvils basically?"[25]

"That's one of the problems the skeptics have," Tom admits cheerfully, "that there are no fashioned tools, no flaked stone tools, that there are no knives, no scrapers, no choppers."

"But if I'm correct, you're arguing that can be explained—because what these ancient humans were doing was extracting the marrow from the bones.[26] They were smashing up the bones. They didn't particularly need fine tools for this."

"That's what we're saying. We're saying that this was a carcass. It wasn't killed by these humans. It wasn't even butchered by these humans. Most likely it was a carcass at an advanced stage of decomposition but it still had potential for the extraction of marrow from the bones."

"Some critics have claimed it was the backhoe or the grader or other equipment used in the roadworks that broke the bones," I point out.[27] "Others have argued that they were broken by being rolled against rocks carried along in river water when the surrounding sediment was laid down."[28]

Tom raises an eyebrow. "Flow velocities that are strong enough to transport rocks like the big anvil stones are going to carry all the finer material much farther away. And yet we still have all that fine material at the site— small stones, small bone fragments, and obviously the associated silt and sand, too. So there really is a disjunct in terms of the hydrology."

Addressing the suggestion of Cerutti skeptic Gary Haynes that the bones were broken by the roadmaking equipment in 1992,[29] Tom launches into a long and detailed exposition. It's too technical to try the reader's patience with here, but the takeaway is that a recently broken, fossilized bone has a very different appearance to a bone broken when it was still fresh, within a short time of the animal's death. Experiments carried out by Demére's colleague Steve Holen on the bones of a recently deceased African elephant showed that the characteristic spiral fractures that occur when you deliberately and systematically break fresh bone between a stone hammer and a stone anvil in no way resemble the fractures caused by the teeth of scavengers or predators and simply cannot occur in fossilized bones.[30] The presence of spiral fractures among the bones of the Cerutti mastodon therefore leads to the inevitable conclusion that they must have been broken 130,000 years ago, when they were fresh.[31]

Meanwhile, the presence of the hammer and anvil stones, and the evidence of how they were used to break the bones, makes it equally certain that humans were involved.[32]

"Because," I muse, "nothing else is going to smash up those bones and take out the marrow in that way."[33]

"That's how we see it," Tom confirms, "but I'm a scientist so I'm open to alternative explanations if they fit the data better than ours. And so it's possible that we are wrong. But the evidence suggests to us that the only explanation for the taphonomic data at this site is that humans were responsible."

Taphonomy is the study of the circumstances and processes of fossilization, a field that is generally better understood by paleontologists like Tom than by archaeologists.

IF YOU DON'T LOOK, YOU WON'T FIND

AFTER WE'VE COMPLETED OUR TOUR of the exhibits Tom takes us behind the scenes at the museum into areas off-limits to the public. As we ride the elevator up to the fourth floor I ask him if it was a struggle to get the *Nature* paper accepted.

"Well, it was a yearlong review process," he replies, "rigorous, which you'd expect. I've tried publishing in *Nature* before. It's not an easy journal to get into. So we were excited when they sent it out for review. That's really the first hurdle—if it gets off the editor's desk. Then we went through several rounds of revisions and re-review and re-revision but eventually it was accepted. So that was really exciting. It's a terrific journal. And that's the other thing, of course, it's *Nature*, it's not some third- or fourth-tier publication."

"Absolutely top tier," I agree as we step out of the elevator, "which is why it's had such a huge impact. . . . I've been following the story of the peopling of the Americas and for a very long while there was extreme resistance around the so-called Clovis First model. I mean, that was it. It was almost dangerous career-wise to propose anything else."

"Apparently," Tom says.

"And then the evidence starts to come in and starts to just overwhelm that paradigm. We begin to open up to the possibility of 14,000, 15,000, 18,000, 25,000 years. And you can see the archaeological community kind of reluctantly embracing that, but then you come along with 130,000 years and that is a time bomb. Literally. It's a huge explosion."

Tom's expression is rueful. "It wasn't our intention. It was just where the evidence led us."

We enter The Nat's archives where the larger part of the Cerutti mastodon collection is permanently stored in a secure room in three huge cabinets. An Indiana Jones moment follows as Tom grabs a four-spoked steel wheel and spins it. Soundlessly the cabinets slide apart, avenues appear between them and then Tom is opening drawers and showing us mastodon bones and mastodon teeth and more pieces of rock and stone while Santha takes photographs and we continue talking.

The more I see, the more persuaded I am and the better I understand why *Nature* published Tom's paper. Despite the whines and quibbles of the skeptics, the evidence, once it's laid out in front of you, once you actually look at the bones and stones, and once the technical details are properly considered, is absolutely solid and convincing.

"What's next?" I ask. "How do you take this further?"

"Well, of course one of the things we've said all along to our critics is that if you don't look in deposits of this age with the idea in mind that evidence of humans could be there, then you're not going to find anything. So we're suggesting, as a challenge, that people should start considering, should start to look in these deposits, as a way of testing this hypothesis. I know that's a lot of work, but there are unexamined deposits of this age throughout the US."

"It's also good science," I comment. "I mean, not just to rest on a paradigm but to try to look for other possibilities. Again I'm struck by the emotional nature of the reaction your paper has provoked. Some people are quite reasonable but others almost insultingly reject the whole thing."

"Dismissive! So . . . I guess the reaction I was looking for was healthy skepticism but with the idea of—well, let's look at this now, let's consider this and what the implications are and what sort of predictions can we make about testing this. . . . But that's been a minority of the reactions. We've seen the extremes of both. Some people say this is pure garbage and others say this is the find of the century, but what we're saying to everyone, really, is open your mind to the possibility that instead of the peopling of the Americas being associated with the last deglaciation event [the so-called Bølling-Allerød interstadial, dated from around 14,700 years ago to around 12,800 years ago[34]] what we should actually be looking at is the deglaciation event *before that*— between 140,000 and 120,000 years ago. You get the same sort of scenario with a land bridge and ice sheets retreating and you get that same sweet spot between really low sea levels and a blockage by ice sheets, and ice sheets gone and the flooding of the land bridge."

"And yet," I reflect, "so much else changes if you're right. The peopling of the Americas becomes a whole different story—much more complicated."

"Well," Tom suggests, "it becomes richer. . . ."

"A much richer and longer story. So much so, in fact, that it's really hard for a lot of archaeologists to swallow when they're committed to a shorter time frame." I hesitate before raising my next point: "Look . . . I know we're not supposed to talk about this but your date of 130,000 years ago raises the possibility that it might have been Neanderthals who were at your site, or Denisovans, or anatomically modern humans—because they were all in the world at that time."

With this comment I've taken us into territory I'd specifically agreed would be off-limits when my request for an interview was accepted, but Tom seems happy to express his point of view. "As a paleontologist," he muses, "I ask the question—why *weren't* there humans here earlier? I mean, we have dispersal of Eurasian animal species into North America and dispersal of North American species into Eurasia at earlier times. So why *shouldn't* humans have been here as well?"

"And now it looks like they were."

"I'm certain of that from our evidence."

"Which raises the question of why in 150 years of professional study archaeologists have failed to find similar evidence."

"There's always the possibility," Tom offers, "that our site witnesses a failed colonization attempt. So you had this dispersal event. It didn't take, maybe because population size wasn't great enough, and they quite quickly died out—in which case they would have left almost no trace of their presence for archaeologists to find. Then thousands of years later there was a successful colonization by other migrants and naturally they dominate the archaeological record."

"It could be like that," I concede. "But on the other hand, it could be there were people here all along and they've just been invisible to archaeology because of the particular way archaeology works and the particular things archaeology looks for."

"You'd have to ask the archaeologists." Tom shrugs. "But like I say, if you go to a place and you absolutely rule out in advance that humans were there 130,000 years ago, then you're clearly not going to find evidence that they were. But if you go with an open mind"—an impish smile—"and dig deep enough in the right places, then who knows what you might turn up?"

6

MILLENNIA
UNACCOUNTED FOR

WHEN TOM DEMÉRÉ DUG DEEP enough he turned up evidence of humans in North America 130,000 years ago that was sufficiently robust to make it through *Nature*'s rigorous peer-review process and into print in April 2017.

By then it was no longer news that the New World had been peopled long before Clovis. In chapter 4 we saw that Monte Verde, Meadowcroft, and Bluefish Caves had already pushed back the date of the "First" Americans from around 13,000 years ago to at least 24,000 years ago. These, however, are only three sites among a growing number that suggest a vast, complex, textured antiquity for the human presence in the Americas across ages when hitherto we've been asked to picture an uninhabited wilderness awaiting the arrival of Man. No matter how long it exists, an uninhabited wilderness will not produce a civilization, and it would make no sense to look for one there. But with new evidence continuing to pour forth, it's increasingly obvious that humans were in the Americas not just for thousands of years before Clovis, but for tens of thousands of years—all the way back to the Cerutti Mastodon Site or earlier—and thus had vast expanses of time at their disposal to develop in any direction they chose.

Wanting to get a better feeling for the time-depth of this mystery leads me, through various contacts and connections, to a walk in the South Carolina woods. It's early November, a sunny yet cold morning. There's a mulch of fallen leaves underfoot but the trees around us are still in foliage, mostly green with muted hints of autumnal reds and yellows beginning to mottle the canopy. I'm with Albert "Al" Goodyear, professor of archaeology at the University of South Carolina. Around 70 years of age, cheerful and in rubicund good health, he's wearing a South Carolina Gamecocks baseball cap, a navy check shirt, a tweed jacket, and tough outdoor pants tucked into his hiking boots to keep ticks carrying Lyme disease at bay. Our ramble takes us close to the Savannah River, which here forms the border between the states of South Carolina and Georgia.

Al is a world expert on the Clovis culture and back in 1998, having excavated an extensive Clovis layer in these woods, he dug deeper. In the end, what he found was evidence that humans had been here 50,000 years ago, not as old as the Cerutti mastodon by any means, but still a good 37,000 years before Clovis. Unsurprisingly, Clovis Firsters were adamantly opposed and launched a campaign to discredit the find.[1]

The site is now called Topper, after David Topper, a local forester. In 1981 he spotted stone tools on the ground here.[2] He notified Al, who a couple of years later launched a comprehensive archaeological survey of the Savannah River watershed. As part of this larger project, excavations began at Topper in 1986 and it was immediately obvious that Native Americans had been coming here for many thousands of years. Obvious, too, was the reason why—a huge outcrop of easily accessible chert, the raw material of a form of flint ideal for making stone tools.[3]

Al suddenly stoops and picks up a small, almost translucent piece of reddish flint from the ground at our feet. It is recognizably a fragment of an arrowhead, with a notch near the base. Al confirms my guess that it's not Clovis. "It's a nice piece," he says. "It's been heat treated. It's probably about 8,000 years old."

He draws my attention to an area off the path relatively free of fallen leaves where there's quite a scatter of stones, mostly small broken pieces like this one. Al refers to them as "debitage" (the technical term for lithic debris and discards found at sites where stone tools and weapons were made). "Every flake on the ground was struck off by a human," he says, "and you can roughly tell the age. With strong coloration they're more recent, but if they're white and creamy, they're weathered and older."

Our next stop is the chert quarry, the reason so much was going on around Topper for so long. "For them this was like aluminum bauxite or iron ore for our culture," Al explains. "They didn't have jackhammers. They didn't have crowbars. They just had to work what they could get off the surface; maybe set a fire or something to push it out. So we call this 'Topper Chert'—the chert source for the Topper site."

"I find it amazing," I say, "that there are still broken points 8,000 years old just lying around on the surface whereas you have to excavate to reach other materials from that horizon."

The earth is a dynamic place, Al explains, with multiple different processes of deposition and erosion under way at all times. You can make guesses based on style and weathering, but fragments of worked stone that have been in the open for an unknown period can't be dated by their archaeological context, because there is none. Carbon-dating organic materials in the sediment in which they were found won't work, either, because they were never entombed and preserved in sediment. And in fact no other objective and widely accepted method of dating can tell us how old they are. For these reasons archaeologists have to discount artifacts found on the surface when coming to any conclusions about the age of a site, even though the artifacts themselves may obviously be ancient. Their presence, however, does serve as a clue that much more might be awaiting discovery underground—which was precisely why Al followed up on David Topper's 1981 suggestion to take a look.

THERE'S A FIRST TIME
FOR EVERYTHING

AFTER THEIR FIRST SEASON OF excavation at Topper in 1986, Al and his team methodically worked their way down during the next dozen years through the levels of what was turning out to be a *very* extensive, detailed, and time-consuming excavation. There were a number of archaeological "horizons" here, stacked one above the other in nice, easily datable layers of sediment, containing the leavings of different cultures at different, and increasingly more ancient, periods of the past. "We found pottery down to about 2,000 years ago," Al says. "Below that there was no pottery but there were plentiful artifacts from the period we call the Archaic. So we kept on going down and we got into the Early Archaic [around 8,000 to 10,000 years ago[4]]. They made these beautiful little notched points. And then below that, in 1998—bingo!—we found Clovis."

Topper is the only Clovis site to be excavated on the coastal plains of Georgia and the Carolinas.[5] As though by way of compensation, however, the Clovis level at Topper turned out to be so massive that the excavations there would not be complete until 2013. As he tells me about the treasure trove of more than 40,000 Clovis artifacts that he and his team uncovered, Al radiates excitement. And rightly so! It was a tremendous achievement that continues to enjoy renown among archaeologists.[6]

The same, however, cannot be said for what happened next. "So we got down to the bottom of the Clovis level," Al continues, "and then we all voted to go deeper." For the next half meter or so there was just sand and small gravels, devoid of any evidence of human presence, and then suddenly the excavators found themselves among artifacts again.

I ask if there was a particular aha moment.

Al laughs. "My aha was more of an uh-oh! Everybody else was going aha but they weren't going to have to stand up at national conferences and defend what we'd found."

"Which was evidence of the presence of humans in America tens of thousands of years before Clovis?"

"Exactly. After we'd done a thorough lab analysis we were certain we were dealing with artifacts."

I ask when he began to feel the inevitable wrath of the Clovis First lobby.

"Immediately!" he replies. "It began with 'we don't believe in pre-Clovis. There's no such thing as a pre-Clovis culture.' Then I think when it was realized we'd made a strong case that many of our flake-tool artifacts had been produced by the 'bend-break' technique, and that the media were already onto the potential significance of what we'd found, the critics moved the goalposts and said things like 'Okay, we understand bend-breaks but we don't know of an assemblage anywhere that has so many bend-breaks.'"[7]

But the key issue remained the antiquity of the site:

The *New York Times* was here, CNN, they were all holding their stories until the dates came back. And I was thinking maybe they'll come back at 20,000 years ago maybe even 25,000 years ago, and I'll be out of here clean. This is going to be easy. But the date that came back was 50,000[8]—ancient beyond all imagining and right at the limits of radiocarbon.[9] Since then we have OSL-dated the deposit and those dates also came back in the range of 50,000.[10] So we've got it dated two ways, but still the skeptics keep saying that what we've found can't be a human site and that our artifacts must be works of nature because they're so different from the artifacts found at other sites. To which my response is: "Well . . . you've never dug a 50,000-year-old site in America, right? There's a first time for everything."

THEY UNDERSTOOD THE PROPERTIES OF STONE

AFTER OUR PLEASANT HIKE WE'VE reached the main excavation area, a large rectangular pit about 12 feet deep, 40 feet wide, and around 60 feet long, where the majority of the archaeology trenches have been left open, in their original condition, and the entire area covered over with a roofed shelter. It's tastefully done, allowing in plenty of light but keeping out rain, and it's an education to see the stratigraphy through which Goodyear and his team dug to reach the controversial pre-Clovis levels.

Although Topper is located on land owned by a specialty chemicals company and not open for public access, Al does occasionally bring interested groups here to explain the site to them, and to this end signs have been set up identifying the different levels. My eyes are drawn immediately to one that says "Clovis Level: 13,000 years." Farther down another reads "Pleistocene Alluvial Sands, 16,000–20,000 years." We step down again to the excavation floor and I see the thick band of clay where the pre-Clovis artifacts were found, labeled "Pleistocene Terrace: 20,000–50,000 years."

Off to the side, laid out as a display, is a row of three or four chunky fist-size rocks. Al picks one up. "The more abundant pre-Clovis artifacts are fashioned from chert cobbles like this," he tells me, "but they're no good to anybody as they are. They have to be cracked open first. You have to get rid of all this"—he indicates the rough, heavily patinated surface of the cobble—"to get at the stuff inside that can be turned into tools. In experiments we've thrown cobbles like that, slammed cobbles like that against each other, and nothing breaks."

"So what does break them?"

"When we put an 8-pound sledgehammer on them, that did the trick."

"But presumably the pre-Clovis people didn't have 8-pound sledgehammers?"

Al shrugs. "Maybe they did it the way the Australian aborigines used to deal with big slabs of quartzite. They didn't have sledgehammers, either. They would light a small fire underneath a face of the quartzite and they would wait for it to get hot enough till they heard a *tink,* and then they would pull a slab off. So I think you could use fire to prepare the cobble and then maybe break it apart. The point is once you break open a piece of flint like that then you can do anything you want with it. All of the interior surfaces are susceptible to flaking but the cobble in its raw form is not. So when our critics say that cobbles like these maybe got broken by rolling down the slope of the escarpment our answer is no.[11] What you need is heat or something like an eight-pound sledgehammer—and even then we had to hit them several times before they broke."

"In other words, only humans could have done this."

"Right. Human beings who understood the properties of the stone and how to work it. If nature can't break it, it can't make it."

None of the pre-Clovis tools have been left at the excavation, of course, but before we set out for the site this morning Al showed me examples kept at the South Carolina Institute of Archaeology and Anthropology exhibit at its nearby regional campus in Allendale. What quickly became clear, which Al willingly concedes, was that they were, without exception, extremely simple and generally quite small, with unifacial flake tools such as burins and small blades predominating.[12] The vast majority of the burins, more than 1,000 of them,[13] were created by the distinctive flint-knapping technique known as "bend-break,"[14] whereby two edges are "broken off at a 90 degree angle to form a sharp sturdy tip that may have been used in the engraving of bone, antler or wood."[15] Flint cores left over after large flakes had been struck off were also found in close proximity to a large anvil stone.[16] It appears there were several, separate rock-chipping stations like this, resembling workstations.[17]

A VERY LONG TIME

THE EXTENSIVE EVIDENCE FROM THE pre-Clovis levels at Topper clearly does *not* document the handiwork of any kind of lost advanced civilization. What it speaks to me of instead, like the Cerutti Mastodon Site, is a far more complex and nuanced past for the peopling of the Americas than has hitherto been properly contemplated.

I don't propose here to give a blow-by-blow account of the fifty or so sites in the Americas, with more found every year, presently claimed to be of pre-Clovis antiquity.[18] Not all are of the same quality. Some may not be archaeological sites at all, their supposed "artifacts" perhaps being "geofacts." Others are very strong.

A measure of discernment is therefore needed along this continuum, and what I observe is that archaeologists who are open to the notion of greater antiquity (these days the majority apart from a few die-hards) consider the most important pre-Clovis sites in North America in addition to Cerutti and Topper to include: Hueyatlaco, Mexico;[19] Old Crow and Bluefish Caves, Canada; Calico Mountain, California; Pendejo Cave, New Mexico; Tula Springs, Nevada; Meadowcroft Rockshelter, Pennsylvania; Cactus Hill, Virginia; Paisley Five Mile Point Caves, Oregon; Schaefer and Hebior Mammoth site, Wisconsin; Buttermilk Creek, Texas; and Saltville, Virginia.[20] In South America, Pedra Furada in Brazil, Monte Verde in Chile, Taima-taima in Venezuela, and Tibito in Colombia are likewise singled out as convincing pre-Clovis sites of special interest.[21] However, other than some anomalies, indeed some deep mysteries, connected to a select few of these sites—which we'll come to in later chapters—most feature only rudimentary stone-working technologies similar to those of pre-Clovis Topper, although with definite evidence of increasing refinement and improved techniques between early pre-Clovis and late pre-Clovis.[22] Early or late, however, the importance of all these sites, as I view them, has nothing to do with the level of technology they manifest, whether judged to be "low" or "increasingly refined"—or whatever. They really matter in that they offer compelling proof of the enduring presence of humans *of some kind* in the Americas from perhaps as far back as 130,000 years ago until today.

That's a very long time. It might even be long enough—speaking entirely hypothetically, of course—for something that we would recognize as an advanced civilization to have emerged in the Americas alongside the hunter-gatherers, foragers, and scavengers whose simple tools dominate the pre-Clovis horizons so far excavated.

But if such a civilization was indeed present somewhere on the American landmass, how has it escaped the notice of archaeologists up to now while the hunter-gatherers have not? And isn't it grasping at straws in the first place even to suggest that an advanced civilization could have coexisted with hunter-gatherers during the Ice Age?

PRECONCEPTIONS ARE BLINKERS

LET'S CALL TO MIND HOW things are in our own globally connected twenty-first century. Rio de Janeiro, Bogotá, and Lima are, by any standards, advanced technological cities; yet on the same continent, in the depths of the Amazon rainforest, uncontacted tribes of hunter-gatherers remain at a "Stone Age" level of technology.[23] Likewise, in Africa, Johannesburg, Cape Town, and Windhoek are advanced technological cities, yet you can walk from them to the Kalahari desert where San bushmen, though well aware of the technological world, choose to continue a hunter-gatherer and still largely "Stone Age" way of life.

There are no purely logical grounds, therefore, that can rule out the possible coexistence of an advanced civilization with hunter-gatherers during the Ice Age.

Nor can this—at first sight absurd—possibility be ruled out on archaeological grounds. For more than half a century, as we've seen, American archaeology was so riddled with pre-formed opinions about how the past *should* look, and about the orderly, linear way in which civilizations *should* evolve, that it repeatedly missed, sidelined, and downright ignored evidence for *any* human presence at all prior to Clovis—until, at any rate, the mass of that evidence became so overwhelming that it took the existing paradigm by storm.

We thus find ourselves in a place now where "Clovis First" can quite definitely be ruled out, despite the fading protests of a very few zealots still clinging on to that discredited fantasy.[24]

At the same time no new ruling paradigm, let alone consensus, has yet taken its place. Several are vying for the crown, though all remain rooted in the preconception that what they must explain is limited to the presence of relatively "simple" and "unsophisticated" hunter-gatherers in the Americas much earlier than had previously been supposed. None have factored in the possibility—they would be puzzled at the very thought—that a lost civilization might be part of the missing picture as well.

I'm reminded of Tom Deméré's point: "If you go to a place and you absolutely rule out in advance that humans were there 130,000 years ago, then you're clearly not going to find evidence that they were."[25]

By the same reasoning, if we don't ever *look* for a lost civilization—because of a preconception that none could have existed—then we won't find one.

Fortunately, as we'll see in part 3, geneticists have developed sophisticated techniques for studying ancient DNA that have overturned entrenched thinking and opened completely new and unexpected avenues of inquiry.

PART III

GENES

▎▶ ● ◀▎

The Mystery in DNA

7

SIBERIA

CROSS BOTH SOUTH AND NORTH America DNA studies have revealed that at some point in the remote past, in some unknown location or locations, the ancestors of Native Americans interbred with an archaic—and now extinct—human species. Only recently discovered, and closely related to the more famous Neanderthals who also produced offspring with our ancestors, geneticists have named this species "the Denisovans." Insufficient sampling has been done to establish exact levels but the current estimate is that 0.13 to 0.17 percent of Native American DNA is of Denisovan origin[1]—with indications in the data that some indigenous groups, for example, the Piapoco of Colombia and Venezuela in South America and the Ojibwa of northeastern North America, can be expected to have higher levels of Denisovan DNA than others.[2]

We know about the Denisovans because of paradigm-busting discoveries at the eponymous Denisova Cave in a region of rugged highlands known

as the Altai at the extreme south of the Russian Federal District of Siberia. Bordered by Mongolia, China, and Kazakhstan, and extending from the Ural Mountains in the west to the Kamchatka Peninsula and the federal district of Chukotka more that 5,000 kilometers to the east,[3] Siberia covers 13.1 million square kilometers—around 77 percent of the total geographical area of Russia. The Urals form a prominent part of the dividing line between Europe and Asia. Kamchatka and Chukotka stand at the junction of the Pacific and Arctic Oceans, with Kamchatka's coast washed by the waters of the Bering Sea while Chukotka commands the Bering Strait.

Presently 82 kilometers wide between Cape Dezhnev in Chukotka and Alaska's Cape Prince of Wales, during the last Ice Age the Strait was drained by lowered sea levels and a tundra-covered land bridge—"Beringia"—connected Chukotka with Alaska. In other words, at that time, Europe, Asia, and the Americas were one continuous landmass. Should you have had the inclination and the stamina, there were certain periods when it would have been technically possible to walk from the Atlantic coast of what is now Spain, across western and eastern Europe to the Urals, through the Urals, through Siberia, across "Beringia," into Alaska and Canada, down through the "ice-free corridor" dividing the two primary sheets of the North American ice cap, into the United States and thence through Central America into South America as far as Tierra del Fuego before again encountering another ocean—a narrow one during the Ice Age when Antarctica was much larger.[4]

No investigation of the human story in the Americas, therefore, can ignore the role of Siberia as a crossroads in the migrations of our ancestors. Moreover, despite the fact that only a tiny fraction of its vast area has yet been sampled by archaeologists, we already know that anatomically modern humans were present in both western and Arctic Siberia at least as far back as 45,000 years ago.[5] We know, too, that DNA studies have revealed close genetic relationships between Native Americans and Siberians that speak to a deep and ancient connection.[6]

ANOMALIES IN THE DATA

WITH A FEW NOTABLE EXCEPTIONS,[7] it was the consensus view of archaeologists and anthropologists during the period of "Clovis First" dominance that the Americas were settled exclusively by the overland route from Siberia via "Beringia" and southward through the ice-free corridor. Despite the collapse of "Clovis First," this remains the consensus view today; however, it has been finessed to accommodate the discovery of ever more sites in North and South America predating the opening of the ice-free corridor that therefore could not possibly have been settled by migration through it.[8] In addition, several subsequent studies have pointed out that for much of its duration long stretches of the supposed ice-free corridor would have been completely uninhabitable and thus most unpromising territory for a lengthy migration.[9]

To explain how migration might have taken place *at all*, therefore, and to account for the growing mass of archaeological and genetic evidence suggesting that humans had been in the Americas, isolated from Asia, for thousands of years before Clovis, two theories have recently found favor:

1. A "Beringian standstill" model (within which scholars continue to debate) whereby, in the simplest terms, having crossed the land bridge into Alaska perhaps as much as 30,000 years ago, the migrants found their southward progress blocked by the conjoined Cordilleran and Laurentide Ice Sheets. More or less simultaneously their return to Siberia was interdicted by the expansion of glaciers in Siberia's Verkhoyansk Range and in Alaska's Mackenzie River

Valley.[10] Their descendants were therefore obliged to spend between 10,000 and 20,000 years stranded in Beringia before further climate shifts allowed them to spread south into the Americas. During this "incubation period" the now isolated population experienced certain genetic changes that would distinguish them from their northeast Asian ancestors at the level of DNA while at the same time confirming their close ancestral relatedness.[11]

2. A "coastal migration" theory whereby the first migrants were boat people who crossed the narrow island-strewn neck of the North Pacific from northeast Asia into the Americas.[12] This coastal theory relies heavily on the so-called Kelp Highway migration model, which notes that the deglaciation of North America's Pacific Coast presented migrants with a region rich in kelp and other aquatic resources that could support their journeys. The coastal model also relies on the unarguable presence, though scarce, of early Paleolithic northwest American archaeological sites. Such coasting could have been undertaken at any time during lowered Ice Age sea levels, particularly when Beringia was exposed, could have been achieved with extremely simple technology such as rafts and coracles, and often would not have required the migrants to lose sight of land. Since we know that other ancient peoples migrated by sea as much as 65,000 years ago—for example, the crossing of the Timor Straits by the first migrants to Australia[13]—there can be no objection in principle to the Americas being inhabited in the same way.

All this seems thoroughly reasonable and I have no doubt that both things happened. Island-hopping migrants in simple vessels suitable for short open-water crossings did indeed contribute significantly to the peopling of Americas. Similarly, one need look no further than Jacques Cinq-Mars's excavations demonstrating a human presence 24,000 years ago at Bluefish Caves in the Yukon to confirm that there is truth to the Beringian Standstill model, too.[14]

But are these revised and finessed models, currently very much in vogue with archaeologists, sufficient to explain all the complexities and anomalies in the data that science offers on the peopling of the Americas?

SERGEY AND OLGA

IN EARLY SEPTEMBER 2017, A couple of months before visiting Topper with Al Goodyear and a month before meeting Tom Deméré at The Nat in San Diego, Santha and I applied for Russian visas and declared our destination as Denisova Cave in the Altai.

The visas were expensive, the dauntingly opaque application forms took a great while to fill out, and in the general fog of bureaucratic time-wasting we began to wonder if we might have to postpone the trip until the spring of 2018 when the Siberian winter would have come and gone. Russia is more efficient than it looks, however, and we had our visas within a week.

Still, it was going to have to be a very quick visit with a big American journey planned from the end of September through until close to the end of November. There was no time for sightseeing, therefore, when we flew to Moscow on September 12, overnighted at Sheremetyevo, and caught a connecting flight the next morning to Novosibirsk, the Siberian capital, a four-hour flight and four time zones east of Moscow.

After landing and collecting our bags Santha and I were met groundside by our local connection, Sergey Kurgin. I say "connection" because you have to have one if you're going to travel in Russia. You can't just get up and go. Some solid citizen, or business, or tour operator must take responsibility for you and officially invite you, and you must have a prearranged and preplanned

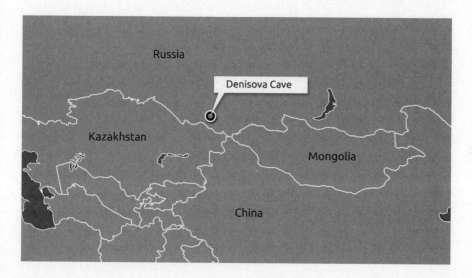

itinerary to preapproved destinations or your visa won't be issued—nor, if you somehow manage to slip through the net, will any hotel accommodate you on your route.

Sergey owns a small private travel business called Sibalp, and I'd contacted him on the internet to help set up the trip. Negotiations were complicated by the fact that he spoke no English—he was perplexed that I spoke no Russian—but various translators got involved and a deal was done. Sergey would drive us the 600 kilometers or so from Novosibirsk to Topolnoye, a township in the Altai, where we would stay with a local family while we visited the cave about 20 kilometers farther on. When we were done he would drive us back to Novosibirsk. He would arrange all accommodation en route and find us an interpreter, without whom we would be unable to speak to anyone. Joining Sergey at the airport to meet us, therefore, was Olga Votrina, the bilingual student from Novosibirsk State University who'd be interpreting for us.

Novosibirsk is a city of monotone drabness with an oppressive, regimented, Soviet-era feel to it. Olga was cheerful and nervous, wanting very much to be a good interpreter and guide. Thickset and grizzled, Sergey was an older man perhaps in his seventies, but solid, gruff, and strong. He owned a four-wheel-drive Mitsubishi minivan that had at some point been imported, used, from Japan and thus had its steering wheel on the wrong side. It was battered and creaky with a pronounced and disconcerting tug to the right, but as he drove us through the geometric grid of Novosibirsk's streets, Sergey assured us it was up to the journey ahead.

Our hotel was in the academic quarter, a stone's throw from the Museum of the Peoples of Siberia. We spent the following morning viewing artifacts from Denisova Cave, and in the afternoon we set off on the long road south beneath leaden, wide-open skies across a remarkably flat landscape relieved by patches of muted color—black earth here, green field there, rank upon rank of hay bales set upon yellowing stubble marching toward the remote horizon. There was something lulling and dreamlike about the whole scene; I drifted off to sleep and when I awoke, darkness had fallen.

Sergey was downing a can of Red Bull and gripping the juddering wheel tightly as he weaved in and out of the surprisingly heavy Siberian traffic. Despite his disadvantageous position on the wrong side of the road he was doing well and by midnight we had two-thirds of the journey behind us and stopped to sleep in the town of Biysk.

We were back on the road again early the next morning—a much brighter and more cheerful day—and drove 65 kilometers farther south to Belokurikha, near which there were rumored to be some intriguing megaliths that Sergey believed he would be able to locate.[15] Quite different from the flatlands of the day before, we were now on the borders of the Altai Mountains, and spent the next several hours in the region of Mt. Mokhnataya[16] driving off-road through fields, circling likely looking hills covered in outcrops of granitic rocks, and asking farmers for directions. Eventually we met a man who knew a man who knew the couple, Vladimir Illych and Raisa Stepenov, both in their late sixties, who were said to have discovered the alleged megaliths. An hour later we were sharing bread and honey with them in their home in the village of Nizhnekamenka. This was followed, quaintly, by a tour of their vegetable garden and an invitation—how could we refuse?—to pick raspberries and blackberries from the briars growing in abundance there.

It was early afternoon by the time Vladimir and Raisa, their daughter Svetlana, and their strapping young grandson Maxim all crammed into Sergey's groaning minivan with us. It seemed we had been in *roughly* the right place all morning, missing the site only by about half a mile. I was excited that we were finally going to see it, but as we set out again on the bumpy off-road drive Vladimir advised me to lower my expectations. In his opinion the media coverage had been much ado about nothing and the so-called megaliths he was about to show us were natural rock formations.

BEHIND THE HEADLINES

THE INFORMATION THAT THERE MIGHT be ancient megaliths here in the Altai, quite close to Denisova Cave, had come to me by way of a news item in the English-language edition of *The Siberian Times* published on May 8, 2017. The rather compelling headline reported the discovery of "Dragon and Griffin Megaliths" dating back to the end of the Ice Age.[17] "Archaeological researchers" named Aleksandr and Ruslan Peresyolkov were cited suggesting the enigmatic monuments were likely to be at least 12,000 years old but that precise dating would be impossible until "the culture that created them is identified."[18]

This is always a problem with monuments carved out of stone. The cutting and shaping of the stone itself cannot be directly dated. What is needed is an archaeological context in which the monument is set—preferably with carbon-datable organic materials in situ—and from these the age of the monument may then usually be inferred. Since there was no excavation at Mt. Mokhnataya, however, no context had yet been established and the archaeological researchers were surely right that precise dating was presently impossible.

But what sort of "archaeological researchers" had even these provisional assessments reported in *The Siberian Times* come from? The news item gave no information about their credentials, nor could I find any online. The only clue, and not necessarily a reliable one, was in the comments section where Ruslan Peresyolkov was described as "a little-known web-designer and not an archaeologist (not even an amateur)."[19]

We humans are hardwired for pattern recognition, so it's not surprising that people all over the world frequently detect patterns in nature that they believe are the work of men but later, on closer examination by cooler and more experienced heads, prove to be entirely natural. This happens particularly often with eroded outcrops of rock, notably with certain types of granite that can crack and weather in ways that seem obviously designed but in fact are not.

Archaeologists are trained to be skeptical of such simulacra and their default position will be that a rock is just a rock until there is really hard and compelling evidence that humans shaped it. Needless to say, if the rock in question ended up as a granite statue of Ramesses II, the context and the style, plus any hieroglyphs engraved upon it, would tell you all you need to know. Granite boulders that have been sitting on an unexcavated hillside in the Altai for unknown thousands of years, however, are an entirely different proposition, and I wasn't inclined to take any opinion of them on trust whether expressed by a fully qualified archaeologist or by a web designer or, for that matter, by Vladimir.

I was just curious, and literally "in the area"—so why not take a look for myself?

MESSAGES OF EARTH AND SKY

WE DROVE AS CLOSE AS possible to a rugged hill that I recognized from our earlier search, and trudged across a field to get to it. Raisa, who'd recently had hip replacement surgery, remained behind in the Mitsubishi, but Vladimir, Svetlana, and Maxim joined us—the young man kindly offering to carry Santha's weighty bag of cameras.

We reached the base of the hill and began a long clamber up a steep slope thickly carpeted with wild grasses, heather, and clinging brambles. Svetlana warned us that the area was infested with snakes. "Always look before you step," she said.

The afternoon was sunny and surprisingly warm and the sky an eggshell blue with a few soft white clouds up high. At one point, pausing for breath, I turned and looked back. Behind us, dotted with lower mounds and hills, was a patchwork quilt of greens and yellows spread out for 20 miles across the floor of a glorious valley. It was through this valley and around these hills that we had spent the morning fruitlessly driving. Now, from this new vantage point, I saw it was bounded to the east by the humped, tawny backs of a distant range of mountains. I watched for a moment the shadows of the clouds painting their own patterns across the landscape, struck by the poignant, fleeting beauty of it all.

We resumed the climb, close now to our first objective—an outcrop of rough, deeply fissured and fractured natural granitic bedrock, visible because the otherwise omnipresent undergrowth could find no purchase on it. It was red-gray in color, about 50 meters in length and 20 wide, obviously an integral part of the hillside itself, sloping at the same steep angle and surmounted at its upper end by a dense cluster of large boulders. "The tail of the dragon," said Vladimir skeptically, pointing to the downslope sector of the outcrop, "and the head"—he indicated the boulders.

At first I didn't get it, but once we'd climbed above the outcrop and could look back and down on it, a figure began to emerge. I could just about make sense of the tail and I could see the head clearly—but not as the head of a dragon. Viewed very slightly turned in profile from where I stood it seemed to me much more to resemble the head and the left eye of some great serpent.

I was, of course, already sensitized and preconditioned to recognize the form of a serpent in the outcrop, perhaps a little by Svetlana's warning of snakes in the grass in these parts but also, in an even more visceral way, by what I had learned at Serpent Mound in Ohio.

The "language" that Serpent Mound speaks is hard to understand from the technological-materialist point of view. That view, so dominant and widespread today, is one in which there is no such thing as "spirit" and the earth is simply dead "matter" to be mined, exploited, and consumed. By contrast the ancient people to whom Serpent Mound addressed itself in clear and ringing tones not only knew that all things, both animate and inanimate, were imbued with spirit but also lived close to the earth and were in touch with Her rhythms and awake to the manifold messages and signals and ciphers by which She spoke to them.

Among these were perfectly "natural" features of the landscape through which, whether on account of their special appearance, or location, or alignment, or some other remarkable quality, the spirit of the earth could manifest wisdom, beauty, and teachings. Serpent Mound is one of these "Manitou," and we saw how the presence there of a natural serpentine ridge, with a natural serpentlike "head" oriented toward the setting point of the sun on the summer solstice, offered an epiphany to the ancients of the union of earth and Sky and was their cue to create the great effigy mound that now commands the site and still "swallows the sun" on the longest day of the year.

Nearly 3 months had passed since that summer solstice at Serpent Mound. Now the autumn equinox was just a few days away and I was very far from America, yet in a part of the world directly linked to the migrations of the ancestors of the First Americans. I was therefore not averse in principle to considering the possibility that this peculiar formation in the Siberian Altai might be another "Earth Serpent," enhanced and embellished by human beings attentive to the ciphers of nature.

But it equally might be how Vladimir saw it—simply one of those accidents of nature that give the illusion of a human hand at work.

From the rough bearings I was able to take, though I offer no guarantees, it seemed to me that the serpent's head (I could not see it as a "dragon!") was oriented more or less due west and thus aligned to the setting point of the sun on both the spring and the autumn equinoxes. About 2 meters high and 4 meters long to the base of the neck, the head was massive and possessed a distinct brow ridge overlying the firmly defined left eye. Moving forward, I saw

The Altai "dragon/serpent." Graham Hancock at the left side of the "head" with his hand on its lower left eyelid. PHOTO: SANTHA FAIIA. INSET: An enhanced image helps to explain why recent visitors, and the ancients before them, could imagine this natural rocky outcrop as the head of a dragon or serpent.

View of the right side of the same structure. PHOTO: SANTHA FAIIA.

the mouth was present, the jaws clearly demarcated and slightly ajar. There was a peculiar cleft in the front of the lower jaw.

Much of this, apart from that odd gap, was moderately serpentlike—but only on the left side of the serpent's head. When I scrambled around to view the right side it was as though I were suddenly looking at a completely different structure—not a serpent at all but a megalithic wall built from ten hefty eroded but precisely interlinked granite blocks. Somehow, whether by nature or by human beings, a structure had been created that appeared to be a wall on one side and the head of a serpent on the other.

If this was done by humans, I reasoned, then surely they would have wanted to make both sides look the same?

On the other hand, if it was done by nature, how were we to account for the blocks—and, even more difficult—the combination of blocks and serpent simulacrum?

Either on its own might be explained by weathering, but for both to occur together in such a limited area seemed much less likely.

A few hundred meters farther up the hill the so-called griffin shed no greater light on the problem. Another rocky outcrop was involved, this time

The Altai "Griffin." Natural? Or modified by human hands? PHOTO: SANTHA FAIIA.

oriented south, and into its granite face, 3 meters tall from the base of its neck and 5 meters wide from the tip of its beak to the crest on the back of its head, was carved the likeness of some immense, mythical, hook-beaked bird—hence its designation as a "griffin."

Natural? Or modified by human hands?

An argument against it being man-made is the way that the lower part of the beak is unfinished and unseparated from the surrounding bedrock. An argument in favor of human enhancements of the natural bedrock is that directly beneath the crest are three small alcoves set side by side step fashion. It is difficult to envisage how nature alone could have achieved this effect. And, besides, there are similar rock-hewn structures in the high Andes of South America that are indisputably man-made.

As we climbed back down the hill Vladimir remained unpersuaded but I wasn't so sure and a few days later, after returning to Novosibirsk where we had access to fast internet again, I searched for information about the region's snakes.

What I learned was that there are six species of serpent in the Altai and that the largest, most venomous and most respected of these by far is *Gloydius halys,* the Siberian pit viper.

In my opinion its clearly defined eyes, its brow ridges, the general shape of its head, and the way that its forked tongue is sometimes thrust out, allowing it to hang down over the middle of its lower jaw creating the illusion of a cleft in that jaw are all rather closely mimicked by the granite features of the "Earth Serpent" we trudged up and down that hill in the Altai to inspect.

But does that make it a remnant of a megalithic Ice Age civilization? Or even a megalith at all? Certainly not! And the same goes for the "griffin." Yet they are set in the heart of a region of mystery where previously held certitudes about humanity's past have been shattered by the discoveries at Denisova Cave.

After saying our good-byes to Vladimir, Raisa, Svetlana, and Maxim, as evening fell over that sunny Siberian day, we drove the remaining 80 kilometers south to Topolnoye, only 20 kilometers from the cave. There another friendly, down-to-earth couple waited to welcome us into their home and feed us not only bread and honey but milk fresh from the cow and other delicious, nourishing things.

ENTERING THE DENISOVANS'
SECRET VALLEY

OUR NEW HOSTS WERE PAPIN Asatryan, dark-haired and bearded, a migrant to the Altai from Armenia when it was still part of the former Soviet Union, and his blond Siberian wife, Elena Darenskikh. They were both in their fifties, their children long ago grown up and fled the nest. Like most of the other 1,100 inhabitants of Topolnoye they had regular jobs (Papin was a builder, Elena an accountant), but also owned a few cows and goats and a fair-sized vegetable garden, growing enough food, it seemed, to make them self-sufficient in most essentials.

That night over a fantastic dinner I joked that if twenty-first-century civilization were to collapse it would be people like Elena and Papin who would survive—not people like me who've never hunted a deer or grown a cabbage or milked a cow in their lives.

"Don't worry," Elena said, "we will save you!"

Some eye-watering local vodka was served, followed by a surprisingly comfortable night's sleep on bunk beds and a sunlit morning greeted with an ample breakfast of eggs, bread, jams, fruit, coffee, and a jug of clotted cream. Then Sergey fired up the Mitsubishi and we were off along a reasonably good road, graded but not paved, running beside the Anui River, fast-flowing with patches of white water, reminding me of the trout streams my grandfather used to fish in the Scottish Highlands where I would sometimes accompany him when I was a child.

For Santha the landscape had more of a "Tolkienesque" quality. Guarded by distant, soaring peaks, we were in a deep, hidden valley, sometimes darkly shadowed and enclosed, sometimes opening out suddenly and unexpectedly into undulating hills and hummocks where coppices of mixed autumnal woodland overlooked bright meadows at the river's edge.

For geologists the landform here is known as "karst," a special type of topography created by the random dissolution over millions of years of soluble, usually sedimentary rocks—in this case limestone. Like all such landscapes it is characterized by extensive underground drainage systems, sinkholes, and caves, of which Denisova Cave is just one among many. Some are already known to contain ancient human remains and artifacts, but far more have not yet been properly studied, or studied at all, by archaeologists.[20]

Sergey pulled the Mitsubishi over and parked beneath a freshly minted National Monument sign, painted brown and helpfully labeled "Denisova Cave" in both Russian and English. Narrow here between low banks, the river was behind us, forested to its edge on the far side and with a saw-toothed range of mountains rising in the distance beyond. On our bank the trees had been cleared and in front of us, across the road, rising steeply for about 200 meters, was a grassy slope with a wooden stairway constructed on its upper part leading to a rugged silver-gray karst cliff at the base of which gaped the black, almost square mouth of the cave.

It is, arguably, the most important archaeological site in the world, and yet not a soul was here, not a scientist, not a tourist, not even a guard. The whole place was eerily deserted, silent but for birdsong and the gentle rustle of wind through the grass, marking time under the sun as it had done for millennia, the guardian of many mysteries still.

Not that I minded the solitude and the peace.

What a privilege, I thought, what a gift, to be here on this bright morning and to have this ancient place to ourselves.

8

HALL OF RECORDS

D ENISOVA CAVE HAS HAD ITS modern name only since the early nineteenth century when a monk, *Dionisij*—Dennis—lived, meditated, and left his graffiti here.[1] Before that the peoples of the Altai used to call it *Aju-Tasch,* which means "Bear Rock."[2] We have no idea how far that nomenclature may go back. It is certain, however, that Denisova Cave has been used and occupied by various species of human for at least 280,000 years, making it an unrivaled archive—a sort of "hall of records"—of our largely unremembered ancestral story.[3] Since excavations began in 1977 it has proved to be a gift that just keeps on giving as archaeologists have systematically combed out the secrets buried in its successive occupation levels.[4]

At the risk of stating the obvious, in an archaeological excavation through orderly and undisturbed stratigraphy of the kind that Denisova Cave generally exhibits, the upper levels are the youngest and the lower levels get progressively older the deeper down you dig. This, for example, is why archaeologists divide the period they call the Paleolithic (the "Old Stone Age," dating from roughly 3 million years ago until 12,000 years ago) into the Lower, Middle, and Upper Paleolithic, with the latter conventionally dated between 50,000 and 12,000 years ago.[5]

The first two trenches at Denisova Cave, both 4 meters deep, sliced down through the more recent levels and exposed artifacts beneath them dating back to the Upper Paleolithic. In the decades that followed these deposits proved to be rich, various, and well preserved and the cave became recognized as a prehistoric locality of great importance.[6] At certain times during the past 280,000 years, not continuously but at intervals, it had been occupied by Neanderthals[7]—our extinct cousins with whom, as is now widely known, our ancestors interbred and from whom some extant modern human populations have inherited as much as 1–4 percent of their DNA.[8] Neanderthals were probably still using the cave 50,000 years ago. It wasn't until 2010, however, when proof emerged that a human species hitherto unrecognized by science had been present at Denisova—a species now also known to have interbred with our ancestors[9]—that the true global significance of this very obscure and remote place could begin to be fully realized.

The sensational news was broken first in the pages of *Nature* in December 2010 in a benchmark paper, "Genetic History of an Archaic Hominin Group from Denisova Cave in Siberia."[10] Coauthored by a stellar team of biomolecular engineers, geneticists, and biologists, with a couple of anthropologists and archaeologists thrown in for good measure, the paper announced the discovery of "the distal manual phalanx [i.e., the fingertip] of a juvenile hominin. . . . The phalanx was found in layer 11, which has been dated to 50,000 to 30,000 years ago. This layer contains microblades and body ornaments of polished stone typical of the 'Upper Palaeolithic industry' generally thought to be associated with modern humans."[11]

The big surprise, however, following a thorough analysis of DNA from the fingertip, was that it didn't belong to an anatomically modern human, nor a Neanderthal, but to a species that had diverged from the common lineage leading to anatomically modern humans and Neanderthals about 1 million years ago. This previously unknown species was judged to be "a sister group to Neanderthals."[12]

PALEO-CSI

DNA WAS ON MY MIND as we scrambled up to the cave because a good way to get to grips with the challenge of Denisova is to think of it as a crime scene—a very old, neglected, contaminated, and long-unrecognized crime scene from which the physical evidence is mostly gone apart from a few bones and teeth but where just enough genetic material might remain to help us figure out what happened there.

Nonetheless, from the moment I entered the cave it impressed itself upon me first, foremost, and forcefully, as a sacred and mystical space. It faced roughly west, overlooking the steep slope leading down to the Anui River, and that morning, as no doubt on many mornings over many thousands of years, the brightness of the day outside was reflected back through the entrance to illuminate the spacious "Main Gallery" within. Looking up I saw that a narrow natural window opened in the ceiling 10 meters above the gallery's west side close to the entrance, admitting more light but also no doubt in ancient times serving as a chimney.

I paused to breathe in the cave air, cool and moist, and to look around, struck by the way the bone-white walls, stained by lichen and covered in the ugly scrawl of recent graffiti that defaced almost every exposed surface, nonetheless gathered about themselves a kind of somber, ancient magnificence. The effect was enhanced by soaring archways leading into the smaller, more intimate East and South Galleries, the side chapels to this prehistoric basilica. I deploy the analogy deliberately because the Denisova Cave system does have a "cathedral-like" feel about it, but I do not claim that it was ever used for religious or spiritual purposes. It may have been, but what the mass of archaeological evidence suggests is that for extraordinarily long periods of time it functioned as a "factory" or "workshop," and that raw materials were brought here from far-off places to be worked and fashioned.

This became clear during the brief visit we made to the Museum of the Peoples of Siberia in Novosibirsk before setting out for Denisova Cave. Director Irina Salnikova apologized that there was so little for us to see in the Denisova room of her museum, explaining that much of the collection was away at exhibitions or in laboratories for further investigation. What she was able to show us, however, as well as many stone tools at various stages of refinement,

from extremely primitive to sophisticated, were some unusual and beautiful pieces of jewelry including pendants featuring biconical drilled-out holes,
cylindrical beads, a ring carved from marble, a ring carved from mammoth
ivory, and bone tubes perhaps designed to hold bone needles so they could be
carried safely.[13]

Many of the materials employed had been brought considerable distances
to the cave,[14] and now that I had reached the cave itself I could see all three
of the galleries in which they had been found and inspect the open excavation
trenches with little tacks and tags left in place to mark the various occupation levels. It was the gaping rectangular trench in the center of the Main
Gallery, however—I would guess it was 5 meters deep, 4 meters long, and 3
meters wide—that most clearly displayed Denisova's amazing time machine
of stratification, with distinct Ice Age occupation levels numbered from 9,[15]
the youngest, all the way down to 20, the oldest, right at the bottom.

The excavation had descended farther here, down to Level 22, but the
tacks and tags for these last two lower and older levels, visible on early reports
of the progress of archaeology in the cave,[16] were no longer present. According
to studies undertaken by the excavators, man-made tools and artifacts were
found in these two exceedingly ancient layers, dated by radiothermolumi-
nescence to between 155,000 and 282,000 years ago.[17] "The lithic [stone]
industries recovered from strata 22 and 21 are characterized by Levallois and
parallel strategies of stone reduction; the tool kit is dominated by sidescrapers
and notch-denticulate tools."[18]

I knew that artifacts together with Neanderthal and Denisovan remains
had been recovered in the excavations in all three galleries across multiple
Paleolithic occupation levels. That morning, however, my focus was particularly on Level 11 in the East Gallery, where certain unusual and distinctive
tools and pieces of jewelery had been found.

Some of these had the archaeologists scratching their heads.

USUAL THINGS AND UNUSUAL THINGS

ANNOYINGLY, I HAD BEEN UNABLE to view these special items during my
visit to the Museum of the Peoples of Siberia. But I knew from my research

that they'd been retrieved, together with other more "normal" and "usual" objects, from an almost exclusively Denisovan occupation level of the East Gallery, nominated Level 11 by the archaeologists and dated to the Upper Paleolithic between 29,200 and 48,650 years ago.[19]

After the first Neanderthal skeletal remains were identified in Europe in the nineteenth century it was, for a very long while, one of the fundamental unquestioned assumptions of archaeology, a matter taken to be self-evidently true, that other "older," "less-evolved" human species never attained, or even in their wildest dreams could hope to aspire, to the same levels of cultural development as *Homo sapiens*. During more than a century of subsequent analysis, and despite multiple additional discoveries, the Neanderthals continued to be depicted as nothing more than brutal, shambling, stupid subhumans—literally morons by comparison with ourselves.[20] Since the beginning of the second decade of the twenty-first century, however, and with increasing certainty as the evidence has become overwhelming, a new "image" of the Neanderthals as sensitive, intelligent, symbolic, and creative beings capable of advanced thought processes and technological innovations has taken root among archaeologists and is set to become the ruling paradigm.[21]

There should be no objection in principle, therefore, to the notion that the anatomically archaic Denisovans, a close genetic "sister species" to the Neanderthals, might have been capable of creating the sorts of tools and symbolic artifacts that, a few decades ago, would automatically have been assumed to be the work of anatomically modern humans.

Yet a difficulty arises.

Among the more "unusual" and "unique" items excavated from the Paleolithic deposits within the entrance zone of the East Gallery, specifically from Level 11.1,[22] were two broken pieces of a dark green chloritolite bracelet. It would have measured 27-millimeter wide and 9-millimeter thick when intact, with an original complete diameter of about 70 millimeters.[23] A detailed use-wear analysis of the bracelet was undertaken and revealed something odd: "This artifact was manufactured with the help of various technical methods of stone working **including those that are considered non-typical for the Paleolithic period.** . . . The bracelet demonstrates a high level of technological skills."[24]

In their detailed scientific analysis published in the journal *Archaeology, Ethnology and Anthropology of Eurasia,* A. P. Derevianko, M. V. Shunkov, and

P. V. Volkov draw our attention, in particular, to "a hole drilled close to one of the edges" of the bracelet and report that "drilling was carried out with a stable drill over the course of at least three stages. Judging by traces on the surface, the speed of drill running was considerable. Vibrations of the rotation axis of the drill are minor, and the drill made multiple rotations around its axis."[25]

They therefore conclude that the bracelet "constitutes unique evidence of an unexpectedly early employment of two-sided fast stationary drilling during the Early Upper Paleolithic."[26]

This is a big deal!

What the investigators are getting at is how peculiar and misplaced in time the bracelet seems to be. It is not simply that it shows the application of skills and technologies that are "unique for the Paleolithic"[27] (i.e., to state the matter plainly, skills and technologies that had never before been seen in a Paleolithic context in any excavation) but also that at least some of these skills and technologies, like "stationary drilling" with the use of a bow drill that does not leave signs of drill vibration,[28] would not be seen again until the Neolithic many thousands of years later. The bracelet thus refutes what the authors describe as "a common assumption" held by archaeologists that "stone drilling originated during the Upper Paleolithic, but gained the features of a well-developed technology only during the Neolithic."[29]

So not only was this curious bracelet unequivocally the work of anatomically *archaic* human beings—the Denisovans—but also it testified to their mastery of advanced manufacturing techniques in the Upper Paleolithic, many millennia ahead of the earliest use of these techniques in the Neolithic by our own supposedly "advanced" species, *Homo sapiens*. Also made crystal clear was the realization that the Denisovans must have possessed the same kinds of artistic sensibility and self-awareness that we habitually associate only with our own kind—for there can be no doubt that very real, conscious, aware, and unmistakably *human* beings had interacted with this bracelet at every stage of its conception, design, and manufacture, all the way through to its end use.[30]

Though the outward structure of Denisovan skulls might have been rather different from ours (predictable for a "sister species" to the Neanderthals), the sense of style, design, and personal adornment manifested in the bracelet seems completely modern, and archaeological reconstructions show it to have been a beautiful thing.

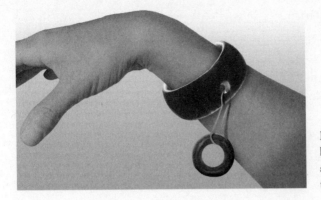

Reconstruction: The
bracelet formed a torque,
slipped sideways onto
the wrist.

Its calculated diameter of just 70 millimeters when intact would have
made it "practically impossible to put even the thinnest hand into it."[31] The
most likely solution, however, since it undoubtedly *was* worn, is that this stone
bracelet originally took the form of a *torque*—not fully circling the wrist, but
with a section removed: "The tips of the bracelet were likely cone-shaped.
Such a shape of the ends of the bracelet makes it easy to put on a hand tangen-
tially. . . . Judging by the size of the artifact and the signs of extensive use-wear
on the interior surface close to the end, the bracelet sat tightly on the wrist."[32]

These signs included evidence of "long contact of the interior surface
with human skin"[33] and, more intimately, "remains of . . . fat from human
skin"[34]—details that reach across the ages and forge a poignant sense of connection. Indeed it dilates the imagination to contemplate the identity of the
person this bracelet was originally made for, who certainly—given the estimated diameter—must have had slim and graceful wrists to wear it well. It is
unlikely to have been the property of a child because of its rarity, artistry, and
high value. As the investigators report: "It brightly shimmers in broad daylight and reveals a rich play of hunter green shades in the light of a campfire.
The bracelet was hardly an everyday item. Fragile and elegant, it was apparently worn on very special occasions. Given the utmost rarity of the material
and the thorough finish, the bracelet was a prestigious ornament attesting to
its owner's high status."[35]

All in all, it seems a fair speculation that the slim-wristed person who
owned this bracelet so many millennia ago was a woman. If so, whoever she
was, whatever position of status she may have occupied, we can also guess
that she had quite an eye for beauty and a whimsical sense of style. A nice

additional detail of the bracelet is that for a long while the drilled hole held a leather strap from which was suspended a pendant.[36] Though neither the pendant nor the strap has survived, their presence left unmistakable polish marks around the hole: "The polished area is limited suggesting that the pendant was rather heavy and caused a strictly set amplitude of oscillation of the strap. The outlines of the polished area suggest the 'up' and 'down' sides of the bracelet and allow us to assume that the bracelet was worn on the right arm."[37]

Again, there is that sense of contact, of intimacy, as though we're separated by no more than a hair's breadth from this ancient human. It must be admitted, however, that even here we're speculating. We might not be dealing with a single individual at all. The bracelet might instead have been a treasured heirloom, passed down from mother to daughter across many generations.

Whatever the truth is, it was eventually broken—not once but twice. On the first occasion the break was evidently accidental and it must still have been cherished because it was carefully repaired, literally put back together again, with some effective but as yet unidentified form of glue.[38]

The second occasion was very different. It appears that the bracelet was deliberately smashed—we can only guess at the motive—"by a blow against a hard surface."[39]

THE EYE OF THE NEEDLE

THE LOWER PART OF LEVEL 11 dates back, as we've seen, to around 50,000 years ago, but the bracelet was found in the upper part, officially designated Level 11.1 and provisionally dated to the Upper Paleolithic about 30,000 years ago[40]—making it, because of its "Neolithic" characteristics, roughly 20,000 years ahead of its time.[41]

The reader will understand, therefore, why it was one of the frustrations of our trip to Siberia in September 2017 that I was not able to see, nor Santha to photograph, this enigmatic, intriguing, and profoundly out-of-place bracelet. Under normal circumstances it is kept at the Museum of the Peoples of Siberia in Novosibirsk, but as luck would have it, during our short visit there, it was out of town—indeed not only out of town but out of Siberia, out of Russia, and in fact in Paris, where it had been on show in an exhibition.

When I said we'd travel there to see it, Irina Salnikova told us that it was no longer on public view and was under investigation by "an international team of archaeologists."[42]

Gone with it was a second anomalous object, an exquisite bone needle 7.6 centimeters in length, with a near-microscopic eye less than 1 millimeter in diameter drilled out at the head.[43] Slightly curved like a modern surgical suture needle, it was excavated from the lower part of Level 11 (Level 11.2) of the central chamber in the summer season of 2016.[44] No detailed analysis had been published before my visit to Novosibirsk in September 2017, but there was some coverage in the Russian media when the discovery was announced. "It is the most unique find of this season, which can even be called sensational," commented Professor Michael Shunkov, coauthor of the report on the bracelet and director of the Institute of Archaeology and Ethnography at the Russian Academy of Sciences.[45] His colleague Dr. Maxim Kozlikin added, "It's the longest needle found in Denisova Cave. We have found needles before, but in younger archaeological layers."[46]

He was referring specifically to the upper part of Level 11 where the bracelet was found and where, indeed, other smaller bone needles had also been excavated some years before.[47] They, too, have fine drilled-out eyes of the type more usually seen in Neolithic than in Paleolithic deposits and provided grounds for skeptics to suggest that the Denisovan dates might have to be revised.[48] The idea was floated that both the bracelet and the small needles must in fact be of Neolithic provenance but had somehow migrated downward through the deposits to end up in Level 11.1—a stratum, from the skeptical point of view, in which they were "obviously" too advanced and "untypical" to belong.

What put an end to such speculation was the discovery of the longer, even finer and more technically perfect needle in 2016 and its location not in the upper—younger—part of Level 11 near its contact with Level 10, but instead in the much older lower part near its contact with Level 12. As we've seen, this lower part of Level 11 has been dated by accelerated mass spectrometry to around 50,000 years before the present[49] (although it may be more ancient, given that 50,000 years is the limit of radiocarbon dating).

By the second half of 2016, therefore, far from proving *younger* as some had expected, the mysterious artifacts of Denisova Cave were beginning to look like they were much, much older. This impression was confirmed in 2017

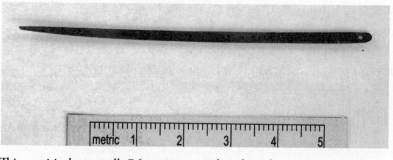

This exquisite bone needle 7.6 centimeters in length, with a near-microscopic eye less than 1 millimeter in diameter drilled out at the head, was found at Denisova Cave in 2016. PHOTO: INSTITUTE OF ARCHAEOLOGY AND ETHNOGRAPHY, SIBERIAN BRANCH, RUSSIAN ACADEMY OF SCIENCES.

with a shocking announcement. Level 11 had been reassessed and its various internal strata reexamined and re-dated. The result of these new investigations was that the bracelet was no longer thought to be 30,000 years old as had originally been supposed, but 50,000 years old![50]

A year later the *Siberian Times* published speculation that it might be even older—perhaps as much as "65,000 to 70,000 years old."[51]

Professor Shunkov did not welcome the speculation and pointed out that the great antiquity of the bracelet was already a matter of global significance, with immense implications for the way archaeologists look at the past.[52] He wasn't about to commit to an older date before all the relevant experts had reached consensus. "Until then, I will refrain from saying anything," he explained, adding that some data was "ambiguous" and required clarification. "If or when we agree, we will have to prepare a publication first."[53]

I could understand his caution. It was the same sort of caution, for pretty much the same reasons, as Tom Deméré had felt for so long before presenting his controversial evidence and conclusions about the Cerutti Mastodon Site in the pages of *Nature*. With discoveries like these that have the potential to disrupt years of comfortable scientific consensus it pays to take care, and to prepare the ground, before you go public.

Persistent rumors filter out of paradigm-busting new discoveries concerning the Denisovans and "multiple big headlines coming up."[54] Meanwhile that beautiful and haunting cave in the Siberian Altai was still, as I write these words in 2018, the only place on earth where physical remains of Denisovans have been confirmed.[55] Those so far recovered are few in number, but such are the wonders of genetic science that the fingertip we spoke of earlier, some teeth, some additional bone fragments, and even some dust from the cave floor allow us to be quite sure that Denisovans were in occupation here at least as early as 170,000 years ago and that they came back 110,000 years ago and again around 50,000 years ago.[56]

Just like the Neanderthals who overlapped with our ancestors and interbred with them, so, too, the Denisovans overlapped the Neanderthals and interbred with them while also, again like the Neanderthals, interbreeding with anatomically modern humans. Viable offspring capable of reproduction resulted from all these liaisons and in August 2018, Denisova Cave obliged yet again by yielding up a bone fragment, more than 50,000 years old and in sufficiently good condition for genome sequencing. It turned out to have belonged to a female, about 13 years of age, who had a Neanderthal mother and a Denisovan father.[57]

In consequence of such liaisons it's a tricky business, tens of thousands of years later, to unravel the tangle of inheritance—with gene flow going in both directions between Neanderthals and Denisovans, Neanderthals and anatomically modern humans, and Denisovans and anatomically modern humans. Thus, where Denisovan DNA is found in human populations today (to give just a single example of the sorts of difficulties faced), researchers must be alert to the possibility that it may not have come directly from a Denisovan but via a Neanderthal who had inherited DNA from an earlier tryst, perhaps dozens of generations back, between a Neanderthal and a Denisovan. Multiple other bewildering combinations are also possible, but using powerful computers geneticists are able to disentangle this cat's-cradle of intertwining genes and lives.

What now appears to be certain is that Neanderthals, *Homo sapiens* (as modern humans are classified taxonomically), and Denisovans all shared and descended from a common ancestor a million years or so ago.[58] The divergence of the Neanderthal line from the modern human line began at least 430,000 years ago, and perhaps as early as 765,000 years ago.[59] The divergence of the Neanderthal line from the Denisovan line occurred between 381,000 and 473,000 years ago.[60] Humans today are therefore, to a greater or lesser degree, hybrids who have inherited genes from Neanderthals, Denisovans, and archaic *Homo sapiens*.

CROSSING THE LINE

THE MODERN INHABITANTS OF THE Altai are notable in that they have inherited virtually no Denisovan DNA at all—just a tiny fraction of a single percent.[61] By contrast, the human populations with the highest percentage of Denisovan DNA today are found among "geographically isolated New Guinean and Australian aborigines (in the range of 3–4%)."[62]

The first detailed investigation went a little higher than this in some cases, concluding, for example, that the archaic Denisovan population "contributed 4–6% of its genetic material to the genomes of present-day Melanesians."[63] Subsequently, varying levels of Denisovan admixture have also been identified in populations from eastern Indonesia, the Philippines, Near and Remote Oceania, and the Americas.[64]

At first this widespread heritage seems strange in view of the location of Denisova Cave itself, deep in the Altai Mountains of southern Siberia, thousands of miles from New Guinea and Australia and even farther from the Americas. But tens of millennia have passed since the Denisovans occupied the cave, occasionally interbreeding with Neanderthals and anatomically modern humans and passing on their genes through all kinds of convoluted liaisons and migrations. We don't even know—on the most recent evidence it seems unlikely—that the cave was in any way central to the Denisovan range. It could equally well have been some peripheral outpost and indeed a number of scientists, notable among them Alan Cooper of the University of Adelaide and Christopher Stringer of London's Natural History Museum, have made a case that the ancient Denisovan homeland was not in Siberia, or indeed in Asia at all, but instead lay "east of Wallace's Line."[65]

A deep oceanic trough, notorious for its fast-flowing currents, Wallace's Line divides Asia to its west from Australia to its east. It is rightly recognized as "one of the world's biggest biogeographic disjunctions"[66] and even during the lowered sea levels of the last Ice Age it would always have confronted migrants seeking to travel in either direction with a challenging maritime crossing. Any who undertook it must not only have been intrepid explorers of unknown realms and lands, but must also have possessed sufficient sailing and navigational skills to cross 30 kilometers of deep and sometimes turbulent open water between Bali and Lombok and, in the case of those who reached Papua New Guinea and Australia, to cross again the wider gulf of the Timor Straits—a formidable barrier of 90 kilometers of open water even at times of lowest sea level.

Coupled with the presence very far to the west in Siberia of Denisovan artifacts as well as Denisovan physical remains yielding a fully sequenced genome, the prominent Denisovan genetic signal among Australian aborigines and Melanesians cannot be explained without invoking these open-water crossings. In remote antiquity **somebody** was certainly undertaking them, and in the process spreading Denisovan genes. What we don't know yet is whether this gene flow was the result of direct interbreeding with the Denisovans themselves, or with some perhaps as yet unidentified people whose own heritage included a significant admixture of Denisovan genes.

We also don't know, and can only guess, at the location of the lost homeland of the Denisovans. Was it east of Wallace's Line, as Cooper and Stringer have argued? Or might it not just as well have been west of the Line on the plains and savannas of the exposed Sunda Shelf during the lowered sea levels of the last Ice Age when the Malaysian peninsula and the islands of Sumatra, Java, and Borneo all formed one continuous landmass?[67]

Wherever it was, we know that 90 kilometers of open water was no barrier to these people—so why not farther? Why should they not even have crossed to the other side of the Pacific Ocean, making landfall in the Americas?

9

THE STRANGE AND
MYSTERIOUS GENETIC HERITAGE
OF NATIVE AMERICANS

BY NO MEANS FULLY UNDERSTOOD yet despite the best efforts of Darwin and his successors, the process we call "evolution" combines continuous change with continuous conservation in an endless, swirling, bewildering dance of almost unbelievable intricacy. Zoom in at sufficiently high resolution to the DNA that choreographs this dance, however, and certain distinct and identifiable patterns begin to emerge. Because we are all members of a single human family, these patterns can then be used to establish the degree of relatedness—and thus to track the prehistoric migrations and liaisons—of seemingly disparate populations, even if they now reside on opposite sides of the globe. It's an endeavor of great technical complexity, deploying the latest advances in twenty-first-century genomic science, but it reveals previously hidden clues to the lost story of our past and—potentially—offers us a way out of the cultural amnesia that has erased tens of thousands of years of ancestral experiences from our collective memory.

This is not a genetics textbook and I don't want us to get bogged down in superfluous details, but here are some essentials we'll need going forward:

1. DNA is the genetic mechanism of inheritance, and the various types of DNA present in our cells have, as a result of scientific advances in the late twentieth and early twenty-first centuries, been subject to close investigation by a range of highly sophisticated techniques.[1] The results of these investigations have shed light on the degree of genetic relatedness that exists between individuals and, on a larger scale, between entire populations.[2]

2. Located in the fluid surrounding the nucleus of every cell in our bodies, mtDNA (mitochondrial DNA) is inherited by both males and females but is passed on to offspring only by females.[3] MtDNA can identify lines of descent from shared maternal, but not paternal, ancestors.[4] What geneticists like about mtDNA is its abundance, being present in multiple copies per cell, giving plenty of material to work with.[5]

3. The same cannot be said of nuclear DNA, inherited equally from both parents, which has only two copies per cell but which encodes far more genetic information than mtDNA, allowing for far more robust and precise analyses of genetic relatedness.[6]

4. Within the cell nucleus are also located the chromosomes— segments of DNA that determine sex. If you have two X chromosomes you're a female; if you have an X and a Y you're male. Y-DNA is passed on only by males, thus facilitating the determination only of shared paternal ancestry, whereas X-DNA is inherited both through the maternal and paternal lines (since males and females both have X chromosomes) and can therefore be useful in isolating shared common ancestors along particular branches of inheritance.[7]

Is it important to understand the technicalities of DNA and DNA analysis as a means of establishing degrees of relatedness?

By all means dig deeper if you wish to, for this whole area of science is a fascinating one. But don't feel you have to—any more, for example, than you might feel you must master plumbing in order to run water from a tap, or the intricacies of mechanical engineering in order to drive a car, or medical studies before undergoing surgery.

In other words, genetics, unlike archaeology, is a hard science where the pronouncements of experts are based on facts, measurements, and replicable experimentation rather than inferences or preconceived opinions. Mistakes *are* made by geneticists, of course, and profound disagreements are routinely thrashed out between colleagues in the professional journals. By and large, however, just as we trust the engineer, or the plumber, or the surgeon for their specialized knowledge (even though they sometimes get things wrong), it will streamline matters greatly here if we trust the conclusions of specialists working with the latest high-tech tools at the cutting edge of analysis of ancient DNA.

TWO SITES, TWO FAMILIES, ONE HUMAN RACE

MIND YOU, "SHOTGUN SEQUENCING" OF long strands of DNA and other similarly esoteric technologies are not required for us to connect—at a basic human level—with the story of our ancestors. Particularly poignant examples of what I mean here are provided at two ancient sites, one in Siberia and one in Montana.

The Siberian site lies to the west of Lake Baikal near the village of Mal'ta on the banks of the Bolshaya Belaya River. As the crow flies (and a great deal farther on foot through winding valleys and over high passes) this is a location more than 1,000 kilometers east of Denisova Cave. Its reach back into the human past does not extend as far as Denisova's. Still it has been recognized for many years as the home of an Upper Paleolithic culture—archaeologists call it the Mal'ta-Buret culture—that left behind many beautiful and mysterious works of art thought to be more than 20,000 years old.[8] Among them, done in bone and mammoth ivory, are carvings of elegant, long-necked water fowl and a collection of thirty human Venus figures that are "rare for Siberia but found at a number of Upper Paleolithic sites across western Eurasia."[9]

The primary excavations at Mal'ta, which took place between 1928 and

1958,[10] also uncovered two burials, both of young children interred with curious and beautiful grave goods including pendants, badges, and ornamental beads.[11] One of these children, a boy aged 3–4 years and now known to archaeologists as MA-I, had been buried beneath a stone slab, there was a Venus figurine beside him,[12] and he was "wearing an ivory diadem, a bead necklace and a bird-shaped pendant."[13] Traces of pigmentation were found on his bones,[14] which presently reside in the Hermitage State Museum in St. Petersburg, where a high-level international team of investigators, prominently featuring geneticists and evolutionary biologists, paid them a visit in 2009. The scientists drilled out a number of small samples from the bones and subjected them to accelerator mass spectrometry C-14 dating that showed them, give or take a few hundred years, to be 24,000 years old.[15] Detailed tests were then carried out on the samples and in due course the investigators announced that they had successfully sequenced MA-1's entire genome—making it, when a full account of the investigation was published in *Nature* in 2014, "the oldest anatomically modern human genome reported to date."[16]

We'll consider the implications of what was found in context also of the second site I mentioned above—located in Montana. Known to archaeologists as the Anzick-1 burial site and dated to 12,600 years ago (which makes it 11,400 years younger than MA-1), it is also a child's grave—in this case a boy aged 1–2 years who was interred with more than 100 tools of stone and antler, all sprinkled with red ochre.[17]

One thing we see for sure in both these ancient burials, separated by thousands of miles and thousands of years, is that the human capacity to love and cherish family members, and to regret and mourn those who pass prematurely, is not diminished by time; indeed, we instantly recognize and identify with it today because we share it. For convenience we'll continue to use the rather dehumanizing archaeological labels "MA-1" and "Anzick-1" here. But let's not forget the bereaved parents and family members as they gathered around those gravesides 24,000 years ago in Siberia and 12,600 years ago in Montana, and the care and thought, the symbolism and emotions, the love and the aching sense of loss that went into the careful preparation of the graves and the choice and placing of the grave goods in both cases.

Across the ages and regardless of geography, in everything that really matters, it bears repeating that we are all members of a SINGLE human family—a family of intrepid adventurers who have been exploring the world in one form or another for the best part of a million years.[18] In the course of this long odyssey we've moved so far apart, across oceans, over mountains, and to the opposite ends of jungles, deserts, and ice caps that we've forgotten how closely related we in fact are. In this sense, like the simple human message of the burials, the message of genetics also speaks to a hidden unity within our apparent diversity—and sometimes in ways that defy our expectations.

ANCIENT EUROPEAN GENES

FEW HAVE COMMENTED ON THE obvious cultural similarities in burial practices, but as to genetics, all authorities agree that MA-1 and Anzick-1 are closely related, sharing large sequences of DNA.[19] Anzick-1, however, "belonged to a population directly ancestral to many contemporary Native Americans" and thus, unsurprisingly—despite his proximity to MA-1—is "more closely related to all indigenous American populations than to any other group."[20]

Just as it was for so long an article of faith that the Americas were peopled exclusively by migrations from Siberia across the Bering land bridge, so, too, it was held to be self-evident that those Siberian migrants must have been most closely related to *east* Asians.[21] What did the Bering land bridge *do,* after all, if not connect the far north*east* of Asia with the far north*west* of North America?

But a surprise awaited the investigative team led by Maanasa Raghavan of the Centre for GeoGenetics at Denmark's Natural History Museum and Pontus Skoglund of Harvard Medical School's Department of Genetics. Instead of confirming the anticipated connection to east Asia, MA-1's Y chromosome (the male sex chromosome) turned out to be "basal to modern-day **western** Eurasians."[22] We have mentioned the limitations of Y-chromosome analysis already, so it is good—and raises the confidence level all around—that this unanticipated and potentially boat-rocking finding was subsequently confirmed with autosomal evidence[23] (the best kind of DNA evidence, derived from the nucleus of the cell). "MA-1," the investigators repeat and reemphasize, "is basal to modern-day western Eurasians . . . with no close affinity to east Asians."[24]

Moreover—and most intriguingly—the investigators discovered that MA-1 also stands "near the root of most Native American lineages,"[25] and "14 to 38% of Native American ancestry may originate through gene flow from this ancient population [the population from which MA-1 stemmed]. This is likely to have occurred after the divergence of Native American ancestors from east Asian ancestors, but before the diversification of Native American populations in the New World."[26]

The final link in the chain of evidence emerged when MA-1's mitochondrial genome was sequenced, revealing the Siberian infant to be a member of "haplogroup U, which has also been found at high frequency among Upper Paleolithic and Mesolithic European hunter-gatherers."[27]

"Our result," the investigators conclude, "therefore suggests a connection between pre-agricultural Europe and Upper Paleolithic Siberia."[28]

A genetic consequence of this previously unsuspected European/Siberian nexus, since as much as 38 percent of Native American ancestry is attributable to gene flow from MA-1's people, is that Native American DNA carries a strong and very ancient "European" signal.[29]

HIDDEN SOUTH AMERICAN ORIGINS OF CLOVIS REVEALED

SOMETHING I HAVEN'T MENTIONED YET—the ochre-dusted stone and antler tools found buried with Anzick-1 were unmistakably Clovis artifacts.[30] There are two reasons why this "Clovis connection" is particularly noteworthy and relevant to our quest.

First, the Anzick-1 burial was originally dated to around 12,600 years ago—or, more exactly, within the limits of resolution of C-14, to between 12,707 and 12,556 years ago.[31] This suggested that the grave was dug and the grave goods placed with the remains of the deceased infant a century or two **after** the abrupt and mysterious disappearance of the Clovis culture from the archaeological record around 12,800 years ago.

That disappearance testifies to a sudden cessation of previously widespread cultural activities, suggestive of interruption by some far-reaching cataclysmic event. What it does **not** mean, however, is that every member of the Clovis population died out overnight. Even if most did there would, undoubtedly, have been survivors—small groups coalescing into scattered, wandering tribes, whose members might have looked back on the achievements of their ancestors with awe.

One possibility that has been considered is that Anzick-1 himself may have belonged to just such a remnant group. This possibility was raised after a small but significant discrepancy was found between the dates of Anzick-1's bones and the dates of certain artifacts buried with him.

The artifacts, known as "foreshafts," are specially cut, shaped, and hollowed sections of red deer antler, each designed to hold a projectile point at one end and to clamp onto the tip of a wooden spear shaft at the other. As we've seen, Anzick-1's bones were initially dated between 12,707 and 12,556 years ago. The antler foreshafts among his grave goods are a century or two **older** than that—in the range of 12,800 to 13,000 years ago[32]—"a much more typical and acceptable age for Clovis," as archaeologist Stuart J. Fiedel observes, than the "age attributed to the infant's bones."[33]

To resolve the discrepancy, Fiedel offers a simple but insightful reading of the evidence. The discordant data, he speculates in a paper published in *Quaternary International* in June 2017, would be reconciled if "the foreshafts were 100 to 200-year-old antique heirlooms interred with the infant by the very last Clovis folks in the region."[34]

Alternatively he suggests that due to contamination of the sample, "the infant bone dates may be slightly too young."[35]

A number of other researchers seized on the apparent temporal discrepancy to discount Anzick-1 as a Clovis individual,[36] but Fiedel's comment on contamination proved prescient. In June 2018, a year after his *Quaternary International* paper, a new study by scientists at the Oxford Radiocarbon Accelerator Unit was published in *Proceedings of the National Academy of Sciences* (*PNAS*) under the headline "Reassessing the Chronology of the Archaeological Site of Anzick."[37] The study reminds us that "in radiocarbon dating, contamination can be a major source of error" but adds that "methodological improvements" since the original dating work at Anzick was done "have seen a significant effect in dating accuracy and reliability."[38] After applying these new methods the study concludes, contrary to previous findings, that

"Anzick-1 is temporally coeval with the dated antler rods. This implies that the individual is indeed temporally associated with the Clovis assemblage."[39]

We'll return to the mysterious end of the Clovis culture in later chapters. Meanwhile there's a second reason why Anzick-1's "Clovis connection" is of immediate relevance to our quest here—which is that although Clovis did, at the limits of its range, extend into some northern areas of South America, its heartland was in North America.[40] Intuitively, therefore, we would expect the Montana infant, a Clovis individual, to be much more closely related to Native North Americans than to Native South Americans. Further investigations, however, while reconfirming that Anzick-1's genome had a greater affinity to **all** Native Americans than to any extant Eurasian population,[41] revealed it to be much more closely related to native **South** Americans than to Native North Americans![42]

Morten Rasmussen of Denmark's Centre for GeoGenetics and Pontus Skoglund of the Department of Genetics at Harvard Medical School seek to explain the anomaly by arguing that the ancestors of the First Americans must have split into two separate groups—they label them "the NA and SA lineages"—before entering the Americas, "with the Anzick-1 individual belonging to the SA lineage."[43]

That seems reasonable enough on the face of things until we stop to consider the spectacle of these two groups, sharing common ancestry but already genetically distinct, racing into the Americas on parallel and nonconverging tracks, one heading straight for South America, the other staying in North America—yet never, throughout this process, making sufficiently enduring contact with one another to compromise their separateness or leave a trace in the genetic record. This seems to deny human nature and simply doesn't make sense in lots of ways even before we get to the fact that Anzick-1, the most ancient representative of the "SA lineage" so far studied by science,[44] wasn't found anywhere near South America but in North America and, indeed, in Montana, which, 12,600 years ago, was about as far north as you could get before you hit the great Cordilleran ice sheet.

A PECULIAR SIGNAL
FROM DOWN UNDER

IN SUMMARY, ANZICK-1 IS A paradox clothed in a conundrum, wrapped up in a mystery—an individual in a North American Clovis culture grave who is closely related to Native South Americans, to the Siberian Mal'ta population, and to ancient western Europeans. Because the South American lineage to which he belonged shared a common ancestor with the North American lineage, the geneticists found nothing in the data to challenge their long-held view that the settlement of the Americas, both North and South, had been accomplished from northeast Asia by a single founding population—albeit one that divided itself into two streams.

A year later, however, in September 2015, Pontus Skoglund, his senior colleague Professor David Reich of the Department of Genetics at Harvard Medical School, and other leading experts in the field announced in the pages of *Nature* that they had found new evidence in South America, and specifically in the Amazon rainforest, that called for a rethink:

> Here we analyse genome-wide data to show that **some Amazonian Native Americans descend partly from a Native American founding population that carried ancestry more closely related to indigenous Australians, New Guineans and Andaman Islanders than to any present-day Eurasians or Native Americans.** This signature is not present to the same extent, or at all, in present-day Northern and Central Americans or in a 12,600-year-old Clovis-associated genome, suggesting a more diverse set of founding populations of the Americas than previously accepted.[45]

We've already done the groundwork on the "12,600-year-old Clovis-associated genome" the researchers speak of here. The reference, of course, is to Anzick-1, that paradoxical infant, swaddled in mystery, who we know was more closely related to Native South Americans than to Native North Americans. What the new study adds to this is that there was a previously unsuspected structure within the SA lineage, including at least one sub-lineage—to which Anzick-1 did **not** belong—that was more closely related to Melanesian

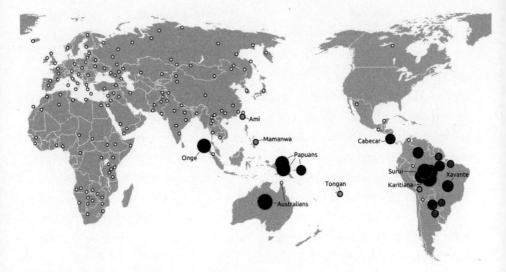

South Americans, notably in the Amazon rainforest, share ancestry with Australasian and Melanesian populations not seen in Mesoamericans or North Americans. (After *Nature,* "Genetic Evidence for Two Founding Populations of the Americas," September 3, 2015).

Papuans and Australian Aborigines than to **any** extant Native American population.

There is no trace of this lineage in most modern Native Americans, and—it's worth driving this point home—no trace either in the ancestral population represented by Anzick-1. Nevertheless, the investigators continued to be confronted by a peculiar and distinctive "Australasian signal," showing genetic relatedness to "indigenous groups in Australia, Melanesia, and island Southeast Asia,"[46] calling attention to itself in the genomes of Native Americans from the heart of the Amazon jungle. The Surui and Karitiana tribes, speaking languages belonging to the Tupi family, proved to have a peculiarly close connection to Australasians, as did the Ge-speaking Xavante of the central Brazilian plateau.[47]

Such a signal was completely unexpected given the vast distance between Australasia and the Amazon and the absence of any overland DNA trail. Skoglund and Reich therefore subjected it to particularly rigorous testing, applying four different methods of statistical analysis to compare the genomes of 30 Central and South American peoples with the genomes of 197 other populations from around the world.[48] "We spent a really long time trying to make this result go away," Skoglund explained, "but it just got stronger."[49]

In the end "a statistically clear signal linking Native Americans in the Amazonian region of Brazil to present-day Australo-Melanesians and Andaman Islanders" was confirmed.[50]

"It's incredibly surprising," commented David Reich. "There's a strong working model in archaeology and genetics, of which I have been a proponent, that most Native Americans today extend from a single pulse of expansion south of the ice sheets—and that's wrong. We missed something very important in the original data."[51]

What was missed, Reich and Skoglund argue, was nothing less than the fingerprints of a lost lineage—a **second** founding population of the Americas. It is very old,[52] in their view, and almost all traces of it have been overwritten almost everywhere by later genetic "noise." That we can still detect it at all among isolated peoples in the Amazon is probably because their genomes have been subject to less admixture and introgression than most.

The investigators have given their "putative ancient Native American lineage" a name: "Population Y" after *Ypykuéra,* which means "ancestor" in the Tupi language family."[53]

And they come to a very clear, if tantalizing, conclusion: "A Population Y that had ancestry from a lineage more closely related to present-day Australasians than to present-day East Asians and Siberians likely contributed to the DNA of Native Americans from Amazonia and the Central Brazilian Plateau."[54]

But how, when, and where did this contribution occur?

One possibility that Skoglund and Reich consider is that the patterns of genomic variation of present-day Amazonians could be explained if a large proportion—up to 85 percent—of their ancestry derived "from a population that existed in a substructured northeast Asia, and was similar to the main lineage that gave rise to other Native Americans while retaining more Australasian affinity."[55]

In other words, congregating in that original northeast Asian—that is, Siberian—melting pot we are now being asked to envisage not only people with European genes and people with east Asian genes, but also people with Australasian genes. Neanderthals were part of the mix, too, interbreeding vigorously with *Homo sapiens,* and there were people carrying Denisovan genes and of course the Denisovans themselves. We're asked to see these groups as essentially divided and separate from one another—despite the obvious evidence of their liaisons—and we're asked to accept that they remained divided and separate, already conveniently prearranging themselves into what would become the "NA" and "SA" lineages, as they trekked across the Bering land bridge.

The endlessly flexible boundaries of such an improbable model seem perfectly adapted to explain away any potentially boat-rocking data. It's not surprising, therefore, to find a hermetically sealed and hitherto invisible "Australasian lineage" being tacked on to the mongrel pedigree of the First Americans as soon as the inconvenient presence of Australasian genes in the midst of the Amazon jungle needed to be explained and normalized. Nor is it surprising to see the hypothetical "Population Y," identified as the bearer of those genes, depicted as heading straight to South America to oblige without leaving any of its DNA along the way among the North American populations with which it would surely have had to mingle.

Perhaps because of the impracticality of some of these ideas, Skoglund and Reich conclude with an offbeat alternative. "The patterns of genomic variation of present-day Amazonians," they point out, seemingly off the cuff, could also be explained "by as little as 2% admixture from an Australasian-related population, that would thus have penetrated deep inside the Americas without mixing with the main ancestral lineage of present-day Native Americans."[56]

In other words, on this view, what has been preserved in those isolated, unadulterated Amazonian genomes that speaks to an ancient connection with Australasia might not be the traces of a full-scale *migration* but something more like a one-off settlement by a relatively small group.

In the next chapter we'll consider the profound implications of this scenario for our understanding of American prehistory.

A SIGNAL FROM THE
DREAMTIME?

S KOGLUND AND REICH'S PAPER IN *Nature* reporting the presence of
Australasian genes in certain populations in the Amazon is titled "Genetic
Evidence for Two Founding Populations of the Americas."[1] It was first pub-
lished online on July 21, 2015 (ahead of the print edition, which appeared on
September 3, 2015).

On precisely the same day (before appearing in print in the journal *Science*
on August 21, 2015), another team of researchers, led by Maanasa Raghavan
and Eske Willerslev, both of the Centre for GeoGenetics at the University of
Copenhagen, published the online version of a paper titled "Genomic Evidence for the Pleistocene and Recent Population History of Native Americans."[2] Unlike Skoglund and Reich, who see two founder populations in the
data, Raghavan and Willerslev see only one, arriving in "a single migration
wave from Siberia no earlier than 23 thousand years ago and after no more
than an 8000-year isolation period in Beringia."[3]

Raghavan and Willerslev several times drive home the point that the data they present "are consistent with a single initial migration of all Native Americans"[4] along a route from Siberia via Beringia and that "from that single migration, there was a diversification of ancestral Native Americans leading to the formation of northern and southern branches."[5]

This is all very neat, tidy, and in certain ways reassuring for those American archaeologists—a majority—still reeling from posttraumatic shock following the collapse of the Clovis First dogma. Of course they would have to be in a state of rigid and unyielding denial to continue to shrug off the perfect storm of evidence from genetics and from sites like Topper, Cactus Hill, and Monte Verde that relegated Clovis to the trash can of history. But at least their favored route—from Siberia, across the Bering land bridge—remains intact and not only that, but Raghavan and Willerslev's paper also endorses the currently fashionable "Beringian standstill" model.

If only the geneticists had ended their paper there, archaeological contentment with it would have been complete. However, because they are good scientists, Raghavan and Willerslev—just like Skoglund and Reich—could not ignore the persistent "Australasian signal" that kept cropping up in the data:

> We found that some American populations—including the
> Aleutian Islanders, Surui, and Athabascans—are closer to Australo-
> Melanesians as compared with other Native Americans, such as North
> American Ojibwa, Cree, and Algonquin and the South American
> Purepecha, Arhuaco, and Wayuu. The Surui are, in fact, one of the
> closest Native American populations to East Asians and Australo-
> Melanesians, the latter including Papuans, non-Papuan Melanesians,
> Solomon Islanders, and South East Asian hunter-gatherers such as
> Aeta.[6]

As we've seen in previous chapters, the archaeological mainstream is an intensely conservative and territorial scholarly community, resistant to change, whose deeply embedded prejudices deny that our "Stone Age" ancestors could have possessed anything other than the most primitive and rudimentary technological abilities. For orthodox thinkers, it is literally **inconceivable** that prehistoric settlers from the general vicinity of Papua New Guinea could have crossed the entire width of the Pacific Ocean to South America, and thence made their way to the Amazon to leave evidence of their presence in the DNA of people still living there today.

What's paradoxical about this position is that—admittedly after a hard-fought struggle—no one in the mainstream now would seriously dispute that our ancient hominid ancestors were capable of undertaking successful open-water voyages to colonize new lands.[7] We've seen how the presence of Denisovan DNA on both sides of the Timor Straits and both east and west of the Wallace Line confirms that migrations across stretches of open water up to 90 kilometers wide were indeed taking place at least 60,000 years ago—a position already supported by a mass of other evidence.[8]

Likewise, and significantly earlier, bones and artifacts of *Homo erectus* dated to 800,000 years before the present have been found on the Indonesian islands of Flores and Timor, again making open-water crossings by these supposed "subhumans" a certainty even during periods of lowered sea level.[9]

All of this has long ago been conceded. Despite the passage of close to a million years since *Homo erectus* first sailed to Flores, however, what archaeology does **not** concede is that the human species could have developed and refined those early nautical skills to the extent of being able to cross a vast ocean like the Pacific or the Atlantic from one side to the other. In the case of the former, extensive transoceanic journeys are not believed to have been undertaken until about 3,500 years ago, during the so-called Polynesian expansion.[10] And the mainstream historical view is that the Atlantic was not successfully navigated until 1492—the year in which, as the schoolyard mnemonic has it, "Columbus sailed the ocean blue."

Indeed, the notion that long transoceanic voyages were a technological **impossibility** during the Stone Age remains one of the central structural elements of the dominant reference frame of archaeology[11]—a reference frame that geneticists see no reason not to respect and deploy when interpreting their own data. Since that reference frame rules out, a priori, the option of a direct ocean crossing between Australasia and South America during the Paleolithic and instead is adamant that all settlement came via northeast Asia, geneticists tend to approach the data from that perspective.

This is the case with Raghavan and Willerslev. First, as we've seen, they concede the presence within the data of "a distant Old-World signal related to Australo-Melanesians and East Asians in some Native Americans."[12] But, second, they go on to downplay the implications of this with the following interpretation:

> The widely scattered and differential affinity of Native Americans to the Australo-Melanesians, ranging from a strong signal in the Surui to a much weaker signal in northern Amerindians such as Ojibwa, points to this gene flow occurring **after** the initial peopling by Native American ancestors.[13]

Here's how they arrive at this interpretation of the data:

1. They trace the source of the strong Australasian signal in the Amazon to "gene flow"—the transfer of genetic variation from one population to another.[14]

2. They propose that this gene flow reached Amazonian peoples such as the Surui from northern Amerindian populations such as the Aleutian Islanders and the Athabascans, and they appear to favor particularly a "route via the Aleutian Islanders," since the latter "were previously found to be closely related to the Inuit who have a relatively greater affinity to East Asians, Oceanians, and Denisovans than Native Americans."[15] They hypothesize that the "complex genetic history" of the Aleutian Islanders perhaps "included input from a population related to Australo-Melanesians through an East Asian continental route [i.e., from Siberia across the Bering land bridge], and this genomic signal might have been subsequently transferred to parts of the Americas, including South America, through past gene flow events."[16]

The problem I have with all this is that these hypothetical "past gene flow events" somehow left a strong DNA signal in the Amazon, one of the remotest and most inaccessible parts of South America, while leaving next to no signal at all in North America, which—whether the genes were carried by people who traveled on foot or by people who island-hopped and coasted from the Aleutians in simple watercraft—would surely have involved interactions with

North American populations before any interactions with South American populations took place—and therefore presumably should have left a DNA signal in North America at least as strong as the signal found in the Amazon.

Seeking clarification, I contacted Professor Willerslev directly at the University of Copenhagen on March 2, 2018, and asked what in his data had led him and his coauthors to conclude that the gene flow bringing the Australasian signal to the Amazon had occurred **after** the initial peopling of the Americas. I also asked why they favored Aleutian islanders as the likely vector and whether it was not counterintuitive to propose such an extreme northern source for this gene flow. If a northern source had indeed been involved, I argued, then:

wouldn't we expect to see a cline in the signal from strongest in the north, nearest the putative source, to weakest in the faraway south and particularly in remote South American regions like the Amazon? But my understanding of the data is that if there is a cline at all it is in the opposite direction—i.e., from strongest in the south to weakest in the north. Am I understanding correctly and if so how do you explain this counterintuitive cline? Are we to imagine Aleutians or Athabascans island-hopping and coasting down the entire Pacific coast of North America, absolutely not intermingling with anyone else or leaving any DNA traces along the way, until they arrive (presumably) at some point on the Pacific coast of South America whence they strike inland for the Amazon?[17]

Professor Willerslev replied:

When you talk about a cline in contemporary data you assume peoples have stayed in the same place since the Pleistocene. We do not know that. Therefore I don't think it's a particularly good argument. A lot of stuff can happen over tens of thousands of years in regard to distribution of peoples. In principle the signature in the north could have been lost by replacement. We simply don't know.[18]

"Dear Eske," I responded (happily we had agreed to switch to first-name terms):

I take your point, absolutely, on all of this. And I certainly don't imagine that peoples have stayed in the same places since the Ice Age. It's part of the essence of being human, I think, to move around, migrate, and explore. Still, will I be misrepresenting the facts if I were to state in my book, **with reference specifically to present-day populations,** that a cline of the Australasian signal is evident with a stronger signal in South America, particularly the Amazon, than anywhere in North America? And further, again with reference specifically to present-day populations, would I be misrepresenting the facts to say that the Australasian signal is stronger amongst the Surui than it is amongst the Aleutians and Athabascans and that the Surui's affinity to East Asians, Oceanians, and Denisovans is stronger than that of the Inuit?[19]

"No!" Eske replied, "I would not call it a cline.[20]. . . It's strongest in the Surui but stronger in Aleutians than in Athabascans . . . but these groups also contain more East Asian so it may simply reflect just that. The Denisovan signal is not stronger in the Surui than in the others (to my knowledge)."[21]

In summary, therefore, taking into account all of the above, the situation seems to be that the Denisovan signal remains at a constant and fairly low level throughout present-day indigenous populations so far sequenced in both North and South America.[22] The Australasian signal, by contrast, is definitely and notably much stronger among populations in the Amazon, such as the Surui, and much weaker among other Native Americans such as the Arhuaco (of non-Amazonian northern Colombia), the Wayuu (of non-Amazonian northern Venezuela), the Purepecha (of Mexico), and the Ojibwa, Cree, and Algonquin of north and northeast North America. While never reaching the high levels found among Amazonian populations, the signal among Aleutian Islanders and Athabascans is relatively stronger than in other Native North American groups and relatively stronger in Aleutian Islanders than it is in Athabascans—though Raghavan and Willerslev warn in their *Science* paper that the Aleutian Islander data must be interpreted with some caution since it "is heavily masked owing to recent admixture with Europeans."[23]

"THE MOST PARSIMONIOUS SOLUTION . . ."

I NEXT REMINDED ESKE OF Skoglund and Reich's papers. In these, as the reader will recall, the authors contemplate the "formal possibility"[24] that the Australasian signal might reflect direct settlement in the Amazon by an Australasian-related population "that would thus have penetrated deep inside the Americas without mixing with the main ancestral lineage of present-day Native Americans."[25] My question to Professor Willerslev, therefore, was whether there was anything in the genetic data that he was aware of that would effectively refute the notion of direct settlement.

His reply got straight to the point:

Currently no one has a good explanation of the Australo-Melanesian signal. All that is put forward as possible explanations are purely speculative. So whether it's an old or a later event is unknown. What we do know is that it's present in some Native American groups particularly from Brazil. We also know it has to be pre-Columbian. We also know that it's not present in any of the ancient skeletons genome sequenced so far. Possible explanations can be: 1) It comes in after the initial peopling of the Americas e.g. by costal migrations that do not leave much trace behind in contemporary populations (e.g. they move quickly), or that we just haven't sequenced the populations in North America that hold the signal; 2) it's an old migration through Beringia before Native Americans but then it's strange they leave no signals in the ancient skeletons sequenced so far; 3) it's a structured initial Native American population moving south into the Americas of which some carry the signal but again then it's strange that there is no evidence of admixture between the two groups; 4) someone holding this signal comes into the Americas not through Beringia but crossing into South America across the Ocean. Based purely on the genetic data this is the most parsimonious explanation but it does not make practical sense; 5) Finally it's a possibility that the signal is a methodical artefact. That the methods are not behaving as we think they should do.[26]

Apart from point 5, which is above my pay grade to assess, it was refreshing to encounter such a straightforward admission that no good explanation has yet been offered for the Australo-Melanesian signal, and such willingness to consider a wide range of possibilities. Since I was already leaning toward the view that the signal is mysterious and might bear witness to a crossing of the Pacific Ocean followed by the settlement in the Amazon of a relatively small group, my eyes were naturally drawn to Eske's point 4. "Based purely on the genetic data," and invoking the parsimony principle (whereby the simplest scientific explanation that fits the evidence is preferred), it looked very much as if this leading figure in the study of ancient genetics agreed with me! Where he and I parted company, however, was over the possibility that anybody could have made an oceanic crossing of thousands of kilometers during the Stone Age. For Eske such a proposition simply didn't make practical sense.

I sent him a follow-up mail to ask if he based this conclusion "on the archaeological consensus that our Upper Palaeolithic and early Holocene ancestors were incapable of undertaking long trans-oceanic voyages?"[27]

He replied, "In regard to crossing the Pacific. I'm not saying it did not happen but there is no evidence suggesting that humans were capable of such a journey until quite late in history (Polynesian expansion). It's a possibility and I'm open to the idea but there's not much evidence supporting it except going for the most parsimonious solution of the genetic data."[28]

So here again is a refreshing openness of mind so rarely seen among archaeologists. The best fit for the genetic data does indeed appear to be a transpacific voyage (or voyages) to South America by a group (or groups) of settlers carrying Australo-Melanesian genes. However, on the matter of the *practicality* of anyone undertaking transpacific voyages in the Stone Age, which has to do primarily with the level of technology attributed to our ancestors at that time, Professor Willerslev accepts, and builds into his own reasoning, the mainstream archaeological consensus that "there is no evidence suggesting that humans were capable of such a journey until quite late in history."

He is not to be blamed for doing so, since it is normal in the sciences for an expert in one field to trust and rely upon the conclusions of experts in other fields. Quite possibly Professor Willerslev is not aware—why should he be?—of how little like a science archaeology really is and how often the mainstream archaeological consensus has proved, after suppressing dissenting opinions for decades, to have been fundamentally wrong all along. Recent examples include the hasty and forced addition of more than 5,000 years to the previously accepted chronology for the earliest megalithic sites after the discovery of 11,600-year-old Gobekli Tepe in Turkey,[29] the collapse of "Clovis First," and the comprehensive debunking of the long-held belief that the Neanderthals were incapable of art.[30] Clearly, the mainstream archaeological consensus is **not** always right in what it agrees upon and it may well turn out that it is not right on the matter of grand oceanic voyages during the Ice Age. Indeed, rather than being ruled out on the basis of a priori assumptions, perhaps that strange Australo-Melanesian genetic signal in the Amazon is part of the **proof** that such voyages must indeed have occurred.

Then there's the matter of the role of the Denisovans in all this. We know from the evidence of Denisova Cave itself that their technology—while undoubtedly "Stone Age"—was far ahead of its time and in some ways much more akin to the Neolithic than to the Upper Paleolithic. We know that they could make sea crossings and that they ranged over a vast area, at least from the Altai Mountains in the west to Australo-Melanesia in the east. Last but not least, we know that their DNA survives most strongly today in people of Australo-Melanesian descent, and there's informed speculation that Australo-Melanesia may have been their original homeland.

It's strange, and evocative, that the mystery of the Denisovans and the mystery of the Australo-Melanesian genetic signal in the Amazon should collide in this way, and all the more so because, as Eske Willerslev makes clear, there's no especially strong Denisovan element in the signal. Perhaps further research will provide us with a higher-resolution picture, but from the data presently in hand it looks like the gene flow to the Amazon involved a population of Australo-Melanesians who had undergone little or no mixing with Denisovans. For such a people to have existed in the very area where the genetic evidence suggests the Denisovans were most strongly congregated is itself somewhat mysterious and suggests some kind of selective process at work.

In previous books, in particular *Fingerprints of the Gods* and *Underworld,* I have given extensive consideration to the intriguing phenomenon of ancient maps that show the world as it looked during the last Ice Age and do so, moreover, with stunning longitudinal and latitudinal accuracy and with the use of complex spherical trigonometry. Though it would be superfluous to reproduce here evidence that I have already presented in such detail elsewhere, I include an appendix—appendix 2—that gives some indication of the richness and the significance of this overlooked material.

However many times by however many hands they have been copied and recopied down the ages, it is my contention that these anomalous maps can be traced back to lost source documents that could only have originated with a civilization at least advanced enough to have explored the world, and to have mapped and measured it, when it was still in the grip of the Ice Age. A civilization capable of such feats must, at the very least, have had its own adepts in the techniques of boat-building, sailing, navigating, cartography, and geometry—none of these being among the skills that archaeologists are normally willing to attribute to Ice Age hunter-gatherers.

It is not inconceivable, however, if such a hypothetical civilization had existed, that it might have sponsored "outreach programs" to the hunter-gatherers who also lived in the world at that time, just as our own twenty-first-century technological civilization has "outreach programs" to hunter-gatherer tribes in the Amazon rainforest, the jungles of New Guinea, and the Namibian desert today—anthropologists, aid workers, resettlement experts, and so on and so forth. It's even conceivable that a hypothetical lost civilization of the Ice Age could have had "resettlement experts" of its own who were interested in the outcomes that might follow from physically removing people from one area—such as Melanesia, for example—and resettling them in far-off places like South America. If a global cataclysm were to loom, threatening the annihilation of the civilization, such "outreach" initiatives might even have been accelerated to prepare hunter-gatherer populations to serve as refuges for the survivors.

This is all pure speculation, of course, but at least it's in good company. As Eske concedes, **all** of the explanations—including his own—that have so far been offered to account for the presence of Australasian DNA in the Amazon are "purely speculative."

And the mystery continues to deepen. In November 2018, two major new studies were published, one in the journal *Cell,* coauthored by Cosimo Posth, David Reich, and others, and the second in *Science,* coauthored by Eske Willerslev, J. Victor Moreno-Mayar, David Meltzer, and others.[31] These new studies found Australasian DNA already present in skeletal remains from Lagoa Santa, Brazil, dated to 10,400 years ago, and confirmed the suspicion of the researchers that the anomalous genetic signal must have reached

South America in the "Late Pleistocene"[32]—that is, near the end of the last Ice Age.

"How did it get there?" wonders geneticist J. Victor Moreno-Mayar, immediately answering his own question as follows: "We have no idea." Similarly, David J. Meltzer expressed amazement at the most peculiar character of the signal, so clearly present in South America yet "somehow leaping over all North America in a single bound."[33]

For the purposes of my own quest, however, that anomalous, unexplained signal had the effect of opening up a new and fruitful avenue of inquiry. With the archetypally North American Clovis culture now known to have South American genetic roots, it was becoming increasingly obvious that to explore the mysteries of one half of the megacontinent I could not be oblivious to what had happened in the other half.

My focus would remain on North America, to which we'll return in part 5, but I had a strong intuition that I might miss an important piece of the puzzle if I failed to investigate the Amazon first.

I resented the intuition, which felt like a diversion, but it was so insistent that ultimately I could not ignore it.

PART IV

MEMES

The Amazon Mystery

11

GHOST CITIES
OF THE AMAZON

I N MY QUEST FOR THE traces of a lost civilization of prehistoric antiquity, the Amazon rainforest at first seemed to have little to offer. Without that teasing, tantalizing Australasian DNA signal I probably wouldn't have given it a second thought. But the signal was there, it was real, it was hugely anomalous, and it cried out for a deeper inquiry.

Along with much of the rest of the Americas, the Amazon entered European consciousness in the sixteenth century—the century of conquest. It was not a primary target. Mexico and Peru were hit first, their armies conquered, their wealth pillaged. Then rumors began to circulate of exotic civilizations rich in gold hidden in the jungles beyond the Andes Mountains. The greed of the Spaniards was aroused and in February 1541 Francisco de Orellana and Gonzalo Pizarro (the latter the brother of Francisco Pizarro, the conqueror of Peru) struck east from the city of Quito in Ecuador on a journey into the unknown.

Their mission was nothing less than to find the fabled El Dorado in the remote interior of South America and to loot the vast wealth they expected to find piled up there. In this they failed but in the grander scheme of things they succeeded mightily, for their expedition left us with the earliest surviving eyewitness account of the Amazon—unfortunately not of the *pre-Columbian* Amazon, which would have been ideal, but of the Amazon so soon after contact that it remained, effectively, in its pre-Columbian state. As such, it has much to tell us about the lost prehistory of the Americas.

At the head of a force of more than 200 Spanish soldiers, Orellana and Pizarro descended from the Andes. Hacking their way through increasingly dense and difficult jungle and fighting multiple engagements with hostile tribes, they eventually reached the banks of the Coca River, a tributary of the Napo River that is, in turn, an important tributary of the great and majestic Amazon itself. The terrain made further overland travel almost impossible and, far from finding and reveling in the supposedly limitless riches of El Dorado, the conquistadors were by now depleted by illness and weak with hunger. Their solution was to build a fair-sized boat, which they named the *San Pedro*. In it, on Pizarro's orders, Orellana then embarked with a force of 50 men to seek out and raid local villages for food.

The agreement was that Orellana would return within 12 days with whatever supplies he could gather. Unfortunately, however, the Amazon River system hadn't been consulted when the plan was made, and the *San Pedro* was swept downstream at such a rate that very soon it was hundreds of miles away and the prospect of a return against the powerful currents was most uninviting. Besides, even if Orellana's force had been able to row the rough-and-ready craft upstream again there was no guarantee that they would ever find their way back to Pizarro through the maze of braided river channels in which one opening looked very much like the next.

They decided, therefore, to press on and, in the process, became the first Europeans ever to navigate the entire length of the Amazon River and to cross the full width of South America from west to east. This was barely 20 years after the Spanish brought smallpox to the "New World"—another first!—and the great pandemics that were to depopulate the Americas had not yet penetrated deeply (if at all) into the remote fastness of the Amazon jungle. The pale horse of death would very soon follow, but Orellana's adventure took place at just about the last time that the cultures and civilizations that had thrived and prospered in the rainforest for thousands of years could ever be seen in something approaching their original form and context.

For that reason we are fortunate that Orellana and his murderous gang of mercenaries—often starving, often having to fight for their lives—were accompanied on this desperate voyage by Brother Gaspar de Carvajal, a literate and sensitive Dominican friar who kept a journal throughout. In it he describes himself as "a man to whom God chose to give a part in such a strange and hitherto never experienced voyage of discovery, such as this one which I shall relate from here on."[1]

The expeditionaries frequently faced extreme privations. On one occasion, for example, Carvajal reports that after many days without food,

> we were eating nothing but leather, belts and soles of shoes, cooked with certain herbs, with the result that so great was our weakness that we could not remain standing, for some on all fours and others with staffs went into the woods to search for a few roots to eat and some there were who ate certain herbs with which they were not familiar, and they were at the point of death, because they were like mad men and did not possess sense; but as Our Lord was pleased that we should continue our journey, no-one died.[2]

Whether by divine intervention or by good luck, or because of Orellana's effective leadership, none of his tough and resourceful men died of starvation on the voyage, and only a handful lost their lives due to infections, disease, and battle wounds. It was, all in all, a 7,000-kilometer journey, the whole of which, from departure from Quito in February 1541 to arrival at Marajo Island in the Amazon estuary on the Atlantic coast of Brazil in August 1542, took 18 months.

More important by far than his descriptions of the risks and dangers of the adventure, the great historical significance of Carvajal's journal is the shockingly counterintuitive picture it paints of a vast and complex Amazon. Certainly there were regions of complete wilderness where the expeditionaries suffered badly—hundreds of kilometers of deserted riverbanks with no people, no crops, and apparently no wildlife. But we discover as we read on that these empty quarters were interspersed with regions of astonishing, heavily populated abundance, where "great cities" more than 20 kilometers from end-to-end, roughly the length of Manhattan, lined the riverbanks.[3] Here Carvajal reports that enormous expanses were given over to productive agriculture[4] and there were signs everywhere of large and well-organized political and economic systems linked to centralized states that were capable of fielding disciplined armies thousands strong.[5]

These last glimpses of the Amazon before the ruination of European contact hint at a glorious, sophisticated, and technologically advanced indigenous prehistory. Carvajal tells of one stretch of the mighty river, 80 leagues—possibly more than 500 kilometers[6]—in length, ruled by a "great overlord named Machiparo." Throughout his territories a single language was spoken and the towns and villages stood so close together that there was usually not more than "a crossbow shot" between them.[7]

A week later the Spaniards came to a "fortified village" and, finding themselves short of food they took it by storm, killing some of the inhabitants and forcing the remainder to flee into the jungle. They then "remained resting, regaling ourselves with good lodgings, eating all we wanted, for three days in this village. There were many roads here that entered into the interior of the land, very fine highways."[8]

Orellana took these latter as an ominous sign—the locals they had driven out of their homes might easily return with reinforcements—and the expedition sailed on, enjoying the abundant and varied foods that they now found everywhere on their route downriver.[9]

The next major halt was at "a village that was on a high bank, and as it appeared small to us the Captain ordered us to capture it, and also because it looked so nice that it seemed as if it might be the recreation spot of some overlord of the inland."[10]

The residents put up a tough fight but were eventually expelled:

And we were masters of the village, where we found very great
quantities of food of which we laid in a supply. In this village there
was a villa in which there was a great deal of porcelain-ware of various
makes, both jars and pitchers, very large, with a capacity of more than
twenty-five arrobas [one hundred gallons], and other small pieces such
as plates and bowls and candelabra of this porcelain of the best that
has ever been seen in the world, for that of Malaga is not its equal,
because this porcelain which we found, is all glazed and embellished

with all colors, and so bright are these colors that they astonish, and, more than this, the drawings and paintings which they make on them are so accurately worked out that one wonders how with only natural skill they manufacture and decorate all these things making them look just like Roman articles; and here the Indians told us that as much as there was made out of clay in this house, so much there was back in the country in gold and silver.[11]

From this village, as from others through which they had passed, "there went out many roads and fine highways to the inland country."[12] Orellena had previously resisted the impulse to explore these enticing jungle thoroughfares but now, wishing to find out where they led to—perhaps even to El Dorado itself!—he took several companions with him and set out. Once again, how-ever, discretion got the better of valor:

He had not gone half a league when the roads became more like royal highways and wider and when the Captain had perceived this, he decided to turn back, because he saw that it was not prudent to go on any further.[13]

No doubt Orellana's prudence was among the reasons that so many of his men survived the perilous 7,000-kilometer voyage from the Andes to the Atlantic, but it is a matter of profound regret that he did not explore those "royal highways" through the jungle. In consequence, today we may only imagine where—and what—they led to.

UNPALATABLE TRUTHS

ALTHOUGH WIDELY DISCUSSED AT THE time, Carvajal's journal, the first eyewitness account of the full length of the Amazon in a near-pristine state, subsequently disappeared from public view for more than 300 years.[14] It only resurfaced in the nineteenth century following an exhaustive archival search by the Chilean scholar José Toribio Medina, who published it in 1895.[15]

Still it seemed that forces were at work to sideline Carvajal's uniquely important contribution to our understanding of the ancient Amazon. No sooner was the journal in print, at any rate, than it began to be "debunked" by scholars.[16]

For example, there were strident objections to a claim made at one point in Carvajal's account that statuesque female archers, whom the friar unhesitatingly calls "Amazons" after the warrior women of classical Greek myth,[17] had participated in an attack on Orellana's expeditionaries.[18] Carvajal also states that many of the other peoples they met on the journey were "subjects of the Amazons" whose dominions were extensive and whose sumptuous capital city had five enormous temples at its heart:[19]

In these buildings they had many gold and silver idols in the form of women, and many vessels of gold and silver for the service of the Sun.[20]

Such descriptions enjoyed wide currency and inflamed the public imagination in the years following the voyage.[21] As a result, the great river system Orellana explored is not today named after him, or some other Spanish adventurer, but called the "Amazon" instead.[22] To the skeptics of a later age, however, the link to the classical world that Carvajal suggested, and the notion of a lavish city in the depths of the jungle, seemed ridiculous.

Nor was this all.

What really stuck in the skeptical craw were the accounts Carvajal gave of the inhabitants of the rainforest, of the general level of their civilization, of the refinement of their arts and crafts, and particularly of the extent of their settlements—not only the fabulous capital of the Amazons but also other "very large cities," including some that "glistened in white."[23] By the 1890s the view had already set in among anthropologists and archaeologists that the Americas as a whole had only been peopled relatively recently—and it was strongly believed that one of the very last places to be settled, in this generally very late migration scenario, would have been the Amazon. As this view tightened its grip in subsequent decades, it began to seem obvious to all serious-minded researchers—so obvious as to be beyond question—that the Amazon could only been have been inhabited for about 1,000 years, and then only by very small groups of hunter-gatherers since the jungle was "resource-poor."[24] Indeed in this same vein, even as late as the 1990s, the rainforest was still being depicted by environmentalists as "a counterfeit paradise whose lush vegetation hid nutrient-poor soils incapable of supporting large populations and complex societies."[25]

The reason Carvajal's account was disbelieved for most of the twentieth century by almost everyone who reviewed it is therefore plain to see. The picture he painted of the pre-contact state of the peoples and cultures of the Amazon flew in the face of a dominant (and domineering) scholarly theory. Predictably, therefore, the first reaction of most archaeologists was not to question the theory in the light of the rediscovery, after long neglect, of an on-the-spot, eyewitness account. Instead they chose to defend the theory and undermine Carvajal by accusing him of lying in order to glorify the achievements of the expedition.

The friar gives us his word—no small matter for such a man—that he wrote only "the truth throughout."[26] But his accounts of cities, huge populations, advanced ceramics ("surpassing those of Malaga"), and enormous, fertile agricultural lands along the course of the Amazon were too subversive to be accepted. Quite simply, if he was right about all this, then the modern "experts" were wrong—and that could not be tolerated.

Indeed the judgment that Carvajal was a fantasist and a liar, and that nothing he had said about the Amazon could be taken seriously, seemed about to be set in stone when the first shreds of the evidence that would ultimately exonerate him, proving that he had indeed told the truth throughout, began to emerge.

DID AMAZONIAN CITIES EXIST?

PROFESSOR DAVID WILKINSON OF UCLA, an authority on long-term and large-scale phenomena in world politics, including empires and systems of independent states, has made a special study of the level of civilization in the Amazon prior to European contact.

The key question for civilizationists is: were there Amazonian cities before European contact? "Civilizations" require "cities," and "cities"

are the defining feature of "civilizations." And by "cities," we mean 4th
magnitude settlements, i.e. settlements with a population of not less
than the order of 10^4 (~10,000) . . . Did Amazonian cities exist?[27]

Judging from the earliest reports of Spanish and Portuguese expeditions,
says Wilkinson, "the answer would certainly have to be in the affirmative."[28]
He draws particular attention to one of the cities, mentioned earlier, that
extended for more than 20 kilometers from end to end,[29] and to another settlement that Carvajal describes as "more than two leagues long."[30] The exact
length of a league, Wilkinson notes, was "not a fully agreed-upon or stabilized
physical distance, but was probably not less than 2.5 English statute miles
nor more than 4."[31] A settlement of close-packed housing covering 2 leagues
would therefore have been between 5 miles (8 kilometers) and 8 miles (13
kilometers) in extent. Here Wilkinson refers us to a study by an international
team of anthropologists and geologists who focused on what is known about
this settlement and calculated that it would have housed "perhaps 10,000
inhabitants."[32] As Wilkinson notes, this therefore makes it, by definition, a
fourth-magnitude settlement—that is, a city, and "hence part of a civilization."[33] It follows that the larger settlement, with an extent of more than 20
kilometers, would likely have had at least twice as many inhabitants, that is,
20,000 or more.

It is instructive to compare these figures with those of "civilized" Europe
in a similar time frame.[34] Certainly London, with a population estimated at
60,000 in the sixteenth century,[35] was larger than either of the two Amazonian cities we are considering here, but the difference was one of degree, not of
kind. The British city of York, an established urban center since Roman times,
had a population estimated at between 10,000 to 12,000 in the sixteenth
century[36]—very much on the same scale as the Amazonian cities—while
in Spain, Toledo did not achieve a population of 13,000 until the mid-
nineteenth century.[37]

On Carvajal's account, therefore, not only did the Amazon have cities but
its cities were comparable in size to those of Europe at the same time. He also
reports that the chieftain Machiparo ruled over "many settlements and very
large ones which together contribute for fighting purposes fifty thousand men
of the age of from thirty years up to seventy, because the young men do not go
to war." Aside from the interesting anthropological observation about the age

at which men in sixteenth-century Amazonian society went to war, this statement has important implications for our understanding of the population of the region. Machiparo's domain was just one among many through which the Orellana expedition passed, yet if Carvajal reported correctly it could muster an army 50,000 strong. This is a greater number than Denmark and Norway combined, or Sweden and Finland combined, or Brandenburg-Prussia, or even the Tsardom of Russia, could field in the same period.[38]

A view of the Amazon as an "uncivilized" and "savage" place—indeed as the very epitome of savagery—has been deeply ingrained in the European psyche for centuries. It is therefore not surprising the Carvajal was disbelieved when his journal finally surfaced in 1895. Also disbelieved were the reports of the two similar adventures that followed—the Ursua expedition, which took place 20 years after Orellana's voyage, and the Teixeira expedition of 1637–38.

There was no official recorder for the Ursua expedition, but one of its officers, a certain Captain Altamirano, provides independent confirmation of Carvajal's observations when he speaks of settlements with populations of around 10,000 in the heart of the Amazon jungle—at the lower end of the urban scale, but again, as Professor David Wilkinson notes, "city-sized."[39]

By the time of the Teixeira expedition the region had been riven by smallpox epidemics that caused depopulation across wide areas, and had also begun to suffer other negative effects of European penetration and exploitation. Nonetheless the expedition's Jesuit priest, Father Cristóbal de Acuña, who, like Carvajal, kept a journal, could report that "the river of Amazons waters more extensive regions, fertilizes more plains, supports more people, and augments by its floods a mightier ocean" than the Ganges, Euphrates, or Nile. Like Carvajal and Altamirano before him, Acuña, too, was still able to speak of an "infinity of Indians" and of inhabited areas hundreds of kilometers in extent where the settlements were packed "so close together, that one is scarcely lost sight of when another comes in view."[40]

"These testimonials," Wilkinson writes, "would seem sufficient. With eyewitnesses reporting the size of settlements and the wealth of surplus food available to support dense populations (and social complexity), there could be, and apparently there was indeed, pre-Columbian civilization in the Amazon basin."[41]

The problem, however, as Wilkinson immediately concedes, is that "serious doubts later arose."[42]

The first element of doubt had to do with the accounts of subsequent penetrations of Amazonia—after the Orellana, Ursua, and Teixeira expeditions. In this regard the observations of Padre Samuel Fritz, a Jesuit preacher, are of particular significance.[43] He lived among the Omaguas, through whose domains along the banks of the Rio Napo, between the Coca and Aguarico, the Orellana expedition passed and which Carvajal (although he does not refer to the Omagua by name) describes as densely populated.[44]

Not so according to Padre Fritz! Between 1686 and 1715 he established thirty-eight Jesuit missions among the Omagua and noted on a map that the important settlements among which he had planted these missions had a combined total population of just 26,000 people[45]—quite a different matter from the hundreds of thousands reported by Carvajal. Let us note in passing—for there is a hint here of what was really going on—that Fritz's main preoccupation, other than preaching, was to advise "these small weak village communities on how to retreat and regroup upriver to evade continual Portuguese slave-raiding."[46]

Likewise, a little later—between 1743 and 1744—the French geographer Charles-Marie de la Condamine traveled through the region and reported no cities or armies in Amazonia, again in stark contrast to Orellana. For Condamine, the Omaguas were "a people formerly powerful" while along the entire river system he found "no warlike tribes inimical to Europeans, all such having either submitted or withdrawn themselves to the interior."[47]

These reports, and many others like them as the eighteenth century merged into the nineteenth and the nineteenth into the twentieth, did serious damage to the credibility of the earlier explorers—to such an extent that Smithsonian Institution archaeologist Betty Meggers was still insisting, before she passed away in 2012, that Carvajal had either misunderstood everything he saw or, more likely, that his entire account was riddled with fantasy and invention.[48]

THE LONG SHADOW OF BETTY MEGGERS

THROUGHOUT HER WORKING LIFE MEGGERS was a passionate advocate of the view that no pre-Columbian Amazonian settlement could ever have supported even 1,000 people, let alone several thousands or even tens of thousands as Carvajal had reported. It was likewise her opinion that the level of sophistication Carvajal had described—the armies, the food storage, the porcelain specialists, and so on—was in fact completely **impossible** given the limitations of the Amazonian environment.[49]

Meggers's *Amazonia: Man and Culture in a Counterfeit Paradise,* published in 1971 (but expanding on work she had done and conclusions she had reached in the 1950s), has been described as possibly "the most influential book ever written about the Amazon."[50] And indeed, it was this book, and the "environmental limitation" movement that it spawned—because many other archaeologists, anthropologists, and ecologists simply followed Meggers without question—that for a long while served as the sole acceptable reference frame through which the prehistory of the Amazon would be understood. As Professor Wilkinson puts it, "the meticulously careful and systematic researches of 20th century cultural-ecologist archaeologists" like Meggers created a consensus that "large-scale settlements and societies" could **never** have existed in what the environmental limitationists saw as the "wet-desert" of Amazonia.[51]

But as was the case with Vance Haynes and the mistaken Clovis First doctrine that kept so many locked in illusion for so long, so it was with the ideas of Meggers and her followers. A dominant individual, with a prestigious position, can delay the progress of knowledge for decades but ultimately cannot stop the buildup of contrary evidence and opinions that will lead to a new paradigm.

Predictably, therefore, as Wilkinson goes on to note in his study of Amazonian civilization:

> Towards the end of the 20th century, the archaeological pendulum began to swing back toward crediting the early explorers' accounts. Even Meggers [in *Amazonia: Man and Culture in a Counterfeit Paradise*] had passed on without comment a report [dated approximately 1662] by Mauricio de Heriarte that the capital of the Tapajós (at today's Santarem) could field 60,000 warriors. Any such number of militia would by . . . comparative-civilizational standards have implied an urban population of 300,000 to 360,000![52]

It is troubling, in retrospect, that Meggers knew of, yet did not consider, the implications of Heriarte's report—but, of course, had she done so, she would have been obliged to rethink her whole thesis. Within twenty years after the publication of *Counterfeit Paradise,* however, other scholars were actively doing the rethinking for her. Notable among them was Anna Curtenius Roosevelt, now professor of anthropology at the University of Illinois at Chicago. In 1993 she presented evidence that some pre-Columbian Amazonian settlements "held many thousands of people . . . from several thousands, to tens of thousands of individuals or more." And in 1999 she wrote, "In Amazonia, non-state societies appear to have organized large, dense populations, intensive subsistence adaptations, large systems of earthworks, production of elaborate artworks and architecture for considerable periods of time."[53]

Likewise, in 1994, anthropologist Neil Whitehead concluded of the prehistoric Amazon, "We are dealing with civilizations of considerable complexity, perhaps even protostates."[54] And in 2001, Michael Heckenberger, James Petersen, and Eduardo Neves, facing criticism from Meggers, strongly defended their own by then well-established position that "there were past Amazonian societies significantly larger than anything reported in the past 100–200 years,"[55] that these societies included "chiefdoms" or "kingdoms,"[56] and that "lost civilizations" were indeed present in some parts of the Amazon before European contact.[57]

What are we to make of all this to-ing and fro-ing?

In summary, "to address the contradictions in the sources and among the authorities," Wilkinson asks, "If there were Amazonian cities, where did they go? And, if there were Amazonian cities, how could they have subsisted?"[58]

He gives two two-word answers to these questions—"recurrent catastrophes" to the first and "exemplary agronomy" to the second.

EXTINCTION AND AMNESIA

WE'LL COME TO THE EXEMPLARY agronomy in a later chapter, but let's deal with the recurrent catastrophes now.

Prior to the Orellana expedition, smallpox may already have found its way to the Amazon overland from Mexico where it had been introduced during the Spanish conquest a few decades earlier.[59] If not, then the direct transmission of the disease to Peru in 1532–33 by Pizarro's conquistadors certainly brought it into the Andes Mountains in force, making it only a matter of time before it descended to the east side of the range and thoroughly infiltrated the rainforest.[60] Quite possibly, although there is no proof, the Orellana expedition may itself have been the first principal vector that carried the scourge into the heart of the Amazon but if so it was certainly not the last—nor was smallpox the only Old World disease to which Europeans possessed significant immunity while Native Americans did not. Measles, influenza, and other viruses also took a ghastly toll.

Wilkinson cites an important study by anthropologist Thomas P. Myers that documents "more than 30 epidemics—smallpox, measles, and other outbreaks—some 'on a massive scale'—in 16th–18th century South America."[61] Myers finds evidence of "very substantial depopulation between the Orellana and Teixeira expeditions" and estimates that in many areas it ran as high 99 percent.[62] This, he further suggests, "may have been the reason why the missionaries later transmitted the idea of a relatively uninhabited Amazon region. The people they found were the survivors of the diseases and epidemics."[63]

The implications of the virtual extinction of the Amazon's pre-Columbian population are immense. If so many died, then we can be sure that much else died with them. As Wilkinson succinctly phrases it, "A small city of 10,000 that loses 99% of its inhabitants becomes a village of 100, that can do far less."[64]

Likewise, by extension, we can imagine what would have happened if that city were just a small part of a great and complex civilization of the Amazon and if that entire civilization were deprived of 99 percent of its warriors, 99 percent of its farmers, 99 percent of its hunters and gatherers, 99 percent of its astronomers, 99 percent of its healers and shamans, 99 percent of its architects, 99 percent of its boat builders, and 99 percent of its wisdom keepers. Of course, across the scale of the whole Amazon basin, this would not have happened overnight; likely it would have extended over a century or two—a creeping cataclysm rather than a single big hit. But the end result, whether it came slow or fast, would have been the same. Once left deserted, the great cities and monuments and other public works of any hypothetical Amazonian civilization would quickly have been encroached upon and soon completely hidden by the jungle while, at the same time, cultural memory banks would have been wiped almost clean and vast resources of skills, knowledge, and potential would have been lost forever.

Little wonder, then, that to this day amnesia, confusion, contradictions, and mystery confound the search for the truth of the Amazon's deep past.

12

THE ANCIENTS
BEHIND THE VEIL

THE DNA EVIDENCE PRESENTED IN part 3 reveals an astonishing anomaly. At some point during the Ice Age, perhaps as early as 13,000 years ago, a group of people carrying Australo-Melanesian genes settled in what is now the Amazon jungle.

The Amazon basin today is a vast and diverse region encompassing almost 7 million square kilometers, of which approximately 5.5 million square kilometers are still covered by rainforest.[1] The figures only become meaningful by comparison. The whole of India, with a total area of 3.29 million square kilometers, is less than half the size of the Amazon basin,[2] but Australia, at 7.7 million square kilometers, is bigger,[3] as are China (9.59 million square kilometers),[4] Canada (9.98 million square kilometers),[5] the United States (9.63 million square kilometers),[6] and Europe (10.18 million square kilometers).[7] All in all, then, it's fair to say that what the Amazon confronts us with is a truly gigantic landmass, on a similar scale to many of the world's largest countries and regions, extending for thousands of kilometers from north to south and thousands of kilometers from east to west.

There has been no lasting scholarly consensus on the climate, environment, vegetation, and tree cover of the Ice Age Amazon (see appendix 3 for details) but the situation is possibly even worse around the issue of the peopling of this immense region—and indeed around the entire vexed question of how and when humans began to settle in South America as a whole.

The reader will recall from part 2 that it was Tom Dillehay, professor of anthropology at Vanderbilt University in Tennessee, who first put the cat among the Clovis pigeons with his excavations at Monte Verde in southern Chile. The excavations began in 1977 and continue to this day, with multiple reports and papers published in scientific journals. The story is therefore a long one, but to make it short let's just say that Dillehay's extensive and meticulous excavations initially revealed, in his own words:

one valid human site (MV-II) dated ~14,500 cal BP. . . . Although bifacial projectile points, flaked debitage, and grinding stones were recovered, most lithic tools were edge-trimmed pebble flakes and sling and grooved bola stones.[8]

Seen through the distorting lens of the "Clovis First" belief system, Dillehay's date looked very threatening—in part because the artifacts, tools, and points found at Monte Verde had nothing to do with Clovis whatsoever but more so because to have reached the far south of South America by 14,500 years ago meant that the ancestors of these settlers must have crossed the Bering land bridge (the full length of two continents away) long before that and therefore, by definition, that Clovis was very far indeed from being "first."

All Dillehay's battles with Vance Haynes and his supporters were over this relatively conservative date of 14,500 years ago—and as we've seen, Monte Verde was vindicated in that fight after a site visit in 1997 when the Clovis Firsters (begrudgingly) conceded defeat.

But the story was far from over and as the excavations at Monte Verde continued, deeper and older occupation levels began to be exposed, yielding increasingly more ancient dates. The results of these new studies were published by Dillehay in November 2015, confirming a revised age for Monte Verde of around 18,500 years[9] and revealing that the site had been reoccupied several times thereafter over a period of more than 4,000 years.[10] Again in Dillehay's own words:

> The new evidence is multiple, spatially discontinuous, low-density occurrences of stratigraphic *in situ* stone artifacts, faunal remains, and burned areas that suggests discrete horizons of ephemeral human activity radiocarbon dated between ~14,500 and possibly as early as 19,000 cal BP.[11]

Nor, it seems, is Monte Verde quite done with surprising us. Even as he was reporting his first paradigm-busting date of 14,500 years ago for MV-II, Dillehay was already drawing attention, in a rather careful, noncommittal way, to the possibility that MV-I, another area of the site, might be older—and not just 18,500 or 19,000 years old but perhaps significantly more than 30,000 years old:

> MV-I dated ~33,000 BP . . . initially defined by scattered occurrences of three clay-lined, possible culturally produced burned areas and twenty-six stones, at least six of which suggest modification by humans. This . . . evidence from MV-I was too meager and too laterally discontinuous to falsify or verify its archaeological validity.[12]

This whole issue, which even the most adamant Clovis Firsters on the 1997 site visit had admitted was "extremely intriguing,"[13] was reexamined by Dillehay and his team in the 2015 study, across several areas of Monte Verde. Dates as tantalizingly ancient as 43,500 years ago were associated with the remains and artifacts unearthed, but Dillehay again carefully judged the finds to be "still too meager and inconclusive to determine whether they represent human activity or indeterminate natural features. At present the latter case is perhaps more feasible given there is presently no convincing archaeological or other data to substantiate a human presence in South America prior to 20,000 years ago."[14]

ONE MORE LINE IN THE SAND CROSSED

DESPITE HAVING FOR SO LONG been a rebel on the subject of First Americans, despite having been vindicated in the end on his first date for Monte Verde, despite having then published new dates pushing the age of the site back further, and despite those "meagre" hints of even greater antiquity, it does sound very much as if Dillehay was imitating his former critics here. Just as they used to argue that there was no convincing archaeological evidence to substantiate a human presence in South America 14,500 years ago, now he was saying there was none prior to 20,000 years ago.

When, I wonder, will archaeologists take to heart the old dictum that absence of evidence is not the same thing as evidence of absence, and learn the lessons that their own profession has repeatedly taught—namely that the next turn of the excavator's spade can change everything? So little of the surface area of our planet has been subjected to any kind of archaeological investigation at all that it would be more logical to regard **every** major conclusion reached by this discipline as provisional—particularly so when we are dealing with a period as remote, as tumultuous, and as little understood as the Ice Age.

I was therefore not at all surprised, after Dillehay had drawn his line in the sand at 20,000 years ago, that later research, published in August 2017, confirmed a human presence in South America even earlier in the Ice Age!

This followed decades of study by a team under the leadership of Denis Vialou of the Muséum National d'Histoire Naturelle in Paris at the Santa Elina rock shelter in the Brazilian state of Mato Grosso.[15] Located at the convergence of two major river basins, and roughly at the geographic center of South America as a whole, the shelter is known for its huge display of around 1,000 prehistoric paintings and drawings.[16] In the long rectangular habitation area nearby, Vialou found and excavated a series of beautifully stratified deposits testifying to different periods of human occupation from 27,600 years ago down to 23,000 years ago.[17] Some very finely worked and drilled bone ornaments were among the objects discovered.[18]

PEDRA FURADA

MORE THAN 2,000 KILOMETERS NORTHEAST of Santa Elina, the eminent archaeologist Nède Guidon has spent 40 years excavating hundreds—literally hundreds!—of richly painted prehistoric rock shelters in Serra da Capivara National Park in the Brazilian state of Piauí. While everyone else is playing catch-up, she has long been confident that humans arrived in South America much earlier than 20,000 years ago. In 1986–3 years before Dillehay first began to offer his own cautious dissent from the Clovis First paradigm—she published a paper in *Nature* boldly titled "Carbon-14 Dates Point to Man in the Americas 32,000 Years Ago."[19] It was a report on her work at a particularly large and richly decorated rock shelter called Pedra Furada where she had excavated "a sequence containing abundant lithic industry and well-structured hearths at all levels" documenting continuous human occupation over the entire period from 6,160 years ago to 32,160 years ago.[20] In addition, she found conclusive evidence that at least one of the spectacular rock paintings was 17,000 years old:

> This pictograph indicates the practice of rupestral art [i.e., rock art]
> at that time and makes the site of Pedra Furada the most ancient
> rupestral art site known in America and one of the most ancient in the
> world.[21]

But this was just the beginning, and in 2003 Guidon and other researchers completed a further study. The results pushed back the date of the human presence at Pedra Furada to 48,500 years ago,[22] and of the paintings themselves, to at least 36,000 years ago.[23]

Most archaeologists—particularly North American archaeologists still partially under the spell of Clovis First—have not embraced Guidon's interpretation of the evidence at Pedra Furada. This, however, does not mean that she is wrong, only that she is willing to think—and thoroughly investigate—outside the box. She is an acerbic critic of what she calls the "climate of scepticism attending old dates"[24] that has haunted American archaeology for so long, and of the unquestioning acceptance of Beringia as "the only realistic route for human entry to the New World."[25]

Guidon does not see any reason why Beringia should have been the only route of entry:

> Everybody is willing to give humans the abilities necessary for voyaging across to Australia about 60,000 years ago. Why then would it have been impossible for them to pass from island to island along the Aleutians, just as one example? We have no justification for converting the humans who peopled the Americas to a single state of being, where they could do nothing but follow herds by a land route.[26]

In another paper anticipating the speculations of geneticists like Skoglund, Reich, and Willerslev by more than a decade, she goes even further, reminding us of the puzzling cranial morphology of certain ancient Brazilian skulls (reviewed in appendix 1) and concluding that, "although little probable":

> the possibility of migration from Australia and surrounding islands across the Pacific Ocean . . . more than 50 k years ago cannot be discarded.[27]

HIDDEN REALMS

IT IS IN THE AMAZON basin that the oddly misplaced Australasian genetic signal beats out its enigmatic pulse. As well as being very far indeed from Australia and Papua New Guinea, however, neither Monte Verde, nor Santa Elina nor Pedra Furada are in the Amazon Basin—though the latter two are closer than the former, being respectively about 515 kilometers and 625 kilometers as the crow flies from the Xingu River, a major southeastern tributary of the Amazon.[28]

The long-standing but now thoroughly discredited archaeological model whereby the Amazon was supposedly uninhabited by humans during the Ice Age and remained so until less than 1,000 years ago inevitably had a chronic impact on research priorities and research funding. The result, relative to its importance in global ecology and its enormous land area, is that very little archaeology has been done in the Amazon basin at all and very little of what has been done—truly a tiny fraction—focuses on Ice Age occupation levels.

A refreshing exception, however, is the work of the ever open-minded Anna Curtenius Roosevelt, currently professor of anthropology at the University of Illinois, whom we encountered in chapter 11. On April 19, 1996, she and a group of coresearchers took to the pages of *Science* to publish the results of their study of Pedra Pintada, another beautifully painted rock shelter in

Brazil but this time located right in the heart of the Amazon basin at the confluence of the Tapajos and Amazon Rivers.[29]

Here Roosevelt and her team excavated multiple occupation layers spanning the Holocene (our current era) and the late Pleistocene (the Ice Age), with the oldest and deepest turning out possibly to be as old as 16,000 years (according to thermoluminescence dating) and 14,200 years (according to radiocarbon dating).[30]

Conclusion?

> The human presence in Caverna de Pedra Pintada during the late Pleistocene is established by numerous artifacts. . . . The dated materials are associated in stratigraphic context at the beginning of a long cultural sequence. There is no pre-human biological material that could have mixed with the cultural remains, which are stratigraphically separated from later Holocene assemblages by a culturally sterile layer. . . . The discovery of Palaeoindians along the Amazon confirms earlier evidence that the Palaeoindian radiation was more complex than current theories provide for.[31]

Indeed so! And even in these days of man-made ecological disaster let us remind ourselves that 5.5 million square kilometers of the Amazon basin is still covered by rainforest. To put that in perspective, picture Mexico, Guatemala, Belize, Honduras, and El Salvador. Taken together they encompass 2.22 million square kilometers[32]—not nearly enough—so we will need to add on India with its 2.97 million square kilometers to get an imaginary realm almost equivalent in size to the Amazon rainforest.[33] My point here is that when we consider the Amazon as an archaeological project, its *scale* is comparable to Mexico, Guatemala, Belize, Honduras, El Salvador, AND India all added together, **and all, in addition, entirely covered by dense rainforest** and therefore difficult and expensive to access. Moreover, unlike Mexico, Guatemala, Belize, Honduras, and El Salvador, where the famous Maya civilization flourished, and unlike India with its ancient cities and temples, there was, as we've seen, no inducement for archaeologists to invest scarce time and money on excavations in the Amazon while it was believed that nothing of great interest would be found there. At the close of the second decade of the twenty-first century no serious archaeologists are still thinking that way! The state of affairs they've inherited, however, means that huge swaths of the Amazon, encompassing millions of square kilometers, have never been subject to any kind of archaeological investigation at all.

This is a wider problem than the Amazon. For example, sea level rose 120 meters when the Ice Age came to an end with the result that 27 million square kilometers of land that was above water at the last glacial maximum 21,000 years ago is under water today.[34] These submerged continental shelves were prime seafront real estate during the Ice Age, yet only a few tiny slivers of them have ever been subject to any kind of marine archaeological investigation. Again, this is because, like the Amazon, access requires special preparations, equipment, and transportation and also because of a similar belief that whatever would be found as a result of these costly investigations would not add greatly to what is already known.

I'll say nothing about Antarctica, with its 14 million square kilometers entirely virgin to the archaeologist's spade.[35] The almost universal agreement that humans could never have lived there in the past might or might not be correct, but we'll never know for sure unless we look.

We do know that the Sahara desert, presently occupying an area of about 9 million square kilometers,[36] had a very different climate during the Ice Age, and in the early millennia of the Holocene, than it experiences today and that there were long periods when it was well watered and fertile, with extensive lakes and grasslands and abundant wildlife.[37] It is near enough to Egypt and the other great centers of early civilization in North Africa and the Middle East to have attracted the attention of archaeologists, but like the Amazon and like the submerged continental shelves, access is difficult and expensive, placing serious practical limits on what can be achieved.

Part of our predicament, therefore, as a species with amnesia, is that huge areas of the planet that we know for sure were used by and lived upon by our ancestors—the submerged continental shelves, the Sahara desert, the Amazon rainforest—have, for a variety of practical and ideological reasons, been badly served by archaeology. The truth is, we know VERY little about the real prehistory of any of these places, and the tiny patches that have thus far been surveyed and excavated within them are no legitimate basis upon which to draw conclusions and express certainties about the vast areas that remain unsurveyed and unexcavated.

Guatemala, in central America, was one of the six countries I suggested we put together to envisage the scale of the Amazon rainforest. Guatemala itself encompasses just under 109,000 square kilometers.[38] It's an indication of how pointless it is to take any so-called facts about the past for granted, however, that even in this tiny country, fifty times smaller than the Amazon, a huge archaeological surprise was unveiled in 2018.

"Everything is turned on its head," commented Ithaca College archaeologist Thomas Garrison on the results of a survey of 2,100 square kilometers of Guatemala's densely forested northern Peten region.[39] Deploying Lidar (Light Detection and Ranging) pulsed laser technology, what the survey revealed, in areas quite close to known and even famous and well-visited Mayan sites such as Tikal, were more than 60,000 previously unsuspected ancient houses, palaces, defensive walls, fortresses, and other structures as well as quarries, elevated highways connecting urban centers, and complex irrigation and terracing systems that would have been capable of supporting intensive agriculture.[40] Previously scholars had believed that only scattered city-states had existed in an otherwise sparsely populated region, but the Lidar images make it clear, as Garrison puts it, that "scale and population density had been grossly underestimated."[41]

Katheryn Reese-Taylor, a University of Calgary archaeologist, adds:

After decades of combing through the forests, no archaeologists had stumbled across these sites. More importantly, we never had the big picture that this data gives us. It really pulls back the veil and helps us see the civilization as the ancient Maya saw it.[42]

When pulling back the veil on the relatively recent Maya civilization in a small part of the tiny country of Guatemala can produce so many surprises, we may begin to imagine what "big picture" might come to light if the vastly larger and more opaque veil that has covered the Amazon rainforest for so long were to be drawn back.

Hopefully the interest will be there and the funds made available for it to be drawn back thoroughly using the latest scanning technologies followed up by site surveys and excavations. Until that happens, however, no archaeologist is in any position to dismiss the possibility that the very old and very troublesome Australo-Melanesian genetic signal that has been detected among Amazonian populations might have gotten there by the "most parsimonious" route—namely, by a direct crossing of the Pacific from Australasia to South America.

That, in turn, would imply a civilization capable of great oceanic voyages and therefore by definition at a much more advanced stage of development than archaeologists are prepared to accept for any branch of humanity during the Ice Age.

13

BLACK EARTH

IT SEEMS TO ME TO be no longer in doubt that civilizations with true cities and mature polities did flourish in the Amazon before the European conquest. Less clear is how far back the story of these civilizations can be traced in this immense region where so little archaeology has been done.

Thanks to Anna Roosevelt's work we know, at the very least, that humans were present at Pedra Pintada at the Tapajoz/Amazon confluence by about 14,000 years ago and possibly significantly earlier.[1] With other more accessible painted rock shelters in Brazil dating back as much as 50,000 years, it is, I suspect, only a matter of time before evidence of at least equally great if not greater antiquity emerges from the Amazon itself.

But greater antiquity of what? Was it foragers and hunter-gatherers all the way back? Or was some advanced but unseen presence capable of spanning the globe at work behind the scenes of prehistory that might help to explain how Australasian genes reached the Amazon during the Ice Age? Again, the problem is complicated by the fact that few archaeologists other than Roosevelt have looked for evidence of humans in the Amazon at all at such a remote period, so we have very little to go on across thousands of years during which the data are sketchy and inconclusive.

But then out of that opaque interlude in the life of the prehistoric Amazon, quite suddenly and unexpectedly, the lineaments of a great mystery begin to materialize. It concerns the "exemplary agronomy" that UCLA's Professor David Wilkinson cites as his two-word explanation for how the cities of the rainforest were able to feed their large populations—because rainforests in general do **not** have good base soils but sustain their fertility in the mulch of plants and leaves above ground.[2] This is why, when areas of the Amazon are cleared for agriculture today—for example, to make way for soybean plantations—they become exhausted, infertile, and useless after only a few years.[3] But Wilkinson is not speaking of the base soils. His "exemplary agronomy," as we shall see, refers to an artificial, **man-made** soil that first suddenly and inexplicably appeared in the Amazon many thousands of years ago but that has such miraculous properties of self-regeneration that it is still in use for agriculture and still incredibly productive today.

It is called *Terra preta*. More than any other single factor, it is now understood by scholars to have been responsible for the astonishing and utterly anomalous agricultural productivity that allowed a population estimated at between 8 and 20 million people[4] to thrive for untold epochs in the Amazon before being overtaken by the cataclysm of the European conquest.

Terra preta feels like the work of scientists, but if there was a civilization in the Amazon, then why should we be surprised to find scientific achievements to its credit?

THE MYSTERY

THE EXISTENCE OF TERRA PRETA was first reported by Europeans in colonial-period Brazil who called it *terra preta de Índio* (Indian Black Earth), "the reference to 'Indians' reflecting the presence of abundant pottery shards of evident pre-Columbian age on the surface of most known exemplars."[5] Today these special soils, described by one nineteenth-century explorer as consisting of "a fine, dark loam, a foot, and often two feet thick,"[6] are more often spoken of as "Black Earth," "Amazonian Anthropogenic Dark Earths,"[7] or simply as "Amazonian Dark Earths"—ADEs for short.[8]

Whatever we call them though, what are they, and why do they matter?

We've seen how, across immense areas, the natural *terra firme* (non-floodplain) soils of the Amazon are too poor to sustain intensive agriculture and thus to feed the large-scale populations that we now know inhabited the region in pre-Columbian times:

> With few available nutrients and having extremely high aluminum concentrations, one could not imagine a worse regime for productive agriculture.[9]

Indeed, the consensus of scholars is that even the floodplains with their better soils are high-risk areas for crop production "because of the unpredictability of the flood regime."[10]

But, and it's a big but, what are we to make of those early explorers' reports of dense settlements extending for kilometers along river bluff edges whence roadways branched out into the interior?

The remnants of some of these settlements are now being investigated by twenty-first-century researchers, no longer blinded by the prejudices of the past, who often refer to them as "garden cities" of the Amazon.[11] Invariably it turns out that they are associated, as one authoritative study puts it, with large acreages of "'Indian black earth' or *terra preta*. The heightened fertility status of these soils, generically termed 'dark earths . . .' has long been recognized by the indigenous inhabitants of the region, as well as by current colonists."[12]

Across the rainforest there are many **thousands** of expanses of terra preta on a similar range of scales, covering a total area that is in all honesty unknown but that various authorities have guesstimated at 6,000 km², 18,000 km², 154,063 km², and "an area the size of France" (i.e., around 640,000 km²).[13] Whatever the true figure, these widely scattered plots of ADE—the rediscovered remnants of a once much more extensive system—are indeed actively sought out and productively cultivated by indigenous people to this day.

In the southeastern Amazon along the Xingu River, to give just one example, a recent study found that existing settlements, though on a much smaller scale than in the past, are still able to survive largely because of the accomplishments of their ancestors who had "continuously occupied, managed and modified" the soils over thousands of years. Almost without exception the riverine people of the Xingu today "inhabit and plant in dark earths," and make use of resources, such as "Brazil nuts, babassu palm, dark earths and vine forests" that are "indicators or products of this earlier occupation." Indeed, as Stephen Schwartzman, the research team leader, maintains, "Contemporary land use and resource management in the Xingu corridor is . . . significantly conditioned or made possible by mostly little-studied prehistoric land-use practices."[14]

Particularly little studied and poorly understood are the practices that resulted in the so far unexplained inception in the Amazon, a very long time ago, of the incredibly fertile ADEs themselves. Nobody doubts that they are "anthropogenic"—man-made in some way[15]—and everyone agrees that they're an amazing success story. So fecund is terra preta, even after thousands of years of use, that it can still regenerate barren soils it is added to, and has been described as "miracle earth."[16]

The important questions therefore, are *how* was terra preta made, *why* was it made, *when* was it made, and *who* made it?

Part of the answer to the first question is often dug up by villagers along the Xingu River. In (and characteristic of) the patches of ancient terra preta where they plant their crops they "regularly encounter potsherds, stone axes, ceramics and figurines."[17]

Such "refuse" left behind by people of the remote past, seems to play an important role in the amazing fertility of the ADEs—but then so do all the other strangely jumbled and juxtaposed ingredients that typically also include compost, the feces and urine of humans and animals, and all sorts of organic "kitchen" waste, including bones, notably fish bones.

Most researchers believe that terra preta soils formed as composted material accumulated via **incidental** human activity (often in debris piles referred to as middens).[18]

University of São Paulo archaeologist Eduardo Neves reportedly favors a scenario in which successive generations could have swept food refuse—especially fish and animal bones—from their dwellings and then added human and animal excrement.[19]

Elsewhere, in a paper published in the *Journal of Archaeological Science* in February 2014, Neves, Michael Heckenberger, and others develop this idea further. Their argument depicts the ancient Amazonians as living amid a shitscape (euphemistically referred to as a "middenscape"),[20] dumping their excretions, rubbish, broken crockery, and fish bones into the middens and—most importantly—burning wet vegetation on top of the middens, and always conscientiously making sure, without any long-term planning or purpose in mind, to keep the fires damped down under a blanket of dirt and straw.[21]

This method of cool-burning, explains Tom Miles, an expert in the combustion and gasification of biomass,[22] is known as "slash-and-char"—to distinguish it from the widely condemned "slash-and-burn":

> In slash-and-burn, dry brush and grass are burned in open fires, spewing vast quantities of carbon dioxide into the atmosphere and leaving only small amounts of nutrients in the ash that's then dug into the ground.
>
> By contrast, slash-and-char involves burning wet vegetation, so it smoulders underneath a layer of dirt and straw. Robbed of oxygen, the fire only partly burns any wood or stalks, leaving most as tiny chunks of charcoal. This bio-char is turned into the soil.[23]

In due course—entirely incidentally and accidentally according to most proponents of such views—these stinking, smouldering middens spread and alchemically transformed themselves into ADE, "the world's most fertile soil,"[24] without any deliberate human intervention at all.

I'd say it's an unlikely story!

I can't prove it but my bet is that terra preta is not an *accidental* by-product of shit, fish bones, broken pots, figurines, stone ax heads, and low-temperature fires. Just because it contains all those things doesn't inevitably make it fortuitous. I think the evidence supports another possibility—that this remarkable soil was *invented,* making excellent use of freely available local resources, as an ingenious, low-tech, and environmentally friendly way to increase agricultural yield in areas that would otherwise not have been able to sustain agriculture, and thus large populations, even for a few decades, let alone for several thousands of years—as the Amazonian Dark Earths have consistently demonstrated a "miraculous" ability to do.

"What has been mysterious about these soils," Professor Antoinette WinklerPrins, director for environmental studies at Johns Hopkins University, admits, "is their ability to persist in a landscape that common ecological knowledge would dictate they could not.[25]. . . Why then have ADE's dated to have formed up to 2500 years ago, continued to exist?"[26]

It is not just a matter of 2,500 years ago—as we shall see, the origin of the Amazonian Dark Earths goes back much farther than that—but here's how Dr. WinklerPrins answers her own question:

> The unique nature of the carbon in these soils is the key to the
> stability of the organic matter in ADE's and the key to the mystery of
> the persistence of ADE's in this landscape.[27]

There appears—exceptionally—to be universal agreement among scientists on one point. This is that the explanation for all the useful qualities of terra preta "lies in large part with the char (or biochar) that gives the soil its darkness" and that is produced, as Tom Miles explained, by the smouldering (rather than hot burning) of organic matter in an oxygen-poor environment. The results are not properly understood, but, according to *Nature*, "The particles of char produced this way are somehow able to gather up nutrients and water that might otherwise be washed down below the reach of roots."[28]

William Balée, professor of anthropology at Tulane University, confirms these observations, adding that "microbial activity leads to increased carbon sequestration," and that "ADE is richer and more diverse in microbes than surrounding soils, even though millions of these species remain to be identified precisely, and literally *a million separate taxa can be contained in only 10 grams of soil*. A significant proportion of the microbes in ADE are different from microbes in the surrounding primeval soils."[29]

Another authoritative study also focused on the surprising microbial vigor and utility for agricultural purposes of ADEs, noting a further connection with the managed use of fire. "Fire contributes charcoal and ash, which increase soil pH, thereby suppressing aluminum activity toxic to plant roots and soil microbiota."[30]

What is more, fire increases the capacity of the soils to retain nutrients, thus maintaining a "synergistic cycle of continued fertility."[31]

In summary, concedes Professor WinklerPrins, the microbial complexes associated with ADEs are "poorly understood" and "quite mysterious actually."[32] Likewise, even the authors of the shitscape/middenscape theory of ADE formation admit that "despite the importance of research on *terra preta,* we still lack a firm understanding of the specific formation processes that led to the diversity inherent in these anthrosols."[33]

Yet all this mystery, all this effectiveness, all this efficiency, and all these remarkable contributions to welfare, we are asked to believe, came about as incidental by-products of human activity? They just *happened*—without any planning, or deliberation, or design at all?

I could see immediately why such ideas would give comfort to archaeologists whose roller-coaster ride thus far has taken them from a position where they had convinced themselves and their students that there could never have been any cities in the Amazon, to a position where they must now accept that the prehistoric rainforest once teemed with cities. This in itself has been a traumatic enough paradigm shift. I'm therefore not surprised that most archaeologists remain unwilling to go the extra mile needed to view terra preta—that "miraculous" agent of fertility—as the product of deliberate, ingenious, organized, focused, *scientific* activity. It causes far less cognitive dissonance, for so naturally conservative and cautious a discipline, to conclude instead that it was the waste and refuse of those previously contested Amazonian cities with their very large populations that had accidentally fertilized the land and made possible the otherwise anomalous boost to agricultural productivity that had kept the stomachs of the otherwise anomalous urban populations full.

But isn't it much more likely that all this happened the other way around?

Surely it makes no sense that the large populations came first. If they did, how did they feed themselves while enough shit and fish bones were being accumulated to create the first patches of terra preta? Isn't it more logical that the settlement and expansion of human populations in the Amazon was a planned affair in which the spread of terra preta was a *precondition* for the development of large settlements rather than a consequence of it?

Professor Balée, not an archaeologist, seems to be thinking somewhat along these lines when he cites the bizarre microbial differences between ADEs and the original, unenhanced soils that surround them as evidence for a deliberate human "contribution to microbial diversity in the Amazon, a remarkably intriguing and still living, even evolving legacy of the pre-Columbian Dark Earth people."[34]

REMARKABLE AND
PRECOCIOUS SCIENCE

AS WITH SO MUCH ELSE that concerns the Amazon, the issue of **when**, exactly, terra preta first began to be created continues to be fogged by confusion and uncertainty.

A casual glance through the scientific literature might leave the reader with the impression that these exceptionally fertile anthropogenic soils are a phenomenon of the past 3,000 years only—with the great bulk of terra preta creation taking place between about 1,000 years ago and the time of the European conquest.[35]

Look closer, however, and you will discover that many of the same authorities are tiptoeing around the edges of another mystery here.

For example, while reemphasizing their satisfaction with the idea that Amazonian Dark Earths are "produced by human habitation but unintentionally,"[36] and noting that ADE formation "ceased in most, if not all, parts of Amazonia during the early Contact period," Eduardo Neves and his colleagues concede that "the initiation of ADE formation has been more difficult to explain so far."[37]

They choose to focus on the period from around 2,500 to 2,000 years ago but caution that earlier sites may have disappeared due to the dynamic landscape processes of the Amazon, or perhaps because "the soil organic matter in most older ADE sites has been mineralized, leaving only inorganic artifacts behind, without coloration of the substrate by organic matter, and thus, early sites are under-represented."[38]

But by no means all of the earlier sites have disappeared. Enough of the older plots remain for several of the leading authorities to agree that 2,500 years ago is nowhere *near* the beginning of the story. Neves himself accepts the existence of much older ADE sites, notably "the sites of the so-called Massangana phase . . . dated ca. 4,800 BP."[39]

These sites, which are about 300 years older than the orthodox date for the construction of the Great Pyramid of Giza, are located in southeast Amazonia in the Jamari River area. Unfortunately, they are no longer accessible, having been flooded by the construction of the Samuel hydroelectric dam.[40] It seems, however, that there are even older ADEs. In the *Proceedings of the Royal Society*, for example, Neves and others report Black Earths that are between 5,000 and 6,000 years old.[41] Elsewhere—in no less august a journal than *Nature*—we read of ADEs that "are thought to be 7000 years old."[42]

Nor does the trail leading back to humanity's time of amnesia quite fade from view even there. Specialists from Cornell University's Department of Crop and Soil Sciences, joined by Eduardo Neves and citing his "unpublished data," conclude in the *Journal of the Soil Science Society of America* that the man-made Dark Earths of the Amazon in fact date back as far as 8,700 years ago.[43]

And again, Neves's own caution must surely apply—that even older sites than this may very well once have existed but have disappeared with the passage of time.

Given the incredible longevity of this soil and its extraordinary ability to regenerate its own fertility through microbial action, it is by no means beyond the bounds of reason to suppose that plots of terra preta dating back to the last Ice Age might *still* exist somewhere in the millions of square kilometers of the rainforest that have never been investigated by archaeologists at all.[44]

What is certain, however, is that a remarkable and precocious skill and competence in soil science—"exemplary agronomy" in Professor David Wilkinson's phrase—leaves its fingerprints in the Amazon at least 8,700 years ago. After that (and for how long *before* that we do not know) its use becomes integrated into the harmonious and successful lifeways of ancient Amazonian civilization. This civilization thrives for millennia, long outlasting ancient Egypt and ancient Mesopotamia, doing very well for itself and for its people in just about every possible way, until the catastrophe of European contact that not only subjects it to genocide by sword and by epidemic, but also conspires to deny its very existence for centuries thereafter.

Reader, please note—when I speak of an "ancient Amazonian civilization" I am not under any circumstances claiming that this was the lost civilization I have spent much of my working life trying to track down! My suggestion, rather, is that, in weighing what happened in the Amazon from the Ice Age until the European conquest, we may find that certain striking anomalies such as the mysterious Australasian genetic signal, and indeed the Amazonian Dark Earths themselves, bear the fingerprints of that world-exploring, world-encompassing, world-measuring lost civilization of prehistoric antiquity. More specifically, the proposition we are presently considering in this context is that the settlement and expansion of human populations in the Amazon was a planned affair in which the spread of terra preta was a *precondition* for the development of large population centers rather than a consequence of it.

It was, in other words, not something random at all but an integral part of a carefully thought-out project.

14

GARDENING EDEN

FURTHER INTRIGUING HINTS THAT SOME sort of intelligent, guided *project* was mounted in the Amazon thousands of years ago are to be found in recent studies of the species of trees that populate the rainforest. These studies demonstrate that far from being a "pristine" natural environment, the Amazon is largely a *human creation*.

Anna Roosevelt, whose sometimes radical views we've already encountered, criticizes other scientists for assuming—all too often—that the Amazon's forests are entirely works of nature "without conducting research to exclude a human influence."[1]

When that research is done, it turns out that while "Amazonian forests in different regions differ significantly from one another in topography, climate, geology, hydrology, structure, seasonality, and history," they nonetheless "often resemble each other" in showing a "pattern of unexpected dominance and density of a small group of plant species. This pattern has been found wherever Amazon forests have been inventoried and has yet to be explained by natural factors."[2]

The best current estimate is that the Amazon is presently home to about 16,000 woody tree species. Out of this total, however, "only 227 hyperdominant species dominate Amazonian forests."[3] These so-called oligarchs (from the Greek for "rule by a few") "make up only 1.4% of all the Amazon forest species but almost half of the trees in any given forest."[4]

In 2017 a large international team of ecologists and archaeologists, led by environmental science researcher Carolina Levis of Wageningen University in the Netherlands, completed a study looking into this peculiar pattern of distribution. What immediately stood out in their data was that, among the oligarchs, "domesticated species are five times more likely than nondomesticated species to be hyperdominant."[5]

Moreover, in almost every case where clusters of hyperdominants were inventoried, ancient archaeological sites were found among them[6]—a correlation so frequent and reliable that the presence and concentration of oligarchs could, in theory, be used to "predict the occurrence of archaeological sites in Amazonian forests."[7]

The team's detailed analysis, published in *Science,* therefore concludes that "modern tree communities in Amazonia are structured to an important extent by a long history of plant domestication by Amazonian peoples. . . . Detecting the widespread effect of ancient societies in modern forests . . . strongly refutes ideas of Amazonian forests being untouched by man. Domestication shapes Amazonian forests."[8]

We've seen that the question of exactly when human beings first arrived in the Amazon remains to be settled. So, too, does the question of exactly when they began to domesticate trees. The team's results suggest that "past human interventions had an important and lasting role in the distribution of domesticated species found in modern forests, despite the fact that the location of many archaeological sites is unknown."[9] On present evidence, however, adds Levis, all that can be said with certainty is that at some point "more than 8,000 years ago," Amazonian people were already focusing attention on certain trees that were particularly useful to them.

They really cultivated and planted these species in their home gardens, in the forests they were managing.[10]

Among the favored species mentioned in the *Science* paper, now all hyper-dominant, are *Bertholletia excelsa* (the Brazil nut tree), *Inga edulis* ("Ice-Cream Bean," a fruit tree), *Pourouma cecropiifolia* ("Amazon Grape," a fruit tree), *Pouteria caimito* (the abiu, a fruit tree), and *Theobroma cacao* (the cocoa tree—chocolate).[11]

Other prized Amazonian species domesticated in ancient times include the açai palm and tucuma palm, the peach palm, the Cupuaçu tree, the cashew tree, and the rubber tree.[12]

A MAJOR CENTER OF CROP DOMESTICATION

AS I RESEARCHED THIS MATERIAL I was initially surprised to learn that cocoa trees and rubber trees, both of which I'd wrongly believed were indigenous to and had been domesticated in Mexico, were in fact originally South American species and had been domesticated in the Amazon. I was equally surprised to learn that capsicum—chili peppers, red and green bell peppers, et cetera—which I had again wrongly thought were Mexican in origin, had likewise first been domesticated in the Amazon.[13]

Indeed, though often overlooked, Amazonia has rightly been described as "a major center of crop domestication" on a global scale.[14] Prior to the European conquest, according to Charles R. Clement of Brazil's National Institute of Amazonian Research, "at least 83 native species were domesticated to some degree, including manioc, sweet potato, cacao, tobacco, pineapple and hot peppers, as well as numerous fruit trees and palms, and at least another 55 imported neotropical species were cultivated."[15]

Pineapples! There was another surprise for me, as I had (again wrongly) always assumed that these tropical fruits grow on trees and had their origins in some Pacific archipelago, perhaps Hawaii. In fact, the pineapple plant with its long, spiky leaves, is not a tree. It grows close to the ground (with each plant producing a single pineapple), belongs to the Bromeliad family, and is indigenous to, and was first domesticated in, the Amazon rainforest.[16]

There is no firm information on *when* domestication was undertaken, but in Charles Clements's view, "The widespread distribution of the pineapple in the Americas at the time of the European conquest, the diversity and quality of the cultivars, not surpassed after one century of modern, intensive breeding, the diversity of uses, the economic and cultural importance of the crop, all point to a very ancient domestication."[17]

Out of the 83 crops native to Amazonia and the 55 "exotic" ones, a total of 138 crops in all, Clements and his colleagues classify 52, including the pineapple, as fully domesticated. Of these, 14 (27 percent) are fruit or nut trees or woody vines. Among the 41 crops classified as semi-domesticated, 35 (or 87 percent) are fruit or nut trees or woody vines. Among the 45 crops classified as incipiently domesticated, all but 1 are fruit or nut trees:[18]

> Overall, 68% of these Amazonian crops are trees or woody perennials. In landscapes largely characterized by forest, a predominance of tree crops is perhaps not surprising. Nonetheless, the most important subsistence crop domesticated in Amazonia is an herbaceous shrub, manioc, and several other domesticates are also root or tuber crops, most of which are adapted to savanna-forest transitional ecotones with pronounced dry seasons.[19]

Think of it. The rainforest was coaxed, shaped, and transformed by what can only be described as scientific practices into a vast garden of useful and productive trees. But trees alone cannot feed large populations, so the prehistoric domestication program was extended on a massive scale to include agricultural species that were then successfully incorporated, through the use of terra preta, into the Amazonian ecology.

THE MANIOC CONUNDRUM

MANIOC, THE KEY STAPLE, "THE most important food crop that originated in Amazonia,"[20] and on which the majority of the population of the Amazon still depend today,[21] is of particular interest for a number of reasons. Molecular analysis has confirmed that this woody shrub, cultivated for its edible roots, was domesticated in the Amazon basin, "most likely in the savannas, the Brazilian *Cerrado,* to the south of the Amazon rainforest,"[22] and more specifically "in northern Mato Grosso, Rondônia and Acre states, in Brazil, and adjacent areas of northern Bolivia. Domestication must have started before 8,000 BP, as that is the earliest date reported from the Zana and Ñanchoc valleys of coastal Peru."[23]

Unlike the Amazon itself, large parts of which remain inaccessible to archaeologists, these two coastal Peruvian valleys have been well studied, yielding, as well as manioc, "evidence for radiocarbon-dated human cultivation of squash (9240 and 7660 yr B.P.), peanut (7840 yr B.P.), quinoa (8000 and 7500 yr B.P.), and cotton (5490 yr B.P.)."[24]

What is notable, however, is that all of these crops had **already** been domesticated elsewhere before being grown in coastal Peru.[25]

As with cocoa and chilies, I'd long been under the impression that the squash plant (*cucurbita*) was first domesticated in Mexico around 10,000 years ago, and indeed there is archaeological evidence to support this.[26] But now here it was turning up in Peruvian coastal valleys 9,240 years ago, and not only there but at similar dates in the nearby sites of Paiján and Las Pircas.[27] An authoritative study published in *Science* suggests that these cultivated Peruvian squash plants may have been from a line that had originally been domesticated not in Mexico but in "southwestern Ecuador and the Colombian Amazon" as early as 10,000 to 9,300 years ago.[28]

What about the peanuts cultivated in the Zana and Ñanchoc valleys 7,840 years ago? They, too, it turns out, were domesticated east of the Andes in a region extending south from the southern edge of the Amazon basin.[29] This is broadly the same region in which manioc was also domesticated,[30] and in both cases we can only go on the dates of the earliest surviving materials— currently put at around 8000 years BP[31]—to guess when domestication in fact took place. Certainly it was before 8,000 years ago, but how long before is a matter largely of conjecture and some authorities are already seeking to push the horizon back to at least 9,000 and perhaps 10,000 years ago.[32]

Manioc, also known as cassava, is a starchy crop, a good staple providing almost twice as many calories as potatoes weight for weight.[33] But it is also so low in protein content that, as one specialist warns, "in manioc-dominated diets, protein-deficiency can lead to malnutrition and also aggravate symptoms related to manioc cyanogenic toxicity."[34]

We'll return to that issue of toxicity in a moment but let's note, meanwhile, that peanuts have a very high protein content that makes them a perfect nutritional "complement to starchy manioc-based diets."[35] Several authorities have noticed the pairing of the two in ancient cultures and British botanist Barbara Pickersgill speculates that the wide prehistoric distribution of peanut cultivation may have accompanied the spread and uptake of manioc.[36]

Again I can't help but wonder if there might not have been something more active and intentional at work behind the scenes of this process than mere "accompanying." What I have in mind is the possibility that a deep knowledge of plants and of their nutritional and other properties might have *preceeded* the first domestication activities that we have evidence for. Surely it is only on the basis of such foreknowledge that crops like groundnuts and manioc could be selected, domesticated, planned, and planted to complement each other's nutritional contribution to human welfare?

This is pure speculation, of course. But it's strengthened somewhat by the curious nature of the manioc roots themselves, which (although there are many varieties) are classified into two main categories—"bitter" and "sweet." All contain compounds known as cyanogenic glucosides, found in low concentrations in the less popular sweet varieties and in very high concentrations in the greatly prized and more widely used bitter varieties.[37] The need-to-know element here is that if you eat any of the "bitter" varieties, without first processing them in the correct way (extracting the glucosides), you will at least suffer from "cyanic intoxication, with symptoms like vomiting, dizziness, and paralysis," if not die of cyanide poisoning.[38]

Ignorant of this, several of the soldiers on Francisco de Orellana's sixteenth-century voyage down the Amazon ate unprocessed manioc roots. They survived but became mightily sick, near to death, as a result.[39] To avoid poisoning they would have had to peel the roots, then grate them, then strain and press the resulting mash to remove the hydrocyanic acid, and at last toast it to produce a fine faintly yellowish flour[40]—simple but absolutely essential procedures that the indigenous peoples of the Amazon have followed for thousands of years to make "bitter" manioc safe.

The fundamental question, however, is exactly how and when this processing system was first devised? Obviously since we have evidence of the cultivation of domesticated manioc by 8,000, or perhaps even as much as 10,000 years ago, it follows that the ability to process it must already have been developed by then. It would make no sense to anybody to go to all the trouble of domesticating a species and then growing crops from that species that nobody could eat without getting horribly, and perhaps lethally, sick. That's why I keep coming back to the haunting possibility that some person or group of people with an interest in the Amazon *already* understood the potentials of manioc— and the exact steps that would have to be taken to avoid its dangers—long before they ever chose to domesticate it and put it under cultivation.[41]

Otherwise, frankly . . . why bother?

PLANT GNOSIS

THE MANIOC ISSUE LOOKS SIMPLE. You just need to peel it, grate it, soak it, strain it, and meticulously cook it to remove the poison, and it is transformed into a useful staple.[42] All steps of the processing seem rather obvious and basic in retrospect, but consider the amount of trial and error—the number of volunteers you would have had to make sick or kill—before you arrived at the right method.

And what would motivate you to start such a project in the first place, unless you already knew the potential of the wild progenitor that would eventually become domesticated manioc?

The same problem looms on an even larger and more complex scale with other plants of the Amazon, the uses to which they are put, and the processing they require. Anthropologist Jeremy Narby, author of *The Cosmic Serpent: DNA and the Origins of Knowledge,* draws attention to curare, the blow-gun and arrow poison, invented—we do not know when—in the ancient Amazon. It produces paralysis and death by asphyxiation as the muscles required for breathing cease to function. It is used, Narby explains, because "it kills tree-borne animals without poisoning their meat while causing them to relax their grip and fall to the ground. Monkeys, when hit with an untreated arrow, tend to wrap their tails around branches and die out of the archer's reach."[43]

A very useful hunting aid, therefore, and one, moreover, that has been adopted into modern medical anesthesiology. But the real mystery, as Narby goes on to show us, is how it was ever invented in the first place. The consensus among scholars is that curare, of which there are forty types in the Amazon made from seventy plant species, was stumbled upon by chance experimentation.[44] Narby doubts this scenario:

ABOVE: Only from the sky does the entire form of the great Manitou of Serpent Mound become visible. BELOW: The Serpent's head appears to seek out the setting sun, but only on the summer solstice. PHOTOS: SANTHA FAIIA.

A marriage of earth and sky: progress of the summer solstice sunset over Serpent Mound. PHOTOS: SANTHA FAIIA.

Winter solstice sunrise as viewed through the kilometer-long axis of the Temple of Karnak, Upper Egypt. PHOTO: SANTHA FAIIA.

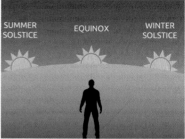

The Great Sphinx of Egypt is an equinoctial marker. At the summer solstice the sun rises far to the north of east and at the winter solstice far to the south of east, but on the equinox the sun rises due east in direct alignment with the gaze of the Sphinx. PHOTO: SANTHA FAIIA.

The temple of Angkor Wat, Cambodia, is perfectly aligned to the cardinal directions so that the rising sun on the equinox sits momentarily at the pinnacle of the central tower, lighting up the whole enchanted structure like a fairy-tale kingdom. PHOTO: SANTHA FAIIA.

ABOVE: Entrance to Denisova Cave, Siberia, where the prehistory of our species is being rewritten. BELOW: View out of the main entrance of Denisova Cave, downslope to the Anui River. PHOTOS: SANTHA FAIIA.

ABOVE: Excavation trench, central gallery, Denisova Cave. BELOW: Although it seems to have served as a workshop where very special objects were made, the arches and the natural clerestory window of Denisova Cave give it a cathedral-like feel. PHOTOS: SANTHA FAIIA.

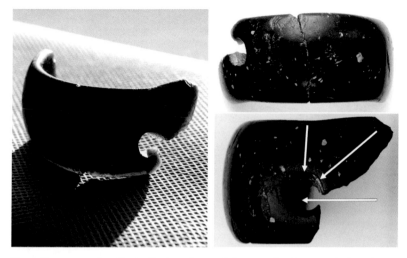

These fragments of a chloritolite bracelet, and the way that it seems designed to catch and transform light, suggest a far higher degree of artistic sophistication among the "anatomically primitive" Denisovans than among anatomically modern humans of the same period. The drill marks—indicated by superimposed arrows—bear witness to a level of technology in the depths of the Ice Age that was thousands of years ahead of its time. PHOTOS: INSTITUTE OF ARCHAEOLOGY AND ETHNOGRAPHY, SIBERIAN BRANCH, RUSSIAN ACADEMY OF SCIENCES.

Graham Hancock with Tom Deméré (left), chief palaeontologist at the San Diego Natural History Museum. The evidence that Deméré and his colleagues have excavated from the Cerutti Mastodon Site, including a single tusk set purposefully upright in the ground as a marker (right), indicates that humans were present in North America 130,000 years ago—ten times as long as had previously been supposed. PHOTOS: SANTHA FAIIA.

In the archives of the San Diego Natural History Museum examining the evidence for a human presence in the Americas 130,000 years ago. PHOTO: SANTHA FAIIA.

At Topper, South Carolina, with archaeologist Al Goodyear (left) who kept on digging below the Clovis level and found evidence of pre-Clovis humans going back 50,000 years. PHOTO: SANTHA FAIIA.

To produce it, it is necessary to combine several plants and boil them for seventy-two hours, while avoiding the fragrant but mortal vapors emitted by the broth. The final product is a paste that is inactive unless injected under the skin. If swallowed, it has no effect. It is difficult to see how anybody could have stumbled on this recipe by chance experimentation.[45]

The whole mystery of the Amazonian plant medicines, notably the vision-inducing brew ayahuasca (which itself is a mixture of several plants that are most unlikely to have been fortuitously brought together) is explored in depth in my 2005 book *Supernatural: Meetings with the Ancient Teachers of Mankind*. In these medicines, as in curare, as in terra preta, and as in the incredible burst of domestication of plants and trees in the Amazon that followed the end of the Ice Age, could we be looking at the cultural DNA not only of a civilization but of a sophisticated civilization that had developed sciences of its own that it began to share with other people—very much including the peoples of the Amazon basin—around the time that the last Ice Age came cataclysmically to its end?

Judging from the clues that lie scattered like tantalizing jewels across the Amazon, this hypothetical lost science of a hypothetical lost civilization would have looked very different from any of our own sciences, employing not only empirical methods but also shamanistic techniques, vision quests, and out of body encounters in the "spirit world" that most modern Western intellectuals would regard as absurd. Again, however, if we go by the evidence of the Amazon, the plain fact is that the remnants and borrowings of this supposedly laughable form of science have again and again produced practical and down-to-earth results—domesticating and processing huge numbers of plants and trees, for example, or creating "miracle" soils that are still fertile after thousands of years of use, or inventing muscle relaxants like curare that inhibit acetylcholine receptors at the neuromuscular junction. Moreover, unlike Western technology, to which the earth is a dead thing, this ancient technology addresses all the needs, spiritual as well as physical, of the human creature. Again, though the skeptics will scoff, none of the many thousands of people who've had their lives transformed by ayahuasca in the past 20 years would deny that something very powerful and very hard to explain is at work here.[46]

SACRED GEOMETRY

F ROM THE TIME OF ITS earliest appearance in the archaeological record (which is absolutely not the same thing as the time that it first took shape) Amazonian civilization is a continuum that does not break from the wisdom and insights of its founders. The same basic principles, defining the relationship between humanity and the cosmos continue to manifest and to be re-expressed over thousands upon thousands of years, in some cases evolving and developing into strange new growths, in others devolving and decaying. But just like that enigmatic Australasian genetic signal still found among Amazonian peoples today, other traces of ancient and mysterious connections, though faint, have also survived.

For example, despite rejecting the old stereotypes of the "savage" and "primitive" Amazon, and despite knowing that prehistoric civilizations of some complexity had once flourished there, scientists at the beginning of the twenty-first century were nonetheless taken aback to be presented with overwhelming evidence of an ancient practice of *geometry* in the rainforest—and on a very ambitious scale.

Let's get one thing straight before we take a closer look at this mystery. Just because people live in a dense jungle, and haven't attended math classes in high school, does **not** mean they have no grasp of geometry—"one of the deepest and oldest products of human reason."[1] On the contrary, though often wrongly attributed to Euclid, there is compelling evidence—mysterious in itself—that "the conceptual principles of geometry are inherent in the human mind."[2] This evidence comes from an isolated region at the heart of the Amazon where scientists from the Cognitive Neuroimaging Unit of the Collège de France led a study in which the indigenous Mundurukú people were tested on basic geometry skills. The study found that:

> Mundurukú children and adults spontaneously made use of . . . the core concepts of topology (e.g., connectedness), Euclidean geometry (e.g., line, point, parallelism, and right angle), and basic geometrical figures (e.g., square, triangle, and circle) . . . and they used distance, angle, and sense relationships in geometrical maps to locate hidden objects.[3]

In summary, therefore, isolated peoples in remote parts of the Amazon today, whose contact with technological civilization is extremely limited,[4] possess innate geometrical knowledge and are able to deploy it "independently of instruction, experience with maps, or measurement devices."[5] No doubt their ancestors, and probably most humans always, have been blessed with the same neurological gift. Indeed, we see it made manifest down the ages in all kinds of man-made structures. Even the simplest wattle-and-daub hovels tend to be rectangular or square rather than randomly shaped. Likewise, from England's Stonehenge, to the Great Pyramid of Egypt, to India's Madurai Meenakshi Temple, to Borobudur in Indonesia, to Angkor Wat in Cambodia, to Tikal in Guatemala, to Tiahuanaco in Bolivia—and to countless other sites too numerous to mention—the design of the sacred architecture of the world is entirely governed by geometry.

The very universality of this geometry, as an innate faculty of the human mind, is not in doubt, but how it has been **expressed** by different civilizations in different epochs is culturally driven. Thus, Angkor Wat is not the Great

Pyramid and the Great Pyramid is not Stonehenge. All three, however, share the same fundamental geometries and connections to the cosmos that—I have long argued—were incorporated into a *system* of architecture central to the beliefs and lifeways of a lost civilization of remotest prehistory. When that civilization was destroyed in the series of cataclysms that brought the last Ice Age to an end, there were survivors who took the system with them, seeking to replant it in the many different parts of the world where they found refuge. In some it took root and flowered early, and over thousands of years it manifested in multiple different ways; in others it lay dormant for millennia before bursting into exuberant life.

Mainstream archaeology recognizes no such universal system, nor even the vestiges of one, and insists that there was no "diffusion" of ideas between these ancient cultures (*How could there be when Angkor is 3,500 years younger than the Great Pyramid?*). The point is fair but irrelevant to my proposition which does not require diffusion within the past 5,000 or even the past 10,000 years. Instead I suggest that the similarities and differences between certain ancient monumental structures, created around the world at different times by different cultures, are best explained by a remote common ancestor civilization that left a legacy of ideas and *knowledge* in which they all shared, which their priests, shamans, and sages sought to preserve, and which they in due course deployed in their own different ways.

One of the hallmarks of this worldwide "system," whether its widespread presence is coincidental or not, is geometry. And, in turn, whenever the geometry manifests on a monumental scale that could only be achieved by skilled specialists and a large, well-organized workforce, the obvious implication is that a fairly advanced civilization must have been involved.

That was why, when giant geometrical earthworks were discovered in the Rio Branco area of the Brazilian state of Acre in the southwestern Amazon in 1977 nobody at first paid much attention. This was the era when the Smithsonian's Betty Meggers still reigned supreme over all things Amazonian. Her *Man and Culture in a Counterfeit Paradise* had been published just 6 years before and her view that the jungle could never have supported large populations or any form of civilization capable of monumental architecture was the full-blown dogma of the day. Little wonder then, although the Smithsonian had sponsored the National Program of Archaeological Research in the Ama-

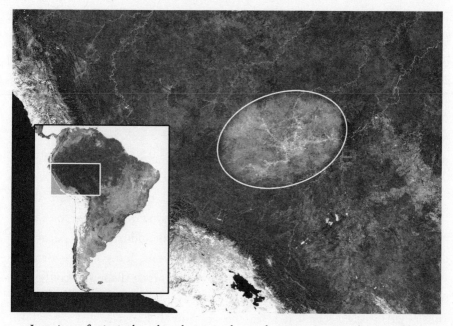

Locations of principal earthwork sites in the southwestern Amazon discovered by 2018.

zon that found the first "geoglyphs," that it did not announce the discovery until 11 years later.[6]

The young man who actually spotted the earthworks from a Smithsonian survey aircraft was Alceu Ranzi, and it was he who named them "geoglyphs."[7] His career took him elsewhere for the next two decades but his interest was sparked again after another overflight in 1999 and, now at the Federal University of Acre, he resumed his research together with colleagues Denise Schaan of the Federal University of Pará and Martti Pärssinen of the University of Helsinki.

Their first detailed results were published in the December 2009 issue of *Antiquity*,[8] which trailed the findings as evidence of the existence in ancient times of "a sophisticated pre-Columbian monument-building society in the upper Amazon Basin on the east side of the Andes. This hitherto unknown people constructed earthworks of precise geometric plan connected by straight orthogonal roads."[9]

At the outset of the paper, Ranzi, Schaan, and Pärssinen described "clusters of these monumental earthworks" mostly located on a 200-meter-high plateau:

> Formed by excavated ditches and adjacent earthen walls . . . the earthworks are shaped as perfect circles, rectangles and composite figures.[10]

But why had these stunning Amazonian geoglyphs first been noticed only a few decades previously?

Ranzi and his colleagues observe that while the geoglyphs were abandoned about 500 years ago, and then heavily overgrown, they have since been revealed by mass clearing of the forest for the cattle industry, thus becoming visible, especially from the sky, over the past 30 years. Indeed, the enormous size of the geoglyphs makes it easier to distinguish their shape and configuration from an aerial perspective than at ground level, and satellite imagery has been made freely available to researchers by Google Earth.[11]

NAZCA–AMAZON CONNECTIONS

TO THE EXTENT THAT THEY are best seen and understood for what they are from the air rather than from ground level, comparisons with the famous "Nazca Lines" of southern Peru were inevitable, and quickly began to be made—particularly so since, in addition to its giant images of animals and birds, the Nazca plateau also features many precise geometrical figures.[12]

Ranzi himself has invited the comparison by asserting that the Amazon geoglyphs are "as important as the Nazca Lines"[13] and, indeed, his own use of the term "geoglyphs" was, according to his colleague and coauthor Denise Schaan, inspired by the figures on the Nazca plateau. This, Schaan argues, is "unfortunate" because the Nazca Lines "are a different phenomenon. In the Nazca desert, geometric and zoomorphic figures were shaped by the displacement of dark, weathered rocks on the surface to expose a lighter subsurface. In Brazil and Bolivia, however, the 'figures' were produced by the excavation of large, continuous ditches forming circles, rectangles, hexagons, octagons and other, nongeometric, shapes."[14]

Nazca geometry. PHOTOS: SANTHA FAIIA.

I'm not persuaded by this distinction. Whether a painter uses oils or watercolors, the end result is still a painting. Likewise, although different techniques and materials were used—unavoidable given the very different environmental conditions of the Amazon and at Nazca—the end result in both cases is still a "canvas" decorated with immense geometric, as well as "nongeometric," shapes.

Though it is now more than quarter of a century in the past, I recall vividly my encounter with Maria Reiche, the venerable "lady of the lines," at her home in the town of Nazca where she had lived since 1945 surrounded by the ancient geoglyphs that it was her fate to study, protect, and introduce to the world. She had recently celebrated her ninetieth birthday when Santha and I met her in June 1993. Although bedridden with advanced Parkinsonism, her mind was sharp and her voice clear when she shared with us her own view of the significance of the lines:

> They teach us that our whole idea of the peoples of antiquity is wrong—that here in Peru was a civilization that was advanced, that had an advanced understanding of mathematics and astronomy, and that was a civilization of artists expressing something unique about the human spirit for future generations to comprehend.[15]

I have already explored the mystery of Nazca in previous books so I won't go over old ground here except to note that among the most iconic of the Nazca geoglyphs, etched into the desert with a single unbroken line extending for more than a mile[16] and occupying an area of approximately 90

TOP RIGHT: Nazca monkey. PHOTO: SANTHA FAIIA. TOP LEFT: Spiral Woolly Monkey tail. PHOTO: STEFFEN FOERSTER, DREAMSTIME.COM [26291981]. BOTTOM: Nineteenth-century illustration of Amazonian spider monkeys.

meters by 60 meters[17] is an image of a monkey. Its prehensile tail, stylized into a spiral, is a diagnostic feature of New World monkeys that distinguishes them from Old World monkeys.[18] However, no monkeys have ever lived in the Nazca desert. The nearest specimens, for example, capuchin monkeys, spider monkeys, and woolly monkeys, are all native to the Amazon rainforest.[19]

Another of the better-known Nazca geoglyphs looks like and is usually referred to as a spider. It has been suggested, however, that the huge 46-meter-long[20] image arguably does not depict a spider but a member of a closely related order of millimeter-sized arachnids, the "tickspiders" called Ricinulei.[21] More than seventy species have thus far been identified worldwide, not one of them in the Nazca desert. Nor should we expect any there. Ricinulei favor "tropical forests and caves"[22] and the nearest populations of this very peculiar creature to Nazca are in the Brazilian Amazon, specifically in central, eastern, and southern Amazonia.[23]

There are many strange things about the Ricinulei order, but strangest of all is a single feature that is regarded as its distinguishing anatomical characteristic.[24] As described by Brazilian arachnologist Alexandre B. Bonaldo, this is its "system of sperm transfer, which is achieved by an elaborate copulatory apparatus in the male third leg."[25] Although barely a millimeter long, and difficult to discern without magnification, it was first pointed out by the late professor Gerald S. Hawkins of Boston University that this unusual reproductive extension, common to all Ricinulei species, is depicted in the correct place on the third leg of the Nazca "spider."[26]

Hawkins, however, was an astronomer, while Bonaldo, a real expert on South American spiders, disagrees, remarking in emails we exchanged in October 2018:

The idea that the Nazca spider is a *Ricinulei* is kind of odd to me, since I always thought it was a myrmecomorphic spider such as the species of *Myrmecium* . . . *Myrmecium* is an exclusive South American genus, being recorded from the Venezuelan Caribbean to southern Brazil, but the majority of the species (28 out of 38) are endemic to the Amazon Basin, including lower parts of the oriental Andean slopes in Peru, Ecuador and Colombia.

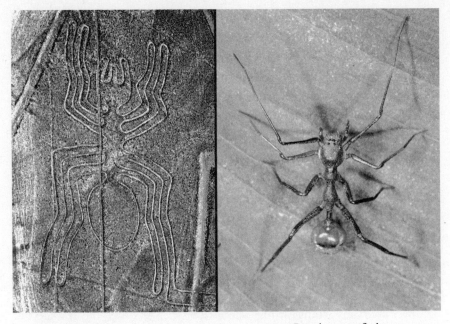

LEFT: Nazca "spider." PHOTO: SANTHA FAIIA. RIGHT: Greatly magnified, Myrmecium from the Amazon. PHOTO: ARTHUR ANKER.

I asked if I could quote him on this and he replied:

Sure, you can quote it, if you want. I would add that that third leg "modification" shows no structures and is not bilateral. It appears to be just an extension of the drawing, as is common in other Nazca drawings.

Bonaldo then kindly referred me to Arthur Anker, a colleague of his who specializes in macrophotography, and Anker in turn provided me with the image of *Myrmecium* from the Amazon (specifically from the Tambopata Reserve, near Puerto Maldonado) that is reproduced here. It is, in my view, a far better candidate for the Nazca spider than Ricinulei—and once again what it suggests to me is that scientists, who observed nature closely, were at work in ancient South America. But let's lower our sights and simply say that the monkey and "spider" figures, with their Amazonian provenance, call, at the very least, for a rethink of Schaan's view that the Nazca Lines and the Amazon geoglyphs are unconnected phenomena.

SOME FACTS AND FIGURES ON THE AMAZONIAN GEOGLYPHS

WHAT IS THE GENERAL STRUCTURE and appearance of the geoglyphs uncovered in the southwestern Amazon in recent decades? In their 2009 paper in *Antiquity*, Schaan, Ranzi, and Pärssinen give us this broad overview:

> In general, the geometric figures are formed by a ditch approximately 11m wide, currently 1–3m deep, with adjacent 0.5–1m high earthen banks, formed by deposition of the excavated soil. Ring ditches have diameters that vary from 90 to 300m. . . . When there are two or more structures, they are usually connected by embanked roads. Some of the single rectangular structures may have short roads coming out of their mid-sides or corners. Composite figures include a rectangle inside a circle or *vice versa*.[27]

Some of the figures are quite roughly executed, others are extremely exact, and in some cases an exact figure is combined with an inexact one in the same geoglyph, as at Santa Isabel, for example, where a large well-made octagon is juxtaposed with an imprecise circle.

By contrast, the geometrically austere Fazenda Parana site is "comprised of two perfect squares (200m and 100m wide) connected . . . by a 20m wide,

Fazenda Parana.
MAP AND PHOTO:
MARTTI PÄRSSINEN.

Fazenda Colorada. MAP AND PHOTO: MARTTI PÄRSSINEN.

100m long causeway. The two squares are further connected to straight roads leading east and west, north and south."[28]

More complex by far is the Fazenda Colorada site. Its geoglyphs consist of:

one circle, a quadrangle and a double ditch structure which forms a three-sided square. The three-sided square double ditch is connected to a trapezoidal structure comprised by linear walls without ditches. Its south-western corner is open and connects to a *c.* 55m broad, avenue-like, road; on both sides of the entrance one can still see two high mounds, standing like towers. The road has embankments which border both sides, and, as it extends away from the entrance, it narrows, vanishing 600m further.[29]

Then consider the site known as Fazenda Atlantica. Here the principal geoglyph forms a square measuring 250 meters along each side. Quadrants are inscribed into the east and west corners and a circle 125 meters in diame-

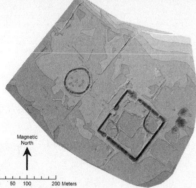

Fazenda Atlantica.
MAP AND PHOTO: SANNA SAUNALUOMA.

ter, connected to the square by a causeway 10 meters wide, lies 150 meters to the northwest.[30]

Defined by the avenue connecting the square and the circle, it is clear that the primary axis of Fazenda Atlantica runs northwest to southeast—an orientation that makes it a candidate for alignment to the setting sun on the June solstice and the rising sun on the December solstice. The reader will recall that Serpent Mound in Ohio is also aligned northwest to southeast to both these events. Its principal focus, signaled by its open jaws, is on the June solstice—midsummer in the Northern Hemisphere, where the Serpent is located, and midwinter in the Southern Hemisphere, where the Amazonian geoglyphs are located. Without an archaeoastronomical survey, however, it is impossible to say whether or not the general northwest to southeast alignment of Fazenda Atlantica is solstitial, and—if it is—whether any aspect of the site indicates priority given to one solstice over the other.

A similar northwest to southeast orientation is seen at Tequinho, another of the great Amazonian geoglyphs. When all its ancillary works were intact it extended over an area of 15 hectares (37 acres). What remains today are its two principal squares, the larger measuring 210-by-210 meters (with two further squares inscribed within it) and the smaller, which has suffered extensive damage, measuring 130-by-130 meters and enclosing one further square. Defining the ruling northwest axis of the site, the main entrance to the larger square is 40 meters wide and opens onto a causeway 1.5 kilometers long.[31] A proper survey will be required to establish whether or not there is any archaeoastronomical significance to the northwest orientation of Tequinho's main entrance and causeway.

Magnetic
North

Scale 1:4.500   0   40   80   160 Meters

Tequinho. MAP: SANNA SAUNALUOMA.
PHOTO: MARTTI PÄRSSINEN.

Fazenda Iquiri II—The mounds form an oval with its long axis oriented to the northwest. MAP AND PHOTO: SANNA SAUNALUOMA. ORIENTATION ARROWS ADDED.

Coquerial: The surviving ten mounds form the remains of an oval with its long axis oriented to the northwest. MAP AND PHOTO: SANNA SAUNALUOMA. ORIENTATION ARROWS ADDED.

What is already certain, however, is that a number of other Amazonian geoglyphs share the same general alignment. An example is Fazenda Iquiri II, which combines a square earthwork measuring 140 meters along each side with an oval earthwork formed by 25 adjoining mounds. The long axis of this oval, paralleling the axis of the square, extends for 180 meters and is oriented to the northwest,[32] making this site, too, a candidate for possible solstitial alignment if and when an archaeoastronomical survey is carried out.

Another candidate is the partially destroyed site of Coqueiral, which also consists of a series of adjoining mounds, of which ten survive out of an original total of eighteen. The remaining mounds form a partial oval with its long axis extending to approximately 100 meters oriented to the northwest.[33] As with Tequinho, as with Fazenda Iquiri II, and as with Fazenda Atlantica, a proper survey will be required before any possible archaeoastronomical significance of the Coqueiral oval can be investigated.

Indeed, as I review the otherwise excellent science so far dedicated to the Amazonian earthworks, it is evident that the most serious and consequential lapse—which must be remedied if further progress is to be made—concerns this consistent blindness to possible archaeoastronomical connections. Not a single one of the many papers on the geoglyphs reviewed in this chapter has a word to say about astronomical alignments and, so far as I am aware at the time of writing, not one of the leading scholars has shown any interest in investigating the possibility that such alignments might exist. Ironically, however, the same scholars all agree:

> The geometric earthworks were constructed on carefully selected,
> elevated yet level surfaces. Their location on intefluvial plateaux
> provided good visible control over the surrounding terrain. . . . The
> carefully planned position of the earthworks in the landscape and
> the recurring geometric forms represented in earthwork architecture
> suggest functions that were part of a tradition of shared collective
> ideology related to the cosmology and/or socio-political concerns of
> the ancient peoples.

The irony is that there's an important clue here, hidden in plain sight. It's true that the choice of "elevated locations" giving "good visible control over the surrounding terrain" could have something to do with "the socio-political concerns of the ancient peoples." But because they offer an unobstructed view of the horizon, such locations are also very often what ancient astronomers looked for when they set out monuments on the ground—aligned, say, to the June solstice sunset or to the March equinox sunrise.

Perhaps it's partly in recognition of this that the passage cited above includes a token reference to "cosmology."

But token references are not enough.

Without a full-scale archaeoastronomical survey of the Amazonian geoglyphs we are, in my opinion, unlikely ever to get to grips with the full range of challenges—and opportunities—that they represent.

AN EVER-RECEDING HORIZON

HOW OLD ARE THE GEOGLYPHS?

In 2009 only a single carbon date had been established for the entire area surveyed, then "250 km across" and constituting "200 known sites with over 210 geometric structures."[34] The date was from Fazenda Colorada and proved to be quite recent—around 750 years before the present but with a margin of error that the investigators chose to average at AD 1283,[35] a date they believed to be "representative of a number of sites" since Fazenda Colorada "exhibits much of the variability seen for the region."[36] This date, they declare, "implies a late occupation . . . only around 300 years before the Europeans' arrival, but is consistent with the development of complex societies in other areas of the Amazon between A.D. 900 and 1400."[37]

As we've seen so often with archaeology, new discoveries can change everything, and after just three more seasons of excavation, Ranzi, Schaan, and Pärssinen were singing a very different song. In a follow-up paper to their 2009 study, published in the *Journal of Field Archaeology* in 2012, they reported a greatly expanded survey area, now encompassing roughly 25,000 square kilometers.[38] Within it, 281 enclosures "formed by continuous ditches, in most cases surrounding a perfectly geometric inner plaza with an area of 1 to 3 ha" had been found "in various shapes," chiefly "circles, ellipses, rectangles and squares."[39]

Then came the first dynamite revelation. Fazenda Colorada had been thoroughly re-excavated and five additional radiocarbon samples, collected from different stratigraphic levels, were analyzed. Again, there are margins of error with C-14 dating, but the bottom line is that the previous date of AD 1283, while fitting with preconceptions about when and where complex societies developed in the Amazon, was found to have been taken from organic materials deposited **very late** in the life of the site. What the new samples indicated was that Fazenda Colorada had been "consistently occupied" from as early as AD 25 until around the end of the fourteenth century.[40]

Organic materials from a number of other geoglyph sites were also excavated and dated, showing a similar profile, and the overall conclusion of the investigators across all the sites was that these "new radiocarbon dates place the initial stage of earthwork construction as early as 2000 BP."[41]

In summary, therefore, just 3 years of research between 2009 and 2012 witnessed a profound change in archaeological understanding of the geoglyphs of the southwestern Amazon. Previously they'd been thought to be just 750 years old; now, without any real attention being drawn to the implications, they'd become 2,000 years old. To put this in context, an error and subsequent correction on a similar scale would certainly attract a great deal of attention if it concerned Western architecture—indeed it would be like discovering that the great Gothic cathedrals of Europe such as Chartres and York Minster were not, in fact, works of the late medieval period but had actually been built by the Romans.

What are we to conclude concerning mistakes of such magnitude, and the tendency of archaeologists to reach and propagate premature conclusions based on limited samples? For instance, the single AD 1283 date from Fazenda Colorada being allowed to stand for 3 years without corroboration as "representative of a number of sites"? And similarly at Serpent Mound in Ohio, where in 2018 a date of around AD 1000 was still being touted in official notices despite firm C-14 evidence, on the public record since 2014, that the structure is more than 1,000 years older than that?[42] Readers will make up their own minds, but the uncertainty and the constant failure of old models (such as Clovis First in North America and Meggers's "counterfeit paradise" dogma about the Amazon) do not fill me with confidence about much else that this discipline has to say.

In particular, I am not persuaded by the new consensus that the geoglyphs of the southwestern Amazon are 2,000 years old. Other C-14 dates mentioned in the 2012 report already hint at a more complicated picture.

Take the site known as Severino Calazans, for example. Curiously, the square geoglyph the archaeologists excavated here has the same massive "footprint"—measuring 230 meters along each side[43]—as the Great Pyramid of Egypt.[44] Both monuments are also cardinally oriented—that is, their sides face the cardinal directions, north, south, east, and west.[45]

Two C-14 dates for Severino Calazans were cited by Ranzi, Schaan, and Pärssinen as further confirmation that the Amazonian geoglyph project began "about 2000 years ago."[46] Margins of error apply, but these dates were 159 BC (from excavation Unit 3) and 171 BC (from Unit 6B).[47] Fitting much less comfortably into the new hypothesis, however, were the two other dates from Severino Calazans. Again, there are margins of error, but these dates were, respectively, 1211 BC (from Unit 5) and **2577 BC** (from Unit 3)[48]—the latter suggesting that this geoglyph might not only have the same footprint as the Great Pyramid of Egypt but might also be about the same age.

We've seen how the existence of true civilizations in the Amazon before European contact has been cautiously embraced by archaeologists in recent years. Even so, few would yet be willing to accept that any Amazonian "civilization" worthy of the name might have existed as early as 2577 BC and certainly not one well-organized and motivated enough to create a cardinally oriented geoglyph on the grand scale of Severino Calazans, where the full perimeter, defined by an enclosure ditch 12 meters wide, measures 920 meters—more than 3,000 feet.[49]

Unsurprisingly, therefore, Ranzi, Schaan, and Pärssinen conclude that the date of 2577 BC "is probably unrelated to the time of initial construction of the earthworks."[50]

All they're prepared to concede is that "this date suggests early human activity at the site."[51] They perhaps stick their necks out further than most of their peers would when they allow the possibility that the second anomalous date from Severino Calazans—1211 BC—"may be related to earthwork construction."[52]

But what is the logic of this? If we have dispensed with our former assertion that a date of AD 1283 was "somehow representative" of the geoglyphs in general, and if we are going to allow a possible start on this great regional project as early as 1211 BC, then why should we be unable to contemplate an even earlier start as far back as 2577 BC? Since so little of the Amazon has been surveyed by archaeologists, and since no theory about the character and constraints of its past cultures and civilizations has been able to explain all the data, it would surely be wiser to keep an open mind.

Besides, as Ranzi, Pärssinen, and Schaan themselves point out, they are working with a very limited sample of the potential data. Pärssinen at one point estimated that as many as 1,500 geoglyphs might ultimately be found,[53] and the authorities are in general agreement that "these earthworks, uncovered by modern deforestation . . . represent only a fraction of the total, which lie undiscovered beneath the intact seasonal southern Amazonian rainforests."[54]

It is therefore perfectly possible that multiple other sites, as yet unknown to archaeologists, will be discovered in the years to come. They might confirm the existing archaeological model that the geoglyphs are about 2,000 years old, or they might turn out to reinforce that anomalous date of 2577 BC— or, who knows, they might even provide much older dates and reveal more sophisticated constructions.

Once again, whatever the facts are on the ground, we won't know for sure unless we look.

CURIOSITIES

IT'S A CURIOSITY—I CLAIM nothing more at this point—that the **square** enclosure ditch at Severino Calazans shares the ground plan, base dimensions, and cardinality of the Great Pyramid of Egypt, as well as a carbon date from the epoch of the Great Pyramid.[55] That epoch, moreover, around 2500 BC, coincides and overlaps with the megalithic epoch in Europe, so another curiosity is the way that the **circular** geoglyphs of Amazonia resemble "henges"—the circular embankments with deep internal ditches that surround the great stone circles of the British Isles. The scale is very similar and the resemblance is so obvious that even the most sober archaeologists, usually wary of cross-cultural comparisons, are willing to remark upon it. For example, Dr. Jennifer Watling of the Museum of Archaeology and Ethnography at the University of São Paulo, author of an important study of the Amazonian earthworks published in the *Proceedings of the National Academy of Sciences* in February 2017, states frankly that the characteristics of the circular geoglyphs with their embankments and ditches "are what classically describe henge sites. The earliest phases at Stonehenge consisted of a similarly laid out enclosure. . . . It is likely that the geoglyphs were used for similar functions to the Neolithic causewayed enclosures, i.e. public gathering, ritual sites."[56]

A point of order here. A "henge" is a prehistoric earthwork formed by a circular embankment surrounding a ditch. Usually the embankment is heaped up from the soil removed to create the ditch. This is the case, for example, at the causewayed enclosure of Avebury, Europe's largest henge, which has a diameter of approximately 420 meters.[57] Walking briskly it takes about half an hour to make a complete circuit of the lip of the Avebury embankment from which you look down, across the ditch, at the immense circular inner plaza that the ditch defines. Disposed at intervals around the outer perimeter of this plaza, set back a couple of meters from its edge, a complete ring of giant megaliths once stood in antiquity, encompassing two other stone circles placed side by side. Very few of the original megaliths now remain—the site having been used as a quarry in later times—but, although Avebury's causeways are almost entirely gone, the henge is still there and it is still possible to make out the form of the great stone circle that it encloses and the remnants of the paired inner circles. What cannot now be seen, but was discovered in

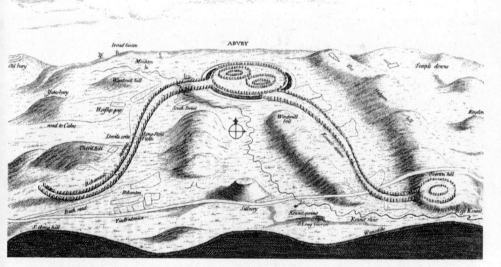

An impression by the antiquarian William Stukeley (early eighteenth century) of the complete Avebury complex as it would originally have appeared in its landscape. Approached by two monumental serpentine causeways, the great henge is top center, with its pair of inner circles clearly shown.

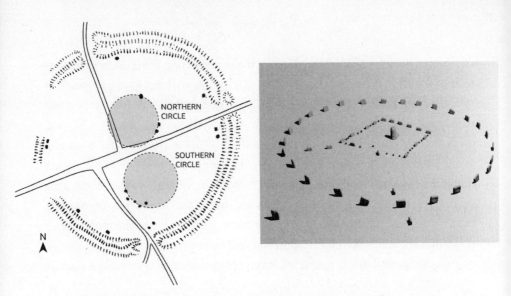

LEFT: Detail of the main henge at Avebury with its two inner circles. RIGHT: Reconstruction of Avebury's southern inner circle showing a composite of multiple phases of activity spanning up to 2,000 years. Based on M. Gillings et al. "The Origins of Avebury," in *Antiquity* (Cambridge University Press) [in press]. IMAGE COURTESY OF PROFESSOR MARK GILLINGS, SCHOOL OF ARCHAEOLOGY AND ANCIENT HISTORY, UNIVERSITY OF UEICESTER.

The Amazon: Squaring the circle at Jacó Sá. PHOTO: RICARDO AZOURY/PULSAR IMAGENS.

2017 by archaeologists using ground-penetrating radar, is the **square formation**, measuring 30 meters along each side, again defined by a perimeter of standing stones, that once occupied the center of the southernmost of the two inner circles.[58]

Strangely enough, at a site called Jacó Sá in the Amazon we also find a geoglyph in which circle and square are combined, but here it is the square that encloses the circle: "The square sides," report Ranzi, Schaan, and their colleagues, "are 140 m long, while the external embankment is 12 m wide and 1.6 m high. The circle contains an internal embankment, and is 100 m in diameter."[59]

This mention of embankments raises a more general point. Though Avebury is a true henge, Stonehenge—despite its name—technically is not. This is because its original great circular ditch was cut *outside,* not inside, its embankment.[60] As Jennifer Watling remarks, it's interesting to note that some of the Amazonian geoglyphs have this same format "with an outer ditch."[61] Some, like Jacó Sá, have both. As with the British henges, however, so with the Amazon. Ranzi, Schaan, and Pärssinen confirm that "the ditches" of the Amazonian geoglyphs "are usually situated *inside* the embankments."[62]

A GLOBAL LEGACY?

JENNIFER WATLING'S PAPER, COAUTHORED WITH Denise Schaan, Alceu Ranzi, and others, describes circular geoglyphs of the Amazon "with ditches up to 11 m wide, 4 m deep, and 100–300 m in diameter."[63] The authors argue that these sites, "some of which have up to six enclosures . . . rival the most impressive examples of pre-Columbian monumental architecture anywhere in the Americas." Their excavations found "an almost complete absence of cultural material . . . within the enclosed areas." They conclude that the earthworks "were built and used sporadically as ceremonial and public gathering sites between 2000 and 650 calibrated years before present, **but that some may have been constructed as early as 3500–3000 BP.**"[64]

I've put the early dates in bold for two reasons.

First, because they are given in the paper at all. What we have here is a group of mainstream archaeologists sticking their necks out a little bit further in the pages of a prestigious journal on what, until now, would have been thought of as an impossible achievement for Amazonian societies 3,500 years ago.

Second, these same archaeologists are still being cautious. The period of 3500–3000 BP that they're prepared to entertain for the construction of at least "some" of the geoglyphs corresponds with Unit 5 at Severino Calazans, where a sample yielded a date, within the usual margins of error, of 1211 BC.[65]

The paper makes no mention, however, of the other much earlier date of 2577 BC that was retrieved from Unit 3[66]—the date that coincides with the epoch of Stonehenge, Avebury, and the Great Pyramid of Egypt.

Before I go further let me reiterate a key point about which it is important to be absolutely clear. It is NOT my purpose here to insinuate that the Amazonian geoglyphs were in any way inspired by Britain's stone circles, or by the Great Pyramid of Egypt or by other known Old World monuments— or, for that matter, vice versa. Where there are similarities, my suggestion is that it might be more fruitful to look for their origins in a remote ancestral civilization that passed down a common inheritance all around the globe— an inheritance of knowledge, an inheritance of science, an inheritance of "earth-measuring" that was then put into practice in many different environments by the many different cultures receiving it.

In some, the inheritance may have been rejected at the outset, or subsequently frittered away and lost. In others, as millennia passed, locally originated differences in expression multiplied to such an extent that they often almost completely obscured the underlying genetic connections to a remote common ancestor.

Nonetheless, dig deep enough and those connections—like recessive genes—sooner or later make themselves felt.

Not all the henges of the British Isles contain stone circles; many are simply gigantic earthworks like the geoglyphs of the southwestern Amazon. No megalithic monuments have yet been found in the Brazilian state of Acre where the geoglyphs proliferate—perhaps because of a lack of good natural materials, or perhaps because so much of the area has yet to be properly surveyed.

There **are** stone circles in the Amazon, however, as we shall see in the next chapter.

16

THE AMAZON'S OWN
STONEHENGE

THE FIRST FOREIGN VISITOR TO mention the existence of megalithic circles in the Amazon was the Swiss zoologist Emílio Goeldi, who traveled up the Cunani River into what is now the northern part of the Brazilian state of Amapá, near its border with French Guiana, in the late nineteenth century.[1] He makes no mention, however, of formations of huge granite blocks, obviously worked upon and moved into place by human beings, overlooking a stream called the Rego Grande.

In the 1920s Curt Nimuendajú, a German-Brazilian ethnologist, also visited megaliths in the region, but he likewise appears to have been unaware of the spectacular formations of Rego Grande. They were seen, however, and noted by Betty Meggers and her colleague Clifford Evans of the Smithsonian Institution in the 1950s[2] and now, at last, with the Smithsonian's resources, came the opportunity for a thorough investigation of the mysterious site.

Predictably, what we might call "the curse of Meggers" descended upon the Rego Grande stone circles. These great formations of megaliths shouldn't have existed at all, according to her prejudices about the ancient Amazon, and were thus deemed unworthy of further excavation.[3]

Thereafter, lacking the Smithsonian's seal of approval, the interesting problem of Rego Grande was quietly set aside and ignored by archaeology **for the next 40 years** while the site itself fell back into its former state of absolute obscurity and was in due course forgotten.

But climates of opinion in scholarship from time to time undergo radical shifts, and forgotten things sometimes cry out to be remembered. Thus, just as the geoglyphs of Acre were first identified back in the 1970s in an area where swaths of formerly dense rainforest were being cleared for use by the cattle industry, so it was with the Rego Grande stone circles. They were redis-covered in the 1990s by ranch foreman Lailson Camelo da Silva, who was clearing land for pasture. "I had no idea that I was discovering the Amazon's own Stonehenge," he later told a reporter. "It makes me wonder. What other secrets about our past are still hidden in Brazil's jungles?"[4]

The publicity around Silva's "discovery," coupled with new insights into the complexity of ancient Amazonian civilization, led to a gradual reawaken-ing of interest in Rego Grande. More research was done and out of roughly 200 prehistoric sites identified across the state of Amapá it was found that 30 had megalithic monuments of one kind or another.[5]

In 2005 archaeologists Mariana Petry Cabral and João Darcy de Moura Saldanha of Amapá's Institute of Scientific and Technological Research set about the task of surveying them all, with a particular focus on Rego Grande. There, the principal stone circle, which has a diameter of 30 meters, con-sists of 127 upright megaliths. Brought from a quarry 3 kilometers away, the megaliths weigh up to 4 tons each and stand between 2.5 meters (just over 8 feet) and 4 meters (just over 13 feet) tall.[6] Areas within the circle were used for elaborate human burials involving funerary urns and vases in a known pottery style of the region.

By 2011 a preliminary age of about 1,000 years was being suggested for the site. This was based, according to Mariana Cabral, on "three date checks on fragments of charcoal" found among pottery in the burial area.[7] Ten other prehistoric sites in the state of Amapá, three of them with megaliths, were also dated in the same way and "all seem to have been occupied between seven hundred and a thousand years ago."[8]

Much more work will have to be done before we can be sure that these dates will not be revised—like the ages of the geoglyphs—in the light of new evidence. Most important, meticulous care will have to be taken to be certain that the stone circle, on the one hand, and the burials from which the C-14 dates were derived, on the other, are works of the same period. The phenomenon of "intrusive burials" is one that archaeologists commonly encounter; particularly where an ancient, sacred site is involved there is a tendency for later people to want to bury and sanctify their dead there (such anachronistic burials have been found, for example, at the Sphinx and at the Third Pyramid at Giza). The danger, therefore, is that an older site will be given a falsely young date based on materials from the intrusive burial.

Indeed, Cabral and Saldanha note that pottery of the same style and type as the pieces at Rego Grande from which the samples of charcoal were taken is common along "all of the northern coast of Amapá and in French Guiana" and has also been "regularly found in prehistoric sites that have no stone monuments."[9]

I'm therefore not convinced by the association of this pottery and carbondatable charcoal with the original construction date of the stone circle at Rego Grande. That being said, however, it makes no difference to me if it **does** turn out to be of the same age as the burials. My argument is not that every mysterious monument now emerging from the depths of the Amazon must date back to the Pleistocene. I'm concerned here, rather, with the manifestation of a legacy of **ideas** that may be of Ice Age antiquity—ideas involving geometry and ideas also very much involving **astronomy**. It's the ideas that matter, whether we encounter them in the Amazon, or at Serpent Mound in Ohio, or at Angkor in Cambodia, or at Stonehenge in the British Isles, or among the monuments of Egypt's Giza plateau. If mechanisms to carry, preserve, and transmit them down the generations have been introgressed into the local cultural DNA, then I see no reason why they should not manifest, and reveal their fundamental similarities, wherever and whenever conducive circumstances arise.

It therefore has to be of interest, whatever the age of the great stone circle

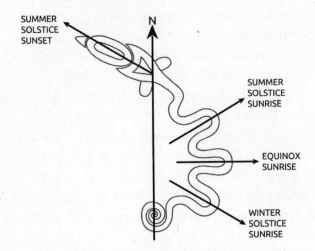

The primary alignment of Serpent Mound is to the summer solstice sunset. But in the reverse direction the same alignment targets—and in a convolution of the Serpent's body recognizes—the winter solstice sunrise. Two other convolutions target, respectively, the equinox sunrise and the summer solstice sunrise.

at Rego Grande ultimately proves to be, that it appears to share a key "meme" with Stonehenge and with Serpent Mound.

Coined by Richard Dawkins in his 1976 book *The Selfish Gene*,[10] the word "meme" refers to "An element of a culture or system of behavior passed from one individual to another by imitation or other non-genetic means."[11]

In the case of Stonehenge, Serpent Mound, and Rego Grande, the meme concerns the orientation of the sites—which in all three cases honors the sun on the June and December solstices. We reviewed these alignments for Stonehenge and Serpent Mound in part 1, and the reader will recall that they are reversible—that is, an alignment to the summer solstice sunrise is also, in the reverse direction, an alignment to the winter solstice sunset, while an alignment to the winter solstice sunrise is also, in the reverse direction, an alignment to the summer solstice sunset.

In the case of Rego Grande, it is the winter solstice that is the primary focus. Cabral and Saldanha point to a megalith that uses shadow effects to track "the sun's path throughout this day."[12] Two other granite megaliths close by, one with an artificial hole cut through it, also line up to track the rising point of the winter solstice sun.[13]

The Rego Grande Stone Circle. PHOTO: MARIANA CABRAL. Stone 3 tracks the path of the sun throughout the day on the winter solstice. Stones 1 and 2 (the former with a sighting hole cut through it—see inset) line up to target the winter solstice sunrise.

The strong foundations of the site make it unlikely that the megaliths would have shifted position. Even blocks lying horizontally, it turns out, have not fallen but were purposefully placed:

> Those lying on the ground never stood upright. Instead, the layer of laterite [beneath them] was carefully dug so that they fit snugly with the ground. Excavations carried out . . . around the bottom of the standing stones also revealed small blocks of granite and laterite which were used to wedge the monoliths at this unusual angle.[14]

Cabral and Saldanha's conclusion is that all the angles were "carefully considered by those who conceived them."[15]

Archaeologist Manoel Calado of the University of Lisbon, an expert on Portuguese megaliths, agrees. "I'm sure," he said after a visit to Rego Grande.

"This is one of the aspects that makes the Amazon megaliths very similar to those in Europe."[16]

Richard Callahan, professor of archaeology at the University of Calgary, is also on Cabral and Saldanha's side:

> Given that astronomical objects, stars, constellations, etc., have a major importance in much of Amazonian mythology and cosmology, it does not in any way surprise me that such an observatory exists.[17]

For Eduardo Neves, too, "the idea of the place being a sort of observatory is a good one," although he adds, quite rightly, that "we still need to test it."[18]

PAINEL DO PILÃO

ONLY THE MOST RUDIMENTARY SURVEY has been undertaken at Rego Grande, enough to reveal the major solstitial focus of the great stone circle, but nothing more. Other, much richer information may or may not be concealed within the multiple alignments of the megaliths, as is the case at Stonehenge and Serpent Mound, but a major archaeoastronomical study will be required to settle the matter. As Jarita Holbrook, associate professor of physics at South Africa's University of the Western Cape, comments: "It takes more than a circle of standing stones to get a Stonehenge."[19]

I would add, however, that a circle of standing stones with a solstitial alignment is a pretty good start!

Moreover, and I suggest of great relevance given the uncertainty over the dates of Rego Grande, a major archaeoastronomical study **has** already been undertaken at another Amazonian site approximately 550 kilometers to the southwest. Named Painel do Pilão, it is located just 400 meters from Pedra Pintada, the painted rock shelter investigated in 1996 by Anna Roosevelt. We saw in chapter 12 how she and her team excavated multiple occupation layers within the shelter, the oldest and deepest of which turned out to be perhaps as old as 16,000 years (according to thermoluminescence dating) and 14,200 years (according to radiocarbon dating).[20]

There has been no serious challenge to these dates but, following further

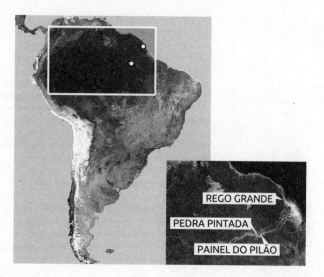

work by Roosevelt, Pedra Pintada's rock art is now usually reported, reflecting the current cautious consensus of the archaeological community, to date between 13,630 and 11,705 years ago.[21]

Dates for the art at the nearby Painel do Pilão rock shelter, excavated by Christopher Sean Davis of Northern Illinois University, are closely similar, being variously given in his 2016 report at between 13,014 and 12,725 years ago, and between 13,135 and 12,810 years ago.[22] All together a total of four samples from two adjacent excavation levels were subjected to C-14 testing. All were found, says Davis, "to be consistent and contemporary to Roosevelt's paleoindian dates from Caverna da Pedra Pintada."[23] His conclusion, therefore, is that the initial artworks of Painel do Pilão were created at "around the time that the area was first inhabited 13,000 years ago, and that those earliest images, which were probably retouched or traced more recently, were positioned in the most prominent wall locations and height."[24]

Davis suggests that the rock wall itself, as well as the floor at its base, were deliberately leveled by the ancients to form a 90-degree angle to one another. The whole ensemble, he says, was "made straight and flat throughout" to configure a "platform stage from which an observer can view the rock art from a specific location."[25]

Once standing in that location, Davis further notes, "the painting most central to the observer's field of view is a grid image that has individual boxes marked with mostly repetitive (but some varying) tallies."[26]

Painel do Pilão "calendar." PHOTO: CHRISTOPHER SEAN DAVIS.

It looks like a calendar—and indeed, some years before Davis, Roosevelt was the first scholar to consider that possibility.[27] While recognizing that "alternative theories not related to astronomy cannot be ruled out," Davis reinvestigated the matter over the course of a solar year and noticed a possible pattern to do with

[t]he intersection of the setting sun to a rocky perch in the near distance above and to the right of the painted outcrop.

The annual movement of the sun relative to the rocky perch allows for the intersection of the setting sun through the center of the perch **approximately 18–20 days before and after the winter solstice** (which currently occurs on December 21). . . . If each box of the painted grid

SUN-CAPTURE WINDOW

Painel do Pilão painted outcrop with its rock art surface in the center-to-left foreground, and a rocky outcrop with a window-like feature at a distance in the top right background of the photo. The sun intersects this "window" in the early afternoon 18 to 20 days before and after the winter solstice. PHOTO: CHRISTOPHER SEAN DAVIS. ANNOTATION ADDED.

image represents one day of observing the setting of the sun relative to the rocky perch, 49 days after the day of the winter solstice, the sun sets too far to the north of the rocky perch, entirely missing the structure. The grid painting has 49 total boxes and the center boxes have tally marks that are simply vertical lines. Most other tally marks are crisscrosses. The rocky perch and the grid image might, therefore, have been **a way for paleoindians to foretell the winter solstice** and the passage of a new year.[28]

What adds to the likelihood that Davis is correct is that he and his team found other alignments at Painel do Pilão. For example, just as the orientation of what they call the "platform stage" suggests an ancient focus on the December solstice sunset, so, too, another prominent cluster of images aligns to the rising point of the sun on the June solstice.[29]

Meanwhile:

A third astronomy alignment occurs with a single red pictograph discovered above the excavation unit on a vertical ledge on the underside of the painted outcrop. The ledge may have been intentionally altered, but further investigation is needed for certainty. The painted circle itself faces 270° [the azimuth of sunset on the equinox], but the shelter walls block all views of the western horizon or sky from this location. However, just beneath the circle and ledge is an opening that allows one to see through to the other side of the outcrop and the horizon beyond. This vantage point beneath the painted circle aligns to ~90°, the position of the rising sun on the equinox, which occurs on March 20 and September 23 currently.[30]

At the very least, says Davis, the rock art and alignments at Painel do Pilão tell us that cultures in the heart of the Amazon 13,000 years ago "engaged and utilized sophisticated knowledge of astronomy maintained through rock art and possibly shared or reimagined by more recent cultures who either inherited or rediscovered the ancient paintings."[31]

He's right to draw attention to the legacy aspect of all this—the possibility, long after the original painters and horizon astronomers of Painel do Pilão were gone, that later cultures might have inherited and reimagined the ancient ideas and obsessions manifested there. This is how we would expect carefully crafted and cleverly designed memes to propagate themselves down the ages, and it appears to echo *exactly* the process at Serpent Mound, which was likewise maintained, renovated, and reimagined by successive cultures down the ages and which likewise signals the solstices and the equinoxes.

Painel do Pilão is important because it tells us that the "meme" of sacred structures aligned to the solstices and equinoxes, found in monumental art and architecture all around the world, has been present in the Amazon for at least 13,000-years and perhaps—we must await future discoveries in the unexplored reaches of the jungle—for far longer than that.

It also has wider implications. If people were capable of carefully marking, recording, and honoring these celestial events in South America 13,000 years ago, then there is no good reason to suppose they should not have done so in North America as well—and therefore no good reason to dismiss the possibility that Serpent Mound's original alignments also go back to that distant epoch.

Archaeology says a firm NO to this, accompanied by guffaws of derision.

As we've seen, however, the archaeology of Serpent Mound is riddled with contradictions and uncertainties and appears to have produced dates marking various episodes of restoration and renovation rather than convincing evidence of when the monument was originally designed and founded.

HYPOTHESIS

IN HIS REPORT CHRISTOPHER DAVIS mentions Rego Grande, "presumed to be more recent" than Painel do Pilão, as another Amazonian site at which archaeoastronomical alignments have been investigated.[32] He draws no specific connection beyond that, but in my view the confirmation of a solstitial focus at both, as also at Serpent Mound in Ohio, and Stonehenge and other megalithic sites worldwide, is noteworthy.

Moreover, although there is no henge at Rego Grande, we've seen that the solstitially aligned stone circle there shares the Amazon basin with huge numbers of hengelike earthworks. We've noted how these, too, have never been subject to any kind of rigorous archaeoastronomical investigation. Meanwhile, the total number of geometric ditched enclosures discovered in the southwestern Amazon survey area had increased from "over 210," the figure on record in 2009, to "over 450" by 2017.[33]

Then in 2018 a further study by Denise Schaan and colleagues reported an extension of the survey area across much of the southern rim of the Amazon basin:

> The results show that an 1800 km stretch of southern Amazonia was occupied by earth-building cultures.[34]

In one area alone, the Upper Tapajos Basin, 81 previously unknown pre-Columbian sites were discovered, with a total of 104 earthworks.[35] Among them were many complex enclosures including one, 390 meters in diameter, featuring 11 mounds circularly arranged at the center of the enclosure.[36]

The researchers suggest that at least 1,300 further sites remain hidden within the jungles of the Amazon's southern rim—a number, they add, that is "likely to be an underestimation"[37] while "huge swaths of the rainforest are still unexplored."[38] They remind us that the *terre firme* forests "that account for ~95% of the Amazon are particularly uncharted" because "these areas have been archaeologically neglected following traditional views that pre-Columbian people concentrated on resource-rich floodplains. However, the discovery of large pre-Columbian earthworks in *terra firme* along the Southern Rim of the Amazon undermines the assumption that these areas were marginal in terms of past human impact and the development of complex societies."[39]

It is undoubtedly the case that many more structures remain to be found than have already presented themselves to science. Our entire understanding of this vast region is being transformed by new discoveries and, indeed, as we've seen, the notion of complex societies in the pre-Columbian Amazon is no longer anathema to archaeologists, some of whom now even dare to describe those societies as "civilizations."

Given that such civilizations existed in ancient Amazonia, and clearly had the capacity to manifest their ideas in great public projects, it is intriguing that the end result was the vigorous, flamboyant, and extensive expression of **the very same** architectural, astronomical, and geometrical "memes" that characterize sacred architecture in many other parts of the world, and at many different periods.

An analogy between genetics and culture—genes and memes—can serve us well here.

Let's say, purely hypothetically of course, that a system of ideas is transferred, by direct teachings, from one culture to another. The recipient society as a whole, however, may not yet be ready to put the teachings into practice. What is required, then, is that some sort of institution be set up that can recruit the brightest and the best from the local population. They, in turn, will draft new talent with each new generation, initiating them and training them in the essential details of the system—which will assume the character of a religion and will in due course integrate itself deeply into every level, even into the habits of thought, of the recipient culture. Eventually, when the right time for the next stage of the project is judged to have arrived—perhaps very soon, perhaps after thousands of years, depending on local circumstances—the religious leaders will mobilize the population to enact the great projects of sacred geometry that had for so long remained encoded, but unexpressed, within their cultural DNA.[40]

It is, I emphasize, only a hypothesis. In this context, though, it's thought-provoking to consider an ethnographic report from 1887 written by a certain Colonel Antonio R. P. Labre after he had ascended the Madeira, the Beni, and the Madre de Dios Rivers and then crossed overland to the Acre River. His journey took him right through the heart of the geoglyph territory of Acre and involved numerous encounters with its inhabitants, the Araona people—who had, by that time, been reduced to a tiny remnant after hundreds of years of devastating epidemics, slave raids, and murderous attacks by commercial rubber tappers seeking to drive them off their land. "It was not uncommon," writes Denise Schaan, "for rubber tappers to capture native women for wives. The encroaching whites would frequently promote raids to enslave the native population for the rubber industry, a situation that 40 years later would result in the near-extinction of tens of thousands of natives."[41]

Since all work on the geoglyphs had ceased hundreds of years previously, we can only guess how much of the past of their once great culture these harried, encroached-upon, and deeply endangered Aroanas remembered by the time of Labre's visit. We cannot even be sure that they were the direct descendants of the geoglyph builders (rather than of more recent migrants to the area).

Nonetheless, what Labre tells us feels significant. He didn't see the geoglyphs, which were then entirely overgrown by jungle, but he was in the midst of them on August 17, 1887, when he stayed overnight at an Aroana village called Mamuceyada. He describes there being, as well as plantations, "about 200 inhabitants . . . a form of government, temples and a form of worship"—from which, together with "knowing the name of the idols," women were excluded. Of particular importance and relevance here is Labre's report:

> The idols are not of human form, but are geometrical figures made
> of wood and polished. The father of the gods is called Epymara,
> his image has an elliptical form, and is about 16 inches high. . . .
> Although they have "medicine-men" charged with religious duties and
> remaining celibates, the chief is nevertheless pontifex of the church.[42]

Consider the improbability of this if it does not arise from some real though forgotten connection. Here in a landscape mysteriously inscribed in antiquity with vast geometrical earthworks, at a time when the earthworks themselves had long since been swallowed by jungle, we find a Native American tribe whose gods take the form of polished wooden "geometrical figures." The tribal chief is the religious leader but there are also "medicine-men" who likewise have religious duties.

It already sounds exactly like the sort of institution for the replication and transmission of geometric memes that I proposed as a hypothesis earlier, but it gets even more interesting when the shamans involved, and often the population, are drinking ayahuasca.

17

THE VINE OF THE DEAD

WHAT ARE THE AMAZONIAN GEOGLYPHS? Why did the ancients go to such trouble to make these colossal earthworks? Why is geometry their most obvious theme? And to what extent, if any, since stone circles are frequently associated with similar earthworks elsewhere, does the presence of stone circles in the Amazon help us to understand the geoglyphs?

So far we have considered only geometry and certain cosmic alignments, but my hypothesis in both cases, and in the case of the extraordinarily similar earthworks of the Mississippi Valley that we'll explore in parts 5 and 6, is that we are dealing with "memes" here. Moreover, it is a phenomenon in itself that the same memes appear again and again among seemingly unrelated cultures of both the Old World and the New World, separated sometimes not only by thousands of miles but by thousands of years.

Much more work will be required to establish **when** the memes of geometry and cosmic alignment first took root in the Amazon. Archaeology on its own is of limited use to us here, since so little has been done even at the sites already discovered and since so much of the region has never been investigated at all. What would help would be a much more thorough and detailed archaeoastronomical survey of Rego Grande, and of other stone circles in its vicinity, than has already been undertaken. In parallel, as I argued earlier, an equally thorough archaeoastronomical survey of the Amazonian geoglyphs is a must if we are to refine not only our understanding of their geometry but also to tease out any cosmic alignments they may contain. Since no such study has yet been undertaken all we can say for sure is that **some** of the geoglyphs reviewed in chapter 15 are, definitely, cosmically aligned.

We've seen, for example, that both Fazenda Parana and Severino Calazans consist of square geoglyphs. The first features two squares, one 200 meters along each side and the second exactly half that size, with an interconnecting causeway. Meanwhile, the second site has side lengths of 230 meters, giving it the same footprint as the Great Pyramid of Egypt. All four of these squares—the two at Fazenda Parana, the one at Severino Calazans, and of course the Great Pyramid itself, are cardinally oriented, that is, their sides face true north, south, east, and west. The most basic and obvious of the cosmic alignments shared across these sites are therefore to the celestial north and south poles (the points on the celestial sphere directly above the earth's geographic north and south poles, around which the stars and planets appear to rotate during the course of the night[1]), and to the points of sunrise and sunset on the spring and autumn equinoxes (when the sun rises perfectly due east and sets perfectly due west).

We've also seen that other great earthworks of the Amazon feature strong northwest-to-southeast orientations. This would put the investigation of possible solstitial alignments and also of "lunar standstill alignments" (of which more in part 5) at the top of the list of priorities if any proper archao-astronomical survey should ever be undertaken.

I think it likely that such a survey of the Amazonian geoglyphs, as of the stone circles, would reveal many more (and far more intricate) cosmic alignments, perhaps even as subtle and complex as the multiple alignments found at the Great Pyramid, Stonehenge, and Serpent Mound. There's little point in speculating further on such matters when we don't yet have the necessary data from the Amazon. For the sake of argument, however, let's assume that the memes of geometry and cosmic alignment **are** part of a connected system there, as they are in so many other parts of the world where the required research has already been done. In that case we can say, on the basis of the equinoctial and solstitial alignments at Painel do Pilão, the single Amazonian site where something approaching a thorough archaeoastronomical study has been undertaken, that the system must have reached Amazonia at least 13,000 years ago. That it should then have later iterations in different media, such as the stone circle at Rego Grande and the great cosmically aligned geoglyphs at Severino Calazans and Fazenda Parana, should not surprise us.

We are dealing, I believe, with **deliberately** created memes here—memes that have a deeply mysterious purpose and that function in ineffable ways. They are transmitted by repetition and replication, which explains their similarities. But cultures, once separated, tend to evolve and develop in their own distinctive and quirky fashion. We can therefore expect that not only the media and materials through which the memes are made manifest, but also their local **interpretation**, will vary greatly through time and between one part of the world and another while nonetheless retaining a constant core of unvarying central ideas.

WESTERN SCIENCE WADES IN

THE FIRST EFFORTS OF WESTERN scientists to interpret the geoglyphs of Amazonia were predictably utilitarian and reductionist, with attempts being made to persuade us that the great geometrical earthworks must have been built for defensive purposes. But with no evidence of warfare around them, with the ditches clearly not "moats" (since so many of them are placed within the earthen embankments rather than outside them), and with no evidence of palisade walls (for example, in the form of postholes or wooden remains), this theory soon lost favor.[2] Not only was there no evidence of warfare, but actually very little at all in the way of archaeological materials—pottery, figurines, refuse, et cetera—that would help to decipher the use, meaning, and purpose of the geoglyphs. The consensus now, therefore, is that they were created for "ritual," "spiritual," "religious," and "ceremonial" purposes.[3]

William Balée, professor of anthropology at Tulane University, is a supporter of this new consensus, but is doing no more than stating the obvious when he suggests that the spiritual/religious role of the Amazonian glyphs must in some way have involved "geometry and gigantism."[4]

Well, yes, professor. Obviously! But in what way? And to what purposes?

If we seek useful answers to such questions, rather than easy inferences or mere descriptions of these gigantic geometric patterns, then we are going to have to do what a very few Western scientists, to their credit, are now doing—and that is to consult indigenous peoples still living in the Amazon today.

Finnish scholars Sanna Saunaluoma and Pirjo Kristiina Virtanen have led the way in this fresh approach. The cultural destruction of the past five centuries has wiped many of the tribal memory banks clean—the ongoing process of imposed amnesia that has left us so bereft of knowledge about the ancient Amazon. It is clear, however, that all is not yet lost.

In 2013, for example, Saunaluoma and Virtanen brought a group of five Manchineri—an indigenous tribe living today in the region of the earthworks—to visit Jacó Sá. This immense geoglyph, depicting a circle within a square, as the reader will recall, is located about 250 kilometers from their territory. The investigators report that the Manchineri "immediately reported feeling sensations of being in an ancient ritual atmosphere." Moreover, "They said that their ancestors had talked about these types of places, although they could not offer any explanation as to why the earthwork ditches were so deep or even why they had been constructed."[5]

A second local tribal group, the Apuriná, "narrated that their parents had advised them to pass by the earthworks quickly and avoid their vicinity when possible because they signify difference, promote avoidance, and are regarded as 'enchanted,' or 'miraculous' places."[6]

Certainly, then, at least the traces of a memory of how significant the earthworks must have been in their prime, and of the awe that they formerly inspired, lingers on in local superstitions and folklore.

But a reservoir of much more detailed information has been stored away in the Amazon and here, too, Saunaluoma and Virtanen are pioneers in finding links to the earthworks.

THE SHAMANISTIC COSMOS

SOME OF THE CLUES THEY have drawn on have been available for more than 130 years.

They're found in the account, given in the last chapter, of the worship of "geometrical" gods by the Aroana people in the vicinity of the geoglyphs when Colonel Antonio R. P. Labre stayed among them in 1887. From Labre we also learn that the Aroanas had "temples and a form of worship" and that their religious officiants were "medicine men."

During the twentieth century the term "medicine men" went out of fashion and, where indigenous systems of spirituality are still practiced in the Amazon today, the majority of ethnographic and anthropological studies define the officiants as "shamans." This word is NOT derived from, or used, in any Amazonian language. It comes, instead, from the Tungus-Mongol noun *saman,* meaning, broadly, "one who knows."[7]

Its widespread use by anthropologists today—not only with reference to religious ritual functionaries in the Amazon but also to similar figures who are found in tribal and hunter-gatherer societies all over the world—has not come about because the Tungus mysteriously contacted and influenced other cultures but because Tungus shamanism was the first example of the phenomenon to be studied by European ethnologists. The Tungus word entered Western languages through their enthusiastic written reports and has subsequently continued to be applied in all parts of the world where systems very similar to Tungus shamanism have been found.

It is the shaman—usually a man but sometimes a woman—who stands at the heart of these systems. And what all shamans have in common, regardless of which culture they come from or what they call themselves, is an ability to enter and control altered states of consciousness. Often, but not always, psychedelic plants or fungi are consumed to attain the necessary trance state. Shamanism, therefore, is not primarily a set of beliefs, nor the result of purposive study. It is, first and foremost, mastery of the techniques needed to attain trance and thus to occasion particular kinds of experiences—shamans call them "visions," Western psychiatrists call them "hallucinations"—that are then in turn used to interpret events and guide behavior:

The true shaman must attain his knowledge and position through trance, vision and soul-journey to the Otherworld. All these states of enlightenment are reached . . . during a shamanic state of consciousness, and not by purposive study and application of a corpus of systematic knowledge.[8]

Such a method of knowledge acquisition seems absurd and fantastical to the "rational" Western mind. And indeed, underlying the whole notion of soul-journeys to the otherworld is a model of reality that is diametrically opposed in every way to the model presently favored by Western science. This remotely ancient shamanistic model holds our material world to be much more complicated than it seems to be. Behind it, beneath it, above it, interpenetrating it, all around it—sometimes symbolized as being "underground" or sometimes "in the sky"—is an otherworld, perhaps multiple otherworlds (spirit worlds, underworlds, netherworlds, etc.) inhabited by supernatural beings. Whether we like it or not, we must interact with these nonphysical beings, which, though generally invisible and intangible, have the power both to harm us and to help us.

THE GEOMETRICAL PULSE

THE BIG PICTURE OF SHAMANISM, altered states of consciousness, and their immensely important place in the human story—was the focus of my 2005 book *Supernatural: Meetings with the Ancient Teachers of Mankind.*[9] I refer the reader to that book for a comprehensive body of data that reinforces and underlines what I have to say in this chapter.

Meanwhile, the key point, standing right at the heart of the matter and nonsensical to "rational" Western minds, is the notion that the human condition requires interaction with powerful nonphysical beings. Across much of the Amazon the nexus that facilitates such interaction is the extraordinary visionary brew ayahuasca, a plant medicine that has been in use among the indigenous peoples of this vast region for unknown thousands of years. Its active ingredient, derived from the leaves of the chacruna shrub (botanical name *Psychotria viridis*) is dimethyltryptamine—DMT—an immensely potent hallucinogen. It is from the other ingredient, however, derived from the *Banisteriopsis caapi* vine, that the brew gets its name. The function of the ayahuasca vine in the brew is to transmit a monoamine oxidase inhibitor into the bloodstream of the recipient so that he or she may gain sustained access to the extraordinary effects of DMT—a substance that is normally neutralized in the gut by the enzyme monoamine oxidase. There are other ways of accessing the visionary power of Amazonian plants rich in DMT—notably by snorting them as snuff—but the effects are short-lasting. Taken orally, in the form of the ayahuasca brew, however, the experience can last up to 6 hours, permitting a much more sustained and immersive trance "journey."

It is, in my view, a remarkable scientific feat that such a highly effective combination of just 2 out of the estimated 150,000 different species of plants, trees, and vines in the Amazon was discovered by mere trial and error. Nor if you ask Amazonian shamans, as I have done, how their ancestors made this discovery, will they admit to trial and error at all—or indeed to any other method that Western science would recognize as rational. What they claim, very simply—but unanimously—is that a variety of "plant spirits," among which ayahuasca is paramount, have taught them everything important they need to know about the properties of other plants in the jungle, thus allowing them to make powerful medicines, to heal the sick, and, in general, to be good "doctors."[10]

Ayahuasca itself is said to be a "doctor," possessing a strong spirit, and is considered to be "an intelligent being with which it is possible to establish rapport, and from which it is possible to acquire knowledge and power."[11] The anthropologist Angelica Gebhart-Sayer, who studied the Shipibo-Conibo people of the Amazon, notes that under the influence of ayahuasca "the shaman perceives, from the spirit world, incomprehensible, often chaotic information in the form of luminous designs."[12] As Gebhart-Sayer sees it, it is the shaman's function to decode and "domesticate" this raw, unprocessed data beamed at him by the plant spirits by "converting it" into therapy for the tribe as a whole.

Very often these luminous designs, rich in data, take the form of **geometry**. I speak from experience, having participated in more than seventy ayahuasca sessions since 2003, continuing to work with the brew for the valuable lessons it teaches me long after *Supernatural* was researched, written, and published. Here's part of my account of the first time I drank ayahuasca in the Amazon:

I raise the cup to my lips again. About two thirds of the measure that the shaman poured for me still remains, and now I drain it in one draught. The concentrated bittersweet foretaste, followed instantly by the aftertaste of rot and medicine, hits me like a punch in the stomach. . . . Feeling slightly apprehensive, I thank the shaman and wander back to my place on the floor. . . .

Time passes but I don't keep track of it. I've improvized a pillow from a rolled-up sleeping bag and I now find I'm swamped by a powerful feeling of weariness. My muscles involuntarily relax, I close my eyes, and without fanfare a parade of visions suddenly begins, visions that are at once **geometrical** and alive, visions of lights unlike any light I've ever seen—dark lights, a pulsing, swirling field of the deepest luminescent violets, of reds emerging out of night, of unearthly textures and colors, of solar systems revolving, of spiral galaxies on the move. Visions of nets and strange ladder-like structures. Visions in which I seem to see **multiple square screens** stacked side by side and on top of each other to form **immense patterns of windows arranged in great banks.** Though they manifest without sound in what seems to be a pristine and limitless vacuum, the images possess a most peculiar and particular quality. They feel like a drum-roll—as though their real function is to announce the arrival of something else.[13]

Other notes I made following my ayahuasca sessions in the Amazon refer to a "geometrical pulse,"[14] to "a recurrence of the geometrical patterns,"[15] to "a background of shifting geometrical patterns,"[16] and to "complex interlaced patterns of geometry. . . . I zoom in for a closer view. . . . They're rectangular, outlined in black, like windows. There's a circle in the centre of each rectangle."[17]

PATHS

THOSE SESSIONS TOOK PLACE IN January and February 2004 some years before I first learned of the existence of the great geometrical geoglyphs of the Amazon. The reader will understand, therefore, that when I began to

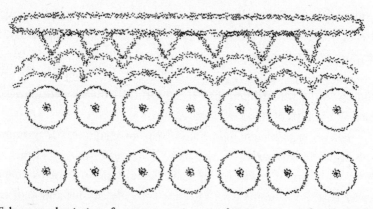

Tukano sand painting of patterns seen in an ayahuasca vision. (After G. Reichel-Dolmatoff, *The Shaman and the Jaguar*, 1975, p. 46.)

research the glyphs in 2017 and to wonder about their meaning to whichever unknown peoples created them, it was natural for me to consider ayahuasca as an inspiration. I can't confirm whether any circles within rectangles are among the more than 550 glyphs discovered by 2018, but Jacó Sá (where the Manchineri group brought by Saunaluoma and Virtanen reported sensations of being in an ancient ritual atmosphere) certainly gives us a circle within a square. And, while the geometrical patterns that I likened to "multiple square screens" and "banks of windows" might be described and manifested using very different materials in very different ways by people from different cultural backgrounds, what seems to stay constant throughout is the geometry.

It is the fundamental motif of the earthworks but it turns up in much else besides—for example in the ayahuasca-inspired art of the Tukano of the Colombian Amazon (where the brew goes by the name of *yajé*).[18]

The Tukano create geometrical patterns and abstract designs in sand, on fabrics and musical instruments, on their houses and on the communal *malocas* where they consume *yajé*.[19] Colombian anthropologist Gerardo Reichel-Dolmatoff reported the results of an intriguing experiment he carried out in which he asked members of a Tukano community to make crayon drawings of what they saw when they were drinking *yajé*. (The drawings were of course made from memory, after the drinkers had returned to everyday consciousness.)

The results, broadly identical to the designs on the houses and fabrics, included a triangle flanked by vertical lines ending in spirals, a rhomboid, a rectangular design filled with parallel lines, patterns of parallel undulating lines drawn horizontally, a number of different oval- and U-shaped elements, rows of dots or small circles, a vertical pattern of little dots, grid patterns, zigzag lines, nested rectangles, nested parallel arcs (catenary curves), and so on.[20] Significantly, the Tukano also paint identical shapes and patterns on rock faces in the hills of the northwest Amazon.[21]

More than seventy different indigenous Amazonian cultures use ayahuasca— many giving different names to the brew (*yajé, natema, caapi, cipo, shori,* etc.).[22] Since almost all report seeing geometrical visions, I wasn't surprised to discover that Saunaluoma and Virtanen were already far ahead of me in contemplating a connection between ayahuasca visions as expressed in indigenous art and the immense geoglyphs now emerging from jungle clearances along the southern rim of the Amazon.

Of the contemporary Manchineri, for example (who live much closer to the ancient earthworks than the Tukano), they note in a 2015 paper that "certain geometric motifs," often expressed in ceramics and body paintings, "have meaning as signs of specific ancestors. Some ancestors possess their own geometric designs that may appear in shamanic *ayahuasca* visions, transmitting ancestral knowledge and power."[23]

They therefore conclude that "not only using but also constructing geometric earthworks may have been important social intra-group or inter-group events."[24]

In a follow-up paper, published in *American Anthropologist* in August 2017, Saunaluoma and Virtanen take their analysis much further, proposing that the geoglyphs "were systematically constructed as spaces especially laden with visible and invisible entities."[25] Their argument is that, regardless of scale or medium, the whole process of materializing visionary iconography, in particular geometric patterns, is "related to the fluid forms inhabiting the Amazonian relational world. Different designs 'bring' the presence of nonhumans to the visible world of humans for a number of Amazonian Indigenous peoples, while perceiving geometric designs in Amerindian art as paths from one dimension to another allows a viewer to shift between different worlds, from the visible to the invisible."[26]

Citing the work of their colleague Luisa Belaunde, Saunaluoma and Virtanen note that for the Shipibo-Conibo of the Peruvian Amazon, "the lines embody a package of ways in which beings move, travel, communicate between themselves, and transmit knowledge, objects, and powers. These paths exist everywhere, from macro to micro scales. Geometric designs are thus about certain ways of thinking, perceiving, and indicating invisible aspects so they can be seen."[27]

Saunaluoma and Virtanen further establish that, to the Shipibo-Conibo, the geometric lines open "a window to the macrocosmos" and allow "macrocosmic order" to be "iconically sketched in the microcosmos here, in landscape designs."[28]

As above, so below.

PORTAL

BY TAKING THE WORLDVIEW, INSIGHTS, and philosophies of indigenous peoples seriously in efforts to understand their past, Saunaluoma and Virtanen's research marks a refreshing change of note for Western science and offers rewarding insights into the realm of ideas underlying the geoglyphs. It is by no means a realm of "primitive" ideas. On the contrary: with its notions of pathways between dimensions, and of making visible the presence of usually invisible entities, there are aspects of thought surrounding the traditional use of ayahuasca that would not be out of place in a quantum physics laboratory.

Once again I suggest we are looking at the remnants of an advanced system that propagates itself through time and across cultures with powerful memes among which geometry and cosmic alignments take a large share. We do not know where or when this system originated. In the ancient Amazon, however, to a greater degree than anywhere else, its dissemination became integrated with the use of vision-inducing plants—and there, up to the present day, the secrets of how to use these plants have been preserved and passed down within indigenous shamanic traditions.

The origin myth of the Tukano speaks of the time, eons ago, when humans first settled the great rivers of the Amazon basin. It seems that "supernatural beings" accompanied them on this journey and gifted them the fundamentals upon which to build a civilized life. From the "Daughter of the Sun" they received the gift of fire and the knowledge of horticulture, pottery-making, and many other crafts. "The serpent-shaped canoe of the first set-

tlers" was steered by a superhuman "Helmsman."[29] Meanwhile other supernaturals "travelled by canoe over all the rivers and . . . explored the remote hill
ranges; they pointed out propitious sites for houses or fields, or for hunting
and fishing, and they left their lasting imprint on many spots so that future
generations would have ineffaceable proof of their earthly days and would
forever remember them and their teachings."[30]

The slow, methodical progress of the serpent canoe, setting down its cargo of
migrants here and there, explains anthropologist Gerardo Reichel-Dolmatoff:

> Was marked not only by the successive spots of debarkation but
> also by an advancing scale of human achievement. . . .
>
> The rules for the initiation into shamanism were laid down,
> accompanied by a large body of prescriptions, regulations and
> prohibitions that, from now on, were to guide and govern the life of
> the people.
>
> But above all . . . if mankind was to prevail and survive as part
> of nature, and was to pass on a true legacy to new generations,
> people had to assume responsibilities and find ways to control the
> organization of society so as to procure a balance between human
> needs and the resources available in nature.[31]

In this period "the spirit-beings prepared the land so that mortal human
creatures might live on it."[32] Once that task had been completed, however,

> the supernatural beings returned to their otherworldly abodes. Before
> leaving . . . they took care to provide mankind with the means of
> communication, of establishing contact with them whenever there
> should be need. Mortal men could not be left alone without the
> possibility of communing with the spirit-world. . . . It was essential,
> then, for the welfare of mankind to have at its disposal a simple and
> effective means by which, at any given moment, an individual or a
> group of people could establish contact with the supernatural sphere.[33]

It is rather brutally to compress many colorful and thought-provoking
details to say that at the end of the lengthy myth, the "effective means" of
contacting the spirit-world turns out to be . . . ayahuasca:

A plant that opened the door into another dimension, a drug that produced visions in which the spirit-beings revealed themselves to men—talking, teaching, admonishing and protecting.[34]

There are multiple different elements intertwined in the Tukano story but three of them stand out for me.

First, what's being described is dressed up in the language and imagery of myth and may of course be "just a myth." What it sounds like, however, is a mythologized account of a settlement mission in the Amazon in which a group of migrants were accompanied by a number of more sophisticated people considered to be "supernatural" or "superhuman."

Though I don't want to put undue weight on it, I would be negligent if I failed to mention in passing that the Tukano, and the closely related Barasana, are among a number of Amazonian tribes whose distinctive "men's cults" are paralleled by virtually identical institutions in Melanesia, on the opposite side of the Pacific Ocean. As the reader will discover in appendix 1, the same secrecy surrounding male initiation rituals is found in both areas, the same exclusive possession of sacred flutes and trumpets that women are forbidden to see,[35] the same belief that there was a time when women dominated men, and the same belief that men, either by trickery or force, had subsequently wrested power from women.

Second, the Tukano origin myth makes it completely clear that the "supernaturals" departed after they had completed their work of preparing the Amazon for settlement by the migrants in the serpent canoe.

Third, we are led to understand that direct contact between humanity and the spirit world would thereafter be broken. However a portal—ayahuasca—through which humans could still travel to the spirit world, and benefit from its teachings, would be left open.

THE LEAP TO THE MILKY WAY

ALTHOUGH ANY MEMBER OF THE Tukano community may drink ayahuasca, the deeper mysteries of the brew are primarily the work of the shaman—the *payé*—whose responsibility it is to travel through the portal whenever required to negotiate with powerful supernaturals on behalf of his community. Where matters of the greatest importance must be resolved, a group of *payé* will work together, consuming massive quantities of ayahuasca until they reach a point, lying in their hammocks, where they

> feel they are ascending to the Milky Way. . . . The ascent to the Milky Way is not easily accomplished. An apprentice will hardly ever be able to rise immediately to this . . . region but rather will learn to do so after many trials. At first he will barely rise over the horizon, the next time perhaps he will reach a point corresponding to the position of the sun at 9 a.m., then at 10 a.m., and so on until at last, in a single, soaring flight, he will reach the zenith.[36]

In summary, therefore, the shaman's visionary journey through the ayahuasca portal involves a leap or, after sufficient practice, a "soaring flight," to the Milky Way. It is not the final goal, however, but a way station. "Beyond the Milky Way" lies the entrance to the Otherworld. As Reichel-Dolmatoff explains:

> It is said that the individual "dies" when he drinks the potion and that now his spirit returns to the uterine regions of the Beyond, only to be reborn there and to return to his ordinary existence when the trance is over. This then is conceived as an acceleration of time, an anticipation of death and rebirth.[37]

HIDDEN HAND

THE TUKANO OTHERWORLD IS DIVIDED into regions or districts and one of these, of particular interest to shamans, is the domain of *Vai-mahase,* the supernatural "Master of Animals." It is a strangely geometrical "hill" in the form of a square with its four sides oriented to the cardinal directions.[38]

Is it an accident that geometry arises spontaneously in ayahuasca visions? And is it an accident that it does so not only among Amazonian peoples in the Amazon itself, but—as my own experiences and multiple scientific studies

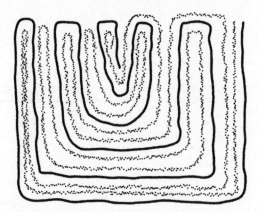

Entrance to the "Otherworld" as depicted in Tukano visionary art. (After G. Reichel-Dolmatoff, *The Shaman and the Jaguar*, 1975, p. 174.)

have proved—among peoples from industrialized cultures as well?[39] Whether you drink the brew in the rainforest, or in New York, London, Frankfurt, or Tokyo, it is a plain fact that sooner or later you are going to see geometry.[40]

Is the presence of some deeper enigma hinted at here—an enigma that the ancients had plumbed when they devised their memes and sent them ringing down the ages? Just because our high-tech civilization has demonized psychedelics for the last 50 years doesn't mean that other societies in the past did so. Indeed it's likely that these powerful agents of transformation were used by ancient civilizations for profound and far-reaching inquiries into aspects of reality about which our own high-tech civilization remains willfully ignorant.[41]

We've seen that ayahuasca has many different names among the many different peoples who use it across the Amazon, but the word *ayahuasca* itself is from the Quechua language of the high Andes overlooking the western edge of the Amazon basin. This is the language that was spoken by the remarkable Inca civilization of Peru in the few short centuries before its destruction by the Spaniards. In that language what *ayahuasca* means is the "Vine of the Dead" or the "Vine of Souls."

The memes of geometry and cosmic alignments are not the only ones to have propagated from a so far unidentified common source. Intimately connected to them are other ideas that went "viral" in both the Old World and the New, and that therefore somehow transcended the Ice Age separation of peoples.

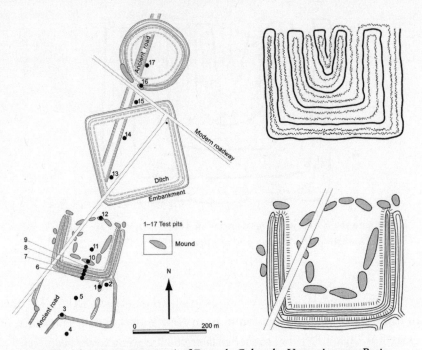

LEFT: Plan (by Martti Pärssinen) of Fazenda Colorada, Upper Amazon Basin geoglyph site (see chapter 16). TOP RIGHT: Tukano visionary art depicting the entrance to the "Otherworld," said to lie "beyond the Milky Way." BOTTOM RIGHT: Detail (rotated) from Fazenda Colorada.

The central focus of all these ideas concerns the mystery of death, and anthropologists have long been aware that the Quechua name ayahuasca is entirely appropriate since "in the indigenous context Ayahuasca is intimately related to death."[42]

In parts 5 and 6 our investigation returns to North America, where eerie doppelgängers of the great earthworks of the Amazon haunt the Mississippi Valley. As we'll see, it's almost as though what we're dealing with are the faint surviving traces of an immensely ancient and deeply thought-through system of knowledge and initiation, perhaps arising from direct investigations using vision-inducing plants, in which profound notions of the afterlife destiny of the soul were stitched together with the geometry and cosmic alignments into a single "blueprint" that was then hastily replicated and urgently distributed to the remotest corners of the earth.

PART V

STUFF JUST KEEPS ON GETTING OLDER

The Mystery of the Primeval Mounds

Six thousand kilometers as an aircraft flies from the heart of the Amazon to the heart of the Mississippi.

SUN

FROM THE CITY OF MANAUS, at the heart of the Amazon River basin in South America, it's a journey of about 6,000 kilometers by air to reach the city of St. Louis in the heart of the Mississippi River basin in North America. On the way you'll cross the Equator and the Tropic of Cancer. Google informs me that the flight time will be about 11 hours, including a stopover in the Dominican Republic.

It wasn't so simple in the ancient world. Although sections of the journey could have been made by sea most of the route would have been overland through some geographically very challenging parts of Central America and involving, ultimately, much more than 6,000 kilometers.

This is not to say that such a great distance must necessarily have ruled out any communication and interchange between the two regions. On the contrary, it is not in dispute that the peoples of South and North America are more closely related genetically to each other than they are to anyone

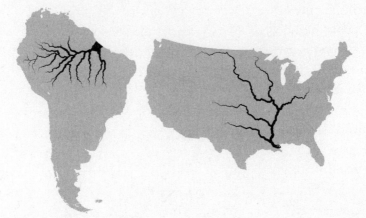

The two giant river basins of the Americas (note, maps not to scale). The Amazon River basin (left) has a total area of 7.5 million square kilometers. The Mississippi River basin (right) has a total area of 2.9 million square kilometers.

else, that there are some linguistic connections, and that crops such as maize or manioc that had been domesticated in one region were also grown in the other—though sometimes with a significant time lag. In summary, the evidence confirms that there were contacts but it also suggests that they were random and infrequent rather than regular and sustained.

What, then, are we to make of the fact that stunningly similar earthworks repeating stunningly similar geometric themes on a stunningly similar scale to those of the Amazon River basin are also found in the Mississippi River basin?

Are the resemblances coincidental?

Or did they arise during one of the random and infrequent episodes of contact?

Or is there some other explanation?

It's June 14, 2017, a week before the summer solstice, and I'm chewing over these questions with Santha while we stand on top of an earthwork called "Monks Mound" at the sacred heart of the ancient Mississippian city of Cahokia.

Looking southwest from this vantage point what stands out, about 8 miles away, are the twin A-shaped support towers and cable ties of the Stan Musial Veterans Memorial Bridge, joining Illinois to Missouri across the Mississippi River, and a couple of miles farther south along the Mississippi waterside the glittering, stainless-steel Gateway Arch of the city of St. Louis. Conceived as "a public memorial to the men who made possible the western territorial expansion of the United States,"[1] the arch reaches a height of 630 feet and is claimed to be the tallest man-made monument in the Western Hemisphere and the tallest arch in the world.

The contrast between old and new is abrupt—for the ancient mounds and earthworks of the Mississippi Valley, even gigantic sites like Cahokia, have an understated quality. They don't radiate the brash and boastful self-importance of so many of our modern structures—such as the skyscraper One Metropolitan Square, which at 593 feet high seems to do battle with the Gateway Arch to dominate the St. Louis skyline. Neither do they overwhelm you with their grandeur and their majesty, like the pyramids of ancient Egypt and Mexico. Nor do they wear their mysteries in full view like the great moai of Easter Island. Instead an elegant synthesis between heaven and earth seems to have been sought out. In consequence even Monks Mound, on the 100-foot-tall summit of which we're now standing, is so seamlessly integrated with its setting that it seems almost as much a work of nature as of man.

Indeed this was precisely the view of Dr. A. R. Crook, director of the Illinois State Museum and a geologist by training, who undertook the first "scientific" investigations of Monks Mound in 1914. His theory, shared by many of his colleagues at the time and perhaps colored by an underlying prejudice that prehistoric Native Americans would not have been capable of building on such a scale, was that the mounds of Cahokia were entirely natural "erosional remnants." In 1914 Crook drilled twenty-five shallow augur holes into the north face of Monks Mound, found nothing to change his view and—as late as 1921—was continuing to declare, as though it were an established and objective fact, that the mounds were merely glacial and alluvial deposits and thus of no archaeological interest.[2]

This mattered because other, wiser, scholars were already absolutely certain that the Cahokia complex was man-made and of outstanding archaeological interest and had mounted a campaign to save the mounds from further destruction at the hands of farmers and industrialists. Crook's claims that they were natural formations were therefore most unhelpful and had to be refuted before further progress could be made.

This challenge was duly taken up by archaeologist Warren T. Moorehead, who joined forces with geologist Morris Leighton to undertake a much more thorough investigation of the mounds in 1922 than Crook had mounted in 1914. After several test pits had been dug on the Fourth Terrace and on the east side of Monks Mound, including auguring to a depth of 20 feet, the results, in the form of artifacts and exposed construction levels, were too conclusive and compelling to be dismissed.[3] Even Crook was convinced and thereafter abandoned his position that the mounds were natural features[4]—a position that today, in the light of subsequent extensive excavations around Cahokia and at Monks Mound, seems absurd.

Nonetheless, there remain many who would seek by one means or another to take Cahokia away from the Native Americans who built it. Since it can no longer be credibly claimed as a natural erosional feature, the fallback position, popular in the late nineteenth and early twentieth centuries but repeatedly returned to even now, is that the great city, and others like it up and down the Mississippi Valley, must have been the work of some superior "master-race" of white-skinned foreigners who reached America in antiquity and built the mounds with their advanced skills and techniques but were then driven off or wiped out by native "savages."[5]

Frequently compounded by rumors of "giants" or "aliens," such reasoning has already been comprehensively refuted by excavations proving to the satisfaction of anyone capable of logical thought that the mounds, including Monks Mound—that "stupendous pile of earth" as one early explorer described it[6]—are indeed the work of Native Americans.[7]

The very name of the great mound, however, demonstrates the effects of the ongoing casual misappropriation of indigenous achievements. It bears that name simply because a group of Trappist monks—immigrants from France—grew vegetables on its terraces for a few years either side of AD 1810,[8] but it was built around AD 1050 by the Native American civilization archaeologists call the Mississippians.[9]

We don't know what the people of that civilization called themselves and we don't know what they called Monks Mound. We do know, however, that they thought and worked on a grand scale, as I shall show, and that they made use of the same kinds of geometry and astronomy deployed at Serpent Mound, 420 miles to the east, and in the great earthworks and mounds of the Amazon thousands of miles to the south.

TWO VALLEYS

DESPITE THE PROMISING CLUES OFFERED by ethnographic research into the likely role played by vision-inducing plants and shamanic experiences, the fact remains that we are confronted across huge expanses of the Amazon by such severely limited archaeological data that it's impossible to give responsible, informed answers to three fundamental questions:

> What motivated the creation of the mounds and geoglyphs?

> When were the very first structures of this kind made?

> Where and how were the requisite design, planning, engineering, and architectural skills developed?

In the Amazon, on all three counts, we simply don't know. Moreover, our ignorance is compounded by the absence of any detailed geometrical or archaeoastronomical surveys of the earthworks and mounds thus far discovered and by the fact that millions of square kilometers of the rainforest have never been studied by archaeologists at all.

It's quite a different story in the Mississippi Valley, which is not veiled by vast areas of near-impenetrable jungle and where mounds and earthworks remarkably similar to those now coming to light in the Amazon have been the subject of more than 170 years of intensive archaeological investigation.[10] Because they were always in plain view, however, and because they often occupied land that was desirable for agricultural or industrial purposes, the vast majority of the immense prehistoric structures of the Mississippi Valley no longer exist. An estimated 90 percent are gone—either partially or completely demolished and cleared away in the obliteration of North America's past that began with the European conquest.

So just as archaeologists in the Amazon have only a limited database from which to construct their theories, because the jungle covers so much, it's also the case that archaeologists in the Mississippi Valley have only a limited database because so much has been destroyed. Still, they've achieved a great deal with the roughly 10 percent of the original total of sites that have survived and it may not be too much to hope that their discoveries could shed light on the mysterious counterpart mounds and earthworks of the Amazon.

EARTH ISLAND, SKY WORLD

FROM CHAPTER 16, THE READER may recall Severino Calazans, an Amazonian earthwork with the same 13-acre footprint and the same orientation to the cardinal directions as the Great Pyramid of Giza. Though rectangular rather than square (910 feet from north to south and 720 feet from east to west), Monks Mound has a 14-acre footprint.[11]

Considered as a pyramid—and it is indeed a form of step pyramid—it comes third in the Americas after the Pyramid of Quetzalcoatl at Cholula and the Pyramid of the Sun at Teotihuacan,[12] both of which are stone-reinforced monuments and significantly taller.

Considered an earthwork, and echoing that early explorer's report, Monks Mound has been described as "stupendous in many ways. It is the tallest mound, covers the most area and contains the most volume of any prehistoric earthen monument in the Americas."[13] It is, moreover, part of a giant complex with multiple different elements including more than 100 subsidiary earthen mounds, the archaeological traces of what was once a spectacular circle of huge wooden posts (known as Cahokia's "Woodhenge"), a spacious central plaza, and an 18-meter-wide, 800-meter-long earthwork causeway running arrow-straight between raised embankments.

Enigmatically, but quite deliberately set to an azimuth of 005 degrees—that is, 5 degrees east of true north—it is this causeway, referred to by archaeologists as the "Rattlesnake Causeway," that defines Cahokia's principal axis,[14] giving the site a certain ambiguity and adding to its air of mystery. Every mound and earthwork is set out upon the ground in strict relation to it, with clusters of structures, dominated by Monks Mound itself, running south to north and other clusters running west to east.

It's easy to understand, then, why the first and most powerful impression I get overlooking this massive ancient site from the top of Monks Mound is of its distinct "cardinality." Exactly as is the case at Giza and Angkor—both of which are aligned within fractions of a single degree to true north—so, too, here at Cahokia. Despite its puzzling 5-degree offset there's no mistaking where to look for the cardinal directions. Something about the place—something intended and carefully thought through by its original designers—immediately connects you to both earth and sky.

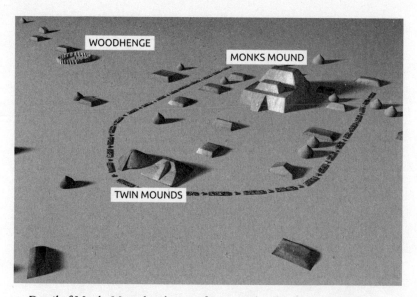

Detail of Monks Mound and some of its immediately adjoining structures.

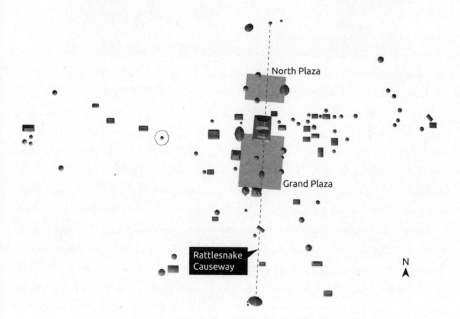

Running through the Grand Plaza and Monks Mound, and extending northward beyond Monks Mound, the Rattlesnake Causeway defines Cahokia's 5 degrees east of north axis.

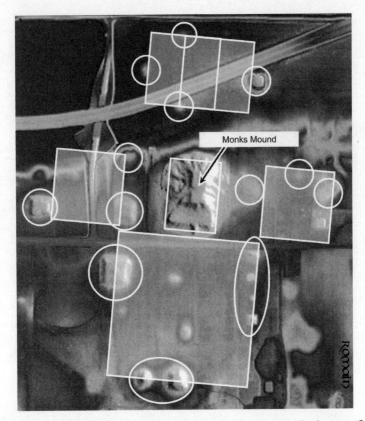

Lidar image reveals how Monks Mound is bounded by plazas and other significant structures on its north, south, east, and west sides. IMAGE BY WILLIAM ROMAIN.

This sense of terrestrial and cosmic connectedness is among several cogently argued reasons why archaeologist William Romain, whose work at Serpent Mound we encountered in part 1, considers Monks Mound to have been conceived by its designers as a true "axis mundi"—intended to serve as a junction point between heaven and earth. He reminds us of the traditional shamanistic spiritual system of the Native American peoples of the Eastern Woodlands—the region of Cahokia. According to this system, the universe is comprised "of an Above World, This World, and Below World. . . . Connecting these realms is a vertical vector . . . the axis mundi that enables shamans to move between cosmic realms. . . . The axis mundi can be symbolically represented by any number of vertical elements such as a pole, tree, column of smoke, mountain, pyramid, or mound."[15]

Monks Mound has the look of a small mountain, Romain observes. It dwarfs everything in the surrounding landscape and utterly dominates Cahokia. This character of "verticality" is enhanced by the local topography of the Mississippi floodplain, which would have ensured that the Grand Plaza was regularly, if shallowly, inundated. Out of the watery, marshy realm thus created, Monks Mound would have seemed to rear up in numinous and mythic power and was perhaps, Romain writes:

> imagined as an earth island. . . . If the Below World as represented
> by the wetlands, swamps, lakes, and man-made water features
> surrounding central Cahokia is a watery world, then it is appropriate
> that in its verticality, Monks Mound would be the structural axis
> mundi linking the watery Below World to the Above Sky World.[16]

Interestingly, and again despite the 5-degree offset from true north so firmly declared by Cahokia's principal axis, the largest known building of the Mississippian civilization was erected on the apex of Monks Mound and in this case was precisely aligned to the cardinal directions.[17] Its long axis, measuring 30.85 meters, was set perfectly east–west; its short axis, measuring 13.85 meters, was set perfectly north–south.[18]

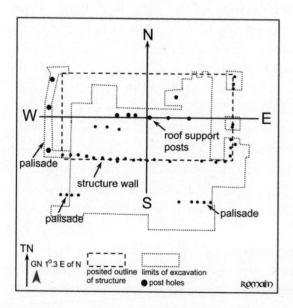

Archaeologists have established that a large structure, perfectly aligned to the cardinal directions, once stood on the summit of Monks Mound. IMAGE BY WILLIAM ROMAIN.

MONKS MOUND

SUMMER SOLSTICE
MARKER POST

WINTER SOLSTICE
MARKER POST

EQUINOX
MARKER POST

CENTER POST

The workings of Cahokia's Woodhenge. PHOTO BY WILLIAM ISEMINGER;
ANNOTATIONS BY WILLIAM ROMAIN.

Romain also draws our attention to "the powerful visual hierophany" that
would have been witnessed at the spring and fall equinoxes when Cahokia
was in its prime, locking the site in to key conjunctions of heaven and earth.
It was in the staging of this hierophany that the site's "Woodhenge" played
its most crucial role. Re-created with a modern simulacrum for the benefit
of the 300,000 tourists who now visit Cahokia each year, and named after
the similar prehistoric circle of huge wooden posts that stood on England's
Salisbury Plain close to the world-famous site of Stonehenge before the stone
circle itself was completed, Cahokia's Woodhenge lies some 850 meters west
of Monks Mound. Its existence remained unsuspected until the 1960s when
archaeologist Warren Wittry found traces of immense postholes. Subsequent
excavations revealed that no fewer than five woodhenges had been built on
the same site over a period of a couple of centuries in order to accommodate
increases in the size and shape of the Mound itself, which affected crucial
solar sight lines.

The objective of every realignment and rededication was that an observer
at the center of the post circle, looking due east across the "front sight" of a
specially placed equinox marker post, should see the sun's disk appear above

Equinox sunrise above the slope of the southern terrace of Monks Mound.
PHOTOGRAPHED FROM WOODHENGE BY WILLIAM ROMAIN.

the slope of the southern terrace of Monks Mound—an arrangement, says Romain, that establishes an east–west solar-oriented line across the entire Cahokia complex:

> The result is that Monks Mound is visually connected to the Above World vis á vis the rising sun and its location on the east–west sightline that intersects the major site axis. In this way, Monks Mound is positioned at a center place.[19]

That assertion and manifestation of centrality is reconfirmed by two other posts at Woodhenge that serve as front sights targeting the horizon azimuths of the summer and winter solstice sunrises.[20]

ENTER THE MOON

THE CIRCLES, RECTANGLES, AND SQUARES of Cahokia, the solstitial and equinoctial alignments, and the perfect cardinality of the large structure that once stood atop Monks Mound are among the hallmarks of the same distinct pattern of geometry and astronomy that we find in the Amazon earthworks.

Unexplained so far, however, is why Cahokia's designers made a deliberate choice **not** to align the main axis of their premier site to the cardinal directions of earth and sky but instead chose to offset it by 5 degrees east of true north?

It's a question to which William Romain offers an intriguing answer. The builders of Cahokia, he argues, were geometricians who made use of a special rectangle, known as a "root-2 rectangle," in planning the layout of the city.

He gives much supporting evidence for this claim, which need not detain us here.[21] Nor do we want to get bogged down in unnecessary technical detail. In brief, however, a root-2 rectangle is constructed by extending the

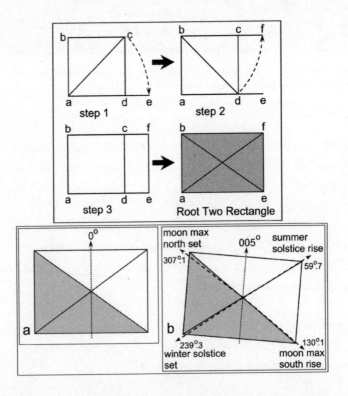

opposite sides of a square to the length of the square's diagonal. If you take such a rectangle, orient it to true north (0 degrees azimuth), and then rotate it eastward by 5 degrees to match the azimuth of Cahokia's principal axis, its diagonals turn out to align closely with important solar and lunar events as viewed from Monks Mound—specifically, **the summer solstice sunrise** at azimuth 59.7 degrees, **the winter solstice sunset** at azimuth 239.3 degrees, **the moon's maximum southern rising position** at azimuth 130.1 degrees, and **the moon's maximum northern setting position** at azimuth 307.1 degrees.

The match, Romain admits, "is not perfect. A couple of the celestial azimuths differ from the diagonals of the root two rectangle by 2 to 3 degrees. But since the rectangle is not intended for observational purposes it is perhaps close enough to symbolically represent the complementary opposite relationships of the sun and moon."[22]

If Romain is right, then it appears that sophisticated astronomical and mathematical ideas, combined with complex and cleverly thought through symbolism, were already present, fully worked out, and in the hands of competent professionals when Cahokia underwent what archaeologists call its "big bang"—an explosive period of expansion and development—around AD 1050.[23]

Is there evidence that such ideas were deployed elsewhere in North America before Cahokia?

MOON

WILLIAM ROMAIN'S CASE THAT NOT only solar but also lunar connections were mediated through geometry in the alignments of Cahokia is strengthened by the fact that other significantly older earthwork sites, most of which were destroyed by "development" in the nineteenth and twentieth centuries, were built in the Mississippi River basin incorporating complex geometries based almost exclusively on lunar alignments. Two of the most significant such sites to have survived, at least in part, into the twenty-first century are the High Bank Works and Newark Earthworks, both in Ohio. High Bank Works is located near the town of Chillicothe, about 40 miles northeast of Serpent Mound, and Newark Earthworks stands about 60 miles farther to the northeast near the town of Newark.

Both are true geoglyphs in the Amazonian sense, being formed by embankments and ditches set out on such a gigantic scale that their shape is not evident at ground level and can only be discerned clearly from the air.

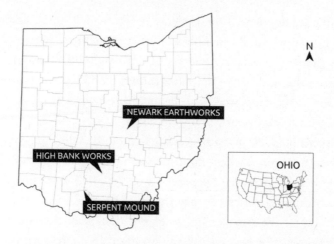

This 1934 aerial photograph shows the Circle-Octagon combination of the Newark Earthworks. Those parts that still survive are now largely contained within a private country club that includes an eighteen-hole golf course and promotes itself as "unlike any other in the world. It is designed around famous prehistoric Native American Earthworks that come into play on eleven of the holes."

Both are dominated by immense octagon-circle combinations linked by short causeways amid assemblies of other geometrical figures. Both are currently thought to date to between AD 250 and 400.[1] Both are attributed to a culture that archaeologists have named the "Hopewell"—after a certain Captain M. C. Hopewell, who happened to own a farm in the right place when excavations began.[2]

Newark and High Bank were first professionally surveyed in the mid-nineteenth century when numerous mounds—most subsequently leveled for plowing or industrial purposes—were reported to be situated within the geometrical earthworks.[3] It may therefore be relevant to recall at this point that many of the Amazonian geoglyphs described in chapter 15 also contain mounds—for example, eleven arranged in a circle within an immense enclosure in the Upper Tapajos Basin,[4] the "two high mounds, standing like towers" at the southwestern entrance of the trapezoidal earthwork at Fazenda Colorada,[5] the twenty-five adjoining mounds of Fazenda Iquiri II,[6] and the ten surviving mounds of Coqueiral.[7]

Whereas no archaeoastronomical survey of the Amazonian earthworks has yet been attempted, Cahokia and Serpent Mound have both been subject to intense scrutiny. Meanwhile, at Newark and High Bank a series of studies since the 1980s have revealed a complex symphony of geometry and astronomy encoding not only familiar solar alignments but also, as we are about to see, much more subtle and esoteric conjunctions of heaven and earth concerned with the complex dance along the horizon of the rising and setting moon.

PCBS

NEWARK AND HIGH BANK HAVE an almost technological feel to them, resembling gigantic printed circuit boards or wiring diagrams from the innards of some immense and ineffable instrument. It's interesting, therefore, that Bradley Lepper, currently curator of archaeology with the Ohio History Connection, believes they may originally have been conceived by their designers as the components in "a monumental engine for world renewal . . . a vast machine, or device, designed and built to unleash primordial forces."[8]

At both sites the principal geoglyph combines a circle with an octagon and

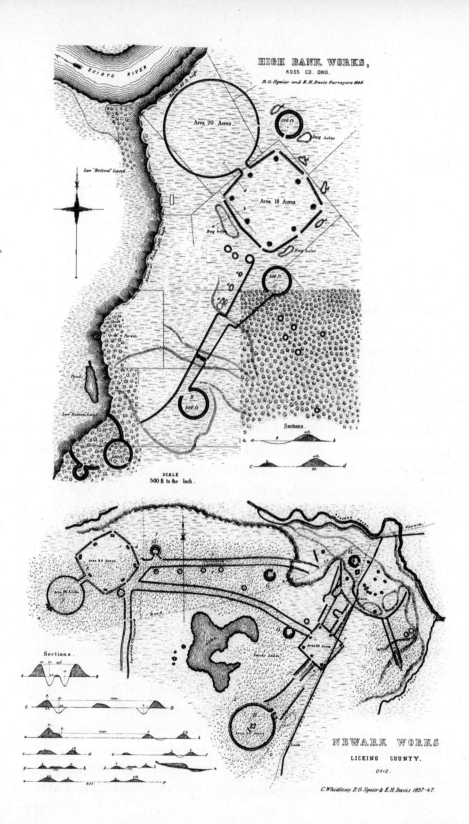

HIGH BANK WORKS,
ROSS CO. OHIO.

E.G. Squier and E.H. Davis Surveyors 1846.

SCIOTO RIVER

Area 20 Acres

250 ft.

Bug holes

Low "Bottom" Land.

Area 16 Acres

Bug holes

Bug holes

500 ft.

Forest.

Pond.

Low Bottom Land.

B.
500 ft.

500 ft.

Sections.

SCALE
500 ft to the Inch.

Area 50 Acres

Area 20 Acres

Sections.

NEWARK WORKS

LICKING COUNTY.

OHIO.

C. Whittlesey E.G. Squier & E.H. Davis 1837-47.

Newark Great Circle, also known as
the Fairground Circle, with its interior
ditch and central three-lobed "Eagle
Mound." The diameter of the circle is
365.9 meters (just over 1,200 feet).

in both cases these figures are formed by large earthen embankments as much
as 12 meters wide at the base and typically about 1.7 meters high.[9]

A striking similarity of general design connects the octagon/circle theme
of Newark and High Bank with the Amazonian geoglyph (see chapter 15)
of Santa Isabel. Although the latter is less geometrically exact than the Ohio
examples, this is by no means always the rule since both regions exhibit numbers of extremely precise and numbers of more mediocre earthworks.

The strict lines of Ohio's Newark Octagon enclose an area of 50 acres and
its eight walls have an average length of 167.7 meters.[10] The adjoining circle,
known since the nineteenth century as the "Observatory Circle," encloses an
area of 20 acres and has a diameter of 321.3 meters.[11] A resurvey of the site,
carried out with modern instruments in 1982, revealed that "the midline of
the embankment walls deviates by no more than 1.2 m at any place from a
perfect circle of diameter 321.3 m. A perfect circle of this diameter would have
a circumference of 1009.4 m, whereas the actual circle has a circumference of
1008.6 m. Thus it is evident that the Observatory Circle very closely approx-
imates a true circle."[12]

Located 2 kilometers southeast of the Observatory Circle is a second,
larger but less geometrically perfect circle known as the Great Circle and formerly as the Fairground Circle, since it was used as the site of the Licking
County Fairgrounds from 1854 to 1933.[13] It encloses an area of 30 acres[14]
and, though much depleted by misuse and the passage of time, its earthwork
walls today, varying between 1.5 meters and 4.3 meters in height and between
11 meters and 17 meters in width,[15] still give a sense of the enormity of the
original enterprise. At its center are the remnants of a three-lobed mound,
usually referred to as "Eagle Mound" because many visitors have seen in it

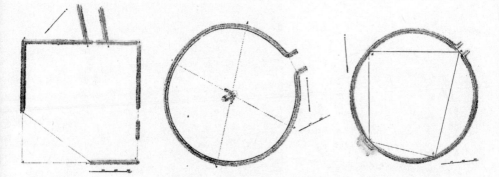

Images from the 1894 Bureau of Ethnology Survey. Badly damaged even then, Newark's Great Square (left), also known as "Wright Square" or "the Wright Earthworks," is almost completely destroyed today, with only a short segment of one of the four walls remaining. The perimeter of the Great Square is equal to the circumference of the Great Circle (center), while its area is equal to the area of the Observatory Circle (right).

a resemblance to a bird with outstretched wings.[16] Archaeologists, however, regard it as "a series of conjoined mounds rather than a specific effigy form."[17]

The diameter of the Great Circle, at 365.9 meters,[18] is of the same order of magnitude as the Neolithic henges in the British Isles. Stonehenge at 110 meters is smaller[19] but Avebury at approximately 420 meters is larger.[20] Moreover, just like Avebury and many of the Amazonian earthworks reviewed in chapter 16, a striking feature of Newark's Great Circle is the massive ditch—as much as 12.5 meters wide and 4 meters deep[21]—that runs *inside* its embankment walls. Indeed, such a ditch, within rather than outside a circular embankment, is the very definition of a henge.

Alongside its circles, and an integral part of the same enormous complex (to the other major elements of which it was joined by causeways), Newark in its prime possessed a square enclosure, "nearly geometrically perfect,"[22] with sides averaging 931 feet in length.[23] Almost nothing of it remains today but fortunately enough was intact when it was surveyed in the nineteenth century, first by Squier and Davis and later by Cyrus Thomas of the Bureau of Ethnology, to establish its measures exactly. These and subsequent surveys have revealed not only that "the perimeter of the square earthwork is precisely equal to the circumference of the Great Circle," but also, as Bradley Lepper notes, that "its area is equal to the area of the Observatory Circle." In these

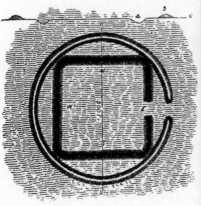 

Variations on a theme. LEFT: Ancient Works, Pike County, Ohio, as mapped by Squier and Davis in 1848. RIGHT: Jacó Sá earthwork, the Amazon. PHOTO: RICARDO AZOURY/PULSAR IMAGENS.

clearly deliberate and carefully thought through harmonies, Lepper rightly finds "indications of the remarkable sophistication of the geometry incorporated into the architecture of the Newark Earthworks."[24]

William Romain is more specific. In his view the creators of this extraordinary and in some ways rather otherworldly site "were intrigued by the variety of possible relationships between a circle and a square. . . . The idea that seems to be expressed is that, for every circular enclosure, a corresponding square . . . can be related to the circle by geometric means."[25]

"Squaring the circle"—constructing a square with the same area as a given circle—was of course a geometrical exercise of great interest to the master mathematicians of ancient Babylon, Egypt, and Greece.[26]

The dominant reference frame of modern archaeology does **not** encourage us to believe that any Native North Americans 2,000 years ago would have possessed the necessary knowledge and skills to perform such an exercise. Yet clearly they did, for the proof is there at Newark—not scratched on some handy-sized clay tablet or papyrus but set out with high precision on the ground in an assembly of truly gigantic and mysterious earthworks.

Many different variations on the same theme, which there is not space to review here, are to be found at other Hopewell sites in Ohio—for example, a square/circle combination that formerly existed in Pike County. Fortunately, it was surveyed by Squier and Davis in 1848 and their rendering, in figure 11 of *Ancient Monuments of the Mississippi Valley,* shows it to have been very similar in concept and plan—and indeed in size—to the earthwork at Jacó Sá in the Amazon described in chapter 15. The two figures are not identical, but they appear to demonstrate the identical geometrical principle.

From chapter 15 the reader will also recall the recent discovery of a squared circle complex within the great henge at Avebury in the British Isles.

Are we to resort once again to the archaeological cover-all of "coincidence" to explain the constant repetition and replication of the same astronomical and geometrical constructs in earthworks as far apart in space and time as Avebury, Newark, and Jacó Sá? Or could it be that some guided and intentional process, as yet undetected by archaeology, was under way behind the scenes of prehistory?

THE CONNECTION TO HIGH BANK

WE'VE SEEN HOW THE DIAMETER of the nearly geometrically perfect Observatory Circle at Newark is 321.3 meters (1,054 feet). Astronomer Ray Hively and philosopher Robert Horn of Indiana's Earlham College, whose comprehensive work at Newark and High Bank in the 1980s provided the foundation for all subsequent studies, realized that the same length of 321.3 meters had also been used by the builders to lay out the Octagon:[27]

> The conclusion suggested by the geometry of the Observatory Circle–Octagon combination is that both figures have been carefully and skilfully constructed from the same fundamental length.[28]

This unit of measure, now known by the unfortunate yet strangely appropriate acronym OCD (for Observatory Circle Diameter), was also deployed at High Bank, which, as Hively and Horn remind us, is "the only other circle-octagon combination known to have been constructed by the Hopewell."[29] It cannot be a coincidence, then, that High Bank turns out to conform to a geometric pattern based on a fundamental length of 0.998 OCD.[30]

Nor is the connection between these two sites limited to their shared unit of measure.

Perhaps most striking of all is the fact, noted by archaeologist Bradley Lepper, that "the main axis of High Bank Works—that is, a line projected through the center of the Circle and the Octagon—bears a direct relationship to the axis of Newark's Observatory Circle and Octagon. **Although built more than 60 miles apart**, the axis of High Bank Works is oriented at precisely 90 degrees to that of Newark earthworks. This suggests a deliberate attempt to link these sites through geometry and astronomy."[31]

In my view it more than merely "suggests!" Given that these are the only two sites in North America with circle-octagon combination earthworks, given that the circles are 99.8 percent identical in size, and given their precise 90-degree orientation to one another, a quite remarkable feat of surveying across a great span of country, I think we can safely say that the designers **did** intend a deliberate connection here. Lepper himself makes a strong case that this connection might have been more than symbolic when he presents evidence for the former existence of a causewayed road with some stretches of its parallel walls still in place as late as the mid-nineteenth century. He calls it "the Great Hopewell Road" and speculates that it was perhaps a pilgrim route that once ran between Newark and High Bank.[32]

As at Newark, a circle-octagon combination forms the dominant glyph at High Bank, and there are adjacent figures and causewayed avenues. When Squier and Davis surveyed the site in the nineteenth century (there has been massive destruction since) they reported that the walls of the High Bank Octagon were "very bold; and where they have been least subjected to cultivation are between eleven and twelve feet in height, by about fifty feet base. The wall of the circle is much less, nowhere measuring over four or five feet in altitude."[33] Despite its once "bold" walls, the High Bank Octagon, enclosing 18 acres,[34] is a much smaller figure than the Newark Octagon, which, as we've seen, encloses 50 acres.[35]

Why, since otherwise the circle-octagon motifs of the two sites are so similar, since their circles are of identical size, and since it seems the earthwork-makers did nothing by chance, should there be this marked reduction in scale of the High Bank Octagon?

The answer, as we shall see, has to do with eerily precise, indeed scientific, observations of the moon.

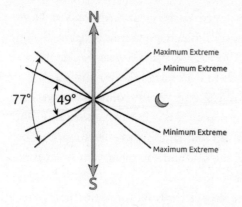

Extreme rise and set points of the moon over its 18.6-year cycle as viewed from Newark, Ohio. When the moon is at a position for maximum extremes, the extreme north and south moonrises and moonsets in a given month are separated by 77 degrees; at the position for minimum extremes, the extreme moonrises and moonsets are separated by 49 degrees.

SKY KNOWLEDGE

LIKE OTHER SACRED SITES SCATTERED around the world, the geometrical mounds and earthworks of North America don't give up their secrets easily. They have ways of grabbing your attention but they're going to force you to do some work before they allow you to understand them. Thus, for example, getting to grips properly with Serpent Mound requires knowledge of what a solstice is and of how the rising and setting points of the sun change according to a predictable cycle throughout the year.

Such knowledge, archaeologists argue, would have had immediate utility in the pre-industrial world, reminding farmers, in the words of Ecclesiastes, that for "every thing there is a season . . . a time to plant and a time to pluck that which is planted."

As a motive for the memorialization of solstitial and equinoctial alignments, however, the arguments in favor of a practical immediate agricultural payoff don't adequately account for the enormous effort involved in the construction of many of the sites. After all, the same calendrical functions could have been realized almost as effectively and much less expensively with pairs of aligned poles.

The notion that a reliable agricultural calendar was the primary motive for skywatching also fails to explain why we find the same focus on the rising and setting sun on the solstices and the equinoxes in distinctly **pre**-agricultural sites such as Painel do Pilão in the Amazon, dating back more than 13,000 years.[36]

Likewise, though they can only have been the product of detailed observations of the heavens and would have required meticulous record-keeping over many generations, the lunar alignments manifested in the great earthworks at Newark and High Bank have no obvious practical function in terms of harvests—or, indeed, of any other utilitarian pursuit. Once again, though, what they do require of those who seek deeper knowledge of them is a study of the heavens.

Nothing beats direct observation of the sky over the course of the year—except observing it over the course of many years—but these days excellent free astronomical software can speed up and simplify the learning task by showing us the exact rising points of the sun and the moon at any location and over any interval we choose.

If we make use of such software to observe the behavior of the moon over, say, a period of a century, we will quickly notice that its rising and setting points along the eastern and western horizons are locked to a cycle shifting from farthest north to farthest south and back to farthest north again **every month**. As more time passes, however, we will also observe that these monthly "boundaries" on the moon's rising and setting points aren't fixed from year to year but instead widen and narrow over an 18.6-year cycle. If they are at their widest ("Maximum Extreme") today, then they will be at their narrowest ("Minimum Extreme) in 9.3 years and at their widest again 9.3 years after that.

Eight prominent directions are therefore implicated in these celestial events. Four target the maximum and minimum monthly boundaries north of east and the maximum and minimum monthly boundaries south of east between which the moon can rise during its 18.6-year cycle. The other four do the same for moonset on the western horizon. On each occasion as it reaches one of its extremes the moon's constant motion stops—literally comes to a standstill—before it reverses the direction of its oscillation for the next 9.3 years.

The geometry of the Newark Earthworks—and of High Bank, too—turns out to be very closely fitted to these obscure celestial events, known to astronomers as "lunar standstills," knowledge of which would appear to have no practical contribution to make to the necessities of everyday life.

NEWARK'S LUNAR CODE

IT'S LARGELY THANKS TO RAY Hively and Robert Horn that we know of these lunar connections at all.

When they began work at Newark in 1975 their purpose was to conduct "a field exercise in data collection and analysis for an undergraduate inter-disciplinary course."[37] Although cosmology and the astronomical knowledge of prehistoric and ancient cultures were within the scope of the course, they make clear that they "did not expect to find any particular geometrical or astronomical pattern" at Newark.[38] "Indeed, given the difficulty of showing that any such pattern was intentional rather than fortuitous, we doubted any persuasive hypothesis regarding design of the earthworks could be formed."[39]

To their surprise, however, as they admitted in 2016:

Our continued analysis . . . has revealed repetitive patterns of earthwork and topographical features oriented or aligned to the extreme rise and set points of both the sun and the moon on the horizon. These alignments, combined with the massive scale, geometrical symmetry and regularity of the earthen enclosures suggest that the Newark Earthworks were built to record, celebrate, and connect with celestial actors or large-scale forces that appear to govern relations among earth, sky and the human mind.[40]

In their initial study, published in the journal *Archaeoastronomy* in 1982,[41] Hively and Horn did not recognize any solar alignments at Newark.[42] What grabbed their attention instead was the intricate cat's cradle of lunar alignments uncovered by their detective work.[43]

Some were obvious, indeed unmissable once the lunar concerns of the site were admitted—for example, the fact that "the avenue axis of the Octagon points to the maximum northern extreme rising point of the moon with an error of 0.2°."[44]

Such an "error," amounting to less than two-tenths of a single degree, represents remarkable precision for any epoch and far exceeds the level of science generally assumed by archaeologists to have existed in the pre-Columbian Americas. Moreover, "the avenue axis and four sides of the Octagon mark five of the eight extreme lunar rise-set points with a mean accuracy of 0.5°."[45]

The three remaining alignments, accurate to within 0.4 degrees, 0.7 degrees, and 0.8 degrees, respectively, are also shown in the diagram following.

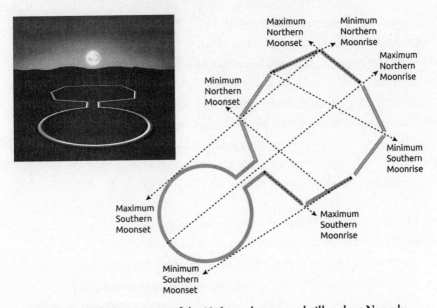

RIGHT: The eight key stations of the 18.6-year lunar-standstill cycle at Newark. The central axis and four walls target, respectively: (1) maximum northern moonrise; (2) maximum northern moonset; (3) minimum northern moonrise; (4) minimum southern moonset; and (5) maximum southern moonrise. The three remaining alignments identified by Hively and Horn are (6) maximum southern moonset; (7) minimum northern moonset; and (8) minimum southern moonrise. **TOP LEFT:** Simulation of maximum northern moonrise at Newark, as viewed along the Observatory Circle–Octagon axis.

Hively and Horn reinforce their case with another observation. The four sides of the Newark Octagon that are **not** aligned to significant lunar events form closely parallel pairs and are highly symmetrical. By contrast the four sides that **do** align to lunar standstills are neither parallel nor symmetrical. The obvious deduction to be made from this is that the geometrical symmetry of the Octagon was deliberately distorted to achieve more accurate lunar alignments.[46] Moreover,

the requirements of (1) octagonal symmetry and of (2) alignment with lunar extrema uniquely define the Newark Octagon. Of the infinity of possible octagons which could have been constructed at this site, the one we find is precisely the one which matches the lunar extrema most closely. In fact we have been unable to design an equilateral polygon

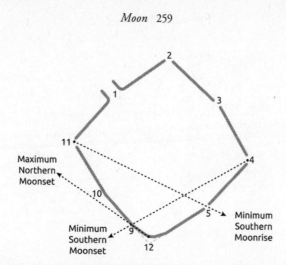

In the High Bank Octagon wall 11 → 1 is 16 percent longer than wall 10 → 11, displacing vertex 11 from its ideal position in such a way as to produce a lunar alignment, targeting the minimum southern moonrise between vertices 11 and 5. Likewise, there is no gap at the position of the ideal vertex at position 12. Instead the gap has been moved northward to position 9. A line between points 4 and 9 aligns with the minimum southern moonset. A further alignment, made possible by deviations in linearity, targets the maximum northern moonset at maximum standstill.

with eight or fewer sides which incorporates the same lunar points more efficiently and accurately than does the Newark Octagon.[47]

SUN AND MOON AT HIGH BANK

THE GREAT CONTRIBUTION OF HIVELY and Horn's 1982 paper in *Archaeoastronomy* was that it demonstrated how precisely, and how cleverly, Newark celebrates and embraces the lunar standstills. In a follow-up paper published in the same journal in 1984, the same investigators go on to prove that the High Bank structures embody equally unequivocal alignments to the extreme north and south rise points of the moon.[48] And just as at Newark, where deliberate asymmetries were introduced into the side lengths and angles of the Octagon to achieve more perfect lunar alignments, so, too, we find that one of the eight walls of High Bank's octagon is 16 percent longer than it "should" be to preserve perfect geometrical symmetry. This "error,"

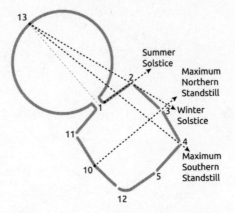

Targeting of the northern extreme moonrise and the southern extreme moonset at High Bank—both at maximum standstill. In addition, the summer solstice sunrise is targeted within 0.5 degrees by wall 1 → 2 while the alignment 13 → 2 targets the winter solstice sunrise.

however, alters the angle to the neighboring vertex, thus opening up an alignment to the **southern extreme moonrise** at minimum standstill within a margin of just 0.6 degrees. If the wall had been the "correct" symmetrical length no lunar alignment would have been possible.[49] A second such "error" facilitates an alignment with the **southern extreme moonset**, again at minimum standstill.[50]

A further alignment, in this case made possible by deviations in linearity, targets the **northern extreme moonset** at maximum standstill.

Clearly, therefore, High Bank and Newark have much in common and in some ways seem almost like twins. Why then, as we asked earlier, does the octagon of one of these "twins" enclose 50 acres while the octagon of the other encloses just 18 acres?

The answer offered by Hively and Horn is that not only does the 50-acre Newark octagon match the lunar extrema more closely than any other possible octagon, but also that it was designed to do so within the specific latitude band—measuring 44.5 kilometers from north to south—in which Newark is located.[51] In other words, the purpose of accurately aligning the earthwork to the lunar standstills would **not** have been served if the Newark octagon, like the circle, had been reproduced with an exact duplicate at High Bank more than 90 kilometers to the south.[52] The 18-acre figure with different vertex angles that we find at High Bank is perfectly suited to the task at High Bank's latitude.

Among other differences between the two sites, perhaps the most notable is that no alignment to any significant solar event, whether to the equinoxes, or to the solstices, or to the so-called cross-quarter days in between, has yet been satisfactorily identified at Newark in the earthworks themselves.[53]

But there's a context to this.

Recent research by Hively and Horn has raised the intriguing possibility that the very reason Newark's earthworks are where they are is that four prominent "high-elevation overlooks" in the surrounding landscape serve as natural front and back sights targeting sunrise and sunset on the winter and summer solstices.[54] It's unlikely to be an accident that the point of intersection of these natural alignments "lies in the central region of the earthworks and is equidistant (within 2 percent) from the centers of the Observatory Circle and the Great Circle."[55]

Just as with its latitude, therefore, though the matter cannot be proved, the choice of Newark's natural setting feels designed and deliberate.

Meanwhile, at High Bank, Hively and Horn's 1984 study not only confirmed key lunar alignments to southern extreme moonrise, southern extreme moonset, and northern extreme moonset, as we've seen, but also to the **northern extreme moonrise** and to the **southern extreme moonset**—both at maximum standstill. In addition, the **summer solstice sunrise** is targeted within 0.5 degrees by wall 1 → 2 while the alignment 13 → 2 targets the **winter solstice sunrise**[56]—the same familiar memes of cosmic mystery and geometric magic that manifest in earlier sites such as Serpent Mound and later sites such as Cahokia.

We've seen that these memes can be traced in the Amazon at least as far back as Painel do Pilão some 13,000 years ago.

Before Cahokia, before Newark and High Bank, before Serpent Mound, how far back can we follow their trail in North America?

THE POVERTY POINT
TIME MACHINE

DEAR READER, I DO NOT propose to take you on a tour of every mound and earthwork site in the United States, nor even of every mound or earthwork site I've visited personally. But if you were to rent a car in New Orleans and drive the 800 or so miles north through the Mississippi Valley as far as Cincinnati or a little farther, with time on your hands for some significant side trips east and west, you could plan an interesting journey. Despite the wanton destruction during the past 200 years, some outstanding sites have been saved in Louisiana,[1] Mississippi,[2] Alabama,[3] Tennessee,[4] Illinois,[5] and Ohio,[6] and there are also significant sites in Florida,[7] Georgia,[8] Texas,[9] Arkansas,[10] Kentucky,[11] and Indiana.[12] Other states have mounds and earthworks, too. But in antiquity the North American mound-building phenomenon was centered on the Mississippi River, and on its great Ohio and Missouri tributaries, and this is reflected in the distribution of the surviving sites today.

A number of different "mound-building cultures" have been identified by archaeologists, who have assembled them into categories based on period, location, types of pottery, types of tools, arts and crafts, and other criteria. We've already met some of the leading lights in this typology, such as the "Adena" (roughly 1000 BC to 200 BC), presently thought to have been the builders of Serpent Mound, the "Hopewell" (roughly 200 BC to AD 500), who were responsible for Newark and High Bank, and the "Mississippians" (roughly AD 800 to 1600), who built Cahokia.

Archaeologists make routine use of all these labels but also interpolate them with others that filter out of the classroom and into general consciousness, causing confusion all around. Thus, for example, you will not go far in learning about the mound-builders without encountering references to the Woodland Period, which is in turn divided into Early Woodland (1000 BC to 200 BC), Middle Woodland (200 BC to AD 600–800) and Late Woodland (AD 400 to AD 900–1000).[13] Allowing for some oversimplification of a complicated picture, the Adena culture built its mounds and earthworks during the Early Woodland period. The Hopewell culture built its mounds and earthworks during the Middle Woodland period. The Coles Creek culture was prominent during the Late Woodland period. The Late Woodland period in turn overlaps with the Early Mississippian period.

But these are no more than artificial constructs that help tidy-minded archaeologists preserve a sense of order and control over otherwise dangerously unruly data—and, besides, we must question how much the types of utensils and tools used by a culture actually tell us anything of value. We wouldn't expect to gather crucial information about modern cultures from their knives, forks, hammers, and screwdrivers, so why should we suddenly set different standards when we try to understand the ancient world?

Undoubtedly many different Native American cultures, speaking many different languages, were involved in the construction of the mounds. Undoubtedly their arts and crafts and tools and pottery differed. Undoubtedly they expressed themselves in many different ways. Yet when it came to their earthworks, for some mysterious reason, they all did the **same** things, in the **same** ways, repeatedly reiterating the **same** memes linking great geometrical complexes on the ground to events in the sky.

It represents a catastrophic loss of memory for our species, something akin to a madman smashing his own brains out, that there was such wholesale destruction of the Native American earthworks during the rapid growth of the United States in the nineteenth and twentieth centuries. To give credit where credit is due, it is entirely because of the excellent, dedicated, meticulous surgery of archaeologists that anything has been salvaged from the wreck at all—and as it turns out, quite a lot has been salvaged.

In consequence, whether we are viewing the handiwork of the Adena, such as Serpent Mound, or of the Hopewell, such as Newark and High Bank, or of the Mississippians, such as Cahokia, no sentient person can doubt the prodigious scale of this Native American achievement. There can be no doubt either that geometers and astronomers were in every case central to the enterprise. Nor is there doubt about when the enterprise came to an end—around AD 1600 in yet another catastrophic consequence of the European conquest of North America.

But when did it begin?

DEFYING EXPECTATIONS

I'M OUT NEAR THE WESTERN edge of Poverty Point, a very mysterious archaeological site in northeast Louisiana, climbing the second biggest earthwork mound in North America. Built around 1430 BC,[14] a century before the pharaoh Tutankhamun took the throne in ancient Egypt, it's often referred to as "Bird Mound," because of a supposed resemblance to a bird with outstretched wings flying east. Slumped and ruined in places, it does have something of that appearance today, particularly when viewed from the air, but an archaeological reconstruction of how the entire mound would have looked in antiquity does not support the bird interpretation. More prosaically and more usually, therefore, it's known simply as Mound A.

It reaches 72 feet in height.[15] Monks Mound at Cahokia, 500 miles to the north, is taller by 28 feet, and also more massive, but 2,500 years younger and the work of a settled agricultural civilization. Mound A, on the other hand, was made by hunter-gatherers,[16] as was the entire Poverty Point complex, where the oldest element of the site, Mound B, has been dated as early as 1740 BC.[17]

The sides of Mound A at its base measure 710 feet east to west and 660 feet north to south (as compared to 720 feet east to west and 910 feet north to south for Monks Mound). Mound A's volume is estimated at 8.4 million cubic feet, a number hard to visualize, but Diana Greenlee, station archaeologist at Poverty Point, offers a good analogy. "Take a standard American football field," she suggests, "and make it 146 feet tall. It's that much dirt."[18]

Some archaeologists still give credence to the notion that Mound A is an enormous bird effigy since "birds are important within the iconography of Native Americans past and present of the southeastern United States."[19] But not so long ago, just as was the case with Monks Mound, the experts felt they didn't need to invoke Native Americans, or indeed any human agency, to explain Mound A. It and Motley Mound (2 kilometers north of the Poverty Point complex) were judged to be:

Of natural origin, solitary outliers, the only ones for many miles in any direction, of the geological formations found in the bluffs to the east and the west of the Mississippi river; islands left by the drainage which cut the present river valley. Their appearance would easily deceive someone who was not somewhat familiar with such deposits.[20]

This confident piece of misinformation, put out in 1928 by respected archaeologist Gerard Fowke, was among a number of factors that delayed proper investigation and recognition of Poverty Point. And again, as happened at Monks Mound, when the amazing structure could no longer be shrugged off as natural there were still many who sought to deny Native Americans the credit for it, attributing it instead to some imaginary group of prehistoric Caucasian settlers who in the course of time were overrun by "savage" Native Americans.[21]

All archaeologists now agree that the half dozen mounds and other earthworks at Poverty Point are man-made. All agree likewise that Caucasian settlers (no matter how appealing the idea continues to prove with the general public) were NOT in any way involved, and that Native Americans made them. Such disputes and debates as did occur on the road to reaching these conclusions were more around the level of sophistication of the site, the amount of manpower thought necessary to build it, and the degree of socio-economic complexity that would have been required to see it through.

We'll not go into detail here, since we've seen already that the mainstream view for much of the nineteenth and twentieth centuries was that large-scale monumental constructions like Mound A at Poverty Point could only have been made by equally "large-scale, centralised and hierarchical societies" that had "the administrative means to carry out such achievements and to organise the large, settled populations whose labour is required."[22] Hunter-gatherers, the prevailing theory proclaimed, could never have generated sufficient surpluses, nor put the necessary hierarchical organization in place, to make such projects viable. Living from hand to mouth, their concerns were entirely focused on survival. Productive agricultural societies, by contrast, were wealthy enough to lift the burden of the daily struggle to survive from the shoulders of talented individuals, thus allowing a class of specialists—architects, surveyors, engineers, astronomers, and others—to emerge and to master their skills.

It was realized from the first archaeological surveys in the 1950s that Poverty Point was ancient, but it was not initially assumed to be **very** ancient. Hitherto the oldest mounds in America north of Mexico were thought to be Early Woodland (e.g., Adena) in origin, dating between 1000 BC and 200 BC—although clustered toward the latter end of that period. Two initial C-14 dates, explains Professor Jon L. Gibson of the University of Louisiana, "seemed to indicate that the Poverty Point mounds were not only contemporary with Early Woodland but overlapped the earliest part of the Middle Woodland Hopewellian mound-building period."[23] In consequence, "pushing the mounds back to the time of Poverty Point was not that drastic a conceptual jump."[24]

Indeed, despite being older than any other mounds previously encountered by archaeologists in North America, the evidence from Poverty Point was accepted with relative ease. That it was not the subject of the usual catfights and rival claims, Gibson suggests, was in part because of the general assumption of the profession in the 1950s and 1960s that "mound building, pottery, agriculture, sedentism, and large populations were . . . an integrated complex. . . . This all or nothing association . . . promoted the assumption of an agricultural base for Poverty Point despite the lack of direct evidence."[25]

Nor would direct evidence of agriculture ever be forthcoming, for, as subsequent excavations have proved, Poverty Point was not the work of agriculturalists, but of hunter-gatherers.[26] This was paradigm-busting in its way, but archaeologists do hate a busted paradigm, so some wriggle room was found. "Planned large-scale earthworks," commented *Science* magazine in 1997,

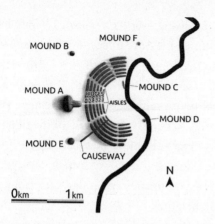

Schematic of Poverty Point indicating
principal mounds and geometric ridges.

"were previously considered to be beyond the leadership and organisational skills of seasonally mobile hunter-gatherers. Poverty Point was considered the exception, and its extensive trade was cited as evidence for sophisticated socio-economic organisation."[27]

The notion that trade rather than agriculture fostered a sufficiently complex and prosperous society to get the mounds built proved satisfactory to most archaeologists. The two younger ("Hopewellian") dates turned up in the initial excavations subsequently proved to be out of context. No one now disputes that the oldest structures at Poverty Point go back to around 1700 BC—fully 1,500 years earlier than the first Hopewell earthworks—that the site flourished for 600 years, and that it was abandoned and left deserted at around 1100 BC.[28]

THE WORLD'S LARGEST PREHISTORIC SOLSTICE MARKER?

THERE ARE SIX MOUNDS AT Poverty Point, labeled A, B, C, D, E, and F. Of these Mound B is the oldest, perhaps as old as 1740 BC, as we've seen. Mound F, where construction began sometime after 1280 BC,[29] is the youngest. And Mound D (also known as "Sarah's Mound") was not the work of the Poverty Point culture at all, but was a much later addition by the Coles Creek culture some time after AD 700.[30]

Thus it is the four mounds, A, B, C, and E, that form the key elevations of old Poverty Point. Mound A looms massively over all of them. Despite its huge presence, however, it is not the definitive feature of the site, and neither are any of the other mounds. That role is reserved for a complex earthwork consisting of a series of six concentric ridges, originally up to 9 feet high, forming together a gigantic geometrical figure resembling a half octagon or the letter C, with a diameter of ¾ of a mile. When the lengths of all the ridges are added together they total almost 7 miles.[31] The ridge crests are up to 100 feet wide, as are the ditches between the ridges, but they were much damaged by plowing in the nineteenth and twentieth centuries and today vary from a few inches to at the most about 6 feet in height.[32]

When archaeology began at Poverty Point in 1952, the ridges were so insignificant that they went unnoticed for about a year. The late William G. Haag, one of the original excavators, gave a candid account[33] of his reaction when he saw them for the first time in aerial photographs shown to him in 1953 by his colleague James Ford—who didn't initially reveal where the photographs had been taken:

"You know where that site is?" Ford asked.

"Well, it's got to be in the Ohio River Valley," Haag replied. "No place, except that area in the East where you get complex earthworks like that."

Simulation of Poverty Point's geometric ridge system in its prime.

Haag clearly had in mind the geometrical earthworks of Ohio, such as High Bank and Newark, reviewed in the last chapter, but he was in for a surprise.

"You've walked all over that site," said Ford.

"Not I," insisted Haag. "I've never been to that site."

But then doubt set in, he looked closer and finally exclaimed: "That's Poverty Point!"

Haag may have been a little slow in recognizing the ridges, but he was decades ahead of everyone else when he joined forces with astronomer Kenneth Brecher[34] in 1980 to coauthor a paper in the *Bulletin of the American Astronomical Society* titled "The Poverty Point Octagon: World's Largest Prehistoric Solstice Marker."[35]

Haag and Brecher supposed the ridges had once formed a complete octagon but that the eastern half had been "washed away." However:

The western half is intact and well-defined. It is intersected in four places by broad avenues, radiating out from a common center. . . . The west-northwest and west-southwest avenues have astronomical azimuths of approximately 299° and 241° respectively, accurately pointing to the summer and winter solstice sunset directions at the latitude of the site (32°37' N).[36]

Subsequent research proved Haag and Brecher wrong in their assumption that the Poverty Point ridges had originally formed an octagonal shape,[37] a matter that anyway has no bearing on their solstice thesis, which depends exclusively on the angles of the avenues in what survives of the figure today.

If they're right about this, then it would confirm a much deeper lineage for the astronomical and geometrical memes that we've followed back in time through the Mississippian and Hopewell and Adena earthworks.

MASTER PLAN

IN THE JANUARY 1983 ISSUE of *American Antiquity* the alignments along the avenues that Haag and Brecher had proposed were questioned by Robert

Purrington, an astronomer at Tulane University. He agreed that in the epoch of Poverty Point, "the sun would have set, at the solstices, at azimuths of 241° and 299°."[38] He disagreed, however, that these were the azimuths of the west-southwest and west-northwest avenues, which he put at 239 degrees and 290 degrees, respectively. He concluded that these avenues "very poorly mark the solstices. . . . There are no obvious solar alignments."[39]

Haag and Brecher responded in the same issue that the discrepancy between their azimuths and those of Purrington appeared "to arise mainly from the difference in the location of the center of the earthwork. "Purrington," they complained, "has located the viewing center at least 100 m to the east-northeast of the center we have found."[40] They repeated their assertion that "for the latitude of Poverty Point, the summer and winter solstice sunset azimuths are 241° and 299°, respectively, in good agreement with the orientatons of the southwest and northwest avenues. Such a solstitial alignment, while not surprising, seems hard to doubt in the Poverty Point earthwork."[41]

Purrington continued to *sound* like he doubted it, yet in a confusing and self-contradictory manner. In 1989 he published a paper in *Archaeoastronomy* titled "Poverty Point Revisited: Further Consideration of Astronomical Alignments."[42] In it he recalculated the azimuth of the west-southwest avenue from his previous figure of 239 degrees to a revised figure of 240 degrees that, he now stated, gave "an excellent match to the setting of the sun at the winter solstice (241°)."[43] His azimuth for the west-northwest avenue, however, remained the same as before at 290 degrees, thus missing "the summer solstice setting azimuth by as much as 9°" and therefore "almost certainly not intended to mark this solar standstill. The symmetry of the site then suggests that *neither* is a solar solstice alignment."[44] As a final equivocation, however, Purrington conceded that "a counter-argument would take into account the special importance attached to the winter solstice standstill by the native American Indians."[45]

There the matter rested until 2006, when archaeologists launched a magnetic gradiometer survey at Poverty Point. Completed in 2011, the survey revealed the traces of no fewer than thirty great circles of wooden posts that had once stood in the plaza east of the geometric ridges, "some built only inches away from the previous ones, as if the posts were erected, removed sometime later, moved a slight distance, then rebuilt."[46]

According to archaeologist Diana Greenlee, who was closely involved in all aspects of the investigation, the postholes located were straight-sided and flat-bottomed, nearly 1 meter wide and 2 meters deep, while the circles they formed varied in diameter from 6 meters to 60 meters.[47] Unfortunately, though, as Greenlee concedes, the project was confined almost exclusively to remote sensing:

> We didn't excavate a complete circle, or even a significant arc of one. So there is a lot we don't know about the circles. We don't know how many different kinds of post circles are represented. We don't know how high the posts were. We don't know if there were walls between the posts. We don't know if they had roofs. We don't know what, if anything, they did inside the circles. We don't know how many post circles were visible in the plaza at any one time. Someday I hope to excavate a larger area of the plaza circles so that we can find answers to these questions.[48]

One possibility, surely worthy of further investigation, is that what the survey found were the archaeological fingerprints of a series of "woodhenges" at Poverty Point. Very much like the Woodhenge at Cahokia—also constantly moved and adjusted, as we saw in chapter 18—they were perhaps used in conjunction with other features to create sight lines that would manifest sky-ground hierophanies at the solstices and equinoxes.

At any rate, even without the circles, the case for significant solar alignments at Poverty Point was greatly strengthened when Ohio archaeologist and archaeoastronomer William Romain, one of the sharpest thinkers in this field, rolled up his sleeves and got involved. His paper on the subject, coauthored with Norman L. Davis and published in *Louisiana Archaeology* in 2011, used newly acquired Lidar data, and refined archaeoastronomical calculations, to conclude that "Brecher and Haag were right in their assessment more than thirty years ago—i.e. Poverty Point does incorporate solstice alignments . . . [and] may indeed be the world's largest solstice marker."[49]

The alignments, however, turn out not to be those that Brecher and Haag originally proposed. Instead, with the advantage of the new data, Romain and Davis were able to identify two locations "of special importance in the design of Poverty Point." Referring to these locations as Design Point 1 (DP1) and Design Point 2 (DP2) they note:

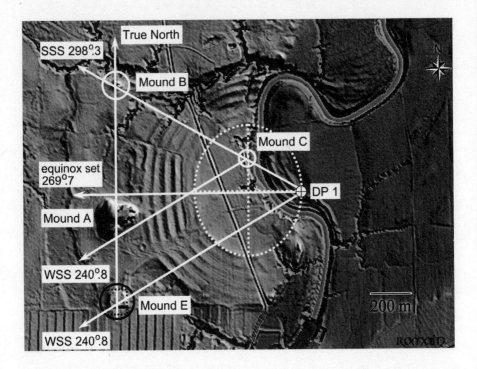

> Line DP1 to Mound B is aligned to the summer solstice sunset.

> Line DP1 to Mound E is aligned to the winter solstice sunset.

> Viewed from Mound C, the summer solstice sun will set over Mound B.

> Viewed from Mound C, the winter solstice sun will appear to set not over but rather into the side of Mound A. The placement of Mound C . . . allowed for a long sight line to Mound A, but also resulted in the location for Mound A in a place that seems not-symmetrical with the overall site plan.

> A line from DP1 through the central plaza of the site marks the azimuth of the equinox sunset along the northern edge of Mound A.[50]

According to Davis, an eyewitness to the latter phenomenon, the sun appears to "roll down the northern edge of Mound A before sinking into the western horizon."[51]

Together with the monkey and spider figures
(see chapter 15), the hummingbird is another of
the geoglyphs of the Nazca plateau that represents
Amazonian species. PHOTO: SANTHA FAIIA.

The geometric theme of Nazca is expressed not only in pure geometrical figures (lower left and right) but also in effigies such as the "Condor" (top). PHOTOS: SANTHA FAIIA.

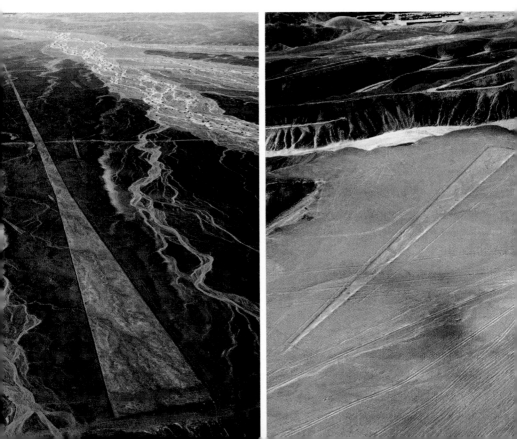

The English megalithic sites of Stonehenge (above) and Avebury (below) combining sacred geometry, earthworks, and stone circles. PHOTOS: SANTHA FAIIA.

ABOVE: The Great Pyramid of Egypt with the Pyramid of Khafra to its left, both perfectly oriented to the cardinal directions. PHOTO: SANTHA FAIIA.
BELOW: The Amazonian earthwork site of Fazenda Parana with its principal square also perfectly oriented to the cardinal directions. PHOTO: MARTTI PÄRSSINEN.

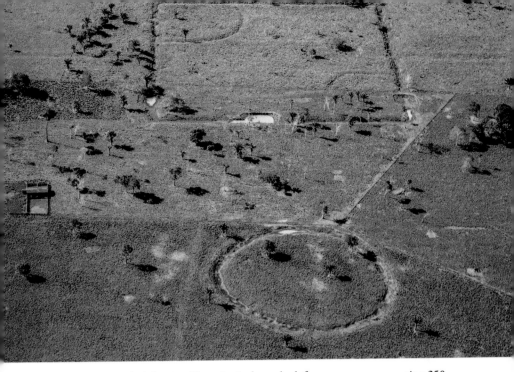

ABOVE: Fazenda Atlantica. The principal geoglyph forms a square measuring 250 meters along each side and is oriented northwest to southeast—an alignment that makes it a candidate for alignment to the setting sun on the June solstice and the rising sun on the December solstice. As yet no archaeoastronomical survey has been carried out on the Amazonian geoglyphs. BELOW: The Amazonian geoglyphs frequently combine two or more geometrical forms. Here, at Fazenda Cipoal, a square inscribed within an octagon with rounded corners. PHOTOS: MARTTI PÄRSSINEN.

ABOVE: The colossal Amazonian geoglyph of Tequinho once extended over an area of 15 hectares (37 acres). What remains today are its two principal squares, the larger measuring 210-by-210 meters (with two further squares inter-nested within it) and the smaller, which has suffered extensive damage, measuring 130-by-130 meters and enclosing one further square. Defining the ruling northwest axis of the site, the main entrance to the larger square is 40 meters wide and opens onto a causeway 1.5 kilometers long. BELOW: The principal geoglyph of Jacó Sá earthwork complex, here seen in context, intriguingly "squares the circle," as discussed in chapter 15. PHOTOS: MARTTI PÄRSSINEN.

ABOVE: As well as its spectacular geometrical earthworks, the Amazon is home to an unknown number of megalithic sites, such as the great stone circle of Rego Grande, shown here and discussed in chapter 16. PHOTO: MARIANA CABRAL.
BELOW: Paired circle geoglyph at Ramal do Capatará, western Amazon.
PHOTO: RICARDO AZOURY/PULSAR IMAGENS.

The complex arrangement of geoglyphs at Fazenda Colorada includes a large open square that may have been connected to ancient Amazonian beliefs about the mystery of death and the afterlife journey of the soul. See discussion in chapter 17. PHOTO: MARTTI PÄRSSINEN.

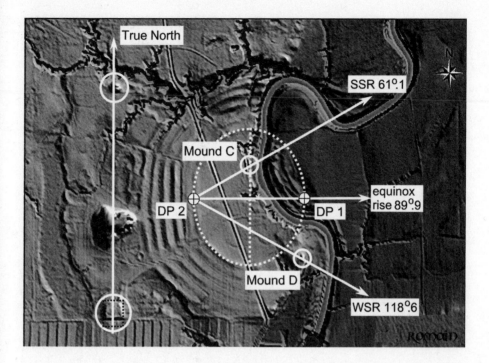

Poverty Point is "a center place," Romain and Davis assert, "and also a place of balance in the sense that, in addition to the sunset alignments . . . conceptually opposite sunrise alignments are also found."[52] These they detail as follows:

> ❯ Viewed from DP2, the summer solstice sun will rise over Mound C.

> ❯ Viewed from DP2, the winter solstice sun will rise over Mound D. If in fact Mound D was constructed more than 2,000 years after the Poverty Point florescence, then the implication is that the people of the Coles Creek culture understood, incorporated, and further expanded upon the Poverty Point design for their own purposes.

> ❯ Viewed from DP2, the equinox sun will rise in alignment with DP1.[53]

The overall achievement—the "seamless integration of site orientation, celestial alignments, bilateral symmetry of design points, internal geometry

[and] regularities in mensuration"[54]—leads Romain and Davis to conclude that "Poverty Point was built according to a preconceived master plan . . . or design template . . . that integrated astronomical alignments, geometric shapes and local topography."[55]

In their view, the question that begs to be answered is, "Why? Why was Poverty Point designed in such a way that it connects geometric earthen forms to celestial bodies and events at such a massive scale?"[56]

It's an excellent question, but another should be asked first.

If there was a "preconceived master plan," where did it come from?

CONTINUITY

THE SOUTHERNMOST OF THE POVERTY Point mounds is Mound E, also known as "Ballcourt Mound." Just 2.6 kilometers farther south, however, is another mound, once thought to have been part of the Poverty Point complex. Known as Lower Jackson Mound, excavations by archaeologists Joe Saunders and Thurman Allen have established that it is in fact extremely ancient—not from the Poverty Point era around 1700 BC at all, but from fully 3,000 years earlier, specifically between 3955 and 3655 BC.[57]

"That Poverty Point builders were aware of ancient mounds is beyond doubt," comments John Clark, professor of anthropology at Brigham Young University:

The entire layout of Greater Poverty Point is calibrated to the position of Lower Jackson, a Middle Archaic mound. All principal measuring grids pass through Lower Jackson, and calculated space appears to have commenced from there.[58]

What Jon L. Gibson of the University of Louisiana makes of the same evidence is that there must have been "an enduring traditional, if not direct ancestral, connection between the Old People and later groups."[59] This connection, he argues, is "demonstrated by the incorporation of the Middle Archaic Lower Jackson Mound into the principal earthwork axis at Poverty Point. Actually, Lower Jackson Mound was not merely incorporated—it fur-

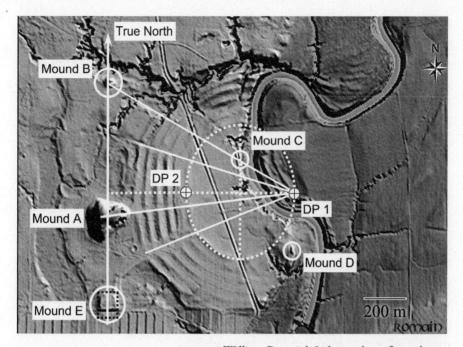

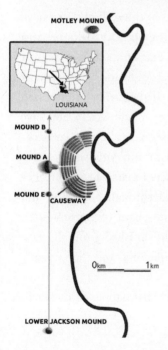

ABOVE: William Romain's Lidar work confirms that Mound E ("Ballcourt Mound"), Mound A, and Mound B are all aligned to true north. LEFT: Lower Jackson Mound, 3,000 years older, is on the same azimuth.

nished the alpha datum, the anchor, a vivid case of material or implicit memory."[60]

The suggestions, made by Clark in 2004 and Gibson in 2006, were followed up in 2011 by William Romain. The results of his Lidar survey greatly strengthen the case that "Poverty Point was intentionally oriented to true north" along "the sightline between Mounds E-A-B and the Lower Jackson Mound."[61]

The implications of a connection between the Lower Jackson mound-builders and their successors at Poverty Point are intriguing for many reasons.

The "intrusive" Mound D, built by the Coles Creek culture at least 1,800 years after

Poverty Point was abandoned, and more than 2,000 years after works peaked there, appears to have been deliberately located to create an alignment to the winter solstice sunrise. In William Romain's view, as we've seen, this suggests that the people of the Coles Creek culture "understood, incorporated, and further expanded upon the Poverty Point design."

The suggestion, therefore, is that below the radar of archaeology more than 2 millennia of continuously transmitted knowledge connected the Coles Creek culture to the Poverty Point culture.

Now, going much further back in time, Gibson proposes continuity across the earlier 2,000-year gap between the builders of Lower Jackson Mound and Poverty Point.

These are long periods of time to maintain any kind of connection, but such a feat is by no means impossible. The Judaic faith, for example, carries down a body of traditions and beliefs that are at least 3,000 years old.[62] Hinduism has roots going back to the Indus Valley civilization more than 5,000 years ago.[63] Both religions also create architecture, the design of which is directly influenced by their beliefs and traditions.

There's no reason in principle why the same sort of thing should not have happened in North America. The notion that Lower Jackson Mound and Poverty Point are each manifestations in different eras of a single system of ideas is the only way, other than coincidence, to account for the obviously deliberate axial relationship between the two sites. If the earlier mound had **not** been significant for the later builders, then they surely would not have used it to "anchor" the great enterprise on which they were about to embark.

But there's a problem. In the cases of Hinduism and Judaism we have unimpeachable evidence of continuity. Through sacred texts, through teachings passed from one generation to the next, and through cherished and vibrant traditions, there are no broken links in the chain of transmission. Neither Hinduism nor Judaism have ever abruptly vanished from the face of the earth, left zero traces of their presence for millennia, and then equally abruptly reappeared in full flower.

As we'll see, however, this appears to be exactly what happened in North America.

21

GLIMPSES BEHIND THE VEIL

THE REMOTE EPOCH BETWEEN 6,000 AND 5,000 years ago out of which Lower Jackson Mound emerges is an important one in the story of civilization. It was toward the end of this same millennium that the civilizations of ancient Mesopotamia and ancient Egypt took their first confident steps on the stage of history. They, too, built mounds—for example, Egypt's predynastic *mastabas* or the *tells* of Uruk-period Mesopotamia. They, too, deployed geometry and astronomical alignments in the project of sacralizing architectural spaces. And they, too, participated in an extraordinary and seemingly coordinated burst of early construction—for just like the mounds of ancient Egypt and ancient Mesopotamia, Lower Jackson Mound is not an isolated case but part of what may once have been a very numerous and widespread group of monuments.

Just how numerous and widespread we may never hope to know because of the wholesale destruction of thousands of mounds and earthworks across North America in recent centuries. No doubt most of those ancient monuments, sacrificed to the modern gods of agriculture and industry, were from the more recent periods—Mississippian, Hopewell, and so on—but chances are that some, and perhaps many, were from the much earlier episode of mound- building dating back to 5,000 years ago and more.

From what remains we can begin to gauge the extent of the loss and by 2012, despite the destruction of ancient sites, archaeologists had identified as many as 97 surviving mounds and earthworks in the Lower Mississippi Valley, with several others found as far afield as Florida, thought to be in the range of 5,000 years old.[1] Very few of these sites have yet been subject to radiometric dating, but of the 16 that have, with a combined total of 53 mounds and 13 causeways, all are more than 4,700 years old[2]—and many are much older than that.

As a result, says Joe Saunders, a leading specialist in this field, "the existence of Middle Archaic mound-building is no longer questioned."[3]

Why there should be such a concentration of these archaic sites in the Lower Mississippi Valley is unclear. It could be an accident of history—that is, purely by chance more old sites survived destruction in this area than elsewhere. Or it could be that many more sites were built here in antiquity than elsewhere and this is why more have survived. Who knows? Perhaps future research will reveal very ancient mounds much farther afield in North America. For the present, however, the Lower Mississippi Valley is where the action is.

It's unnecessary to describe every site. Indeed only one, Watson Brake, need concern us in any detail. For the rest, the map and the minimal listing below, substantiated by references for readers who wish to dig deeper, will serve the purpose.

The **Banana Bayou Mounds** and the so-called **LSU Mounds** (because they are on the grounds of Louisiana State University) date to around 2700 BC,[4] which, in a global context, makes them about 200 years older than the Great Pyramid of Giza.

After that, the mounds of the Lower Mississippi Valley just keep on getting older. We've already spoken of **Lower Jackson Mound** (3955 to 3655 BC). Here are some of the others:

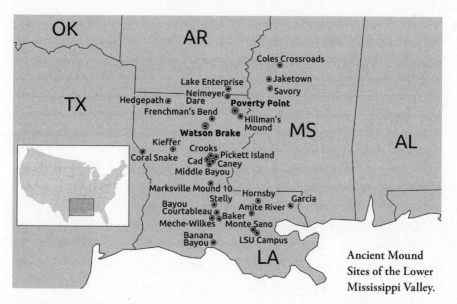

Ancient Mound Sites of the Lower Mississippi Valley.

WATSON BRAKE

One C-14 date suggests that mound-building may have begun as early as 3590 BC; others suggest a range of 3400 to 3300 BC.[5]

CANEY MOUNDS

C-14 dates range from 3600 to 3000 BC.[6]

FRENCHMAN'S BEND

C-14 supports a date of 3570 BC.[7] A significantly older date of 4610 BC—almost 7,000 years ago—was derived from an excavated hearth.[8]

HEDGEPETH MOUNDS

The earliest mound date is 4930 BC—again, very close to 7,000 years ago.[9]

MONTE SANO

A charcoal sample from a cremation platform within one of the mounds yielded a date of 4240 BC.[10] Two other charcoal samples from a small platform mound produced dates of 5030 to 5500 BC[11]—moving past 7,000 years ago and toward 7,500 years ago.

CONLY

Eight radiocarbon dates securely locate the site between 7,500 and 8,000 years ago.[12]

THE SITE THAT CHANGED THE GAME

BOTH IN TERMS OF QUANTITY and of quality, Watson Brake has been the subject of more thorough, sustained, and wide-ranging scientific scrutiny than any of the other sites that are 5,000 years old or older. Moreover, it is only at Watson Brake that the excavations and archaeological research have been accompanied by detailed archaeoastronomical assessments, allowing comparison with the later Adena, Hopewellian, and Missippian sites reviewed in previous chapters.

So it is Watson Brake we'll focus on here.

First, and it is good the reader should harbor no illusions in this regard, not a single item has been excavated at Watson Brake that in any way suggests the presence of an advanced material culture. The people who built the mounds and lived at the site intermittently—or perhaps more permanently—over a period of many hundreds of years used stone tools and points that are typical of the Middle Archaic period. They were hunter-gatherers, not agriculturalists, and although they did gather plants that would later be domesticated, they did not domesticate these plants themselves. In other words, they lived simply, close to the earth, and were in every way a normal and representative population for this part of North America 5,000 or 6,000 years ago.[13]

In every way, that is, except one.

They built mounds.

Referring to the sites listed above (and a handful of others I didn't list), Joe Saunders writes:

> The earliest . . . earthworks in the Lower Mississippi Valley appear to have been made by autonomous societies. Practically speaking, it is difficult for 16 Middle Archaic mound sites spanning 1,000 years of prehistory in three subregions of Louisiana . . . not to look autonomous.
>
> But there must have been some communion among the autonomous societies because there are too many shared traits that cross the vast expanses of the Lower Mississippi Valley, and there is no evidence of other monuments being made elsewhere. If all Middle Archaic mound sites were spontaneous creations, would they not occur spontaneously elsewhere as well?[14]

Sadly, Saunders passed away on September 4, 2017. Formerly regional archaeologist and professor of geosciences at the University of Louisiana, he was the acknowledged expert on Watson Brake and its lead excavator. It was his paper, "A Mound Complex in Louisiana at 5400–5000 Years Before the Present," published in *Science* on September 19, 1997,[15] that effectively put Watson Brake on the map, preempting arguments that might otherwise have arisen around the dates of the site with a meticulous, comprehensive, and wide-ranging body of evidence.

"There's just no question about it," said Jon Gibson at the time. "Saunders has come at it from too many different angles."[16]

And Vincas Steponaitis of the University of North Carolina commented: "It's rare that archaeologists ever find something that so totally changes our picture of what happened in the past, as is true for this case."[17]

Certainly Watson Brake did change the picture archaeologists had of the past, delivering the death blow to the tired old prejudice, already mortally wounded by Poverty Point, that hunter-gatherer societies were somehow constitutionally incapable of complex large-scale constructions.

And as it turns out, despite its low-maintenance material culture, the site itself is sophisticated and precociously clever.

SACRED OVAL

LIKE SERPENT MOUND, WATSON BRAKE was built on a natural elevation, in this case a terrace dating back to the depths of the Ice Age overlooking the 12,000-year-old floodplain of the Ouachita River with its tributary stream the Watson Bayou.[18] And in just the way that Serpent Mound stands above Brush Creek, Watson Brake stands above Watson Bayou,[19] creating the illusion that the mounds are 5 or 10 meters higher than they actually are.[20]

In the case of Serpent Mound, in front of the effigy's gaping jaws, the reader will recall the presence of an earthwork enclosure in the form of a great oval. Although complicated by the integration of mounds into the figure, and on a much larger scale, Watson Brake is also an earthwork enclosure forming a distinct and unmistakable oval, with a long axis of 370 meters and a short axis of 280 meters.[21]

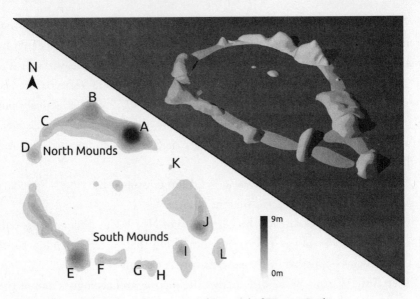

LEFT: Watson Brake site plan. RIGHT: 3D model of Watson Brake.

There is some disagreement as to whether the total number of mounds at Watson Brake should be counted as eleven or twelve because one, designated Mound L, requires further archaeological verification. It also lies outside the border of the oval formation so firmly demarcated by the other eleven mounds and their interconnecting embankments—these latter being in the range of 20 meters wide and about 1 meter high.[22] The plaza contained within the embankments covers an area of 9 hectares (about 22 acres)[23] and appears to have been artificially leveled.[24] The excavators found it to be almost completely sterile of artifacts or debris, "suggesting its use as ritual space."[25]

"Apparently daily activities did not occur in the enclosure," comments Saunders.[26] By contrast, however, "daily activities," suggestive of resident populations, certainly did occur on the wide embankments surrounding the enclosure, particularly on the northeastern side.[27]

In a major study published in *American Antiquity* in 2005 Saunders reports that the initial occupation of the site took place as early as 4000 BC[28] and that:

The first occupants came to Watson Brake to fish, hunt deer and gather plants in every season of the year. Prolonged visits probably occurred. . . . The construction of the first minor earthworks began around 3500 BC, with Mounds K and B (and possibly A) followed by midden accumulations where Mounds D and C, and to the south I and J, and E were subsequently built. This suggests that the shape of the complex was deliberately laid out by 3500 BC. Major building projects then commenced ca. 3350 BC and existing earthworks may have been heightened and extended along the north mound row. Mound J was erected on the south side at around 3000 BC. Site occupation was concentrated along the terrace escarpment before construction began and continued after the earthworks were completed.[29]

The relative "residential stability and autonomy" evidenced at Watson Brake, Saunders concludes, were made possible by "the diversity and abundance of resources" in the local area.[30]

It seems almost superfluous to state, however, that those resources and the stability they promoted could have been exploited efficiently **without** the mounds. Indeed they **were** exploited for the 500 years when humans were present at the site who built no mounds at all between 4000 BC and 3500 BC.

And then, suddenly . . . mounds.

Why? What could have prompted this colossal architectural enterprise? What was its purpose?

"I know it sounds pretty Zenlike," Saunders speculated when he was asked this question in 1997, "but maybe the answer is that building them was the purpose."[31]

TRIANGULATION

MAYBE. BUT I'M TRYING TO envisage how the community leaders or influencers would have sold that to the population. Somehow, "We want you to build these mounds because building them will be a good thing for you to do" doesn't sound like a winning line to me. And when we remember that in the same period mounds and earthworks were also being built at other scattered sites belonging to separate, autonomous communities across the Lower

Mississipi Valley, it becomes increasingly obvious that a powerful and far-reaching social phenomenon must have been at work.

After years of field research, excavations, and on-site measurements, Kenneth Sassman of the Laboratory of Southeastern Archaeology, and Michael Heckenberger of the University of Florida are convinced that at least three of these sites—Watson Brake, Caney Mounds, and Frenchman's Bend—share the same basic design:[32]

> The plan we infer from the spatial arrangement of Archaic mounds consists of a series of proportional and geometric regularities, including (1) a "terrace" line of three or more earthen mounds oriented along an alluvial terrace escarpment; (2) placement of the largest mound of each complex in the terrace-edge group, typically in a central position; (3) placement of the second-largest mound at a distance roughly 1.4 times that between members of the terrace-edge group; (4) a line connecting the largest and second-largest . . . mound (herein referred to as the "baseline") set at an angle that deviates roughly 10 degrees from a line orthogonal to [i.e., at right angles to] the terrace line; and (5) an equilateral triangle oriented to the baseline that intercepts other mounds of the complex and appears to have formed a basic unit of proportionality.[33]

I won't attempt to describe Frenchman's Bend or the several other sites that Sassman and Heckenberger believe may also fit this pattern.[34] Watson Brake and Caney can stand for them all. Again a long story must be cut short since these two sites tick all the boxes listed above, but perhaps the most striking outcome of Sassman and Heckenberger's study is the clear evidence they've produced for a shared geometrical plan involving the mounds designated A, E, I, and J at Watson Brake and mounds B, F, E, and D at Caney.

In both cases the line that Sassman and Heckenberger call the "baseline" between the largest and second-largest mounds (A and E at Watson Brake; B and F at Caney) forms one side of an equilateral triangle. In both cases the lines that form the other two sides of the triangle extend through a second pair of mounds (I and J at Watson Brake; E and D at Caney) before intersecting. And in both cases a line emanating from the "baseline" evenly bisects the gap between a second pair of mounds (B and K at Watson Brake; A and C at Caney).[35]

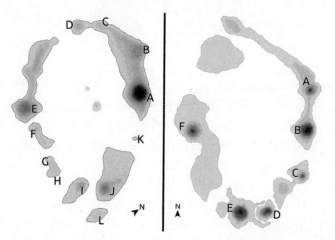

A comparison of the overall layout, design, and orientation of Watson Brake (left) and Caney Mounds (right).

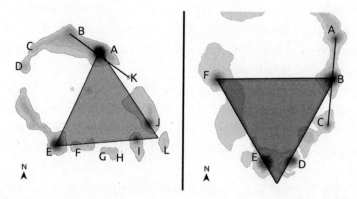

Evidence for a shared geometrical system at Watson Brake (left) and Caney Mounds (right).

All equilateral triangles have internal angles of 60 degrees, but why, asks Norman Davis in a review of Sassman and Heckenberger's findings, "did Middle Archaic Builders use a 60° triangle? Why not a 45°, or a 65 or a 75° triangle?"[36]

The answer to this question, he suggests, has everything to do with the sun:

It is probably not a coincidence that at Watson Brake the distance along the horizon from where the sun rises (or sets) on the winter solstice to where it rises (or sets) on the summer solstice defines an arc of 59 degrees. . . . Their triangle was probably derived from [this].[37]

THE DIRECTORS

AS AT SERPENT MOUND, AS at Cahokia, as at Newark, as at High Bank, and as at Poverty Point, the primary concern of the designers of Watson Brake seems to have been to manifest, memorialize, and consummate the marriage of heaven and earth at key moments of the year. This notion of sky/ground communion—summarized in the Old World in the Hermetic dictum "as above so below" but part of a universally distributed package of astronomical and geometrical memes—can involve the moon and the earth, specific stars or constellations and the earth, other planets and the earth, the Milky Way and the earth, and the sun and the earth.

At Watson Brake, it's the sun and the earth that take center stage, as Norman Davis ably demonstrated in 2012 across 18 pages of the journal *Louisiana Archaeology*.[38] The principal assertions concerning solstitial and equinoctial alignments that he makes there have stood the test of time and won the support of leading archaeoastronomers.[39]

In brief, Davis includes the twelve recognized mounds, A through L, in his survey but he also takes note of two natural mounds "possibly modified"[40] that in his view were intentionally left near the center of the oval in antiquity when the rest of the plaza was artificially leveled. These he designates Mounds 1 and 2.

Among his key findings the most immediately striking is that no fewer than five separate alignments running through the site each independently and redundantly target the summer solstice sunset. "Even if the alignments were not to the sun," Davis writes, "the ability to establish five perfectly parallel, nearly equidistant sightlines across several hundred meters would be remarkable. The sightlines had to have preceded construction. Their pattern suggests a master site plan, with construction to the plan taking years, or perhaps centuries, to complete."[41]

Impressively, the alignments target the sun not exactly where it rises and sets today but rather precisely where it would have risen and where it would have set in the epoch of 3400 BC—which, at the latitude of Watson Brake, was at azimuth 119 degrees for the winter solstice sunrise and at azimuth 299 degrees for the summer solstice sunset.[42] As the reader will recall, solstice alignments are reciprocal. If you are facing the setting sun on the summer

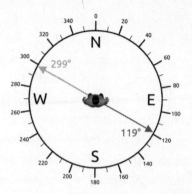

The "azimuth" of an object is its distance from true north in degrees counting clockwise. North is nominated as 0 degrees, so azimuth 90 degrees is due east, azimuth 180 degrees is due south, and azimuth 270 degrees is due west. An azimuth of 299 degrees will therefore be 29 degrees north of west. An azimuth of 119 degrees is 29 degrees south of east.

solstice, then 6 months later on the winter solstice the sun will rise in the exact opposite direction, 180 degrees around the "dial" of the "azimuth clock."

There are no alignments to the **summer solstice sunrise** or to the **winter solstice sunset** at Watson Brake. But the clear alignments to the **summer solstice sunset** (azimuth 299 degrees) and the **winter solstice sunrise** (azimuth 119 degrees) identified by Davis are as follows:

>   From Mound A to Mound B.

>   From Mound J to Mound 2.

>   From Mound D to Mound L.

>   From Mound I to the southern edge of Mound D.

>   From Mound E to the outside edge of the double bulge on the Mound E platform.[43]

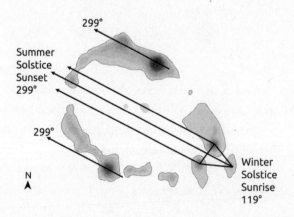

"The Mound J to Mound 2 sightline," Davis adds, "continues on and passes through the center of the gap between Mounds C and D. The Mound D to Mound L sightline passes through the center of the gap between Mounds I and J. The sightlines have azimuths of 119 degrees and 299 degrees."[44]

Could Watson Brake's multiple alignments to the summer solstice sunset and the winter solstice sunrise have come about by chance? It already seems vanishingly unlikely, but what settles the matter is that the site's concerns turn out to be not only with the solstices but also with the spring and autumn equinoxes—those special times of balance around March 21 and September 21 when night and day are of equal length and the sun rises perfectly due east and sets perfectly due west. Davis has identified four equinoctial alignments at Watson Brake, as follows:

> From Mound A to Mound C.

> From Mound 1 to Mound 2.

> From Mound E to Mound F.

> From Mound G to Mound H.[45]

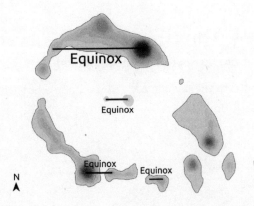

In addition, several of these equinox sight lines, notably Mounds E–F and mounds G–H, extend to other mounds and features of the earthwork in such a way, Davis notes, that their east to west alignment "had to have preceded construction. This suggests that equinox alignments were . . . used to engineer this site."[46]

And not only the equinox alignments.

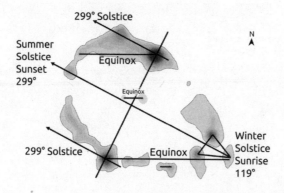

The length of the Watson Brake earthworks is defined by the alignment to the summer solstice sunset of the two ends of its principal axis, Mound L in the southeast and Mound D in the northwest. Its breadth is defined on one side by the Mound E to Mound E-platform alignment, and on the other by the Mound A to Mound B alignment, both also solstitial.[47]

All in all, Davis makes a strong case that the entire design of the site is an artifact of its solstitial and equinoctial alignments. They came first; everything else followed. The question that remains unanswered, however, is . . . why? Davis sidesteps it, stating that his purpose is only "to demonstrate that solstice and equinox alignments are present at Watson Brake."[48] There's no doubt he has succeeded in this enterprise, as his findings regarding the

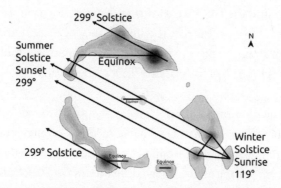

Joining earth to sky. All equinox and solstice sight lines at Watson Brake.

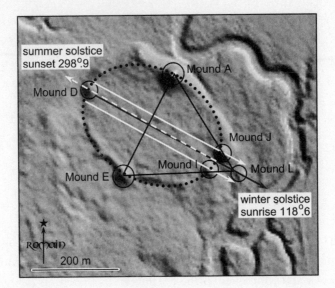

summer solstice
sunset 298°.9

Mound A

Mound D

Mound J

Mound E

Mound I

Mound L

winter solstice
sunrise 118°.6

Romain

200 m

Lidar confirmation and refinement of the solstitial alignments in the Davis survey
by William Romain.

site's solstice alignments have subsequently been confirmed at a higher level of
technical precision in a Lidar survey by archaeoastronomer William Romain.

Building on the discoveries made by Davis, Romain's conclusions are
striking:

> Watson Brake incorporates sophisticated geometric designs tied to
> astronomical sightlines in multiple ways. As someone who has worked
> mostly in the field of Hopewell archaeology, I am still trying to wrap
> my head around the fact that all this anticipates Adena and Hopewell
> by thousands of years. Indeed, the significance of these findings is
> that Watson Brake appears to be the earliest-known celestially-aligned
> mound complex in North America. That's a big deal.[49]

The fact that it's a big deal only makes the unanswered "why" question
more urgent, but Davis admits he's unable to think of any "practical reason
why the site should have been designed and engineered around solar sightlines. In fact it must have added to the difficulty of construction."[50]

The logical conclusion, he suggests, is that "using solar azimuths to design
and build Watson Brake may have had more to do with cosmology [beliefs

about the origin and nature of the universe] than astronomy [the scientific study of the heavens]."[51]

None of the other Middle Archaic sites have yet had the benefit of the sort of thorough archaeoastronomical survey that Davis, and subsequently Romain, have been able to carry out at Watson Break. However, Davis estimates from map analysis, within a margin of error of plus or minus 2 percent, that the Caney Mounds site has "one equinox alignment and two summer and winter solstice alignments. Frenchman's Bend has one equinox alignment and one winter solstice alignment."[52]

The mystery, although the sites so far investigated "show no evidence for the development of astronomical knowledge over time,"[53] is that "the people who directed the construction of Watson Brake . . . had an advanced knowledge of the solar and probably lunar cycles, and they used this knowledge to design and engineer their sites. Who were these directors, and how did they get others to build the sites one container of earth at a time?"[54]

REINCARNATIONS

OTHER QUESTIONS SHOULD BE ASKED.

How were these "directors" able to manifest geometrical and astronomical knowledge, and advanced combinations of the two, more than 5,000 years ago when no prior evidence of the existence of such abilities has been found in North America at such an early date? Set aside for a moment the issue of the organizational competence necessary to motivate and manage the workforce. The bigger problem is that the scientific skills and the knowledge required to create the earthworks just seem to appear out of nowhere, with no evolution and no buildup.

One minute they're not there. The next, almost magically, they are. And then, at once, the Middle Archaic mound-building phenomenon bursts into full bloom.

We know it starts earlier, but for convenience let's take the florescence of Watson Brake around 3400 BC as a benchmark.

What follows, there and at the other sites, is roughly 700 years of stability, continuity, and—we must assume given the similarities—communications and connections. As noted earlier, these were all different cultures, but they all shared the same mound-building obsession and continued to express it in the same ways.

Until sometime around 2700 BC.

That was when, for some unexplained reason, the ancient sites were all abandoned and the whole mound-building enterprise came to an abrupt and complete halt. I'll let Joe Saunders, the acknowledged expert on the subject, take up the story of the mysterious end of Middle Archaic mound-building:

> New radiometric data indicate a sudden and widespread cessation of mound building in northeast Louisiana. The clustering of the ten youngest dates from seven mounds at four sites is remarkable. The median probability for seven of the ten samples falls between 2884 BC and 2739 BC. Equally remarkable is that the cessation of mound construction may have lasted up to 1,000 years, or until the emergence of the Poverty Point culture. . . . To date, not one mound site dating to the Late Archaic (2700 BC to 1700 BC) has been identified in the Lower Mississippi Valley.[55]

Saunders declines to speculate in any depth about the reasons for this precipitous end to the precocious early mound-building phenomenon in North America. He's open to the possibility, suggested by some, that climate change might have been involved, but states his own view that "the 'synchronous' event may be better understood as a social phenomenon. The abandonment of an ideology or change in ethos can occur simultaneously within a diverse range of environments. Also the absence of environmental change would be consistent with the documented continuity in economy from Early to Late Archaic periods—before, during, and after mound building."[56]

Whatever the reason, the facts are not in doubt. Mound-building, with all its sophisticated geometry and astronomy, stopped dead in its tracks around 2700 BC. For the next thousand years not a single mound was built and not a single earthwork was raised. There's not a hint of geometry or of monumental architecture. The only reasonable conclusion is that those skills had been utterly lost.

But then, as suddenly and mysteriously as the "mound-building movement" had vanished, it appeared again, at around 1700 BC, in the spectacular and sophisticated form of Poverty Point.[57] All the old geometrical and astronomical skills were redeployed there—and by practiced hands—as though they'd been in regular use all along.

Poverty Point thrived for the next 600 or so years, only to be abandoned in its turn at around 1100 BC. Then it seems that mound-building was interrupted again until relatively late in the development of the culture archaeologists call the Adena. The label "Adena" is in fact the name of the country estate in Ohio on which the "typesite" was found.[58] We have no idea what that culture called itself. Its origins can be traced back to around 1000 BC.[59] However, no early Adena mounds exist and those that have been dated, such as the Adena Mound typesite,[60] cluster around 200 BC or, in the case of Serpent Mound, 300 BC,[61] but not significantly earlier.[62]

It looks very much as if there was another hiatus, perhaps not of 1,000 years—let's say 800 years—between the end of Poverty Point and the rebirth of the mound-builder movement late in the Adena period. Thereafter it grew again to full force in its Hopewell and later Mississippian manifestations until finally being brought to an end by the European conquest.

Despite the fact that different cultures were involved at different periods, every resurgence of mound-building was linked to the reiteration and reimagination of the same geometrical and astronomical memes.

This was not "chance" or "coincidence."

Witness, for example, the way that Lower Jackson Mound was used as the base datum from which the entire geometry of Poverty Point was calculated.

Or, at a more human level, consider the case of the highly polished hematite plummet—a valuable item—that was made at Poverty Point at around 1500 BC but that some pilgrim carefully carried to the by then long-abandoned and deserted site of Watson Brake and deliberately buried half a meter deep near the top of Mound E.[63]

This kind of behavior—the incorporation of ancient sites into younger ones, pilgrimage, an offering—has the feel of a religion about it. Religious institutions have proved themselves throughout history to be extremely efficient vehicles for the preservation and transmission of memes across periods of thousands of years.

It's not unreasonable, therefore, to suppose that some kind of cosmic "sky-ground" religion lay behind the alignments to the solstices and the equinoxes at Watson Brake and at the other early sites—a religion sufficiently robust to ensure the continuous successful transmission of a system of geometry, astronomy, and architecture over thousands of years.

John Clark is in no doubt. "The evidence," he says, "suggests very old and widely disseminated knowledge about how to build large sites. The building lore persisted remarkably intact for so long that I think we can, and must, assume that it was part of special knowledge tied to ritual practice."[64]

Where did this special knowledge come from before it appeared at Watson Brake?

How old is it really?

And why, like the serpent that changes its skin or the phoenix reborn from the ashes, does it possess the extraordinary ability to vanish for millennia and then to reappear, as Clark puts it, "with no apparent distortions, loss of measurement accuracy, or shifts in numeration?"[65]

If it was carried in religious ritual among the ancient civilizations of the Mississippi Valley, then perhaps there will be clues to its origins, and its purpose, in what survives of the spiritual ideas of those long-lost people.

PART VI

EQUIPPED FOR JOURNEYING

〉 ● ᠁

The Mystery of Death

22

QUIETUS?

I N MAY 2017, ON A research trip for this book across the American Southwest, I awoke in my hotel room in the small town of Bloomfield, New Mexico. It was deep in the night and very dark. I felt nauseous and assumed I'd picked up a stomach bug somewhere along the way. I didn't imagine it was anything serious. I remember getting out of bed without disturbing Santha, who was sleeping deeply after a long day of photography in the sun. I found my way to the bathroom, switched on the light, and stood hunched over the toilet, waiting to throw up.

The next thing I knew I was returning to consciousness, deeply confused, wired to a drip and lying in a hospital bed. It was full daylight and Santha was standing over me, looking scared.

"Where am I?" I asked. My voice sounded slurred, my tongue thick in my mouth. I had difficulty forming words. "What the fuck happened?"

"You had a seizure, my love," Santha replied, "but they say you're going to be okay."

The hospital was the San Juan Regional Medical Center in Farmington, New Mexico, about 15 miles west of Bloomfield. I recall nothing of the paramedics coming, or the ambulance journey, or what happened in the emergency room. What I do know, because Santha subsequently told me, is that at around 3:30 am she had awakened, sensed my absence, seen that the light was on in the bathroom, and called my name. I didn't answer so she called again, and when there was still no reply she hurried from the bed to find me lying on the floor, half in the bathroom and half out of it, writhing uncontrollably with powerful muscular convulsions and blood pouring from my mouth where I'd bitten my tongue.

After turning me on my side to stop me from choking, Santha called 911 and woke our traveling companions, Randall Carlson and Bradley Young, who were staying in neighboring rooms.

I remember none of this. It seems, however, that I'd been stabilized in the ER and then transferred to the bed where I regained consciousness and quite rapidly began to get my wits back. That evening I was discharged and was able to return to our hotel in Bloomfield, where I read my medical notes. It turned out I was suffering from a previously undetected heart condition known as atrial fibrillation and was now to take anticoagulant medication daily to prevent a possible recurrence of what was diagnosed as a transient ischemic attack—in other words, a "mini stroke." I suffered some loss of memory of events that had taken place in the weeks before the attack but there was no obvious neurological damage visible on the scans. The medical staff at Farmington were absolutely brilliant. I'm deeply grateful for their rapid and effective intervention.

I do indeed have atrial fibrillation, which can and does cause strokes (the blood pools and clots in the heart). I'm still taking anticoagulants. However, the diagnosis I'd been given was very far from complete, as became clear around noon on Monday, August 14, 2017, when I suffered further, far more severe, seizures at my home in Bath, England.

Again I was rushed to the emergency room and then to the ICU. Again the medical staff, now at the Royal United Hospital in Bath, were completely brilliant, caring, and engaged with my case far above and beyond the call of duty. This time the convulsions racking my body were exceptionally violent and continuous and Santha was taken aside by the neurologist who advised her she must prepare herself for the worst. The medical team was having no success in stopping the seizures and it was possible I would die or end up so badly brain damaged that I would effectively be a vegetable.

As a last resort I was put into an induced coma, intubated on a ventilator. My condition settled over the next 48 hours and eventually the doctors were able to withdraw the tube and start me breathing for myself again. It was the evening of Wednesday, August 16, when I began to return to some form of consciousness, baffled to see that Sean and Shanti, two of my grown-up children, had flown from Los Angeles and New York to be with Santha at my bedside, together with Leila and Gabrielle, two more of our grown-up children, who live in London. For quite some time I couldn't understand what had happened, why I'd been fitted with a catheter, why my brain was so foggy.

Little by little consciousness increased. I was moved to the neurology ward and on Thursday night, August 17, much to my relief, the catheter was removed. All day Friday the 18th I remained in the neurology ward, very wobbly but able to totter to the toilet with the aid of a stick. By Friday night I was feeling much better. Finally, on Saturday, I was discharged and came home.

Tests carried out established pretty clearly (although there is still some mystery over what exactly is going on) that the epileptic seizures were not caused by blood clots deriving from my atrial fibrillation, but rather by long-term overuse of a migraine medication called sumatriptan, delivered by injection; I was taking up to a dozen of these shots a month and had been doing so for more than 20 years. Turns out having migraines is itself a risk factor for epilepsy, and research has established a link between triptans (especially when overused) and seizures. It's almost certain it was the sumatriptan that had brought me to death's door, and it is now obvious that I must simply suffer the hideous and mind-numbing pain of my migraines or end up comatose or dead. As I write this in 2018 I'm still on massive daily doses of the anticonvulsant medication levetiracetam. As long as I keep on taking it there's a good chance the condition won't recur.

OUT OF BODY

THE 48 HOURS OF INDUCED coma, though utterly harrowing for Santha, for our children, and for myself, raised interesting questions. Where was "I" during these missing 48 hours? I do remember the ventilator tube being stuffed down my throat and the powerful sense that I was being invaded and asphyxiated. But what happened after that?

A few confused recollections return from time to time to haunt me, but they're so muddled and fragmentary I can't put them into place. I don't think they're memories of near-death experiences because—after all—I wasn't dead. It was simply that my consciousness had been switched by medication to standby mode and the more I look back on it the more I realize that I was just absent, just gone, during those 48 hours. If I try to visualize that strange interlude what I see and what I feel is . . . darkness.

Claustrophobic, enclosed, thick darkness.

It wasn't like that the last time I "died," which was in May 1968, pretty much exactly 49 years earlier, following a massive electric shock.

I was seventeen then and still living at home with my parents. I'm an only child. One of my siblings, a boy, was carried to term but born dead a couple of years before I was conceived. My two other siblings, first a girl—Susan—and then a boy—Jimmy—each lived for nearly a year before they died. When my parents went away to their holiday cottage that weekend in May 1968 I was home alone. Naturally, I seized the opportunity to throw a party on Saturday night.

The house was semidetached with a small garden off a quiet, close-packed street, not an ideal location for 300 rowdy teenagers, loud music, and public drunkenness. It turned into an all-night event. The last stragglers didn't leave until the early afternoon on Sunday and visits from irate neighbors left me in no doubt how fortunate I was that the police had not been called. Certainly my parents would be informed about what had happened when they returned that evening.

In a state of some anxiety I spent the afternoon cleaning up. The house had been trashed so it took me hours to make it presentable, but by nightfall I was left only with the kitchen. I didn't expect my parents back until late. There was still time. So I rolled up my sleeves and started in on the huge pile of dishes, cups, glasses, and empty bottles littered around the sink. A lot of water had been spilled on the floor. I would find a mop and deal with that as soon as the dishes were done.

I was barefoot, hands and arms wet, and standing in the water around the base of the sink, when it occurred to me to check whether the refrigerator was properly plugged in. I'm quite obsessive and often push the back of a plug to make sure it is securely in its socket. The plug was close, I knew exactly where it was—having done this many times before—and without looking I reached for it.

What I didn't realize was that the back of the plug had been smashed off during the night and the live terminals were exposed. When I touched them with my wet hand while standing in a pool of water there was a tremendous *BANG*, a huge searing jolt lashed through my body, and I was thrown across the kitchen, hitting the wall behind me and slumping down to the floor.

I knew I was slumped on the floor because I saw my body clearly but from a completely new perspective. I was no longer "in" that body! I was up around the light, hovering like a bird, looking down on myself.

"Hmm," I remember thinking, "how interesting." My body lying there below me seemed a heavy, cumbersome thing now. Quite unnecessary, really. It was no great loss to be rid of it, and I liked the feeling of lightness and freedom.

"What happens next?" I wondered.

But then just as suddenly as I'd left my flesh, with just as little choice in the matter, I was within it again, stirring, groaning, coming back to consciousness on the floor.

I was okay. Just fine, in fact! I'd had a nasty electric shock, that was all.

I was young and strong then, and quite soon I was back on my feet. I finished the dishes, mopped the kitchen floor, and did a final check of the whole house. Finally, around 10 pm, with my parents still not returned, I took Rusty, my Irish terrier, for a walk. The moon was full and huge in the sky, dimming the stars with its cold, clear light and casting eerie shadows on the ground. Although I don't remember the exact date in May 1968 on which I was electrocuted, a quick internet search confirms it could only have been the night of Sunday, May 12, when the moon was indeed full.

My migraines began quite soon after that and have continued ever since. I think there's a pattern where they occur more frequently around the time of the full moon than at other times of the month, but I've never bothered to keep a detailed record that would confirm or refute that theory. I could just as easily be imagining the connection.

One thing my near-death experience in 1968 and my experiences of seizure and induced coma in 2017 have taught me, however—one thing I'm sure of—is that the borderline between life and death is filmy, fragile, and as permeable as a breath of air.

We feel firmly fixed in our lives but any of us may cross over at any time. Sometimes, very rarely, we come back.

But when we don't? What happens then? Is that the end of us, or is it possible—as every religion in the world asserts—that some part of us, some immaterial essence, survives the grave?

A faction of scientists (Richard Dawkins and Daniel Dennett are notable members), scoff at the very suggestion that there might be anything more to us than our material, mortal parts—and they could be right. It may really be the case that there is no transcendent meaning in the universe, no purpose to the human experience, no such thing as the soul, and therefore no possibility of any kind of "life after death." It's important to be clear, though, that such ideas are **not** proven, evidence-based, scientific "facts" arising from experiments and empirical research. On the contrary, they are unproven assumptions and as such, even if voiced by eminent figures like Dawkins and Dennett, they're of no greater or lesser value than the unproven assumptions that underlie all religions.

Regardless of one's own opinions on such matters, moreover, there is one undeniable fact on which I think everyone can agree, and this is that ancient civilizations, just like our own, had religions and that these religions, just like our own, concerned themselves very deeply with the problem of death.

REALM OF THE DEAD

I WAS RAISED IN A Christian family, and being by nature rebellious I committed myself to atheism at around age fifteen.

After that, I think can safely say that I took no interest in spiritual matters whatsoever until I encountered the *Ancient Egyptian Book of the Dead* in my early forties. I was ready for it then, in a way I wouldn't have been in my twenties or thirties, and I was so intrigued by its contents that over a period of years I also delved extensively, with growing fascination, into the more ancient Pyramid Texts and the less well known Coffin Texts, *Book of Gates, Book of What Is in the Netherworld,* and *Book of the Breaths of Life.*

I'll refer to these texts in what follows sometimes by their specific titles and sometimes, collectively, as the "books of the dead" or as the "funerary texts." They are the surviving treasures of an ancient and profound inquiry into the mysterious nature of reality. I first began to describe what I drew from them in *Fingerprints of the Gods,* published in 1995, and then had the opportunity to go into greater detail in two subsequent books, *Message of the Sphinx* (titled *Keeper of Genesis* in the United Kingdom), published in 1996, and *Heaven's Mirror,* published in 1998.

An enigma that I explore in all those books, but in the greatest detail in *Heaven's Mirror,* is that traces of the same spiritual concepts and symbolism that enlighten the Egyptian texts are found all around the world among cultures that we can be certain were never in direct contact. Straightforward diffusion from one to the other is therefore not the answer, and "coincidence" doesn't even begin to account for the level of detail in the similarities. The best explanation, in my view, is that we're looking at a legacy, shared worldwide, passed down from a single, remotely ancient source.

There are many aspects to this legacy, but I believe its hallmark, as the reader knows by now, is a system of ideas in which geometry, astronomy, and the fate of the soul are all strangely entangled. The geometrical and astronomical memes by which the system replicates itself across cultures and epochs are plentifully represented in the circles, squares, rectangles, and triangles, and in the solstitial, equinoctial, and lunar alignments, of the great mounds and geoglyphs of the Amazon and the Mississippi River basins.

But what about the fate of the soul?

For the entire span of more than 3,000 years that it endured, this question was the preeminent focus of the astonishing high civilization of ancient Egypt and of the remarkable religion that seems to have been born fully formed with it in the Nile Valley in the late fourth millennium BC. Within that religion, expressed in the books of the dead, certain key symbols and ideas stand out, involving most prominently the constellation of Orion, the Milky Way, and the notion, intimately connected to beliefs about both, that the soul must make a perilous postmortem journey on which it will face challenges and ordeals and be judged on the choices that it made during life.

The constellation Orion, on the west bank of the Milky Way, was seen in ancient Egypt as the celestial image of the god Osiris, Lord of the Realm of the Dead. A narrow shaft cut though the body of the Great Pyramid targets Zeta Orionis, the lowest of the three stars of Orion's belt. IMAGE: ROBERT BAUVAL.

Seemingly with the intention of preparing its initiates for this afterlife journey, as Robert Bauval and I showed in our coauthored book *Message of the Sphinx,* the funerary texts also called for the construction of large-scale geometrical and astronomically aligned structures that were to "copy" or imitate on the ground a region of the sky known as the *Duat*—the ancient Egyptian name, often translated as "Netherworld," for the realm of the dead.[1]

The ruler of this Duat realm was the god Osiris, Lord of the Dead, whose figure in the sky was the majestic constellation that the ancient Egyptians called *Sahu,* and that we know as Orion.[2] It is therefore not surprising, as a manifestation of this "as above so below" cosmology, that the three great pyramids of Egypt's Giza necropolis are laid out on the ground in the form of the three stars of the belt of Orion. This correlation was first discovered and put on the public record by my dear friend Robert Bauval in his ground-breaking

1994 book *The Orion Mystery*.[3] As early as the mid-1960s, however, Egyptologist Alexander Badawy and astronomer Virginia Trimble had recognized that a mysterious narrow shaft constructed at an angle of about 45 degrees through the body of the Great Pyramid would have pointed at the belt of Orion at meridian transit some 4,500 years ago.[4] With the use of accurate inclinometer data provided by a robotic exploration in 1992, Robert Bauval was able to refine Badawy and Trimble's work and to confirm that in the Pyramid Age, circa 2450 BC, the shaft had been precisely targeted on Zeta Orionis, the first of the three stars of Orion's belt, counterpart in the sky of the Great Pyramid on the ground.[5]

This, too, makes perfect sense from the perspective of ancient Egyptian beliefs. An invocation often repeated in the Pyramid Texts states of the deceased pharaoh:

> O King, you are this great star, the companion of Orion, who
> traverses the sky with Orion, who navigates the Netherworld with
> Osiris. . . . O King, navigate and arrive.[6]

Since the shaft emanates from the so-called King's Chamber of the Great Pyramid, within meters of an empty granite sarcophagus, it's therefore difficult to disagree with what is now the prevailing scholarly opinion concerning its purpose—namely that it must have been designed to serve as a portal, a "star-shaft," through which the soul of the deceased could ascend to Orion and thence begin its navigation of the Duat.[7]

ANCIENT EGYPT IN ALABAMA?

FOLLOWING MY FIRST BOUT OF seizures in New Mexico in May 2017, Santha and I flew to New Orleans and enjoyed a few days of rest, recreation, and good Cajun food in one of the most laid-back cities in the world while I recovered my strength. Then we were on the road again, driving north to explore the mound-builder sites of the Lower Mississippi Valley, heading ultimately for Serpent Mound in Ohio on the summer solstice.

We stopped first about 4 hours north of New Orleans at the incredible geometrical and astronomical earthworks of Poverty Point, described in chapter 20.

We then went on to visit Emerald Mound, also in Louisiana, and the Winterville Mounds in Mississippi, and on the fourth day of our journey reached Moundville in Alabama.

Here, in addition to the geometry and astronomy I'd come to expect, I found myself plunged most unexpectedly into an ancient Egyptian déjà vu moment after we'd climbed to the top of Mound B. A good vantage point for Santha's photography, this mound is pyramidal in form, 18 meters high, and dominates the whole rather spectacular site that extends southward from the Black Warrior River. The expansive grand plaza lay at our feet, edged by more than twenty mounds laid out, somewhat like Watson Brake, in the pattern of a great ellipse. At the center of the plaza, presently the focus of Santha's camera, stood a large rectangular platform mound—Mound A—and while she photographed it I stepped aside to read the official archaeological marker.

Much of what it had to say was standard stuff about the building of the site, most of which apparently had been completed over a period of about 100 years in the twelfth and thirteenth centuries. There was some predictable speculation that religion must have been used to coerce, cajole, or convince the population to do all that work. But then suddenly things got interesting. "At Moundville," I read,

an excellent example of a powerful religious image was the hand
and eye motif. Moundville's "Rattlesnake Disk," pictured on this
noticeboard, offers us the best-known version, although numerous
variations occur in pottery, copper, stone and shell artifacts.

Stories passed down among various tribes tell of the dead entering
the afterlife through an opening marked by a great warrior's hand
in the sky. One account describes that hand as the constellation we
know as Orion with Orion's belt as the wrist, its fingers pointing
downwards. A faint cluster of stars in the center of the palm is a
portal to the path of souls or path to the land of the dead. Researchers
speculate that the hand and eye represent this constellation.[8]

I was nonplussed. I try to prepare thoroughly, but it looked like I'd missed something important in my background reading before starting out on this

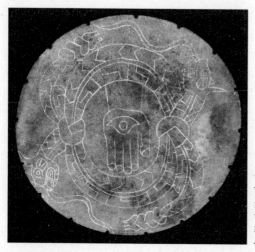

Moundville: Rattlesnake Disk
with "Hand-and-Eye" symbol.
PHOTO: COURTESY OF THE
UNIVERSITY OF ALABAMA
MUSEUMS, TUSCALOOSA,
ALABAMA.

trip. The connection of the constellation of Orion to the land of the dead was a fundamental aspect of the ancient Egyptian religion and it felt weirdly like coming home—that comfortable intimacy of familiar territory—to find it here in a Native North American religion.

But I should have known about this!

The Rattlesnake Disk was in the museum we'd passed through briefly on our way into the site, intending to see the exhibits properly at the end of our visit.

Now suddenly it was top priority, so 10 minutes later we were standing in front of its display case.

It's a mysterious, complex image on a disk of dark gray sandstone, 32 centimeters (just over 12 inches) in diameter. Seventeen notches, creating a coglike effect, are chiseled at equal distances around the perimeter of the disk. Next, intaglio, come two intertwined rattlesnakes, their long tongues flicking forward, their bodies knotted together. Curiously, these serpents have horns. An oval enclosure formed by their coils frames a human hand with what indeed appears to be an eye engraved at its center.

"The hand and eye," I read in the accompanying description:

is a prominent Moundville motif and is thought to represent a part of the constellation that we identify as Orion. As a group the knotted serpents and the hand and eye are believed to be a representation of the night sky. The serpents are the ropes that join the earth and sky.

In the palm of the hand is the portal or doorway through which the spirits of the dead can ascend the path of souls . . . a road or ribbon of light, the Milky Way, stretching out before the traveling souls. This river of light . . . deposits the souls, after a series of trials, into the realm of the dead. Families from all over the Moundville chiefdom brought and buried their dead here because they believed that Moundville was the appropriate place for the spirit to start its journey along the path of souls. Thus over time Moundville became, in the minds of its people, not only the symbolic gateway to the realm of the dead but also the materialized image of that sacred domain on earth.[9]

So not only was the constellation of Orion part of the Moundville story, not only was a journey to the realm of the dead part of it, too, but now I knew also that a series of trials would have to be faced on that journey, that the Milky Way was involved and, last but by no means least, that Moundville itself had been thought of as an image, or copy, of the realm of the dead on earth. Every one of these were important symbols, concepts, and narratives in the ancient Egyptian funerary texts that I'd been fascinated by for more than 20 years. It would be striking to find even two of them together in a remote and unconnected culture, but for them all to be present in ancient North America in the same way that they were present in ancient Egypt, and serving the same ends, was a significant anomaly.

In the museum there were other superb examples of the art and iconography of Moundville. It is all indisputably Native American art, the work of the same Mississippian culture responsible for Cahokia. Every piece on show in the display cases had been produced between about AD 1150 and 1500 when Moundville was abandoned, and the archaeologists had done their work so well that there could be no doubt whatsoever about the dates. This ruled out any possibility of direct influence since ancient Egypt breathed its last under Roman occupation in the fifth century AD, at least 500 years before the Mississippian culture came into existence.

How, then, to explain the fact that some of the fundamental symbols and ideas of the religions practiced at Moundville and in ancient Egypt—ideas and symbols specifically concerning the afterlife journey of the soul—appear to be the same?

23

THE PORTAL AND THE PATH

THE BOARD AT THE TOP of Mound B said there was "one account" linking the constellation that we know as Orion to traditions of "a great warrior's hand in the sky." This turned out not to be the case. There are in fact dozens of such accounts specifically referencing an ancient Native American constellation in which the stars of Orion's belt form the wrist of this hand— sometimes said to belong to a great warrior chieftain and sometimes to a malevolent celestial being called "Long Arm," who used it in an attempt to block a portal between earth and sky but lost the hand when it was chopped off by a human hero.[1]

Other than their underestimation of the sheer numbers of such accounts, it took me no more than an hour on Google to confirm that the information about the Mississippian afterlife beliefs displayed at Moundville, though scant, was based on solid research and accurately reflected the views of leading scholars in the field.

The Milky Way, the connection with Orion, the perilous afterlife journey of the soul, and the notion of creating an image or copy of the realm of the dead on the ground were all genuinely present in the Mississippian religion, just as they were in the ancient Egyptian religion. No one familiar with the Pyramid Texts and the Book of the Dead could fail to notice these obvious resemblances. I'm not the first to do so. Andrew Collins and Gregory Little made passing mention of them in 2014 and there was earlier brief recognition of the same issue by others in 2012.[2] To my knowledge at the time of this writing, however, no in-depth comparative study has ever been undertaken to determine whether there's a real connection between these two otherwise very different cultures, separated not only by geography but also by time.

Is it all just coincidence?

Or can coincidence be ruled out?

The issue, it seemed to me, was important enough to justify a thorough investigation, and I already had a head start since the ancient Egyptian funerary texts, though never "easy," were home turf for me. I'd been through them so often while researching previous books that I had no difficulty in reengaging with them. As a bonus I still had hundreds of pages of detailed notes I'd made on all the key recensions over the years and most of those notes, with page references to the heavily underlined and tagged print editions in my shelves, were in searchable electronic form.

The ancient Egyptians left us immense numbers of documents in their beautiful hieroglyphic script and we've been able to read them since Champollion deciphered the Rosetta Stone in the nineteenth century. We also have historical accounts of the ancient Egyptians and their religious beliefs written in antiquity by eyewitnesses to their civilization such as Herodotus. So we have a lot to go on.

In the case of North America, on the other hand, there are no eyewitness reports to provide a pre-Columbian historical record, and since Native North Americans possessed no written languages, they left no documents. Even had they done so, if the example of the organized burning of the Mayan codices during the Spanish conquest of Mexico is anything to go by,[3] precious few of them would remain for us to study today. Such wholesale destruction was visited upon the indigenous cultures of North America that it is a miracle any of their painted and engraved images on pottery, stone, copper, shell, and bone have survived at all.

We can only guess at what has been lost and work with what remains. In this respect, as anthropologist Mark Seeman explains, while sites like Watson Brake, Serpent Mound, and even the Hopewell earthworks are so old that "historical connections are extremely difficult to make," it's quite a different matter with the Mississippian culture, which is "close enough in time to connect it to the religious practises and oral traditions of historical groups such as the Chickasaw, Creek, Caddo and Osage."[4]

Similar connections with the Lakota, Mandan, Hidatsa, Crow, Arapaho, Oglala, and other Siouan speakers, as well as with the Ojibwa and other speakers of Algonquian languages, have added further vital information to the inquiry.[5]

With these resources at hand, and through a sustained exercise of interdisciplinary detective work involving archaeologists, anthropologists, and ethnologists, the code of Mississippian ideas and iconography has been comprehensively broken. The crucial realization, as anthropologists Kent Reilly and James Garber inform us, is that much of the imagery "has a linkage to ethnographic material that describes the location of the realm of the dead and the journey of dead souls to the underworld."[6]

There is "variation in ethnographic details from one tribal group to another, as might be expected," adds Professor George Lankford, an internationally recognized authority on Native American folklore, anthropology, religious studies, and ethnohistory.[7] Nonetheless:

There is a unifying metaphor which argues for a common core of belief across the Eastern Woodlands and Plains, and probably far beyond that area. That unifying notion is an understanding of the Milky Way as the path on which the souls of the deceased must walk.[8]

Elsewhere Lankford reiterates that this belief system was by no means confined to the Plains, the Eastern Woodlands, and the Mississippi Valley. It is better understood, he argues, as part of "a widespread religious pattern" found right across North America and "more powerful than the tendency towards cultural diversity."[9] Indeed, what the evidence suggests is the former existence of "an ancient North American international religion[10] . . . a common ethnoastronomy . . . and a common mythology. Such a multicultural reality hints provocatively at more common knowledge which lay behind the façade of cultural diversity united by international trade networks. One likely possibility of a conceptual realm in which that common knowledge became focused is mortuary belief [and] . . . the symbolism surrounding death."[11]

SOULS OF ANCIENT EGYPT

IN BOTH ANCIENT NATIVE NORTH America and ancient Egypt the universe was believed to be "layered"—with This World, the everyday material realm, inhabited by humans, sandwiched between an Underworld below (often with powerful Underwater aspects) and an Upper World, or Sky World, above. In both ancient Native North America and ancient Egypt the afterlife journey was envisaged as unfolding in the Sky World, among the stars. But in both this apparently celestial setting had contradictory Below World characteristics, including bodies of water and other obstacles to cross, architectural spaces to navigate, and monstrous adversaries to face.

Ancient Egyptian notions of the soul can seem extremely complex at first glance. Indeed, according to the great authority on the subject, Sir E. A. Wallis Budge, formerly Keeper of Egyptian Antiquities at the British Museum, it's not just a matter of one soul but of multiple souls—all of them separate from but in some way connected to the *khat,* or physical body—"that which is liable to decay."[12]

In Budge's summary, these separate, nonphysical "souls"—perhaps "aspects of the soul" would be a better description—include notably:

> The *Ka,* or "double," that stays earthbound after death in the immediate vicinity of the corpse and the tomb.

> The *Ba,* depicted as a bird or human-headed bird that can fly freely "between tomb and underworld."

> The *Khaibit,* or shadow.

> The *Khu,* or "spiritual soul."

> The *Sekhem,* or "power."

> The *Ren,* or "name."

The *Ba* soul flying free of the physical remains of the deceased.

>   The *Sahu,* or "spiritual body," which formed the habitation of the
    soul.

>   The *Ab,* or heart, "regarded as the center of the spiritual
    and thinking life. . . . It typifies everything which the word
    'conscience' signifies to us." The heart, and what its owner has
    imprinted upon it by his or her choices during life, is the specific
    object of judgment in the Netherworld.[13]

It would be possible to write an entire book, perhaps several, on the complexities of ancient Egyptian soul beliefs. In my opinion, however, once the
baroque flourishes, dramatic elements, and multiple iterations are dispensed
with, the eight "souls" or "soul aspects" listed above can be boiled down to
two, reflecting the ancient Egyptian view of the fundamentally dualistic
nature of the human creature as both a spiritual and as a material being.

On the one hand, there is that nonphysical, spiritual aspect of ourselves
that is potentially eternal and immortal, aspiring to the "life of millions of
years," as the funerary texts put it. Having worn the body like a suit of clothes,
it is this "soul" that is liberated from it at death and can ascend to the stars,
specifically to the constellation of Orion, to begin the next stage of its journey.

On the other hand, there is the physical body and the animating force believed to have attended to the vital functions of that body during life. Also seen as a kind of "soul," a supernatural entity in its own right, it is the lot of this ghostly, nonphysical presence—combining most notably the characteristics of the *Ka* ("double") and of the *Khaibit* ("shadow")—to remain on earth with the corpse.

Inevitably in such a system of ideas, earth and sky become opposed dualities symbolizing the material realm that is to be left behind and the spiritual realm to which the potentially immortal, nonphysical aspect of the deceased ascends. Thus we read in the Pyramid Texts:

Earth is this King's detestation. . . . This King is bound for the sky.[14]
The spirit is bound for the sky, the corpse is bound for the earth.[15]
The King is one of those . . . beings . . . who will never fall to the earth from the sky.[16]

In a similar vein, with some complexity regarding the activities of the "shadow," the *Book of What Is in the Duat* has this to say:

Let thy soul be in heaven . . . let thy shadow penetrate the hidden place, and let thy body be to the earth.[17]

Many other examples could be cited but the summary is that the ancient Egyptians believed in two souls, or two fundamental aspects of the soul. One of these (let us not quibble about its several different avatars) remained bound to the physical remains and the tomb. The other, again in its several forms, was free to ascend to the sky and begin the journey to the realm of the dead.

SOULS OF ANCIENT AMERICA

WHAT NOW OF NATIVE NORTH AMERICAN conceptions of the soul?
Here, too, we find at first a bewildering multiplicity.
The Quileute people of the US northwest coast believe that within every liv-

ing human body there reside several souls that "look exactly like the living being and may be taken off or put on in exactly the manner as a snake sheds its skin."[18]

These souls are an inner soul, called the "main, strong soul," an outer soul, called the "outside shadow," a life-soul, referred to as "the being whereby one lives," and the "ghost" of the living person, "the thing whereby one grows."[19]

Let's note in passing that the *Ancient Egyptian Book of the Dead* declares in chapter 164:

I have made for thee a skin, namely a divine soul.[20]

Returning to North America, it was believed among the Yuchi of Oklahoma that the individual "possesses four spirits . . . one of which, at death, remains on the spot where the disembodiment took place, while two others hover in the vicinity of tribesfolk and relatives. . . . The fourth starts upon a four-days" journey . . . to the haven of souls.[21]

In other accounts gathered from among the widely spread Ojibwa people of northeastern North America, the ethnographer Vernon Kinietz was told that humans have seven souls—only one of which, "the real soul," goes to the realm of the dead.[22] Another Ojibwa group reported that, according to their traditions, the human being consists of three parts:

The body (*wiyo*), which decays after death, the soul (*udjitchog*), which at death departs for the realm of the dead in the West, and the shadow (*udjibbom*), which after death becomes a grave-ghost.[23]

Expressing the same idea in a slightly different way, the Menominee of Wisconsin say there are two souls in every human being:

One, which is called "a shade across," resides in the head and is the intellect; after death it becomes a grave ghost. The other is the real soul, *tcebai*, which has its seat in the heart and at death betakes itself to the realm of the dead.[24]

For the Choctaw, also, humans have two souls—the *shilombish*, "the outside shadow," and the *shilup*, "the inside shadow," or ghost, which at death goes to the land of ghosts. The *shilombish* remains on earth.[25]

And indeed, when the unnecessary details and confusingly ambiguous terminology are stripped away, it becomes clear that the fundamental Native North American belief across a vast geographical area, like the fundamental belief of the ancient Egyptians, was in the existence of two souls, one bound to the body and the earth, the other free to ascend to the sky. "Soul dualism," concludes renowned Swedish anthropologist Ake Hultkrantz in his immense and still widely cited 1953 study, *Conceptions of the Soul Among North American Indians,* "constituted the predominant type of soul belief in North America."[26]

At the heart of this widespread belief system stand twin concepts defined by Hultkrantz as the "free-soul" and the "body-soul." The latter, also sometimes referred to as the "life soul," represents "the forces that keep the body vital and active." The "free-soul," on the other hand, represents "the person himself in his extracorporeal form" but with the added power of limitless movement.[27]

To what end was this freedom of movement used?

Among ancient Native North Americans, as George Lankford explains, it was believed that

at a crucial point in the dying process the "free-soul," the one that is self-aware and has an identifiable personality in relation to the deceased, separates from the body, leaving behind the life-soul, a mindless force which can be dangerous to the living, trapped in or near the physical remains. The free-soul remains present in the vicinity for a brief time, then . . . sets off towards the west on its final journey. . . . If at any time along the route the free-soul gains the power or will to return to earthly life, then it may retrace its steps and re-enter its body. . . . Mortuary rituals must therefore include at least two different tasks, taking care of two different souls."[28]

Exactly the same care and attention paid to two different "souls," and for the same reasons, also characterized ancient Egyptian mortuary rituals.[29] It seems clear that these separate ancient Egyptian "souls" are essentially identical to, and interchangeable with, Native American notions of the "body-soul" and the "free-soul."

THE ROAD TO THE WEST

IN THE ANCIENT EGYPTIAN PYRAMID Texts, line 1109, a soul reaches the realm of the dead only to hear a voice telling him:

> Turn about, O you who have not yet come to the number of your days.[30]

A legend of the Ottawa, a Native American people who lived in Michigan and Ohio before migrating to Oklahoma where most members of the tribe are now found, tells of a person who enters the realm of the dead although he himself still lives. A voice, "as if it were a soft breeze," whispers in his ear:

> Go back to the land from whence you came. Your time has not yet come.[31]

The free-soul can become detached from the body not only in death, but also in dreams, visions, and comatose states. From the Native American perspective, "death" has therefore not definitively occurred until there is certainty that the absent free-soul will not return. It is for this reason, explains Lankford, that "the 'dead' are almost never buried immediately, and most people have a ritually specified time of waiting."[32] The Ojibwa were particularly known for their "habit of keeping the dead four days, in the hope that the soul in the spirit world would return and the person come back to life."[33]

But when the soul does not return, where has it gone and how did it get there?

A legend of the Native American Tachi Yokut people tells of a husband whose deeply cherished wife had died. Grieving, he went to her grave and dug a hole near it:

> There he stayed watching, not eating. . . . After two nights he saw that she came up, brushed the earth off herself, and started to go to the [land] of the dead.[34]

Similarly, in the ancient Egyptian Pyramid Texts, lines 747–48, we read the following invocation to the deceased:

Arise, remove your earth, shake off your dust, raise yourself that you may travel in company with the spirits.[35]

In ancient Egypt the first stage of the journey to the realm of the dead was to ensure that the mortuary rites were properly observed. The purpose of these rites, Wallis Budge explains, was to enable the "disembodied spirit . . . to pass through the tomb out into the region which lies immediately to the west of the mountain chain on the west bank of the Nile, which we may consider as one mountain and call Manu, or the mountain of the sunset."[36]

In the case of the Native American afterlife journey, likewise, as Lankford summarizes:

The path leads towards the west, the place of the setting sun, the end of the east-west cosmic passage, the point of transition from day to night.[37]

Returning to ancient Egypt, it is clear that the first stage of the afterlife journey unfolds on the earth plane and brings the soul to a special location in the west, described as beyond "the mountain of sunset." At this place, Budge continues,

are gathered together numbers of spirits, all bent on making their way to the abode of the blessed; these are they who have departed from their bodies during the day.[38]

In Native America, too, a place is reached at the western edge of the "earth-disk" where the dead gather and where they, too, must await the right moment, after nightfall, to make the transition from the earth plane to the Sky World. "There may be a camping-place for the free-soul," Lankford tells us:

For there may be a wait until conditions are right to continue the journey.[39]

ORION, THE "LEAP," AND THE PORTAL IN ANCIENT AMERICA

IN ANCIENT EGYPT, THE CONSTELLATION of Orion, located prominently on the west bank of the Milky Way, was seen as the celestial figure of the God Osiris, Lord of the Realm of the Dead, and the funerary texts explicitly and repeatedly urge the soul to ascend to the sky and unite itself with Orion. A few examples:

> You shall reach the sky as Orion.[40]
> May a stairway to the Netherworld be set up for you in the place where Orion is.[41]
> I have gone upon the ladder with my foot on Orion.[42]
> The Netherworld has grasped your hand at the place where Orion is.[43]
> May Orion give me his hand.[44]

The intention, confirmed in architecture by the star-shaft of the Great Pyramid (see previous chapter) is unmistakable. After completing its westward journey on the earth plane, and gathering with other souls at a staging point, the spiritual form of the deceased must find a way to gain access to the "place where Orion is" from whence the remainder of its journey to the realm of the dead will unfold.

But how to get to Orion?

The means suggested in the utterances quoted above include a stairway, a ladder, and the "hand" of the constellation itself. Another utterance tells us more vaguely, "There is brought to him a way of ascent to the sky"[45] and fifty lines later we read:

> Here comes the ascender, here comes the ascender! Here comes the climber, here comes the climber! Here comes he who flew up, here comes he who flew up.[46]

How was the transition to the Sky World achieved in the Native American afterlife journey when the soul had reached the staging point at the edge of the earth-disk? Lankford draws on his vast store of knowledge of the ethnography surrounding this subject when he tells us that in order to continue its journey to the realm of the dead:

> What the free-soul must do . . . is to make a terrifying leap. The realm
> of the dead . . . can only be reached by walking the Path of Souls,
> the Milky Way, across the night sky. To get to the path, however, one
> must leave the earth-disk and enter the celestial realm. The portal
> that is appointed for the free-soul at death is to be seen on the edge of
> the Path of Souls. It is a constellation in the shape of a hand, and the
> portal is in its palm.[47]

As I learned at Moundville, this Native American "Hand" constellation is none other than the constellation we know as Orion, with the three prominent belt stars forming the wrist. Beneath these stars, identified as part of Orion's sword by the Greeks, is a bright sky object known as Messier 42, or the Orion Nebula. In the "hand-and-eye" motif it is this nebula, regarded

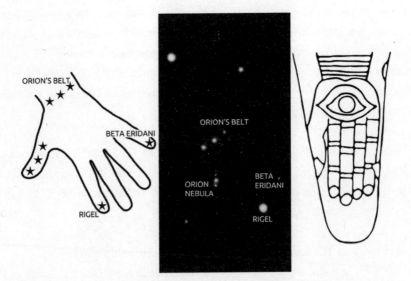

LEFT: Native American "Hand" constellation in which the three stars of Orion's belt form the wrist. CENTER: Orion's belt and the Orion Nebula. RIGHT: An example of the Moundville "hand-and-eye" motif. The Orion Nebula is represented by the "eye," and was conceived of as a portal through which the soul must leap on its afterlife journey.

by modern astronomers as a "stellar nursery" where new stars are constantly born,[48] that represents the "eye." Its description as such is, however, a misleading and long outdated label that only remains in use out of habit. The truth, as scholars are now agreed, is that in Mississippian iconography it does not represent an eye at all but "a hole in the sky, a portal,"[49] through which the free-soul must pass in order to reach the realm of the dead.

George Lankford clarifies the muddle:

> The hole in the sky is indicated as a slit being pulled apart, and the fact that it is celestial is frequently elaborated by the inclusion of a star circle or dot. The resulting double sign thus gives the appearance of being an eye, but . . . it is a coincidental similarity. The "eye" is but a portal with a star at its center. The hand-and-eye combination thus indicates the beginning of the spirit journey, the entry of the soul into the Milky Way at Orion.[50]

In ancient Egypt the hieroglyphic representation of the Duat Netherworld (likewise accessed via Orion and the Milky Way) made use of exactly the same concepts expressed in locally appropriate symbolism. Whereas in Mississippian art it was customary to depict a star in the form of a circle or dot, the star symbol in ancient Egypt was very much like the five-pointed version we still use today. Likewise, in Mississippian art the sky portal was depicted as an aperture in the form of an open slit while in ancient Egypt it was represented by a circle.

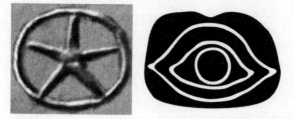

LEFT: ANCIENT EGYPT: The hieroglyph for the Duat Netherworld depicts a hole in the sky with a star at its center. RIGHT: ANCIENT NATIVE AMERICA: "The hole in the sky is indicated as a slit being pulled apart, and the fact that it is celestial is frequently elaborated by the inclusion of a star circle or dot."

ORION, THE "LEAP," AND THE PORTAL IN ANCIENT EGYPT

THE TOP HALF OF "ORION" above the belt stars is important in the ancient Egyptian *Sahu* constellation but isn't part of the "Hand" at all. The stories behind the imagery that were told in the Nile Valley and the Mississippi Valley are also very different. Nonetheless, it's bizarre that the same constellation plays such a key role in both Native American and ancient Egyptian beliefs concerning the afterlife journey.

Moreover, although ladders and stairs are among the "means of ascent" suggested to the soul in the ancient Egyptian funerary texts, they are by no means the only ones. Particularly close to the Native American notion of a "leap" for the portal is Utterance 478 of the Pyramid Texts, line 980, in which the deceased states:

I leap up to the sky into the presence of the god.[51]

Likewise in Utterance 467, lines 890–91, we read:

Someone flies up. I fly up from you, O men; I am not for the earth, I am for the sky.[52]

And again, almost technologically, in Utterance 261:

The King is a flame moving before the wind to the end of the sky.[53]

Such references, and numerous other examples that could be cited, leave little room for misinterpretation. As with the Native Americans, so, too, with the ancient Egyptians—a "leap" by one means or another from the earth-plane to Orion was an essential stage in the afterlife journey.

It might be objected that the constellation *Sahu*/Orion for the ancient Egyptians was the celestial figure of Osiris, Lord of the Realm of the Dead, and therefore in no way a "portal" in the Native American sense. That, however, does no justice to the possibility, in so subtle a system as the ancient Egyptian funerary texts, that symbols might be encoded with multiple levels of meaning. A close study of the texts reveals that the passage of the soul through a portal in the sky was indeed a fundamental stage of the ancient Egyptian afterlife journey.

The Pyramid Texts again:

> Portal of the Abyss, I have come to you; let this be opened to me.[54]
> The doors of the sky are opened for you, the doors of the starry sky are thrown open for you.[55]
> The doors of iron which are in the starry sky are thrown open for me, and I go through them.[56]
> Open the gates which are in the Abyss.[57]
> The aperture of the sky-window is open to you.[58]
> The celestial portal to the horizon is open to you.[59]
> I am he who opened a door in the sky.[60]
> The door of the sky at the horizon opens to you.[61]

"The Orion Nebula," clarifies Susan Brind Morrow in a new study of the Pyramid Texts, "is in the door of the sky."[62]

And in case there is any remaining doubt, the celestial address of this portal through which the deceased must pass in order to enter the Duat Netherworld is also repeated on multiple occasions in the Pyramid Texts, for example:

> The *Duat* has grasped your hand at the place where Orion is.[63]

And, as we've seen:

> May a stairway to the Netherworld be set up for you in the place where Orion is.[64]

THE TIMING OF THE "LEAP"

FOR THE ANCIENT EGYPTIANS, ARRIVAL at the top of the metaphorical "stairway," the accomplishment of the "leap" to the sky "in the presence of the god," was to be timed to coincide with the moment when:

Orion is swallowed up by the *Duat*.[65]

According to R. O. Faulkner, translator of the Pyramid Texts, this occurs when "the stars vanish at dawn."[66] More broadly the "swallowing" of Orion by the Duat can be linked to the setting of the constellation in the west at whichever time of day or night this happens.

Let's now return to George Lankford's authoritative account of the Mississippian afterlife journey and the soul's leap to the portal in the Orion Nebula in the constellation that Native North Americans called the "Hand." The leap can only be attempted when that constellation makes its closest approach to the edge of the earth-disk, setting low in the west under the Milky Way just before it vanishes beneath the horizon—the precise moment, for both ancient Egyptians and ancient Native Americans, when the door of the sky, "the celestial portal to the horizon," was believed to stand open. As Lankford makes clear:

> The portal in the Hand must be entered by a leap at the optimum time, which is a ten-minute window which occurs once each night from November 29, when the Hand vanishes . . . in the West just at dawn, to April 25, when the Hand sinks at dusk, not to be seen again for six months. During that winter period the portal is on the horizon

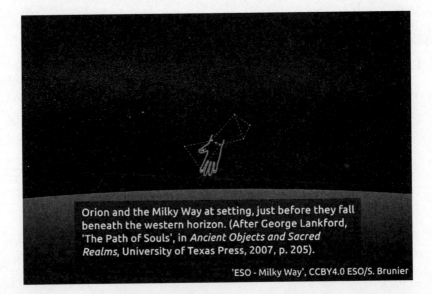

Orion and the Milky Way at setting, just before they fall beneath the western horizon. (After George Lankford, 'The Path of Souls', in *Ancient Objects and Sacred Realms*, University of Texas Press, 2007, p. 205).

for a breathless few minutes each night, and the free-souls must enter at that time or be lost. Free-souls who do not make the transition remain in the West and can eventually become unhappy threats to the realm of the living.[67]

Likewise in ancient Egypt, Budge informs us, it is the fate of those who have not prepared adequately for the afterlife journey to remain trapped on the earth plane—where their lot, "having failed to present themselves in the Judgment Hall of Osiris," is an unhappy one.[68]

And in both ancient Egypt and ancient North America it was also believed that those souls that had successfully ascended to Orion must then continue their long and arduous journey, now transposed from the earth plane to the Sky World. On that journey they would meet monsters and terrors for which it appears that the ancient Egyptian books of the dead and the parallel oral and iconographic traditions of the Mississippian civilization were designed to prepare them.[69]

Before we explore these further similarities between the supposedly entirely unconnected religions of the Mississippi and the Nile, let's reflect in passing on the spiritual system that has evolved in the Amazon rainforest around the use of ayahuasca, the "Vine of the Dead." The reader will recall that it has that name because in the "indigenous context" ayahuasca is "intimately related to death."[70] The visions received in the ayahuasca trance are considered to resemble death and to give foreknowledge of the death process and thus, at the level of experience rather than of study, the "Vine of the Dead" appears to be performing the same function as a "Book of the Dead."

Ayahuasca shamans in the Amazon speak of "dying" when they drink the brew. It's again suggestive of hidden connections that thereafter, as we saw in chapter 17, they experience "ascent to the Milky Way" in a "single soaring flight" (which sounds very much like a "leap") in order to reach the "Otherworld" that lies "beyond the Milky Way."

Sometimes, as they make these journeys, the shamans encounter trials and adversaries that will test them:

Terrifying monsters . . . jaguars and serpents that approach and threaten to devour the person who, terror stricken, will call out in anguish.[71]

TERRORS AND OBSTACLES OF THE ANCIENT EGYPTIAN NETHERWORLD

NO ONE IN THE NORTHERN Hemisphere who pays any attention to the sky can fail to notice the presence of the majestic constellation of Orion during the winter months or the fact that it stands at the western side—indeed one could say on the west bank—of the glowing band of supernal light that is our own disk-shaped galaxy viewed from within. We call that band of light the Milky Way. To the ancient Egyptians it was the "Winding Waterway,"[72] the great celestial river that, as Wallis Budge informs us,

> flowed through the Duat much as the Nile flowed through Egypt.
> There were inhabitants on each of its banks, just as there were human
> beings on each side of the Nile.[73]

Moreover, the soul's leap to Orion was not an end in itself, but simply its means of entry to the Sky World. Once there, it was the Winding Waterway that would provide the setting for the next stage of the afterlife journey. "May you take me and raise me to the Winding Waterway," as the Pyramid Texts put it.[74]

It is therefore intriguing that in ancient North America the Milky Way was most widely known as the "Path of Souls,"[75] and it was on this path, after passing through the Orion portal, that the spirits of the deceased found themselves. Lankford takes up the story again:

> When the free-soul has entered the celestial realm, the Path of Souls
> stretches out before it. By most accounts it is a realm much like the
> earthly one left behind, but some describe it as a river of light with
> free-souls camped alongside. The free-soul must journey down the
> Path to the realm of the dead.[76]

Inevitably, with a great river flowing through it, the Duat "had the shape of a valley."[77] However, unlike the Nile Valley, which it otherwise resembled, this ancient Egyptian realm of the dead was "shrouded in the gloom and darkness of night . . . a place of fear and horror."[78]

It was, moreover, a place filled with obstacles and fearsome challenges including:

> abysses of darkness, murderous knives, streams of boiling water, foul stenches, fiery serpents, hideous animal-headed monsters and creatures, and cruel, death-dealing beings of various shapes.[79]

A few hours with the vignettes and tomb paintings and you begin to get the idea.

The Duat is an utterly eerie parallel universe that is at once a starry "otherworld" and a strange physical domain with narrow passageways and darkened galleries and chambers populated by fiends and terrors. There are entities whose work is "to hack souls in pieces." There are serpents of enormous size, serpents with legs and feet, serpents with multiple heads, serpents with wings. There are serpents that breathe fire and that are depicted as flooding corridors with fire. There is in particular the monstrous serpent Apep and a specially dedicated company of nine gods whose work is to slay Apep. There are firepits where souls are roasted, in some cases head down. There are bodies of water to cross and "abysmal depths of darkness." There are torture blocks. There

Vignette from the *Book of What Is in the Duat*. E. A. Wallis Budge offers no direct translation of the relevant hieroglyphs, merely describing the scene thus: "[A] goddess standing upright with her hands stretched out to the top of the head of a man who is kneeling before her, and is cutting open his head with a hatchet." LEFT: Detail of the vignette. RIGHT: The vignette in context.

are gods armed with knives who will kill inadequately prepared souls.[80] And one particularly curious vignette shows "a goddess standing upright with her hands stretched out to the top of the head of a man who is kneeling before her, and is cutting open his head with a hatchet."[81]

The vignette[82] captured my attention for reasons that I will explain below. Budge expresses no opinion in his description and since I don't read hieroglyphs I couldn't be sure exactly what was going on. One interpretation that occurred to me was that the goddess was trying to **stop** the kneeling man from bashing his own brains out. But the scene had an uncanny, rather ominous, quality that suggested a very different possibility. From the way the outstretched arms and hands of the goddess were portrayed it looked more to me as though she was **encouraging** him to take that hatchet to his own head—or even perhaps exerting some kind of divine will to **force** him to do it.

Since there are repeated references to a menacing female figure, usually called the "brain-smasher" or the "brain-taker" in accounts of the Native American afterlife journey, it occurred to me there was an opportunity here to test the mettle of my evolving theory of a deep structural connection between the spiritual systems of ancient Egypt and the ancient Mississippi Valley. All I had to do was find an Egyptologist to translate the hieroglyphs in the vignette for me. If the translation showed no relationship whatsoever between the goddess in this vignette and the Native American "brain-smasher," then my theory would be weakened. If, on the other hand, a clear relationship emerged, then my theory would be strengthened.

Egyptologists in general avoid me, but I was fortunate that Louise Ellis-Barrett at the British Museum was prepared to accept the commission. She was curious as to why I wanted a translation at all but I was determined that this should be a proper blind test, in which no preconceptions were inserted into the translator's mind before she began work, so I declined to tell her.

A few weeks later, after investigating the matter thoroughly, Louise came back to me with her translation of the group of hieroglyphs describing the role of the goddess in the scene:

> She lives from the blood of the damned
> And from what these gods provide her
> That Ba-soul who belongs to the damned
> The demolishing one, who cuts the damned to pieces.

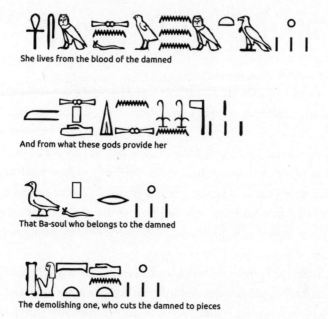

She lives from the blood of the damned

And from what these gods provide her

That Ba-soul who belongs to the damned

The demolishing one, who cuts the damned to pieces

For clarification Louise added that the *Book of What Is in the Duat* is "divided into Hours—each of which is a unit of text and illustration." The vignette occurs in the Fifth Hour of the journey through the Duat (often also referred to as the "Fifth Division of the Duat") where, as we shall see, the ancient Egyptian judgment scene was also set. Moreover, although the vignette itself is not a formal part of the judgment, the entire burden of the Fifth Hour, as Louise expressed it in the document she prepared for me, is:

> its indication of the turning point in life. Here, life will either be
> renewed or annihilated. The last scene of the upper register [where
> the vignette is located] demonstrates the task of the deities whose
> responsibility is annihilation, the goddess demonstrating how the
> damned will be dealt with.

They will be dealt with, in other words, just as in the ancient Native American belief system, by having their brains smashed out.

TERRORS AND OBSTACLES OF THE ANCIENT AMERICAN NETHERWORLD

ANTHROPOLOGIST AKE HULTKRANTZ NOTES TRADITIONS among the Ojibwa and the Huron of northeastern North America concerning:

> the so-called brain-smasher [who] . . . deprives travellers to the land of the dead of their brains. . . . There is in general something demoniac about the brain-catching guardian. . . . In the eschatological conceptions of the Sauk and Fox Indians . . . the deceased perishes altogether if he is unable to save himself from the "brain-smasher."[83]

George Lankford gives an overview of such myths across North America and confirms the very widespread nature of the "fearsome image of a 'brain-smasher,' usually a woman, whose task is to destroy memory (and humanity?) by removing or smashing the brain."[84]

An interesting variant, documented by the ethnologist Alanson Skinner in the early 1920s, comes from the Sauk people, who speak of an obstacle on the Path of Souls where the celestial river must be crossed:

> A log serves for a bridge, and this is guarded by a being called *Po'kitapawa,* "Knocks-a-hole-in-the-head," or "Brain Taker." Brain taker has a watch-dog who barks the alarm whenever a new soul approaches and the fleeting spirit must be swift indeed to avoid having his brains dashed out. If this happens, he is destroyed or lost forever.[85]

It seems, therefore, that the Native American "brain smasher" and the ancient Egyptian goddess in the vignette from the Fifth Hour of the Duat both serve exactly the same function, namely, the annihilation and permanent destruction of unworthy souls on the afterlife journey. There are differences in the traditions, to be sure, as one would expect if they descended from a remote common ancestor many millennia ago and then evolved separately, but the fundamental similarities of the role are unmissable.

A further point arising from this material has to do with the more general issue of the trials and tribulations faced by the soul on its postmortem

Monstrous winged serpents of the ancient American Netherworld.

journey. That the precise character of these obstacles should vary between ancient Egypt and ancient Native America is only to be expected. Even so, the striking similarities in the core structure of the "story"—physical death, a journey of the soul on land, a leap to the sky involving Orion followed by a further journey with perils and challenges to be faced, through the valley of the Milky Way—all argue for some as yet unexplained connection.

In the case of Native America a bridge, sometimes shaky, sometimes thin as a blade, from which the soul can easily fall and be lost forever in the raging torrent below, is one among several ordeals consistently documented in the ethnographic accounts.[86] Another regular character (who, along with the bridge, appears in one of the recensions of the brain smasher tradition cited above) is a dog, often monstrous and ferocious, described by the Algonquin as "the dog with the bloody mouth that devours the souls."[87]

In some accounts the bridge has the power to transform into a serpent,[88] thus further challenging spirits on the Path. Indeed the Native American afterlife journey is almost as filled with monster serpents as the ancient Egyptian Duat. Most notable in this respect is the presence of the Great Horned Water Serpent, sometimes described as "Master of the Beneath World" and sometimes as "the Great Serpent with the Red Jewel in its Forehead:"[89]

If the free soul knows how to deal with the Serpent and is permitted to pass, then it enters the realm of the dead.[90]

In the ancient Egyptian tradition, too, the guardians of various gates and passageways in the Duat, often in serpent form, would permit the soul to pass so long as it had "knowledge of certain formulae, or words of power, and magical names."[91]

THE UNDERWATER PANTHER
AND THE GREAT SPHINX

OTHER NOTABLE CURIOSITIES INCLUDE THE fact, noted earlier, that the serpents of the Duat are very often winged[92] and, in addition, are sometimes depicted with legs and feet.[93] The same goes for the Great Horned Water Serpent, almost always winged,[94] and in addition, in a Sioux account, described as a "water monster which . . . resembled a rattlesnake, but he had short legs."[95]

Because we have the benefit of copious documentation and painted and engraved images, the descriptions of the Duat that have come down to us from ancient Egypt are more vivid and detailed than the descriptions of the Path of Souls that have survived from the Native American oral tradition. Nonetheless, enough remains to confirm that as well as serpents, many of the other monsters and fiends of the Duat also have their counterparts in the Native American afterlife journey.[96]

Of particular interest in this respect is the Underwater Panther, a bizarre hybrid figure, described by the Ojibwa as "a curious combination of cougar, rattlesnake, deer and hawk"[97] and understood to be an avatar, or alter ego, of the Great Horned Water Serpent.[98]

Different Native American peoples gave different names and aspects to the Underwater Panther—*Mishebeshu* and *Michibichi* are the most common—

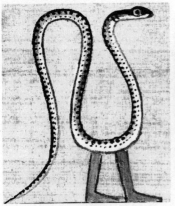 

Monstrous serpents of the ancient Egyptian Netherworld—winged (right), and with legs (left).

but it was also known among the Algonquian-speaking tribes as *Pizha*, mean-ing "panther."[99] On account of this latter name, and of an ancient image of it that was once visible painted on a bluff above the Mississippi at Alton, Illinois, the Underwater Panther became known to interested European travelers as the "Piasa" and was described confusingly both as a "tiger" and as an "animal of the dragon species."[100] In 1839 Arenz and Company of Düsseldorf pub-lished a line drawing of it "taken on the spot by artists from Germany," which is reproduced above. The original petroglyph no longer exists, as the whole face of the bluff on which it was depicted was quarried away in 1846–47.[101]

Other imagery of the Underwater Panther, long since lost, was seen by Nico-las Perrot in 1664, who called it the "Great Panther," while the Ojibwa today describe it as a "sea tiger," preserving its watery associations, and as a "huge brown cat."[102] In some accounts it is said that the Piasa has "a human head."[103]

If the variety of descriptions is bewildering we should not be surprised, for we are dealing with the Netherworld and its shape-shifting denizens here. That the Underwater Panther was seen as having feline characteristics, how-ever, is certain from a number of surviving images of the creature.

Among them is a pottery figure, reproduced in the collage below, that I was able to see for myself in the museum at Moundville. Although the scale is completely different, I suggest that it bears more than a passing resemblance to the Great Sphinx of Giza. The Sphinx, of course, has a human head, not the head of a feline, but let's keep in mind those traditions in which human-headed Piasas are described. Also possibly of relevance here is the evidence that the original prehistoric Sphinx, perhaps more than 12,000 years old, had the head, as well as the body, of a lion. After suffering severe erosion over several millennia the leonine head was recut into human form during the early Dynastic period.[104] Last but not least, Native American traditions of

TOP: Underwater Panther, Moundville. Note tail position and paws. PHOTO: SANTHA FAIIA. BOTTOM RIGHT: The Great Sphinx of Giza. PHOTO: ALBI, DREAMSTIME.COM [21951]. Note tail position and paws. BOTTOM LEFT: Detail of the tail of the Great Sphinx. Compare with tail of Underwater Panther.

the Underwater Panther speak of a time when "four Piasas existed, each associated with its own cardinal direction."[105] Is it a coincidence that the Great Sphinx of Giza, with its strong family resemblance to the Underwater Panther, is an equinoctial marker, oriented precisely to one of the four cardinal directions to face the sun as it rises due east on the equinox?

DOGS AND OTHER "COINCIDENCES"

FEROCIOUS DOGS THAT APPEAR AS obstacles and challenges on the Native American afterlife journey have their counterparts among the monsters of the Duat described in the ancient Egyptian books of the dead. "That god who lives by slaughter," for example, in Spell 335 of the Coffin Texts, "whose face is that of a hound."[106]

Nor is that the only curious nexus involving dogs.

As an exception to the general rule among Native American peoples, the Cherokee do not describe the Milky Way as the "Path of Souls" but refer to it, rather, as "Where the Dog Ran."[107] This is on account of a myth of a giant mill standing on one side of the earth-disk where corn was ground into meal. The store of flour was kept in a great bowl and on several mornings the people who attended the mill found that some of the flour was missing. When the thefts continued they investigated and found the tracks of a dog. The next night:

They watched, and when the dog came . . . and began to eat the meal out of the bowl they sprang out and whipped him.[108]

At this, the dog, who lived on the opposite side of the earth-disk, leapt to the sky and fled "howling" across it to his home,

with the meal dropping from his mouth as he ran, and leaving behind a white trail where now we see the Milky Way, which the Cherokee call to this day *Gi'li-utsun' stanun' yi,* "Where the dog ran."[109]

What's strange is that in ancient Egypt, too, where the Milky Way was the Winding Waterway, there is an exception. It's found in a curious "spell" from the Coffin Texts in which no dogs are mentioned but where the deceased declares:

I am made a spirit. . . . I am he who is in charge of secret matters. . . . I have come equipped with magic, I have quenched my thirst with it. I live on white emmer, filling the Winding Waterway.[110]

White emmer is, of course, one of the domesticated varieties of wheat, and one, moreover, that was particularly favored in ancient Egypt.[111] As with maize in the Americas, it must be milled to produce usable flour. In this variant ancient Egyptian tradition, as in the variant Cherokee tradition, the path in the sky on which the afterlife journey unfolds is likened to a white trail of milled flour.

There are other curiosities.

Take the case of the hero-deity known as the "Birdman," of whom multiple depictions have survived in the Mississippi Valley. He is unmistakably part falcon, part man, just like the god Horus of the Nile Valley. Just like Horus, the Birdman's celestial associations include both the Morning Star and the Sun.[112] And just like Horus, the fundamental role of the Birdman is to symbolize the triumph of life over death. "Although everyone must die eventually," explains Professor James Brown of Northwestern University,

> life is the victor through the survival of one's descendants. The avatar of this struggle of life to reassert itself in the face of inevitable death is the falcon, and one of his guises is the Morning Star. In the pre-dawn light the Morning Star beats back the darkness to make way for the life-sustaining sun. The fact that the [Native American myth of the] Birdman has embedded within it the diurnal progress of night and day, the passage of the heavenly bodies and the cardinal directions tells us that they are properties of a particular cosmology. These elements are not loosely connected.[113]

This is not the place to elaborate further on the Birdman myth, or on the extensive traditions surrounding the god Horus, one of the most famous and complex figures in the ancient Egyptian pantheon. Entire books could be, and have been, written about each and there are great differences between the two as well as some rather striking similarities. What remains to be resolved is whether these similarities are purely coincidental or whether there is some deep, hidden, and previously undetected connection.

Then there's the question of pygmies and dwarfs. They enjoyed special favor in ancient Egypt, where their mummified remains have survived in a number of tombs. They were regarded as possessing more than human powers—there is even a pygmy god named Bes—and they were given positions of importance in the funerary texts.[114] For example, in a vignette to chapter 164 of the Book of the Dead we see a goddess flanked by two dwarfs, each of whom is depicted with two heads, one of a man and one of a falcon.[115] And in the Pyramid Texts, the deceased on his afterlife journey declares:

ABOVE: Woodhenge, Cahokia. Alignment of the center post and equinox-marker post to the equinox sunrise over the southern face of Monks Mound. PHOTO: WILLIAM ISEMINGER. BELOW: Woodhenge overview. A modern reconstruction of an ancient astronomical device. PHOTO: SANTHA FAIIA.

ABOVE: Monks Mound, Cahokia, from the air. PHOTO: WILLIAM ISEMINGER.
BELOW: Monks Mound, that "stupendous pile of earth," the third largest
pyramid in the Americas after the Pyramid of Quetzalcoatl at Cholula and the
Pyramid of the Sun at Teotihuacan. PHOTO: SANTHA FAIIA.

ABOVE: Artist's impression, by William Iseminger, of Cahokia in its prime. BELOW: "Bird Mound," also known as "Mound A," Poverty Point—the second largest earthwork mound in North America after Monks Mound. PHOTO: SANTHA FAIIA.

Moundville, Alabama: Mound A viewed from Mound B, with three of the mounds of the outer ellipse also visible. PHOTO: SANTHA FAIIA.

The hand-and-eye symbol is everywhere at Moundville—here on pottery. PHOTO: SANTHA FAIIA.

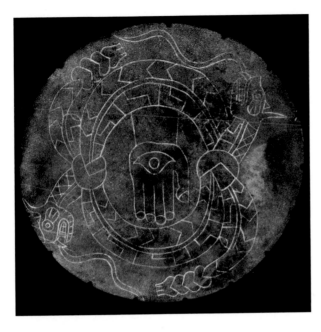

Moundville's "Rattlesnake Disk," a powerful representation of the hand-and-eye symbol. The hand is the Mississippian depiction of the constellation of Orion, and the "eye" represents a portal in the sky, identified with the Orion Nebula, through which it was believed that the souls of the dead must travel on their afterlife journey. See discussion in chapters 22 and 23. PHOTO: COURTESY OF THE UNIVERSITY OF ALABAMA MUSEUMS, TUSCALOOSA, ALABAMA.

Utterances from the ancient Egyptian Pyramid Texts in the tomb chamber of the Pyramid of Unas (5th Dynasty) at Saqqara in Upper Egypt. The progenitor of the more famous Book of the Dead, the Pyramid Texts seek to prepare the deceased for an afterlife journey that is eerily similar to the afterlife journey envisaged by the ancient Mississippians. PHOTO: SANTHA FAIIA

The god Osiris, seated. In the ancient Egyptian system of religion Osiris was identified with the constellation of Orion. As in the case of the hand-and-eye symbol of the Mississippians, the constellation of Orion was seen as a portal to the afterlife journey. PHOTO: SANTHA FAIIA.

In the ancient Egyptian system, Amit, the "Eater of the Dead," with his slavering jaws, served as the agency of permanent annihilation for those souls not justified in the judgment. PHOTO: SANTHA FAIIA.

In the Mississippian system the Underwater Panther, with his slavering jaws, served an identical purpose. PHOTO: SANTHA FAIIA.

FACING PAGE: The weighing of the soul against the feather of Truth in the ancient Egyptian judgment scene. Both the ancient Egyptians and the ancient Mississippians believed that the soul must face judgment after death. PHOTO: SANTHA FAIIA.

The Temple of Horus at Edfu preserves ancient archives, the "Edfu Building Texts," that tell the story of a great and godlike civilization, destroyed in a global cataclysm in remote prehistory. Though Egyptologists are unwilling to make the connection, the destroyed "Island of the Gods," the "Homeland of the Primeval Ones" spoken of in the Edfu Building Texts, shares many common elements with Plato's story of Atlantis—which was said to be derived from an ancient Egyptian source. PHOTO: SANTHA FAIIA.

The Edfu Building Texts report that there were survivors of the cataclysm that destroyed the "Homeland of the Primeval" ones. We are told that these survivors set about "wandering" the world in the desperate hope that their high civilization could be restarted, or that at least something of its knowledge, wisdom, and spiritual ideas could be passed on so that mankind in the post-cataclysmic world would not be compelled (Plato's words concerning the aftermath to the fall of Atlantis) to "begin again like children, in complete ignorance of what happened in early times." PHOTOS: SANTHA FAIIA.

LEFT: Engraved whelk shell depicting the ancient Mississippian hero-deity referred to by archaeologists as the "Birdman." PHOTO: THE NATIONAL MUSEUM OF THE AMERICAN INDIAN (NMAI), SMITHSONIAN INSTITUTION [18/9121]. RIGHT: Statue of the ancient Egyptian hero-deity Horus. The fundamental role of both was to symbolize the triumph of life over death. PHOTO: RAOUL KIEFFER.

I am deemed righteous in the sky and on earth. . . . I am that pygmy of "the dances of god" who diverts the god in front of his great throne.[116]

Likewise, dwarfs and pygmies enjoyed special favor and respect among ancient Native Americans. Hultkrantz reports "a widespread belief in dwarves on the land, at times associated with the concept of a more or less extinct 'prehistoric' race, at times linked to the concept of spirit beings."[117]

As in ancient Egypt, the skeletons of dwarfs have been found in ancient Native American tombs, and as in ancient Egypt, dwarfs were believed to possess superhuman and magical powers. There is even evidence of the existence of dwarf shamans in the Mississippi Valley.[118]

Also worthy of note is the appearance and manifestation of souls, and we have seen already how, in ancient Egypt, the free-flying *Ba* soul was depicted as a bird or as a human-headed bird. "He opens for you the doors of the sky," the Pyramid Texts declare:

he throws open for you the doors of the firmament, he makes a road for you that you may ascend by means of it into the company of the gods, you being alive in your bird shape.[119]

In the case of ancient Native America, the free-soul was likewise very often pictured and spoken of as a bird. Among the Modoc tribe, for example, a boy training to become a shaman fell into a deathlike trance. In this condition he met a female spirit who took out his heart. The boy then heard the spirit talking to his heart, which she held in her hand:

After a while she opened her hand and let go of the heart. Then the little boy thought he saw a bird coming from the west. It came to him and lighted on his breast. That moment he jumped up.[120]

Hultkrantz reports that among the White Knife Shoshoni the soul has the appearance of a bird while "the Huichol identify it as a little white bird and the Luiseno know that it is a dove. The Kootenay believe that the free-soul can show itself as a tomtit or a jay."[121] . . . The free-soul of the Bella Coola is like a bird enclosed in an egg [the physical body]; if the shell of the egg breaks and the soul flies away its owner must die."[122]

Once again, then, it seems that some of the fundamental ideas and imagery of the death process were held in common in ancient Native America and in ancient Egypt and once again the only question we must decide is whether this is a coincidence or not.

JUDGMENT

BOTH THE ANCIENT EGYPTIAN AND the ancient Native American afterlife journeys involve a strong element of judgment. Indeed, in a sense, the entire ordeal in both cases concerns the judgment of the soul for its choices—for what it has done and not done, for the use that it made of the gift of life—during its physical incarnation. In both cases the unworthy soul can face annihilation by gods, demons, and monsters at any point on the journey (for example, at the hands of the "brain-smasher" figure) but in both cases also, for those who have progressed thus far through the Netherworld, a specific judgment awaits.

In the ancient Egyptian system the judgment scene occurs in the Fifth Division (or "Hour") of the Duat, in the Judgment Hall of Osiris, also known as the Hall of Maat—a location that can be reached only by those who are sufficiently provided with spiritual protection to make it through the first four divisions.

I have described the scene at length in previous books, and will not repeat all the details here. In summary, however, the deceased is ushered into a great hall or chamber at the head of which, in partially mummified form, sits Osiris, the high god of death and resurrection, identified in the ancient Egyptian sky religion with the constellation Orion. Also present, wearing a feather headdress, is Maat, the goddess of truth and cosmic justice, and forty-two dispassionate figures, crouched in the manner of scribes poring over papyrus, each wearing the feather of Maat, which symbolizes truth. These are the forty-two Assessors of the Dead, before each of whom the deceased must be able to declare himself innocent of certain acts of moral wrongdoing—notably the act of murder.

Having completed this stage of its examination the soul now finds itself confronted by an immense pair of scales beneath the arms of which are to be seen representations of Anubis, the jackal-headed guide of souls, and Horus, the falcon-headed son of Osiris. One pan of the scales contains an object, shaped like a small urn, symbolizing the heart of the deceased, "considered to be the seat of intelligence and thus the instigator of man's actions and con-

science."[123] In the other pan is placed the feather of Maat, symbolizing, once again, Truth.

If the soul is to triumph in the judgment, heart and feather must stand poised in equilibrium and the prize of eternal life in the Osirian kingdom of the dead beckons. But if the heart is heavy with wickedness and willful waste of the gift of life, if it does not balance with the feather of Truth, then eternal annihilation awaits. To remind us of this, beyond the scales in every depiction of the judgment scene we see the agency of the soul's extinction—a monstrous hybrid, part crocodile, part lion, part hippopotamus, who is known as Amit, the "Devourer," the "Eater of the Dead," in whose slavering jaws the "unjustified" soul is utterly destroyed.[124]

In the ancient Native North American afterlife journey the judgment scene is nowhere so formalized and elaborate as it is the ancient Egyptian version but there is nonetheless—and unmistakably so—a judgment. In the early 1900s, for example, Francis La Flesche, a member of the Omaha tribe of Nebraska and Western Iowa, cooperated with Alice C. Fletcher of Harvard's Peabody Museum to record the traditions of his people. The result, published by the Bureau of American Ethnology in 1911, includes the following account of a crucial moment in the afterlife journey:

> It was said that at the forks of the path of the dead (the Milky Way) there "sat an old man wrapped in a buffalo robe, and when the spirits of the dead passed along he turned the steps of the good and peaceable people toward the short path which led directly to the abode of their relatives, but allowed the contumacious to take the long path, over which they wearily wandered. . . ." The simple and ancient belief seems to have been that the Milky Way is the Path of the Dead. It was said also that the spirit of a murderer "never found his way to his relatives but kept on endlessly searching but never finding rest."[125]

Likewise the late Joseph Epes Brown, founder of the Native American Studies Program at Indiana University, gives this account of the afterlife journey of the Sioux:

> It is held . . . that the released soul travels southward along the "Spirit Path" (the Milky Way) until it comes to a place where this

way divides. Here an old woman, called *Maya owichapaha,* sits; "She who pushes them over the bank," who judges the souls; the worthy ones she allows to travel on the path which goes to the right, but the unworthy she "pushes over the bank," to the left.[126]

In 1967 Ake Hultkrantz joined Fletcher and Brown in linking such traditions to the fact that:

the path of souls is not always one and undivided. In the northern hemisphere the Milky Way splits into two streaks. Not unexpectedly, the Indians have associated this phenomenon with concepts of different passageways to the other world and of dissimilar fates after death. Tradition has it that one road . . . leads to the blessed land of the dead and the other brings downfall and annihilation.[127]

To this George Lankford adds a crucial insight that Hultkrantz missed, namely that there is "a bright star—Deneb—that is placed right at the fork in the path and thus could serve as a marker for the decision point or a figure who does the deciding."[128]

Again a long story must be cut short here, but what Lankford goes on to demonstrate is that a ferocious bird, a raptor with a hooked beak, is a very distinctive "opponent" or "adversary" on the afterlife journey, as portrayed in Moundville pottery. In his view this "Moundville Raptor" is the Mississippian equivalent of the old woman who pushes souls over the bank or the old man who condemns the souls of murderers to endless wandering without rest. And to reinforce his argument, he draws our attention to the Alabamas and the Seminoles, "two groups who are major candidates for descendants of the prehistoric inhabitants of Moundville," who indeed place an eagle in the role of an adversary on the Milky Way path of souls.[129]

Deneb is of course Alpha Cygni, the first-magnitude master star of the Cygnus constellation, which the Greeks identified as a bird, and specifically as a swan. "It is a satisfying coincidental possibility," writes Lankford, "that the people of Moundville saw it the same way, but with the identity of an eagle rather than a swan."[130]

Since his specialty is Native American religions, there is no reason why Lankford should have studied the ancient Egyptian Pyramid Texts. Had he

The star Deneb in the constellation we know as Cygnus, the Swan, is positioned on the bank of the Milky Way exactly at the fork where a second "path," a dead end, branches off. George Lankford identifies Deneb—and Cygnus as a whole—with the Moundville Raptor figure (inset), an adversary on the journey of the soul.

done so, however, he would surely have been struck by Utterance 304, in which the soul on its journey through the Duat is confronted by a bird adversary that apparently has the power to block its path. It's difficult to give any other interpretation to this encounter since the soul is made to declare:

Hail to you, Ostrich which is on the bank of the Winding Waterway! Open my way that I may pass.[131]

An ostrich is not a swan and a swan is not an eagle. Nonetheless, it is surely noteworthy that in both the ancient Egyptian and the ancient Mississippian religions we encounter a bird, with the power to block the further progress of the soul, poised on a bank of the Milky Way.

What else but recognition of the same fork in the Milky Way that was regarded as so ominous in Native American myth can be expressed in Utterance 697 of the Pyramid Texts, where we read:

Do not travel on those western waterways, for those who travel thereon do not return, but travel on the eastern waterways.[132]

ASTRONOMER CHIEFS

IN THE COFFIN TEXTS, IN a passage that addresses the deceased, we read:

> May you recognise your soul in the upper sky while your flesh, your corpse, is in *On*."[133]

The latter location, now a suburb of Cairo 12 miles to the northeast of the immense Old Kingdom burial fields and world-famous pyramids of Giza, was the center of the religious cult that served the Giza necropolis in antiquity. It was the Biblical Hebrews who called this cult center *On*—there are references to it in Genesis, Jeremiah, and Ezekiel.[134] Its original name in the ancient Egyptian language, however, was *Innu*—"the pillar"—and the Greeks would later know it as *Heliopolis,* "the City of the Sun."[135]

The Pyramid Texts, from which the Coffin Texts and all the later funerary texts descended, are often referred to as the "Heliopolitan Recension of the Book of the Dead"[136] because they are thought to have originated in the archives of the cult center of Heliopolis. The archives have not survived the millennia, but the texts themselves are convincing evidence that something such must have existed since they "contain formulae and paragraphs which, judging from the grammatical forms that occur in them, must have been composed, if not actually written down, in the earliest times of Egyptian civilization."[137]

Let's note in passing that the High Priest of Heliopolis bore the title "Chief of the Astronomers" and is represented in tomb paintings and statuary wearing a mantle adorned with stars.[138] It is therefore of interest, when ethnographers recorded the customs and beliefs of the Skidi Pawnee of Oklahoma in the nineteenth century, that they were reported to have shamans, raised to the rank of chiefs, who specialized in astronomy. In the archives of the Smithsonian Institution there is a photograph of one of these individuals, named His Chiefly Sun, and notably he is shown wearing a mantle adorned with stars.[139] It was also the custom of the Skidi Pawnee to wrap a newborn baby in a speckled wildcat skin. This, ethnographers were told,

> was equivalent to saying, "I wrap the child with the heavens," for the hide represented the sky and stars.[140]

LEFT: In ancient Egypt priests wearing a leopard-skin mantle, on which the spots represented stars, played a key role in mortuary ceremonies to prepare the deceased for the afterlife journey. IMAGE FROM TUTANKHAMUN'S TOMB. CENTER: The High Priest of Heliopolis, the cult center of the Giza pyramids, was titled the "Chief of the Astronomers" and wore a mantle like this one adorned with stars. PHOTO: FEDERICO TAVERNI AND NICOLA DELL'AQUILA/MUSEO EGIZIO. RIGHT: Skidi, Pawnee Astronomer Chief. PHOTO: THE NATIONAL ANTHROPOLOGICAL ARCHIVES (NAA), SMITHSONIAN INSTITUTION [BAE GN 01285].

In the case of the Heliopolitan "Chief of the Astronomers" we can see clearly from surviving depictions that the mantle he wore, upon which stars were embossed, was in fact a leopard skin. When the leopard skin was left undecorated the spots of the leopard itself were believed to have symbolized stars.[141] A specialized class of priests, the Sem Priests, also wearing leopard-skin mantles, played a key role in mortuary ceremonies for the deceased.[142]

There is no dispute that the great Mississippian religious centers like Cahokia and Moundville were primarily focused on a cult of the dead, and while not every mound in these sites contains a burial, or multiple burials, the vast majority do. This is also the case at many other mound and earthwork sites in North America. Even some of the very earliest, such as Monte Sano, contain evidence of the postmortem processing of bodies.[143] The Adena mounds are largely burial mounds.[144] And as to the Hopewell earthworks, William Romain writes:

By far the vast majority of known . . . remains are interred in mounds located within the geometric enclosures. Necessarily, then, the physical relationship between the remains of the dead and the enclosures tells us that the Hopewell did, indeed, associate the geometric enclosures with the passage of the individual from life to death.[145]

It may even be, Romain adds,

that the Hopewell considered the geometric enclosures to be actual gateways, or doorways, to the otherworld. Certainly the idea of architectural structures being used to create entrances to the otherworld was known throughout North America. The circular hole in the top of the Ojibway shaking tent, for example, was specifically meant to allow for "soul-flight travel to the Hole in the Sky and across the barrier to the spirit realm."[146]

Though different in degree in terms of the engineering required, there is no difference in kind between the hole in the Ojibwa tent and the star-shaft in the Great Pyramid—which likewise appears to have been intended to facilitate soul-travel to the sky across the barrier to the spirit realm.

Similarly, although there is again a marked difference of degree, there is no difference in kind between the geometric, astronomically aligned structures of the Giza plateau and the geometric, astronomically aligned structures of the Mississippi Valley. All of them seem bound together by the single purpose of the triumph of the soul over death and by the means deployed to achieve that purpose.

But why were structures required at all? And why these specific kinds of structures?

24

ASTRONOMY AND GEOMETRY
IN THE AFTERLIFE

I'M NOT SUGGESTING THAT THE religion of ancient Egypt was brought
from there to ancient North America and I'm **not** suggesting that the religion of ancient North America was brought to ancient Egypt. I accept the
scientific consensus that the Old World and the New World have been isolated from one another, with no significant genetic or cultural contacts, for
more than 12,000 years. Also, the similarities between the religious systems
practiced in ancient Egypt and ancient North America are not such as could
be explained by direct "missionary" or "conversion" activities at any time,
whether relatively early or relatively late. There are too many stark and obvious differences, too deeply adapted to local conditions and local cultural circumstances, for this to be the case.

What, then, are we to make of the striking package of shared beliefs and
symbols reviewed in the previous chapter? In both cases we have a journey
of the soul to a staging ground in the west, a "leap" to a portal in the con-

stellation Orion, transition through that portal to the Milky Way, a journey along the Milky Way during which challenges and ordeals are faced, and a judgment at which the soul's destiny is decided.

Just as the differences rule out direct influence so, too, in my view, the similarities are too many and too obvious to be dismissed as mere "coincidences." A better explanation needs to be sought and in this respect it's helpful to remember that analogous situations arise in genetics. Sometimes, for example, two seemingly completely different groups of people, separated by huge distances and formidable geographic barriers and with zero opportunity to trade DNA, nevertheless turn out to share certain distinct clusters of genes. In these cases the answer very often lies in an earlier population, perhaps with no living members today—a "ghost" population—that was the remote common ancestor of both otherwise unrelated populations in which the surprising genetic resemblances have been found.

In the realm of archaeology, E. A. Wallis Budge faced a comparable problem with similarities he had identified between the Mesopotamian deity Sin, a moon god, and the ancient Egyptian deity Thoth, also associated with the moon. The resemblances, in Budge's view, are "too close to be accidental. It would be wrong to say that the Egyptians borrowed from the Sumerians or the Sumerians from the Egyptians, but it may be submitted that the literati of both peoples borrowed their theological systems from some common but exceedingly ancient source."[1]

Walter Emery, late Edwards Professor of Egyptology at the University of London, also looked into similarities between ancient Egypt and ancient Mesopotamia. He found it impossible to explain them as the result of the direct influence of one culture upon the other and concluded:

The impression we get is of an indirect connection, and perhaps the existence of a third party, whose influence spread to both the Euphrates and the Nile. . . . Modern scholars have tended to ignore the possibility of immigration to both regions from some hypothetical and as yet undiscovered area. [However] a third party whose cultural achievements were passed on independently to Egypt and Mesopotamia would best explain the common features and fundamental differences between the two civilizations.[2]

What I'm suggesting is essentially the same. The hypothesis that best explains the puzzling common features and fundamental differences between the religions of ancient Egypt and ancient North America is that an even more ancient religion, of as yet unidentified provenance, was ancestral to both. The presence of its "DNA" in Egypt and North America also has chronological implications. In view of the evidence that the Old and New Worlds were isolated for more than 12,000 years, from the end of the Ice Age until the time of Columbus, the remote common ancestor of the religions that would later blossom in the Nile and Mississippi River valleys must therefore be more than 12,000 years old. I suggest that this ancestral religion—perhaps *system* would be a better word—used astronomical and geometrical memes expressed in architectural projects as carriers through which it reproduced itself across cultures and down through the ages, and that it was a characteristic of the system that it could lie dormant for millennia and then mysteriously reappear in full flower.

The ayahuasca-inspired art of the Shipibo, in the Peruvian Amazon, is noted for its complex geometrical imagery. PHOTOS: TOP LEFT AND BOTTOM: LUKE HANCOCK. TOP CENTER: NMAI. SMITHSONIAN INSTITUTION [19/5940]. TOP RIGHT: "DADEROT."

Though it is not my purpose to argue this case here, the possibility that the system still hibernates in some form or another in the twenty-first century cannot be ruled out, nor the possibility that it might at some point be awakened again in a garb suited to its time.

Indeed, might we not already be seeing the first intimations of this with the explosion of interest all around the world in ayahuasca as a teacher plant, and in the parallel growth in public exposure to the initiating geometries of ayahuasca-inspired art?

The notion that human agents were behind the spread of the system is not contradicted by this suggestion. On the contrary, the system may itself have had its origins in visionary experiences, in which case those responsible for its spread would surely have made use of "plant allies" wherever they could find them.

ANSWERS IN UNEXPECTED PLACES?

BECAUSE OF THE BURNING OF the library of Alexandria and the frenzied despoiling of the temples by fanatical Christian mobs in the fifth and sixth centuries, much of the legacy of wisdom that made ancient Egypt the "light of the world" has been lost. Nevertheless, because they carved so much in stone, and wrote so much down on papyrus and other media, and because they were enormously prolific artists and builders for more than 3,000 years, the ancient Egyptians have left us a vast legacy of knowledge about their spiritual ideas.

The immense destruction, genocide, and near-total obliteration of indigenous cultures unleashed in North America during the European conquest was a matter of an entirely different order—a full-blown, fast-moving cultural cataclysm, as a result of which we're left often with no record at all or with huge gaps in the record. Thus, although we can be sure the great earthworks and mounds of the Mississippi Valley were connected to beliefs about death and the afterlife, no myths or traditions have survived to explain why it was essential to these beliefs that geoglyphs and mounds should be built or why these structures should incorporate complex geometry and astronomical alignments.

After all a vast expenditure of energy, effort, ingenuity, manpower, and organizational skills was required to create a Cahokia or a Moundville or a Newark Earthworks or, for that matter, a Watson Brake, so it makes no sense that such projects would have been undertaken without some enormously important motive that inspired all the participants. In the absence of surviving evidence of what that motive was in North America, could it be possible that the ancient Egyptian funerary texts might provide an answer?

SQUARES, RECTANGLES, ELLIPSES, AND CIRCLES

I REMEMBERED FROM MY EARLIER encounters with the texts that they included references to geometry and sought out those references now.

A few examples.

In chapter 108 of the Book of the Dead we read of the "Mountain of Sunrise . . . in the eastern heaven. It hath dimensions of 30,000 cubits in length and 15,000 cubits in breadth."[3]

That's a perfect 2-by-1 rectangle, no matter what system of measure you convert it into, equivalent roughly to 15,000 meters by 7,500 meters.

Strange "mountain!"

In chapter 81 there's an obscure geometrical reference to "four sides of the domain of Ra and the width of the earth four times."[4]

Ra is the Sun God and it is the business of "geometry"—literally "earth-measuring"—to know the "width of the earth."

Turning to chapter 110 of the Book of the Dead, we read:

The god Horus maketh himself to be strong like unto the Hawk which is one thousand cubits in length and two thousand cubits in width.[5]

It seems a scribe copying from an older source document mixed up the concepts of length and width but what is defined here is nonetheless a 2-by-1 rectangle with dimensions of approximately 1,000 meters by 500 meters.

In the *Book of What Is in the Duat* another rectangular district is men-

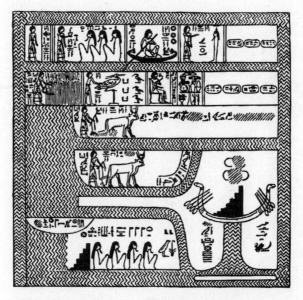

Sekhet-Hetepet (Papyrus of Nebseni, BRITISH MUSEUM).

tioned. Named Sekhet-Hetepet, its long and short dimensions are so close that it is almost, and in the vignettes appears visually to be, a square. Its shape is defined by an unbroken water-filled moat. The land within it is intersected by canals.[6]

A second district of the Duat, named "Tchau," is "440 cubits in length and 440 cubits in width."[7]

That's a perfect square, no matter what system of measure you convert it into, equivalent to roughly 220 meters by 220 meters.

Later, in the Seventh Division of the Duat, another square enclosure of identical dimensions is encountered.[8]

In the Land of Sokar, part of the Fifth Division, and the location of the Judgment scene, we meet a "goddess of the apex."[9] In that same division we also encounter "the god of his angle" whose hieroglyph incorporates a right triangle,[10] fundamental for surveying and trigonometry. The heart of the Land of Sokar, which rests on the backs of two man-headed lion sphinxes set tail to tail, is formed by an elongated ellipse over the top of which looms a pyramid with its apex in the form of the head of a goddess.[11]

Pyramid over elliptical enclosure in the Land of Sokar.

Turning to the Coffin Texts, we find a gigantic ship or "bark" described with the following dimensions:

A million cubits are half the length of the bark; starboard, bow, stern and larboard are four million cubits.[12]

That's around 500 kilometers for "half the length of the bark" and a combined total of 2,000 kilometers for its other listed parts, a geometrical progression with a ratio of 4.

Among the squares, rectangles, and ellipses of ancient Egypt's starry Netherworld there are also perfect circles everywhere.

Staying with the Coffin Texts, we read of "the circle of the Pillar of Horus which is north of the opening of darkness."[13]

In the Book of the Dead we meet "the gods of the *Querti*"—literally the "Circles"—to whom the soul on its afterlife journey was obliged to sing hymns of praise.[14]

In the *Book of What Is in the Duat*, in the Fifth Division and associated with Ra, the Sun God, we are told of a "Circle" that "unites itself with the roads of the Duat."[15] In the Seventh Division a journey is made "in the path of the Circle of Osiris,"[16] while in the Eighth Division we learn of "the Circles of the hidden gods who are on their sand."[17] In addition, five "Circles of the Duat," each entered through a "door," are described.[18]

And throughout the texts we hear repeatedly of "the hidden Circle of the Duat,"[19] a location of great significance, as we shall see. There are indications that the Duat itself was considered to be circular in form. As Wallis Budge points out, there is a scene in the *Book of Gates* that depicts "the body of Osiris bent round in a circle and the hieroglyphics enclosed within it declare that it is the Duat."[20]

SUN AND MOON

AS WELL AS MULTIPLE REFERENCES to stars and constellations, too numerous and all-pervasive in the funerary texts to require special mention here,[21] the moon is frequently encountered on the journey through the Duat. In the Second Division, for example, a vignette shows a boat, the purpose of which, as Budge describes it, is "to support the disk of the full moon. . . . By the disk kneels a god who is 'supporting Maat,' which is symbolized by a feather, and is described by the word MAAT."[22]

Central to the ancient Egyptian judgment scene described in the previous chapter, the concept of Maat enshrines notions of cosmic justice, harmony, and balance. Its association with the moon is appropriate since the moon indeed plays a key "balancing" or "stabilising" role for the earth.[23]

The sun is also often figured as being carried aboard a boat and also features prominently in the Duat, blazing an indomitable path through its terrors each night, a symbol of hope and resurrection in whose company, if they are fortunate, the souls of some of the deceased might be permitted to ride. That much might be expected, but what is interesting are passages in the texts that help us to understand the special attention paid by the ancient Egyptians to the solstices, with several of the greatest temples of the Nile

Valley, notably the Temple of Karnak at Luxor, incorporating spectacular solstitial alignments.

A defining characteristic of the solstices, around June 21 and December 21 when the sun reaches its northernmost and southernmost rising and setting points, is that the pendulum swing of the solar disk along the horizon appears to pause or "stand still," without further northward or southward movement, for an interval of 3 days. In this connection let's recall the peculiarly geometrical "Mountain of Sunrise." The passage concerning it in chapter 108 of the Book of the Dead that I cited earlier continues as follows:

> There is a serpent on the brow of that Mountain, and he measureth 30 cubits in length; the first 8 cubits of its length are covered with flints and with shining metal plates. . . . Now after Ra hath stood still he inclineth his eyes towards him and a stoppage of the boat of Ra taketh place, and a mighty sleep cometh upon him that is in the boat.[24]

It's difficult to interpret this passage in any other way than a colorful, lyrical, poetic description of a solstice.

Similarly, in the Coffin Texts we read:

> I am here from the lifting up of the horizon that I may show Ra at the gates of the sky. . . . A path is prepared for Ra when he comes to a halt.[25]

Again, what else but a solstice could possibly bring Ra, the almighty Sun God, to a halt?

EARTHWORKS

THERE ARE CAUSEWAYS IN THE ancient Egyptian Netherworld.

"I will travel on that great causeway," proclaims the deceased in Spell 629 of the Coffin Texts, "on which those whose shapes are great travel."[26]

In Utterance 676 of the Pyramid Texts, in a passage that calls to mind a pilgrimage with relics, we read:

Do for him what you did for his brother Osiris on that day of putting
the bones in order, of making good the soles, and of traveling the
causeway.[27]

And in Utterance 718:

The Mourning Woman summons you as Isis, the Mooring-post calls
to you as Nepthys, you having appeared upon your causeway.[28]

Very frequently when causeways are mentioned it's in specific association
with mounds. The above passage continues:

May you travel around your Horite Mounds [i.e., mounds consecrated
to the god Horus], may you travel around your Sethite Mounds [i.e.,
mounds consecrated to the god Seth]. You have your spirit, O my
father the King . . . make yourself into a spirit.[29]

In Utterance 470 the deceased informs the soul of his mother, the "Lady
of the Secret Land:"

"I am going to the sky that I may see my father."
"To the High Mounds?" she asks, "or to the Mounds of Seth?"
"The High Mounds," the deceased replies, "will pass me on to the
Mounds of Seth."[30]

It's a very curious, obviously coded language, beyond the reach of straightforward translation, that continues throughout the funerary texts.

As well as Horite Mounds and Sethite Mounds there are the Mounds of
Osiris,[31] and also the Southern Mounds and the Northern Mounds that the
soul must travel to and traverse on its journey through the Duat.[32] And the
structure in the Fifth Division of the Duat that Budge refers to as a pyramid is
also sometimes described as a "hollow mound,"[33] and as a "mound of earth."[34]

In the Coffin Texts we hear of "the gods on their mounds,"[35] and later that
"mounds will be towns and towns will be mounds."[36]

There are also frequent references to "cities of the gods," as in:

A divine city hath been built for me; I know it and I know the name
thereof. Sekhet-Aaru is its name.[37]

Or:

I come from the city of the god, the primeval region.[38]

I mention these "city" references because if towns can be mounds and
mounds can be towns, then "cities" presumably can also be towns and therefore mounds as well? Moreover, the whole picture immediately becomes
much more complicated when we read of a god who "setteth the stars in their
places"[39] only for the translator to immediately qualify that the word he's
chosen to render as "places" actually means "towns." What this god is doing,
therefore—though it seemed an impossible concept to the translator—is
literally setting stars down to earth in "towns."

And we already know that towns can be mounds and mounds can be towns.
That both should also be stars is not at all a contradiction if you just . . . think
like an Egyptian!

HOW TO EQUIP A SPIRIT FOR JOURNEYING

THE ANCIENT EGYPTIANS SAW THEIR lives as their opportunity to prepare
for the trials of the journey through the Duat that they would have to confront
as souls after death. The stakes were high, with both eternal annihilation and
immortality being possible outcomes of that journey. There was undoubtedly
an ethical aspect to the Judgment, as we've seen, but something else was also
required, some gnosis, some deep understanding, and very strangely it turns out
to be the case that those who truly sought the prize of immortality—"the life of
millions of years"—were called upon first to build on the ground perfect copies
"of the hidden circle of the Duat in the body of Nut [the sky]."[40]

Whoever shall make an exact copy of these forms, and shall
know it, shall be a spirit well-equipped both in heaven and earth,
unfailingly, and regularly and eternally.[41]

Whosoever shall make a copy thereof, and shall know it upon earth, it shall act as a magical protector for him both in heaven and upon earth.[42]

If copies of these things be made according to the ordinances of the hidden house, and after the manner of that which is ordered in the hidden house, they shall act as magical protectors to the man who maketh them.[43]

He who hath no knowledge of the whole or part of the secret representations of the Duat shall be condemned to destruction.[44]

Whosoever shall know these secret images shall be in the condition of a spirit who is equipped for journeying.[45]

Wrapped up in the colorful archaic language is a belief—or perhaps the inculcation of a belief—that the immortal destiny of the soul can be influenced by an architectural project to copy on the ground a "hidden" or "secret" part of the Duat sky region, the coordinates of which are set down in archives in the "hidden house."

Egyptologists already accept that the Milky Way and the constellation Orion on its west bank are key markers in the celestial geography of the Duat, and in 1996 Robert Bauval and I made the case in our book *The Message of the Sphinx* that the constellation Leo was very much part of the Duat as well. To cut a long story short, our argument, which we stand by today, is that the ideas expressed in the funerary texts were indeed manifested in architecture in Egypt in the form of the Great Pyramid, the leonine Sphinx, and the underground corridors and chambers beneath these monuments.

The complex was constructed, we believe, as a three-dimensional replica, model, or simulation of the intensely geometrical Fifth Division of the Duat, also known as the "Kingdom of Sokar" and always regarded as an especially hidden and secret place.[46] Moreover, we suggest that what motivated the population to support this gigantic project was precisely the promise of thus obtaining that "magical protection," that power to become "a spirit equipped for journeying," that would ensure a successful afterlife passage through the Duat.

It is not necessary, for the sake of my argument, to enter into any debate about the merits or demerits of such beliefs. It is enough to say that they were clearly held in ancient Egypt over an immensely long span of time and that the proof of this is in the books of the dead and in the Giza architectural complex. Nor is it controversial to add that it was around the belief system expressed in those texts and monuments that the entire extraordinary civilization of the ancient Nile Valley was organized and mobilized from the very beginning—and since that civilization endured and fed its people and nourished their spirituality for more than 3,000 years, it's also obvious that at some fundamental level something about the system *worked*.

QUESTIONS AND ANSWERS

SO WE RETURN TO THE question of why, over a period of many thousands of years, sometimes punctuated by long, culturally barren intervals, huge numbers of architectural projects were undertaken up and down North America's Mississippi Valley linked to a very distinctive set of beliefs about the afterlife journey of the soul that shared many core elements with the spiritual cosmology of ancient Egypt.

If the resemblances are coincidental, we would not expect the ancient Egyptian funerary texts to provide immediate, sensible answers to some outstanding questions about the monuments of the Mississippi Valley. The fact that they do, in my view, increases the likelihood that we're looking at a real connection.

Why are the Mississippi Valley sites built on such a gigantic scale and why are celestial alignments of such importance within them?

For the same reasons given in the ancient Egyptian funerary texts for the construction of the sky-ground architecture of the Nile Valley— that the sky is gigantic and the purpose of the architecture is to honor, connect with, and above all "resemble the sky."

Why are the Orion constellation and the Milky Way so important in the funerary symbolism of the Mississippian culture? And why is the Milky Way the "Path of Souls"?

For the same reason given in the ancient Egyptian funerary texts— that within the general frame of the starry sky it is specifically Orion that hosts the portal through which the soul must pass to reach the "Winding Waterway" that in turn leads the soul onward on its journey through the Land of the Dead.

Why is geometry, and its particular manifestation in the form of rectangular, square, circular, and elliptical enclosures, such a significant element of the Mississippi Valley sites?

For the same reasons given in the ancient Egyptian funerary texts for the distinct geometrical character of the sky-ground architecture of the Nile Valley—geometry is a foundational characteristic of the Land of the Dead and the rectangular, square, circular, and elliptical enclosures are the typical forms of celestial "districts" through which the soul must pass on its afterlife journey.

Why do the Mississippi Valley sites feature causeways and mounds?

For the same reasons given in the ancient Egyptian funerary texts for the incorporation of causeways and mounds in the sky-ground architecture of the Nile Valley—namely, that causeways and mounds are prominent features of the celestial Land of the Dead that it is the purpose of the architecture to replicate on earth.

Why were the peoples of the Mississippi Valley willing to expend such great quantities of treasure and energy on the creation of spectacular sites such as Moundville, Cahokia, and the Newark Earthworks, and why did they take such care to imbue every one of them with intense geometrical characteristics and to ensure that each in its own way "resembled" and formed intimate connections with the sky?

For the same reason given in the ancient Egyptian funerary texts—the belief that if the sky, or some "hidden" or "secret" aspect of it, were NOT copied on the ground (and in some way explored, navigated, and *known* prior to death), then those souls who had failed to do this necessary work, and thus were not equipped with the knowledge of "the secret representations," would be "condemned to destruction."

SKY AND GROUND

WHEN IT COMES TO MOTIVATIONAL techniques, as the Roman Catholic Church demonstrated throughout the Middle Ages, the prospect of eternal damnation can be very effective. I suggest that in ancient Egypt it was the equivalent prospect of "destruction" or "annihilation" of the soul, and the possibility of avoiding such a fate—as spelled out in the funerary texts—that motivated the construction of the sky-ground temples and pyramids of the Nile Valley. They were all, in a sense, gigantic books of the dead in stone and some–the Giza complex in particular—were undoubtedly seen as "actual gateways, or doorways, to the otherworld."

That phrase, "actual gateways, or doorways, to the otherworld," is William Romain's, cited at the end of the previous chapter with reference to the Hopewell earthworks. I quote it again here to emphasize the peculiar interchangeability of spiritual beliefs in the Nile Valley and the Mississippi Valley. Although widely separated in time and space, the ancient inhabitants of these two regions seem to have shared a core set of ideas about the afterlife destiny of the soul and seem, moreover, to have been largely in agreement not only that those ideas should be manifested in architecture, but also on many of the specific characteristics of that architecture, and on the purpose that the architecture was intended to serve.

Thus, while one reproduced Orion's belt and the constellation of Leo and the other orchestrated complex architectural dances aligned to lunar and solar standstills, the fundamental objective of both was to open portals between sky and ground through which the souls of the dead could pass.

I'm not ruling out the possibility that some of the monuments of the Mississippi Valley are "constellation diagrams"—or constituent parts of "constellation diagrams"—much like the Giza monuments. Indeed Ross Hamilton, as we saw in part 1, has long been of the opinion that Serpent Mound is a terrestrial figure of the constellation Draco. George Lankford, on the other hand, makes a strong case that it represents the constellation Scorpius.[47] The point is not whether one is right or wrong, but that both see the possibility that the mounds and earthworks could have been used to represent constellations.

Perhaps we'll never know for sure, since so much of North America's pre-Columbian heritage has been destroyed. Nevertheless, efforts are already being made.

Stepping back in time from the Mississippian civilization, for example, William Romain's detailed studies of the Hopewell lead him to conclude that, in the minds of those who made them:

> the Newark Earthworks were a portal to the Otherworld that allowed for interdimensional movement of the soul during certain solar, lunar and stellar configurations.[48]

He also argues that the "Great Hopewell Road," an ancient causeway that once ran straight for more than 60 miles between Newark and High Bank (see chapter 20), "was the terrestrial equivalent of, or metaphor for the Milky Way Path of Souls providing a directional component for soul travel to the Realm of the Dead."[49]

Further, Romain joins George Lankford in linking Serpent Mound to Scorpius and in concluding that "Serpent Mound was a cognate for the Great Lowerworld Serpent which guarded the Realm of the Dead."[50]

What confronts us with the Hopewell, then, as with ancient Egypt and as with the Mississippian civilization, is a Realm of the Dead in the sky and its representation by architectural structures on the ground. It is part of the brilliance of such structures that they can play multiple roles in the cosmic drama. Thus, while the Great Sphinx may be the terrestrial counterpart of the constellation Leo, its gaze also sacralizes the union of heaven and earth at sunrise on the equinoxes. And while Serpent Mound may indeed be the earthly twin of the constellation Scorpius, its open jaws and the oval earthwork between them also serve to unite ground and sky at sunset on the summer solstice.

In this connection, let's reconsider the reference cited earlier from the Book of the Dead concerning a great serpent on the brow of a mountain that brings the boat of the Sun God Ra to a halt, plunging that deity into a "mighty sleep" with nothing more than a glance.[51] It may, of course, be a coincidence, but this description resonates curiously with the situation of Serpent Mound. For what do we encounter there on the bluff above Brush Creek if not a massive serpent effigy with its gaze targeted on the sun at its midsummer standstill?

That's indeed a time, as we've seen, when the setting point of the solar disk appears to remain fixed at the same place on the horizon for 3 days, an event that might appropriately be expressed, in mythical language, as a "mighty sleep" brought on by the precisely aimed gaze of the Serpent.

Then, too, the great serpent in the Book of the Dead is described as having "the first 8 cubits of its length"—its head and neck, in other words—"covered with flints and with shining metal plates."[52] The resonance here is with George Lankford's study of Native American traditions of the Great Horned Water Serpent (see chapter 23), sometimes described as the "Master of the Beneath World" and sometimes as "the Great Serpent with the Red Jewel in its Forehead"—a notion not so very far away from the ancient Egyptian representation in which the creature's head and neck glitter "with flints and with shining metal." It is this Great Jeweled Serpent, Lankford concludes, represented as an adversary on the Path of Souls, that is depicted very frequently in Moundville designs where it is directly linked to other imagery associated with the afterlife journey. He also makes a strong case that Serpent Mound is a three-dimensional representation of the same supernatural entity[53] and draws an interesting comparison with myths of the Cherokees describing the Uktena, "a great snake, as large around as a tree-trunk," with:

> a bright blazing crest like a diamond on its forehead, and scales
> glittering like sparks of fire.[54]

The same myths also tell us that the gaze of this serpent had the power to "daze" people so that they were stopped in their tracks and could not escape from it,[55] and again there is a notable parallel here with the great serpent of the Book of the Dead whose gaze plunges even the Sun into a "mighty sleep."[56]

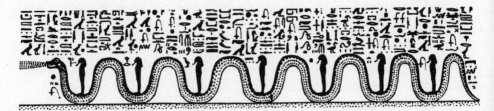

Kheti, a serpent of the Duat.

RENEWAL AND REBIRTH

SCHOLARS ARE IN NO DOUBT that the ideas about the afterlife journey of the soul expressed in the ancient Egyptian funerary texts are much older than the surviving inscriptions and extend far back into the oral traditions of the pre-dynastic, pre-literate period before 5,500 years ago.[57]

Likewise, although we have no hieroglyphs or inscriptions from North America, it's noteworthy that the same geometrical concerns and the very same alignment to the summer solstice sunset that we see at Serpent Mound, supposedly from the "Adena" period around 2,300 years ago, are also present at Watson Brake 5,500 years ago. And indeed we may say that the sudden burst of mound-building and earthwork construction across the Lower Mississippi Valley between 6,000 and 5,000 years ago is mysterious and unexplained. Like the sudden and fully formed appearance of the high civilization of Egypt, it seems just to have come out of nowhere, with no apparent antecedents, yet already in possession of advanced knowledge.

The earliest mound sites we know of in North America may possibly date back as far as 8,000 years.[58] After that the trail goes cold.

But then why should we be surprised? The trail goes cold for a full 1,000 years between the end of the Watson Brake epoch and the beginning of Poverty Point, and it goes cold again several times thereafter, only to reappear reborn and renewed on the far side of each lacuna. The same stop-start process, however, also means that we can't date the inception of the tradition to its oldest manifestations so far found.

First, the archaeology is very far from complete, and given the destruction of so much of the evidence from prehistory, will never be complete—so our ability to figure out what really happened in the North American past is deeply compromised. It may be that there was no mound-building at all before 8,000 years ago, but it could equally well be that the evidence of an earlier mound-building episode has simply been lost.

Second, because we are dealing with a system of ideas that has a proven ability to appear and disappear and reappear again fully formed, we must consider the possibility that it is such a "reappearance" that the archaeological record has identified at the supposed "earliest" mound sites—in other words, that the skills manifest in those already very ancient sites were, as my friend the late John Anthony West used to put it about the civilization of ancient Egypt, "a legacy not a development."

But a legacy of what? And when? And how is it that it keeps on turning up all around the world, in different places at different times, but always expressing and manifesting the same core ideas?

Once again, the ancient Egyptian texts offer some suggestive answers.

REBIRTH OF A LOST WORLD

THIS TIME IT'S NOT THE funerary texts I'm referring to, but the Edfu Building Texts, so called because they are inscribed on the walls of the Temple of Horus at Edfu in Upper Egypt.

These texts take us back to a very remote period called the "Early Primeval Age of the Gods"[59]—and these gods, it transpires, were not originally Egyptian,[60] but lived on a sacred island, the "Homeland of the Primeval Ones," in the midst of a great ocean.[61] Then, at some unspecified time in the past, an immense cataclysm shook the earth and a flood poured over this island, where "the earliest mansions of the gods" had been founded,[62] destroying it utterly, submerging all its holy places, and killing most of its divine inhabitants.[63] Some survived, however, and we are told that this remnant set sail in their ships (for the texts leave us in no doubt that these "gods" of the early primeval age were navigators[64]) to "wander" the world.[65] Their purpose in doing so was nothing less than to re-create and revive the essence of their lost homeland,[66] to bring about, in short:

> The resurrection of the former world of the gods . . .[67]
> The re-creation of a destroyed world.[68]

For those readers not already familiar with the enigma of the Edfu Building Texts, and who would like to know more, I give a detailed analysis in my book *Magicians of the Gods*. I won't repeat here the case I made there, nor support it with the evidence presented there. The takeaway is that the texts invite us to consider the possibility that the survivors of a lost civilization, thought of as "gods" but manifestly human, set about "wandering" the world in the aftermath of an extinction-level global cataclysm. By happenstance it was primarily hunter-gatherer populations, the peoples of the mountains, jungles, and deserts—"the unlettered and the uncultured," as Plato so eloquently put it in his account of the end of Atlantis—who had been "spared the scourge of the deluge."[69] Settling among them, the wanderers entertained the desperate hope that their high civilization could be restarted, or that at least something of its knowledge, wisdom, and spiritual ideas could be passed on so that mankind in the post-cataclysmic world would not be compelled to "begin again like children, in complete ignorance of what happened in early times."[70]

In this Edfu account of the wandering civilizers am I wrong to be very strongly reminded of the Tukano origin myth, given in chapter 18? It tells of how "Helmsman" and "Daughter of the Sun" brought the gifts of fire, horticulture, pottery-making, and other skills to the first humans to enter the Amazon while other "supernaturals" traveled over all the rivers, explored the remote hill ranges, identified the best places for settlement, and "prepared the land so that mortal human creatures might live on it."

Before returning whence they had come these so-called supernaturals:

Left their lasting imprint on many spots so that future generations would have ineffaceable proof of their earthly days and would forever remember them and their teachings.[71]

These same spots, very frequently marked with petroglyphs, are still held sacred by the Tukano today, anthropologist Gerardo Reichel-Dolmatoff confirms, as "proof of the divine origin of the cultural heritage, the foundations of which had been laid down by the spirit beings who, at that time, still dwelled upon earth."[72]

Returning to ancient Egypt and to the Edfu texts, we're told that the survivors of the Island of the Primeval Ones:

journeyed through the . . . lands of the primeval age. . . .[73] In any place in which they settled they founded new sacred domains.[74]

We may deduce, therefore, that part of their mission was to repromulgate the lost religion of the days before the flood.

Next we learn that architecture, initially in the form of earthen mounds, was also central to their mission. Indeed it was so central that they carried with them a book, *The Specifications of the Mounds of the Early Primeval Age,* that literally "specified" the locations in the Nile Valley upon which every mound was to be situated, the character and appearance of each mound, and the understanding that those first, foundational mounds were to serve as the sites for all the temples and pyramids that would be built in Egypt in the future.[75]

Little wonder then that included among the company of the "gods" of Edfu were the *Shebtiw,* a group of deities charged with a specific responsibility for "creation,"[76] the "Builder Gods" who accomplished "the actual work of building,"[77] and the "Seven Sages" who, in addition to dispensing wisdom, as their name suggests, were much involved in the setting out of structures and in laying foundations.[78]

My argument has long been that the Edfu Building Texts reflect real events surrounding a real cataclysm that unfolded between 12,800 and 11,600 years ago, a period known to paleoclimatologists as the Younger Dryas and that the Texts call the "Early Primeval Age." I have proposed that the seeds of what was eventually to become dynastic Egypt were planted in the Nile Valley in that remote epoch more than 12,000 years ago by the survivors of a lost civilization and that it was at this time that structures such as the Great Sphinx and its associated megalithic temples and the subterranean chamber beneath the Great Pyramid were created. I have further proposed that something resembling a religious cult or monastery, recruiting new initiates down the generations, deploying the memes of geometry and astronomy, disseminating an "as-above-so-below" system of thought, and teaching that eternal annihilation awaited those who did not serve and honor the system, would have been the most likely vehicle to carry the ideas of the original founders across the millennia until they could be brought to full flower in the Pyramid Age.

TURTLE ISLAND

IF WE TAKE THE EDFU Building Texts seriously, with their depiction of seafaring missions sent all around the world to attempt to restart a civilization after a global cataclysm, and if ancient Egypt is the distant descendant of one of those missions, then we would expect to find other distant descendants elsewhere in the world.

It is my case in this book that we do indeed find such a descendant civilization in the Mississippi Valley and that, like ancient Egypt, it carries the DNA of a "ghost" civilization of remote prehistory. At sites such as Cahokia and Moundville, and 1,000 years earlier at Newark and High Bank, and 1,000 years before that at Poverty Point, and again 2,000 years before that at Watson Brake, we see the same sky-ground geometrical and astronomical system at work, with origins that keep on receding deeper and deeper into the past until the trail fades from view around 8,000 years ago. In the case of the older sites in this continuum—despite early evidence of a special place granted to the constellation Orion across North America[79]—there is insufficient information for us to be sure of the afterlife beliefs of the people who made them and whether they were linked to the "Path of Souls" complex that we find so amply demonstrated in the later sites. But the fact that such beliefs are confirmed at Cahokia and Moundville, and other relatively recent Mississippian sites where the archaeological evidence can be enriched with ethnographic data, and the fact that they are also strongly implicated in Hopewell and Adena sites such as Newark, High Bank, and Serpent Mound, suggest strongly that the same "cultural package" of sky-ground geometry and astronomy, linked to the same set of beliefs about the afterlife journey of the soul, is likely to have been at work from the beginning to the end of the mound-building enterprise in North America.

Then there's the matter of the Amazon, where earthworks incorporating geometrical and astronomical memes identical to those manifested in the ancient Nile and Mississippi River Valleys are now emerging from the jungle hand in hand with traditions of "geometrical gods" and evidence of an ancient quest using vision-inducing plants to gain knowledge of the realm of the dead.

At the same time, the whole story of the peopling of the Americas is up for grabs. We know that the New World has been separated from the Old—a gigantic island—since the epoch of sea-level rise at the end of the Ice Age between 12,800 and 11,600 years ago. We know that there were subsequently no significant transfers of culture or genes between the two regions until about 500 years ago, when the European conquest of the Americas began. We may safely conclude, therefore, that anything held in common culturally or genetically between the Old World and the New that is not the result of mixing in the past 500 years is either a coincidence or has to date back at least 11,600 years—and could, of course, be far older than that.

The extraordinary similarities we've considered between ancient Egypt and ancient North America are far beyond the power of coincidence to explain and yet the differences, and the physical and temporal separation of the Nile and Mississippi Valley civilizations, mean direct influence also must be ruled out.

What's left is a remote third party—a lost civilization, perhaps even the "island" that the Edfu texts call the Homeland of the Primeval Ones destroyed in the global cataclysm of 12,800 years ago.

North America—"Turtle Island" in Native American tradition—is always, almost automatically, assumed to be a place to which culture was brought from elsewhere, but let's shift the reference frame. What if North America itself was the Homeland of the Primeval Ones? What if the distinctive system of ideas involving the afterlife journey of the soul and the building of very specific types of structures thought to facilitate that journey weren't **brought** to North America but originated there?

Now that the "Clovis First" nonsense has finally been laid to rest we know for sure that humans have been in the Americas for at least 25,000 years, with compelling evidence for an even earlier presence 50,000 years ago or more. Indeed if, Tom Deméré and his team have correctly read the clues at the Cerutti Mastodon Site, the real First Americans may have inhabited the New World—as far south as San Diego—as much as 130,000 years ago.

Even if the continent wasn't inhabited until 25,000 years ago, however, we're still left with an immense span of time before the earliest evidence of mound-building in North America around 8,000 years ago. That's an interval quite long enough for great innovations in human culture to have occurred, yet if they did occur, why do we find no trace of them?

We've already seen, and I think there's no dispute about it, that a vast heritage of truth about Native American cultures, and what they really knew and believed, was utterly obliterated by the European conquest in the past 500 years. That's one reason why the record is so patchy, with great chunks simply missing.

The second reason, as Tom Deméré explained (see part 2), is that archaeologists have, until recently, been unwilling to investigate older deposits because of a preexisting conviction that nothing would be found in them.

But there's a third factor that may prove to be of far greater significance than the other two, and this has to do with the extinction-level cataclysm that the earth experienced 12,800 years ago. Although the entire globe was affected, all the evidence indicates that the epicenter was in North America. It's giant ice cap, 2 kilometers deep and extending in that epoch as far south as Minnesota, was massively destabilized, and the destruction that followed was near total across an immense area where the archaeological record was effectively swept clean.

What happened in North America?

PART VII

APOCALYPSE THEN

The Mystery of the Cataclysm

25

ELOISE

IT'S EARLY OCTOBER 2017, A roasting-hot midmorning, and we've just left Tucson, Arizona, for the 80-mile drive to Murray Springs, a very rich and complex Clovis site about 14 miles southwest of the town of Tombstone and 20 miles north of the Mexican border. Our route takes us via I-10 and AZ-90 through increasingly sere scrub and semidesert under a merciless sky, but when we arrive at Murray Springs itself, park, say hello to the rangers at the gate, and walk the couple of miles of the trail around the archaeological site we find ourselves in a sort of oasis with abundant mesquite growing tall enough along the edges of a sinuous arroyo—a flood channel—to offer some welcome shade. Although flash floods still rip through here from time to time it's rumored that the present lush environment owes more to treated sewage being dumped in the area.

Santha and I are accompanied by geophysicist Allen West and his wife, Nancy. Working with Jim Kennett, an earth scientist and oceanographer at the University of California, and Richard Firestone, a nuclear analytical chemist at Lawrence Berkeley National Laboratory, West is one of the principal investigators in a loose alliance of more than sixty scientists from many different fields who have joined forces since 2007 to try to solve a profound mystery. It concerns the Younger Dryas, the interlude of cataclysmic global climate change coinciding with the Late Pleistocene Extinction Event in which thirty-five genera of North American megafauna (with each genus consisting of several species) were wiped out around 12,800 years ago. Sharing their fate were the Clovis people and their distinctive culture with its characteristic "fluted-point" weaponry.

We climb down to the floor of the arroyo, which is about 2 meters deep and 12 meters wide at this point, and begin to walk along it. After a few moments Allen stops. "It's around here that they excavated Eloise," he says. He's referring to one of the mammoths ambushed and butchered at Murray Springs by the Clovis people some 12,800 years ago. He describes how Eloise's skeleton was found intact except for the hind legs, which had been chopped off right after she was killed. One was moved up and placed alongside her head. Archaeologists found the other a few hundred meters away, close to the residue of an ancient campfire. Part of a broken Clovis point was also found by the campfire, while the rest of it was "in Eloise."

The archaeologist who excavated the mammoth in the 1960s, and who would bring Allen West and Richard Firestone to the site many years later, was Vance Haynes, Regents Professor Emeritus at the University of Arizona and a senior member of the National Academy of Sciences. The reader will recall that his adamant defense of "Clovis First" was a significant factor in extending the life of that now thoroughly discredited theory and in inhibiting other research indicating a much earlier peopling of the Americas.

As the discoverer and principal excavator of Murray Springs, however, Haynes deserves credit for drawing attention to a very curious aspect of the site—a distinct dark layer of soil draped "like shrink-wrap," as Allen West puts it, over the top of the Clovis remains and of the extinct megafauna—including Eloise.

Haynes has identified this "black mat" (his term) not only at Murray Springs but at dozens of other sites across North America,[1] and was the first to acknowledge its clear and obvious association with the Late Pleistocene Extinction Event. He speaks of the "remarkable circumstances" surrounding the event, the abrupt die-off on a continental scale of all large mammals "immediately before deposition of the . . . black mat," and the total absence thereafter of "mammoth, mastodon, horse, camel, dire wolf, American lion, tapir and other [megafauna], as well as Clovis people."[2]

Haynes notes also that "The basal black mat contact marks a major climate change from the warm dry climate of the terminal Allerød to the glacially cold Younger Dryas."[3]

From roughly 18,000 years ago, and for several thousand years thereafter, global temperatures had been slowly but steadily rising and the ice sheets melting. Our ancestors would have had reason to hope that earth's long winter was at last coming to an end and that a new era of congenial climate beckoned. This process of warming became particularly pronounced after about 14,500 years ago. Then suddenly, around 12,800 years ago, the direction of climate change reversed and the world turned dramatically, instantly cold— as cold as it had been at the peak of the Ice Age many thousands of years earlier. This deep freeze—the mysterious epoch now known as the Younger Dryas—lasted for approximately 1,200 years until 11,600 years ago, at which point the climate flipped again, global temperatures shot up rapidly, the remnant ice sheets melted and collapsed into the oceans, and the world became as warm as it is today.[4]

In addition to Murray Springs, Vance Haynes reports finding:

At least 40 other localities in the United States with Younger Dryas age black mat deposits. . . . [5] This layer or mat covers the Clovis-age landscape or surface on which the last remnants of the terminal Pleistocene megafauna are recorded. Stratigraphically and chronologically the extinction appears to have been catastrophic, seemingly too sudden and extensive for either human predation or climate change to have been the primary cause. This sudden . . . termination . . . appears to have coincided with the sudden climatic switch from Allerød warming to Younger Dryas cooling. Recent evidence for extraterrestrial impact, although not yet compelling, needs further testing because a remarkable perturbation occurred . . . that needs to be explained.[6]

Haynes published these thoughts in the *Proceedings of the National Academy of Sciences* in May 2008. The "extraterrestrial" impact that he mentions (and finds "not yet compelling") has nothing to do with "aliens" but refers to a serious scientific theory, the "Younger Dryas Impact Hypothesis," that had received its first formal airing—also in *PNAS*—in October 2007.[7] The paper was coauthored by Allen West, Richard Firestone, James Kennett, and more than twenty other scientists and presents evidence that multiple fragments of a giant comet—a swarm of fragments—struck the earth with disastrous consequences around 12,800 years ago. The effects were global but the epicenter of the cataclysm was over the North American ice cap, which the impacts destabilized, triggering the Younger Dryas deep freeze and the megafaunal extinctions.[8]

Haynes was right to say, in 2008, that this radical hypothesis needed further testing. It would receive it in the years ahead and become the focus of a furious debate that has divided scientists and continues to this day. On one side, many highly qualified and experienced specialists from many different fields are convinced that a comet swarm was indeed encountered around 12,800 years ago and that the result was a global catastrophe, with its most extreme effects felt in North America. On the other side is a smaller but more vocal and highly influential group of skeptics who reject the theory. I reported the debate between the two factions in some detail in my book *Magicians of the Gods* so won't repeat myself here. As I write these words in 2018, and despite a decade of unrelenting criticism and focused attempts at refutation, the upshot is that the Younger Dryas Impact Hypothesis [YDIH] has stood the test of time, gained increasingly wide acceptance among scientists, and remains by far the best single, coherent explanation for the cataclysmic events and extinctions— the "remarkable perturbation"—that did indeed occur around 12,800 ago.

Allen West is at the cutting edge of the research into this colossal mystery and the coauthor of more than forty scientific papers looking into it in depth. I'm privileged to have him join me at Murray Springs.

BLACK MAT

ALLEN LEADS US OVER TO the side wall of the arroyo, explaining, as we walk, that the area would have had a very different appearance 12,800 years ago. In particular it would have been "much wetter," with "a string of lakes" serving as watering holes for the megafauna that the Clovis hunters came here to kill. The arroyo itself is a relatively recent feature but a useful one because it slices vertically through a couple of meters of sediment laid down before and after the onset of the Younger Dryas and thus functions something like an archaeological trench, revealing the layers—and what's in them—stacked one on top of the other.

A distinct black stratum, running horizontally like a layer in a cake, is visible on both walls of the arroyo about a meter below present ground level. It obviously lies across the whole landscape and has been exposed here by the flash floods that cut the arroyo—as though, to extend the analogy, a "slice" of the cake has been removed, allowing us a glimpse of its interior.

The stratum is about a hand's-breadth thick.

"That's the black mat," Allen confirms.

It doesn't look like a cataclysm, but appearances can be deceptive.

The first and most obvious sign of an impact by an asteroid or comet is a crater—or multiple craters in the case of a swarm. However, the earth's surface is dynamic and craters can be obliterated by erosion or other geological processes, or covered over by later sediments or submerged by rising sea levels. In the case of impacts on the 2-kilometer-deep North American ice cap, as envisaged in the YDIH, the craters would have been excavated in ice that would have subsequently melted away, leaving little or no evidence on the ground beneath.

Scientists have therefore developed other measures, more subtle than looking for craters, to detect cosmic impacts in the geological record. Nanodiamonds, for example, are microscopic diamonds that form under rare conditions of great shock, pressure, and heat, and are recognized as being among the characteristic fingerprints—"proxies" in scientific language—of powerful impacts by comets or asteroids.[9] Other proxies include meltglass (resembling trinitite), tiny carbon spherules that form when molten droplets cool rapidly in air, magnetic microspherules, charcoal, soot, platinum, carbon molecules containing the rare isotope helium-3, and magnetic grains with iridium.[10]

Certain of the glassy and metallic proxies require temperatures in excess of 2,200 degrees C to form and there is nothing in nature other than the heat and shock of a cosmic impact that can instantly generate such temperatures.[11] Alternative explanations might be offered for some of the other proxies but when they occur together, and in abundance, a cosmic impact again fits the evidence better than anything else.[12]

Moreover, to this day, scientists know of only two layers of sediment "broadly distributed across several continents that exhibit coeval abundance peaks in a comprehensive assemblage of cosmic impact markers, including nanodiamonds, high-temperature quenched spherules, high-temperature melt-glass, carbon spherules, iridium and aciniform carbon."[13]

These layers are found at the Cretaceous-Paleogene Boundary 65 million years ago, when it has long been agreed that a gigantic cosmic impact in the Gulf of Mexico caused the mass extinction of the dinosaurs, and at the Younger Dryas Boundary 12,800 years ago.[14]

I have a question for Allen. "Since the black mat was found draped directly on top of Eloise—like 'shrink-wrap,' you said—then presumably it must have begun to form very shortly after she was killed and butchered with most of her remains left lying on the spot?"

"What we see is that at the bottom of that black-mat layer, literally the first thing touching those bones, are spherules, iridium, platinum, and small pieces of melt-glass from the event. So it doesn't mean the animal was alive when the event happened, but she had to have been alive very, very shortly, at most a few weeks, before it."

I ask Allen to explain the black mat to me. "I understand that the lowest part of it is full of impact proxies laid down at the time the mat began to form but clearly they're not the mat itself . . ."

"The black mat formed on top of the layer of proxies," Allen replies. "Down here it has a lot of charcoal in it. But it also has algal remains so it's not just fire. The Younger Dryas changed the climate and made the area much wetter. Algae began to grow along the edges of the lakes." He puts a hand on the black stripe along the arroyo wall: "So the remains of about 1,000 years of dead algae, charcoal, and a lot of other stuff are all embedded in here, and at the bottom of it, where the impact happened, we find iridium, platinum, and a layer of melted spherules where the temperatures must have been so high that they would have melted a modern car into a pool of metal."

"So are you saying that there was an impact right here? At Murray Springs?"

Allen replies that it's not as simple as that. "The bigger impacts were farther north. Down here it's more likely to have been an airburst—a fragment of the comet that literally blew up in the sky before hitting the ground . . ."

"And the effect of that would have been . . . what?"

"If you'd been standing here it would have seemed like the whole sky caught on fire with the center of it brighter than the sun. And the thing is it would have been totally silent. They would have heard nothing at first. Because the speed of sound is a lot slower than the speed of light."

My imagination has gone into overdrive. "Could it have happened," I ask, "while the Clovis hunters were actually butchering Eloise?"

Allen shakes his head. "We know it didn't happen instantaneously," he reminds me, "because they chopped her legs off and hauled one of them away and cooked it. But it could have happened later the same day and like I say it certainly happened within a couple of weeks. That's based on modern data from elephant kills in Africa. The scavengers come in quickly and disarticulate the skeleton, and that didn't happen with Eloise."

This kill site sounds like unfinished business to me.

"That other haunch left up by Eloise's head," I reflect, "and the rest of her intact. Doesn't that suggest that the hunters were still in the vicinity and meant to come back to finish butchering her, but for some reason never did?"

Allen joins in with the spirit of the thought. "Okay," he says. "It's pure speculation, obviously, because we'll never know for sure the exact sequence of events here 12,800 years ago, but based on the evidence it's not unreasonable to envisage the hunters sitting around, cooking mammoth haunch over their campfire when all of a sudden the sky explodes . . ."

"And that's why they never go back for the rest of Eloise? Because they're all dead?"

"Could be," Alan agrees. He jabs a finger into the base of the black mat and continues.

"But what we can be certain of was that this moment marked the end of their story, and the end of an epoch, really. There's not a single Clovis point found anywhere in North America that's above that black mat. They're all in it or below it. And there's not a single mammoth skeleton anywhere in North America that's above it. A huge part of the die-off could have been as a direct result of the impacts themselves, but impacts and airbursts south of the ice cap, particularly as far south as New Mexico, would also have set off wildfires. There's overwhelming evidence that gigantic wildfires raged at the onset of the Younger Dryas—in fact, more soot has been found at the Younger Dryas Boundary than at the Cretaceous-Paleogene Boundary. We did the calculations and it looks like as much as 25 percent of the edible biomass and around 9 percent of the total biomass of the planet was on fire and destroyed within days or weeks of the YDB. So in many areas if the animals weren't killed outright they wouldn't have been able to forage enough food afterwards to survive. The grass would have burned up, leaves on trees were gone. . . . And you know, the other thing is that when comet fragments come in they're traveling incredibly fast and they literally punch a hole in the atmosphere. They actually push the air aside and they bring in that super cold from space, and when they explode in the air that cold plume continues to the ground and you literally have things frozen in place if they were close enough to where the plume came down. It's possible they were fried and then frozen all within a matter of seconds."

MULTIPLE INJECTIONS OF PLATINUM

I ASK ALLEN HOW LONG, in his opinion, the multiple impacts that kicked off the Younger Dryas were sustained for. Was it an overnight affair? Was it a matter of days? Was it weeks?

He replies that there are levels of uncertainty, variables that will probably never be properly resolved, but that within those limits what the evidence points to is not days or weeks but a **21-year** period of utter devastation, horror, and cataclysm unfolding between 12,836 years ago and 12,815 years ago, with a peak around 12,822 years ago.

This ability to zoom in at very high resolution on a time window just 21 years wide and almost 13,000 years in the past comes to us courtesy of an amazing scientific resource consisting of ice cores from Greenland. Extracted with tubular drills that can reach depths of more than 3 kilometers, these cores preserve an unbroken 100,000-year record of any environmental and climatic events anywhere around the globe that affected the Greenland ice cap. What they show, and what Allen is referring to, is a mysterious spike in the metallic element platinum—"a 21-year interval with elevated platinum," as he puts it now—"so we know that was the length of the impact event because there's very little way, once platinum falls on the ice sheet, that it can move around. It's pretty well locked in place."

The backup to what Allen's saying is in a paper I'm already familiar with by Michail Petaev of Harvard University's Department of Earth and Planetary Sciences and his colleagues Shichun Huang, Stein Jacobsen, and Alan Zindler. Published in the *Proceedings of the National Academy of Sciences* in August 2013, the self-explanatory title of the paper is "Large Pt Anomaly in the Greenland Ice Core Points to a Cataclysm at the Onset of Younger Dryas."

Platinum is, of course, an element found on earth, but analysis of the platinum in the ice core by Petaev and his colleagues reveals a composition quite unlike terrestrial platinum and leads the scientists to conclude that "an extraterrestrial source," perhaps "a metal impactor with an unusual composition," is the most likely explanation.[15] They note also that during the 21-year interval—between 12,836 and 12,815 years ago, as indicated by Allen:

> The Pt concentrations gradually rise by at least 100-fold over ~14 y
> and drop back during the subsequent ~7 y. . . . The observed gradual
> ingrowth of the Pt concentration in ice over ~14 y may suggest
> multiple injections of Pt-rich dust into the stratosphere.[16]

Allen's reading of what Petaev's findings point to, shared widely by his colleagues, is that the "impactor" was in fact multiple impactors, all of them fragments of a comet that had wandered in from the outer solar system and taken up a potentially deadly earth-crossing orbit.

Though bound together by ice, comets have rocky cores that are often volatile, and it is in the nature of these cores to undergo fragmentation. Take Comet Shoemaker-Levy 9, for example. It broke apart into twenty-one fragments, all of which smashed into the planet Jupiter over a period of 6 days in July 1994 with spectacular effect, creating huge, fiery explosions and dark scars, in some cases larger than the earth, that persisted on the surface of the gas giant for many months.

Something of the same sort is involved in Allen's vision, again widely shared by his colleagues, of what happened to the earth at the Younger Dryas Boundary. Drawing also on the work of William Napier, professor of astrobiology at the University of Cardiff, what the Younger Dryas Impact Hypothesis proposes, in brief, is a large parent comet in the range of 100 kilometers in diameter. Plunging in from the outer solar system, it enters an earth-crossing orbit around 30,000 years ago and remains intact for the next 10,000 years.

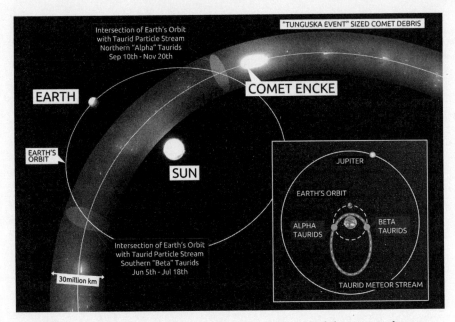

The Taurid Meteor Stream. Remnant of a giant comet 100+ kilometers in diameter, before undergoing fragmentation. The stream includes three known comets or comet-like objects, namely: Enke, Oljiato, and Rudnicki, and nineteen of the brightest near-earth objects.

About 20,000 years ago, due to gravitational forces in the inner solar system it undergoes a massive "fragmentation event" that transforms it from a single deadly and potentially world-killing object into multiple objects varying in diameter from the extremely dangerous kilometer-plus range down to a few tens of meters, down to chunks the size of cars, down to boulder-sized pieces, down to fist-sized rubble, and down beyond that to countless billions of smaller fragments and an immense penumbra of dust. As thousands of years pass, the whole turbulent mass of big and little pieces of the comet orbiting at tens of thousands of kilometers per hour begins to separate into multiple filaments each filled with debris, eventually expanding to form a giant tubular "meteor stream" some 30 million kilometers in diameter and extending more than 300 million kilometers across the entire orbit of the earth—which it cuts in two places so that we must pass through the stream twice a year. Traveling 2.5 million kilometers along its orbital path every day, the earth takes 12 days to complete each passage through the stream.[17]

Because the meteor stream produces showers of "shooting stars" that look to observers on the ground as though they originate in the region of the sky occupied by the constellation Taurus, it's called the Taurid meteor stream. Our planet still passes through it twice a year, negotiating its dangerous inner filaments in late June and early July (when shooting stars are not visible because they are encountered in daylight) and again from late October into November, when a spectacular "Halloween fireworks" display is put on.[18]

On most of these biannual encounters with the Taurids we just get the pretty fireworks, but occasionally we get more. On June 30, 1908, for example, an object thought to have fallen out of the Taurid meteor stream,[19] and estimated to be somewhere between 60 and 190 meters in diameter, penetrated earth's atmosphere. It exploded in the air—fortunately above an uninhabited region of Siberia—flattening 80 million trees across an area of 2,000 square kilometers. To put this in context, Greater London has an area of 1,582 square kilometers and a population of more than 7 million people. "If transferred to London," Professor Napier calculates, the Tunguska airburst:

> would have been heard throughout the UK, north to Denmark and across Europe as far as Switzerland. Topsoil would have been stripped from fields in the north of England, people in Oxford would have been thrown through the air and severely burned, an incandescent column of matter would have been thrown 20 km in the air over London, and the city itself would have been destroyed about as far out as the present-day ring road. Impact energy estimates range from 3 to 12.5 Mt (megatons TNT equivalent).[20]

The consequences if an object of similar size were to explode over a major city today would, in other words, be utterly catastrophic, but because the Tunguska event took place in a remote region before the era of modern mass communications, very few people are aware of how deadly even relatively small chunks of space rock can be.

Professor Napier and his colleague Victor Clube, formerly dean of the Astrophysics Department at Oxford University, go so far as to describe the "unique complex of debris" within the Taurid stream as "the greatest collision hazard facing the earth at the present time."[21] Coordination of their findings with those of Allen West, Jim Kennett, and Richard Firestone, has led both teams—the geophysicists and the astronomers—to conclude that it was very

Tunguska—an airburst at an altitude of 5–6 kilometers. The object was estimated to have had a diameter of between 60 and 190 meters. It flattened 80 million trees across an area of more than 2,000 square kilometers. This is an area larger than London. Had the event occurred over a major city, rather than over an uninhabited area, the loss of life would have been horrendous. PHOTOS: LEONID KULIK.

likely objects from the then much younger Taurid meteor stream that hit the earth around 12,800 years ago and caused the onset of the Younger Dryas. These objects, orders of magnitude larger than the one that exploded over Tunguska, contained extraterrestrial platinum, and what the evidence from the Greenland ice cores seems to indicate is an epoch of 21 years in which the earth was hit *every year,* with the bombardments increasing annually in intensity until the fourteenth year, when they peaked and then began to decline before ceasing in the twenty-first year.

"It's as though after dodging the bullet for thousands of years," I say to Allen as we walk back along the baking floor of the arroyo, "the earth finally intersects a particularly lumpy and rocky filament of debris and we get hit really hard, over and over again, year after year, until we've passed through it."

"Petaev himself says 'multiple injections of platinum,'" Allen reminds me. "I think those were pretty much his exact words in the paper, so that's an

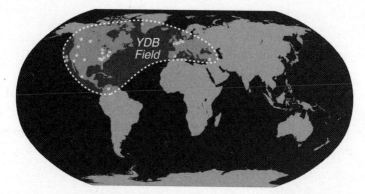

The Younger Dryas Boundary strewn field. The area enclosed by the dotted line defines the current known limits of the YDB field of cosmic impact proxies spanning more than 50 million square kilometers.

independent assessment of the idea. There's something else, too, from new research we've been working on. In the ice core, at the exact same moment we see this big onset of platinum at the beginning of the 21 years, we also see a sudden rise in dust."

"Which tells you what?"

"Which tells us that along with everything else that was going on at the time there were also **very** high winds blowing. There are certain proxies of that windiness that end up in the ice sheet. When it's windier the winds will pick up continental dust, and, number one, it's colder so there's less plant cover, so when it gets windier and there are less plants to hold the sediment down, you get huge dust storms. We can see that buildup in the Greenland ice sheet. We see magnesium and calcium, a huge increase in them, and those are indicative of terrigenous dust, continental dust, and we see an increase in sodium and chlorine which are from sea salt—so the winds are so strong they pick up more sea salt and deposit it in Greenland. The levels of these windiness proxies continue to climb for nearly 100 years. At the same time we see one of the biggest peaks in the entire ice core in all the biomass-burning proxies, and those occur within less than a 10-year window of the start of that 21-year interval—so you look at that and the best explanation is the impact occurred, that it triggered immense biomass burning, and that it changed the climate radically, resulting in high winds and immense dust storms."

"So it was a combination of really horrible things?"

"A cascade of bad things. It must have felt like the end of the world for those who lived through it."

"And particularly bad here in North America—the epicenter of the disaster?"

"Much worse here than anywhere else! A true calamity. But it wasn't only North America. We've traced evidence of further impacts from the same swarm in the exact same period in Europe and as far east as Syria and even into South America. The strewn field extends across more than 50 million square kilometers of the earth's surface."

NEW EVIDENCE

I HAVE WRITTEN EXTENSIVELY ABOUT the Younger Dryas Impact Hypothesis in *Magicians of the Gods*. There I present evidence that the impacts changed the world completely and wiped from the record almost all traces not only of the Clovis people but also of an advanced civilization of the Ice Age.

The fact that North America was the epicenter of the cataclysm, though acknowledged, has profound implications for our understanding of the human past that archaeologists have never thought through—in part because the scale of the cataclysm is only now beginning to be fully mapped out.

After completing *Magicians,* therefore, I made sure I stayed up to date with the steady stream of new evidence released by Allen and his group in the scientific journals. There was a visible quickening in the pace of the research, and in 2017 and 2018 two major studies revealed how truly devastating the cataclysm at the onset of the Younger Dryas really was.

If there was ever a time when a significant chapter in the story of human civilization could have been lost, this, surely, was it.

26

FIRE AND ICE

A LLEN WEST AND THE TEAM of scientists working on the Younger Dryas Impact Hypothesis established themselves as a formal research organization, the Comet Research Group, in 2015.[1] The group (hereafter CRG) presently numbers sixty-three leading scientists from fifty-five universities in sixteen countries.[2] Many other scientists are also directly and indirectly associated as coauthors of papers written by CRG members.

This is the case with a paper, published in *Nature*'s sister journal *Scientific Reports* on March 9, 2017, titled "Widespread Platinum Anomaly Documented at the Younger Dryas Onset in North American Sedimentary Sequences."[3]

The lead author is geoarchaeologist and CRG member Dr. Christopher Moore of the University of South Carolina. His coauthors and fellow CRG members are geophysicist Allen West, whom we met in the last chapter, anthropologist Randolph Daniel of East Carolina University, archaeologist Albert Goodyear, whom we met in chapter 6, earth scientist James P.

Kennett of the University of California, geologist Kenneth B. Tankersley of the University of Cincinnati, and geologist Ted Bunch of Northern Arizona University. The non-CRG coauthors are planetary and atmospheric scientist Malcolm LeCompte of the University of South Carolina, geomorphologist Mark J. Brooks, also of the University of South Carolina, environmental scientist Terry A. Ferguson of Wofford College, South Carolina, geoscientist Andrew H. Ivester of the University of West Georgia, luminescence-dating expert James K. Feathers of the University of Washington, and physicist Victor Adedji of Elizabeth City State University.[4]

All in all, therefore, a very distinguished assembly of scientists—and the task that they set themselves was also in the finest tradition of good science, namely, to test an important prediction made by other scientists. From the previous chapter, the reader will recall the research by Michail Petaev and his colleagues showing elevated levels of platinum in the Greenland ice cores over a 21-year period between 12,836 and 12,815 years ago. Petaev reports what appear to have been "multiple injections" of platinum-rich dust into the stratosphere over this period and predicts that if the source of the dust was cometary, asteroidal, or meteoroidal, then the fallout should have extended far beyond Greenland and would be "expected to result in a global Pt anomaly."[5]

The coauthors of the 2017 platinum paper chose North America, the suspected epicenter of the Younger Dryas cataclysm—and also their home turf—to test this prediction by establishing "whether or not a Pt anomaly exists in terrestrial sediments of YD age that is similar to that reported from the GISP2 ice core."[6]

It sounds low-key, but much was at stake. If soil samples showed platinum to be at normal background levels in the YDB layer across North America, then Petaev's prediction would be false and the Younger Dryas Impact Hypothesis would suffer serious collateral damage. On the other hand, if elevated levels of platinum were found, it would vindicate Petaev and give further strong support to the hypothesis that cosmic impacts caused the Younger Dryas cataclysm.

Eleven archaeological sites—see map below—all with good stratification and well-established YD-age sediments were selected as the focus of the study: 1. Arlington Canyon, Santa Rosa Island, California; 2. Murray Springs, Arizona; 3. Blackwater Draw, New Mexico; 4. Sheriden Cave, Ohio; 5. Squires Ridge, North Carolina; 6. Barber Creek, North Carolina; 7. Kolb, South Car-

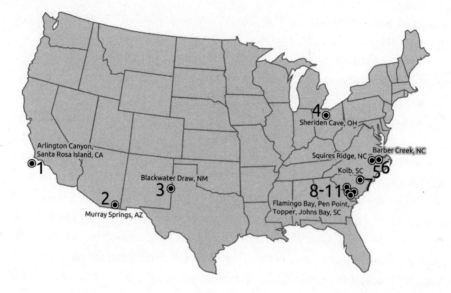

olina; 8. Flamingo Bay, South Carolina; 9. Pen Point, South Carolina; 10 Topper, South Carolina; and 11. Johns Bay, South Carolina.

The project began by testing soil samples from Arlington Canyon, Murray Springs, Blackwater Draw, and Sheriden Cave, four sites with particularly "well-defined and well-dated YDB age sediments containing peaks in YDB impact-related proxies."[7] What the tests revealed was:

> a large above-background Pt anomaly at each site in the identical
> sample previously identified as the YD boundary layer containing
> abundance peaks in YDB proxies, including micro-spherules,
> meltglass, and nanodiamonds.[8]

The team then extended the Pt analysis to soil samples from the seven other sites. In summary, across all eleven sites, they conclude that their results

> provide strong evidence for above-background enrichment in Pt
> within sediments that date to the onset of YD climate change at
> ~12,800 Cal B.P. Pt abundances from our study sites averaged 6.0
> parts per billion (ppb) . . . compared to background abundances above
> and below the YDB layer averaging 0.3 ppb. Average background
> Pt concentrations are all lower than crustal abundance of 0.5

ppb, whereas average YDB concentrations are 12× higher. These concentrations are also higher than the peak Pt concentration (~80 parts per trillion [ppt] or 0.1 ppb) reported at high chronological resolution from the GISP2 ice-core in Greenland by Petaev et al. All study sites contain significant Pt peaks that are ~3 to 66× higher than in Greenland.[9]

The technical language and abbreviations make it difficult to stay focused on the grave implications of all this. In a layer in the earth that already contains abundant evidence of a cataclysmic cosmic impact around 12,800 years ago, a mass of new corroborative evidence has now been discovered. In parallel, the much greater strength of the Pt signal in the United States than in Greenland joins multiple other indicators pointing to North America as the most severely affected locus of the cataclysm. If this were a homicide investigation in which the prosecution were hesitating to charge the suspect, new evidence of this quality would be decisive, and a winnable case could be brought to court. Moore and his colleagues are cautious and modest, however, claiming only that:

> the consistent presence of anomalous Pt concentrations within sediments from multiple archaeological sites across North America that date to the onset of the YD Chronozone is compelling. . . . This study finds no evidence to contradict the conclusions of Petaev et al. that the Greenland Pt enrichment most likely resulted from an extraterrestrial source. . . . In addition, our findings show no contradiction with the Younger Dryas impact hypothesis.[10]

After completing their own investigation, Moore et al. combed the scientific literature for indications of how far beyond North America and Greenland the YDB platinum anomaly extends. Though not central to any investigation prior to Petaev's, they found that platinum group elements had been discovered and mentioned in passing in other earlier studies of the Younger Dryas Boundary at locations as far afield as Belgium, the central Pacific, Venezuela, the southwest of England, and the Netherlands—"important information," hinting at a truly global picture, that they hope "may encourage further research."[11]

In the Supplementary Information to their main paper, Moore and his colleagues also provide detailed evidence ruling out either volcanic activity or processes in the mantle of the earth as the sources for the enriched platinum at the YDB.[12] By contrast, after compiling geochemical data for 167 meteorites, including chondrites, achondrites, irons, and ureilites, they found very high average Pt abundances, "making all four classes of meteorites possible sources of YDB Pt enrichment."[13]

They also note, "If a Pt-rich meteorite or comet impacted Earth, the target rocks would have become a melted mix of meteoritic and terrestrial material, and so should be Pt-enriched."[14]

The coauthors therefore compiled geochemical data from eighty-six examples of such "impactites" from three major impact layers spread out over a period of more than two billion years. In every one of them they found elevated Pt abundances in a range including all the values in the Pt-rich YDB layers from around 12,800 years ago.[15]

FOLLOWING THE TRAIL OF CLUES

THE CORROBORATING EVIDENCE KEEPS COMING in.

When we met at Murray Springs in October 2017, Allen West told me about new CRG research that had identified an extended episode of extreme windiness, dustiness, and large-scale "biomass burning" at the onset of the Younger Dryas. He mentioned that "around 9 percent of the total biomass of the planet was on fire and destroyed within days or weeks of the YDB"—an astonishing statement—but I'd been so focused on other aspects of what he was saying that I hadn't really considered the implications.

In February 2018 the *Journal of Geology* published the massive two-part study on which Allen's off-the-cuff remarks were based. The title speaks for itself: "Extraordinary Biomass-Burning Episode and Impact Winter Triggered by the Younger Dryas Cosmic Impact ~12,800 Years Ago."[16] CRG member Wendy Wolbach, professor of inorganic chemistry, geochemistry, and analytical chemistry at Chicago's De Paul University, led the study, in which she was joined by Allen West and twenty-five other top researchers.[17]

Confirmation of the figure of 9 percent of terrestrial biomass comes on the first page, with the calculation that this would have meant that plant matter covering an area of no less than 10 million square kilometers would have been consumed by the inferno.[18]

To imagine a world in which 10 million square kilometers of vegetation is in flames is to imagine a world in which an area roughly twice the size of the Amazon rainforest is burning. That would be about the same as the entire area of China or the entire area of Europe or the entire area of North America in flames.

No matter how many separate wildfires there were, or how spread around the planet, a conflagration on this scale, hand in hand with the cascade of other disasters that marked the onset of the Younger Dryas, can only be described as hell on earth.

Once again, although records from lake sediments also provide vital clues, it is the Greenland ice cores, together with ice cores from other Arctic regions, that contain decisive evidence of the large-scale wildfires that raged across the world 12,800 years ago. This is not least because the upper (i.e., most recent) levels of these extremely long cores contain the traces of biomass wildfires that occurred and were recorded in the historic period, thus allowing identification and calibration of specific combustion aerosols, notably oxalate, ammonium, nitrate, acetate, formate, and levoglucosan, that serve as distinct signals—or proxies—of biomass-burning.[19] Wherever an abundance of these combustion aerosols shows up in the ice cores we can be certain that they mark the atmospheric fallout from extensive wildfires, we can date those wildfires, and it is often possible to identify where on the planet they occurred.

Here are some important pieces of the Younger Dryas puzzle winnowed from the dense pages of the 2018 paper:

> GISP2 Ice Core: Ammonium (NH_4), a biomass-burning proxy, displays one of the highest peaks in the 120,000-year record in an interval dating to 12,830–12,828 years ago. This overlaps the platinum-rich interval dating to 12,836–12,815 years ago and coincides with the onset of the Younger Dryas.[20]

> NGRIP Ice Core: A single high NH_4 peak, traced to biomass burning across North America, begins at the YD onset. It is the largest biomass-burning episode from North American sources in the entire record.[21]

> The GRIP concentrations of combustion aerosols began to increase sharply around 12,816 years ago, correlating with the GISP2 Pt anomaly (12,836–12,815 years ago). At the onset of the Younger Dryas, concentrations of oxalate and formate reached their highest known concentrations in the ~386,000-year core, with acetate abundances ranking among the highest in the entire core.[22]

> These GRIP data reveal that massive wildfires occurred at the onset of the Younger Dryas, representing the most anomalous episode of biomass burning in at least 120,000 years and possibly in the past ~386,000 years.[23]

> The Taylor Dome (Antarctica) ice-core record exhibits a small but distinct peak in NO_3 that closely correlates with the Younger Dryas onset. The base of the Belukha, Siberia, ice core exhibits a major peak in NO_3 [nitrate], indicating that a major episode of biomass burning occurred at the Younger Dryas onset.[24]

> Several ice-core sequences (GISP2, NGRIP, GRIP, Taylor Dome and Belukha) confirm that the onset of the Younger Dryas was intimately associated with one of the highest and most pervasive late Quaternary peaks in each of NH_4, NO_3, formate, oxalate, and acetate. These peaks occurred synchronously with the abrupt cooling and other climatic effects marking the onset of the Younger Dryas episode.[25]

> Investigation of "black mats" at nineteen sites in North America, Central America, Europe, and the Middle East: Peak abundances of black carbon (BC)/soot and other biomass-burning proxies were found in the Younger Dryas Boundary layers. . . . Concentrations of levoglucosan from within the black-mat layer in Ohio were around 125 times higher than those in the layer below it, signalling a significant peak in biomass burning.[26]

> Analysis of charcoal in lake sediments from nine countries in South and Central America: One of the highest peaks in the record occurs at the Younger Dryas onset around 12,850 years ago.[27]

> Analysis of charcoal in lake sediments from seven countries across Asia: There is a conspicuous peak in mean charcoal abundances at

around 12,950 years ago (plus or minus 225 years) . . . followed by a sharp decline in biomass burning and then a peak at 12,400 years ago.[28]

❯ A 24,000-year sequence recorded in a marine core from the Santa Barbara Basin, off the coast of California, exhibits the highest peak in biomass burning precisely at the onset of the Younger Dryas. . . . This anomalously high peak correlates with intense biomass burning documented from the nearby Channel Islands. . . . The peak also coincides with the extinction of pygmy mammoths on the islands and with the beginning of an apparent 600–800-year gap in the archaeological record, suggesting a sudden collapse in island human populations.[29]

❯ A marine core from the western Pacific, 1,500 kilometers north of Papua New Guinea, provides a biomass-burning record spanning a period of 368,000 years. This core is unusual in providing a record not only of charcoal but also of black carbon, which includes AC/ soot. The core exhibits a high black-carbon peak spanning the period between 13,291 and 12,515 years ago and overlapping the Younger Dryas onset at around 12,800 years ago. In addition, the YDB peak in black carbon coincides with an above-average charcoal peak at around 12,750 years ago.[30]

❯ Evidence from widely separated ice records and sediment records demonstrates that a major, widespread peak in biomass burning occurred on at least four continents at the warm-to-cold transition marking the YD onset. This peak is synchronous with the cosmic-impact layer at the Younger Dryas Boundary as recorded by multiple impact-related proxies, including peak abundances of platinum, high-temperature microspherules, and meltglass.[31]

In summary, the earth and all life upon it endured and was devastated by what can only be described as a globally distributed firestorm at the onset of the Younger Dryas around 12,800 years ago. In this planetary debacle, 10 million square kilometers of trees and other plant matter burned.

To put that in perspective, the United Kingdom was in a state of traumatic shock in late June and early July 2018 after 4,942 acres of Lancashire moorland were consumed by wildfires. That's an area of just 20 square kilometers, but firefighters and emergency services from seven counties were utterly overwhelmed by the blaze and the military had to be brought in to assist.[32]

Meanwhile, a report in the *Sacramento Bee* dated July 2, 2018, opined that California's wildfire season had started early, with two "major fires" already fought at huge expense and requiring evacuation of local residents. These two fires were estimated to have consumed 85,000 acres,[33] which sounds an awful lot but in fact converts to just 344 square kilometers.

The previous year, 2017, was California's most destructive wildfire season then on record, with a total of 1.25 million acres burned.[34] The cost of dealing with the disaster, including fire suppression, insurance, and recovery expenditures, was estimated at US$180 billion.[35] Yet 1.38 million acres converts to just 5,585 square kilometers—an insignificant fraction (around 0.05 percent—that is, a twentieth of 1 percent) of the 10 million square kilometers destroyed in the Younger Dryas wildfires.

It seems, therefore, that the United States and Britain, two of the world's wealthiest, most technologically advanced, and most powerful countries, face great difficulties in confronting what are, in the grand scheme of things, relatively minor wildfires. Imagine, then, the consequences for all living things of the great inferno that consumed 9 percent of the earth's biomass around 12,800 years ago and that left an indelible record of its climatic and atmospheric impact in lake sediments and Arctic ice.

IMPACT WINTER

NEWS FOOTAGE OF THE US AND UK summer wildfires shows smoke everywhere. Close up it seems foggy or misty. In the longer view there's an obvious gloom, a darkening of the skies, where the pall obscures incoming sunlight. It's a local effect, of course. Fifty miles away the air is clear and the skies are blue.

The 2018 *Journal of Geology* study reports that matters would have been very different at the onset of the Younger Dryas, when the smoke from 10 million square kilometers of burning biomass would have enshrouded the entire earth, creating what Wendy Wolbach and her coauthors describe as an "impact winter."[36]

This is a concept derived directly from research in the early 1980s revealing previously unexpected consequences of a nuclear war in the form of a "nuclear winter." The findings of that research were first put before the public in October 1983 in an article by esteemed astrophysicist Carl Sagan under the headline **"In a Nuclear Exchange, More Than a Billion People Would Instantly Be Killed, But the Long-Term Consequences Could Be Much Worse."**

Appearing in a mass-circulation magazine, Sagan's article showed that the immense quantities of dust and smoke arising from multiple nuclear explosions, and from the wildfires they sparked off, would significantly reduce the amount of sunlight reaching the surface of the earth, causing a steep and sustained fall in global temperatures, widespread failure of crops, and devastating famines. Nor would a full-scale war between superpowers be required to bring on the terrible, and potentially terminal, consequences of a nuclear winter. Even a regional nuclear conflict could do it.[37] "We have placed our civilization and our species in jeopardy," Sagan concluded.[38]

In the case of the Younger Dryas, the jeopardy that humanity faced was not from nuclear missiles but from the incoming fragments of a disintegrating giant comet, traveling at tens of kilometers per second, with the larger fragments as deadly as hundreds of nuclear warheads. Indeed, it is estimated that the total explosive power of the comet fragments that struck the earth in repeated episodes over a period of 21 years some 12,800 years ago would have been of the order of 10 million megatons[39]—1,000 times greater than all the nuclear devices stockpiled in the world today.[40]

The Younger Dryas is already recognized as an epoch of extreme, anomalous cold that lasted for approximately 1,200 years, setting in fast and suddenly around 12,800 years ago and ending, equally suddenly, around 11,600 years ago. The *Journal of Geology* study greatly enriches this picture with compelling new evidence that the onset of this 1,200-year "deep-freeze" was marked by a brief period of extremely intense and large-scale wildfires triggered by "the radiant and thermal energy from multiple explosions" as fragments from the comet swarm pelted the earth:

This widespread biomass-burning generated large amounts of long-lived, persistent AC/soot that blocked nearly all sunlight, rapidly triggering an impact winter that transitioned into the YD cool episode.[41] . . .

The negative effects of AC/soot might have persisted for 6 wk or more at the YD onset, blocking all sunlight and causing rapid cooling. Reduced insolation is also expected from the injection of comet dust to the upper atmosphere. If so, the lack of sunlight would have had widespread and catastrophic biotic effects, including insufficient light for plant photosynthesis and growth. At the same time, North Atlantic deep-water formation ceased, thus throttling the so-called ocean conveyor and triggering a sustained decrease in near-global temperatures.[42]

THE MAMMOTH IN THE ROOM

IT HAS LONG BEEN UNDERSTOOD that an interruption of the warm Atlantic current known as the Gulf Stream correlates with YD cooling, and it is generally agreed that

a great gush of cold freshwater derived from the melting Laurentide ice sheet . . . swept across the surface of the North Atlantic. It prevented warm, salty water from the southern ocean flowing deep below the surface (the Gulf Stream) from rising to the surface. The normal overturning of the ocean water stopped. As a consequence the atmosphere over the ocean, which would normally have been warmed, remained cold and so, in consequence, did the air over Europe and North America.[43]

It's revealing, looking back through the scientific literature, to see how long explanations of this sort were simply taken for granted. That there had been a cold-water flood was not in doubt, so the detective work that at first interested scientists most was **WHERE** all the water had come from.

The reader will recall that the North American ice cap had two distinct segments consisting of two separate ice sheets, the Cordilleran in the west and the Laurentide in the east, which were often joined, but which in the later stages of the Ice Age were separated by the famous "ice-free corridor" that for a long while was erroneously believed to have been the sole route for human

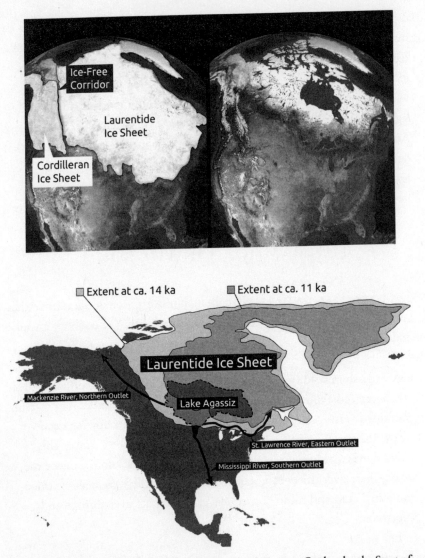

After *Geology,* "Opening of Glacial Lake Agassiz's Eastern Outlets by the Start of the Younger Dryas Cold Period," January 4, 2018.

migration into the Americas. Along the southern margins of these ice sheets, enormous glacial lakes formed and were prone to flooding—most famously glacial lake Missoula in the west and glacial lake Agassiz in the east. Flood-waters out of Lake Missoula would have had no access to the Atlantic Ocean (they would have been routed into the Pacific). Lake Agassiz was therefore thought to be the most likely source, and a study published in *Geology* in January 2018 confirms that its floodwaters "could have been routed eastward to the North Atlantic at the Younger Dryas onset and caused the canonical abrupt climate shift."[44]

So we know that a cold-water flood poured into the Atlantic ocean around 12,800 years ago on a scale sufficient to stop the Gulf Stream in its tracks; we know that glacial lake Agassiz has been implicated in it; and we know that this "great gush of cold freshwater" has been connected to the plunge in global temperature—the "deep freeze"—that defines the Younger Dryas cold event.

The issue that most of the scientists are skirting, however—the mammoth in the room—is **why** such a flood would have occurred at the onset of the Younger Dryas "deep freeze" around 12,800 years ago rather than, say, 800 or 1,000 years earlier at the height of the warm phase—known as the Bølling—Allerød interstadial—that immediately preceded the Younger Dryas.[45] Intuitively one feels the meltwater floods should have been at their peak during the warming phase. Why, therefore, **in this case only**, do we see them at the onset of an extremely cold phase? I raised this problem in *Magicians of the Gods* in 2015,[46] and it is raised again by Wolbach et al. in their 2018 paper, where they present evidence that deepens the mystery. "Unlike for typical warm-to-cold climate transitions," they report, "global sea levels **rose** up to 2–4 m within a few decades or less at the YD onset, as recorded in coral reefs in the Atlantic and Pacific Oceans."[47]

The point is understated, but this is a very big deal. Two to 4 meters of global sea-level rise within "a few decades or less" of the onset of the Younger Dryas is an IMMENSE amount of water, a cataclysmic world flood by any standard.

What makes it all the more remarkable, however—and all the more puzzling—is the evidence from Wolbach's study that in the exact same period the planet suffered a spectacular episode of biomass burning and an associated "impact winter" that "caused warm interglacial temperatures to abruptly fall to cold, near-glacial levels within less than a year, possibly in as little as 3 months."[48]

Meanwhile, in the process of absorbing that sudden massive flood of icy water into the North Atlantic, the world ocean had reacted by shutting off the Gulf Stream, thus sustaining freezing temperatures in Europe and North America and setting in process the entire Younger Dryas cold episode.

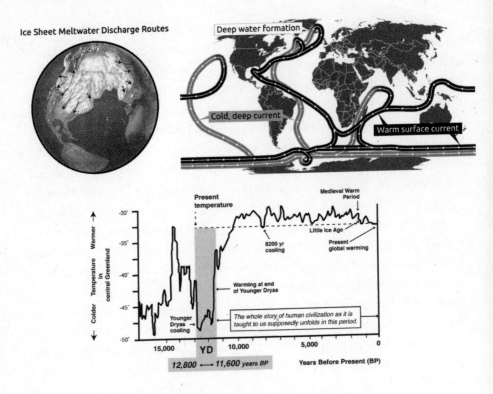

What we are looking for, therefore, is an agent capable—simultaneously and almost instantaneously—of bringing about all of the following:

> a global flood

> wildfires across an area of 10 million km²

> 6 months of icy darkness followed by more than 1,000 years of glacially cold weather

> a stratum of soil across more than 50 million km² dated to the Younger Dryas Boundary (YDB) and infused with a cocktail of nanodiamonds, high-temperature iron-rich spherules, glassy silica-rich spherules, meltglass, platinum, iridium, osmium, and other exotic materials

> a mass extinction of megafauna

Wolbach and her coauthors are forthright in their conclusion:

Multiple lines of ice-core evidence appear synchronous, and this synchroneity of multiple events makes the YD interval one of the most unusual climate episodes in the entire Quaternary record. . . . A cosmic impact is the only known event capable of simultaneously producing the collective evidence.[49]

A VIOLENT HURRICANE OF BOLIDES

WHAT KIND OF COSMIC IMPACT?

From quite early in the research, since the first strong impact-proxy evidence was analyzed, it's been the consensus view of CRG members that the agent responsible for the Younger Dryas cataclysm was a comet. Wolbach's study strengthens that position, noting:

Comets are a compositionally variable mix of volatile ices, meteoritic material, and presolar dust. . . . Wide ranges of elemental ratios confirm that cometary material is heterogeneous, similar to the YDB samples. Although the type of YDB impactor remains unclear, the current evidence does not support any specific meteoritic type as source. Instead, the broad extent of biomass burning at the YD onset is more consistent with Earth's collision with a fragmented comet[50] . . . [resulting in a] violent hurricane of bolides[51] . . . [that] detonated above and/or collided with land, ice sheets, and oceans across at least four continents in the Northern and Southern Hemispheres.[52]

This scenario, the study argues, explains all the anomalous and synchronous evidence:

Vaporization of cometary materials, and platinum-group-element–rich target rocks, injected Pt, Ir, Os, and other heavy metals into the stratosphere, accompanied by impact-related nanodiamonds, meltglass, and microspherules.[53]
Airburst fireballs and the ejection of molten rocks . . . triggered

many individual wildfires over wide areas, producing one of the largest concentrations of combustion aerosols deposited in the Greenland ice sheet during the past 120,000–368,000 years. In the higher midlatitudes, atmospheric and oceanic temperatures abruptly decreased from warm interglacial to near-glacial conditions within a few months to a year. Atmospheric and cometary dust, along with AC/soot, triggered the rapid onset of an impact winter. This blocking of sunlight led to a die-off of vegetation. Damage to the ozone layer likely led to an increase in ultraviolet-B radiation reaching Earth's surface, damaging flora and fauna. Increases in nitrogen compounds, sulfates, dust, soot, and other toxic chemicals from the impact and widespread wildfires likely led to an increase in acid rain. Increased production of organic matter and burn products from environmental degradation and biomass burning contributed to algal blooms and the subsequent formation of widespread black mats.[54]

In my view, however, by far the most significant finding of the study, fitting perfectly with the scenario of a disintegrating comet, is:

The impact event destabilized the ice-sheet margins, causing extensive iceberg calving into the Arctic and North Atlantic Oceans. The airburst/impacts collapsed multiple ice dams of proglacial lakes along the ice-sheet margins, producing extensive meltwater flooding into the Arctic and North Atlantic Oceans. Destabilization of the ice sheet also may have triggered extensive subglacial ice-sheet flooding, leaving widespread, flood-related landforms across large parts of Canada. The massive outflow of proglacial lake waters, ice-sheet meltwater, and icebergs into the Arctic and North Atlantic Oceans caused rerouting of oceanic thermohaline circulation. Through climatic feedbacks, this, in turn, led to the YD cool episode.[55]

In other words, the long-established and widely accepted evidence linking the onset of the Younger Dryas cold interval to a freshwater flood off the North American ice cap and consequent changes in oceanic circulation is fully accepted by Wolbach. What she and her coauthors add, however, is:

an additional key element . . . suggesting that **these climate-changing mechanisms did not occur randomly but rather were triggered by the YDB impact event.** After shutdown of the ocean conveyor, the YD episode persisted . . . not because of continued airburst/impacts but because, once circulation stopped, feedback loops and inertia within the ocean system maintained the changed state of circulation until it reverted to its previous state.[56]

Indeed so. No one is suggesting that impacts and airbursts continued throughout the entire 1,200 years of the Younger Dryas cold interval. Wolbach and her colleagues leave us in no doubt that their study is focused on the **beginning** of that interval and specifically on the sudden and mysterious climatic reversal from warm to cold around 12,800 years ago that they attribute to an "impact event." They remind us at several points in their *Journal of Geology* paper, however, that when they speak of an "event" they do not mean to imply a one-off "hurricane of bolides" striking the earth over a single day or two in a single year. What the evidence points to, instead, is a series of such brief but deadly encounters recurring biannually over the full period of 21 years of platinum enrichment identified in the Greenland ice cores.[57]

Many of the individual impactors would have been Tunguska-meteor-size or smaller, but they would have come in vast swarms capable of doing enormous damage, and there is evidence that at least once during these 21 years the biannual "hurricane of bolides" may have contained comet fragments with diameters of a kilometer or more.

This is what was specifically proposed in the very first scientific paper to outline the Younger Dryas Impact Hypothesis. Coauthored by Wendy Wolbach, Richard Firestone, Allen West, and more than twenty others, and published in *Proceedings of the National Academy of Sciences* in October 2007, it raised the possibility that "multiple 2km objects struck the 2km thick Laurentide Ice Sheet."[58]

Subsequently, in September 2013, Yingzhe Wu, Mukul Sharma et al. drew attention to the Gulf of St. Lawrence, Canada, where a submerged impact crater with a diameter of 4 kilometers—the Corossol Crater—has been dated to the Younger Dryas Boundary. Looking at a range of other evidence they concluded there had been multiple impacts in this region "that were closely associated in time."[59]

Separately, Richard Firestone and Allen West reported evidence of an airburst at the Younger Dryas Boundary "near the Great Lakes of an object unusually enriched in titanium and other incompatible elements. Terrestrial-like ejecta fell close to an impact site near Gainey while projectile-rich ejecta fell farther away. High water content in the ejecta favors an airburst over the Laurentide Ice Sheet north of Gainey."[60]

Now perhaps we are getting closer to an explanation of how a single cause could account both for plunging the earth into a 1,000-year "deep freeze" and for melting sufficient quantities of glacial ice to raise global sea level by up to 4 meters. The immense meltwater pulse that entered the North Atlantic and Arctic Oceans was of course **not** the result of anomalous global warming in an epoch of global cooling but a direct consequence of the "destabilization" of the ice sheet by impacts and airbursts of multiple comet fragments—indeed of a swarm of comets. The thermal energy and blast wave radiated out southward beyond the ice margin all across North America, accompanied by additional local airbursts and impacts that set immense areas of the continent's primeval conifer forests ablaze,[61] followed by "aerial detonations or ground impacts by numerous relatively small cometary fragments, widely dispersed across several continents."[62]

Wolbach et al. looked into a series of seven episodes of meltwater release that occurred during the Ice Age, of which the Younger Dryas was the last. Named "Heinrich Events" (after Hartmut Heinrich, the marine geologist who first identified them), such episodes are distinguished by massive armadas of icebergs calving off the continental glaciers. These icebergs carry rocks, rubble, and other debris that as the bergs melt are deposited on the ocean floor where geologists can identify them, measure them, and derive estimates of scale and chronology.

It's therefore notable that,

> even though the YD is considered a Heinrich event (designated
> H0), the anomalously high peak in wildfire activity at the YD
> onset is completely opposite to that of six previous Heinrich events,
> which showed low levels of biomass burning. . . . This is a crucial
> observation: the presence of high peaks in biomass burning at the YD

onset is completely contrary to very low levels of biomass burning observed at previous similar climatic transitions, making the YD climate episode highly anomalous and unexplainable by the natural processes that created previous warm-to-cold transitions.[63]

Again, the hypothesis of repeated encounters with the fragments of a disintegrating comet over the 21 years from 12,836 to 12,815 years ago provides a straightforward explanation for this apparently anomalous state of affairs. The Younger Dryas Heinrich Event was not triggered by normal climatic changes but by the impacts of comet fragments on the North American ice cap.

We cannot say exactly when within that 21-year period the impact-related destabilization of the ice cap occurred. It might have been right at the beginning, or right at the end, or somewhere in the middle, and it might have happened more than once. What the data from the Greenland ice cores definitely do indicate, however, as we saw in the previous chapter, is that the ferocity and intensity of the bombardment, with its accompanying rain of platinum, increased year-on-year for the first 14 years, reached a peak around 12,822 years ago, and then declined over the next 7 years until ceasing as abruptly as it had begun.

It's a good guess, therefore—nothing more scientific than that—that the peak of the comet's interaction with the North American ice cap, and most likely the time when the really big fragments came in, would be around 12,822 years ago.

Allen West and fellow CRG scientist Richard Firestone think as many as eight such kilometer-scale fragments[64] may have struck the ice cap, excavating their craters in the 2-kilometer-deep ice that subsequently melted away, leaving little or no permanent trace on the ground beneath, or leaving craters that are hard to find, for example, four suspiciously deep holes in lakes Superior, Michigan, Huron, and Ontario.[65]

Encounters with *any* fragments of this size, let alone multiple fragments, would already constitute a planetary disaster on an almost unimaginable scale, wherever they occurred. What we must keep in mind, however, although North America was the epicenter, is that the terrible impacts experienced there were only part of a much wider event that left a trail of devastation across at least three other continents.

WHAT WAS LOST

EXTINCTIONS OF ANIMAL SPECIES TOOK place all around the world at the onset of the Younger Dryas but were particularly fast, savage, and severe in North America, where thirty-five genera of large mammals were wiped out.[66]

Offering evidence from seventy-three sites across twenty-three US states, Wolbach et al. document the synchroneity of these megafaunal extinctions with the Younger Dryas impact.[67] Three examples—one of which, Murray Springs, was the subject of the last chapter—can stand for the rest:

> ❭ BLACKWATER DRAW, NEW MEXICO: At this site, a distinctive black-mat layer, dating to the onset of YD climate change, is in direct contact with peaks in magnetic spherules, Pt, Ir, and biomass-burning proxies, including charcoal, glass-like carbon, fullerenes, and PAHs [polycyclic aromatic hydrocarbons]. These proxies are draped conformably over the last known bones of mammoths killed by Clovis hunters, who then abandoned the site for hundreds of years. The evidence from Blackwater Draw suggests that the YDB impact event is coeval with the megafaunal extinctions and a human population decline, along with a peak in biomass burning and with YD climate change.

> ❭ MURRAY SPRINGS, ARIZONA: Peaks in magnetic spherules, meltglass, nanodiamonds, Pt, and Ir [are located] immediately beneath a distinctive black mat that dates to the YD onset. Peaks in YDB biomass-burning proxies include charcoal, carbon spherules, glass-like carbon, AC/soot, fullerenes, and PAHs. At this site, several mammoths were killed by Clovis hunters, after which the black mat formed atop the bones and humans abandoned the site for ~1000 y. Thus, the evidence supports the synchroneity of the YDB impact event, increased biomass burning, YD climate change, megafaunal extinctions, and a major human population decline.

> ❭ SHERIDEN CAVE, OHIO: There are YDB peaks in magnetic spherules, meltglass, nanodiamonds, Pt, and Ir. A charcoal-rich black mat dates to the YD onset and contains peak abundances of

charcoal, AC/soot, carbon spherules, and nanodiamonds that are closely associated with the last known Clovis artifacts in the cave. The black-mat layer is in direct contact with the wildfire-charred bones of two mega-mammals, the flat-headed peccary (*Platygonus compressus*) and the giant beaver (*Castoroidies ohioensis*), that are the last known examples anywhere in the world of those extinct species.[68]

Horses, camels, mammoths, mastodons, giant ground sloths, saber-tooth tigers, short-faced bears, and dire wolves are among the other iconic creatures of the Ice Age that disappear from the record at this time. "This represents a major extinction," James Kennett and Allen West remind us in a paper published in 2018 by the Florida Museum of Natural History:

Not only because so many large and well-known animals were lost, but also because many of the extinct taxa had resided for millions of years in North America. Horse evolution had continued without a break in North America since the Eocene (~55 million years ago) with the only known absence beginning at around ~12,800 years ago until their return from Europe ~500 years ago. Clearly such extinctions are highly anomalous.[69]

All in all, Kennett and West conclude:

Sufficient geologic and chronologic data now exists to support the hypothesis that megafaunal extinctions were caused by continental-scale ecosystem disruption, resulting from the cosmic impact at the onset of the YD. . . . The megafaunal extinction would not have occurred at or close to the YD onset without the YDB cosmic impact at ~12,800 years ago. Instead many of the now extinct animals would have survived much longer, even to modern times.[70]

The archaeological evidence is scarce, perhaps precisely because so much was swept away and covered over by the Younger Dryas earth changes. Nonetheless, it's clear that along with the disruption of animal life in North America, the cataclysm also had severe consequences for human beings.

Top of the list, of course, is the abrupt, mysterious disappearance of the entire successful, technically accomplished, and geographically widespread Clovis culture right around 12,800 years ago.[71] Then, in the centuries following, if we take the case of the southeast as an example, we see a sudden anomalous 50 percent drop in the numbers of projectile points being made.[72] A similar trend is seen in many other parts of North America at the same time,[73] and in California there is evidence of a cessation of human activity between roughly 12,800 years ago and 12,200 years ago.[74]

A study of almost 700 cultural carbon-14 dates from across North America by David Anderson, Albert Goodyear, and others shows "a rapid decline" in human activities "at the beginning of the YD that reached its lowest level early in the YD . . . a 200-year-long 80 percent decline in the number of cultural carbon-14 dates, implying a major decrease in population . . . followed by a gradual rebound for ~900 years."[75]

We do not possess a time machine. We cannot place ourselves physically in North America 12,800 years ago. But all the evidence suggests the continent passed through a tremendous, earthshaking cataclysm, and we know that at least one ancestral North American culture—Clovis—became every bit as extinct 12,800 years ago as the mammoths and the dire wolves.

What else went the way of Clovis in that time of burning darkness and icy floods?

27

CAPE FEAR

IMAGINE A WORLD WHERE GOOD, honest, hardworking, inquisitive scientists live in fear of ruining their careers, perhaps even of losing their jobs and incomes, if they investigate certain subjects that have been judged by a dominant elite to be "taboo."

Is such a climate of fear-based conformity likely to result in *good* science that breaks new ground? Or is it likely to keep science stuck in a rut, endlessly refining and reconfirming established models while rejecting any evidence that suggests those models might be wrong or in need of fundamental revision?

These are not rhetorical questions, because it turns out that this "imaginary" world is the very world we live in today. Science in the twenty-first century does NOT encourage scientists to take risks in their pursuit of "the facts"—particularly when those facts call into question long-established notions about the human past.

The controversy surrounding the Younger Dryas Impact Hypothesis is an example. Since it was first proposed formally in 2007 the scientists behind it have endured an unrelenting barrage of deeply unpleasant and self-serving attacks from a small but influential group of other scientists whose work and opinions are challenged by the notion of a comet-induced global cataclysm 12,800 years ago.

In my 2015 book, *Magicians of the Gods,* I give a detailed account of the major studies supporting the YDIH coupled with an equally detailed evaluation of the attacks made on the hypothesis up to that point.[1] I will not repeat the same information here since it is on record and can easily be consulted. My conclusion at the time was that the attacks were generally unjustified, misleading, and propagandistic, and that the YDIH constitutes the best possible explanation for the earthshaking events of 12,800 years ago. Now, as I write these words in 2018, my desk is covered with papers published during the past 3 years presenting a great mass of new evidence that very strongly reinforces, extends, and develops the original Younger Dryas Impact Hypothesis. The biomass-burning and platinum studies mentioned in chapter 26 are the jewels in the crown, which is why I focused on them in the limited space available here. The other studies are referenced in the notes.[2]

I'm more confident than ever that the Comet Research Group scientists are on the right track, and I hold them in the highest regard for speaking truth to power and being willing to stick their necks out. I was therefore excited when George Howard, not a scientist but an environmental restoration specialist and a supporter of CRG who edits the online magazine *Cosmic Tusk,* contacted me to suggest a meet-up with some of the leading members of the group during my fall 2017 research trip across the United States. On the same trip I met Al Goodyear and Allen West, and now here was an opportunity to exchange views with some of their other colleagues.

The meet-up was scheduled for Wilmington, North Carolina, on November 13 and 14, 2017. Chris Moore and Malcolm LeCompte, coauthors of both the platinum and the biomass-burning papers, would join us from the University of South Carolina, together with their colleague Mark Demitroff of Stockton University in New Jersey, coauthor of several earlier papers providing solid support for the YDIH.[3]

I invited my friend and colleague Randall Carlson to drive in from Atlanta to be part of the discussions. His work connecting impacts on the North

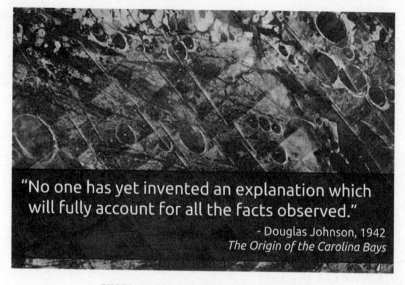

"No one has yet invented an explanation which will fully account for all the facts observed."

- Douglas Johnson, 1942
The Origin of the Carolina Bays

PHOTO: FAIRCHILD AERIAL SURVEYS, 1930.

American ice cap 12,800 years ago to the immense flood damage in the Channeled Scablands of eastern Washington State is discussed extensively in *Magicians of the Gods*.[4]

And I was pleased to learn that George Howard had also asked Antonio Zamora to be there. An independent researcher, a chemist, and a computer scientist,[5] Zamora is not a member of CRG and has nothing whatsoever to do with the group, but I had recently read an intriguing paper he had published earlier in 2017 in the peer-reviewed journal *Geomorphology* tracing the origins of the Carolina Bays to the Younger Dryas impacts.[6]

Around 500,000 peculiar elliptical ponds, depressions, and lakes with raised rims pock much of the US Atlantic seaboard from Delaware to Florida. Since it was in the Carolinas that scientists first noticed them in the late nineteenth century, they became known as Carolina Bays and from quite early on there were theories that they had been created by an immense swarm of meteorites striking the earth.[7] Several CRG members have explored the possibility that the Younger Dryas impacts might be connected to the mystery,[8] but the majority of the group have since distanced themselves from such notions. Dating studies indicate that the Bays were not all created simultaneously, as the YDIH would require, but are of widely varying ages separated by tens of thousands of years.[9]

Antonio Zamora's 2017 paper in *Geomorphology* put the cat among the pigeons by raising an interesting scenario whereby the bays could, after all, have resulted from YD impacts. I had naively assumed that Malcolm LeCompte and Mark Demitroff (who were then both CRG members but have since resigned) would welcome this new research.

I couldn't have been more wrong.

GLACIER ICE IMPACT HYPOTHESIS

LET'S START BY TAKING A proper look at the controversial proposals behind the "Glacier Ice Impact Hypothesis" that Antonio Zamora puts on the table in his *Geomorphology* paper.[10]

He begins by recognizing earlier evidence that discounts the Carolina Bays as impact features but then draws our attention to an intriguing mystery—the so-called Nebraska Rainwater Basins. Other than being oriented from northeast to southwest instead of from northwest to southeast (an important piece of evidence in itself), these curious elliptical geological formations more than 2,000 kilometers west of the Carolinas greatly resemble the bays:

> The Nebraska Rainwater Basins are not as well known as the Carolina Bays but their elliptical shape is so similar that it is necessary to consider that they formed contemporaneously with the Carolina Bays by the same mechanisms. . . . The objective of the Glacier Ice Impact Hypothesis is to examine the characteristics of the Carolina Bays and Nebraska Rainwater Basins to determine whether these geomorphological features could have been created by secondary impacts from terrestrial material, such as glacier ice, ejected by an extraterrestrial impact.[11]

Zamora is the first to acknowledge that his "Glacier Ice Impact Hypothesis" depends heavily on prior work done by two other investigators, Michael E. Davias[12] and Thomas H. S. Harris,[13] the former a specialist in "geospatial big data, data mining, computer graphics and algorithms" and the latter a dynamics and flight science expert at Lockheed Martin Corporation.

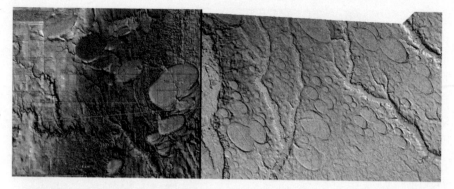

LEFT: Nebraska Rainwater Basins. RIGHT: Carolina Bays. IMAGE: ANTONIO ZAMORA; LIDAR FROM CINTOS.ORG.

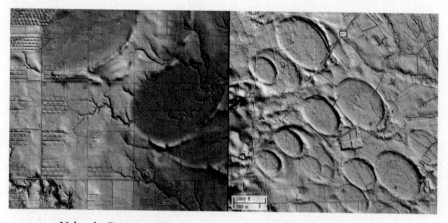

LEFT: Nebraska Rainwater Basins. RIGHT: Carolina Bays. Note orientation from northwest to southeast in the case of the Carolina Bays and from northeast to southwest in the case of the Nebraska Rainwater Basins. IMAGE: ANTONIO ZAMORA; LIDAR FROM CINTOS.ORG.

Michael Davias accompanied Zamora to Wilmington and shared with us there the evidence that he and Harris had first presented in May 2015 at the 49th Annual Meeting of the Geological Society of America.[14]

Published as a conference paper, their proposal is that a cosmic impact during the Ice Age in Michigan's Saginaw Bay (which was then solid land covered by deep glacial ice) would have produced ejecta and secondary impacts in a "butterfly-wing" pattern precisely over the Nebraska Rainwater Basins, where they would be oriented northeast to southwest, and the Carolina Bays, where they would be oriented northwest to southeast.[15]

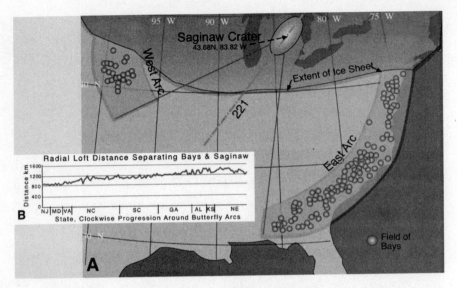

Radial Loft Distance Separating Bays & Saginaw

State, Clockwise Progression Around Butterfly Arcs

IMAGE: MICHAEL DAVIAS, CINTOS.ORG.

While he has no quarrel with Allen West, Richard Firestone, and other CRG scientists who suspect that there may have been a total of eight impacts on the North American ice cap,[16] Zamora focuses his investigation on the Michigan event proposed by Davias and Harris to have been specifically responsible for the simultaneous creation both of the Carolina Bays and of the Nebraska Rainwater Basins.

Saginaw Bay, the suggested impact site, is "commonly attributed to erosion by the Saginaw glacial lobe penetrating through the Mississippian and Pennsylvanian Cuestas," Davias and Harris concede, but propose instead that it is "the footprint of an oblique impact arriving at an azimuth of 222°. . . . Given 1 kilometer of ice over this footprint, 45,000 cubic kilometres of water would have been instantly ionized or vaporized."[17]

Meanwhile, the shock effects of the impact, although somewhat mitigated by the ice cover, would have bulldozed into the ancient promontory of bedrock then beneath the ice at the center of the Michigan Basin, plowed out the gap in the "mitten" that we now call Saginaw Bay, and sent up a mass of ejecta consisting of pulverized Michigan sandstone (from the bedrock) and water (from the vaporized ice).[18] Blasted into suborbital space, this ejecta would then have reentered the atmosphere and fallen back to earth—with the end result being a sort of slurry that splattered down across much of the continen-

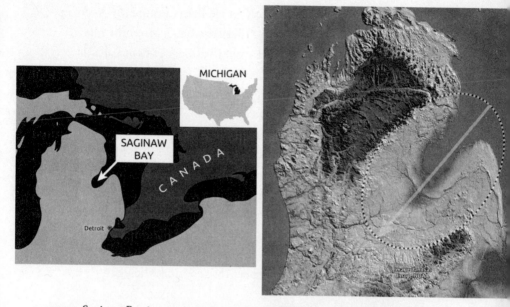

LEFT: Saginaw Bay is an enigmatic, now water-filled, depression in Michigan's distinctive "Mitten," separating the "hand" of the mitten, to the left, from its "thumb," to the right. RIGHT: Instead of erosion by glacial ice, Davias and Harris propose that Saginaw Bay is the footprint of a massive impact of a cosmic object that struck ancient Michigan at an oblique angle. IMAGE: MICHAEL DAVIAS, CINTOS.ORG.

tal United States south of the ice sheet but that only left impressions, such as the Carolina Bays and the Nebraska Rainwater Basins, on suitably soft and "unconsolidated" ground.[19]

When Davias and Harris gave their paper at the Geological Society of America in 2015 they tentatively suggested an age of 786,000 years for the formation of Saginaw Bay.[20] While drawing on their excellent ballistics and triangulation work, Zamora's presentation of his own Glacial Ice Impact Hypothesis in his 2017 paper in *Geomorphology* rejects so great an age and offers a compelling case that Saginaw Bay was scooped out just 12,800 years ago by one of the fragments of the Younger Dryas comet.[21] On technical grounds to do with "the thermodynamics of water in a liquid state" he also rejects Davias and Harris's notion that the ejecta would have consisted of a "foam of sand and water."[22] According to Zamora's calculations, massive quantities of solid glacial ice would instead have been blasted aloft:

Experiments of high-speed impacts on ice sheets using NASA's Ames Vertical Gun demonstrate that ice shatters when a projectile hits it. Pieces of ice are ejected, radiating from the impact site in ballistic trajectories.[23]

"The Laurentide Ice Sheet," writes Zamora,

> covered the convergence point determined by Davias and Harris in Saginaw Bay with a thickness of approximately 1500 to 2000 m of ice during the Pleistocene. . . . Ballistic equations, scaling laws relating crater size to impact energy, geometrical analysis and statistical analysis provide a mathematical foundation for explaining the shape of the bays and their origin from secondary impacts of glacier ice ejected from the Laurentide Ice Sheet that covered Michigan.[24]

It's important to be clear on this.

Just as Zamora does not support Davias and Harris's idea that the ejecta consisted of pulverized sandstone and water, so, too, he adamantly does NOT suggest that hundreds of thousands of fragments of the original Younger Dryas comet bombarded North America's Atlantic seaboard, creating the

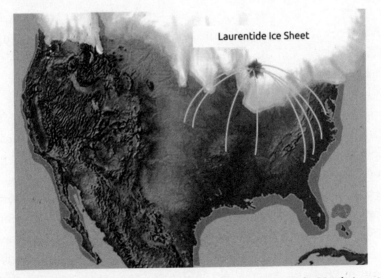

Ballistic trajectories of glacier ice ejecta after a cosmic impact on the North American ice cap. IMAGE: ANTONIO ZAMORA.

phenomenon of the Carolina Bays. Neither is he suggesting that the Nebraska Rainwater Basins were the result of direct hits by comet fragments. Instead he accepts the CRG's long-established position that the epicenter of the impacts was the North American ice cap.

In his view all the damage in the Carolinas and Nebraska was done by the stupendous mass of icy ejecta, varying in size from basketballs to "ice boulders" tens or even hundreds of meters across, that fell back to earth following the Saginaw Bay impact.

AN APOCALYPTIC VISION

I REFER THE READER TO Zamora's paper itself for the detailed evidence behind his findings. In summary, however, having first reviewed and rejected all other explanations for the formation of the bays and basins, and having given special consideration to the longer-term evolution of impact craters on viscous surfaces, Zamora concludes as follows:

> The radial orientation of the Carolina Bays and Nebraska Rainwater Basins toward a convergence point in Michigan, and the elliptical shapes of the bays with specific width-to-length ratios can be better explained by impact mechanisms than by terrestrial wind and water processes.
>
> The Glacier Ice Impact Hypothesis . . . has been supplemented with an experimental model demonstrating that oblique impacts on viscous surfaces can reproducibly create inclined conical cavities that are remodeled into shallow elliptical depressions by viscous relaxation. This makes it possible to model the Carolina Bays and Nebraska Rainwater Basins as conic sections whose width-to-length ratio can be explained by the angle of impact.[25]

Zamora addresses the issue of the great diversity of dates for the Carolina Bays obtained by Optically Stimulated Luminescence (OSL), noting that this has hitherto been the most significant barrier to acceptance of any form of impact hypothesis with reference to the bays. As he rightly points out, however,

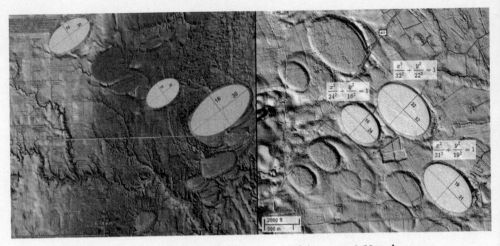

The width-to-length ratios of the Carolina Bays (right) average 0.58 and are very consistent for bays of different sizes. The bays in Nebraska (left) are indistinguishable from the bays on the East Coast based on their width-to-length ratios. IMAGE: ANTONIO ZAMORA; LIDAR FROM CINTOS.ORG.

the fundamental assumption behind the use of OSL has been that the subsurface of the Carolina Bays was exposed to light at the time of bay formation. His experimental model refutes this by demonstrating that impacts on viscous surfaces are plastic deformations that do not expose the subsurface to light:

> Therefore, OSL can only determine the date of the terrain, but not the date of formation of the bays. If all the Carolina Bays and Nebraska Rainwater Basins formed contemporaneously, it will be necessary to find a different way of dating them.
> The Glacier Ice Impact Hypothesis explains all the features of the Carolina Bays and Nebraska Rainwater Basins, including their elliptical shape, radial orientation, raised rims, undisturbed stratigraphy, absence of shock metamorphism, overlapping bays, and the occurrence of bays only in unconsolidated ground.[26]

Finally, and chillingly, Zamora's paper in *Geomorphology* notes:

> The great surface density of the bays indicates that they were created by a catastrophic saturation bombing with impacts of 13 KT to 3 MT that would have caused a mass extinction in an area with a radius of

The Glacier Ice Impact Hypothesis

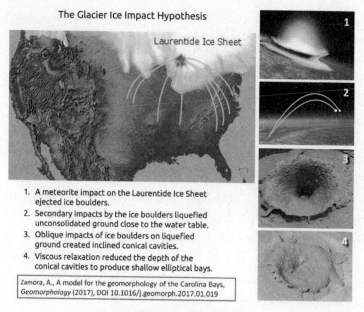

Laurentide Ice Sheet

1. A meteorite impact on the Laurentide Ice Sheet ejected ice boulders.
2. Secondary impacts by the ice boulders liquefied unconsolidated ground close to the water table.
3. Oblique impacts of ice boulders on liquefied ground created inclined conical cavities.
4. Viscous relaxation reduced the depth of the conical cavities to produce shallow elliptical bays.

Zamora, A., A model for the geomorphology of the Carolina Bays, *Geomorphology* (2017), DOI 10.1016/j.geomorph.2017.01.019

IMAGE: ANTONIO ZAMORA.

1500 km from the extraterrestrial impact in Michigan. This paper has considered mainly the ice boulders ejected by an extraterrestrial impact on the Laurentide Ice Sheet during the Pleistocene, but the impact would also have ejected water and produced steam. Taking into consideration the thermodynamic properties of water, any liquid water ejected above the atmosphere would have transformed into a fog of ice crystals that would have blocked the light of the sun. Thus, the time of formation of the Carolina Bays and Nebraska Rainwater Basins must coincide with an extinction event in the eastern half of the United States and the onset of a period of global cooling. This combination of conditions is best met by the disappearance of the North American megafauna, the end of the Clovis culture and the onset of the Younger Dryas cooling event at 12,800 cal. BP. The report of a platinum anomaly typical of extraterrestrial impacts at the Younger Dryas Boundary supports this scenario.[27]

In his book *Killer Comet*, Zamora elaborates on the extent and true horror of the Younger Dryas cataclysm. He considers how the effects of the primary impact over Michigan would have been massively compounded across North

America by the secondary impacts of glacier ice boulders. It's instructive to spend a few moments with the disturbing picture he paints:

> All living things within 100 kilometers of the [Michigan] impact died instantly. They were either burned by the heat blast or killed by the shock wave. On the East Coast, 1000 kilometers from the impact zone, the blinding flash on the horizon was followed by a sky that darkened ominously as it filled with the giant ice boulders ejected by the impact. Three minutes after the flash, the dark sky advanced relentlessly, and the ground shook as the first seismic waves from the extraterrestrial impact site arrived traveling at 5 km/sec.
>
> By this time, all animals and humans were aware that something terrible was happening. The sky continued to darken, and then filled with bright streaks as the ice boulders in suborbital flights re-entered the atmosphere at speeds of 3 to 4 km/sec. . . . [As] the giant ice boulders started falling . . . the thumping of the impacts sent shock waves through the ground that traveled at 5 to 8 km/sec. . . . The shaking ground started to liquefy, trapping everyone. The ground had turned to quicksand, making it impossible to walk or run . . .
>
> At the peak of intensity, a hail of glacier ice chunks, many as big as a baseball stadium, left steam trails in the sky as they re-entered the atmosphere at supersonic speeds and crashed into the liquefied ground accompanied by the thunder of sonic booms.
>
> The impacts created oblique, muddy, conical craters . . . with diameters of one to two kilometres . . . that swallowed whole villages and buried all the vegetation. The vibration of the ground quickly reduced the depth of the conical craters and turned them into [the] shallow depressions [that we know today as the Carolina Bays]. . . . The comet itself had not killed the megafauna. The saturation bombardment by the ice boulders that were ejected when the comet struck the Laurentide ice sheet caused the extinction event. . . . The landscape of the Eastern Seaboard had been transformed into a barren wasteland full of huge, shallow mud holes. . . .
>
> The Carolina Bays have remained as evidence of the glacier ice impacts on the soft, sandy soil of the East Coast.
>
> No such evidence remains of the ice chunks that must have fallen

on harder ground, but the ice impacts in the central and Midwestern states were equally merciless. When the colossal chunks of glacier ice hit the hard terrain, they shattered and sent out ice fragments at high speed. Any creature or vegetation in the path of the fast-moving ice shards was destroyed.

When the ice finally came to rest, the ejecta blanket had covered one-half of the contiguous United States with a thick layer of crushed ice . . . that increased the albedo of the Earth and reflected a significant portion of the dimmer light from the Sun back into space. The combined effect of the increased ice cover and the orbiting ice crystals would make the land cold and inhospitable for many years. . . .

The buried vegetation would freeze or remain dormant under the ice. Grazing animals that had survived the glacier ice bombardment had no access to their normal food sources and would soon starve. Predators that were still alive would also soon die without their herbivorous prey. . . .

Eventually, North America would be repopulated by new land animals and new humans, but the megafauna, and the ingenious Clovis people that had crafted such fine stone projectiles were gone forever.[28]

It's an apocalyptic vision to be sure, and we must remind ourselves that it deals with the widespread consequences of just **one** of the major impacts on the North American ice cap.

ATTACK AND DESTROY

AS WE'VE SEEN, ALLEN WEST and Richard Firestone propose that there may have been as many as **eight** significant impacts on the North American ice cap during the 21 years of the peak Younger Dryas bombardments.[29] Together with the other scientists from the Comet Research Group, they have focused, with great success, on gathering the evidence for these bombardments in the form of impact proxies scattered across 50 million square kilometers of the earth's surface.

What none of the group has yet done, however, is investigate the full implications **for North America itself** of the hypothesized impacts on the ice cap.

Why Antonio Zamora matters, and why his work deserves serious evaluation, is that he is the first to undertake such an exercise—albeit focused on only one out of the possible eight impacts. In addition, he offers testable hypotheses and opens up new vistas for inquiry and discussion. I was therefore expecting to spend 2 constructive and thought-provoking days at Wilmington, sharing ideas with big thinkers and giving proper consideration for the first time to the implications of the icy fallout across North America that Zamora rightly calculates would have been the outcome of impacts on the ice cap.

The opposite happened. It was clear from the outset that the only reason Malcolm LeCompte and Mark Demitroff were with us at Wilmington at all was to attack and destroy the Glacier Ice Impact Hypothesis at birth. There was no interest whatsoever in a discussion of the wider implications of Zamora's thinking. Their entire focus was to demonstrate that he was completely wrong to link the Carolina Bays to any kind of cosmic impacts, and to the Younger Dryas impacts in particular.

At one level this was all good. For science to progress it is important that all ideas be tested in the fire of peer review. And while Zamora's hypothesis had already been through that fire once in order to have appeared in *Geomorphology* at all, here were other scientists who disagreed.

Excellent! Bring it on, guys!

I was at Wilmington to learn, and such constructive disagreements would surely only help me gain a better understanding of what no scientist today can yet claim to understand fully—namely, the cause and true extent of the cataclysmic events that shook the earth at the onset of the Younger Dryas 12,800 years ago.

Because I'd gone into the meeting with the mind-set that we were all colleagues here trying to figure out a solution to one of the greatest mysteries of the past, I didn't initially expect the level of antagonism, hostility, scorn, and downright unpleasantness with which Zamora's impact hypothesis was received by LeCompte and Demitroff—who are themselves proponents of an impact hypothesis at the receiving end of a great deal of antagonism, hostility, scorn, and unpleasantness.

But that was naivete on my part. Over the following months I was to get a much clearer understanding of what was really going on.

"EXTREMELY REGRETTABLE . . ."

AFTER THE WILMINGTON MEETING, SANTHA and I flew to Little Rock, Arkansas, where I had a presentation to give at a conference before we returned to the United Kingdom. During my talk, which was filmed, I showed a photograph of myself with Chris Moore on a field trip to a Carolina Bay—Johns Bay—where platinum had been found. I outlined the platinum research and other YDIH research in my presentation and then moved on to a discussion of Antonio Zamora's Glacier Ice Hypothesis. I did not connect his work to the work of the Comet Research Group and I did not suggest he was a member of the Comet Research Group or had anything to do with it.

The video was released on YouTube on January 26, 2018.[30] A little over a month later I found myself embroiled in heated email correspondence with Malcolm LeCompte and Mark Demitroff.

The first salvo was fired on March 9, 2018, with an email from LeCompte to Zamora, cc'd to me, titled "Paper by Antonio Zamora: *Geomorphology* 282 (2017) 209–216."

That email accused me of providing "extraordinary coverage" of Zamora's "speculative theory" in my Little Rock presentation and of giving it exposure "in juxtaposition" with my "discussion of the YDB Impact Hypothesis." Describing my alleged "association" of Zamora's work with the work of the Comet Research Group as "extremely regrettable," LeCompte added a postscript specifically addressed to me:

Graham, I find Antonio's work to be unsupportable, not because impact proxies aren't found in the bay rims, as you apparently have been told and are now saying, but for the variety of reasons listed in the attached letter, first and foremost of which: because there was no ice in Saginaw Bay or anywhere within 200 km of where Antonio believes his impact occurred.

My bad about the impact proxies!

I had indeed incorrectly stated in that hastily-put-together segment of my presentation that none were found in the Carolina Bay rims and that this was part of the long-established dismissal of any impact connection to the bays. I got that wrong. Platinum is an impact proxy, as I knew very well, and Chris Moore had found it in the Carolina Bays. Multiple other proxies, including "magnetic grains and microspherules, carbon spherules and glass-like carbon," have also been found, as a 2010 study reports, "throughout the rims of 16 Carolina Bays."[31]

What I don't see, however, is how this helps LeCompte's claim that impacts did not make the bays. On the contrary, it seems to me that the presence of the proxies there only strengthens the case that the bays are impact-related. I shall certainly speak of this in future presentations.

Much more significant is the second statement in the postscript, to the effect that 12,800 years ago there was no ice in Saginaw Bay or anywhere within 200 kilometers of the proposed impact site. LeCompte elaborates on this point in the longer letter attached to his mail, formally addressed to the Editor of *Geomorphology*, where he refers to "a large body of literature" providing evidence that Zamora's proposed point of impact had been deglaciated for more than 1,000 years before the onset of the Younger Dryas and that not only Saginaw Bay but all of Lake Huron had been ice-free when the Younger Dryas began.

This seemed to be a fatal criticism of the Glacier Ice Impact Theory—but Zamora gave an immediate response to LeCompte:

> In your note to the editor of *Geomorphology* you say "Dyke (2004), and Larson and Schaetzl (2001), provide graphical depictions of the retreat of the Laurentide Ice Sheet with sufficiently high spatial and temporal resolution to make clear that not only Saginaw Bay, but all of Lake Huron was ice-free at the time of the Younger Dryas onset."
>
> Let us say that no evidence can be found for glaciers at the point where the axial projections of the bays converge. Geologists usually determine the extent of glacier coverage by examining glacial striations on the terrain and by identifying deposits of erratic boulders. Would you expect the site of an extraterrestrial impact to retain these markers? Wouldn't the impact of a 3 km asteroid obliterate striations and erratic boulders? The subsequent melting of the glaciers would then flood the impact point and wash away the last traces of the crater. The Carolina Bays do exist, and because they are conic sections, it is very likely that

they originated as conical impact cavities. . . . The Nebraska Rainwater Basins are now intimately related to the Carolina Bays through their geometry. Any modern publication about the Carolina Bays that ignores the Nebraska basins is incomplete and inadequate. . . . In my paper, I mentioned that an ET impact on hard ground would have sent rocky ejecta only one third as far as an impact on ice. Moreover, an impact on land, rather than on ice, would have left a typical ET crater. My bet is that there was an ice sheet wherever the meteorite hit, otherwise someone would already have found the crater.

Frankly, I thought that Zamora had returned Malcolm's hardball quite well, and soon afterward he followed through by sending me a paper I hadn't come across before, published in *Quaternary Science Reviews* in 1986, titled "Correlation of Glacial Deposits of the Huron, Lake Michigan and Green Bay Lobes in Michigan and Wisconsin."[32] The paper, by Donald Eschman and David Mickelson, concludes that following an earlier retreat there was a re-advance of the ice sheet during the so-called Port Huron stade around 13,000 years ago and that at this time both Saginaw Bay and Lake Huron were indeed covered with ice.[33]

Once again, therefore, as so often in science, statements touted as facts turn out to be opinions contradicted by other opinions that are also touted as facts. The truth of the matter is that there remains great uncertainty and confusion around exactly what happened in North America—and across the whole world—at the onset of the Younger Dryas. While that uncertainty persists, alleged "certainties" of almost any kind are inappropriate and it is wise to keep an open mind to all possibilities.

Beyond the issue of the absence (or presence?) of an ice sheet at the proposed point of impact, LeCompte's dismissal of the Glacier Ice Impact Theory is of course supported by other evidence and reasoning, but my purpose here is not to get into these minutiae. I concede the possibility that LeCompte may be right while remaining open to the possibility that he may be wrong. Either way, the real importance of Zamora's contribution has been to raise new questions around the matter of the Younger Dryas impacts. Only time and further research will tell whether his theory really solves the mystery of the Carolina Bays and the Nebraska Rainwater Basins, but he has undoubtedly done scholarship a service by exploring the ballistics and dynamics of explosive cosmic impacts on the North American ice cap, and by looking into the potentially disastrous consequences in terms of the subsequent storm of icy ejecta.

"YOU WERE REPEATEDLY WARNED . . ."

THE STORM OF EJECTA FROM the Wilmington meeting was far from over. My exchange of emails with Malcolm LeCompte continued, Mark Demitroff joined the conversation as well, and both of them were clearly very annoyed with me! Chris Moore was cc'd but did not comment. What became clear from all this was that LeCompte's objection to the video was not that I had misrepresented the Comet Research Group in any way, or that I had misrepresented Chris Moore's recent research, but simply that right after what I had to say about the Comet Research Group, ending up with the visit I'd just made with Chris Moore to Johns Bay, I had gone on to talk about Zamora's Glacier Ice Impact Theory.

On March 21, 2018, therefore, because I sensed there was something going on here that was worthy of reporting, and wanted no one involved to be in any doubt that I intended to report it, I began a new thread of emails under the subject line FOR THE RECORD:

> I speak about the work of many scientists [in the video]. The fact
> that what I have to say about the work of one scientist follows what
> I have to say about the work of another scientist does not mean I am
> connecting the two—unless I specifically do so, which I don't do here.
> I am therefore really perplexed as to why this video has caused offence.

I have no hesitation in sharing the bulk of LeCompte's reply because of the light it sheds on a growing problem within science in general—the problem of enforced conformity.

The passages that I have placed in bold type were not in bold in the original but I choose to emphasize them in the extracts below because of the insights they provide into the ways this problem can manifest and the states of mind it engenders.

MALCOLM LeCOMPTE TO GRAHAM HANCOCK, MARCH 23, 2018:

You were . . . repeatedly warned that any association of Carolina Bay genesis linked to a discussion of the YDB impact event would likely be harmful to the progress of the YDIH research and to the reputations of its investigators.

You may not be aware of the time and energy spent to largely neutralize the distracting effects and hostility created by the early Carolina Bay related assertions made in the non-peer reviewed book: *Cycle of Cosmic Catastrophes.* [This is a book coauthored by Richard Firestone and Allen West, the original formulators of the YDIH, and published in 2006, a year before the first formal paper appeared in *PNAS.*] The association of bay impact genesis with the YDIH created an early perception in some scientific communities that the YDB impact research was both unprofessional and bordering on pseudoscientific. Those original, naive Bay genesis claims still haunt the research and contribute to hobbling its acceptance as a legitimate research activity for a new generation of scientists. **We have few, relatively younger and seasoned tigers like Chris Moore willing to disregard the real and perceived risks to their careers and reputations, and even fewer younger, newly-trained scientists following in his footsteps to adopt what is still considered a somewhat controversial line of research. His participation in this research is noticed and monitored by his many colleagues.**

Nevertheless, only a week after our meeting, where Mark [Demitroff], with Chris' endorsement, had presented an evidence-based alternative to Zamora's proposed Bay impact genesis, you gave a video presentation that juxtaposed YDIH research with Zamora's very controversial claim of Bay impact genesis. . . .

Less than a month [later] . . . Chris Moore, probably the most important current and hopefully future investigator of the YDB event, received a call from a colleague who had seen your You Tube video and posted it on his anti-pseudoscience website that is apparently visited by some of Chris' peers. Your presentation juxtaposing YDIH research with Zamora's claims certainly endowed them with some unwarranted credibility but also contaminated the YDIH by the association. **Chris achieved some unwanted negative-**

celebrity among his colleagues. He was challenged about the
wisdom of hosting you and suffered the indignity of wondering
about the effect the . . . video might have on his career and
reputation.

It is obvious to me that distribution of your video presentation
has put Chris's reputation, career and participation in the YDIH
research in potential jeopardy . . . the resulting harm . . . has yet
to be completely comprehended. Fortunately Chris made the brave
decision to continue the YDIH research, despite that video's presence
on you tube for the foreseeable future.

Wow! All this stress, drama, and defensiveness over a video of a presentation I gave at a conference! I have to confess, I was taken aback by the vehemence of LeCompte's reply and the suggestion that I might have harmed the career of that very likable and diligent scientist Chris Moore.

But at a deeper level what this whole exchange revealed to me was something disturbing about the way science works. I hadn't quite grasped the role of **fear** before. But I could see it in action everywhere here: fear of being "noticed and monitored by colleagues," fear of unwanted negative celebrity, fear of indignity, fear of loss of reputation, fear of loss of career—and not for committing some terrible crime but simply for exploring unorthodox possibilities and undertaking "somewhat controversial research" into what everyone agrees were extraordinary events 12,800 years ago.

Worse still, this pervasive state of fear has somehow ingrained itself so deeply into the fabric of science that those who have embraced unorthodox possibilities themselves are often among the least willing to consider unorthodox possibilities embraced by others—lest by doing so they "contaminate" their own preferred unorthodoxy.

How will it ever be possible to discover the truth about the past when so much fear gets in the way?

PART VIII

SURVIVE!

The Mystery of the Invisible Man

28

HUNTER-GATHERERS AND
THE LOST CIVILIZATION

UTTERLY HORRIFIC, TROUBLING, AND CONFUSING events took place at the onset of the Younger Dryas, and more than a decade under the scientific spotlight has repeatedly confirmed that the best explanation of all the evidence is that the earth underwent a series of interactions with the remnants of the disintegrating giant comet that spawned the Taurid meteor stream. These encounters are thought to have reached a peak 12,822 years ago but were sustained over a span of 21 years beginning 12,836 years ago and ending 12,815 years ago. There were other episodes of bombardment around the time of the Younger Dryas onset, but this was the worst.

Perhaps it was not a comet after all. Perhaps in the next decade some other even more compelling theory with even more evidence to back it up will be advanced—or perhaps some decisive new discovery will be made that vindicates one of the existing nonimpact theories. Until that time, however, the

Younger Dryas Impact Hypothesis continues to make complete sense to me and to a great many scientists, and its 21-year window of maximum devastation, peaking around 12,822 years ago, deserves special attention.

Archaeological evidence from this period is scarce in North America, but what there is suggests that widely scattered populations of Native American hunter-gatherers were badly mauled at the Younger Dryas onset. Amid indications of sudden population collapses, many previously inhabited areas were abandoned entirely, as we saw in chapter 26, with no return for hundreds of years. Clovis ceased to exist—an entire vibrant, widely distributed culture obliterated—but other humans survived and bounced back, something our species has a talent for. I'd stayed in touch with Al Goodyear since Topper and he confirmed that in his view, while there was evidence for a "possible demographic crash/depression," there had been no "extermination post Clovis."[1]

We shouldn't be surprised.

Hunter-gatherers are hard to exterminate!

They roll with the punches and they bounce back.

In the technology-dominated twenty-first century, the majority of humans live in cities fed by intensive agriculture, but in the world today there still exists a tiny minority of hunter-gatherers. Many of the urbanites enjoy great wealth and abundance while the hunter-gatherers possess very little. If a cataclysm on the scale of the Younger Dryas impacts were to strike in our lifetimes, however, I predict it would be these few remaining groups of hunter-gatherers—in the Kalahari desert, for example, or in the Amazon rainforest—who would have the best chance of surviving the devastating consequences, and it would be their descendants, not ours, who would carry the human story forward. Unlike most city dwellers who have no idea how to live off the land, hunter-gatherers are masters of survival, they know how to deal with environmental setbacks, and no matter how tough things get they can usually improvise a workaround. By contrast the masses in the cities, suddenly discovering that technology can't fix everything, would be psychologically traumatized and largely helpless.

Almost the opposite of our twenty-first-century world, the world as I imagine it 12,800 years ago is one in which the vast majority of humans are hunter-gatherers while a minority have taken another, more complex, path. The hunter-gatherers form populations recognized by modern archaeologists, and their stone tools, weapons, and ornaments speak of an effective but fairly

ABOVE: Graham Hancock with geophysicist Allen West of the Comet Research Group examining the black-mat deposit at Murray Springs, Arizona. Packed with impact proxies such as melt glass, carbon spherules, and nanodiamonds, the black mat is the global signature of the giant series of impacts by the fragments of a disintegrating comet that sparked a global cataclysm 12,800 years ago. The scale of the event was so immense that it interrupted human history and wiped from the record almost all traces of an advanced civilization of the Ice Age. However, some hints and clues as to the nature of that civilization remain. BELOW: Take the case of the massive beams, quarried from solid granite and weighing in the range of 70 tons each, incorporated into the core of Egypt's Great Pyramid in the series of "relieving chambers" stacked on top of the "King's Chamber" more than 50 meters (164 feet) above ground level. None of the wishful scholarly claims of megaliths somehow being slid "easily" into place on wooden rollers or on lubricated sand will work at this elevation. The fact of the matter is that the hulking beams forming the floors and ceilings of the relieving chambers are where they are—and that in order to get there they had to be lifted more than 50 meters into the air. Leverage, mechanical advantage, and the simple technologies attributed to the ancient Egyptians by archaeologists are incapable of achieving such a feat. Are we confronted by the achievements of a lost science? PHOTOS: SANTHA FAIIA.

ABOVE: The Trilithon at Baalbek. The uppermost section of the wall, with the gap, is a relatively recent reconstruction. But under it sit the three ancient blocks of the Trilithon, with the contact between first and second blocks directly under the gap while the contact between the second and third blocks, farther to the left, is too tight to be visible. Each of these three blocks weighs around 900 tons—about the weight of 450 large SUVs. Again, simple technologies of leverage and mechanical advantage seem inadequate to account for the achievement of raising such immense blocks and fitting them perfectly into place. BELOW: Sacsayhuaman, Peru. These colossal megalithic walls are arranged in a series of zigzags and consist of intricately formed polygonal blocks. No two blocks among the thousands at Sacsayhuaman are the same shape and all are so tightly interlocked in all dimensions that the edge of a piece of paper cannot be slipped between the joints. Efforts by archaeologists to reconstruct how the work at Sacsayhuaman was done have proved ludicrous because the only reference frame deemed acceptable, involving leverage and mechanical advantage, is unable to account for many of the more complex anomalies. PHOTOS: SANTHA FAIIA.

The estimated weight of this enormous polygonal block is 360 tons. Archaeologists attribute the construction of Sacsayhuaman to the Incas but there are no records of the Incas moving such immense weights successfully and according to one account disaster followed when they attempted to do so. PHOTO: SANTHA FAIIA.

ABOVE: Sacsayhuaman: detail of block jointing, with indications that the stone had been softened like putty before being put into place. Traditions speak of meditating sages, the use of certain plants, the focused attention of initiates, miraculously speedy workmanship, and special kinds of chanting or tones played on musical instruments in connection with the lifting, placing, softening, and moulding of megaliths all around the world. Confronted by the global distribution of such narratives, and by the stark reality of the sites themselves, we're obliged to ask if we're dealing with the reverberations of an ancient technology we don't understand, operating on principles that are utterly unknown to us. BELOW: The almost unbelievable Kailasa Temple, hewn in a single piece out of solid basalt at Ellora in the Indian state of Maharashtra. Traditions speak of magic used in its construction but, as has been said, "any sufficiently advanced technology is indistinguishable from magic." PHOTOS: SANTHA FAIIA.

ABOVE: With its stone walls, enclosures, and crumbling earthen pyramid, the ancient megalithic site of Tiahuanaco in the high Andes echoes the austere geometries of the earthworks now emerging from the Amazon jungle. BELOW: Teotihuacan, Mexico, "the place where men became gods." With its principal pyramids of the Moon (foreground) and the Sun (mid left) arranged along the immense axis of the "Way of the Dead," the site is rich in geometry and cosmic alignments. PHOTOS: SANTHA FAIIA.

Uncelebrated, and frequently defaced by modern graffiti, large numbers of anomalous megalithic structures await proper study in the forests of New England. Without good evidence archaeologists seek to attribute all of them to the colonial period of the last few centuries, and to deny that Native Americans were involved in their construction. PHOTOS: SANTHA FAIIA.

The megalithic character of the New England structures (above and overleaf) and the fact that their entrances are frequently oriented to solstitial sunrise points (below) argues for their great antiquity and refutes the "colonial root cellar" fantasy of archaeologists. PHOTOS: SANTHA FAIIA.

rudimentary technology. The minority who have taken a different path are not recognized and I contend that this is primarily because the destruction of their civilization was near-total, and because the few, faint, tantalizing clues to their technology that have reached us across the ages hint at a level of science far in advance of anything believed by scholars to have been possible at such a remote period of prehistory.

It is for this reason that ancient maps incorporating scientifically accurate latitudes and longitudes and depicting the world as it looked during the lowered sea levels of the last Ice Age have been dismissed by the mainstream as mere curiosities with no bearing on our understanding of the origins of civilization.

I looked into the mystery of these maps in *Fingerprints of the Gods* (1995) and again in *Underworld* in 2002, and refer the reader to appendix 2 for details. Contrary to the mainstream, my broad conclusion is that an advanced global seafaring civilization existed during the Ice Age, that it mapped the earth as it looked then with stunning accuracy, and that it had solved the problem of longitude, which our own civilization failed to do until the invention of Harrison's marine chronometer in the late eighteenth century. As masters of celestial navigation, as explorers, as geographers, and as cartographers, therefore, this lost civilization of 12,800 years ago was not outstripped by Western science until less than 300 years ago at the peak of the Age of Discovery.

Suppose there was an earlier "Age of Discovery" in the centuries before the onset of the Younger Dryas, when the fleets of the lost civilization set out to open interaction with tribes of hunter-gatherers all around the world and either passed themselves off as, or were mistaken for, "gods." I'm just offering food for thought here, a pure speculation, but I submit this might have followed a period of severely restricted involvement with other peoples—such as the Ming dynasty imposed on China in the late fourteenth century—and I suggest that the renewed outreach may have been motivated by foreknowledge of the impending Younger Dryas cataclysm. This lost civilization, after all, appears to have evolved a sophisticated religion deploying powerful symbolism that emphasized the connection between heaven and earth and that envisaged an afterlife journey through specific well-charted regions of the celestial vault. Its astronomer-priests are therefore most unlikely to have missed the signs in the sky as our planet began its long journey toward intersection with a particularly lumpy and debris-filled filament of the Taurid meteor stream where the menacing serpentlike tails of the outgassing larger fragments might have served as visible omens of the terrors to come.

The astronomers and mathematicians of our hypothetical lost civilization would surely have set to work calculating trajectories and orbits and would have learned in due course that collisions with fragments of the disintegrating comet, though not an immediate threat, were unfortunately inevitable during the centuries ahead. It was not yet certain how large and how sustained the bombardments would be, or where and when the first fragments would strike. Multiple outcomes were possible, from escaping relatively unscathed, at one end of the scale, to a worst-case scenario in which civilization itself would be snuffed out. And although the worst would probably never happen, a contingency plan would certainly have been prepared on the off chance that it did.

My bet is the planners would have seen from the outset that the superior survival skills of hunter-gatherer populations might potentially make them the inheritors of the earth in the event of a true planetary cataclysm. An important strand of any contingency plan, therefore, would have been to establish connections with hunter-gatherers, to teach them, to learn from them, and in so doing to ensure that these populations were willing and able—if called upon—to offer refuge to the "gods" of the lost civilization.

It would not be until weeks or even days before the bombardments began that the areas likely to be worst hit could be pinpointed with any certainty. There must have been hope that by some miracle the impacts might be avoided altogether, but until the centuries of danger passed it was best to regard the whole world as a target and therefore to prepare safe havens on many different continents so that if some were destroyed others would survive. I speculated in chapter 10 that this process of preparation might even have involved the experimental resettlement of groups of hunter-gatherers far from their home regions with the intention that they should create places of refuge for the "gods" in their new surroundings. Such a project might account for that strange Australasian DNA signal stranded in the genes of certain Amazonian tribes.

In this scenario, therefore, hunter-gatherer populations all around the world were deliberately recruited by people from a different, more scientifically advanced culture to prepare for a coming cataclysm, to offer refuge to the "gods" should they require it, and perhaps even to serve as duplicate archives—either in oral tradition or in the safekeeping of physical records—for some of the scientific knowledge of the "gods."

In North America the evidence is that hunter-gatherers bounced back quite successfully within less than a millennium of the onset of the Younger Dryas, and thereafter there is a thin but fairly continuous archaeological record. What is mysterious is not so much the early appearance of mound-building in this new age—perhaps as early as 8,000 years ago, as we've seen—or the sophistication of sites such as Watson Brake 5,500 years ago, nor even their obvious astronomical and geometrical connections to later vast earthworks such as Moundville and Cahokia, but that in this early monumental architecture of the New World memes of geometry, astronomy, and solar alignments consistently appear that are also found in the early monumental architecture of the Old World at iconic sites such as Stonehenge and the Great Pyramid of Giza. A tremendous leap forward in agricultural know-how, coupled with the sudden uptake of eerily distinctive spiritual ideas concerning the afterlife journey of the soul, also often accompanies the architectural memes. It's therefore hard to avoid the impression that some kind of "package" is involved here.

Something designed.

Something deliberately and carefully contrived to engage future generations in specific courses of action, regarded as religious duties, that would also educate them deeply in the cycles of the heavens and in the measurement and nurturing of the earth.

It's almost as though a guiding hand has been at work behind the scenes of prehistory. If so, whether through secret groups of insider initiates or by some other means of cultural transmission, this hidden influence appears to have been active in the Americas since before the onset of the Younger Dryas, to have undergone long periods of inactivity, and to have reemerged again and again at crucial junctures to shape the direction of civilization.

CLOVIS GIVEN A HELPING HAND?

KNOWLEDGE OF THE TRUE GLOBAL extent of the Younger Dryas impacts continues to grow. We've focused on the evidence from North America, but recent research published in *Studia Quaternaria* in 2018 presents evidence of a cometary airburst over Mount Viso in Europe's Western Alps around 12,800 years ago that raised temperatures instantly, in a brief pulse, to above 2,200

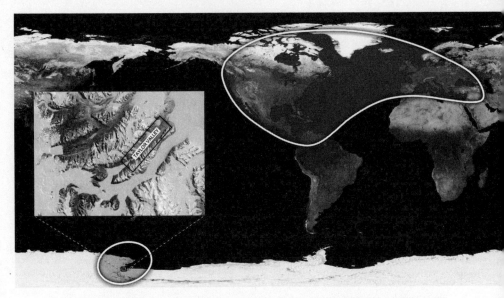

As of late 2014, the Younger Dryas Boundary strewn field of impact proxies had
been traced across 50 million square kilometers of the earth's surface (above).
Since then YDB impact proxies have been found much more widely distributed
than previously reported in South America, and a 2018 study reports their
discovery in Antarctica's Taylor Valley (inset) linked to evidence of an impact or
airburst around 12,800 years ago.

degrees C—almost 1,000 degrees hotter than the melting point of steel.[2] Another
2018 study, published in the *Journal of Geology,* reports evidence from Antarctica's New Mountain, near the Taylor Glacier, that an "impact/airburst of the
same time line as the Younger Dryas Boundary may have reached across South
America and the Pacific Ocean to the Dry Valley Mountains of Antarctica."[3]

As more evidence of this quality continues to pour in, two significant
observations thrust themselves to the fore.

First, this cataclysm, which we know to have been drawn out over 21 years
between 12,836 and 12,815 years ago, was truly global, affecting regions as
far apart as Greenland, the Pacific, the Americas, Europe, and Antarctica.

And second, it was just the luck of the draw that North America, rather
than some other region, found itself at the epicenter of the peak bombardment. However, this had profound implications for the world because so
much of the continent was then still covered by ice that was radically destabilized, releasing the meltwater flood that shut down the Gulf Stream and

ushered in the Younger Dryas. The fact that Greenland and Europe were also severely hit and also ice covered compounded the problem by adding to the deluge of icy meltwater pouring into the Atlantic Ocean. There is no doubt, however, that it was the continental landmass of North America that suffered the worst effects of the impacts, airbursts, shock waves, and wildfires and finally, perhaps early in that 21-year episode of bombardment, of Antonio Zamora's proposed storm of icy ejecta. The latter, we might speculate, could even have played a role in extinguishing the wildfires, thus accounting for the fact that a single massive episode of biomass burning, the largest in the entire NGRIP Ice Core, is documented for North America right at the onset of the Younger Dryas, and then rapidly dies down, never to recur on such a scale.[4]

Once all this is taken into account, the severity of the extinctions in North America seems less surprising and we can begin to understand how it was that the Clovis people passed from abundance to nonexistence virtually overnight.

Moreover, the Clovis phenomenon is, itself, an intriguing mystery. We've already seen that no archaeological background has ever been found to the beautiful and sophisticated fluted points used by these remarkably successful hunter-gatherers to spear mammoths like Eloise at Murray Springs. From the moment we meet them around 13,400 years ago to the moment of their disappearance from the record about 12,800 years ago, they're equipped with their extremely effective signature "toolkit" of which the points are part. These Clovis tools and weapons appear suddenly and fully formed in archaeological deposits across huge expanses of North America with no evidence, **anywhere**, of experiments, developments, prototypes, or, indeed, of any intermediate stages in their evolution.[5]

My guess is there's a connection between Clovis and the lost civilization, not least because studies of ancient DNA show the Clovis genome to be much more closely related to Native South Americans than to Native North Americans (see part 3). Indeed, there's a parallel between the rather sudden and inexplicable way that Australasian genes turn up in the Amazon basin and the equally sudden and inexplicable way that Clovis fluted-point technology turns up in North America.

Could both have the same cause?

Could the same hidden hand that transported a population of Australasian setters across the Pacific Ocean from New Guinea to the Amazon also have given technical assistance to one group among the many that we now know inhabited North America before the onset of the Younger Dryas? And since the whole Clovis First nonsense has finally been relegated to the dustbin of history, perhaps it's time to consider another possibility—let's call it "Clovis Most Favored" or "Clovis Given a Helping Hand."

Though in no way "high-tech" in twenty-first-century terms, the Clovis toolkit is far superior to anything else Native Americans are thought to have been capable of 13,400 years ago when the first fluted points begin to appear south of the ice cap. I'm not proposing that these stone tools were part of the technology of the lost civilization itself—any more than jet aircraft were part of it. I've argued already that a more realistic parallel for the level of science and technology attained would be with Europe and the newly formed United States in the late eighteenth and early nineteenth centuries.

Other than that, the civilization I envisage was very different from our own, founded upon entirely different principles. Much of its science may remain opaque to us not because it is absent but because we are unable to recognize it for what it is. Nor is there any reason to suppose it would have shared its own "high-tech" with other peoples; quite possibly there were even specific stipulations against doing so. But there might have been less hesitation around the idea of devising better, more efficient stone tools to put into the hands of favored groups of hunter-gatherers, thus conferring a competitive advantage upon them.

Suppose Clovis was such a group, already present alongside many other groups that we now know to have inhabited the Americas before the Younger Dryas onset. The connection to the southern lineage of Native Americans is interesting. Perhaps it might even have been in those 5 million square kilometers of Amazon rainforest where archaeologists have not yet ventured that fluted-point technology was initially taught to Clovis ancestors who then migrated north, bringing "their" expertise with them.

In so doing they burst in upon—and in a brief few centuries radically changed—a cultural landscape that archaeologists are now beginning to realize had previously been stable and continuous for thousands of years. Just as Al Goodyear discovered at Topper when he took the decision to dig down below the lowest Clovis occupation level (see chapter 6), recent excavations at the extremely prolific Clovis site of Gault, Texas, have likewise revealed deeper, pre-Clovis levels. Reported in the journal Science Advances in July 2018, these levels contain an assortment of stone tools—"the Gault Assemblage"—so far confirmed to be at least 2,000 years older than Clovis. Significantly, what archaeologists have identified in the assembly is "a previously unknown, early projectile point technology unrelated to Clovis."[6]

Of note also is that:

> There is a ~10-cm-thick zone of decreased cultural material between the Clovis and Gault components. This suggests a reduction in site activity or possible occupational breaks between . . . cultural depositions.[7] . . . The distinct technological differences between Clovis and Gault Assemblage, together with the stratigraphic separation between the cultural depositions, indicate a lack of continuity between the two complexes.[8]

In other words, Clovis just rather inexplicably appears and replaces preexisting native North American cultures, and pretty soon its occupation levels are imposed over other, earlier occupation levels all across the continental United States until suddenly, and mysteriously, in the big bang of the Younger Dryas onset, Clovis itself is gone—dead and buried beneath the black mat.

Yet in the brief few hundred years of its florescence, Clovis sparkled and shone as the most successful and widespread hunter-gatherer culture thus far seen in the Americas. Archaeologists and flint knappers who have studied the matter are in no doubt that the distinctive points, and the way that fluting was deployed in their manufacture, would have given the Clovis people a significant technological edge over other hunter-gatherers.[9] The question, therefore, has to be why they were wiped out while other less prominent and capable cultures were able to emerge from the shadows of archaeological invisibility and survive.

Perhaps they grew too close to the "gods" of the lost civilization and shared their fate?

This is a serious proposition, not a frivolous question, and we may anticipate the skeptical response. If Clovis benefited from contact with a more advanced civilization, then we should find the skeletal remains of those more advanced people intermingled with the Clovis remains, and we do not—therefore, there was no advanced civilization. Similarly, if Clovis benefited from contact with the people of a more advanced civilization, then we should find at least some traces of their higher tech among the Clovis assemblages, and we do not—therefore, there was no advanced civilization.

I've already responded to the second argument. There might have been very good reasons why people from a more technologically advanced civilization would have decided **not** to share their high-tech with hunter-gatherers, while at the same time choosing to favor a particular group with the know-how to work existing raw materials like stone, antler, and bone into more efficient hunting weapons and tools than they'd ever made before.

As to the first argument, although Clovis were not the "first Americans," their culture has been the subject of intensive archaeological study for more than 80 years and we've seen that Clovis artifacts have been discovered in great quantities at sites scattered far and wide across North America.

But how many Clovis bones have been found alongside the artifacts? How many skeletons, crania, tibia, phalanges, or teeth? I had imagined there must be quite a collection for such a famous and well-understood culture. I was therefore surprised to learn during the research for this book that **apart from the incomplete skeleton of a single individual**—the Anzick-1 child excavated in Montana and discussed in chapter 9—**there are no human remains at all from the Clovis period.**[10] Even in the case of Anzick-1, as we've seen, the Clovis provenance was questioned by some until sophisticated dating techniques in 2018 resolved an apparent discrepancy between the age of the infant's bones and the age of the Clovis tools found with him, placing both firmly at the onset of the Younger Dryas around 12,800 years ago and confirming the Clovis identity of the buried child.[11]

Here then is the conundrum. At locations scattered all across North America from Alaska to New Mexico and from Florida to the state of Washington, more than 1,500 Clovis sites have been found. These sites have yielded more than 10,000 Clovis points[12] and tens of thousands of other artifacts from the Clovis toolkit (40,000 at Topper alone, as we saw in chapter 6). Yet among all these archaeological riches, it bears repeating that the sum total of Clovis human remains found in 85 years of excavations is limited to the Anzick-1 partial skeleton.[13]

In short, if the homeland of our hypothetical advanced civilization were in America, and if it became a lost civilization during the tumultuous earth changes of 12,800 years ago, then the Clovis case suggests that a dearth of skeletal remains is a normal state of affairs by which we should not be surprised. Certainly it does not constitute disproof of the lost civilization hypothesis.

By contrast, the sudden appearance of Clovis fluted-point technology with no evidence of prior trial and error, buildup of skills, experimentation, or prototypes[14] cries out for an explanation. So, too, does the Australasian DNA signal in the heart of the Amazon rainforest. So, too, the shared geometry and astronomy, and the shared earthwork designs across the Old World and the New. So, too, the incredible overlaps of symbolism, spiritual inquiry, and beliefs.

The only viable explanation is a remote common source behind them all—a lost civilization, in my view. And although that civilization had established self-perpetuating memes that would keep the flame of its influence burning for thousands of years, it is clear that it did not survive the Younger Dryas cataclysm itself.

Let's look at North America, therefore, with the possibility in mind that it might be the "crime scene" from which a great civilization of prehistoric antiquity—the stuff of myth and legend all around the world—vanished without a trace.

29

UNKNOWN UNKNOWNS

A LOST ADVANCED CIVILIZATION OF the Ice Age with global navigational and mapmaking skills equivalent to our own in the late eighteenth and early nineteenth centuries would have had the capacity to establish outposts on every continent but must also have had a homeland.

Since that homeland has not been found after 200 years of diligent archaeology, most diligent archaeologists conclude—quite reasonably on the face of things—that it did not exist.

But there are other options.

It might be underwater now—the immense Sunda Shelf around Indonesia, for example, submerged by sea-level rise at the end of the Ice Age.

It might be under ice, perhaps in Antarctica, if we're willing to accept that some rather extraordinary geophysical events occurred in the past 100,000 years.

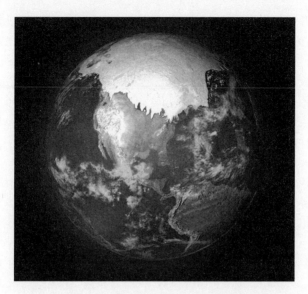

IMAGE: EARTH 18K BCE BY DONALD L. EDWARDS.

It might await rediscovery in the unexplored heart of the Amazon rainforest.

It might lie beneath the sands of the Sahara desert.

Or perhaps its homeland has all along remained hidden in plain view in the very last place that anyone has thought to look—North America?

There are surprisingly few "known knowns" in American prehistoric archaeology and good reasons why there are so many "known unknowns"—reasons that in turn suggest that the third Rumsfeldian category,[1] of "unknown unknowns," the "things we don't know we don't know," may ultimately prove to be far larger and more significant than either of the other two.

First and foremost, the Younger Dryas impacts, and subsequent sustained cataclysm, changed the face of the earth completely and wrought particularly significant havoc across North America. We have considered the question of huge volumes of meltwater released into the Arctic and Atlantic Oceans from the destabilized ice sheet and looked at the effects on global climate. But keep in mind that those enormous floods also devastated the rich North American mainland to the **south**, perhaps the best and most bounteous real estate then available anywhere.

This immense and extraordinary deluge, "possibly the largest flood in the history of the world,"[2] swept away and utterly demolished everything that lay in its path. Jostling with icebergs, choked by whole forests ripped up by their roots, turbulent with mud and boulders swirling in the depths of the current, what the deluge left behind can still be seen in something of its raw form in the Channeled Scablands of the state of Washington today—a devastated blank slate (described at length in *Magicians of the Gods*) littered with 10,000-ton "glacial erratics," immense fossilized waterfalls, and "current ripples" hundreds of feet long and dozens of feet high.[3]

If there were cities there, before the deluge, they would be gone.

If there was any evidence of anything that we would recognize as technology there, before the deluge, it would be gone.

And if an advanced antediluvian civilization had flourished anywhere within 500 kilometers of the southern edge of the ice cap, not only in the Channeled Scablands but all the way along the ice margin, the flood alone might have been sufficient to ensure that not a trace of it would be left for archaeologists to misrepresent 12,800 years later.

Washington displays flood-ravaged scablands, but so, too, does New Jersey much farther to the east. Washington is notable for its fields and hillsides strewn with huge ice-rafted erratics, but so, too, is the state of New York. Interestingly also, just as Washington has its coulees, New York State has its

Scablands, WA

St. Croix River, MN

Finger Lakes, NY

Finger Lakes. These latter were long thought to have been carved by glaciers, but their geomorphology closely parallels that of the coulees of the channeled scablands, and some researchers now believe they were cut by glacial melt-water at extreme pressures—a process linked by sediment evidence to "the collapse of continental ice sheets."[4]

Likewise in Minnesota, on the Saint Croix River, there is a spectacular array of more than eighty giant glacial potholes. One is 10 feet wide and 60 feet deep, making it the deepest explored pothole in the world. Others, as yet unexcavated, are even wider, and probably deeper as well. And all of them, without exception, were formed by turbulent floods at the end of the Ice Age.

We are looking then at vast expanses of North America that were literally *scoured*.

And this is before we get to the other effects of the Younger Dryas impacts explored in previous chapters—including direct hits on populated areas, searing heat and shock waves from airbursts, continent-wide wildfires, an impact winter, icy ejecta, and so on and so forth.

All in all, if North America is where a lost civilization of prehistoric antiquity vanished, then by far the most significant problem we face in investigating it is the way that the "crime scene" was systematically "wiped down" by the cataclysmic events at the onset of the Younger Dryas.

WIPING DOWN THE CRIME SCENE: CONQUEST

THE EUROPEAN INVASION OF THE American mainland began 500 years ago with the Spanish conquest of Mexico. In 1519, when Hernán Cortés first set foot on the shores of the Yucatán, more than 30 million people lived in Mexico. A century later, after the brutal genocide of the conquest itself and immense loss of life to smallpox epidemics, the population had fallen to just 3 million.[5]

The entire pre-Columbian literature of Mexico, a vast library of tens of thousands of codices, was carefully and systematically destroyed by the priests and friars who followed in the wake of the conquistadors. In November 1530, for example, Bishop Juan de Zumarraga, who had shortly before been appointed "Protector of the Indians" by the Spanish crown, proceeded to "protect" his flock by burning at the stake a Mexican aristocrat, the lord of the city of Texcoco, whom he accused of having worshipped the rain god. In the city's marketplace Zumarraga "had a pyramid formed of the documents of Aztec history, knowledge and literature, their paintings, manuscripts, and hieroglyphic writings, all of which he committed to the flames while the natives cried and prayed."[6]

More than 30 years later, the holocaust of documents was still under way. In July 1562, in the main square of Mani (just south of modern Merida in the Yucatan), Bishop Diego de Landa burned thousands of Maya codices, story paintings, and hieroglyphs inscribed on rolled-up deer skins. He boasted of destroying countless "idols" and "altars," all of which he described as "works of the devil, designed by the evil one to delude the Indians and to prevent them from accepting Christianity."[7] Noting that the Maya "used certain characters or letters, which they wrote in their books about the antiquities and their sciences" he informs us:

> We found a great number of books in these letters, and since they
> contained nothing but superstitions and falsehoods of the devil we
> burned them all, which they took most grievously and which gave
> them great pain.[8]

Any of us today interested in the truth about the past share the pain of those horrified Native Americans—for what, we cannot help but wonder, was written in their lost books concerning "the antiquities and sciences" of the ancients? What exactly went up in smoke there?

I have explored the mysteries of the Maya, and of their predecessors the Olmec, in my earlier work, so I have not retold their extraordinary story here. I will mention in passing, however, that in 1998, long before I knew of the Mississippi Valley civilization and its afterlife beliefs concerning the constellation Orion and the Milky Way, I drew attention in *Heaven's Mirror* to a discovery by archaeologists Jose Fernandez and Robert Cormack establishing that the settlement core of the Maya city of Utatlan was designed "according to a celestial scheme reflected by the shape of the constellation of Orion."[9]

Fernandez was also able to prove that all of Utatlan's major temples "were oriented to the heliacal setting points of stars in Orion,"[10] and noted that the Milky Way, alongside which Orion stands, "was thought of as a celestial path connecting the firmament's navel with the centre of the underworld."[11]

This should be familiar territory to the reader by now and hopefully you can guess what comes next. "Very much like the ancient Egyptians," I reported in *Heaven's Mirror,* the Maya regarded the Milky Way as a particularly important feature of the heavens:

> They conceived of it as the road that led to their netherworld, *Xibalba* which, in common with other Central American peoples, they located in the sky.[12]

I also commented on Mexican traditions of the postmortem journey of the soul in which the deceased, just as in the ancient Egyptian Duat, would face a series of ordeals and "a final judgment in the terrifying presence of the death god."[13] Noting numerous other striking similarities in beliefs and symbolism around the mysteries of death and the afterlife, I concluded:

> In Egypt, as amongst the Maya, the stellar context involves Orion and the Milky Way. In Egypt as in Mexico a journey through the netherworld must be undertaken by the deceased. In Egypt as in Mexico religious teachings assert that life is our opportunity to prepare for this journey—an opportunity that should under no circumstances be wasted.[14]

Such correspondences led me to speculate that both ancient Egypt and ancient Mexico had shared in the legacy of an even more ancient cosmological religion, "wrapped up in sophisticated astronomical observations" and specifically focused on the afterlife journey of the soul. Neither Egypt nor Mexico had originated this religion, nor had they transmitted it directly to one another. Rather each of them had inherited it from a third, as yet unidentified, civilization.[15]

It was a hypothesis. What would help to strengthen it, and perhaps even confirm it, would be evidence of other civilizations with no direct relationship in which the same legacy could be identified.

This evidence, I submit, now exists in the astonishing proximity of the religious beliefs, iconography, and symbolism of the Mississippi Valley to the religious beliefs, iconography, and symbolism of ancient Egypt outlined in part 6. These deep structural connections are, in my view, unexplainable by any means other than a shared legacy from a very ancient source—a source predating the separation of peoples when the Americas became isolated from the "Old World" by the rising oceans at the end of the Ice Age.

Let's take a brief look at the most ancient Native American book still in existence—the Dresden Codex, so called because it's kept in a museum in the German city of Dresden.[16]

It is a thought-provoking document for many reasons, not least the scientific character of the mathematics and astronomy incorporated in it. For example, the eminent Mayanist Sylvanus Griswold Morley noticed that on pages 51–58 of the codex, "405 revolutions of the moon are set down; and so accurate are the calculations involved that although they cover a period of nearly 33 years, the total number of days recorded (11,959) is only 89/100th of a day less than the true time computed by the best modern method."[17]

Also of great interest is the way that numbers set out in the Dresden Codex keep on getting longer and longer in the final pages:

Until, in the so-called "serpent numbers," a grand total of nearly twelve and a half million days (thirty-four thousand years) is recorded again and again . . .

Finally, on the last page of the manuscript, is depicted the Destruction of the World, for which these highest numbers have paved the way.

Here we see the rain serpent, stretching across the sky, belching forth torrents of water. Great streams of water gush from the sun and the moon. The old goddess, she of the tiger claws and forbidding aspect, the malevolent patroness of floods and cloudbursts, overturns the bowl of the heavenly waters. The crossbones, dread emblem of death, decorate her skirt, and a writhing snake crowns her head.

Below, with downward-pointing spears symbolic of the universal destruction, the black god stalks abroad, a screeching bird raging on his fearsome head. Here, indeed, is portrayed with graphic touch the final all-engulfing cataclysm.[18]

Dresden Codex—the final page of the manuscript depicting the Destruction of the World. PHOTO OF PUBLIC DOMAIN ARTWORK: THE SAXON STATE LIBRARY [MSCR.DRESD.R.310].

It's curious—this mixture of science, cataclysm, and time. "Calculations far into the past or lesser probings of the future occur in many a Maya hieroglyphic text," notes archaeologist J. Eric S. Thompson:

> On [a] stela at Quiriga a date . . . over 90 million years ago is computed; on another a date over 300 million years before that is given. . . . These are actual computations, stating correctly day and

month positions, and are comparable to calculations in our calendar
giving the month positions on which Easter would have fallen at
equivalent distances in the past. The brain reels at such astronomical
figures, yet these reckonings were of sufficient frequency and
importance to require special hieroglyphs for their transcription.[19]

All that can be said for sure is that embedded in the Mayan material, together
with core religious beliefs very similar to those of the ancient Egyptians—
and now we know very similar to those of the ancient Mississippians also—
is evidence of an interest in complex scientific calculations and immense
expanses of time. I'm reminded of the passage from the *Ancient Egyptian Book
of the Dead,* quoted in chapter 3, in which the Sun God Ra is praised for
his travels through the "untold spaces" of the cosmic void "requiring millions and hundreds of thousands of years to pass over"—a chronology on a
similar order to the Mayan scheme of things but, one would have thought,
irrelevant to the concerns of agricultural societies. And the same goes for the
immense geometrical mounds and enclosures of the ancient Egyptian Duat
that are matched by the immense geometrical mounds and enclosures of the
Hopewell of Ohio and the immense geometrical mounds and enclosures now
emerging from the Amazon rainforest.

What the evidence suggests to me is that something extraordinary, something that the theories of mainstream archaeology cannot account for, was
going on behind the scenes of prehistory. All the indications are that Mexico,
with its ancient tradition of literacy, was once a vast archive of the "antiquities
and sciences" of former times and that the records the Spaniards destroyed in
their zealous stupidity may have been as integral to the memory of humanity
as the library of Alexandria. I think it is very possible, had the Mayan documents survived in sufficient quantities, that they would have shed light on the
mystery of the lost common source of inspiration that appears to have kick-
started civilizations in both the Old World and the New.

In the event, however, out of the tens of thousands of Mayan codices in
existence in 1519 just **four** are still with us in the twenty-first century.[20]

After the Spanish conquest of Mexico, the conquest of Peru soon followed,
again accompanied by the destruction of a high civilization—in this case the
Inca—in the lineage of the First Americans. Though they had their *quipus*
(a means of communication and calculation using knotted string), the Inca

were not a literate people like the Maya and thus possessed no documents for the Spaniards to destroy. As in Mexico, however, a sustained and determined effort was made to stamp out local religions and traditions and replace them with Roman Catholicism. Once again, this effort, officially sanctioned as "the extirpation of idolatry," called for cultural destruction on a grand scale, calculated to erase the memory banks of the population within a generation or two and replace their deep connection to their own past with the new dispensation.[21]

The Spaniards did venture into North America, of course—most eccentrically and unproductively in the form of an expedition led by Hernando de Soto, who landed in Florida in 1539 with more than 600 men.[22] After losing half his force along the way, de Soto spent the next 3 years until his own death in Louisiana in 1542 wandering all over the southeast and deep south of what is now the United States, passing many of the great mound sites, and engaging in ruinous pitched battles with the locals. The most disastrous by-product of his visit, however, may have been smallpox, which his expeditionaries appear to have brought with them and which afterward devastated the indigenous population of the region.[23]

We may say, therefore, that from its earliest days the European conquest of the Americas was an agent of chaos, genocide, and cultural extinction for Native Americans and that this, too, was very much part of the process that wiped down the "crime scene," leaving us scratching our heads trying to make sense of the few clues left behind.

WIPING DOWN THE CRIME SCENE: WITNESS AMNESIA

THE EXTIRPATION OF VITAL EVIDENCE concerning the past of our species across huge swaths of the Americas was by no means limited to the effects of the Younger Dryas cataclysm, or to the subsequent much later cataclysms of militant Christianity and smallpox. Once the calamitous century of the initial encounters was over, a more insidious but equally deadly process of erosion began to grind down the little of the past that the previous millennia had spared. During the sixteenth century, apart from a few failed raids like de Soto's, North America was not much affected, but from the early seventeenth century onward, following the first European settlements in Virginia and Massachusetts, everything changed.

Thereafter, with monotonous, depressing regularity, either for their agricultural potential or for the prospect of gold, lands held sacred in the possession of Native American tribes for eons were snatched from them and their inhabitants driven off or slaughtered. These murderous land grabs only accelerated and became crueler as the seventeenth century was followed by the eighteenth and as the eighteenth century rolled on into the nineteenth:

> From the time Europeans arrived on American shores, the frontier—the edge territory between white man's civilization and the untamed natural world—became a shared space of vast, clashing differences that led the U.S. government to authorize over 1,500 wars, attacks and raids on Indians, the most of any country in the world against its indigenous people. By the close of the Indian Wars in the late 19th century, fewer than 238,000 indigenous people remained, a sharp decline from the estimated 5 million to 15 million living in North America when Columbus arrived in 1492.[24]

In his important book *American Holocaust,* which documents the genocide, David Stannard, professor of American studies at the University of Hawaii, reminds us that scholarly estimates of the size of the pre-Columbian population of the Americas have changed radically in recent decades:

> In the 1940s and 1950s conventional wisdom held that the population of the entire hemisphere in 1492 was little more than 8 million—with fewer than 1 million people living in the region north of present-day Mexico. Today few serious students of the subject would put the hemispheric figure at less than 75 million to 100 million (with approximately 8 million to 12 million north of Mexico), while one of the most well-regarded specialists in the field recently has suggested that a more accurate estimate would be around 145 million for the hemisphere as a whole and about 18 million for the area north of Mexico.[25]

Gone forever—and good riddance—is the long-held myth of North America as a pristine wilderness inhabited by a handful of "savages" when the first settlers from Europe arrived.

Nothing could be further from the truth.

The new picture, derived from a combination of archaeology, ethnography, genetics, and the reports of early travelers, is of a busy and boisterous continent with a growing population, widespread trade networks, and abundant resources.

Like the Inca, though lacking their centralized, structured state, the Native North Americans were people of the spoken word who carried their wisdom and their records not in documents but in oral traditions carefully nurtured, memorized, and passed on from generation to generation. Today we grope in the dark when we try to discover what they knew, what they taught, and what they had preserved from primeval times because the genocide inflicted upon them radically disrupted and in many cases completely destroyed the normal intergenerational processes of transmission.

The accounts of the genocide are repulsive; reading the details today leaves one stunned, nauseated, and horrified. Professor Stannard holds nothing back in *American Holocaust,* a comprehensive record of European wickedness in the Americas, but it's not my purpose here to zoom in on the many massacres and betrayals he describes, or to dwell on the horrific symptoms of the imported infectious diseases that killed indigenous people by the millions.

The point I wish to make is simply that **this happened**, that it was both physical and cultural genocide, and that its long-term effect on the descendants of those who survived was to sever their connections to the traditions, wisdom, memories, and even the languages of their ancestors.

Lest there be any doubt that cultural annihilation was always the purpose, hand in hand with the continent-wide theft of land, we need only consider the shameful history of the so-called Indian boarding schools. The National Native American Boarding School Healing Coalition sets out the bare facts:

> Between 1869 and the 1960s, hundreds of thousands of Native American children were removed from their homes and families and placed in boarding schools operated by the federal government and the churches. Though we don't know how many children were taken in total, by 1926, the Indian Office estimated that nearly 83% of

Indian children were attending boarding schools. The U.S. Native children that were voluntarily or forcibly removed from their homes, families, and communities during this time were taken to schools far away where they were punished for speaking their native language, banned from acting in any way that might be seen to represent traditional or cultural practices, stripped of traditional clothing, hair and personal belongings and behaviors reflective of their native culture.[26]

A founder and advocate of the boarding schools movement, US army captain Richard Henry Pratt, summarized the spirit of the whole enterprise in a speech in 1892:

A great general has said that the only good Indian is a dead one. In a sense, I agree with the sentiment, but only in this: that all the Indian there is in the race should be dead. Kill the Indian in him and save the man.[27]

This, then, was an ethnically targeted brainwashing exercise on a gigantic scale—an exercise deliberately designed to make Native Americans forget their ancient heritage. For the purposes of our inquiry here, if it were indeed from North America that a lost civilization vanished, then not only has the crime scene been thoroughly wiped down but also—to extend the analogy—the principal witnesses have been badly beaten about the head and are suffering from amnesia.

WIPING DOWN THE CRIME SCENE: LAND GRABS

EVEN AS THE GENOCIDE AND imposed "unremembering" gathered pace during the nineteenth and twentieth centuries, a parallel force was also active removing many prominent physical traces—notably the great mounds and earthworks—that Native Americans of former ages had left. This parallel force was primarily greed for land, where the fate of the monuments was either to be plowed down for agriculture or demolished to make way for industry, housing, or commerce. Among the unknown unknowns of North American prehistory, therefore, is how many of the mounds and earthworks were *already* gone—plowed under, demolished, ransacked—before responsible and thorough surveyors began to investigate them from about the mid-nineteenth century onward.

Renowned among these early surveyors were Ephraim Squier and Edwin Davis, whose classic *Ancient Monuments of the Mississippi Valley,* the first-ever publication of the Smithsonian Institution, appeared in print in 1848. In their preface they note of the mounds and earthworks that:

> The importance of a complete and speedy examination of the whole
> field cannot be over-estimated. The operations of the elements,
> the shifting channels of the streams, the levelling hand of public
> improvement, and most efficient of all the slow but constant
> encroachments of agriculture, are fast destroying these monuments of
> ancient labor, breaking in upon their symmetry and obliterating their
> outlines. Thousands have already disappeared, or retain but slight and
> doubtful traces of their former proportions."[28]

One of the reasons that *Ancient Monuments* is still useful today is that it provides the locations of many important mounds and earthworks that no longer exist. In 2011, in a paper published in *American Antiquity,* Jarrod Burks and Robert Cooke looked into the specific case of Ohio, where Squier and Davis had reported "approximately 88 earthwork sites" in 1848. Perhaps because of the fame brought to them by *Ancient Monuments,* 16 of these sites—18 percent of the total—are "now preserved whole or in part within parks." Another 18 sites (20 percent) "are mostly or completely destroyed, with urban development and gravel mining being the primary destructive processes." The remaining 54 sites (62 percent) are "now invisible at the surface."[29]

So, to summarize, out of 88 Ohio sites put on record in 1848 by Squier and Davis, 54 are now "invisible," 18 more are "destroyed," and only 16 (just 18 percent of the total) are still in place–implying an effective loss of 82 percent or, in plain English, 82 out of every 100 sites.

What, then, are we to make of David J. Meltzer's presumably authoritative introduction to the 150th anniversary reissue of *Ancient Monuments,* which informs us that Ohio's Ross County *alone* was estimated by Squier and Davis in 1848 to contain "one hundred enclosures and five hundred mounds"?[30]

If that's the correct figure, then all the other numbers change. Sixteen sites remaining out of 600 is quite a different matter from 16 out of 88 and amounts to a 97 percent loss.

On July 23, 2018, wanting to get to the bottom of this, I emailed Jarrod Burks, coauthor of the 2011 *Antiquity* paper.

His first point was to remind me that the focus in his paper was not on earthworks in Ohio in general but only on those "depicted in Squier and Davis—88 sites. There are many hundreds of earthwork sites (those with enclosures) in Ohio . . . and we keep finding more."

As to the specific issue of the discrepancy between Meltzer's figures and his own, Burks explained:

> I was counting actually sites with enclosures depicted in maps in Squier and Davis. This comes from individual maps of sites, like the map of High Bank Works, and from unique sites depicted on their composite maps of select areas—like the area around Chillicothe. For example, they show the Steel Group site on that map but they do not have a separate, more detailed map of Steel.
>
> So, when I say "enclosure site" I am referring to places with one through X enclosures. Hopewell Mound Group is one site though it has several enclosures. Cedar Bank is one site that has only one enclosure. Following this approach, Squier and Davis depict 88 sites with enclosures in their maps. There is no way there are 100 enclosure sites in Ross County, but there may be 100 enclosures. So far I have only found solid evidence for 37–38 enclosure sites in Ross County, and this includes some previously undocumented ones we have found in aerial photos and subsequently surveyed with geophysics. In fact, most of the 37–38 have been surveyed. . . . Still working on getting access to a few of them.
>
> *The Archaeological Atlas of Ohio* (William C. Mills 1914) reports 586 enclosure sites in Ohio. Many of these are unconfirmed and/or lost since 1914, but we are working to find many of them. We have also found more not recorded in 1914. So, the total number of

enclosure sites once in Ohio conservatively is 500–1000. It could be double or more.

I had also asked Burks if he knew where I might find estimates of the sort that he had made in Ohio for the Mississippi Valley as a whole—that is, how many mounds and earthworks remain and how many have been destroyed since the mid-nineteenth century.

"Getting numbers for all of the Mississippi Valley is a daunting task," he replied, "especially if you include mounds. There are/were many tens of thousands of mounds in the eastern US. You might start by contacting the state historic preservation office in each state."

I was surprised that no archaeologist had yet done this basic legwork and that there was no authoritative volume or paper I could immediately be referred to—since presumably at least some measure of what has been lost must be fundamental to the correct assessment of what remains. I therefore asked for confirmation that I would be representing the facts correctly if I were to "tell my readers that reliable figures simply don't exist for the whole Mississippi Valley and that no archaeologist or other researcher has ever attempted to estimate what has been lost across the whole region as a result of agricultural, industrial and other encroachments since the mid-19th century."

Burks replied immediately:

That's a pretty broad statement. I don't know that "no archaeologist or other researcher" has done that. George Milner produced a book on mounds 10–15 years ago. Perhaps he makes a statement like that? But I doubt it given how nearly impossible it is to track that. For example, in Ohio we say there once were 10,000+ mounds (a 19th century estimate). The state has only about 2000 that have been recorded in the modern list. Many have been destroyed but we are constantly recording new ones, many of which likely were known in the 19th century. So, hard to put numbers to it, but it's true that many, many mounds have been destroyed.[31]

George R. Milner's book *The Moundbuilders* arrived on my desk the following morning, but contains no information that adds significantly to what we already know about the loss of mound sites since the nineteenth century. Nor was David Meltzer able to come up with a figure, observing in reply to my query that "200+ years ago there was no systematic count of these earthworks, so we have no idea what the denominator should be for the equation of sites still extant / sites once present."[32]

The good news is that sites are still being discovered (or probably more often rediscovered). The bad news is that it may be "nearly impossible" to track the "many, many" that have been destroyed.

All estimates are guesswork, but I suspect that Gregory Little's diligent and thoroughly researched *Illustrated Encyclopedia of Native American Mounds and Earthworks,* though not a mainstream source, is close to the truth when it calculates that 90 percent of all the Mississippi Valley sites have been destroyed and that only 10 percent remain.[33]

And lest such a ballpark figure sound too extreme let us remember, despite the conservationist rhetoric of our supposedly more enlightened age, that mounds and earthworks are **still** being destroyed in the twenty-first century.

Walmart seems to have a penchant for this. In 2001, for example, the Fenton Mounds, a pair of Native American burial mounds in Fenton, Missouri, dated between AD 600 and 1400, were leveled to make way for a Walmart Supercenter.[34] A few years later, in August 2009, city leaders in Oxford, Alabama, approved the destruction of a 1,500-year-old Native American ceremonial mound because, once again, Walmart wanted the location.[35] The developers began work, removing a substantial section of the mound, but a month later, following a public outcry, the media reported a change of heart:

> A re-consecration ceremony was held this past weekend at a damaged
> Indian mound in Oxford, Alabama. . . . The 1,500-year-old sacred
> and archaeologically significant site was partially demolished during
> a taxpayer-funded economic development project, with the excavated
> dirt to be used as fill for construction of a Sam's Club, a retail
> warehouse store owned by Walmart.[36]

What's indicated here is a state of mind across a segment of the American population that sees no inherent cultural value in antiquities and believes firmly that the past has nothing to teach us that outweighs our need for yet another large store. I don't mean to pick on Americans. Exactly the same state of mind exists in Britain, France, China, and virtually every other country in the world.

By encouraging disdain for the past, however, the cost of such an outlook in fast-growing America since the nineteenth century has been the mass destruction of ancient sites, notably including the loss of many thousands of the mounds and earthworks of the Mississippi Valley. Exactly how **many** thousands will probably remain a "known unknown" forever. But whatever the true number, it represents yet another level at which the "crime scene" of ancient America has been wiped down.

WIPING DOWN THE CRIME SCENE: BAD ARCHAEOLOGY

THOSE OF US WHO EXPLORE alternative approaches to prehistory are frequently accused by archaeologists and their friends in the media of being "pseudoscientists." What, however, could provide a better example of truly damaging and misleading pseudoscience than the "Clovis First" paradigm that ruled American archaeology for more than 40 years with a wholly false doctrine taught to generations of students as fact? We saw in part 2 how this pseudoscientific theory of the peopling of the Americas, based on wildly irresponsible extrapolations from tiny data sets yet promoted by a powerful lobby of leading archaeologists, was, for a very long while, held to be so **right**, so **correct**, and so self-evidently **true** that any researchers who questioned it faced ridicule, ostracism by their colleagues, withdrawal of research grants, and ruined careers.

This kind of behavior in scholarship not only fails to serve the truth but actively undermines the search for it and, as such, has also played a significant part in wiping down the ancient American "crime scene." How much was missed, and has since been built over or plowed under during those 40-plus years when it was considered heresy to investigate deposits older than Clovis for signs of a human presence? And how much wide-ranging and open-minded investigation into the true age and origins of the First Americans was postponed or entirely nipped in the bud at the same time? How many unexplored avenues do we owe to the absurd Clovis First dogma? How many doors did it close on how many promising initiatives? And how much public interest and curiosity in other possibilities did the pat answer "Clovis First" snuff out?

It's been the same problem with another archaeological theory—the so-called Pleistocene Overkill theory whereby all the megafauna were supposedly slaughtered by those same ruthlessly efficient Clovis hunters (who nevertheless proved insufficiently ruthless and efficient to survive the Younger Dryas onset). I've not gone into the details here—just too much academic bickering to impose upon the reader—but this theory, also, though not yet quite as dead as "Clovis First" (since it still has some advocates), has been "conclusively rejected" by increasing numbers of scholars in recent years.[37]

Although he lists archaeology and North American prehistory among his fields of study, Terry Jones, professor and department chair of social sciences at California Polytechnic State University, brings the benefit of an outsider's perspective when he observes:

The Paleoindian Period (often defined as anything pre-dating 10,000 cal BP [i.e., 10,000 years ago]) is basically the domain of a small number of specialists who interpret it for everyone else. For the last 40 years these researchers have focused their interpretations on two closely related and intricately inter-connected theories: Clovis First and Pleistocene Overkill. During this time, Paleoindian research has also deteriorated into an intense if not hostile debate over these two competing but not mutually exclusive ideas. Much of the energy in this protracted dialog has been devoted to debunking or nullifying alternative hypotheses associated with these two theories. While this is standard practice in science, **the degree to which the Paleoindian debate has been focused on deconstruction of opposing ideas rather than development of empirically solid, new ones has been extreme.**[38]

This, too, is part of the wiping down of the North American "crime-scene." Some limited but perhaps case-breaking clues to what really happened here around 12,800 years ago may remain. To the extent that the "detectives" involved in this paleo-CSI are more interested in ego contests than the truth, however, the truth may take a very long time to emerge.

Besides, there's another aspect to the problem in the visceral resistance shown by a number of influential scholars to **any** suggestion that a cataclysm of **any** kind ushered in the onset of the Younger Dryas. These scholars them-selves apparently believe, and so far as possible would like us to believe, that nothing really bad happened at the Younger Dryas Boundary—that, yes, there were extinctions, and yes, Clovis abruptly disappeared, but there is no mystery here, just a fairly routine and predictable combination of overkill and climate change. Terry Jones, a member of the Comet Research Group, refutes such reasoning at length in a paper in the *Journal of Cosmology*[39] and strongly advocates the Younger Dryas Impact Hypothesis, which, he points out:

> has been introduced into North American archaeology at a time when the failings of the overkill model have been acknowledged by the majority of researchers. . . . Alternatives to overkill have long been focused on climate change associated with the Pleistocene-Holocene transition, but this idea has always been problematic because large animal populations had lived through previous interglacials without massive die offs. Something different seems to have happened in North America at the end of the Pleistocene, and that something was not a blitzkrieg by human hunters.
>
> An extraterrestrial impact event seems to provide an exceptionally parsimonious explanation for a variety of patterns in the archaeological and paleontological records that are not accommodated by overkill.[40]

IN THE CROSSHAIRS

ANOTHER "PATTERN" FOR WHICH THE YDIH provides a parsimonious explanation is formed by the deep structural connections demonstrated in part 6 between the spiritual beliefs and "astro-geometry" of the ancient Egyp-tians and the spiritual beliefs and "astro-geometry" of the ancient Mississippi-ans. The case I've sought to make throughout this book is that these two river valley civilizations were among several in the ancient world that inherited a shared legacy of knowledge and ideas from an earlier, "lost" civilization. Regardless of when that legacy was activated, or how its integrity was pre-served over the many generations before it first manifests in the archaeological record, I've argued that its origins go back to the last Ice Age and predate the physical separation of the Old World from the New. The additional element of parsimony that the YDIH brings to this case, therefore, comes in the form of the impact-related earth changes documented at the Younger Dryas Boundary. These involved not only radical climate change and sea-level rise, not only global wildfires and a subsequent "impact winter," not only mass extinctions of large animal species and the abrupt disappearance of Clovis but also, in the combination of all these ills, a **realistic mechanism** deadly, substantial, drastic, and sustained enough to devastate and destroy even a technologically advanced civilization.

If a disaster on such a scale were to recur today, our civilization would not survive it and all our works would crumble into ruin within a few millennia. I therefore see no reason in principle why the global cataclysm indicated in the Greenland ice cores that we know unfolded at the onset of the Younger Dryas between 12,836 and 12,815 years ago should not have brought an end to that previous high civilization of the "Early Primeval Age of the Gods"—the civilization of the "Ancient Ones," the civilization of the "First Time"—that is recalled with awe in myths and traditions from all around the world.

Although there were significant impacts in Greenland, the Pacific, South America, Antarctica, Europe, and the Near East, the evidence points conclusively toward North America as the epicenter of the Younger Dryas cataclysm and to the North American ice cap specifically as the target for the largest swarm of comet fragments.

Almost by default, therefore, although the crime scene has been brutally compromised, and although the lead investigators have a priori ruled the possibility out, North America is the most likely location on earth where a civilization could have thrived during the Ice Age and been destroyed at the onset of the Younger Dryas.

Not only that. If the Edfu Texts contain a record of these events, as I have proposed, then we should take seriously the message they transmit, that there were survivors of the cataclysm who made it their mission to bring about:

The resurrection of the former world of the gods. . . . The re-creation of a destroyed world. [41]

These survivors are said to have wandered the earth, setting out and building sacred mounds wherever they went, and teaching the fundamentals of civ-

Turtle Island.

ilization, including religion, agriculture, and architecture. In *Heaven's Mirror* (1998) I speculate that it is perhaps as a result of their efforts that we find the basic doctrines of the same sky-ground religion, essentially the same beliefs about the afterlife journey of the soul, and the same architectural and geometrical principles as far afield as South America, Easter Island, Micronesia, Japan, Cambodia, India, Mesopotamia, Egypt, Malta, Spain, and Britain.

Because the earth is a sphere it is technically true that any point could be selected as central to the radiation of these ideas. As I've been researching this book, however, my perspective has changed and what I see now when I look at the globe are two great oceans, the Atlantic on one side and the Pacific on the other, with the longitudinal sprawl of the Americas running between them and forming, literally, the center of the world.

North America, we now know, was scoured, burned, frozen, and flooded by the Younger Dryas cataclysm and has since been systematically ransacked by Western greed and poorly served by Western scholars. Although less severely affected by the impacts of the Younger Dryas, South America also suffered all these assaults. And just as in North America, where millions of square kilometers have been rendered opaque to archaeologists because the "crime scene" has been so successfully wiped down, so, too, in South America we have 5 million square kilometers of the Amazon rainforest that remain almost as unfamiliar to archaeology as the dark side of the moon.

The two great continents of the Americas are not separate and have never been separate, either before or after the Ice Age. North America is in itself a **huge** landmass, with vast regions where little or no archaeology has ever been done. If a lost civilization was here in the Ice Age we cannot rule out the possibility that its physical artifacts and remains might yet be found. Given that many Native American cultures share myths of the destruction of a former world, a subterranean interval in the womb of the earth, and then an emergence into our present world,[42] the most fruitful direction in which to look might be for places of shelter and refuge deep underground.

The other region with immense scope for further inquiry is the Amazon. When North America passed through that cataclysmic episode between 12,836 and 12,815 years ago, South America would have seemed like the obvious place for survivors of the lost civilization to take refuge. This would have been all the more likely if, as I speculate, South American hunter-gatherers had already been "adopted" and gifted with useful know-how in much the same way that Clovis appears to have been.

Even if the human story is badly broken in North America, with big pieces obviously missing, it's possible that a more complete account awaits us in the Amazon.

I can hear the mainstream protests already: "The whole idea of a lost civilization is nonsense!" "Pseudoscience!" "A waste of research funds!"

But the mainstream, which has wasted research funds for decades fruitlessly pursuing nonsensical fantasies like "Clovis First," should have learned by now to keep an open mind.

THE KEY TO EARTH'S LOST
CIVILIZATION

S INCE I BEGAN WORK ON *Fingerprints of the Gods* in the early 1990s I've been an advocate for the unorthodox notion that an advanced civilization flourished during the Ice Age and was destroyed in the cataclysms that brought the Ice Age to an end. I've written my books to make the case and provide supporting evidence for this possibility. I've suggested a number of locations that I feel would be worth looking into—including, most controversially, Antarctica—and I invested nearly 10 years of my life in arduous and sometimes highly risky scuba-diving adventures searching for man-made structures submerged by rising sea levels at the end of the Ice Age.

So I've walked the walk, but it's been a bit like tracking the Invisible Man. There are signs of his presence everywhere—he has touched this, he has reshaped that, this was how he did mathematics, these were his beliefs—but the Man himself remains concealed. There's not even the option to guess the appearance and character of the lost civilization by wrapping its face in bandages like the hero of the H. G. Wells novel. It's much more elusive. Physical traces that might point to its homeland have either been so completely demolished or so thoroughly hidden from view that they are extremely difficult to find, especially so by an archaeological community already preconvinced of their nonexistence and therefore unwilling to look for them.

What's tantalizing, however, is that the influence of the lost civilization declares itself repeatedly in the commonalities shared by supposedly unconnected cultures all around the ancient world. The deeper you dig, the more obvious it becomes that they did not get these shared features from one another but from a remote common ancestor of them all. We see only the effects and modes of expression of that inheritance, not its source, and all searches for the key to the mystery have thus far been in vain.

My proposal, simply, is that America offers us that key, and that it does so because of the unique circumstances of its prehistory. Unlike the interconnected landmasses of Africa and Eurasia, and unlike Australia, which was relatively accessible by sea from the extreme southeast of Asia, we've seen that the Americas were isolated during much of the Ice Age—a geological epoch that lasted, let us not forget, from around 2.6 million years ago until around 12,000 years ago.[1] In this long geological epoch, however, there were several periods of temporary climate warming when the macro-continent of North, Central, and South America would have become accessible. Two of these periods of enhanced accessibility occurred within the known time frame of past human migrations and it is the most recent (the so-called Bølling-Allerød interstadial, dated from around 14,700 years ago to around 12,800 years ago[2]) that archaeologists focused their attention on for far too long in their attempts to reconstruct the true story of the peopling of the Americas. I think paleontologist Tom Deméré is on to something HUGE with this plea that he makes to the scientific community, discussed in chapter 5:

what we're saying to everyone, really, is open your mind to the possibility that instead of the peopling of the Americas being associated with the last deglaciation event [the Bølling-Allerød interstadial] . . . what we should actually be looking at is the deglaciation event *before that*—between 140,000 and 120,000 years ago.[3] You get the same sort of scenario with a landbridge and ice sheets retreating and you get that same sweet spot between really low sea levels and a blockage by ice sheets, and ice sheets gone and the flooding of the landbridge.

Deméré's suggestion still remains unpalatable to some archaeologists, yet it satisfactorily explains the growing mass of evidence that the Americas were peopled many tens of millennia **before** the Bølling-Allerød interstadial (see chapters 4, 5, and 6). More than that, this hitherto unimagined possibility of a very old (rather than very young) human presence in the New World helps make sense of the complex genetic heritage of Native Americans—explored in chapters 7, 8, 9, and 10. Embedded in this evidence is the mind-dilating mystery of the strong Australasian DNA signal present among certain isolated tribes of the Amazon rainforest. It's a recent discovery and highly significant because it raises the possibility, as discussed in chapter 10, that transoceanic voyages were being undertaken more than 12,000 years ago—a notion hitherto considered impossible by archaeologists. If the technology and geodetic know-how to make such voyages were indeed present in the world during the Ice Age (see appendix 2), then we are, by definition, dealing with a lost civilization.

And this of course brings us to the mystery of the Amazon itself. Was it in some way "touched" by a civilization advanced enough to have explored all the world's oceans during the Ice Age? And if so, has any evidence of that influence remained? In chapters 11 through 17 I address these questions and present evidence that human settlement in the Amazon is extremely ancient, that great cities and large populations once flourished there, that ancient scientific knowledge of the properties of plants persists among Amazonian peoples to this day, that there was very early domestication of useful agricultural species, that the rainforest itself is an anthropocentric, cultivated, ordered "garden," and that a "miraculous" man-made soil—*terra preta*—was developed in the Amazon in deep antiquity, bringing fertility to otherwise agriculturally unproductive lands and imbued with astonishing powers of self-renewal that modern scientists marvel at and do not yet fully understand.

In parallel, and again a recent discovery, is the presence of gigantic geometrical earthworks and astronomically aligned stone circles in the Amazon. I show in chapters 15 and 16 that these remarkable structures share significant scientific "memes" with the henges and stone circles of the British Isles and with other works of ancient, sacred architecture all around the world. I suggest this is not coincidental, nor due to the direct influence of one region upon the other, but that it bears witness instead to a shared legacy, a shared package of sacred geometrical and astronomical blueprints, inherited in both these widely separated regions from an earlier civilization lost to history.

Chapter 17 returns to the theme of plant gnosis in the Amazon, looks into the mysteries of the vision-inducing brew ayahuasca, and hears the words of ayahuasca shamans, who see geometric patterns as portals to other realms of existence—specifically to the afterlife realm or land of the dead.

Indeed, the very name ayahuasca means "Vine of the Dead" or "Vine of Souls."

In chapters 18 through 21 I explore the deep structural similarities between the Amazonian geoglyphs and the great mounds and geometric earthworks of the Mississippi Valley. It's not simply a matter of appearances. Mississippian religious ideas, like those of the ancient Amazon, were focused on the mystery of death and on certain very specific notions concerning the afterlife journey—and destination—of the soul.

I show that these notions are extremely ancient in North America and trace them back into remote prehistory through a succession of sites such as Poverty Point, Lower Jackson Mound, Watson Brake, and Conly, where the same astronomical and geometric "memes" consistently reappear.

Chapter 22 recounts my own close encounter, as a teenager, with the mystery of death and how my interest in this mystery was reawakened when I first studied the *Ancient Egyptian Book of the Dead* many years later. I describe the Duat, the afterlife realm as depicted by the ancient Egyptians, and the soul's ascent to the constellation Orion and thence through a portal, or "doorway in the sky," to a journey along the Milky Way. And I describe my astonishment, on a visit to Moundville in Alabama, to learn that what appeared to be exactly the same system of ideas involving Orion, the Milky Way, and a journey to the realm of the dead was also a predominant motif of the Mississippian civilization.

In chapters 23 and 24 I offer a detailed investigation of Mississippian and ancient Egyptian ideas concerning the afterlife journey—and destiny—of the soul. The parallels, in my view, are too remarkable, too many, and too detailed to be explained by coincidence. Nor do they point to a direct influence of ancient Egypt on the Mississippian civilization or vice versa—chronologically impossible because they existed at completely different times. As with the geoglyphs, what is indicated here is a legacy of ideas inherited in both these widely separated areas from a remote common source as yet unidentified by archaeologists.

Could that common source, that lost civilization, have had its Ice Age homeland in North America?

I set out to answer that question in chapters 25 through 27, where I present detailed evidence of the immense cataclysm that shook the earth around 12,800 years ago—a cataclysm that was global in its consequences but that had its epicenter in North America.

For more than two decades, while eliciting patronizing sneers and sometimes extreme hostility from the scholarly establishment, I've consistently maintained that "my" proposed lost civilization was erased from history in a global cataclysm somewhere around 12,500 years ago. At first, the very suggestion that there had been a cataclysm at all, and that it might be of immense relevance to the past of our species, was singled out for particular ridicule, but then came a mass of new evidence that shifted the balance of the argument decisively. Within the resolution limits of radiocarbon calibration (where at such a remove margins of error of two or three centuries are the norm), the date for the cataclysm of around 12,500 years ago that I first put into print in 1995 is extremely close to the date of around 12,800 years ago that scientists have much more recently established for the impacts of multiple fragments of the giant disintegrating comet that precipitated the catastrophic onset of the Younger Dryas.

It seems, then, that there **was** a global cataclysm—and at more or less the very time I had proposed.

But so what? Just because I got lucky on the timing of the cataclysm doesn't mean I was right that it wiped out an advanced prehistoric civilization. Show us its homeland, the skeptics therefore quite reasonably demanded.

This book is, in part, my response to that challenge.

MORE THAN ENOUGH TIME FOR A CIVILIZATION TO DEVELOP

HITHERTO ICE AGE NORTH AMERICA has been seen as an uninhabited archaeological vacuum, awaiting the arrival of culture with the first human migrations across the Bering land bridge. Because of the entrenched belief that these migrations came relatively late, at a time when our ancestors had been "out of Africa" and already established in Europe, Asia, and Australia for tens of millennia, there was no reason to seek the origins of civilization in such an unlikely place. In the light of the new evidence on the very ancient peopling of the Americas that we have explored, however, and of the Younger Dryas Impact Hypothesis, I suggest that the balance of the argument has once again shifted decisively. Whereas before it was reasonable to ask why the homeland of the lost civilization **should** have been in North America, the more pertinent question today is why should it **not** have been in North America—the continent that suffered more severe disruption than any other and that had so much of its rich prehistory pounded, pulverized, and swept away by the devastating events of 12,800 years ago.

Not for the first time in this investigation I'm reminded of what Tom Deméré told me when he showed me the finds from the Cerutti Mastodon Site at The Nat in San Diego:

> If you go to a place and you absolutely rule out in advance that
> humans were there 130,000 years ago, then you're clearly not going
> to find evidence that they were. But if you go with an open mind and
> dig deep enough in the right places, then who knows what you might
> turn up.

Tom was talking about the conclusion that he and his team had reached concerning the mastodon remains now on show in his museum, namely, as we saw in chapter 5, that they had been scavenged by human beings 130,000 years ago. His point was that an ingrained perception that no humans could have reached the Americas by such an early date had for too long inhibited investigation of alternative scenarios—and that perhaps much more evidence of a very early presence would be found if a more targeted and determined search were made.

Using rocks intelligently to smash mastodon femurs so that the marrow can be extracted is certainly not the work of a lost civilization of any kind. It is the work of ancestral humans, perhaps anatomically modern, perhaps not. But the real importance of the Cerutti Mastodon Site is that it provides the first solid evidence—solid enough to make it into the pages of *Nature*—of a truly **ancient** human occupation of the New World. If humans were in North

America 130,000 years ago (more than twice as long as the span of the known human presence in Europe), that gives them **117,000 years** to have evolved a high civilization before the Younger Dryas cataclysm struck.

And why should they **not** have done so? What is particularly special or inviolable about the so-called march toward civilization that **seems** to begin with the onset of the Neolithic at the end of the Younger Dryas? Why did it happen then and not before? Why shouldn't there have been an earlier "march towards civilization" that began with an earlier peopling of the Americas— not with the last deglaciation event but, as Tom Deméré suggested, with "the deglaciation event *before that,* between 140,000 and 120,000 years ago?"

Thereafter, until the next episode of deglaciation (the Bølling-Allerød interstadial) in the 2,000 years immediately preceding the Younger Dryas, all scholars agree that the vast landmass of the Americas, straddling half the globe, was cut off from the rest of the world by the Atlantic and Pacific Oceans and by mountains of ice. Migrants from Asia, even when Beringia was accessible, could not get in. But for those humans who were already south of the ice cap 120,000 years ago, the Americas must have been a paradise, safe from incursions by any other peoples and blessed with an astonishing abundance and variety of natural resources. The New World offered conditions utterly different from those available on any other continent, so I see no reason why the very first of the First Americans should not also have followed a radically different path from other humans—a path that more rapidly veered away from hunting and gathering and that led ultimately to the emergence of a precociously early civilization.

MYSTERIOUS POWERS

IF THE YOUNGER DRYAS EARTH changes wiped a prehistoric civilization from the record, then can anything useful ever be said about the character of that civilization?

Thus far (extrapolating from the belief systems of its descendants) I've suggested that its spirituality must have involved profound explorations of the mystery of death. I've suggested that accurate ancient maps depicting the earth as it looked during the Ice Age imply that it had developed a level of maritime technology at least as advanced as that possessed by European seafarers in the late eighteenth century. I've suggested that it had mastered sophisticated geometry and astronomy. I've also suggested that such a "lost" civilization, maturing in isolation for tens of thousands of years in North America, might have taken a very different path from our own and might have developed technologies that archaeologists would be unable to recognize because they operated on principles or manipulated forces unknown to modern science.

In his 1920 study *The Interpretation of Radium,* Nobel Prize winner Frederick Soddy, one of the pioneers of nuclear physics, speculated as to the former existence of "a wholly unknown and unsuspected ancient civilization of which all other relic has disappeared."[4] He drew attention to the seemingly limitless stores of nuclear energy that were in his time understood to be possessed by certain elements such as radium and compared these to the fabulous "philosopher's stone" credited in ancient traditions with mysterious powers of transmutation and regeneration. The similarity, he felt, was no coincidence but "an echo from one of many previous epochs in the unrecorded history of the world"[5]:

> Can we not read into [such traditions] . . . justification for the belief
> that some former forgotten race of men attained not only to the
> knowledge we have so recently won, but also to the power that is not
> yet ours? Science has reconstructed the story of the past as one of a
> continuous Ascent of Man to the present-day level of his powers. In
> face of the circumstantial evidence existing of this steady upward
> progress of the race, the traditional view of the Fall of Man from
> a higher former state has come to be more and more difficult to
> understand. From our new standpoint the two points of view are
> by no means so irreconcilable as they appeared. A race which could
> transmute matter would have little need to earn its bread by the sweat
> of its brow. If we can judge from what our engineers accomplish
> with their comparatively restricted supplies of energy, such a race
> could transform a desert continent, thaw the frozen poles and make
> the whole world one smiling Garden of Eden. Possibly they could
> even explore the outer realms of space. . . . The legend of the Fall of
> Man . . . may be all that has survived of such a time before, for some
> unknown reason, the whole world was plunged back again under the

undisputed sway of Nature, to begin once more its upward toilsome journey through the ages.[6]

In the 2020s (as would not have been the case in the 1920s) there's a good chance archaeologists would recognize an ancient technology designed to exploit nuclear power—and if they didn't, they would certainly be able to call in someone who did. This is because our own science has now advanced to a level where nuclear power is familiar to us. By contrast, Soddy's imagining of a lost high civilization of prehistoric antiquity that had fully penetrated the mysteries of the atom was written in the infancy of our risky dance with nukes—25 years before Hiroshima and Nagasaki and 35 years before the first nuclear power stations came online. A man of his time, therefore, when the almost magical potential of the new technology was becoming apparent but when its downsides were largely unknown, Soddy was all idealism. He could not have anticipated that the immense power of the atom, once fully harnessed, would **never** be used to transform deserts, thaw the poles, or "make the whole world one smiling Garden of Eden," but would instead be deployed primarily for destructive purposes in the form of bombs and missiles, or for generating electricity at the long-term cost of poisoning the earth.

It is not necessarily the case that an earlier advanced civilization would have chosen the nuclear path so enthusiastically envisaged for it by Soddy. Nor must it inevitably have taken the path of leverage and mechanical advantage that historical civilizations have so doggedly trudged down for the past few thousand years on their way to the "machine age." I return again to my point. Since we are considering the possibility of "a wholly unknown and unsuspected civilization," we must also consider the possibility that it might have developed wholly unknown and unsuspected ways of manipulating matter and energy—which we might therefore be unable to recognize even if the evidence was right before our eyes.

Perhaps this is why modern archaeologists, trained to analyze ancient construction techniques through the reference frame of leverage and mechanical advantage, are unable to provide convincing explanations for a number of significant architectural problems of the ancient world.

Take the case of the massive beams, quarried from solid granite and weighing in the range of 70 tons each, incorporated into the core of Egypt's Great Pyramid in the series of "relieving chambers" stacked on top of the "King's

Chamber" more than 50 meters (164 feet) above ground level. None of the wishful scholarly claims of megaliths somehow being slid "easily" into place on wooden rollers or on lubricated sand will work at this elevation. The fact of the matter is that the hulking beams forming the floors and ceilings of the relieving chambers are where they are—and that in order to get there they had to be lifted more than 50 meters into the air.

Or consider the Trilithon at Baalbek in Lebanon. Here, 20 feet above the ground, three immense ashlars weighing more than 800 tons each have been placed end to end within a wall of smaller blocks and so tightly fitted that the joints can barely be seen. It wouldn't be an easy feat even with twenty-first-century technology, so how could it possibly have been accomplished thousands of years ago?

Let us also not forget the marvel of Sacsayhuamán, perched on a ridge above the city of Cuzco in the Peruvian Andes at an altitude of 3,700 meters (12,140 feet). I have made the case in previous books that this supposed Inca site was already enormously ancient at the time of the Incas and has been wrongly attributed to them. Of particular relevance here are its colossal megalithic walls arranged in a series of zigzags and consisting of intricately formed polygonal blocks. No two blocks among the thousands at Sacsayhuamán are the same shape, some weigh more than 300 tons, and all are so tightly interlocked in all dimensions that the edge of a piece of paper cannot be slipped between the joints. Efforts by archaeologists to reconstruct how the work at Sacsayhuamán was done have proved as ludicrous as a failed attempt in 1978 to build a midget-size scale model of the Great Pyramid—and once again this is because the only reference frame deemed acceptable, involving leverage and mechanical advantage, is unable to account for many of the more complex anomalies.

There is an answer, but it involves looking outside the box.

At the Great Pyramid, at Baalbek, and at Sacsayhuamán, as well as at numerous other mysterious sites (such as the almost unbelievable Kailasa Temple, hewn out of solid basalt at Ellora in the Indian state of Maharashtra), intriguing ancient traditions persist. These traditions speak of meditating sages, the use of certain plants, the focused attention of initiates, miraculously speedy workmanship, and special kinds of chanting or tones played on musical instruments in connection with the lifting, placing, softening, and moulding of megaliths. My guess, confronted by the global distribution of such narratives and by the stark reality of the sites themselves, is that we're dealing with the reverberations of an ancient technology we don't understand, operating on principles that are utterly unknown to us.

Soddy, imagining a lost civilization that had developed machines powered by nuclear energy, speaks of exploring the outer realms of space and manipulating the global climate, but I beg to differ. I don't think nuclear power was involved and I don't think *machines* were involved, either. As I near the end of my life's work, and of this book, I suppose the time has come to say in print what I have already said many times in public Q&A sessions at my lectures, that in my view the science of the lost civilization was primarily focused upon what we now call *psi* capacities that deployed the enhanced and focused power of human consciousness to channel energies and to manipulate matter.

Although *psi* research is still undertaken at a small number of universities and institutes in Britain, the United States, and Russia, it is generally ridiculed and sidelined by modern mainstream scientists. This categorically does not mean that "there's nothing to psi" but instead speaks volumes about the nature of science today, which is heavily dominated by materialist thinkers whose reference frame has little room for "spooky action at a distance." The phrase (which was Einstein's) refers specifically to the paradoxes of quantum entanglement but applies equally well to other alleged "non-local" phenomena such as:

1. telepathy ("communication from one person to another of thoughts, feelings, desires, etc, involving mechanisms that cannot be understood in terms of known scientific laws");

2. remote viewing ("the practice of seeking impressions about a distant or unseen target, purportedly using extrasensory perception");

3. telekinesis ("the movement of a body caused by thought or willpower without the application of physical force");

4. healing powers (whereby patients are successfully cured of their ailments by nonphysical and nonmedical means)

My speculation, which I will not attempt to prove here or to support with evidence but merely present for consideration, is that the advanced civilization

I see evolving in North America during the Ice Age had transcended leverage and mechanical advantage and learned to manipulate matter and energy
by deploying powers of consciousness that we have not yet begun to tap. In
action such powers would look something like magic even today and must
have seemed supernatural and godlike to the hunter-gatherers who shared the
Ice Age world with these mysterious adepts.

Keep in mind that we are talking about a Native American civilization
growing to maturity at some point during the long interval between the scav-
enging of the Cerutti mastodon 130,000 years ago and the cataclysmic onset
of the Younger Dryas 12,800 years ago. Though we may never know what set
it on its own brilliant, idiosyncratic path, there is every reason to suppose that
its people would have been closely related genetically, linguistically—and at
first culturally—to other early Native American populations who remained
at the hunter-gatherer stage. It follows, therefore, if this hypothetical civilization had sciences, that they should be rooted and grounded in a recognizably
Native American reference frame, and therefore would likely have developed
under the guidance of shamans and using the methods of shamanism.

Telepathy, telekinesis, remote viewing, and healing powers are, of course,
all capacities believed to be within the repertoire of master shamans. Indeed
ayahuasca, which lies at the heart of Amazonian shamanism, first entered
mainstream Western consciousness under the name *Telepathine*. In 1952, for
example, on a quest in Ecuador for the visionary brew, William Burroughs
wrote [his spellings; emphasis mine] that he had failed to "score for Yage,
Bannisteria caapi, **Telepathine**, ayahuasca—all names for the same drug."[7]

He was determined to find it, however, because of its "tremendous implications" and the "mystery" surrounding it, adding, "I'm the man who can dig it."[8]

The reason behind the choice of the name *Telepathine*, which began to be
applied to ayahuasca as early as 1905,[9] was that Amazonian tribes making
regular use of the brew repeatedly stated that it facilitated telepathic communication. The mechanistic Western mind of the twenty-first century scoffs
at such claims, but leading ayahuasca researcher Benny Shanon, professor of
psychology at the Hebrew University in Jerusalem, concedes that "reports of
paranormal experiences with Ayahuasca abound:"

Practically everyone who has had more than a rudimentary exposure
to the brew reports having had telepathic experiences. Many such

reports also appear in the anthropological literature. . . . Similarly many of my informants said that without overt verbal articulation they could pass messages to other people present in the Ayahuasca session. . . . Likewise, many indicated that they received such messages from other persons or beings. Usually, in visions in which drinkers feel that they are receiving messages or instructions from beings and creatures, the communication in question is said to be achieved without words—directly from thought to thought.[10]

In the modern world we are so fixated on our machines and devices that it's almost impossible to imagine life without them. But if telepathy is real—a debate we won't be able to get into here—and if its use and projection could be refined and made reliable, then who would need cell phones or Facebook or any of the other means of communication that are so ubiquitous today? Once again we would own our own conversations rather than having to depend on some intermediary or "platform" to relay them!

Might it not be the case that *psi* powers have always been part of the human heritage? Part of our "Golden Age"? Perhaps these powers atrophied after the Younger Dryas cataclysm broke our connection to our roots? And perhaps, in the aftermath of the cataclysm, the resourcefulness of our species was refocused on techniques of leverage and mechanical advantage and a negative feedback loop developed that ushered in the march of the machines and saw *psi* banished to the margins of human experience?

REVERSE ENGINEERING THE SYSTEM

I'LL NOT SPECULATE FURTHER HERE about the lost technology of a destroyed civilization. There are tantalizing hints and clues but unfortunately even the first archaeological steps that might make solid progress possible have never been taken. There's more to work with, however, when we come to religious and spiritual beliefs that, according to the Edfu Building Texts, it was the duty of the survivors of the lost civilization to preserve and to replicate wherever in the world they could find receptive ground.

In the twenty-first century, Christianity and Islam—upstart religions of the past 2,000 years—exercise effective monopolies over the spiritual lives of more than half the world's population. Their simple formula of one creator god (male, of course), and of a heavenly paradise for His faithful paired with a hellish place of punishment for disbelievers and evildoers, brilliantly removes the need for serious thought. All that's required to join the elect is to tick the right boxes and maintain a state of rigid, abiding, unquestioning BELIEF in the authority of the sacred texts and the utterances of the priests and the mullahs self-appointed to interpret them.

Perhaps it's the easiest option, requiring the smallest quantum of uncomfortable reflection, but it's certainly not the only one, and neither is atheism—which also rests on unproven beliefs—in any way its opposite. The full range of human spiritual potential cannot be brutally reduced to believing that a god exists or to believing that a god does not exist. Agnosticism is often proposed as the only alternative, but there are far more subtle and even "scientific" ways forward, explored confidently by our ancestors many millennia ago, that deserve serious attention. Important elements survive in some of the more esoteric aspects of Hinduism and Tibetan Buddhism—notably in *The Tibetan Book of the Dead,* which bears striking similarities to the *Ancient Egyptian Book of the Dead* and descends, I suggest, from the same common source. There is much among the Maya (reported in *Fingerprints of the Gods* and in *Heaven's Mirror*) that adds to the picture. Meanwhile, Amazonian shamanism and the strangely interlinked religions of the Nile and Mississippi Valleys open further vistas of understanding.

In particular, whether we speak of the visionary "leap" to the Milky Way and to the Underworld that lies beyond it made by Tukano shamans under the influence of ayahuasca, or of Mississippian ideas concerning the "Path of Souls," or of the ancient Egyptian afterlife journey through the Duat, I think the only reasonable conclusion to be drawn from the material presented in previous chapters is that we are dealing with a complex and sophisticated system of shared ideas inherited from a remote common ancestor. And just as our DNA can be "reverse engineered" by geneticists to reveal much about our forebears, so, too, the shared segments of cultural DNA in the religions of the Mississippi Valley and ancient Egypt give us insights into the character of the vastly more ancient predecessor religion that spawned them both. That ancient religion—the religion of the lost civilization—was itself, I would contend, a highly specialized offshoot of Native American shamanism and its primary focus, as is the focus of all shamanism, was the mystery of death.

WHAT HAPPENS TO US WHEN WE DIE?

OUR SOCIETY PREFERS TO IGNORE and marginalize the problem of death. It is an ever-present reality for all of us—much less when we are young, much more as we grow old—and yet we do all we can to avoid it. We know in an abstract sense that it awaits us, but meanwhile we prefer to dwell as little as possible on its implications and to live our lives as though they will never end.

The reference frame out of which such thinking emerges cannot be pinned on any of the Abrahamic religions but belongs to the scientism of the modern age, which holds that we are entirely material creatures, random accidents of chemistry and biology, that there is no transcendent meaning or purpose to our existence, that there is no such thing as the soul, that death is final, and that there is no "afterlife." If those are your beliefs, which are only a subset of wider beliefs that strip the universe of spirit and conceive of it as some sort of gigantic, unconscious automaton, then of course it makes sense to abjure all thoughts of death and to postpone death for as long as possible, even though many ancient traditions, despised by the scientific mind-set, warn that unwillingness to die produces unfavorable results. "As here in America," comments W. Y. Evans-Wentz, the translator of *The Tibetan Book of the Dead*,

every effort is apt to be made by a materialistically inclined medical science to postpone, and thereby to interfere with, the death-process. Very often the dying is not permitted to die in his or her own home or in a normal, unperturbed mental condition when the hospital has been reached. To die in hospital, probably while under the mind-benumbing influence of some opiate, or else under the stimulation of some drug injected into the body to enable the dying to cling to life as long as possible, cannot but be productive of a very undesirable death, as undesirable as that of a shell-shocked soldier on a battlefield. Even as the normal result of the birth-process may be aborted by malpractices, so, similarly, may the normal result of the death-process be aborted.[11]

Matters would have been handled very differently, I propose, in an advanced Native American civilization that had **not** severed its roots with shamanism—as we have done—but had instead evolved forms of science and technology that emerged directly from shamanistic preoccupations and shamanistic experiences. Rather than turning its back on death, I expect that such a civilization would have confronted and investigated every aspect of the mystery, and would certainly have deployed trance techniques with scientific objectivity and discipline to explore and test the reality status of the "Otherworlds" and "Underworlds" encountered in vision.

It is further evidence of a remote common source behind some widespread religious motifs that one of the most famous myths of the ancient Greeks—the tale of Orpheus and Eurydice—was also present, long before European contact, in the ancient pre-Columbian cultures of North America.[12] Some details vary, as of course do the names of the central characters and the general setting, but the underlying structure remains the same[13]—(1) a wife or sweetheart (Eurydice) dies prematurely; (2) her husband or lover (Orpheus) follows her soul to the Underworld and persuades its ruler to let her return with him to the land of the living; (3) Eurydice's release is agreed on condition that she walk behind Orpheus as they make the return journey from the Underworld and that under no circumstances should he set eyes on her until they reach the land of the living; (4) at the last moment, overcome with love, Orpheus cannot resist glancing over his shoulder at his wife and in that instant she is cast back into the Underworld that she can henceforth never leave.

So compellingly similar are the Native American and Greek versions that leading scholar of religions Ake Hultkrantz dedicated an immense monograph to the mystery, published in Stockholm in 1957, titled *The North American Indian Orpheus Tradition*.[14] Meanwhile his contemporary, Canadian ethnographer Charles Marius Barbeau, proposed that the Greek and Native American stories must both be offshoots of some much older core narrative and concluded, "The worldwide diffusion from an unknown source of a tale so typically classical as Orpheus and Eurydice must have required millenniums."[15]

Of course I agree that the wide distribution of localized versions of the Orpheus and Eurydice myth suggests the great antiquity of the common source from which they all descend. But what I find equally interesting is that the foundations of the narrative clearly lie in the concepts of the afterlife journey of the soul and the duality of spirit and matter so central to the religious beliefs of ancient Egypt and the ancient Mississippi Valley. Could it be that what we have in these superficially separate but deeply interconnected systems are the surviving threads from a once immense tapestry of thought about the human condition, our place in the cosmos, and the meaning of life and death?

And just as our own sciences today are capable of highly sophisticated interventions and manipulations in the realm of matter, might it not be that the sciences of the lost civilization were capable of equally effective interventions and manipulations in the realm of spirit—and possibly, therefore, had accumulated veridical information concerning dimensions of reality about which we ourselves are presently entirely ignorant?

For those who believe that all notions of "spirit" are fantasy, that consciousness expires with the physical body, and that any form of life after death is therefore impossible, the notion of investing time, resources, and ingenuity in developing a "science of death"—perhaps better termed a "science of the afterlife" or even a "science of immortality"—sounds like the worst kind of wishful thinking. The consequence, described so eloquently by W. Y. Evans-Wentz, is that from the materialistic perspective the only valid application of science to the problem of death is in the outfitting of hospitals and the preparation of medicines to "ease" the passing and—if the deceased is otherwise in good physical condition—to recycle his or her organs.

But what if our materialist science, which has a pedigree of only a few hundred years since the dawn of the so-called Age of Reason in the late seventeenth century, is fundamentally **incomplete** in its analysis of the nature of reality and of the phenomenon of death? And what if the far older tradition of the afterlife journey of the soul manifested in ancient Egypt and in the ancient Mississippi Valley, and by Amazonian shamans to this day, conceals deep truths?

If that were the case, then Western scientific materialism might have led us down a very dark and dangerous path indeed—one with repercussions across eternity.

In Tibetan Buddhism the afterlife realm is known as the Bardo—literally "the Between." Just like the *Ancient Egyptian Book of the Dead* and the Mississippian oral and iconographic traditions, the purpose of the Tibetan Book of the Dead is to serve as a guidebook and instruction manual for the soul on its postmortem journey through this strange parallel dimension.

"The Between," explains prominent American Buddhist scholar Robert A. F. Thurman, is "a time of crisis after death when the soul (the very subtle mind-body) is in its most highly fluid state."[16] It is a time of extraordinary danger but also of extraordinary opportunity:

> If the good person, who has a strong momentum of good evolutionary action, is unprepared for the Between, he or she can lose an enormous amount of evolutionary progress in the twinkling of an eye by becoming frightened and hiding in darkness. Similarly, a bad person, who has a great weight of negative evolution, if well prepared for the Between, can overcome immense eons of wretched lives by bravely shooting for the light. After all, a tiny achievement on the subtle plane can have a powerful impact on the gross. The soul in the Between can directly modify, just with creative imagination, what the Buddhists call "the spiritual genes" it carries with it. The Between voyager has temporarily an immensely heightened intelligence, extraordinary powers of concentration, special abilities of clairvoyance and teleportation, flexibility to become whatever can be imagined and the openness to be radically transformed by a thought or a vision or an instruction. This is indeed why the Between traveler can become instantly liberated just by understanding where he or she is in the Between, what the reality is, where the allies are, and where the dangers.[17]

Western science possesses unprecedented knowledge of the material realm over which it has achieved extensive mastery. We should not assume, however, that this means it is also automatically in possession of superior knowledge that refutes the Tibetan "Science of Death" (the phrase that Robert Thurman uses to describe the teachings in *The Tibetan Book of the Dead*[18]). On the contrary, since Western science has shunned investigation of the afterlife because of the unevidenced preconception that there is no such thing, we should rather accept that Tibetan Buddhism, which has devoted long centuries of intelligent study to the matter, may be far ahead of us. Moreover, as I've argued, *The Tibetan Book of the Dead* descends from the same vastly older progenitor that also gave rise to the ancient Egyptian and Mississippian systems and therefore might potentially be harnessed, like them, to the task of reconstructing that progenitor.

My sense is that the lost civilization, as might be expected with its proposed shamanic origins, was not much interested in material things. Like many other Native American cultures, its primary goals were not to do with the acquisition of status or wealth but instead were focused, through vision quests and right living, on the perfection of the soul. From the complexity and deep wisdom that still shines through in its offspring religions, I suggest that it took these inquiries very far into regions of mystery that in our culture even quantum physicists and scientists engaged with virtual reality have barely begun to contemplate. In order to prepare its initiates thoroughly so that they might be "well equipped" for the ultimate journey of death—surely a matter of far greater significance than any material concerns—the direct exploration of parallel dimensions would, as noted earlier, almost certainly have been undertaken. Had this investigation been allowed to proceed uninterrupted it might by now have transcended space, time, and matter entirely, but 12,800 years ago a deadly mass of matter in the form of the Younger Dryas comet was flung at it and brought a pause to the great prehistoric quest.

A pause but not a halt—for if I'm right there were survivors who attempted, with varying degrees of success, to repromulgate the lost teachings, planting "sleeper cells" far and wide in hunter-gatherer cultures in the form of institutions and memes that could store and transmit knowledge and, when the time was right, activate a program of public works, rapid agricultural development, and enhanced spiritual inquiry.

As to the fate of the lost civilization itself, I can only guess that its North American homeland, in which it may have evolved in comparative isolation for more than 100,000 years, was located in one or several of the immense areas south of the ice cap, from the Channeled Scablands of Washington State in the west, through Nebraska, Wyoming, and the Dakotas, through the Great Lakes where one of most devastating impacts may have occurred, and east to the Finger Lakes of upstate New York. I've suggested that this was a seafaring civilization, able to map the Ice Age world and spread its influence to remote shores, but if it had harbors on the Atlantic and Pacific coasts of North America 13,000 years ago, they would have been submerged by the rapid rise in sea levels at the onset of the Younger Dryas 12,800 years ago and by the even more massive rise that marked the end of the Younger Dryas 11,600 years ago when the remnant ice caps of North America and Europe simultaneously collapsed into the oceans.

PAST IMPERFECT, FUTURE UNCERTAIN

THERE ARE LITERALLY THOUSANDS OF myths from every inhabited continent that speak of the existence of an advanced civilization in remote prehistory, of the lost golden age in which it flourished, and of the cataclysm that brought it to an end. A feature shared by many of them—the story of Atlantis, for example, or of Noah's flood—is the notion that human beings, by their own arrogance, cruelty, and disrespect for the earth, had somehow brought the disaster down upon their own heads and accordingly were obliged by the gods to go back to basics and learn humility again.

Where does this sense of ancestral guilt come from with its peculiar intimations of a mistaken direction taken by humanity in some remote period and purged by a global catastrophe? These are not the kinds of thoughts one would expect hunter-gatherers to devote much time to. A technologically advanced people, on the other hand, particularly if they had mastered the transmutation of matter, would have had vastly more potential for hubris and overreach. In the event of the cataclysmic downfall of their civilization, those who survived might well have reflected on their history and blamed themselves for what happened.

Who knows? Perhaps some hubristic excesses had occurred that would have justified such speculations?

A drift toward self-indulgent materialism?

The introduction of human sacrifice?

The appearance of a new and vigorously proselytizing cult denying the existence of the soul?

The enslavement and exploitation of hunter-gatherer tribes?

The arming of one group of hunter-gatherers—such as Clovis—to give it a competitive advantage over others?

There could be 1,000 reasons why the humbled survivors of a once powerful but now utterly destroyed civilization seeking refuge among hunter-gatherers might have arrived with a sense of guilt.

An Ojibwa tradition seems relevant. It speaks of a comet that "burned up the earth" in the remote past and that is destined to return:

> The star with the long, wide tail is going to destroy the world some day when it comes low again. That's the comet called Long-Tailed Heavenly Climbing Star. It came down here once, thousands of years ago. Just like the sun. It had radiation and burning heat in its tail . . .
>
> Indian people were here before that happened, living on the earth. But things were wrong with nature on the earth, a lot of people had abandoned the spiritual path. The Holy Spirit warned them a long time before the comet came. Medicine men told everyone to prepare. . . . The comet burnt everything to the ground. There wasn't a thing left . . .
>
> There is a prophecy that the comet will destroy the earth again. But it's a restoration. The greatest blessing this island [Turtle Island] will ever have. People don't listen to their spiritual guidance today. There will be signs in the sun, moon and stars when that comet comes down again.[19]

Our science and technology in the twenty-first century are close to the point where, should we choose to do so and be willing to divert the necessary resources from—say—military expenditures, it would be within our capacity to sweep our cosmic environment clean of asteroids and cometary debris and thus spare future generations the existential threat of further impacts. What is **not** within our scientific and technological competence, however, is to restore the earth and its environment **after** a major impact has occurred. Astronomer William Napier, professor of astrobiology at the University of Cardiff and a world expert on comets and asteroids, reminds us that the consequences of a global celestial catastrophe would far outstrip our capacity to respond:

> A modest impact has the potential to end civilisation, a giant one might put our species into an irreversible decline, like other primate species past and present. It took over three billion years of evolution

to produce the sole terrestrial species capable of understanding the universe, and we do not know whether, if we are removed, intelligence is likely to evolve again. Nor do we know whether there are other intelligent species in our Galaxy. In the event that we are alone, and are removed by some catastrophe, then our Galaxy will return to its former dumb state and may never again leave it. In that sense, the survival of this particular species of ape is a cosmic imperative.[20]

We have already received fair warning from the universe in the form of the cataclysmic earth changes at the onset of the Younger Dryas. No serious researcher disputes that those earth changes occurred and, since 2007, the Younger Dryas Impact Hypothesis has established itself as the most widely accepted explanation for everything that happened. But at first the earth scientists behind the hypothesis could only say that the evidence pointed to a cosmic impactor of some kind, most likely a swarm of fragments from a disintegrating comet.

In 2010, however, in a paper published in the *Monthly Notices of the Royal Astronomical Society,* William Napier added his weight and specific details to the conclusion that a comet had indeed been involved—a giant comet, perhaps 100 kilometers in diameter, according to his calculations, that entered the inner solar system on an earth-crossing orbit somewhere between 30,000 and 20,000 years ago and thereafter underwent the series of fragmentations that spawned the Taurid meteor stream.[21] This is a normal process for comets[22] and it's Professor Napier's case that intersection with the fragmenting debris of this exceptionally large comet around 12,800 years ago "provides a satisfactory explanation" for the postulated celestial origin of the Younger Dryas cataclysm.[23]

It's my case that the hit humanity took then erased a remarkable civilization from the record and that we have remained mired in amnesia ever since. In the process what is being neglected, despite the increasingly urgent warnings of a handful of astronomers, is that **most of the rubble from the ongoing fragmentation of the original comet remains in orbit in the Taurid meteor stream**, including some pieces of enormous size capable of ending civilization again. Indeed, as we saw in chapter 25, it's Napier's conclusion that this "unique complex of debris" represents "the greatest collision hazard facing the earth at the present time."[24]

In September 2017, drawing on imagery captured by the European Fireball Network, important new research on the Taurids, published in the journal *Astronomy and Astrophysics,* gave strong support to Napier's warning. The title of the paper speaks for itself: "Discovery of a New Branch of the Taurid Meteoroid Stream as a Real Source of Potentially Hazardous Bodies."[25] *Halloween*

The newly discovered branch is part of the Southern Taurids, encountered by the earth in late October and the first half of November, and it is just one of many indications that humanity's relationship with the Younger Dryas comet is not over. On the contrary, all the evidence from the close observation and investigation of the Taurids now being undertaken by astronomers is that we may be about to enter—or indeed may already have entered—an episode of enhanced danger. Ahead of us, perhaps still some decades away, lie particularly dense and turbulent filaments of the stream believed to contain "dark" fragments of the original comet, in one case with a possible world-killing diameter of 30 kilometers.[26]

A TIME FOR CHANGE?

THIS BOOK HAS ROOTS IN much of my earlier work, particularly on ancient Mexico, the ancient Andean civilizations of South America, and ancient Egypt. However, it was not until early December 2016, during a visit I made to North Dakota and to the protest camp named Oceti Sakowin situated just beyond the present northern boundary of the Standing Rock Sioux Reservation, that *America Before* crystallized in my mind as a definite concept, coupled with firm intent.

Readers may recall how, from July 2016 onward, a rainbow coalition of Sioux, other Native American tribes, and non–Native American people gathered at Oceti Sakowin in an attempt to stop the laying of an oil pipeline under Lake Oahe on the Missouri River half a mile north of Standing Rock in a location where it not only transgressed traditionally sacred lands, but also threatened the reservation's water supply in the event of a spill.

Although extremely active and impassioned in the face of a clampdown by militarized security police, the protests of those who had become known as the "water protectors" failed to achieve their immediate objective, which was to have construction of the Dakota Access Pipeline (DAPL) halted completely. Quite to the contrary, on February 7, 2017, the official easement was granted,[27] work to complete the DAPL went ahead, and the first oil began to flow on June 1, 2017.[28] There were legal challenges from the Sioux and further protests and controversy following oil spills.[29] In December 2017 some interim restrictions were imposed on the pipeline operator to prevent further spills,[30] but as I write these words in July 2018, oil is still flowing through the pipeline and it seems that commercial interests have once again effectively trumped the interests and concerns of Native Americans.[31]

Central to the entire protest at Standing Rock was the notion that we live at a time when there is an urgent need to change our ways, to adopt a more humble and no longer rapacious approach to the earth, and to receive a spiritual message passed down from the ancients and held in safekeeping by the First Americans.

It's a message that resonates profoundly for me with so much that I've learned while researching this book.

"This is about everyone," Cody Two Bears of the Standing Rock Sioux told me as he explained the larger purpose of the Oceti Sakowin protests:

> It's such an important time today—why people need to know this history. Because, for one, the history books would never tell you the correct story . . . the reason why. I talk to a lot of elders and a lot of spiritual leaders. We had to keep our ceremonies secret. We had to keep our stories a secret for so many years to preserve that. Because the government was fearful of what we had and who we are as a people. The laws will tell you that. There's even a current standing law today in Montana, I don't think they've taken it out of their law book, that if you see three Native Americans all together then you are able to shoot and kill them. Still legal in Montana! Those are the types of laws they created because they don't want to see Native Americans gather because for some reason they were fearful of us.
>
> But little do they know, our ceremonies and our ways of life protected us and *Unci Maka* [Mother Earth]. We prayed even for those people who were afraid of us, to help them . . . to pray for them to make sure they were okay.
>
> That's what our ceremonies are based around. It's not witchcraft . . .

it's not casting spells on anybody, but that's what they thought for many, many years. . . . For example, the Ghost Dances we used to have in Lakota and Dakota country. When we did that, the *Washi'chu* [white people—literally "those who always take the largest portion"] were so fearful. They thought we were casting spells, when all in all we were trying to keep the balance with the Earth and the Stars. We need to keep that in balance, because if we don't start doing that today, we're not going to have anywhere to live in the next hundred years."

Some 12,800 years ago the balance between the Earth and the Stars was lost and a key chapter of the human story was lost with it. If it happens again, if our brief chapter, too, is lost, will all that remains of us at some vast remove in the future be an unhappy myth that tells of how, through our own greed and conceit, through our own recklessness and disregard for the planet in our care, and through our own excess of hate and dearth of love, we conspired in our own downfall?

MELAZONIA, AKA AMANESIA

Although they are "a world apart and separated by forty thousand years or more of human history," certain "striking resemblances" and "remarkable similarities between societies in Amazonia and Melanesia" have kept scholars puzzled for more than a century.[1]

One of these puzzles concerns the skull shapes of indigenous Amazonians and Melanesians and an always unorthodox theory known as the "Paleoamerican hypothesis"[2] that proposes, "on the basis of cranial morphology" (just a fancy name for skull shapes):

that two temporally and source-distinct populations colonized the Americas. The earlier population reportedly originated in Asia in the Late Pleistocene and gave rise to both Paleoamericans and present-day Australo-Melanesians, whose shared cranial morphological attributes are presumed to indicate their common ancestry. The Paleoamericans were, in turn, thought to have been largely replaced by ancestors of present-day Amerindians, whose crania resemble modern East Asians and who are argued to be descendants of later arriving Mongoloid populations. The presence of Paleoamericans is inferred primarily from ancient archaeological specimens in North and South America and a few relict populations of more recent age, which include the extinct Pericúes and Fuego-Patagonians.

The Paleoamerican hypothesis predicts that these groups should be genetically closer to Australo-Melanesians than other Amerindians.[3]

Maanasa Raghavan and Eske Willerslev, both of the Centre for Geo-Genetics at the University of Copenhagen, put the hypothesis to the test at the genetic level as part of their study (discussed in part 3) and found that the ancient and more recent Native American skulls previously identified as having Australo-Melanesian morphology in fact cluster at the genetic level "with other Native American groups" and show no affinity to Australo-Melanesians.[4]

Their data joined a mass of preexisting genetic evidence pointing to the same conclusion.

For example, another study found that even the most ancient skulls displaying "traits attributable to Paleoamerican crania" turned out, after genetic sequencing, to "present the same mtDNA haplogroups as later populations with Amerindian morphology."[5]

A third comparative study of morphometric and molecular mtDNA haplogroup data from ancient and more recent Native American skeletal remains likewise concluded that "human populations inhabiting the Americas during archaic times cannot be considered as belonging to two different groups on the basis of analyzed data."[6]

In other words, although their skulls indeed might *appear* different, and much more like Australo-Melanesian skulls than more recent Amerindian skulls, "Paleoamericans" turn out to be genetically indistinct from more recent Amerindian populations. Since genotype trumps phenotype every time as evidence for relatedness, the "Paleoamerican hypothesis" has therefore been regarded for some years as disproved.

Following their own study, however, discussed in chapter 9, Pontus Skoglund and David Reich (both of the Department of Genetics, Harvard Medical School) seem open to reconsidering the whole question when they describe their hypothetical "Population Y" that "likely contributed to the DNA of Native Americans from Amazonia and the Central Brazilian Plateau" as "a lineage more closely related to present-day Australasians than to present-day East Asians and Siberians."[7] They go on to add:

> This discovery is striking in light of interpretations of the morphology of some early Native American skeletons, which some authors have suggested have affinities to Australasian groups. The largest number of skeletons that have been described as having this craniofacial morphology and that date to younger than 10,000 years old have been found in Brazil, the home of the Surui, Karitiana and Xavante groups who show the strongest affinity to Australasians in genetic data.[8]

What has never been substantially in dispute is that the craniometric similarities between ancient populations from the Brazilian Amazon and Australo-Melanesian populations are real and quantifiable.[9] Moreover, while equally real and quantifiable, the genetic data suggesting that these similarities are not evidence of relatedness but must be coincidental, or perhaps the result of some sort of bizarre parallel evolutionary process, seems to me—and clearly to Skoglund and Reich as well—to be directly contradicted by that Australo-Melanesian signal sending out its rather compelling message of relatedness from Brazil.

In view of this I'd say, at the very least, that the earlier craniometric data needs to be revisited, particularly a study by Walter A. Neves and Mark Hubbe published in December 2005 in the *Proceedings of the National Academy of Sciences* in which "the largest sample of early American skulls ever studied"—eighty-one skulls from Brazil's Lagoa Santa region—is compared "with worldwide datasets representing global morphological variation in humans, through three different multivariate analyses."[10]

In their paper Neves and Hubbe point out:

> Whereas late prehistoric, recent, and present Native Americans tend to exhibit a cranial morphology similar to late and modern Northern Asians . . . the earliest South Americans tend to be more similar to present Australians, Melanesians, and Sub-Saharan Africans.[11]

After conducting detailed measurements and analyses of their collection of eighty-one ancient Brazilian skulls and running their global comparisons, Neves and Hubbe are confident that "the results obtained from all multivariate analyses confirm a close morphological affinity between South-American Paleoindians and extant Australo-Melanesian groups."[12]

They then go on to offer two different hypotheses to explain "the morphological differences observed between early and late Native South Americans:"

One is a local microevolutionary process that transformed, *in situ*, the Paleoamerican morphology into that prevailing today among Native Americans. The other is that the Americas were successively occupied by two morphologically differentiated human stocks, with the Paleoamerican morphology entering first.

We believe the second hypothesis is more plausible for three reasons: first, it would be very unlikely that the same evolutionary event . . . happened in the Americas and in East Asia in parallel at approximately the same time; second, because in South America, at least, the transition between the two morphological patterns was, as far as we know, abrupt; and third, cranial morphology has recently been shown to respond adaptively only to extreme environmental conditions, being therefore much less plastic than originally thought.[13]

In short, as Neves and Hubbe summarize elsewhere in their paper, their results support the hypothesis "that two distinct biological populations could have colonized the New World in the Pleistocene-Holocene transition."[14]

This, of course, is a conclusion arrived at from the craniometric data, but it is also precisely the conclusion arrived at by Skoglund and Reich from their reading of the genetic data; namely, as the title of their 2015 *Nature* paper indicates, that there is "genetic evidence for two founding populations of the Americas."[15]

On the other hand, as we've seen, Raghavan and Willerslev disagree. In their *Science* paper they favor, instead, a single founding population.[16]

Clearly in a state of affairs like this where the experts come to radically different conclusions based on nuances within essentially the same data, it would be unwise to go with one side or the other. Whether in the form of skulls or genes, though, it seems to me that the clues so far point in the direction of—to say the least!—some sort of forgotten connection.

There's more.

TWO TOWERS OF BABEL

Several researchers have noted that Australo-Melanesia and the Americas both manifest extraordinary "linguistic diversity" featuring much greater numbers of languages than in all other parts of the world. An implication of this, argues anthropologist German Dziebel, is that:

> measured by the number of independent linguistic stocks, linguistic divergence in the Americas must have taken at least 35,000 years. Of course, this figure cannot be taken literally but there's a marked contrast between language diversity in the Americas (and in places like Papua New Guinea, with human archaeological record of some 40,000 years) and language diversity in Africa.[17]

Austin Whittall, an author and regular blogger on ancient South American genetics and anthropological issues, also comments on the surprising phenomenon of high levels of linguistic diversity in Australo-Melanesia and the Americas:

> Why do Native American people speak so many languages? They supposedly reached the New World recently . . . yet evolved over 40% of the global languages! A figure higher than that found in Africa, the "Cradle of Mankind."
> Africans have had the time . . . and the advantage of not going through bottlenecks . . . . so they should have evolved more languages than any other group of humans. But they have not.[18]

New Guinea, Whittall points out next, has "the highest language diversity in the whole world."[19] Indeed, authority on world languages *Ethnologue* confirms that there are 841 living languages in Papua New Guinea, which make up 11.85 percent of living languages in the world.[20]

Whittal finds this quite reasonable:

> the island is a jungle, with many mountain ranges that isolate populations and keep them from mixing. New Guinea has been considered as one of the first places reached by mankind during our epic trek out of Africa.
>
> But America is different. . . . The Papuans had 50 ky to develop their languages, the Amerindians had less than 15 ky. So how do we explain this?[21]

The linguistic diversity of the Americas **is** an anomaly—Whittall is absolutely right about this—and its parallels with the linguistic diversity of New Guinea and Australasia in general are intriguing. The following table,[22] reproduced in Whittall's blog, makes the anomaly clear:

Total numbers of separate language families by macrocontinent

AFRICA & EURASIA	87	(25%)
AUSTRALASIA	110	(32%)
AMERICAS	144	(42%)

Source: The Autotyp database (Bickel and Nichols 2002ff; Nichols et al. 2013)

"I do believe," Whittall concludes, "that we should look into language diversity as an indicator of an older origin for mankind as a whole and for an earlier date for the peopling of America."[23]

It's an excellent point but, for me, the more immediate takeaway is the two clusters of **especially abundant** linguistic diversity that the table highlights, one in Australasia and the other in the Americas. Moreover, we've already seen that within Australasia it's Melanesian New Guinea that has by far the highest level of linguistic diversity—indeed higher than anywhere else in the world. Likewise, within the Americas, South America has more than double the linguistic diversity of North America,[24] with the greatest abundance of all found in lowland Amazonia where no fewer than 350 of South America's total of 448 languages are spoken.[25]

	Number of language families	Number of languages	Average number of languages per family
NORTH AMERICA	13	220	16.9
CENTRAL AMERICA	6	273	45.4
SOUTH AMERICA	37	448	12.1

Once again, therefore, Melanesian New Guinea and Amazonia seem to parallel one another. Each has the highest level of linguistic diversity within its own macrocontinent and together they occupy first and second place among the world's most linguistically diverse regions.[26]

NOW SOME WEIRD STUFF . . .

Melanesia and Amazonia are divided by the full width of the Pacific Ocean, so ethnographers of the late nineteenth and early twentieth centuries were perplexed when they found that certain distinctive customs and patterns of behavior occurred in almost exactly the same forms in both places.

For example, the practice of organizing society around so-called men's houses, where:

the men conducted secret rituals of initiation and procreation, excluded the women, and punished those who would violate the cult with gang rape or death. In both regions, the men told similar myths that explained the origin of the cults and gender separation. The resemblances were such as to convince anthropologists of the day, including Robert Lowie, Heinrich Shurtz, and Hutton Webster, that they could only have come about through diffusion. Lowie flatly declared that men's cults are "an ethnographic feature originating in a single center, and thence transmitted to other regions."

The parallels included not only men's cults but also similar systems of ecological adjustment; egalitarian social organization; flexibility in local- and descent-group composition and recruitment; endemic warfare; similar religious, mythological and cosmological systems; and similar beliefs relating to the body, procreation and the self. [27]

The scholarly puzzlement at these sorts of similarities has continued into the twenty-first century, for example, in a detailed study, "Gender in Amazonia and Melanesia," published by the University of California Press in 2001,[28] which followed an international symposium organized by the Wenner-Gren Foundation. The symposium was "inspired by the suggestion often made by anthropologists that the cultures of Amazonia and Melanesia seem to display startling resemblances even though they are historically, linguistically, and geographically unrelated."[29]

I do not wish to overload the reader with detail from this important in-depth study, but a few examples will give the general flavor of the results.

The Mundurukú of the Brazilian Amazon and the Avatik of the Sepik River in northern Papua New Guinea both, traditionally, visited "random, indiscriminate violence" on outsiders "as an internal requirement of the village's male cult." In both cases raids were seen as a special kind of hunting. In both cases cult members sought prestige in the eyes of fellow villagers by taking trophy heads during their raids. In both cases the heads were not brought back to the village until the men had undergone a ritual period of seclusion and sexual abstinence. And in both cases the heads were believed to enhance and renew fertility.[30]

Among the Sambia of eastern Papua New Guinea, as among the Arawete, Jivaro, and Mehinaku of the Amazon, a war leader would traditionally exhibit his erect penis as a sign of his aggression.[31]

Among the Alambak, the Sawos, and the Sepik Wape of Papua New Guinea, as among the Cashinahua of the Amazon, domestic conflict prior to a hunt or raid was believed to bring "bad luck" to the endeavor.[32]

In both Melanesia and Amazonia blood is seen as the main agent of growth and vitality. In both regions it is blood—especially menstrual blood—that is seen as the mother's contribution to conception or gestation. In both regions semen is considered closely related to blood or interactive with blood, and many believe, more specifically, that a fetus "is formed from the combination of female blood and male semen."[33]

In both Melanesia and Amazonia "the central symbols of the men's cults" are bullroarers, flutes, and trumpets, and in both regions the myths recall a time when "women discovered, invented, or possessed" these powerful cult objects. In both regions the myths say that the former control of these objects by women allowed them to dominate men. In both regions the myths also say that the men joined forces and compelled or deceived the women into handing the cult objects over to them, resulting in a reordering of society and the dominance of men. Moreover, in both regions "the men share a strategic secret: the sounds of the trumpets, flutes and other instruments associated with the cult are not the voices of spirits but are produced by the men themselves."[34]

Anthropologist Pascale Bonnemère draws attention to certain "striking similarities" in initiation rituals as performed among the Angans of New Guinea and by tribes in the Vaupés region of the Colombian Amazon. These "involve the playing of musical instruments that are hidden from women and that were owned by them in mythic times; they imply the consumption of substances that are symbolically associated with reproduction; they are interpreted in a similar way, as a rebirth of the young boys into the world of men; and myths offer keys for understanding the ritual."[35]

In both Amazonia and Melanesia there are dire consequences for women, including subjection to gang rape and murder, if they see the cult instruments.[36] There is also disruption to society as a whole. Among the Gimi of Papua New Guinea, for example, as among the Barasana of the Amazon, there is a belief that chaos and social disintegration will follow if the men's sacred bamboo flutes are seen by women.[37] Nonetheless, in both Amazonia and Melanesia, the men do not hesitate to "parade and play" the instruments "in public areas such as gardens and plazas that are normally open to women. As such, the men must be extraordinarily vigilant in sequestering the women during rituals"—which in practice, in both regions, means forcing them to remain indoors.[38]

In summary, as Thomas A. Gregor and Donald Tuzin, editors of *Gender in Amazonia and Melanesia,* conclude, "The similarities of men's institutions in Amazonia and Melanesia is one of the great riddles of culture that has not received the attention that it deserves."[39] In their view it is quite noteworthy enough that the "men's house complex"[40] obtains in both regions, but "what is even more striking is that the details of the cult also bear close comparison."[41]

They're right about the magnitude of the riddle but, in my view, the solution they offer is singularly disappointing. Just like the quacks who each year conjure a new mental illness from thin air to add to the already morbidly obese *Diagnostic and Statistical Manual of Mental Disorders,* so, too, Gregor and Tuzin are convinced that the whole weird complex of behavior around

men's cults in Melanesia and Amazonia is best understood using the tools of
psychoanalysis:

> We need the insights of psychology and especially that of personality
> dynamics to explain the emotional content and the remarkable
> regularities in men's conduct in such different cultures.[42]

Though writing in 2001, they particularly recommend the approach taken
in a 1959 paper by Robert Murphy on the Mundurukú men's cult:

> Murphy pointed out that the psychological roots of the cult draw
> on the universal emotional conflicts associated with the Oedipus
> complex. The simultaneous fear of women and antagonism toward
> them and the associated myths of matriarchy are reflections of
> the dark side of the family romance. Since the Oedipus complex
> is universal, Murphy wondered, "why are we not all swinging
> bullroarers?" His answer is that men's cults appear to flourish in social
> environments where the unity of groups of men and groups of women
> is not blurred by competing modes of role allocation such as derive
> from political hierarchy or kinship. The small horticultural societies of
> Amazonia and Melanesia fit this description.[43]

Do you see what's being sold to us here? Wrapped up in the same package
of ideas that portrays the cults as the outcome of deep-rooted psychological
complexes, we're also being asked to accept that these complexes manifest in
the same distinctive ways in Melanesia and Amazonia **because** of the state of
economic development of these societies.

Both propositions are profoundly reductionist. The first seeks to reduce
the remarkably similar details of male behavior in both regions to underlying
psychiatric issues. The second seeks to reduce the cultural expression of such
issues to the specific socioeconomic circumstances of small horticultural societies—as though flutes, trumpets, bullroarers, initiation ceremonies, ritual
prohibitions, and gang rape and murder for those who break them can be
expected to appear, almost automatically, in such societies.

There are other options, and the most obvious that immediately springs to
mind is diffusion. Throughout human history, ideas, religions, cults, and rit-

uals have always traveled far. Why, therefore, should they not have done so in prehistory as well? As we've seen, Gregor and Tuzin do admit that at one time leading anthropologists were convinced that diffusion of ideas "from a single center" was the best explanation for the strange cultural similarities between Melanesia and Amazonia. Other than adding that subsequently "the diffusionist school of anthropology waned,"[44] however, Gregor and Tuzin barely give the notion a second thought. Their whole focus remains throughout on psychological and sociological explanations.

Who knows? They could be right. They have certainly done a wonderful job of assembling the comparative cultural data, and if I were assessing that data in isolation, if it were just the bizarre and idiosyncratic similarities that keep on cropping up, *if that were all there were to it,* then I might be impressed by their proposed sociological psychodrama.

But that's by no means all there is to it.

First and foremost, there's that totally unexpected Australo-Melanesian genetic signal among Amazonian peoples, discovered in 2015, which Gregor and Tuzin could not have been aware of in 2001. The very fact that it's there at all means that diffusion of some kind can no longer be ruled out.

Second, there's more than a hint of a connection from cranial morphology.

Third, Australo-Melanesia and Amazonia constitute the world's largest surviving reservoirs of linguistic diversity, suggesting that their languages have extremely ancient roots.

And now, fourth, we find complex and multilayered similarities in cultural institutions and beliefs in both these widely separated regions.

It stretches credulity to put the simultaneous occurrence of all these factors down to coincidence.

A more "parsimonious explanation," I believe, is that something else must have been going on, some other process must have been under way behind the scenes, *some other hand must have been at work,* that hasn't yet been accounted for.

APPENDIX 2

ANCIENT MAPS OF THE ICE AGE

The Waldseemüller World Map of 1507 (**next page**) is notable for the apparent extreme inaccuracy with which sixteenth-century Southeast Asia and Australia are represented.

By contrast the map offers a much closer match to the region as it appeared in the depths of the Ice Age around 21,300 years ago, when Sahul and Sunda (modern Southeast Asia and Australia) formed an almost continuous landmass.

Waldseemüller's and other similar maps of the sixteenth century were produced by copying from older source maps while attempting to incorporate into them information from the voyages of discovery of Columbus and other later mariners.

Deriving from the discarded and lost older source maps, the portrayal of

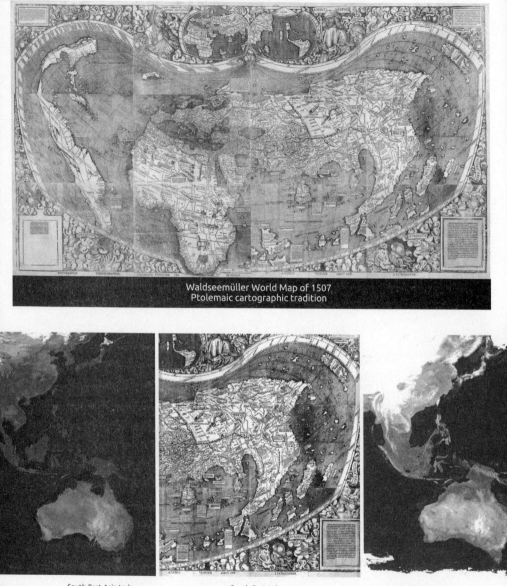

Waldseemüller World Map of 1507
Ptolemaic cartographic tradition

South-East Asia today

South-East Asia,
Waldseemüller 1507

South-East Asia,
21,300 years ago

geographical features last present during the Ice Age hints at the existence of a lost civilization that was capable of exploring and mapping the earth in remotest prehistory.

ANTEDILUVIAN CARTOGRAPHY?

It is the—at first surprising—hypothesis of Professor Robert Fuson of the University of South Florida that the island named "Satanaze" on the 1424 Pizzagano Chart, though incorrectly located in the Atlantic Ocean, is, arguably, the earliest-surviving representation of Japan in European cartography. Professor Fuson's 1995 book *Legendary Islands of the Ocean Sea*,[1] in which he makes this case with a mass of corroborative evidence, came to my attention while I was researching my own book *Underworld*, published in 2002.

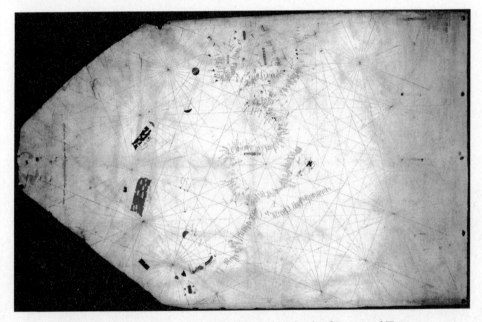

The 1424 Pizzagano Chart incorrectly locates the islands of Japan and Taiwan (respectively nominated as Satanaze and Antilia) in the Atlantic Ocean. Santanaze is the northernmost of the two dark landmasses shown at mid-left on the Chart.

I'm convinced by Professor Fuson's argument, but what I suggest is equally significant about it is a matter that Fuson himself does not comment on, leaving open the opportunity for me to explore it at some length in *Underworld*—namely that "Satanaze"/Japan is **not** depicted as the principal Japanese islands would have looked in 1424, when details from older source maps were copied onto the Pizzagano Chart, but rather as Japan would have

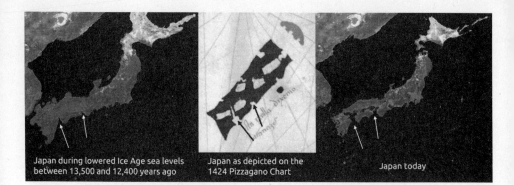

Japan during lowered Ice Age sea levels between 13,500 and 12,400 years ago

Japan as depicted on the 1424 Pizzagano Chart

Japan today

appeared during the lowered sea levels of the last Ice Age, in a very specific interlude, between 13,500 and 12,400 years ago, spanning the cataclysmic onset of the Younger Dryas.[2]

During that interlude the three principal Japanese islands, Honshu, Kyushu, and Shikoku, (**above right**) were all conjoined to form a single large island, as depicted in the sea-level-rise map (**above left**), based on modern geological studies.[3] The depiction of "Satanaze" on the Pizzagano Chart (**above center**), also shows Honshu, Kyushu, and Shikoku as one island and accurately depicts the inlets that existed between 13,500 and 12,400 years ago southwest and northeast of what would later become the island of Shikoku.

A similar state of affairs presents itself on the other side of the world in a representation of Ireland and its surrounding waters in the *Ptolemaeus Argentinae* map of 1513 (**below left**). **Below right** is a bathymetric map of Ireland

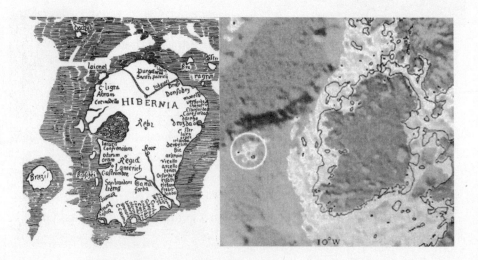

and the surrounding seas with a resolution of 2 minutes. Depth can be gauged through the shading as well as by the contour line, which is placed at 55 meters beneath today's sea level. The bathymetry reveals that around 13,000 years ago, during the lowered sea levels of the Ice Age, a significant island, with an area of perhaps 100 square kilometers, occupied the exact location where the supposedly "legendary" island named "Brazil" appears on the *Ptolemaeus Argentinae* map of 1513.[4]

The implication, again, is that some unknown civilization explored the earth during the Ice Age and that copies of copies of scraps of the maps made by its seafarers and navigators survived to be used as sources of reference by cartographers in the late Middle Ages.

A clear line of transmission through the library of Alexandria via Constantinople and thence into Europe during the era of the Crusades is traced in *Fingerprints of the Gods* for those who wish to follow the matter further.[5]

THE HOLE AT THE BOTTOM OF THE WORLD

Antarctica remained undiscovered by the seafarers and navigators of our civilization until the year 1819, and accordingly does not feature on early-nineteenth-century maps, such as the Pinkerton map of 1818 (**below left**). **To the right of it**, for comparison, is a modern map of Antarctica.

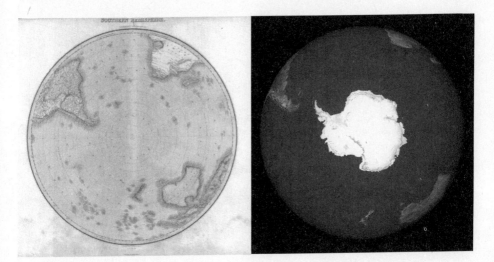

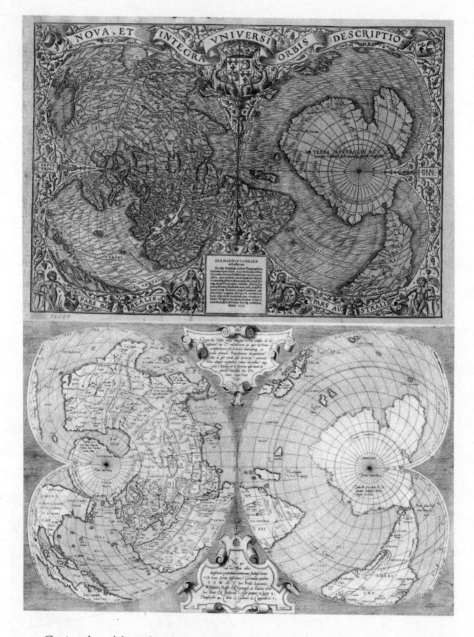

Curiously, although supposedly undiscovered at that time, Antarctica does appear on several maps from the sixteenth century, such as the Oronteus Finnaeus world map (**top**), and **below it** the Mercator world map, which in turn were copied from older source maps now lost.[6]

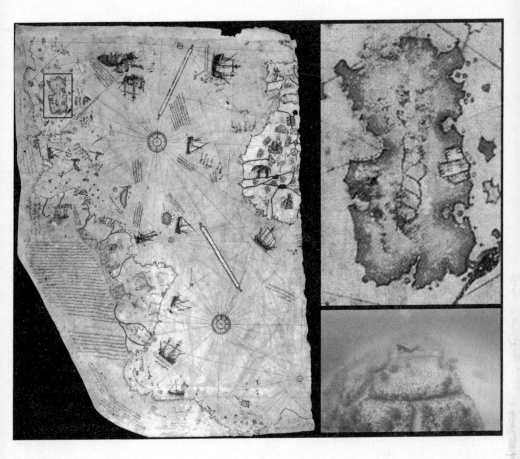

ISLAND OF MEGALITHS

The Piri Reis map of 1513 features the western shores of Africa and the eastern shores of North and South America and is also controversially claimed to depict Ice Age Antarctica—as an extension of the southern tip of South America. I report this claim in *Fingerprints of the Gods*.[7]

The same map (**above left and top right**) depicts a large island lying east of the southeast coast of what is now the United States. Also clearly depicted running along the spine of this island is a "road" of huge megaliths. In this exact spot during the lowered sea levels of the Ice Age a large island was indeed located until approximately 12,400 years ago. A remnant survives today in the form of the islands of Andros and Bimini. Underwater off Bimini (**above,**

lower right and below) I have scuba-dived on a road of great megaliths exactly like those depicted **above water** on the Piri Reis map.

Again, the implication, regardless of the separate controversy of whether the so-called Bimini Road is a man-made or natural feature, is that the region must have been explored and mapped before the great floods at the end of the Ice Age caused the sea level to rise and submerged the megaliths.

FIRST THERE WAS A FOREST,
THEN THERE WAS NO FOREST,
THEN THERE WAS . . .

What sort of place was the Amazon during the Ice Age? What was its climate? And what about the environment, vegetation, and trees?

Given the enormous importance of the world's largest surviving rainforest in global ecology today, I had assumed the subject would have been well studied and that the experts would long ago have reached a consensus. In the case of the former I was correct but in the case of the latter I was not—for there is an ever-shifting consensus that, when you get right down to it, is pretty much the same thing as no consensus at all.

Here's a brief timeline of the debate as I see it:

1. Prior to and into the 1990s, the scientific consensus supported the view that the Amazon had been largely arid during the Ice Age, with isolated rainforest "refugia" broken up by extensive areas of savanna and open vegetation.

2. From the mid-1990s onward, into the early years of the twenty-first century, this entire view came under attack and, out of the dispute, a new consensus emerged in which the Amazon had "always" (anyway for millions of years) been a rainforest, much as it is now.

3. Finally, in the past decade or so the consensus appears to have shifted again and we are told that actually, yes, much of the Amazon was savanna during the Ice Age, and that the tropical rainforest we see today has been present for at most 7,000 or 8,000 years—and barely 2,000 years in some areas.

It's instructive to spend a few moments sampling the flavor and character of this shifting consensus. Let's start with a paper by P. A. Colinvaux, P. E. De Oliveira, and M. B. Bush, published in January 2000 in *Quaternary Science Reviews,* that confirms the overthrow of the earlier, pre-1990s paradigm of an arid savanna interspersed with rainforest refugia:

Our conclusion that the Amazon lowlands were forested in glacial times specifically refutes the hypothesis of Amazonian glacial aridity.[1]

A few months later, Katherine Willis and Robert Whittaker of Oxford University published similar conclusions in *Science*:

The evidence clearly indicates that the lowland tropical forests were not extensively replaced by savanna vegetation during the glacial periods, but rather that the forests dominated throughout.[2]

In the following year, 2001, a study published in *Palaeogeography, Palaeoclimatology, Palaeoecology* concluded:

In the later Pleistocene the whole of the Amazon lowlands were under closed-canopy forest throughout all stages of a glacial cycle, contrary to the biogeographical consensus of the last thirty years.[3]

A 2003 study published in the journal *Geology* reinforced this view:

The current tropical rainforest vegetation has been a permanent and dominant feature of the Amazon River watershed over the past 70 k.y. Specifically, we found no evidence for the development of large savannas that had been previously postulated as indicators of increased glacial aridity in Amazonia.[4]

A further study, published in November 2004 in *Palaeogeography, Palaeoclimatology, Palaeoecology,* investigated the Hill of Six Lakes in the Northwest Brazilian Amazon and concluded:

The data indicate the continuous presence of mesic forest throughout the last ice age. . . . Even during lowstand episodes, pollen is well preserved and provides a clear signal of uninterrupted forest cover.[5]

But now let's jump forward to 2013, when a follow-up study of the Hill of Six Lakes, published in *Quaternary Sciences Reviews,* lamented the great length of time that "Six Lakes was erroneously used as an emblematic locality to illustrate the permanence of the rainforest in the Amazon basin"[6] because:

all of the proxies seem to indicate that the present-day vegetation dates back to the middle-late Holocene, around 6 cal ka BP.[7]

And a year later, in July 2014, a study in the *Proceedings of the National Academy of Sciences* reduced the inception of the present-day forest cover of some parts of the Amazon to just 2,000 years ago or less. Focusing on southern Amazonia, the study concluded that:

the inhabitants exploited a naturally open savanna landscape that they maintained around their settlement despite the climatically driven rainforest expansion that began ~2,000 years ago across the region.[8]

Last, in *Quaternary Science Reviews* of October 1, 2017, Professor Diana Fontes and Professor Renato Cordeiro published a study titled "Paleoenvironmental Dynamics in South Amazonia, Brazil, during the Last 35,000 Years Inferred from Pollen and Geochemical Records of Lago do Saci." Their conclusion, although they state that "the rainforest always existed in this region," is that it underwent "expansion and regression" over time.[9]

There are many other papers I could cite reflecting the shifting consensus, but I'm sure the reader has got my point by now. When leading scientific authorities are in such a state of disagreement that prevailing paradigms abruptly change every decade or two, we cannot be at all sure of the solidity and merits of the current paradigm—according to which the Amazon rainforest in its present form is less than 8,000 years old, and in some areas less than 2,000 years old.

Reviewing the literature, I felt that the conclusion of Fontes and Cordeiro, that there was always rainforest in the area they studied but that it was subject to periodic expansions and contractions, might help to explain why consensus on this subject has been so elusive. The Amazon basin is, after all, a vast and diverse region encompassing more than 7 million square kilometers, of which approximately 5.5 million square kilometers are presently covered by rainforest.[10] The figures only become meaningful by comparison. The whole of India, with a total area of 2.97 million km², is less than half the size of the Amazon basin, but Australia, at 7.68 million km² is bigger, as are China (9.38 million km²), Canada (9.09 million km²), the United States (9.15 million km²), and Europe (10.18 million km²).[11] All in all, then, it's fair to say that what the Amazon confronts us with is a truly gigantic landmass, on a scale similar to many of the world's largest countries and regions, extending for thousands of kilometers from north to south and thousands of kilometers from east to west. It's unrealistic to suppose that, across such enormous distances over great expanses of time, the climate and environment in all areas would always remain the same. Of course there would be significant variations among the different regions and from epoch to epoch, and thus a danger of overenthusiastic extrapolation from particular instances to general conclusions.

On March 12, 2018, therefore, I contacted Renato Cordeiro about the whole issue of the shifting consensus and what conclusions I might legitimately draw from it. "I must confess," I told him, "that expert opinion on the Ice Age Amazon is very confusing and contradictory! I want to try to sort out the facts for my readers, as those facts are understood now, if they are indeed subject to any kind of consensus today."[12]

Professor Cordeiro teaches geoeconomics at Brazil's Universidad Federal Fluminense. His rather technical reply, set out in full in the note, essentially restated the conclusions of his 2017 paper, that the Amazon basin has always contained rainforests, that the gallery forests along the rivers remained "relatively well preserved" even in drier periods, but that in other areas tree cover has undergone considerable fluctuation over time.[13]

It was as close as I was able to get to some kind of answer to what I had thought would be a simple question, namely, what sort of climate, environment, vegetation, and trees characterized the Amazon during the Ice Age? The scholars did not agree among themselves and many different pictures had been painted, but perhaps this was largely because of the immensity of the region and the complex, constantly changing, and often contradictory nature of the data.

Indeed, there is only one thing I have been able to find that all the involved scientists appear to be in complete agreement on, and this is that the region was significantly cooler during the Ice Age—5 or 6 degrees C cooler—than it is now.[14] The year-round average temperature of the Amazon rainforest today is 80 degrees F (26.6 degrees C) so, if anything, a reduction of 5 degrees to 21.6 degrees C/75 degrees F would have been a bonus for prospective settlers.

So . . . forests? Savanna? A mixture of both? Like so much else about the ancient Amazon, it seems there is no certain answer.

NOTES

INTRODUCTION

1. Samuel Noah Kramer, *History Begins at Sumer: Thirty-Nine Firsts in Man's Recorded History* (University of Pennsylvania Press, 1991).
2. Plato, *Timaeus and Critias* (Penguin Books, 1977), 131.
3. Ibid., 37.
4. See, for example, Lewis Spence, *Atlantis in America* (Ernest Benn, 1925); Frank Joseph, *Atlantis in Wisconsin: New Revelations about the Sunken City* (Galde Press, 1995); Ivor Zapp and George Erikson, *Atlantis in America: Navigators of the Ancient World* (Adventures Unlimited Press, 1998).

PART I

1: AN ENCHANTED REALM

1. "Around 12,000 years ago" is, of course, an approximation, a ballpark figure that I will use throughout to allow for margins of error in the data that are constantly being adjusted in the light of ongoing research. From the point of view of my argument, 1,000 years in either direction makes no difference—that is, the point is that the Americas have been isolated from the rest of the world for a VERY long time and my position does not alter whether that time is 13,000 years, 12,000 years, or 11,000 years. Recent work suggests that the Bering land bridge may not have been fully inundated until around 11,000 years ago. See M. Jakobsson et al., "Post-Glacial Flooding of the Bering Land Bridge Dated to 11 cal ka BP Based on New Geophysical and Sediment Records," *Climate of the Past* 13, no. 8 (2017), 991. Also see p. 105 of B. M. Pelto et al, "Oceanographic and Climatic Change in the Bering Sea, Last Glacial Maximum to Holocene," *Paleoceanography and Paleoclimatology* 33, no. 1 (2018), 93–111.

2. Robert V. Fletcher et al, "Serpent Mound: A Fort Ancient Icon?" *Midcontinental Journal of Archaeology* 21 (Spring 1996), 105.

3. Keith A. Milam, "A Revised Diameter for Serpent Mound Impact Crater in Southern Ohio," *Ohio Journal of Science* (Ohio Academy of Science) 110, no. 3 (June 2010), 34–43; see also William F. Romain, "LiDAR Views of the Serpent Mound Impact Crater," *Current Research in Ohio Archaeology* (2011), www.ohioarchaeology.org.

4. See, for example, C. Bull, C. E. Corbato, and J. C. Zahn, "Gravity Survey of the Serpent Mound Area, Southern Ohio," *Ohio Journal of Science* 67, no. 6 (1967), 359.

5. Mark C. Hansen, "Return to Sunken Mountain: The Serpent Mound Cryptoexplosion Structure," *Ohio Geology* (Winter 1994), 1–7.

6. Richard W. Carlton et al., "Discovery of Microscopic Evidence for Shock Metamorphism at the Serpent Mound Structure, South-central Ohio: Confirmation of an Origin by Impact," *Earth and Planetary Sciences Letters* 162, issues 1–4 (October 1998), 184. Also see, for example, Andrew Schedl, "Applications of Twin Analysis to Studying Meteorite Impact Structures," *Earth and Planetary Science Letters* 244 (2006), 530–540, and geologist Mark Baranoski cited in Bill Meyer, "Unearthing Clues at Serpent Mound: Geologists Find Evidence of a Meteor Crash Near Prehistoric Monument in Adams County," *Plain Dealer,* April 12, 2009, online here: http://blog.cleveland.com/pdextra/2009/04/unearthing_clues_at_serpent_mo.html.

7. Hansen, "Return to Sunken Mountain," 4. See also p. 1.

8. See, for example, Schedl, "Applications of Twin Analysis to Studying Meteorite Impact Structures," 530.

9. See, for example, Romain, "LiDAR Views of the Serpent Mound Impact Crater," 4.

10. Mark Baranoski cited in Bill Meyer, "Unearthing Clues at Serpent Mound: Geologists Find Evidence of a Meteor Crash Near Prehistoric Monument in Adams County," *Plain Dealer,* April 12, 2009, http://blog.cleveland.com/pdextra/2009/04/unearthing_clues_at_serpent_mo.html.

11. Raymond Anderson, cited in ibid.

12. See, for example, D. R. Watts et al., "The Serpent Mound Magnetic Anomaly: Fingerprint of a Meteorite Impact?" *Online Journal for E&P Geoscientists* 90930 (1998), http://www.searchanddiscovery.com/abstracts/html/1998/eastern/abstracts/1776a.htm.

13. William Romain, "Terrestrial Observations of the Serpent Mound," *Ohio Archaeologist* 38, no. 2 (Spring 1988), 15–16.

14. Hansen, "Return to Sunken Mountain," 2.

15. Ross Hamilton, *The Mystery of the Serpent Mound* (North Atlantic Books, 2001).

16. The steps have since been removed. Personal communication from Ross Hamilton, August 24, 2018.

17. Robert C. Glotzhober and Bradley T. Lepper, *Serpent Mound: Ohio's Enigmatic Effigy Mound* (Ohio Historical Society, Columbus, Ohio, 1994), 3.

18. Charles C. Willoughby, "The Serpent Mound of Adams County, Ohio," *American Anthropologist,* New Series 21, no. 2 (April–June 1919), 157–158.

19. Herman Bender, "The Spirit of Manitou Across America," *Archaeology Experiences Spirituality?* ed. Dragos Gheorghiu (Cambridge Scholars Publishing, 2011), 143.

20. Ibid., 143–144.

21. In 1900 Harvard's Peabody Museum, which had formerly managed the Serpent Mound site, deeded it to the Ohio Archaeological and Historical Society (more recently the Ohio Historical Society, now the Ohio History Connection), http://worldheritageohio.org/serpent-mound/. In its 2015 *Historic Site Management Plan for Serpent Mound,* the following statement is made by the Ohio History Connection on pp. 41–42: "There is debate as to the number of solar, lunar, and planetary alignments that were intended by the original architects of Serpent Mound. Until there is additional study and agreement regarding these other possible alignments, trees will not be moved or trimmed to accommodate viewing them. Tree shade is critical for visitors' enjoyment of the site."

22. Ephraim G. Squier and Edwin H. Davis, *Ancient Monuments of the Mississippi Valley* (Smithsonian Institution, Washington, DC, 1848, reprinted and republished by the Smithsonian, with an introduction by David J. Meltzer, in 1998), 97.

23. Ibid., 97.

24. Ibid., 97–98.

25. Ibid., 98.

2: A JOURNEY IN TIME

1. J. T. Faith and T. A. Surovell, "Synchronous Extinction of North America's Pleistocene Mammals," *Proceedings of the National Academy of Sciences* 106, no. 49 (2009), 20641–20645. See p. 20641: "Results favor an extinction mechanism that is capable of wiping out up to 35 genera across a continent in a geologic instant." Faith and Surovell give dates in **uncalibrated radiocarbon years** (rather than in calendar years) as occupying a broader range between roughly 12,000 and 10,000 radiocarbon years before the present. Please note that "radiocarbon years" and actual calendar years drift further apart the farther back in time we go, hence the introduction of techniques of calibration.

2. Ibid. See also R. B. Firestone et al., "Evidence for an Extraterrestrial Impact 12,900 Years Ago That Contributed to the Megafaunal Extinctions and the Younger Dryas Cooling," *Proceedings of the National Academy of Sciences* 104, no. 41 (October 9, 2007), 16016.

3. M. P. Pearson, "The Sarsen Stones of Stonehenge," *Proceedings of the Geologists' Association* 127, no. 3 (2016), 363–369, esp. 364.

4. M. Pitts, "Stonehenge Special," in *British Archaeology* (Council for British Archaeology) (2018), 10–12, https://reader.exacteditions.com/issues/62211/spread/1.

5. Ibid.

6. The Sphinx/yardang theory was first proposed by Farouk El-Baz, research professor and director of the Center for Remote Sensing at Boston University, in "Gifts of the Nile," *Archaeology* 54, no. 2 (March/April 2001), 42–45. See also Ted A. Maxwell of the Smithsonian Institution, "Inspired by Nature," *Archaeology* (November/December 2001), 6.

7. El-Baz, "Gifts of the Nile," 45.

8. Clarke Hardman Jr. and Marjorie H. Hardman, "The Great Serpent and the Sun," *Ohio Archaeologist* 37, no. 3 (Fall 1987), 34–39.

9. Ephraim G. Squier and Edwin H. Davis, *Ancient Monuments of the Mississippi Valley* (Smithsonian Institution, Washington, DC, 1848, reprinted and republished by the Smithsonian, with an introduction by David J. Meltzer, in 1998), 97.

10. Hardman and Hardman, "The Great Serpent and the Sun," 35.

11. William F. Romain, "Serpent Mound Revisited," *Ohio Archaeologist* 37, no. 4 (Winter 1987), 5.

12. *The Astronomical Almanac* (2018), "Glossary: Obliquity": http://asa.usno.navy.mil/SecM/Glossary.html#_O.

13. J. D. Hays, John Imbrie, and N. J. Shackleton, "Variations in the Earth's Orbit: Pacemaker of the Ice Ages," *Science* 194, no. 4270 (December 10, 1976), 1125.

14. Anthony F. Aveni, *Skywatchers of Ancient Mexico* (University of Texas Press, 1980), 103.

15. Romain, "Serpent Mound Revisited," 5. Based on Anthony F. Aveni, "Astronomical Tables Intended for Use in Astro-archaeological Studies," *American Antiquity* 37 (4), (1972), 531–540, and assuming 1-degree horizon elevation and observation of the center of the sun.

16. Robert Fletcher and Terry Cameron, "Serpent Mound: A New Look at an Old Snake-in-the-Grass," *Ohio Archaeologist* 38, no. 1 (Winter 1988).

17. Romain, "Serpent Mound Revisited," 5.

18. William F. Romain, *Mysteries of the Hopewell: Astronomers, Geometers and Magicians of the Eastern Woodlands* (University of Akron Press, 2000), 247.

19. Ibid., 248.

20. Ibid.

21. Robert V. Fletcher et al., "Serpent Mound: A Fort Ancient Icon?" *Midcontinental Journal of Archaeology* 21(Spring 1996), 105.

22. Ibid., 105–143.

23. Ibid.

24. Ibid.

25. The process is reflected in uncritical coverage given to the new dates in the archaeological press. See, for example, Jessica E. Saraceni, "Redating Serpent Mound," *Archaeology* 49, no. 5 (November/December 1996), https://archive.archaeology.org/9611/newsbriefs/serpentmound.html.

26. See, for example, Bill Meyer, "Unearthing Clues at Serpent Mound: Geologists Find Evidence of a Meteor Crash Near Prehistoric Monument in Adams County," *Plain Dealer*, April 12, 2009: "Lepper has new evidence of the mound's age. Originally it was thought to have been built sometime between 800 BC and AD 100. That estimate was moved up after two pieces of charcoal recently collected at the mound were subjected to radiocarbon dating. 'It came out to around 1070 A.D,'

Lepper said." http://blog.cleveland.com/pdextra/2009/04/unearthing_clues_at_serpent_mo.html.

27. See image of Serpent Mound visitors' information plaque, by "Stetshep," filed on Wikimedia Commons, https://commons.wikimedia.org/wiki/File:Serpent_Mound_Plaque.jpg.

28. Fletcher et al., "Serpent Mound: A Fort Ancient Icon?" 105.

29. Ibid., 115.

30. Ibid., 122.

31. Ibid., 124–125.

32. Ibid., 132.

33. Ibid., 133.

34. Ibid.

35. Cited in Saraceni, "Redating Serpent Mound."

36. Cited in Meyer, "Unearthing Clues at Serpent Mound."

37. William F. Romain, "LiDAR Views of the Serpent Mound Impact Crater," *Current Research in Ohio Archaeology* 2011(www.ohioarchaeology.org), 1.

38. Edward W. Herrmann et al., "A New Multistage Construction Chronology for the Great Serpent Mound, USA," *Journal of Archaeological Science* 50 (October 2014), 119.

39. Ibid., 121.

40. Ibid., 122.

41. Bradley T. Lepper, "On the Age of Serpent Mound: A Reply to Romain and Colleagues," *Midcontinental Journal of Archaeology* 43, no. 1 (February 2018), 62–75. And in the same issue, pp. 76–88, see William F. Romain and Edward W. Herrmann, "Rejoinder to Lepper Concerning Serpent Mound."

42. See, for example, ancient American snake symbolism documented in R. H. Hall, *An Archaeology of the Soul: North American Indian Belief and Ritual* (University of Illinois Press, 1997), 92: "In the ritual language of the Winnebago Medicine Rite we know that reincarnation was referred to as 'skin shedding.' This is easy to understand from the example of serpents that shed their skin periodically and emerge symbolically reborn. It is but one short step to actually shedding the skin of a sacrificial victim to represent rebirth in the manner of Xipe Totec." See also S. Linda and D. Freidel, *A Forest of Kings: The Untold Story of the Ancient Maya* (William Morrow, 1990), 359. The Mayan serpent similarly served as a symbol of birth and renewal.

43. Herrmann et al., "A New Multistage Construction Chronology for the Great Serpent Mound, USA," 121, 124.

44. Ibid., 124.

45. Ibid.

46. Ibid.

47. Fletcher et al., "Serpent Mound: A Fort Ancient Icon?" 132–133.

48. Ibid., p. 133.

3: THE DRAGON AND THE SUN

1. Ross Hamilton, *The Mystery of the Serpent Mound* (North Atlantic Books, 2001).

2. D. W. Mathisen, "How to Find the Four Important Heavenly Serpents," on The Mathisen Corollary (blog) (05/18/17), "The fourth of the important heavenly serpents . . . is the Dragon of Draco:"https://mathisencorollary.blogspot.com/2017/05/. For ancient cultures that depicted Draco as a serpent or dragon, see the interpretation of ancient Greek and Roman cosmic symbolism in D. Ogden, *Drakon: Dragon Myth and Serpent Cult in the Greek and Roman Worlds* (Oxford University Press, 2013); see, for example, p. 164: "The constellation of Draco was taken to recall various *drakōn* fights. The sixth-century BC Epimenides told that when Zeus was attacked by Cronus, he hid by transforming himself into a *drakōn*, and his nurses into bears, and subsequently celebrated this by installing the adjacent constellations of Draco and the Bears in the heavens."

3. Giorgio de Santillana and Hertha von Dechend, *Hamlet's Mill: An Essay Investigating the Origins of Human Knowledge and Its Transmission Through Myth* (Nonpareil Books, 1977, reprinted 1999), 59.

4. Ibid.

5. See, for example, E. N. Kaurov, "The Draco Constellation: The Ancient Chinese Astronomical Practice of Observations," *Astronomical and Astrophysical Transactions* 15, nos. 1–4, (1998), 325–341, esp. 325: "The Draco constellation is one of the oldest ancient constellations. It is apparently connected with the very archaic practice of observations and with an ancient Chinese astronomical observational practice during the most ancient times."

6. The quotation is from Erasmus Darwin's *The Botanic Garden*, 1791:

With vast convolutions Draco holds
Th' ecliptic axis in his scaly folds.
O'er half the skies his neck enormous rears,
And with immense meanders parts the Bears.

7. Charles C. Willoughby, "The Serpent Mound of Adams County, Ohio," *American Anthropologist,* New Series 21, no. 2 (April–June 1919), 153.
8. W. H. Holmes, *Science* 8, no. 204 (December 31, 1886), 627–628. I have taken the liberty of altering Holmes's original spelling of *manito* to the more usual *manitou.*
9. Hamilton, *The Mystery of the Serpent Mound,* 22.
10. Ibid.
11. *The Ancient Egyptian Book of the Dead,* trans. E. A. Wallis Budge (first published in Great Britain in 1889, reprinted by Arkana, London and New York, 1985), 14.

PART II

4: A PAST NOT SO MUCH HIDDEN AS DENIED
1. Email from Rebecca Handelsman dated September 20, 2017.
2. Steven R. Holen, Thomas A. Deméré, et al., "A 130,000-Year-Old Archaeological Site in Southern California, USA," *Nature* 544 (April 27, 2017), 479ff.
3. More on Professor Grayson can be found here: https://anthropology.washington.edu/people/donald-k-grayson.
4. Interviewed by *BuzzFeed News* for its April 26, 2017, article "Don't Believe the Big Story About Humans Roaming America 130,000 Years Ago," https://www.buzzfeed.com/danvergano/mastodon-mash.
5. Cited in the *Guardian,* London, April 28, 2017, "Could History of Humans in North America Be Rewritten by Broken Bones?" https://www.theguardian.com/science/2017/apr/26/could-history-of-humans-in-north-america-be-rewritten-by-broken-mastodon-bones.
6. Cited in Thomas Curwen, "Archaeology as Blood Sport: How the Discovery of an Ancient Mastodon Ignited Debate over Humans' Arrival in North America," *Los Angeles Times,* December 22, 2017, http://www.latimes.com/local/california/la-me-cerutti-mastodon-20171222-htmlstory.html.
7. Cited in Gary Haynes, "The Cerutti Mastodon," *PalaeoAmerica* 3, no. 3 (June 21, 2017), 196ff. See also Lizzie Wade, "Claim of Very Early Human Presence in Americas Shocks Researchers," *Science* (April 28, 2017).
8. Cited in Curwen, "Archaeology as Blood Sport."
9. Email exchange of September 26, 2017.
10. Ibid.
11. Email exchange of October 10, 2017.
12. Cited in Christopher Hardaker, *The First American* (New Page Books, 2007), 183. See also David E. Stannard, *American Holocaust* (Oxford University Press, 1992), 261, who states a figure of 6,000 years: "Until the 1930's it generally was believed that the earliest human inhabitants of the Americas had moved from the Alaskan portion of Beringia to what is now known as North America no more than 6,000 years ago."
13. For evidence pertaining to anatomically modern human presence in Asia at c. 65,000 years ago see, for example: Chris Clarkson et al., "Human Occupation of Northern Australia by 65,000 Years Ago," *Nature* (July 20, 2017); Kira. E. Westaway et al., "An Early Modern Human Presence in Sumatra by 73,000–63,000 Years Ago," *Nature* (August 17, 2017); Sue O'Connor et al., "New Evidence from East Timor Contributes to Our Understanding of Earliest Modern Human Colonisation East of the Sunda Shelf," *Antiquity* (September 1, 2007); Qiaomei Fu et al., "Genome Sequence of a 45,000-Year-Old Modern Human from Western Siberia," *Nature* (October 23, 2014); Israel Hershgovitz et al., "The Earliest Modern Humans Outside Africa," *Nature* (January 26, 2018); Wu Liu et al., "The Earliest Unequivocally Modern Humans in Southern China," *Nature* 526 (October 29, 2015); Fabrice Demeter et al., "Anatomically Modern Human in Southeast Asia (Laos) by 46 ka," *Proceedings of the National Academy of Sciences* 109, no. 36 (September 4, 2012).
14. See discussion in Charles C. Mann, *1491: New Revelations of the Americas Before Columbus,* 2nd ed. (Vintage Books, 2011), 167–174. See also Anthony T. Boldurian and John L. Cotter, *Clovis Revisited: New Perspectives on Paleoindian Adaptions from Blackwater Draw, New Mexico* (University Museum, University of Pennsylvania, 1999), 2.

15. Frank H. H. Roberts Jr., "Developments in the Problem of the North American Paleo-Indian," *Essays in Historical Anthropology of North America Published in Honor of John R. Swanton, Smithsonian Miscellaneous Collections* 100 (May 25, 1940), 52. See also Gordon G. Wiley and Jeremy A. Sablof, *A History of American Archaeology* (W. H. Freeman, 1993), 50.

16. Boldurian and Cotter, *Clovis Revisited,* xviii. See also A. T. Boldurian, "James Ridgley Whiteman Memorial," *Plains Anthropologist* 49, no. 189 (2004), 85–90, esp. 87.

17. In 1934, on the strength of his work at Blackwater Draw, he became a research associate of the Carnegie Institution in Washington, DC. See J. Alden Mason, "Edgar Billings Howard, 1887–1943," *American Antiquity* 9, no. 2 (October 1943), 230–234.

18. Eastern Mexico University, "Blackwater Draw," https://web.archive.org/web/20080523174557/http://www.enmu.edu/services/museums/blackwater-draw/index.shtml.

19. Edgar B. Howard, *Evidence of Early Man in North America* (University Museum, Philadelphia, 1935), and review by Florence M. Hawley in *American Anthropologist,* New Series 39 (1937), 139–140.

20. Academy of Natural Sciences Philadelphia, *Nature,* January 16, 1937, 103–104.

21. Cited in Mann, *1491,* 173.

22. Charles C. Mann, "The Clovis Point and the Discovery of America's First Culture," *Smithsonian,* November 2013, https://www.smithsonianmag.com/history/the-clovis-point-and-the-discovery-of-americas-first-culture-3825828/.

23. David B. Madsen, "A Framework for the Initial Occupation of the Americas," *PalaeoAmerica* 1, no. 3 (2015), 218–219.

24. Ibid.

25. Gary Haynes, *The Early Settlement of North America* (Cambridge University Press, 2002), 2–3 and 265. See also Kaitlyn A. Thomas et al., "Explaining the Origin of Fluting in North American Pleistocene Weaponry," *Journal of Archaeological Science* 81 (May 2017), 23ff.

26. Thomas et al., "Explaining the Origin of Fluting in North American Pleistocene Weaponry," 24. See also Michael R. Waters, Steven L. Forman, et al., "The Buttermilk Creek Complex and the Origins of Clovis at the Debra L. Friedkin Site, Texas," *Science* 331 (March 25, 2011), 1599.

27. Madsen, "A Framework for the Initial Occupation of the Americas," 219. See also Daniel S. Amick, "Evolving Views on the Pleistocene Colonization of North America," *Quaternary International* 431, Part B (February 28, 2017), 125ff.

28. Mann, "The Clovis Point and the Discovery of America's First Culture." See also: Ohio History Connection, "Clovis Culture 9000 B.C. to 8000 B.C.," http://www.ohiohistorycentral.org/w/Clovis_Culture?rec=2044.

29. Mann, "The Clovis Point and the Discovery of America's First Culture:" "Most researchers believe that the rapid dissemination of Clovis points is evidence that a single way of life—the Clovis culture—swept across the continent in a flash. No other culture has dominated so much of the Americas."

30. See, for example, Kirk Bryan, *Geological Antiquity of the Lindenmeier Site in Colorado,* Smithsonian Miscellaneous Collections 99, no. 2 (Washington, DC, 1940), "It is believed by the writers that the age be much nearer 25,000 years than 10,000." The reference is to the Folsom culture, already established by that time to be younger than the Clovis culture.

31. C. Vance Haynes Jr., "Fluted Projectile Points: Their Age and Dispersion," *Science* 145 (September 25, 1964), 1408–1413. **Important note:** Haynes published his paper in 1964, before improvements in radiocarbon dating, notably "calibration," which takes account of different amounts of C-14 formed in the earth's atmosphere at different periods of the past and derives calendar years from radiocarbon years according to a sliding scale. Going back as far as the last Ice Age, dates in calendar years turn out to be increasingly older than dates given in radiocarbon years so that, for example, a radiocarbon age reading of 12,000 years ago corresponds, after calibration, with a calendar date of 13,800 years ago (see J. Tyler Faith and Todd A. Surovell, "Synchronous Extinction of North America's Pleistocene Mammals," *Proceedings of the National Academy of Sciences* 106, no. 49 (December 8, 2009), 20641). I have therefore taken the liberty in my text of replacing the dates given by Haynes in his 1964 paper with the dates most recently agreed and accepted by archaeologists.

32. Haynes, "Fluted Projectile Points," 1412.

33. Ibid., 1410–1411.

34. Ibid., 1412.

35. Ibid., 1411–1412.

36. Waters et al., "The Buttermilk Creek Complex and the Origins of Clovis at the Debra L. Friedkin Site, Texas," 1599.
37. Haynes, "Fluted Projectile Points," 1411–1412.
38. Ibid., 1412.
39. Mann, *1491*, 178: "The fractious archaeological community embraced his [Haynes's] ideas with rare unanimity; they rapidly became the standard model for the peopling of the Americas."
40. Hardaker, *The First American*, 9.
41. "Young Americans," *Nature* 485 (May 3, 2012), 6.
42. Tom Dillehay et al., "New Archaeological Evidence for an Early Human Presence at Monte Verde, Chile," *PLoS One* (November 18, 2015).
43. Mann, *1491*, 186, reports that fifty studies were dismissed. It is important to add, however, that Haynes's dismissals were often entirely justified. For example, in 1951 a crucial piece of evidence that Hrdlička had suppressed during his tenure at the Smithsonian was—commendably—brought to light by his successor T. Dale Stewart. The disclosure was low-profile, appearing only in the "Comments and Communications" section of the journal *Science* (April 6, 1951, 391), and it did not outright accuse Hrdlička of any malfeasance. The fact remained, nonetheless, that in Hrdlička's own files Stewart had found a paper published in the *American Naturalist* in 1895, that Hrdlička had "failed to mention" when he published his *Skeletal Remains Suggesting or Attributed to Early Man in North America* (Bureau of American Ethnology, Bulletin 33, 1907). "This might be expected, Stewart wrote: "Because Wilson's conclusions are contrary to those of Hrdlička. The latter concluded on morphological grounds that the Natchez pelvic bone was that of a recent Indian, whereas Wilson concluded from the fluorine content that this bone was as ancient as an associated Mylodon bone."
   Fossil bones absorb fluorine from soil and water, so fossils that have been in the same soil for the same length of time should have roughly the same amount of fluorine. The reason the paper caught Stewart's eye in 1951 was that two years previously, a fluorine test carried out on the remains of so-called Piltdown Man had proved them to be hundreds of thousands of years younger than they were supposed to be and set in motion the investigation that would lead in 1953 to the exposure of this embarrassing archaeological fraud. For the latest research on the Piltdown Man hoax see Isabelle De Groote et al., "New Genetic and Morphological Evidence Suggests a Single Hoaxer Created Piltdown Man," *Royal Society Open Science* 3, no. 8 (August 1, 2016).
   For Hrdlička to have ignored the compelling implications of the fluorine test results on the Natchez human pelvic bone, cutting-edge science in his day, was, to say the least, distinctly odd. He was vindicated, however, in April 1990 when C. Vance Haynes was sent a sample of the Natchez bone for radiocarbon dating and reported a relatively recent age of around just 5,000 years (see John L. Cotter, "Update on Natchez Man," *American Antiquity* 56, no. 1 (1991), 38). This turned out to be about 12,000 years younger than the associated mylodon fossil (now redesignated as *Glossotherium harlani,* a giant extinct ground sloth), which was radiocarbon dated to more than 17,000 years before the present (pp. 38–39).
   How had the two deposits of entirely different age become so muddled up that the younger one actually lay beneath the older one?
   The answer, and perhaps Hrdlička had noticed it, giving him what he would probably have regarded as sufficient justification to ignore the 1895 fluorine paper, was that the Natchez bone, together with the associated fossils of extinct megafauna, had been excavated in a ravine from a deposit of clay, "the talus of a neighboring cliff on of which were some old Indian graves." When the famed British geologist Sir Charles Lyell visited the site, he expressed the opinion that "although the human bone may have been contemporaneous with those of the extinct animals with which it had been found, he thought it more probable it had fallen from one of the Indian graves and had become mingled with the older fossils which were dislodged from the deeper part of the cliff. . . . In the wear of the cliff the upper portion, with the Indian graves and human bones, would be likely to fall first and the deeper portion with the older fossils subsequently on the latter" (Leidy cited in Cotter, "Update on Natchez Man," 37).
44. Cited by James Adovasio, *The First Americans: In Pursuit of Archaeology's Greatest Mystery* (Modern Library, paperback edition, 2003), 217.
45. Ibid.
46. Ibid., 219.
47. David J. Meltzer et al., "On the Pleistocene Antiquity of Monte Verde, Southern Chile," *American*

Antiquity 62, no. 4 (October 1997), 659–663. The reference to the 33,000 years BP date is on p. 662.

48. Adovasio, *The First Americans,* 217–230.
49. Ibid., 225.
50. J. M. Adovasio et al., "Meadowcroft Rockshelter, 1977: An Overview," *American Antiquity* 43, no. 4 (October 1978), 632–651.
51. Adovasio, *The First Americans,* 223.
52. National Historic Landmark Nomination, Meadowcroft Rockshelter, https://www.nps.gov/nhl/find/statelists/pa/Meadowcroft.pdf; Lauren Selker, "Meadowcroft: Peering into America's Ancient Past," Spring 2010, http://pabook2.libraries.psu.edu/palitmap/Meadowcroft.html.
53. Heather Pringle, "From Vilified to Vindicated: The Story of Jacques Cinq-Mars," *Hakai Magazine,* March 7, 2017, https://www.hakaimagazine.com/features/vilified-vindicated-story-jacques-cinq-mars/?xid=PS_smithsonian and at http://www.smithsonianmag.com/science-nature/jacques-cinq-mars-bluefish-caves-scientific-progress-180962410/#A1zGtDKtgySyduU6.99.
54. William Josie, director of natural resources at the Vuntut Gwitchin First Nation in Old Crow, cited in Pringle, "From Vilified to Vindicated."
55. Lauriane Bourgeon, Ariane Burke, and Thomas Higham, 'Earliest Human Presence in North America Dated to the Last Glacial Maximum: New Radiocarbon Dates from Bluefish Caves, Canada," *PLoS One* (January 6, 2017).
56. Examples of papers that convincingly document pre-Clovis sites in the Americas are: A. C. Goodyear, "Evidence of Pre-Clovis Sites in the Eastern United States," *Paleoamerican Origins Beyond Clovis* (2005), 103–112; M. R. Waters et al., "The Buttermilk Creek Complex and the Origins of Clovis at the Debra L. Friedkin Site, Texas," *Science* 331, no. 6024 (March 25, 2011), 1599–1603; M. R. Waters et al., "Pre-Clovis Mastodon Hunting 13,800 Years Ago at the Manis Site, Washington." *Science* 334, no. 6054 (2011), 351–353; D. L. Jenkins et al., "Clovis-Age Western Stemmed Projectile Points and Human Coprolites at the Paisley Caves," *Science* 337, no. 6091 (2012), 223–228; T. D. Dillehay et al., "New Archaeological Evidence for an Early Human Presence at Monte Verde, Chile," *PLoS One* 10, no. 11 (2015), e0141923; J. J. Halligan et al., "Pre-Clovis Occupation 14,550 Years Ago at the Page-Ladson Site, Florida, and the Peopling of the Americas," *Science Advances* 2, no. 5 (2016), e1600375; and A. C. Goodyear and D. A. Slain, " The Pre-Clovis Occupation of the Topper Site, Allendale County, South Carolina" in A. C. Goodyear and C. R. Moore, *Early Human Life on the Southeastern Coastal Plain* (University Press of Florida, 2018).
57. Holen et al., "A 130,000-Year-Old Archaeological Site in Southern California, USA," 479ff.

5: MESSAGE FROM A MASTODON

1. Balboa Park History, https://www.balboapark.org/about/history.
2. Bob Yirka, "Researchers Suggest Comet Most Likely Cause of Chicxulub Crater." *PhysOrg* (March 25, 2013), https://phys.org/news/2013-03-comet-chicxulub-crater.html.
3. "Story of the Discovery," San Diego Natural History Museum, http://www.sdnhm.org/search-results/?search_paths%5B%5D=&query=Cerutti+mastodon.
4. Ibid.
5. Ibid.
6. Ibid.
7. Ibid.
8. J. Tyler Faith and Todd Surovell, "Synchronous Extinction of North America's Pleistocene Mammals," *Proceedings of the National Academy of Sciences* 106, no. 49 (December 8, 2009), 20631–20645.
9. "Story of the Discovery."
10. San Diego Natural History Museum, "FAQs," "What Were the Early Signs That Indicated the Cerutti Mastodon Site Was Different from a Typical Paleontological Site?" http://www.sdnhm.org/consulting-services/paleo-services/projects/cerutti-mastodon/cerutti-mastodon-faqs/.
11. Ibid.
12. Fifty thousand years is the "worldwide" limit of C-14 radiocarbon dating. See, for example, CalPal at the University of Cologne: http://monrepos-rgzm.de/research-103/amenities.html.
13. "Story of the Discovery."
14. Cited in Thomas Curwen, "Archaeology as Blood Sport," *Los Angeles Times,* December 22, 2017, http://www.latimes.com/local/california/la-me-cerutti-mastodon-20171222-htmlstory.html.
15. Ibid.

16. Ibid.
17. Ibid.
18. Although the decisive shift came in 2014, Tom Deméré states that the tide really began to turn in 2008 when archaeologists Steve Holen and Kathleen Holen made their initial research visit to The Nat to examine the Cerutti Mastodon materials. A full timeline is available here: https://www.sdnhm.org/consulting-services/paleo-services/projects/cerutti-mastodon/cerutti-mastodon-dis covery-timeline/.
19. "Story of the Discovery." Complete details are given in Steven R. Holen et al., "A 130,000-Year-Old Archaeological Site in Southern California," *Nature* (April 27, 2017).
20. Other members of the team were George Jefferson, Paleontologist Emeritus with the Colorado Desert District Stout Research Center; Kathleen Maule Holen, M.S., M.A., Administrative Director at the Center for American Paleolithic Research; Jared Beeton, Professor of Earth Science at Adams State University; Adam Rountree of the University of Michigan's Museum of Paleontology, and Lawrence Vescera, Paleontologist at California State Parks Colorado Desert District Stout Research Center in Borrego Springs. For further details, see https://www.sdnhm.org/consul ting-services/paleo-services/projects/cerutti-mastodon/cerutti-mastodon-discovery-timeline/.
21. The range of 140,000 to 120,000 years ago is approximate, and Deméré himself (personal correspondence) prefers 130,000 years down to about 115,000 years ago. There are nuances, as usual. For full details of recent discussions around the dating of the Eemian, see "Eemian Interglacial Reconstructed from a Greenland Folded Ice Core," *Nature* 493 (January 24, 2013), 489–494.
22. Like our understanding of the origins of civilization, our understanding of human origins is undergoing somewhat of a paradigm shift. Around the time of the publication of Holen et al.'s Cerutti Mastodon paper in April 2017, multiple studies have pushed the timing of the initial migration of *Homo sapiens* out of Africa back so far that the "Out of Africa" paradigm—which has been firmly in place since 1924 when the first *Australopithecus* fossils were found in South Africa—has been questioned and alternative theories explored. In the same month as the Cerutti paper was published, the Dali skull from China was dated to 260,000 years ago, thus reviving the question of whether *Homo sapiens* originated in isolation in Africa. [Xuefeng Sun et al., "TT-OSL and Post-IR IRSL Dating of the Dali Man Site in Central China," *Quaternary International* 434 A (April 1, 2017), 99–106.] June 2017 saw the results of Hublin et al.'s study on the 315,000–360,000-year-old modern human skeleton in Jebel Ihroud, Morocco, thus making East Africa's status as the "cradle of mankind" redundant. [Jean-Jaques Hublin et al., "New Fossils from Jebel Ihroud, Morocco and the pan-African origin of *Homo sapiens*," *Nature* 546 (08 June 2017), 289–292.] July 2017 saw Clarkson et al.'s publication on the occupation of northern Australia by 65,000 years ago, which altered the minimum date of 60,000–50,000 years ago for the dispersal of anatomically modern humans out of Africa [Chris Stringer and Peter Andrews, "Genetic and Fossil Evidence for the Origin of Modern Humans," *Science* vol. 239, no. 4845 (March 11, 1988), 1263–1268.] or made more likely the possibility that humans migrated from Australia to Africa at that time. [Bruce R. Fenton, *The Forgotten Exodus: The Into Africa Theory of Human Evolution* (Independently Published, April 7, 2017).] In August 2017, the Dali skull was confirmed as being a hybrid *Homo sapiens* and *Homo erectus* hominin that has contributed significantly to the evolution of Chinese *Homo sapiens*, thus further complicating the story and entrenching East Asia as a focal point of human origins. [Sheela Athreya and Xinzhi Wu, "A Multivariate Assessment of the Dali Hominin Cranium from China: Morphological Affinities and Implications for Pleistocene Evolution in East Asia" *American Journal of Physical Anthropology* vol. 164 no. 4 (December 2017), 679–701.] In September 2017, Schlebusch et al.'s study of ancient southern African genomes deepened the divergence of modern humans from archaic humans to 350,000–260,000 years ago, thus supporting a much earlier initial migration event through Asia to southern China. [Carina M. Schlebusch and Helena Malmström et al., "Southern African Ancient Genomes Estimate Modern Human Divergence to 350,000 to 260,000 years ago," *Science* 10.1126/science.aao6266 (September 28, 2017).] In light of all this, on December 8, 2017, Bae, Douka, and Petraglia wrote a review in *Science* calling for the official revision of anatomically modern human migrations to account for the Eurasian findings:

> The identification of Neanderthals and Denisovans in Siberia . . . along with growing fossil and archaeological evidence for the presence of early modern humans in East and Southeast Asia, much earlier than originally thought, places the spotlight on the evolutionary history of our species in Asia over the last 125,000 years. Exciting and unanticipated new discoveries call for a need to critically reexamine the Asian record.

[Christopher J. Bae, Katerina Douka, Michael D. Petraglia, "On the Origin of Modern Humans:

Asian Perspectives," *Science* vol. 358 no. 6368 (December 8, 2017).] Shortly after, on January 18, 2018, a team led by evolutionary geneticist Deigan Yuang published a landmark paper suggesting that the Y chromosome and mitochondrial DNA originated in East Asia, thus calling for a serious reconsideration of the multiregional model of human origins. [Dejian Yuang et al., "Modern Human Origins: Multiregional Evolution of Autosomes and East Asia Origin of Y and mtDNA," *bioRxiv* (May 1, 2018).] Since then, archaeological findings revealing characteristics of early middle Paleolithic culture in India around 385–172 ka has made certain that the traditional "Out of Africa" model must at least be reframed. [Kumar Akhilesh et al., "Early Middle Palaeolithic Culture in India Around 385–172ka reframes Out of Africa Models," *Nature* 554 (February 1, 2018), 97–101.] The current consensus among those interpreting human origins from within the "Out of Africa" framework is marked by the publication of a paper written by twenty-five scholars from institutions around the world entitled, "Did Our Species Evolve in Subdivided Populations Across Africa, and Why Does It Matter?" The abstract reads:

> We challenge the view that our species, *Homo sapiens*, evolved within a single population and/or region of Africa. The chronology and physical diversity of Pleistocene human fossils suggest that morphologically varied populations pertaining to the *H. sapiens* clade lived throughout Africa. Similarly, the African archaeological record demonstrates the polycentric origin and persistence of regionally distinct Pleistocene material culture in a variety of paleoecological settings. Genetic studies also indicate that present-day population structure within Africa extends to deep times, paralleling a paleoenvironmental record of shifting and fractured habitable zones. We argue that these fields support an emerging view of a highly structured African prehistory that should be considered in human evolutionary inferences, prompting new interpretations, questions, and interdisciplinary research directions.

[Eleanor Scerri et al., "Did Our Species Evolve in Subdivided Populations Across Africa, and Why Does it Matter?" *Trends In Ecology & Evolution* vol. 33, no. 8 (August 2018), 582–594.] Also see the somewhat convincing, albeit controversial, interpretation of anthropologist German Dziebel, "The End of Out-of-Africa: A Copernican Reassessment of the Patterns of Genetic Variation in the Old World" (November 13, 2013), http://anthropogenesis.kinshipstudies.org/blog/2013/11/11/the-end-of-out-of-africa-a-copernican-reassessment-of-the-patterns-of-genetic-variation-in-the-old-world/.

23. Tom Demére adds (personal communication): "The site was excavated over a 5 month period and eventually unearthed 50m² of the bone-and-stone-bearing bed. The resulting bone and stone distribution map presented a pattern of 2 work stations with concentrations of objects."
24. Tom Demére adds (personal communication): "The 'work station' hypothesis is based on the pattern of bone and stone distribution revealed after 5 months of hard excavation of the bone bed."
25. Tom Demére adds (personal communication): "Actually, we suggest that there are 'tools' at the CMS—the hammerstones and anvils are expedient tools not manufactured tools. Such 'tools' were probably the 'first' tools used by hominins."
26. Tom Demére adds (personal communication): "We also suggest that the bones were broken to provide raw materials for the making of bone tools."
27. See Gary Haynes, "The Cerutti Mastodon," *PaleoAmerica* 3.3 (2017), 196–199 and Donald Grayson quoted in D. Vergano, "Don't Believe the Big Story About Humans Roaming America 130,000 Years Ago" (Buzzfeed, April 26, 2017). Also see Joseph V. Ferraro and Katie M. Binetti., "Contesting Early Archaeology in California," *Nature* 554 (February 8, 2018).
28. See David Meltzer quoted in "Don't Believe the Big Story About Humans Roaming America 130,000 Years Ago" (Buzzfeed, April 26, 2017).
29. G. Haynes, "The Cerutti Mastodon."
30. S. R. Holen et al., "Supplementary Information" for "A 150-Year-Old Archaeological Site in Southern California," *Nature* (April 27, 2017), 13–25.
31. Ibid., 4. Also see pp. 14–15, "Weathering": "Evidence indicating weathering of bone at the CM site is variable. The majority of limb bones do not exhibit extensive weathering cracks (i.e., weathering stage 0 or 110), while ribs and vertebrae exhibit some cracks that represent wetting and drying processes and/or diagenetic processes related to formation of pedogenic carbonate (caliche). All weathering-like features appear to post-date the disarticulation and burial of CM bones. In addition, some limb element fragments (e.g., CM-288) with unweathered surfaces are spirally-fractured, with smooth curvilinear fracture planes indicating that the bone was broken while it was still fresh."
For visual 3D evidence of the limb element fragments on CM-288 go to the University of

Michigan, "Online Repository of Fossils," Museum of Paleontology, "The Cerutti Mastodon Site," "Bone Fragments," "Specimen: SDSNH 49926, Taxon: *Mammut americanum*, Element: CM 288; bone fragment: https://umorf.ummp.lsa.umich.edu/wp/wp-content/3d/viewer.html?name= 1244&extension=ctm.

See also "Supplementary Information," pp. 15–16, "Geologic Processes of Proboscidean Limb Bone Modification:" "Post-depositional dry-bone fracturing, as evidenced by longitudinal and perpendicular fracture planes with rough surfaces is distinguished from the spiral fracture patterns produced by dynamic fracturing of fresh bone noted on the majority of CM limb bone fragments. There is no evidence at the CM site that geological processes caused breakage of fresh mastodon limb bones" and, "Two biologic processes, carnivoran gnawing and trampling by large mammals, are known to fracture bone. However, fresh cortical proboscidean limb bone is rarely broken by either agent."

See also p. 18: "Fracturing of proboscidean limb bones while still fresh is rare in modern single-elephant death sites, and no sites have been documented like the CM site, where fresh elephant limb bone is broken into numerous small spirally fractured fragments with evidence of multiple impacts. . . . The femoral diaphyses found at the CM site are broken into small spirally-fractured pieces, whereas more fragile bones like ribs and vertebrae are complete, or more complete than the heavier and denser limb bones. This pattern of differential breakage is exactly the opposite of what is found where proboscidean bones have been extensively trampled. Under trampling, the lightest bones (e.g., ribs and vertebrae) are broken first and into much smaller pieces than the limb bones that have thicker cortical walls resistant to breakage."

Also see "Extended Data," Figure 4a–e: Diagnostic anvil wear on CM bone, https://www.nature.com/articles/nature22065/figures/8, as well as Supplementary Video 3 and Extended Data Figure 8: Experimental hammerstone percussion of elephant bone: https://www.nature.com/articles/nature22065/figures/12.

32. Ibid., 13–25.
33. Tom Deméré adds (personal communication): "Again, marrow extraction is only one possible reason for breaking up the long bones—another possible/probably reason is to produce bone 'blanks' from which to fashion bone tools."
34. Thomas M. Cronin, *Principles of Climatology* (New York: Columbia University Press, 1999), 204.

6: MILLENNIA UNACCOUNTED FOR

1. See, for example, Michael Collins quoted in E. A. Powell, "Early Dates, Real Tools?" Archaeological Institute of America (November 17, 2004), https://archive.archaeology.org/online/news/topper.html: "I don't believe those are artifacts. . . . They're geofacts—not manmade."
2. M. Rose, "The Topper Site: Pre-Clovis Surprise," Archaeological Institute of America (July/August 1999), https://archive.archaeology.org/9907/newsbriefs/clovis.html.
3. See discussion in J. M. Adovasio and David Pedler, *Strangers in a New Land* (Firefly Books, 2016), 276.
4. The Southeast-American Early Archaic period is conventionally dated to 10,000 to 8,000 BP. The beginning of the period, at 10,000 BP, was marked in accordance with conventional geological dating of the Pleistocene/Holocene boundary, while the end of the period, 8,000 BP, is usually equated with the Hypsithermsal warming episode. See M. F. Johnson et al., *The Paleoindian and Early Archaic Southeast* (University of Alabama Press, 1999), 15.
5. Adovasio and Pedler, *Strangers in a New Land*, 275. Also see the Paleoindian Database of the Americas (PIDBA), "Total Number of Reported Clovis Projectile Points." The lack of Clovis points found at coastal regions of the southeast (North Carolina, South Carolina, Georgia, and Florida) is clearly illustrated in these two maps: http://web.utk.edu/~dander19/clovis_continent_647kb.jpg and http://web.utk.edu/~dander19/clovis_southeast_569kb.jpg.
6. Adovasio and Pedler, *Strangers in a New Land*, 275: "The renown of its massive Clovis deposit is very well deserved."
7. Some skeptics resorted to arguing that bend-breaks can be made by natural forces or accidental breakage. See for example Stuart. J. Stewart, "Is That All There Is? The Weak Case for Pre-Clovis Occupation of Eastern North America," *In the Eastern Fluted Point Tradition*, (eds.) J. A. M. Gingerich (University of Utah Press, 2013), 333–354. Skip to note 11 of this chapter for a list of studies that have since rendered this argument in association with the Topper Palaeolithic terrace untenable.
8. It was in November 2004 that the radiocarbon results of carbonized plant remains where artifacts

excavated in May from along the Savannah River in Allendale County first came back. See "New Evidence Puts Man in North America 50,000 Years Ago," *Science Daily* (November 18, 2004), https://www.sciencedaily.com/releases/2004/11/041118104010.htm.

The Pleistocene antiquity of the site and artifacts found within it were then reaffirmed in 2009 by a team led by Michael R. Waters, in a paper titled "Geoarchaeological Investigations at the Topper and Big Pine Tree Sites, Allendale County, South Carolina," in the *Journal of Archaeological Science*. See, for example, p. 1305: "Six samples of wood, nutshell, and humic acids were dated from unit 1a (Figs. 4 and 5). These dates represent minimum ages for unit 1a and indicate that this unit dates in excess of 50,000 14C yr B.P. A date of >54,700 14C yr B.P. (CAMS-79022) was obtained on a Hickory (Carya) nutshell and a date of >55,500 14C yr B.P. (CAMS-19023) on a piece of fir wood (Abies) from an organic horizon within unit 1a underlying the reported oldest cultural horizon at the Topper site." It was from unit 1a of the Pleistocene terrace that distinctive bend-break tools were recovered.

9. Albert C. Goodyear, "Evidence of Pre-Clovis Sites in the Eastern United States," *Paleoamerican Origins Beyond Clovis* (2005), 103–112.

10. A. C. Goodyear and D. A. Slain, "The Pre-Clovis Occupation of the Topper Site, Allendale County, South Carolina," in A. C. Goodyear and C. R. Moore, *Early Human Life on the Southeastern Coastal Plain* (University Press of Florida, 2018), S30.

11. The natural vs. human creation of the materials excavated from a Pleistocene terrace at Topper was evaluated by Douglas Slain and presented at the 81st Annual Meeting of the Society for American Archaeology (SAA) in Orlando, Florida, on April 8, 2016. The content of this presentation is documented in D. Slain, "Pre-Clovis at Topper (38AL23): Evaluating the Role of Human Versus Natural Agency in the Formation of Lithic Deposits from a Pleistocene Terrace in the American Southeast," *The Selected Works of Douglas Slain* (April 8, 2016). In this paper, Slain concludes, "The weathering simulations produced lithic detachments that fit the morphological description of bend breaks. However, as these detachments did not have technological attributes consisting of either compression rings, bulbs of force, or impact markers, these items should not be mistaken for the byproducts of intentional biface, or bipolar technologies. In other words, detachments resulting from natural weathering processes often exhibit morphological similarity to cultural debitage, but lack the technological attributes of a chipped stone reductive technology" (p. 7). Consequently, "Evidence from this study supports King's (2012) findings and demonstrates a human origin for the pre-Clovis flake assemblage at the site" (p. 8). The M. King study, "MA Thesis Title: The Distribution of Paleoindian Debitage from the Pleistocene Terrace at the Topper Site: An Evaluation of a Possible Pre-Clovis Occupation (38Al23)" (University of Tennessee, 2012) is indeed consistent with Slain in concluding that "the data supports the notion that the pre-Clovis debitage was manmade" (p. 137).

12. Adovasio and Pedler, *Strangers in a New Land*, 284; see also J. M. Adovasio and Jake Page, *The First Americans: In Pursuit of Archaeology's Greatest Mystery* (Modern Library, 2003), 272.

13. Adovasio and Pedler, *Strangers in a New Land*, 284.

14. A. C. Goodyear, "Evidence of Pre-Clovis Sites in the Eastern United States," 110.

15. Wm Jack Hranicky, *Bipoints Before Clovis: Trans-Oceanic Migrations and Settlement of Prehistoric Americas* (Universal Publishers, 2012), 50.

16. Ibid, 283. And see also Adovasio and Page, *The First Americans*, 272.

17. Adovasio and Page, *The First Americans*, 272.

18. This list, from Wikipedia, gives some idea of the number of claimed sites, but, as its failure to include the Cerutti Mastodon Site indicates, it is by no means complete: https://en.wikipedia.org/wiki/Category:Pre-Clovis_archaeological_sites_in_the_Americas. Probably the most useful source is Adovasio and Pedler, *Strangers in a New Land*, which devotes many chapters to the more credible pre-Clovis sites. But see also http://scienceviews.com/indian/pre_clovis_sites.html and https://www.thoughtco.com/pre-clovis-sites-americas-173079.

19. For a fascinating and extensive discussion of Hueyatlaco, a site that we will consider further, see Christopher Hardaker, *The First American: The Suppressed Story of the People Who Discovered the New World* (New Page Books, 2007).

20. Adovasio and Pedler, *Strangers in a New Land*.

21. Ibid. For Pedra Furada, see also N. Guidon and G. Delibrias, "Carbon-14 Dates Point to Man in the Americas 32,000 Years Ago," *Nature* 321 (June 19, 1986), 769, and Marvin W. Rowe and Karen L. Steelman, "Comment on 'Some Evidence of a Date of First Humans to Arrive in Brazil,' *Journal of Archaeological Science* 30 (2003), 1349.

22. Adovasio and Pedler, *Strangers in a New Land*. Compare, for example, the Topper Assemblage going back 50,000 years or more (p. 279ff.), with the relative sophistication of the Miller Lanceolate projectile point and bone tools found at Meadowcroft (dated between about 17,000 years ago and 13,000 years ago) (pp. 211–212), or with the chert "El Jobo" projectile points from Monte Verde (dated to around 14,500 years ago) (p. 225), or with the Cactus Hill points, dated roughly 18,000 years ago (p. 235).

23. In 2011, there were over 100 uncontacted tribes worldwide. See, for example, Joanna Eede, "Uncontacted Tribes: The Last Free People on Earth," National Geographic Blog: Changing Planet (April 1, 2011), https://blog.nationalgeographic.org/2011/04/01/uncontacted-tribes-the-last-free-people-on-earth/.

24. For example, Stuart J. Fiedel, "The Anzick Genome Proves Clovis Is First, After All," *Quaternary International* 44 (2017), 4–9.

25. As King reminds us with regard to Topper, "Prior to 1998, no units were taken deeper than the Clovis age level since the project director thought it was the oldest possible occupation. However, the 1997 reporting on the discoveries at Monte Verde in South America and discoveries at Cactus Hill, Virginia, in 1998 prompted Goodyear and his research team to excavate below what was known to be Clovis-age sediments." ("MA Thesis Title: The Distribution of Paleoindian Debitage from the Pleistocene Terrace at the Topper Site: An Evaluation of a Possible Pre-Clovis Occupation (38Al23)," 15.) If you don't look, you won't find!

PART III

7: SIBERIA

1. Pengfei Qin and Mark Stoneking, "Denisovan Ancestry in East Eurasian and Native American Populations," *Molecular Biology and Evolution* 32, no. 10 (2015), 2671.

2. Ibid., 2669, Figure 4.

3. A. Briney, "Geography of Siberia," ThoughtCo. (last updated March 17, 2017), https://www.thoughtco.com/geography-of-siberia-1435483.

4. Reconstructions of global sea level over the past 470 ka suggest it was possible to walk from Asia to Alaska via the Bering land bridge from **approximately** 370 to 337 ka, 283 to 240 ka, 189 to 130 ka, and 75 to 11 ka. See for example Mark Siddall et al., "Sea Level Fluctuations During the Last Glacial Cycle," *Nature* 423 (June 19, 2003), 855, Figure 2.

5. Qiaomei Fu et al., "Genome Sequence of a 45,000-Year-Old Modern Human from Western Siberia," *Nature* 514 (October 23, 2014), 445ff; and Vladimir V. Pitulko et al., "Early Human Presence in the Arctic: Evidence from 45,000-Year-Old Mammoth Remains," *Science* 351, no. 6270 (January 15, 2016), 260ff.

6. M. Raghavan et al., "Upper Paleolithic Siberian Genome Reveals Dual Ancestry of Native Americans," *Nature* 505 (January 2, 2014), "The Y chromosome of MA-1 [an ancient 24kya Siberian individual] is . . . near the root of most Native American lineages. Similarly, we find autosomal evidence that MA-1 is . . . genetically closely related to modern-day Native Americans" (p. 87). See also M. Rasmussen et al., "The Genome of a Late Pleistocene Human from a Clovis Burial Site in Western Montana," *Nature* 506 (February 13, 2014), "Gene flow from the Siberian Upper Paleolithic Mal'ta population into Native American ancestors is also shared by the Anzick-1 [ancient American/Montanan] individual and thus happened before 12,600 years BP. . . . Our data are compatible with the hypothesis that Anzick-1 belonged to a population directly ancestral to many contemporary Native Americans" (p. 225).

7. There have been a few theories, generally regarded by the academic establishment as "zany," "lunatic," or worse, that have attempted to argue that prehistoric settlement also occurred from Europe by boat across the Atlantic Ocean. Among these, the most credible is the so-called Solutrean theory of Clovis origins put forward by Dennis J. Stanford, curator of archaeology and director of the Paleoindian Program at the Smithsonian's National Museum of Natural History, and his fellow researcher and coauthor Bruce A. Bradley, associate professor in archaeology and director of the Experimental Archaeology program at the University of Exeter. See Dennis J. Stanford and Bruce A. Bradley, *Across Atlantic Ice: The Origin of America's Clovis Culture* (University of California Press, 2012).

   To cut a very long story very short indeed, Stanford and Bradley strongly resist what they call "the preconceived notion of geneticists and archaeologists that the Americas must have been settled by Asians" (p. 246). Their argument, instead, is that "Clovis predecessors were immigrants from southwestern Europe" and that this wave of immigration took place during the last glacial maximum (p. 247), in other words, somewhere around 22,000 years ago. Their claim is based on the—admittedly stunningly close—morphological resemblances between bifacial projectile points made by the "Solutrean" culture of Upper Paleolithic western Europe between roughly 22,000 and 17,000 years ago, and almost identical bifacial projectile points made with an almost identical technique by North America's "Clovis" culture over a period of less than 1,000 years beginning roughly 13,400 years ago.

The gap of several thousand years between the end of the Solutreans and the beginning of Clovis is one among many reasons why the majority of archaeologists reject Stanford and Bradley's unusually daring theory, while more recent genetic research claims to have refuted it completely. See Morten Rasmussen et al., "The Genome of a Late Pleistocene Human from a Clovis Burial Site in Western Montana," 228. See also Jennifer A. Raff and Deborah Bolnick, "Genetic Roots of the First Americans," *Nature* 506 (February 13, 2014), 162. Indeed Raff and Bolnick of the University of Texas have such confidence in this new research that they conclude: "Unless proponents offer evidence of direct European ancestry in other securely dated ancient American genomes, the Solutrean hypothesis can no longer be treated as a credible alternative for Clovis (or Native American) origins. It is time to move on to more interesting questions."

8. See part 2 of *America Before*.

9. A major multidisciplinary study published in 2016 in *Nature* pointed out that the supposed "ice-free" corridor would have been completely uninhabitable until 12,600 years ago (Mikkel W. Pedersen et al., "Postglacial Viability and Colonization in North America's Ice-Free Corridor," *Nature* 537 no. 7618 (2016), 45). The authors demonstrate this by means of ancient DNA from the bottom of glacial lakes. This suggests that the "first" Americans did not arrive by land, but by sea. This is supported by a study undertaken by a team from the University of California, who reconstructed family trees for bison that lived in the "ice free" corridor and demonstrated that it wasn't habitable until 13,000 years ago (Peter. D. Heintzman et al., "Bison Phylogeography Constrains Dispersal and Viability of the Ice Free Corridor in Western Canada," *Proceedings of the National Academy of Sciences* 113, no. 29 (2016), 8057–8063). Though these studies do not rule out the possibility that the "first" Americans reached the Americas via the Bering land bridge and ice-free corridor as Clovis proponents contend, they do enhance the likelihood that early Americans favored sea over land crossings.

10. Kris Hirst, "The Beringian Standstill Hypothesis: An Overview," August 14, 2017, https://www.thoughtco.com/beringian-standstill-hypothesis-first-americans-172859.

11. S. L. Bonatto and F. M. Salzano, "A Single and Early Migration for the Peopling of the Americas Supported by Mitochondrial DNA Sequence Data," *Proceedings of the National Academy of Sciences* 94, no. 5 (1997), 1866–1871. The authors suggest, on the basis of mitochondrial DNA results, that the collapse of the ice-free corridor between ~14,000 and ~20,000 years ago isolated the people south of the ice sheets, who gave rise to the Amerind, from those still in Beringia; the latter originated the Na-Dene, Eskimo, and probably the Siberian Chukchi.

12. L. Wade, "On the Trail of Ancient Mariners," *Science* 357, no. 6351 (2017), 542–545.

13. C. Clarkson et al., "Human Occupation of Northern Australia by 65,000 Years Ago," *Nature* 547, no. 7663 (2017), 306.

14. Heather Pringle, "From Vilified to Vindicated: The Story of Jacques Cinq-Mars," *Hakai Magazine,* March 7, 2017, https://www.hakaimagazine.com/features/vilified-vindicated-story-jacques-cinq-mars/?xid=PS_smithsonian and at http://www.smithsonianmag.com/science-nature/jacques-cinq-mars-bluefish-caves-scientific-progress-180962410/#A1zGtDKtgySyduU6.99.

15. "Found: Dragon and Griffin Megaliths 'Dating Back 12,000 Years to End of Ice Age, or Earlier,'" *Siberian Times,* May 8, 2017, http://siberiantimes.com/other/others/features/found-dragon-and-griffin-megaliths-dating-back-12000-years-to-end-of-ice-age-or-earlier/.

16. Location here: https://mapcarta.com/25567370/Map.

17. "Found: Dragon and Griffin Megaliths 'Dating Back 12,000 Years to End of Ice Age, or Earlier.'"

18. Ibid.

19. Ibid.

20. Confirmed by emails between my research assistant Holly Lasko and Maxim Kozlikin, May 4–7, 2018. **Excerpt from email of May 4—HL to MK:**
    To what extent can we say that we've gained a good archaeological understanding of the Altai during the Palaeolithic? Or, in other words, approximately how much of the Altai region remains

to be excavated? From what I can see, our understanding is limited to approximately 15 **main** sites out of a possible very many more.

Thank you so much for your time.

May 5: Dear Holly, To be brief, then indeed, the key multi-layered well-studied sites are about 20. In total, more than 100 objects are known.

Yours sincerely, Maxim.

May 7: Thanks so much Maxim! By "objects" do you mean Palaeolithic artifacts?

May 7: Dear Holly, I meant the number of Paleolithic sites.

8: HALL OF RECORDS

1. Christy G. Turner et al., *Animal Teeth and Human Tools: A Taphonomic Odyssey in Ice Age Siberia* (Cambridge University Press, 2013), 79.
2. Denisova Cave, Useful Information, http://www.showcaves.com/english/ru/caves/Denisova.html.
3. David Reich et al., "Genetic History of an Archaic Hominin Group from Denisova Cave in Siberia," *Nature* 468 (December 23–30, 2010), 1053.
4. Turner et al., *Animal Teeth and Human Tools,* 79.
5. N. Zwyns, "Altai: Paleolithic" in *Encyclopedia of Global Archaeology*: "Based on the Eurasian system of division, three main periods can be recognized during the Paleolithic of the Altai: the Lower, Middle, and Upper Paleolithic. The Lower Paleolithic corresponds to the first human occupation of the Altai that would start c. 800 ka. The Middle Paleolithic would start sometime at the end of the Middle Pleistocene and last until c. 50 ka. The Upper Paleolithic covers a time range from c. 50 ka to the end of the Pleistocene" (p. 150). Note that while this is the commonly discerned time frame among Altai archaeologists, the time frame for the Paleolithic era varies by region and academic discipline.
6. Turner et al., *Animal Teeth and Human Tools,* 79.
7. A. Gibbons, "Who Were the Denisovans?" *Science* 333 (August 26, 2011). Svante Pääbo comments, "The one place where we are sure all three human forms have lived at one time or another is here in Denisova Cave." In 2010, a Neanderthal toe bone was discovered in Denisova Cave. The results of its morphological analysis are documented in M. B. Mednikova, "A Proximal Pedal Phalanx of a Paleolithic Hominin from Denisova Cave, Altai," *Archaeology, Ethnology and Anthropology of Eurasia* 39, no. 1 (2011). Radiocarbon dating of the organic material found above the toe revealed that the Neanderthal roamed the cave at least 50,000 years ago. In S. Brown et al., "Identification of a New Hominin Bone from Denisova Cave, Siberia, Using Collagen Fingerprinting and Mitochondrial DNA Analysis," *Scientific Reports* 6, no. 25339 (March 29, 2016), a sample taken from layer 12 from the East Gallery of the cave was found through mtDNA analysis to be from a >50,000-year-old Neanderthal. Then, in 2017, researchers successfully sequenced soil samples from the Cave for DNA; Neanderthal DNA was detected in layer 15 from the Main Gallery, and layer 14 from the East Gallery at a depth deeper than any fossilized remains or artifacts have been found (V. Slon et al., "Neanderthal and Denisovan DNA from Pleistocene Sediments," *Science* 356, no. 6338 [May 12, 2017]: 605–608). Frequent occupations of Denisova Cave by Neanderthals are supported by the Mousterian artifacts, generally associated with Neanderthals, that have been excavated there. The editors of *Encyclopaedia Britannica*, in "Denisova Cave," https://www.britannica.com/place/Denisova-Cave (last updated February 8, 2018), state that there is "evidence of 13 separate occupations occurring between 125,000 and 30,000 years ago . . . supported by the presence of artifacts from the Acheulean, Mousterian, and Levalloisian stone-flaking industries," all of which are associated with Neanderthals.
8. The first conclusive evidence that anatomically modern humans interbred with Neanderthals was established in 2010 by R. E. Green et al., "A Draft Sequence of the Neanderthal Genome," *Science* 328, no. 5979 (May 7, 2010), 710–722. The investigators conclude, on the basis of remains from Croatia, that "between 1 and 4% of the genomes of people in Eurasia are derived from Neandertals" (p. 721). Then, an investigation by K. Prüfer et al., "The Complete Genome Sequence of a Neanderthal from the Altai Mountains," *Nature* 505 (January 2, 2014), concluded that "the proportion of Neanderthal-derived DNA in people outside Africa is 1.5–2.1%" (p. 45). All these results are consistent with Q. Fu et al.'s findings in "An Early Modern Human from Romania with a Recent Neanderthal Ancestor," *Nature* 524 (August 13, 2015), 216–219, in which the 37,000–42,000-year-old was confirmed as having 6–9 percent of its genome derived from Neanderthals (p. 216). The most recent and accurate investigation on modern human and Neander-

thal interbreeding was, however, led by K. Prüfer, "A High-Coverage Neanderthal Genome from Vindija Cave in Croatia," *Science* 358 (November 3, 2017), 655–658. In this study, non-African populations outside Oceania are found to carry between 1.8 and 2.6 percent Neanderthal DNA, East Asians are found to carry 2.3–2.6 percent Neanderthal DNA, and Western Eurasians carry 1.8–2.4 percent. The amount of Neanderthal DNA carried by current modern humans can therefore be estimated as being in the realm of 0–4 percent.

9. Reich et al., "Genetic History of an Archaic Hominin Group from Denisova Cave in Siberia," 1053.

10. Ibid., 1054–1060.

11. Ibid., 1053.

12. Ibid., 1053–1054, 1059.

13. Information provided by Irina Salnikova. For further details on what the excavators call "the art collection," see A. P. Derevianko, M. V. Shunkov, and P. V. Volkov, "A Palaeolithic Bracelet from Denisova Cave," *Archaeology, Ethnology and Anthropology of Eurasia* 43, no. 2 (June 2008), 15.

14. Some of the raw materials came from as much as 200 kilometers away. Ibid., 17.

15. Ibid., 14. Holocene levels are designated 0–8.

16. "First Glimpse Inside the Siberian Cave That Holds the Key to Man's Origins," *Siberian Times,* July 28, 2015, http://siberiantimes.com/science/casestudy/features/f0135-first-glimpse-inside-the-siberian-cave-that-holds-the-key-to-mans-origins/. See photo captioned "The wall, showing all the 22 layers of Denisova cave," and compare with Santha Faiia's photo taken in September 2017.

17. Derevianko, Shunkov, and Volkov, "A Palaeolithic Bracelet from Denisova Cave," 14.

18. Ibid., 16.

19. Ibid.

20. The historical explanation for this is unsurprisingly rooted in early-twentieth-century interpretations of human origins. See, for example, Smithsonian National Museum of Natural History, "La Chapelle-aux-Saints," http://humanorigins.si.edu/evidence/human-fossils/fossils/la-chapelle-aux-saints (accessed March 12, 2018), "The original reconstruction of the 'Old Man of La Chapelle' by scientist Pierre Marcellin Boule led to the reason why popular culture stereotyped Neanderthals as dim-witted brutes for so many years. In 1911, Boule reconstructed this skeleton with a severely curved spine indicative of a stooped, slouching stance with bent knees, forward flexed hips, and the head jutted forward. He thought the low vaulted cranium and the large brow ridge, somewhat reminiscent of that seen in large apes such as gorillas, indicated a generally primitive early human and a lack of intelligence."

The Neanderthal discovery took place within the Victorian epoch in which the Western white man sought to excuse his domination and colonization of the world by means of cultural and racial hegemony, namely "scientific racism" (also termed "eugenics"). It is unsurprising that Neanderthals, a species considered more primitive than the most "primitive" early-twentieth-century humans, were instantly assumed to be intellectually and creatively incapable and totally unable to enjoy abilities reserved for "civilised" white modern humans.

21. Archaeologist Ralph Solecki's 1971 book, *Shanidar: The First Flower People,* was seminal in the consensus change on Neanderthal intelligence. Solecki's article based on the book is available in *Science* 190 as "Shanidar IV, a Neanderthal Flower Burial in Northern Iraq" (880–881). The abstract reads: "The discovery of pollen clusters of different kinds of flowers in the grave of one of the Neanderthals, No. IV, at Shanidar Cave, Iraq, furthers our acceptance of the Neanderthals in our line of evolution. It suggests that, although the body was archaic, the spirit was modern."

Since then, a stream of studies supporting this hypothesis have been published, establishing Neanderthals as not only socially intelligent, compassionate, and sensitive humans, but also as culturally and technologically advanced and artistic. For evidence of Neanderthal social intelligence, compassion, and sensitivity, see Penny A. Spikins, Holly E. Rutherford, and Andy P. Needham, "From Homininity to Humanity: Compassion From the Earliest Archaics to Modern Humans," *Time and Mind* 3.3 (2010), 303–325; William Rendu et al., "Evidence supporting an intentional Neandertal burial at La Chapelle-aux-Saints," *Proceedings of the National Academy of Sciences* 111.1 (2014), 81–86; Penny Spikins et al., "The cradle of thought: growth, learning, play and attachment in Neanderthal children," *Oxford Journal of Archaeology* 33.2 (2014), 111–134; Erik Trinkaus and Sébastien Villotte, "External auditory exostoses and hearing loss in the Shanidar 1 Neandertal," *PloS one* 12.10 (2017), e0186684; Penny Spikins et al., "Calculated or caring? Neanderthal healthcare in social context," *World Archaeology* (2018), 1–20; A. Gómez-Olivencia et al, "La Ferrassie 1: New Perspectives on a 'classic' Neandertal," *Journal of Human Evolution* 117 (2018), 13–32.

For Neanderthal cultural and technological advancement, art, and symbolism see Karen Hardy et al. "Neanderthal medics? Evidence for food, cooking, and medicinal plants entrapped in dental calculus," *Naturwissenschaften* 99.8 (2012), 617–626; Ruggero D'Anastasio et al., "Micro-biomechanics of the Kebara 2 hyoid and its implications for speech in Neanderthals," *PLoS One* 8.12 (2013), e82261; Jacques Jaubert et al., "Early Neanderthal constructions deep in Bruniquel Cave in southwestern France," *Nature* 534.7605 (2016), 111; A. C. Sorensen et al., "Neandertal fire-making technology inferred from microwear analysis," *Scientific reports* 8.1 (2018), 10065; Ana Majkić et al., "A decorated raven bone from the Zaskalnaya VI (Kolosovskaya) Neanderthal site, Crimea," *PloS one* 12.3 (2017), e0173435; Biancamaria Aranguren et al., "Wooden tools and fire technology in the early Neanderthal site of Poggetti Vecchi (Italy)," *Proceedings of the National Academy of Sciences* (2018), 201716068; Dirk L. Hoffmann et al., "U-Th dating of carbonate crusts reveals Neandertal origin of Iberian cave art," *Science* 359.6378 (2018), 912–915; Dirk L. Hoffmann et al., "Symbolic use of marine shells and mineral pigments by Iberian Neandertals 115,000 years ago," *Science advances* 4.2 (2018), eaar5255.

The recent and pivotal turning point in our understanding of Neanderthals as intelligent beings is marked by A. Lawler, "Neanderthals, Stone Age People May Have Voyaged the Mediterranean," *Science* (April 24, 2018), "The recent evidence from the Mediterranean suggests purposeful navigation," the article reads. "The orthodoxy until pretty recently was that you don't have seafarers until the early Bronze Age," adds archaeologist John Cherry of Brown University, an initial skeptic. "Now we are talking about seafaring Neandertals. It's a pretty stunning change."

22. Derevianko, Shunkov, and Volkov, "A Palaeolithic Bracelet from Denisova Cave," 3.
23. Ibid., 15.
24. Ibid., 24. Emphasis added.
25. Ibid., 18.
26. Ibid., 24.
27. Ibid.
28. Ibid.
29. Ibid.
30. See also Alexandra Buzhilova, Anatoly Derevianko, and Michael Shunkov, "The Northern Dispersal Route: Bioarchaeological Data from the Late Pleistocene of Altai, Siberia," *Current Anthropology* 58, Suppl. 17 (December 2017), S500: "Archaeological data suggest that the first Denisovans arrived in the Altai around 300 ka, with continuous cultural development for a long time. The genetic data confirm that Denisovans were present in the area at least twice and possibly over a long period of time. Thus, we have adequate data to evaluate the hypothesis of continuous cultural and physical development of Denisovans over time. The similar morphology of two upper hominin molars from Denisova Cave, separated by a thick deposit and tens of thousands of years, also supports this idea."
31. Derenanko, Shunkov, and Volkov, "A Paleolithic Bracelet from Denisova Cave," 22.
32. Ibid., 22–23.
33. Ibid., 17.
34. Ibid., 20.
35. Ibid., 24.
36. Ibid., 21.
37. Ibid.
38. Ibid., 21–22.
39. Ibid., 33–34.
40. Ibid., 13 and 15. See also 16: "a date of 29,200 ± ± 360 BP (AA-35321) on charcoal from the border zone between strata 11 and 10."
41. Ibid., 24.
42. This conversation took place at the institute on September 14, 2017.
43. M. Kozlikin quoted in "World's Oldest Needle Found in Siberian Cave That Stitches Together Human History," *Siberian Times*, August 23, 2016, http://siberiantimes.com/science/casestudy/news/n0711-worlds-oldest-needle-found-in-siberian-cave-that-stitches-together-human-history/.
44. Email correspondence with Maxim Kozlikin on February 21, 2018: "The needle you're talking about was found in the Central Chamber of the cave in 2016. So far, these materials have been published only in Russian."
45. "World's Oldest Needle Found in Siberian Cave That Stitches Together Human History."
46. Ibid.

47. Derevianko, Shunkov, and Volkov, "A Palaeolithic Bracelet from Denisova Cave," 15.
48. A. P. Derevianko and E. P. Rybin, "The Oldest Evidence for Symbolic Behavior of the Palaeolithic Men in Gorny Altai," *Archaeology, Ethnology, and Anthropology of Eurasia* 3, no. 15 (2003), 27–50.
49. Or, to be more precise, to 48,650 years old plus or minus somewhere between 2,380 and 1,840 years ago. Derevianko, Shunkov, and Volkov, "A Palaeolithic Bracelet from Denisova Cave," 15.
50. "World's Oldest Needle Found in Siberian Cave": "The bracelet was exhibited in Paris this year, carrying a label showing it to be 50,000 years old with the approval of scientists."
51. "Is This Stunning Bracelet Made by Paleolithic Man for His Favourite Woman Really 70,000 Years Old?" *Siberian Times*, August 2, 2017, http://siberiantimes.com/science/casestudy/features/could-this-stunning-bracelet-be-65000-to-70000-years-old/.
52. Ibid.
53. Ibid.
54. Ibid.
55. Which Middle Pleistocene species of human the Sima de los Huesos (SH) hominins of Spain belonged to—either the Denisovans of southern Siberia or the Neanderthals of western Eurasia—adds an interesting nuance to the archaeological evasiveness of the Denisovans, however. While the SH hominins share morphological features and nuclear DNA with Neanderthals, the mtDNA of one SH individual is more closely related to the mtDNA of Denisovans than to that of Neanderthals. Whether or not the Denisovans can be termed a separate species to the Neanderthals and SH hominins has therefore been put to doubt.

   For studies concluding upon the morphological affinity of the SH hominins to Neanderthals, see I. Martínez and J. L. Arsuaga, "The Temporal Bones from Sima de los Huesos Middle Pleistocene Site (Sierra de Atapuerca, Spain): A Phylogenetic Approach," *Journal of Human Evolution* 33 (1993), 283–318; M. Martinón-Torres et al., "Morphological Description and Comparison of the Dental Remains from Atapuerca-Sima de los Huesos Site (Spain)," *Journal of Human Evolution* 62 (2012), 7–58; J. L. Arsuaga et al., "Neanderthal Roots: Cranial and Chronological Evidence from Sima de los Huesos," in *Science* 44, no. 6190 (2014); R. Quam et al., "The Bony Labyrinth of the Middle Pleistocene Sima de los Huesos Hominins (Sierra de Atapuerca, Spain)," *Journal of Human Evolution* 90 (2016), 1–15.

   For sequencing results that link the nDNA of the SH hominins to Neanderthals, see M. Meyer et al., "Nuclear DNA Sequences from the Middle Pleistocene Sima de los Huesos Hominins," *Nature* 531 (March 24, 2016).

   For results that link the mtDNA of SH hominins with Denisovans, see M. Meyer et al., "A Mitochondrial Genome Sequence of a Hominin from Sima de los Huesos," *Nature* 505 (January 16, 2014). There has also been speculation surrounding the mysterious 105–125 ky skulls excavated in Xuchang, China, which from the perspective of Martinón-Torres "definitely" fit what one expects from Denisovans: "something with an Asian flavor but closely related to Neandertals." But because the investigators have not extracted DNA from the skulls, "the possibility remains a speculation" (Martinón-Torres quoted in A. Gibbons, "Ancient Skulls May Belong to Elusive Humans Called Denisovans," *Science* News [March 2, 2017]).
56. See Anne Gibbons, "Siberian Cave Was Home to Generations of Ancient Humans," *Science* (September 15, 2015), http://www.sciencemag.org/news/2015/09/siberian-cave-was-home-to-genera tions-mysterious-ancient-humans.
57. Viviane Slon et al., "The Genome of the Offspring of a Neanderthal Mother and a Denisovan Father," *Nature* (August 22, 2018).
58. Reich et al., "Genetic History of an Archaic Hominin Group from Denisova Cave in Siberia," 1053. And see J. Krause et al., "The Complete Mitochondrial DNA Genome of an Unknown Hominin from Southern Siberia," *Nature* 464 (2010), 894–897.
59. The earlier date of 430,000 years ago is based on the fossil record (Arsuaga et al., "Neanderthal Roots"), whereas genomic results have indicated a divergence window of between 550,000 and 765,000 years ago (Prüfer et al., "The Complete Genome Sequence of a Neanderthal from the Altai Mountains").
60. Martin Kuhlwilm et al., "Ancient Gene Flow from Early Modern Humans into Eastern Neanderthals," *Nature* 530 (February 25, 2016), 429.
61. Qin and Stoneking, "Denisovan Ancestry in East Eurasian and Native American Populations," 2665, Figure 4.
62. A. Cooper and C. B. Stringer, "Did the Denisovans Cross Wallace's Line?" *Science* 342 (October 18, 2013), 321.

63. Reich et al., "Genetic History of an Archaic Hominin Group from Denisova Cave in Siberia," 1053.

64. Qin and Stoneking, "Denisovan Ancestry in East Eurasian and Native American Populations," 2665. See also Sharon Browning et al., "Analysis of Human Sequence Data Reveals Two Pulses of Archaic Denisova Admixture," *Cell* 173 (March 22, 2018), 1–9. Apart from Papuans, highest levels of introgressed Denisovan DNA have been found in Southern Han Chinese, Chinese Hai, Han Chinese, Bengali, Gujarati Indian, Japanese, Kinh individuals (all East, Southeast, and Central Asia). See p. 7, Figure. 5. Also see p. 7: "We found evidence for two waves of Denisovan admixture, one from a population closely related to the Altai Denisovan individual, and one from a population more distantly related to the Altai Denisovan. The component closely related to the Altai Denisovan is primarily present in East Asians, whereas the component more distantly related to the Altai Denisovan forms the major part of the Denisovan ancestry in Papuans and South Asians."

65. Cooper and Stringer, "Did the Denisovans Cross Wallace's Line?" 322.

66. Ibid.

67. See G. Hancock, *Underworld: The Mysterious Origins of Civilization* (Three Rivers Press, 2002) and S. Oppenheimer and I. Syahrir, *Eden in the East* (Ufuk Press, 2010).

9: THE STRANGE AND MYSTERIOUS GENETIC HERITAGE OF NATIVE AMERICANS

1. Particularly by the Human Genome Project from 1990 to 2003. For accessible information on DNA sequencing technologies, see J. U. Adams et al., "DNA Sequencing Technologies," Scitable (Nature Education, 2008), https://www.nature.com/scitable/topicpage/dna-sequencing-technologies-690.

2. For a good overview of the influence of DNA studies on ancient population history, see S. Subramanian, "Ancient Population Genomics," in *Encyclopaedia of Life Sciences* (Wiley, 2001).

3. M. M. Houck and J. A. Siegel, "Chapter 11—DNA Analysis," in *Fundamentals of Forensic Science*, 3rd ed. (Academic Press, 2015), 261–290, esp. 282.

4. Ibid.

5. Ibid., 283.

6. Ibid.

7. For further discussion, see National Human Genome Research Institute, "Chromosomes" (last updated June 16, 2015), https://www.genome.gov/26524120/chromosomes-fact-sheet/. Also see Genetics Home Reference, "What Is Genetic Ancestry Referencing?" (May 15, 2018), https://ghr.nlm.nih.gov/primer/dtcgenetictesting/ancestrytesting.

8. Christy G. Turner et al., *Animal Teeth and Human Tools: A Taphonomic Odyssey in Ice Age Siberia* (Cambridge University Press, 2013), 177G; I. Medvedev, "Upper Paleolithic Sites in South-Central Siberia" in *The Paleolithic of Siberia: New Discoveries and Interpretations*, ed. A. P. Derev'ianko, D. B. Shimkin, and W. R. Powers (University of Illinois Press, 1998), 122–132.

9. Maanasa Raghavan et al., "Upper Palaeolithic Siberian Genome Reveals Dual Ancestry of Native Americans," *Nature* 505 (January 2, 2014), 87.

10. Ibid.

11. Turner et al., *Animal Teeth and Human Tools*, 173; Peter N. Peregrine and Melvin Ember (eds.), *Encyclopedia of Prehistory: Volume 2: Arctic and Subarctic*, Volume 6, p. 194.

12. BBC News, "Ancient DNA from Siberian Boy Links Europe and America," http://www.bbc.co.uk/news/science-environment-25020958.

13. "24,000-Year-Old Body Shows Kinship to Europeans and American Indians," *New York Times*, November 21, 2013, http://www.nytimes.com/2013/11/21/science/two-surprises-in-dna-of-boy-found-buried-in-siberia.html.

14. Peregrine and Ember, *Encyclopedia of Prehistory: Volume 2: Arctic and Subarctic*, 194.

15. Specifically between "24,423–23,891 calendar years before present;" see Raghavan et al., "Upper Palaeolithic Siberian Genome," 87.

16. Ibid.

17. Morten Rasmussen et al., "The Genome of a Late Pleistocene Human from a Clovis Burial Site in Western Montana," *Nature* 506 (February 13, 2014), 225ff; Stuart J. Fiedel, "The Anzick Genome Proves Clovis Is First After All," *Quaternary International* (June 20, 2017), 4ff.

18. As of July 2018, it has been known that a species of *Homo* reached central China by 2.12 million years ago (Z. Zhu et al., "Hominin Occupation of the Chinese Loess Plateau Since About 2.1 Million Years Ago," *Nature* [July 11, 2018]). Whether this species of *Homo* migrated there from Africa or originated somewhere in East Asia, perhaps even China, is up for debate. What is for certain,

is that evidence for the advanced exploratory abilities of the most ancient hominins like *Homo erectus* is mounting and becoming harder to deny. For the most comprehensive documentation of *Homo erectus* and other early hominin technological—most notably maritime—abilities, see R. Bednarik, "The Maritime Dispersal of Pleistocene Humans," *Migration and Diffusion* 3, no. 10 (2002), 6–33; R. G. Bednarik, "The Beginnings of Maritime Travel," *Advances in Anthropology* 4, no. 4) (2014), 209; and R. G. Bednarik, "An Experiment in Pleistocene Seafaring," *International Journal of Nautical Archaeology* 27, no. 2 (1998), 139–149.

For the viability of early hominin maritime dispersal, consult work by Sue O'Connor, for example, S. O'Connor et al., "Hominin Dispersal and Settlement East of Huxley's Line: The Role of Sea Level Changes, Island Size, and Subsistence Behavior," *Current Anthropology* 58, no. S17 (2017), S567–S582; S. Kealy, J. Louys, and S. O'Connor, Reconstructing Palaeogeography and Inter-Island Visibility in the Wallacean Archipelago During the Likely Period of Sahul Colonization, 65–45,000 Years Ago," *Archaeological Prospection* 24, no. 3 (2017), 259–272.

Finally, for conclusive evidence of ancient hominin marine capability, see T. F. Strasser et al., "Dating Palaeolithic Sites in Southwestern Crete, Greece," *Journal of Quaternary Science* 26, no. 5 (2011), 553–560. Crete has been separated from mainland Greece since the Miocene 6 million to 5 million years ago, so the presence of Pleistocene-age arteiacts there proves conclusively that early hominins were able to—and indeed did—make substantial sea crossings and explore more of the world than we hitherto gave them credit for.

Also see T. Ingicco et al., "Earliest Known Hominin Activity in the Philippines by 709 Thousand Years Ago," *Nature* 557, no. 7704 (2018), 233. This paper "pushes back the proven period of colonisation of the Philippines by hundreds of thousands of years, and furthermore suggests that early overseas dispersal in Island South East Asia by premodern hominins took place several times during the Early and Middle Pleistocene stages."

19. "About 1/3 of the genome of all native Americans comes from Mal'ta or a population closely related to it. Importantly however Anzick is just like other Native Americans in this regard, not anything special." Personal communication (by email) from Professor Eske Willerslev, Prince Philip Professor of Ecology and Evolution, Department of Zoology, University of Cambridge, February 23, 2018. See also Rasmussen et al., "The Genome of a Late Pleistocene Human," 225–226; Raghavan et al., "Upper Palaeolithic Siberian Genome Reveals Dual Ancestry," 87–88.
20. Rasmussen et al., "The Genome of a Late Pleistocene Human," 225.
21. Ibid.
22. Ibid. Emphasis added.
23. Raghavan et al., "Upper Palaeolithic Siberian Genome Reveals Dual Ancestry," 87.
24. Ibid.
25. Ibid.
26. Ibid.
27. Ibid.
28. Ibid.
29. Ibid.
30. Fiedel, "The Anzick Genome Proves Clovis Is First After All," 4.
31. Rasmussen et al., "The Genome of a Late Pleistocene Human," 225.
32. Fiedel, "The Anzick Genome Proves Clovis Is First After All," 5.
33. Ibid.
34. Ibid.
35. Ibid.
36. Lorena Becerra-Valdivia et al., "Reassessing the Chronology of the Archaeological Site of Anzick," *Proceedings of the National Academy of Sciences* (June 18, 2018), 1. And see D. J. Stanford and B. A. Bradley in *Across Atlantic Ice: The Origin of America's Clovis Culture* (University of California Press, 2012), 180.
37. Becerra-Valdivia et al., "Reassessing the Chronology of the Archaeological Site of Anzick."
38. Ibid., 2.
39. Ibid., 1.
40. D. S. Miller, V. D. Holliday, and J. Bright, "Clovis Across the Continent," in *Paleoamerican Odyssey,* ed. Kelly E. Graf, Caroline V. Ketron, and Michael R. Waters (Texas A&M University, 2014), 207–220.
41. Rasmussen et al., "The Genome of a Late Pleistocene Human," 226.

42. Ibid.
43. Ibid.
44. Ibid., 225; Raff and Bolnick, "Genetic Roots of the First Americans," 162.
45. Pontus Skoglund et al., "Genetic Evidence for Two Founding Populations of the Americas," *Nature* 525 (September 3, 2015), 104. Emphasis added.
46. Ibid.
47. Ibid., 104–105.
48. "A DNA Search for the First Americans Links Amazon Groups to Indigenous Australians," *Smithsonian Magazine,* July 21, 2015, http://www.smithsonianmag.com/science-nature/dna-search-first-americans-links-amazon-indigenous-australians-180955976/.
49. Ibid.
50. Pontus Skoglund and David Reich, "A Genomic View of the Peopling of the Americas," *Current Opinion in Genetics and Development* 41 (December 2016), 31.
51. Cited in Stephanie Dutchen, "Genetic Studies Link Indigenous Peoples in the Amazon and Australasia," July 21, 2015, https://phys.org/news/2015-07-genetic-link-indigenous-peoples-amazon.html.
52. Skoglund et al., "Genetic Evidence for Two Founding Populations of the Americas," 107. See also David Reich, *Who We Are and How We Got Here* (Oxford University Press, 2018), 154, where a tentative "Date uncertain" age for the arrival of "Population Y" in the Americas is put at "20,000 years ago."
53. Skoglund and Reich, "A Genomic View of the Peopling of the Americas," 31.
54. Skoglund et al., "Genetic Evidence for Two Founding Populations of the Americas," 107.
55. Ibid.
56. Skoglund and Reich, "A Genomic View of the Peopling of the Americas," 31.

10: A SIGNAL FROM THE DREAMTIME?

1. Pontus Skoglund et al., "Genetic Evidence for Two Founding Populations of the Americas," *Nature* 525 (September 3, 2015).
2. Maanasa Raghavan et al., "Genomic Evidence for the Pleistocene and Recent Population History of Native Americans," *Science* 349 (August 21, 2015).
3. Ibid., aab3884-1.
4. Ibid, aab3884-8; see also "Genomic Evidence for the Pleistocene and Recent Population History of Native Americans," Research Article Summary, *Science* 349 (August 21, 2015), 841.
5. Raghavan et al., "Genomic Evidence for the Pleistocene and Recent Population History of Native Americans," aab3884-8.
6. Ibid., aab3884-7.
7. The challenge posed to scholars of the "deliberate voyaging" school is the unconvincing argument that ancient hominins were "accidentally" transported across the sea by natural events like storms and tsunamis. See, for instance, comment from archaeologist Matthew Sprigs in R. Bednarik, "The Maritime Dispersals of Pleistocene Humans," p. 55: "Given Bednarik's ongoing search to find out how sea barriers cannot be crossed, one wonders on what basis he can be so certain that colonization cannot have been accidental, by being caught up in strong currents."

   Among a mass of evidence is a paper by T. F. Strasser et al., "Dating Palaeolithic Sites in Southwestern Crete, Greece," *Journal of Quaternary Science* 26, no. 5 (2011), 553–560. Crete has been separated from mainland Greece since the Miocene 6–5 million years ago, so the presence of Pleistocene-age artifacts there proves conclusively that early hominins made sea crossings (unless one is willing to argue that ancient hominins were "accidentally" transported the approximate 500 miles there from mainland Greece or 600 miles there from mainland Turkey via islands).

   The recent analysis of rock art in Asphendou Cave, Crete, fashioning a species of deer, *Candiacervus,* that has been extinct on the island for at least 11,000 years, indicates that hominins conclusively reached Crete at least 11,000 years ago: if they could create art then why could they not create boats? See T. F. Strasser et al., (2018). "Palaeolithic Cave Art from Crete, Greece," *Journal of Archaeological Science: Reports* 18 (2018), 100–108, esp. p. 103, "if *Candiacervus,* then they date earlier than the end of the Palaeolithic at least 11 thousand years ago," and p. 107, "The last occurrence of the Cretan dwarf deer Candiacervus sometime after 21,500 years ago provides a terminus ante quem for the earliest layer of the Asphendou Cave rock carvings and confirms them as the oldest figural art found in Greece."

   Also see T. Ingicco et al., "Earliest Known Hominin Activity in the Philippines by 709 Thousand Years Ago," *Nature* 557, no. 7704 (2018), 233. This paper "pushes back the proven period of colonisation of the Philippines by hundreds of thousands of years, and furthermore suggests that early overseas dispersal in Island South East Asia by premodern hominins took place several times during the Early and Middle Pleistocene stages."

8. For evidence of Denisovan contribution to the genes of present-day Oceanians, see D. Reich et al., "Genetic History of an Archaic Hominin Group from Denisova Cave in Siberia," *Nature* 468 (2010), 1053–1060, and D. Reich et al., "Denisova Admixture and the First Modern Human Dispersals into Southeast Asia and Oceania," *American Journal of Human Genetics* 89 (2011), 516–528.

   For a reasonable explanation of this genetic signal see Alan Cooper and Chris Stringer, "Did the Denisovans Cross Wallace's Line?" *Science* 342 (2013), 321, esp. p. 332: "The source of the Denisovan gene flow appears to have been east of Wallace's Line, with a lack of Denisovan DNA in mainland populations explained by Wallace's Line limiting the reverse dispersal of introgressed populations."

   For evidence of lesser Denisovan contribution to the genes of present-day East Asians, see K. Prüfer et al., "The Complete Genome Sequence of a Neanderthal from the Altai Mountains," *Nature* 505 (2014), 43–49; P. Skoglund and M. Jakobsson, "Archaic Human Ancestry in East Asia," *Proceedings of the National Academy of Sciences* 108 (2011), 18301–18306; S. R. Browning et al., "Analysis of Human Sequence Data Reveals Two Pulses of Archaic Denisovan Admixture," *Cell* 173, no. 1 (2018), 53–61.

   Also see Robert G. Bednarik, "The Beginnings of Maritime Travel," *Advances in Anthropology* (January 2014), 209: "The maritime history of humanity commenced not a few thousand years ago, as traditional nautical archaeology has tended to assume, but more than a hundred times as long ago . . . Archaeological data from Wallacea (Indonesia) have shown that the history of seafaring began in the late part of the Early Pleistocene, at least 900 ka (900,000 years) ago. To understand better the technological magnitude of these very early maritime accomplishments, expeditions are currently engaged in a series of replicative experiments."

9. Bednarik, "The Beginnings of Maritime Travel," 210–211. Also see results of the experiment made in R. G. Bednarik, "An Experiment in Pleistocene Seafaring," *International Journal of Nautical Archaeology* 27, no. 2 (1998), 148: "The [800km] voyage from Timor or Roti to Australia was made by a marine people whose accumulated knowledge derived from a history of seafaring spanning at least 700,000, and quite probably a million, years."

   For *Homo erectus'* colonization of Flores, also see Paul Y. Sondaar, "Middle Pleistocene Faunal Turnover and Colonization of Flores (Indonesia) by Homo erectus," *Comptes Rendus de l'Academie des Sciences* 319 (1994), 1255: "Several stone artefacts have been found in a uvial sandstone layer belonging to the Ola Bula Formation, near Mata Menge in the Ngada District, West Central Flores, Indonesia . . . indicating an age of slightly less than 0.73 Ma BP. is relatively old age suggests that the artefacts are the work of *Homo erectus*." Also see Ingicco et al., "Earliest Known Hominin Activity in the Philippines by 709 thousand Years Ago," 233.

10. The two papers that established the consensus of 3,500 years ago for the Polynesian expansion are I. D. Goodwin, S. A. Browning, and A. J. Anderson, "Climate Windows for Polynesian Voyaging to New Zealand and Easter Island," *Proceedings of the National Academy of Sciences* 111, no. 41 (2014), 14716–14721, and D. A. Johns, G. J. Irwin, and Y. K. Sung, "An Early Sophisticated East Polynesian Voyaging Canoe Discovered on New Zealand's Coast," *Proceedings of the National Academy of Sciences* 111, no. 41 (2014), 14728–4733.

11. Having said that, mainstream academia has begun to change its tune. Quoted in a *Science* news article from April 24, 2018, is "initial skeptic" of prehistoric human seafaring abilities John Cherry of Brown University: "The orthodoxy until pretty recently was that you don't have seafarers until the early Bronze Age. . . . Now we are talking about seafaring Neandertals. It's a pretty stunning change." Quoted in the same article is Curtis Runnels of Boston University, co-leader of the 2008 and 2009 Crete excavations: "We severely miscalculated. . . . The seas were more permeable than we thought" (A. Lawler, "Neanderthals, Stone Age People May Have Voyaged the Mediterranean," *Science* [April 24, 2018], doi:10.1126/science.aat9795).

12. Raghavan et al., "Genomic Evidence for the Pleistocene and Recent Population History of Native Americans," aab3884–7.

13. Ibid. Emphasis added.

14. Ibid., 841.

15. Ibid., 841, aab3884–7.

16. Ibid.

17. Email exchange with Professor Eske Willerslev, March 2, 2018.

18. Ibid.

19. Ibid.
20. But for an opposing interpretation, see Skoglund et al., "Genetic Evidence for Two Founding Populations of the Americas," 104: "The coefficients for which non-American populations contribute the most to the signals **separate Native Americans into a cline with two Amazonian groups (Surui and Karitiana) on one extreme and Mesoamericans on the other**. . . . Among the outgroups, the most similar coefficients to Amazonian groups are found in Australasian populations: the Onge from the Andaman Islands in the Bay of Bengal (a so-called 'Negrito' group), New Guineans, Papuans and indigenous Australians." (Emphasis added.)
21. Ibid.
22. The Denisovan signal across Native American populations is presently estimated to be between 0.13 and 0.17 percent, not so much on the basis of genomic surveys but of more estimations: "As it was previously estimated that the Denisovan-related ancestry in . . . [Native American] populations is 3.8 percent to 4.8 percent of that in Oceania . . . combining this information with our new estimate of approximately 3.5 percent Denisovan ancestry in New Guinea and Australia leads to estimates of Denisovan ancestry in . . . [Native American] populations of 0.13 percent–0.17 percent." See Pengfei Qin and Mark Stoneking, "Denisovan Ancestry in East Eurasian and Native American Populations," *Molecular Biology and Evolution* 32, no. 10 (2015), 2671.
23. Raghavan et al., "Genomic Evidence for the Pleistocene and Recent Population History of Native Americans," aab3884–7.
24. Skoglund et al., "Genetic Evidence for Two Founding Populations of the Americas," 106.
25. See Skoglund and Reich, "A Genomic View of the Peopling of the Americas," 31, as well as P. Skoglund et al., "Genetic Evidence for Two Founding Populations of the Americas," *Nature* 525 (2015), 106.
26. Email exchange with Professor Eske Willerslev, March 2, 2018.
27. Ibid.
28. Ibid.
29. The dating of Gobekli Tepe, and its implications, is discussed in Graham Hancock, *Magicians of the Gods: The Forgotten Wisdom of Earth's Lost Civilization* (2015), chapter 1.
30. Ian Sample, "Neanderthals—not modern humans—were first artists on Earth, experts claim," *Guardian,* February 22, 2018, https://www.theguardian.com/science/2018/feb/22/neanderthals-not-humans-were-first-artists-on-earth-experts-claim. The two studies that conclusively posit Neanderthals as artists are D. L. Hoffmann et al., "Symbolic Use of Marine Shells and Mineral Pigments by Iberian Neandertals 115,000 Years Ago," *Science Advances* 4, no. 2 (2018), eaar5255, and D. L. Hoffmann et al., "U-Th Dating of Carbonate Crusts Reveals Neandertal Origin of Iberian Cave Art," *Science* 359, no. 6378 (2018), 912–915.
31. See J. Victor Moreno-Mayar et al., "Early Human Dispersals Within the Americas, *Science* (First Release, without page numbers), November 8, 2018. See also Cosimo Poth et al., "Reconstructing the Deep Population History of Central and South America," *Cell* 175 (November 15, 2018), 1–13. And see summary in Lizzie Wade, "Ancient DNA Confirms Native Americans' Deep Roots in North and South America," *Science* (November 8, 2018).
32. Moreno-Mayar et al., "Early Human Dispersals Within the Americas."
33. Cited in Wade, "Ancient DNA Confirms Native Americans' Deep Roots in North and South America."

PART IV

11: GHOST CITIES OF THE AMAZON
1. H. C. Heaton (ed.), *The Discovery of the Amazon According to the Account of Friar Gaspar de Carvajal and Other Documents* (American Geographical Society, 1934), 169.
2. Ibid., 172.
3. Ibid., 198: "There was one settlement that stretched for five leagues without any intervening space from house to house, which was a marvellous thing to behold." Commenting on this observation, Professor David Wilkinson of UCLA notes that the exact length of a "league" was "not a fully agreed-upon or stabilized physical distance, but was probably not less than 2.5 English statute miles nor more than 4." See David Wilkinson, "Amazonian Civilization?" *Comparative Civilizations Review* 74, no. 74 (Spring 2016), 96. At the minimum measure, therefore, 5 leagues equals 12.5 miles (20.1 kilometers), while at the maximum measure, 5 leagues equals 20 miles (32.2 kilometers). It seems safe, therefore, to summarize the extent of this settlement as "more than 20 kilometers."

4. Ibid, 198, where the "territory of the great overlord Machiparo," all inhabited, with "a wealth of natural resources," is said to extend for 80 leagues. See also p. 188 for a second cultivated area of similar extent. And see p. 217: "This land is as good, as fertile, and as normal in appearance as our Spain. . . . Already the Indians were beginning to burn over their fields. It is a temperate land, where much wheat may be harvested and all kinds of fruit trees may be grown; besides this, it is suitable for the breeding of all sorts of livestock." See note above on the length of a league.

5. For example, see ibid., 190: "This Machiparo has his headquarters near the river upon a small hill and holds sway over many settlements and very large ones which together contribute for fighting purposes fifty thousand men of the age of from thirty years up to seventy." See also pp. 194–195, 197–199, 204, 213, and 218–219.

6. See note 3 above on the length of a "league."

7. Heaton, *The Discovery of the Amazon According to the Account of Friar Gaspar de Carvajal and Other Documents*, 198.

8. Ibid., 200.

9. Including: "meats, partridges, turkeys, and fish of many sorts;" "turtles and parrots in abundance;" "turtles . . . manatees and other fish, and roasted partridges and cats and monkeys;" "turtles in pens and pools of water, and a great deal of meat and fish and biscuit . . . in such great abundance that there was enough to feed an expeditionary force of one thousand men for one year;" "pineapples and [avocados] and plums and custard apples and many other kinds of fruit;" "a very great quantity of very good biscuit which the Indians make out of maize and yucca, and much fruit of all kinds," and fish drying "to be transported into the interior to be sold;" "turtles . . . turkeys and parrots . . . bread and . . . very good wine resembling beer;" a tapir; "snails and crabs; yams and maize." Ibid., 175, 180, 182, 192, 200, 203, 207, 210, 211, 230, 231, 232.

10. Ibid., 201.

11. Ibid.

12. Ibid., 202.

13. Ibid.

14. J. T. Medina, *The Discovery of the Amazon According to the Account of Friar Gaspar de Carvajal and Other Documents*, vol. 17 (American Geographical Society, 1934), 8.

15. Ibid., 9.

16. See, for example, Spanish historian Francisco Lòpez de Gomara, quoted in Medina, *The Discovery of the Amazon According to the Account of Friar Gaspar de Carvajal and Other Documents*, 25–26, who in 1552 described Carvajal's journal as being "full of lies." However, Carvajal actually visited the Amazon, whereas Gomara did not. Furthermore, Gomara was evidently more criticized by his sixteenth-century contemporaries for distorting historical truth than Carvajal was; on November 17, 1553, Prince Phillip of Spain imposed a penalty of 200,000 maravedis on anyone who would reprint Gomara's historically inaccurate work.

17. Heaton, *The Discovery of the Amazon According to the Account of Friar Gaspar de Carvajal and Other Documents*, 214: "Our Lord was pleased to give strength and courage to our companions, who killed seven or eight (for these we actually saw) of the Amazons, whereupon the Indians lost heart." Carvajal clearly distinguishes between the "women warriors" or "the Amazons" and "the Indians" here.

18. Ibid., 214.

19. Ibid., 212–214, 220–221.

20. Ibid., 221.

21. By 1541 the fierce Amazonian women warriors had made an especially significant appearance in literary culture and were becoming embedded in the European imagination. For example, they featured heavily in "Las sergas de Esplandan," a sequel to the Amadis of Gaul cycle, which was first published in 1510 and widely circulated. For a good documentation of European imagination of the Amazons, see E. Pink, "The Amazons of the Americas: Between Myth and Reality," available here via Newcastle University: https://www.societies.ncl.ac.uk/pgfnewcastle/files/2015/03/Pink-The-Amazons-of-the-Americans.pdf.

22. Heaton, *The Discovery of the Amazon According to the Account of Friar Gaspar de Carvajal and Other Documents*. Most agree that the Amazon got its name from the women of the Tupya tribe against whom Orellana battled, as they reminded him of the female Amazon warriors of Greek legend. This is evident in Carvajal's account, for he explains, "In the years which followed Orellana's expedition the name Marañón . . . was abandoned, and the river began to more generally be known as

the River of the Amazons." At times, also, it was referred to under the name of its discoverer. An instance of this may be seen in the articles of agreement drawn up by order of the king, under the date of August 11, 1552, empowering Gerónimo de Aguayo "to go to the provinces of the Aruacas **and of the Amazons**," who are located, as this document reads, "[in a region stretching away] from the mouth of the Orellana River, called by another name The Amazons" (162–163). (Emphasis added.) Supporting this are words of the fiercest critic of Carvajal, López de Gómara, who is quoted by Medina in his introduction to Carvajal's account as saying, "Among the extravagant statements which he made was his claim that there were Amazons along this river with whom he and his companions had fought. . . . Because of this imposture, already many write and say 'River of the Amazons,' and there have gathered together so many parties to go there" (26).

23. Heaton, *The Discovery of the Amazon According to the Account of Friar Gaspar de Carvajal and Other Documents*, 217.
24. See, for example, A. C. Roosevelt et al., "Paleoindian Cave Dwellers in the Amazon: The Peopling of the Americas," *Science* 272, no. 5260 (1996), 373–384, esp. 373: "The tropical rainforest was thought to have been an ecological barrier to Paleoindians because it provided only scarce resources for human subsistence, and anthropologists have theorised that people could not survive there before the development of slash and burn cultivation."
25. M. W. Palace et al., "Ancient Amazonian Populations Left Lasting Impacts on Forest Structure," *Ecosphere* 8, no. 12 (December 2017), 2.
26. Heaton, *The Discovery of the Amazon According to the Account of Friar Gaspar de Carvajal and Other Documents*, 235.
27. Wilkinson, "Amazonian Civilization?" 81.
28. Ibid., 81–82.
29. Heaton, *The Discovery of the Amazon According to the Account of Friar Gaspar de Carvajal and Other Documents*, 198.
30. Ibid., 202.
31. See Wilkinson, "Amazonian Civilization?" 96.
32. Thomas P. Myers et al., "Historical Perspectives on Amazonian Dark Earths," in Johannes Lehmann et al. (eds.), *Amazonian Dark Earths* (Kluwer Academic Publishers, 2010), 15.
33. Wilkinson, "Amazonian Civilization?" 83.
34. See for example the population estimates of Jan De Vries in *European Urbanisation, 1500–1800* (Methuen, 1984), 28: "Of the perhaps 3000–4000 settlements in Europe that were vested with city rights of one form or another, or were otherwise acknowledged to be urban places around 1500, only 154 were inhabited by 10,000 or more people, and only 4 contained as many as 100,000. . . ." Also of note is that the whole of Scandinavia is estimated as having had a total urban population of 13,000 in 1500, which is just over half the size of Wilkinson's largest estimated Amazonian settlement (30).
35. Admittedly, the population of London is estimated as having fallen by a third following the bubonic plague. Even so, its estimated population of 60,000 in 1500 is revealing in the context of contemporaneous Amazonian urbanity. Figure taken from Bruce Robinson, "London: Brighter Lights, Bigger City" (BBC, 02/07/2011), http://www.bbc.co.uk/history/british/civil_war_revolution/brighter_lights_01.shtml.
36. Figure taken from Tim Lambert, "A Short History of York, Yorkshire, England," http://www.localhistories.org/york.html.
37. Figure taken from "Alterations to the Municipalities in the Population Censuses since 1842: Toledo," Instituto Nacional de Estadística (Spain), http://www.ine.es/intercensal/.
38. Figures taken from aggregate sources on Wikipiedia: https://en.wikipedia.org/wiki/Military_Revolution.
39. Wilkinson, "Amazonian Civilization?" 83–84.
40. Ibid., 83.
41. Ibid., 85.
42. Ibid.
43. Samuel Fritz and George Edmundson, *Journal of the Travels and Labours of Father Samuel Fritz in the River of the Amazons between 1686 and 1723* (printed for the Hakluyt Society, London, 1922).
44. See the discussion in Heaton, *The Discovery of the Amazon According to the Account of Friar Gaspar de Carvajal and Other Documents*, 62–63.
45. Wilkinson, "Amazonian Civilization?" 85.

46. Ibid.
47. Ibid.
48. In conversation with Charles Mann. See Charles C. Mann, *1491* (Vintage Books, 2011), 330.
49. See, for example, Betty J. Meggers and Clifford Evans, "Archaeological Investigations at the Mouth of the Amazon," *Bureau of American Ethnology Bulletin* 167 (1957), 1–664.
50. Mann, *1491*, 328.
51. Wilkinson, "Amazonian Civilization?" 85.
52. Ibid., 88.
53. Anna Curtenius Roosevelt, "The Rise and Fall of the Amazon Chiefdoms," *L'Homme* 33, no. 126 (1993), 255–283, and Anna C. Roosevelt, "The Development of Prehistoric Complex Societies: Amazonia, a Tropical Forest," *Archeological Papers of the American Anthropological Association* 9, no. 1 (1999), 13–33, cited in Wilkinson, "Amazonian Civilization?" 88.
54. Neil Lancelot Whitehead, *The Ancient Amerindian Polities of the Lower Orinoco, Amazon and Guayana Coast: A Preliminary Analysis of Their Passage from Antiquity to Extinction* (Wenner Gren Foundation for Anthropological Research, 1989), cited in Wilkinson, "Amazonian Civilisation?" 89.
55. Michael J. Heckenberger et al., "Lost Civilizations and Primitive Tribes, Amazonia: Reply to Meggers," *Latin American Antiquity* 12, no. 3 (September 2001), 331.
56. Ibid., 329.
57. Ibid., 332.
58. Wilkinson, "Amazonian Civilization?" 89.
59. The smallpox epidemic, to which the Aztecs had no immunity, was probably the single key factor that ensured Spanish victory in the conquest. By the time Cortes and his conquistadors finally captured Tenochtitlan, the Aztec capital, most of its inhabitants were already dead—from smallpox. It is thought likely that the Inca emperor Huayna Capac died of smallpox in 1528, four years before the arrival of Pizarro's forces in Peru, indicating strongly that the virus had traveled on trade networks from Mexico. If those networks were exclusively coastal, then smallpox might not have reached the Amazon until 1542. If they had been inland, then it is possible it could have done so a decade or so earlier. See, for example, D. R. Hopkins, *The Greatest Killer: Smallpox in History* (University of Chicago Press, 2002), 208–211: "The rumours of the Inca Empire that lured Balboa south were also evidence of communication, by land and by sea, between the Indians of Peru and those living in Central America." The author goes on to say that when smallpox struck the land of the Incas sometime around 1524–1527, it was almost certainly smallpox imported from Central America.
60. Ibid.
61. Wilkinson, "Amazonian Civilization?" 89.
62. Thomas P. Myers, "El efecto de las pestes sobre las poblaciones de la Amazonía Alta," *Amazonía Peruana* 8, no. 15 (1988), cited in Wilkinson, "Amazonian Civilization?" 89.
63. Ibid.
64. Ibid.

12: THE ANCIENTS BEHIND THE VEIL

1. M. Goulding, R. B. Barthem, and R. Duenas, *The Smithsonian Atlas of the Amazon* (Smithsonian Books, 2003), 19: "Approximately 85 per cent of the South American rainforest . . . is found in the Amazon Basin."
2. S. Adams, A. Ganeri, and A. Kay, *Geography of the World: The Essential Family guide to Geography and Culture* (DK, 2006), 170.
3. Ibid., 260.
4. Ibid., 176.
5. Ibid., 24.
6. Ibid., 30.
7. Ibid., 78.
8. Tom D. Dillehay et al., "New Archaeological Evidence for an Early Human Presence at Monte Verde, Chile," *PLoS One* (November 18, 2015), 3. The finds were "associated with the remains of a long tent-like dwelling, the foundation of another structure, hearths, human footprints, economic plants, and wood, reed, bone, and stone artifacts."
9. Ibid.
10. Ibid., 1.
11. Ibid., 2.

12. Ibid., 4.
13. David J. Meltzer et al., "On the Pleistocene Antiquity of Monte Verde, Southern Chile," *American Antiquity* 62, no. 4 (October 1997), 662.
14. Dillehay et al., "New Archaeological Evidence for an Early Human Presence at Monte Verde, Chile," 12.
15. Denis Vialou et al., "Peopling South America's Centre: The Late Pleistocene Site of Santa Elina," *Antiquity* 91 (August 2017), 865–884.
16. Ibid., 867.
17. Ibid., 870. In later millennia, during the Pleistocene/Holocene transition and into relatively recent times, Santa Elina rock shelter was reoccupied by humans on multiple occasions.
18. Technically they are osteoderms—literally "bony skin," from the extinct megafaunal ground sloth *Glossotherium*. Ibid., see esp. p. 875.
19. N. Guidon and G. Delibrias, "Carbon-14 Dates Point to Man in the Americas 32,000 Years Ago," *Nature* 321 (June 19, 1986), 769–771.
20. Ibid., 769.
21. Ibid., 771.
22. Shigueo Watanabe et al., "Some Evidence of a Date of First Humans to Arrive in Brazil," *Journal of Archaeological Science* 30 (March 2003), 351.
23. Ibid., 353–354.
24. N. Guidon and B. Arnaud, "The Chronology of the New World: Two Faces of One Reality," *World Archaeology* 23, no. 2 (October 1991), 167.
25. Ibid., 168.
26. Ibid., 168–169.
27. Watanabe et al., "Some Evidence of a Date of First Humans to Arrive in Brazil," 354. The authors, who see the skulls as having "Negroid charactaristics," are also open to the possibility that the migration might have come "from Africa across the South Atlantic Ocean."
28. Distances calculated using Google Maps "distance from" tool. a) Nearest point of Xingu River to Santa Elina: https://www.google.co.uk/maps/place/15%C2%B019'58.8%22S+56%C2%B057'00. 0%22W/@-12.986961,-55.1104767,7z/data=!4m6!3m5!1s0x0:0x0!7e2!8m2!3d-15.333!4d-56.95.

    b) Nearest point of Xingu River to Pedra Furada: https://www.google.co.uk/maps/place/ Pedra+Furada/@-11.5025045,-53.4068848,7z/data=!4m5!3m4!1s0x93309f3f46300909:0x13635e bcbb173337!8m2!3d-10.8772297!4d-47.3858913.
29. A. C. Roosevelt et al., "Palaeoindian Cave Dwellers in the Amazon: The Peopling of the Americas," *Science* 272 (April 19, 1996), 373–384.
30. Ibid., 380.
31. Ibid., 381.
32. Data taken from the World Bank: "Land area (sq.km):" Mexico 1,943,950.0; Guatemala 107,160.0; Belize 22,810.0; Honduras 111,890.0; El Salvador 20,720.0; Total = 2,206,530. https://data.world bank.org/indicator/AG.LND.TOTL.K2
33. Ibid., + India 2,973,190.0 = 5,179,720.
34. See G. Hancock, *Underworld: The Mysterious Origins of Civilization,* (Michael Joseph, 2002), 629–630.
35. "Antarctica's Location and Geography" on Polar Discovery: Woods Hole Oceanographic Institution, http://polardiscovery.whoi.edu/antarctica/geography.html.
36. Kerry H. Cook and Edward K. Vizy, "Detection and Analysis of an Amplified Warming of the Sahara Desert," *Journal of Climate* 28 (2015), 6560, esp. 6561.
37. See, for example, Nick A. Drake and Roger M. Blench, "Ancient Watercourses and Biogeography of the Sahara Explain the Peopling of the Desert," *Proceedings of the National Academy of Sciences* 108 (January 11, 2011), 458–462.
38. Adams, Ganeri, and Kay, *Geography of the World,* 46.
39. "Sprawling Maya Network Discovered Under Guatemala Jungle," BBC, February 2, 2018, https:// www.bbc.com/news/amp/world-latin-america-42916261.
40. Ibid. See also "Exclusive: Laser Scans Reveal Maya 'Megalopolis' Below Guatemalan Jungle," *National Geographic,* February 1, 2018, https://news.nationalgeographic.com/2018/02/maya-la ser-lidar-guatemala-pacunam/.
41. Ibid.
42. Ibid.

13: BLACK EARTH

1. A. C. Roosevelt et. al., "Palaeoindian Cave Dwellers in the Amazon: The Peopling of the Americas," *Science* 272 (April 19, 1996), 380: "The luminescence dates ~ 16,000 to 9500 B.P. overlap the possible range of calendar dates estimated for the radiocarbon dates, ~ 14,200 to 10,500 yr B.P." See also M. Michab et al., "Luminescence Dates for the Paleoindian Site of Pedra Pintada, Brazil," *Quaternary Science Reviews* 17, no. 11 (1988), 1041–1046, esp. p. 1045: "While the luminescence dates lack the precision of the radiocarbon dates they confirm the fact that the cave was occupied between about 13,500 and 10,000 calendar years ago."
2. M. C. Castro and B. H. Singer, "Agricultural Settlement and Soil Quality in the Brazilian Amazon," *Population and Environment* 34, no. 1 (2012), 22–43, esp. p. 23. Most Amazon base soils are weathered and lack good fertility. As a result, 75 percent of the agriculture practiced across the Amazon basin today requires the help of chemicals and machine technology to yield sustainable annual crops.
3. Ibid., 40.
4. Crystal N. H. McMichael et al., "Ancient Human Disturbances May Be Skewing Our Understanding of Amazonian Forests," *Proceedings of the National Academy of Sciences* 114 (January 17, 2017), 522.
5. Manuel Arroyo-Kalin, *Steps Towards an Ecology of Landscape: A Geoarchaeological Approach to the Study of Anthropogenic Dark Earths in the Central Amazon Region, Brazil* (University of Cambridge Department of Archaeology, 2008), 11.
6. Herbert Smith (1879) cited in Emma Morris, "Putting the Carbon Back: Black Is the New Green," *Nature* 442 (August 10, 2006), 624.
7. Arroyo-Kalin, *Steps Towards an Ecology of Landscape,* 11.
8. See, for example, Morris, "Putting the Carbon Back," 624, and Cornell University's Department of Crop and Soil Sciences information page on terra preta, http://www.css.cornell.edu/faculty/leh mann/research/terra%20preta/terrapretamain.html, which states: "'Terra Preta de Indio' (Amazonian Dark Earths; earlier also called 'Terra Preta do Indio' or Indian Black Earth) is the local name for certain dark earths in the Brazilian Amazon region."
9. B. Glaser and W. I. Woods (eds.), *Amazonian Dark Earths: Explorations in Space and Time* (Springer Verlag, 2004), 1.
10. Ibid.
11. Michael J. Heckenberger et al., "Pre-Columbian Urbanism, Anthropogenic Landscapes, and the Future of the Amazon," *Science* (August 29, 2008), 1214–1217. The phrase "garden city" is applied to residence patterns adopted by the prehistoric urban settlements of the Upper Xingu—see p. 1217. See also the *Daily Telegraph* (London), August 28, 2008, which reports the contents of the *Science* paper under the headline "Amazon Rainforest Was Giant Garden City," https://www.tele graph.co.uk/news/science/science-news/3350474/Amazon-rainforest-was-giant-garden-city.html.
12. Glaser and Woods, *Amazonian Dark Earths,* 3.
13. Figures from Beata Golińska, "Amazonian Dark Earths in the Context of Pre-Columbian Settlements," *Geophysics, Geology and Environment* 40, no. 2 (2014), 220, and Antoinette M. G. A. WinklerPrins, "Terra Preta: The Mysterious Soils of the Amazon," in G. Jock Churchman and Edward R. Landa (eds.), *The Soil Underfoot: Infinite Possibilities for a Finite Resource* (CRC Press, 2014), 238.
14. Stephen Schwartzman et al., "The Natural and Social History of the Indigenous Lands and Protected Areas Corridor of the Xingu River Basin," *Philosophical Transactions of the Royal Society B* (April 22, 2013), 3.
15. See, for example, M. W. Palace et al., "Ancient Amazonian Populations Left Lasting Impacts on Forest Structure," *Ecosphere* 8, no. 12 (December 2017), 3; Eduardo G. Neves et al., "Dark Earths and the Human Built Landscape in Amazonia: A Widespread Pattern of Anthrosol Formation," *Journal of Archaeological Science* 42 (February 2014), 153; Charles R. Clement et al., "The Domestication of Amazonia Before European Conquest," *Proceedings of the Royal Society B* (July 22, 2015), 1, 3; and Arroyo-Kalin, *Steps Towards an Ecology of Landscape,* 11, 13.
16. Ute Scheub et al., *Terra Preta: How the World's Most Fertile Soil Can Help Reverse Climate Change and Reduce World Hunger* (Greystone Books, 2016), xv. See also Bruno Glaser and Jago Jonathan Birk, "Stage of Scientific Knowledge on Properties and Genesis of Anthropogenic Dark Earths in Central Amazonia (*terra preta de Índio*)," *Geochimica et Cosmochimica Acta* 82 (2012), 49: "The existence of terra preta even several thousand years after their creation unambiguously shows that improvement of highly weathered tropical soils by human actions is possible." For a quick overview, see also "Terra Preta: The Secret of the Rainforest's Fertile Soil," *Facts Are Facts Magazine,* https://www.facts-are-facts.com/article/terra-preta-the-secret-of-the-rainforests-fertile-soil.

17. Schwartzman et al., "The Natural and Social History of the Indigenous Lands and Protected Areas Corridor of the Xingu River Basin," 3.

18. WinklerPrins, "Terra Preta: The Mysterious Soils of the Amazon," 236. Emphasis added. See also Glaser and Woods, *Amazonian Dark Earths,* 4: "Most researchers believe that these soils formed in cultural deposits created through the accretion of waste and occupation debris around habitation areas."

19. Eduardo G. Neves et al., "Historical and Socio-cultural Origins of Amazonian Dark Earth" in Johannes Lehmann eds., *Amazonian Dark Earths: Origin Properties Management* (Springer, 2003), 29–50. See p. 40: "Possible sources of ADE in the context of habitation may be associated with burial activities (human remains, urns, cloth, etc.), food preparation (fire remains such as soot, ash, charcoal; food processing remains such as fish waste or waste from game, blood from hunted animals, inedible parts of fruit, vegetables and nuts, etc.; cooking and storage vessels, etc.), eaten food waste (human excrement, processed food waste such as bones of fish and game), housing (debris of housing materials such as straw or palm leaves, wood, skin), and various other activities (dyes, oils, fiber from palms and bark, etc.)."

20. Neves et al., "Dark Earths and the Human Built Landscape in Amazonia," 161.

21. Ibid.

22. "Thomas R. Miles has designed, developed, installed and tested agricultural and industrial systems for fuel handling, air quality, and biomass energy since 1975. An expert in combustion and gasification of biomass, he has designed and developed many systems to make biochar. He has sponsored and hosted internet discussions on biomass energy since 1994 including biochar@yahoogroups.com listservs and www.biochar.bioenergylists.org since 2006." See http://2012.biochar.us.com/profile/116/thomas-r-miles.

23. Tom Miles, "Amazon's Mysterious Black Earth: Soil Found Along Region Riverbanks; Rich in Nutrients, Stores More Carbon," BioEnergy Lists: Biochar Mailing Lists, January 20, 2007, http://terrapreta.bioenergylists.org/forestsorg.

24. The fertility of terra preta is discussed at length in Scheub et al., *Terra Preta,* 6.

25. WinklerPrins, "Terra Preta: The Mysterious Soils of the Amazon," 236. The quoted passage continues: "In the generally high humidity and high rainfall environments such as found in the Amazon basin, most nutrients in the soil mineralize and are leached out of the system quickly, and because of this, the vegetation of the region typically absorbs nutrients quickly from the soil once these have been released in the soil through decomposition or other processes."

26. Ibid.

27. Ibid. "The carbon found in ADE's is aromatic carbon (also known as black or pyrogenic carbon) that is likely a consequence of the incorporation of charcoal into the soil. . . . Soils with this type of carbon are able to retain, even attract nutrients, resulting in more plant-available phosphorus, calcium, and nitrogen, as the aromatic carbon acts as a carrying agent for nutrients. Aromatic carbon is also known to be highly resistant to degradation."

28. Morris, "Putting the Carbon Back," 625. The cited passage continues: "They become homes for populations of microorganisms that turn the soil into that spongy, fragrant, dark material that gardeners everywhere love to plunge their hands into. The char is not the only good stuff in *terra preta*—additions such as excrement and bone probably play a role too—but it is the most important factor. Leaving aside the subtleties of how char particles improve fertility, the sheer amount of carbon they can stash away is phenomenal."

29. William Balée, "Amazonian Dark Earths," *Tipiti: Journal of the Society for the Anthropology of Lowland South America* 8, no. 1 (2010), 5. Emphasis in the original. The cited passage goes on to state: "Biochar is believed to be the principal source of the color of the Amazon Dark Earths as well as the reason for retention of nutrients. Microbial activity leads to increased carbon sequestration. That is what makes ADEs of interest in research on climate change. The higher and more diverse the microbial activity, the better the soil, and ADE is richer and more diverse in microbes than surrounding soils, even though millions of these species remain to be identified precisely and literally *a million separate taxa can be contained in only 10 grams of soil.* A significant proportion of the microbes in ADE are different from the microbes in the surrounding primeval soils."

30. Glaser and Woods, *Amazonian Dark Earths,* 4. The cited passage continues: "The consequent increase in microbiological activity adds colloidally sized organic decomposition products to the soil matrix."

31. Ibid., 4.

32. WinklerPrins, "Terra Preta: The Mysterious Soils of the Amazon," 236.

33. Neves et al., "Dark Earths and the Human Built Landscape in Amazonia," 153.
34. Balée, "Amazonian Dark Earths," 5.
35. See, for example, A. C. Roosevelt, "The Amazon and the Anthropocene: 13,000 Years of Human Influence in a Tropical Rainforest," *Anthropocene* 4 (December 2013), 79, 80; Clement et al., "The Domestication of Amazonia Before European Conquest," 3; Lizzie Wade, "Searching for the Amazon's Hidden Civilizations," *Science* (January 7, 2014), http://www.sciencemag.org/news/2014/01/searching-amazons-hidden-civilizations.
36. Neves et al., "Historical and Socio-Cultural Origins of Amazonian Dark Earths," 38.
37. Ibid.
38. Ibid.
39. Ibid.
40. Ibid., 37–38.
41. Clement et al., "The Domestication of Amazonia Before European Conquest," 3.
42. Morris, "Putting the Carbon Back," 624.
43. B. Liang et al., "Black Carbon Increases Cation Exchange Capacity in Soils," *Soil Science Society of America Journal* (September 1, 2006), 1719 and 1720. See also Jennifer Watling et al., "Direct Archaeological Evidence for Southwestern Amazonia as an Early Plant Domestication and Food Production Centre," *PLoS One* (July 25, 2018), 2: "New radiocarbon dates associated with Massangana phase deposits of lithic artefacts in what appear to be Anthropogenic Dark Earths, or terra preta, matrices at Garbin and Teotonio sites have also pushed regional ADE formation as far back as ca 7,000–6,790 to 8,600–8,420 cal BP . . . which makes the dark earths of the Upper Madeira some 3,500 years older than the rest of Amazonia."
44. See, for example, Palace et al., "Ancient Amazonian Populations Left Lasting Impacts on Forest Structure," 3: "The quest to map ADE locations has been stymied by the immense size of Amazonia, remoteness in many areas, dense forest, and lack of archaeological field surveys."

14: GARDENING EDEN

1. A. C. Roosevelt, "The Amazon and the Anthropocene: 13,000 Years of Human Influence in a Tropical Rainforest," *Anthropocene* (May 27, 2014), 82.
2. Ibid.
3. C. Levis et al., "Persistent Effects of Pre-Columbian Plant Domestication on Amazonian Forest Composition," *Science* 355 (March 3, 2017), 926.
4. Roosevelt, "The Amazon and the Anthropocene," 82.
5. Levis et al., "Persistent Effects of Pre-Columbian Plant Domestication on Amazonian Forest Composition," 925.
6. Ibid., 927.
7. Ibid., 927–928.
8. Ibid., 925, 931.
9. Ibid.
10. Carolina Levis interviewed in *The Atlantic*, March 2, 2017, https://www.theatlantic.com/science/archive/2017/03/its-now-clear-that-ancient-humans-helped-enrich-the-amazon/518439/. See also Levis et al., "Persistent Effects of Pre-Columbian Plant Domestication on Amazonian Forest Composition," 925: "In Amazonia, plant domestication started earlier than 8000 BP."
11. See also Levis et al., "Persistent Effects of Pre-Columbian Plant Domestication on Amazonian Forest Composition," 926.
12. See, for example, Clement et al., "The Domestication of Amazonia Before European Conquest," *Proceedings of the Royal Society B* (July 22, 2015), 2, and Annalee Newitz, "The Amazon Rainforest Is the Result of an 8,000-Year Experiment," *ArsTechnica* (March 6, 2017), https://arstechnica.com/science/2017/03/the-amazon-forest-is-the-result-of-a-8000-year-experiment/. See also Charles R. Clement et al., "Origin and Domestication of Native Amazonian Crops," *Diversity* (March 2010), 72–186.
13. Clement et al., "Origin and Domestication of Native Amazonian Crops," 84–85 and 92, and Barbara Pickersgill, "Domestication of Plants in the Americas: Insights from Mendelian and Molecular Genetics," *Annals of Botany* 100, no. 5 (October 2007), 929.
14. Clement et al., "The Domestication of Amazonia Before European Conquest," 1. See also Jennifer Watling et al., "Direct Archaeological Evidence for Southwestern Amazonia as an Early Plant Domestication and Food Production Centre," *PLoS One* 13, no. 7 (2018), e0199868.
15. Clement et al., "The Domestication of Amazonia Before European Conquest," 2.
16. Pickersgill, "Domestication of Plants in the Americas," 930, and Clement et al., "Origin and

Domestication of Native Amazonian Crops," 72–73, 85–87. See also Chanie Kirschner, "Do Pineapples Grow on Trees?" April 8, 2012, https://www.mnn.com/your-home/organic-farming-gardening/questions/do-pineapples-grow-on-trees. Potted pineapple plants are now sold in super markets as houseplants: https://www.housebeautiful.com/uk/lifestyle/shopping/news/a2807/asda-selling-pineapple-plants.

17. Clement et al., "Origin and Domestication of Native Amazonian Crops," 86.
18. Ibid., 73.
19. Ibid.
20. Ibid., 76.
21. Ibid., 73 and 75.
22. Christian Isendahl, "The Domestication and Early Spread of Manioc: A Brief Synthesis," *Latin American Antiquity* 22, no. 4 (December 2011), 452.
23. Clement et al., "Origin and Domestication of Native Amazonian Crops," 77.
24. Tom D. Dillehay et al., "Preceramic Adoption of Peanut, Squash, and Cotton in Northern Peru," *Science* 316, no. 5833 (June 29, 2007), 1890.
25. Ibid., 1891.
26. Spencer P. M. Harrington, "Earliest Agriculture in the New World," *Archaeology* 50, no. 4 (July/August 1997), https://archive.archaeology.org/9707/newsbriefs/squash.html.
27. Dillehay et al., "Preceramic Adoption of Peanut, Squash, and Cotton in Northern Peru," 1890–1891.
28. Ibid.
29. Ibid.; see also Pickersgill, "Domestication of Plants in the Americas," 930.
30. Pickersgill, "Domestication of Plants in the Americas," 930: "One important legume, the peanut or groundnut (*Arachis hypogaea*), a tetraploid annual, was domesticated east of the Andes, probably close to the area in which cassava was domesticated. It became widespread prehistorically, possibly spreading in association with cassava." See also Clement et al., "Origin and Domestication of Native Amazonian Crops," 93, Figure 3, which includes peanuts among "native Amazonian crops."
31. For manioc, see Clement et al., "Origin and Domestication of Native Amazonian Crops," 77 and 92. For peanuts, see Dillehay et al., "Preceramic Adoption of Peanut, Squash, and Cotton in Northern Peru," 1891.
32. Isendahl, "The Domestication and Early Spread of Manioc," 452. See also Watling et al., "Direct Archaeological Evidence for Southwestern Amazonia as an Early Plant Domestication and Food Production Centre," 19: For manioc, "genetic evidence points to a domestication event sometime between 8,000 and 10,000 BP."
33. Isendahl, "The Domestication and Early Spread of Manioc," 454.
34. Ibid.
35. Dillehay et al., "Preceramic Adoption of Peanut, Squash, and Cotton in Northern Peru," 1890.
36. Pickersgill, "Domestication of Plants in the Americas," 930.
37. Isendahl, "The Domestication and Early Spread of Manioc," 455.
38. Ibid.
39. See, for example, H. C. Heaton (ed.), *The Discovery of the Amazon According to the Account of Friar Gaspar de Carvajal and Other Documents* (American Geographical Society, 1934), 172.
40. "Manioc Processing Amongst Brazil's Canela Indians," https://anthropology.si.edu/canela/manioc.htm.
41. And see Watling et al., "Direct Archaeological Evidence for Southwestern Amazonia as an Early Plant Domestication and Food Production Centre," 21–22: "The pervading view is that the early Holocene inhabitants of the upper Madeira were simple hunter-gatherers from a 'pre'-landscape domestication age. However, this scenario seems unlikely if we think about the following: we know manioc was domesticated—and therefore cultivated—by societies in the same region during the Girau phase, and probably, we have argued, by the Girau-period inhabitants themselves. In domesticating manioc, people not only improved various aspects such as the size and production of its tubers, photosynthetic rates and seed functionality, but they did this by repeated cycles of recombination and selection which involved clonal propagation as a viable reproductive mechanism (wild manioc cannot reproduce from stem cuttings). This process, which was completed by 8,000 years ago, required highly sophisticated knowledge of the natural world."
42. F. F. F. Teles, "Chronic Poisoning by Hydrogen Cyanide in Cassava and Its Prevention in Africa and Latin America," *Food and Nutrition Bulletin* 23, no. 4 (2002), 407–412, esp. p. 410.

43. Jeremy Narby, *The Cosmic Serpent: DNA and the Origins of Knowledge* (Victor Gollancz, 1995), 39.

44. Ibid., 40.

45. Ibid.

46. Examples of studies revealing the transformative power of ayahuasca and its contribution to the Western Consciousness Revolution are psychologist Rachel Harris's *Listening to Ayahuasca* (New World Library, 2017); medical doctor Joe Tafur's *The Fellowship of the River: A Medical Doctor's Exploration into Traditional Plant Medicine* (Joseph Tafur, 2017); and ex-veteran Alex Seymour's *Psychedelic Marine: A Transformational Journey from Afghanistan to the Amazon* (Park Street Press, 2016), among very many more.

15: SACRED GEOMETRY

1. Stanislas Dehaene et al., "Core Knowledge of Geometry in an Amazonian Indigene Group," *Science* 311 (January 20, 2006), 381.

2. Ibid.

3. Ibid., 381, 384.

4. Ibid., 381.

5. Ibid.

6. Charles Mann, "Ancient Earthmovers of the Amazon," *Science* 321 (August 29, 2008), 148.

7. Martti Pärssinen, Denise Schaan, and Alceu Ranzi, "Pre-Columbian Geometric Earthworks in the Upper Purús," *Antiquity* 83, no. 322 (December 1, 2009), 1087.

8. Ibid., 1084–1095.

9. Ibid., 1084.

10. Ibid., 1085.

11. Ibid., 1087.

12. See discussion and photographs in Graham Hancock and Santha Faiia, *Heaven's Mirror: Quest for the Lost Civilization* (Penguin, 1998), 257–269.

13. Cited in Mann, "Ancient Earthmovers of the Amazon," 1148.

14. Denise P. Schaan, *Sacred Geographies of Ancient Amazonia* (Routledge, 2012), 142–143.

15. Maria Reiche interviewed by Graham Hancock and Santha Faiia, June 12, 1993, reported in *Heaven's Mirror*, 261.

16. Anthony F. Aveni, *Between the Lines: The Mystery of the Giant Ground Drawings of Ancient Nasca, Peru* (University of Texas Press, 2000), 34.

17. New World Encyclopedia, "Nazca Lines" (accessed July 23, 2018), http://www.newworldencyclo pedia.org/entry/Nazca_Lines.

18. J. G. Fleagle, *Primate Adaptation and Evolution*, 2nd ed. (Academic Press, 1998), 172.

19. Aveni, *Between the Lines*, 34.

20. Dimensions from Maria Reiche, *Mystery on the Desert* (Editorial E Emprenta Entoria, 1949, reprinted 1996), 24.

21. Firm identification of the Nazca spider with Ricinulei was first made by Professor Gerald S. Hawkins. See Gerald S. Hawkins, *Beyond Stonehenge* (Arrow Books, 1977), 143–144. For their categorization as "tickspiders," see British Arachnological Society, "Hooded Tickspiders (*Ricinulei*)," http://britishspiders.org.uk/wiki2015/index.php?title=Category:Ricinulei.

22. Ricardo Pinto-da Rocha and Renata Andrade, "A New Species of *Cryptocellus* (Arachnida: Ricinulei) from Eastern Amazonia," *Zoologica* 29, no. 5 (October 2012), 474–478. See also Joachim U. Adis et al., "On the Abundance and Ecology of Ricinulei (Arachnida) from Central Amazonia, Brazil," *Journal of the New York Entomological Society* 97, no. 2 (1989), 133–140.

23. See, for example, Alexandre B. Ronaldo and Ricardo Pinto-da Rocha, "On a New Species of *Cryptocellus* from the Brazilian Amazon (Arachnida, Ricinulei)," *Revista Ibérica de Aracnología* 7 (June 30, 2003), 103–108; and Pinto-da Rocha and Andrade, "A New Species of *Cryptocellus* (Arachnida: Ricinulei) from Eastern Amazonia," 474–478.

24. Ronaldo and Pinto-da Rocha, "On a New Species of *Cryptocellus* from the Brazilian Amazon (Arachnida, Ricinulei)," 103: "Like the spider pedipalp, the ricinuleid third leg offers numerous species-specific features that are very important in the recognition of individual species."

25. Ibid.

26. Hawkins, *Beyond Stonehenge*, 144.

27. Pärssinen, Schaan, and Ranzi, "Pre-Columbian Geometric Earthworks in the Upper Purús," 1087. See pp. 1090–1091 for some specific examples cited in the paper, for example, "a 250m wide

quadrangular structure, crossed by a 12m wide NE-SW oriented road, leading after 1300m to [a] geoglyph site . . . which is comprised of a rectangular structure with rounded corners, measuring 200 × 260m. . . . Another rectangular structure . . . is a 100m wide square, with a road leaving it in the south direction, vanishing after 120m. The fourth example . . . is a double ditched square, with roads leaving from the centre of its north, east and south sides."

28. Ibid., 1091.
29. Ibid., 1087–1088.
30. Sanna Saunaluoma, Martti Pärssinen, and Denise Schaan, "Diversity of Pre-colonial Earthworks in the Brazilian State of Acre, Southwestern Amazonia," *Journal of Field Archaeology* (July 9, 2018), 5–6.
31. Ibid., 5.
32. Ibid., 7–8.
33. Ibid., 10–11.
34. Pärssinen, Schaan, and Ranzi, "Pre-Columbian Geometric Earthworks in the Upper Purús," 1094.
35. Ibid., 1089.
36. Ibid., 1090.
37. Ibid., 1089.
38. Denise Schaan et al., "New Radiometric Dates for Pre-Columbian (2000–700 BP) Earthworks in Western Amazonia, Brazil," *Journal of Field Archaeology* 37 (2012), 132–142.
39. Ibid., 133.
40. Ibid., 137–138.
41. Ibid., 132.
42. E. W. Herrmann et al., "A New Multistage Construction Chronology for the Great Serpent Mound, USA," *Journal of Archaeological Science* 50 (2014), 117–125.
43. Schaan et al., "New Radiometric Dates for Precolumbian (2000–700 BP) Earthworks in Western Amazonia, Brazil," 135.
44. J. H. Cole, Survey of Egypt Paper No. 39, *Determination of the Exact Size and Orientation of the Great Pyramid of Giza* (Government Press, Cairo, 1925), 6.
45. For the accuracy of the Great Pyramid's cardinal alignments, see I. E. S. Edwards, *The Pyramids of Egypt* (Penguin Books, 1993), 99–100. For the cardinal orientation of the Severino Calazans geoglyph, see Schaan et al., "New Radiometric Dates for Precolumbian (2000–700 BP) Earthworks in Western Amazonia, Brazil," 135, Figure 3. These authors do not provide precise survey details and note (on p. 136) that the site has been damaged by modern intrusions. Nonetheless, from the information they do provide, its general cardinal orientation is not in doubt.
46. Schaan et al., "New Radiometric Dates for Precolumbian (2000–700 BP) Earthworks in Western Amazonia, Brazil," 136.
47. Ibid., 136, Table I.
48. Ibid.
49. Ibid., 135.
50. Ibid., 136.
51. Ibid.
52. Ibid.
53. According to Mann, "Ancient Earthmovers of the Amazon," p. 1148, at a time when more than 150 geoglyphs had been found Pärssinen estimated this number to represent "less than 10%" of the total.
54. John Francis Carson et al., "Environmental Impact of Geometric Earthwork Construction in the Pre-Columbian Amazon," *Proceedings of the National Academy of Sciences* 111, no. 29 (July 22, 2014), 10497.
55. Schaan et al., "New Radiometric Dates for Precolumbian (2000–700 BP) Earthworks in Western Amazonia, Brazil": A date of 2577 BC was retrieved from excavation unit 3 (p. 136, Table I); it measures 230 meters along each side; and its full perimeter, defined by an enclosure ditch 12 meters wide, measures 920 meters—more than 3,000 feet (p. 135). The Great Pyramid has almost the same footprint; see Cole, *Determination of the Exact Size and Orientation of the Great Pyramid of Giza*, 6. For the accuracy of the Great Pyramid's cardinal alignments, which are the same as those given by Severino Calazans, see Edwards, *The Pyramids of Egypt*, 99–100.
56. Interviewed in Sarah Knapton, "Hundreds of Ancient Earthworks Resembling Stonehenge Found in Amazon Rainforest," *Daily Telegraph,* February 6, 2017, http://www.telegraph.co.uk/science/2017/02/06/hundreds-ancient-earthworks-resembling-stonehenge-found-amazon/.

57. L. Falconer, "Interactive Virtual Archaeology: Constructing the Prehistoric Past at Avebury Henge," International Conference on Ubiquitous Computing and Communications and 2016 International Symposium on Cyberspace and Security (IUCC-CSS), December 2016, 153–158, esp. p. 155.

58. "'Secret Square' Discovered Beneath World-Famous Avebury Stone Circle," University of Southampton, June 29, 2017, https://www.southampton.ac.uk/news/2017/06/avebury-square.page. See also: "Avebury Neolithic Stone Circle Is Actually Square" (BBC, June 28, 2017), http://www.bbc.co.uk/news/uk-england-wiltshire-40431673 and "Avebury Square Discovered Beneath Neolithic Stone Monument" (Live Science, June 30, 2017), https://www.livescience.com/59668-avebury-circle-once-a-square.html.

59. Schaan et al., "New Radiometric Dates for Precolumbian (2000–700 BP) Earthworks in Western Amazonia, Brazil," 138.

60. T. Darvill et al., "Stonehenge Remodelled," *Antiquity* 86, no. 334 (2012), 1021–1040, esp. p. 1028: "Stonehenge first consisted of a circular bank and external ditch with an overall diameter of about 110m. This earthwork was entered by a main access from the north-east and a smaller entrance to the south. It is not technically a henge, because henges have a bank outside the ditch, but it conforms to the emergent class of 'formative henges' constructed in the late fourth and early third millennia cal BC."

61. Interviewed in Knapton, "Hundreds of Ancient Earthworks Resembling Stonehenge Found in Amazon Rainforest."

62. Pärssinen, Schaan, and Ranzi, "Pre-Columbian Geometric Earthworks in the Upper Purús," 1089.

63. Jennifer Watling et al., "Impact of Pre-Columbian "Geoglyph" Builders on Amazonian Forests," *Proceedings of the National Academy of Sciences* 114, no. 8 (February 21, 2017), 1868.

64. Ibid. (Emphasis added.)

65. Schaan et al., "New Radiometric Dates for Precolumbian (2000–700 BP) Earthworks in Western Amazonia, Brazil," 136, Table I.

66. Ibid.

16: THE AMAZON'S OWN STONEHENGE

1. Marcos Pivetta, "The Sun Stones," *Revista Pesquisa* (August 1, 2011), http://revistapesquisa.fapesp.br/en/2011/08/01/the-sun-stones/.

2. Ibid. However, the article appears to be inaccurate in that it has both Goeldi and Nimuendajú visiting Rego Grande. According to Mariana Cabral—the leading modern scientific expert on the site—neither of them did so, and I therefore report accordingly.

3. Simon Romero, "A 'Stonehenge,' and a Mystery, in the Amazon," *New York Times,* December 14, 2016, https://www.nytimes.com/2016/12/14/world/americas/brazil-amazon-megaliths-stonehenge.html.

4. Ibid.

5. Pivetta, "The Sun Stones."

6. Ibid. Other estimates, giving the total number of megaliths at 127, giving a range of heights including 3 meters and 4 meters, and giving the 3 km distance to the quarry can be found, variously, in Romero, "A 'Stonehenge,' and a Mystery, in the Amazon"; http://www.blueplanetheart.it/2017/04/rego-grande-chi-ha-eretto-la-stonehenge-dellamazzonia-era-molto-piu-avanzato-di-quanto-im maginiamo/;https://stanflouride.com/2016/12/21/amzonian-stonehenge-the-rego-grande-sun-ston es/; and https://en.wikipedia.org/wiki/Parque_Arqueol%C3%B3gico_do_Solst%C3%ADcio. Several of these sources also put the diameter of the circle at 30 meters.

7. Pivetta, "The Sun Stones."

8. Ibid.

9. Ibid.

10. Richard Dawkins, *The Selfish Gene,* 2nd ed. (Oxford University Press, 1989), 192: "We need a name for the new replicator, a noun that conveys the idea of a unit of cultural transmission, or a unit of imitation. 'Mimeme' comes from a suitable Greek root, but I want a monosyllable that sounds a bit like 'gene.' I hope my classicist friends will forgive me if I abbreviate mimeme to meme. If it is any consolation, it could alternatively be thought of as being related to 'memory,' or to the French word même. It should be pronounced to rhyme with 'cream.'"

11. Oxford Dictionary definition: https://en.oxforddictionaries.com/definition/meme.

12. Pivetta, "The Sun Stones."

13. Ibid., and see "Amapá: Cradle of the Brazilian 'Stonehenge,'" *Ceticismo,* March 16, 2010, https://ceticismo.net/2010/03/16/amapa-berco-do-stonehenge-brasileiro/.

14. Guianas Geographic, "Solstice Megaliths: Calçoene, Amapá, The Amerindian Stonehenge," http://

www.guianas-geographic.com/article-en/solstice-megaliths-calcoene-amapa-the-amerindian-stonehenge/.
15. Pivetta, "The Sun Stones."
16. Ibid.
17. "Another 'Stonehenge' Discovered in Amazon," NBC News, June 26, 2006, http://www.nbcnews.com/id/13582228/ns/technology_and_science-science/t/another-stonehenge-discovered-ama zon/#.WrUQRdPFLUI.
18. Gibby Zobel, "Will Amazon's Stonehenge Rewrite History?" June 27, 2006, http://www.meta-re ligion.com/Archaeology/Southamerica/will_amazon_stonehenge.htm.
19. Romero, "A 'Stonehenge,' and a Mystery, in the Amazon."
20. A. C. Roosevelt et al., "Palaeoindian Cave Dwellers in the Amazon: The Peopling of the Americas," *Science* 272 (April 19, 1996), 380: "The luminescence dates ~ 16,000 to 9500 B.P. overlap the possible range of calendar dates estimated for the radiocarbon dates, ~ 14,200 to 10,500 yr B.P."
21. See, for example, Christopher Sean Davis, "Solar-Aligned Pictographs at the Paleoindian Site of Painel do Pilão Along the Lower Amazon River at Monte Alegre, Brazil," *PLoS One* (December 20, 2016), 2: "Anna Roosevelt and her team (1996) excavated at Caverna da Pedra Pintada, the largest and closest painted cave to the Amazon River, on a hill called Serra da Paituna. There they unearthed evidence of a Late Pleistocene paleoindian occupation period associated with numerous paint drops and lumps of pigment, artifacts, black soil, and other food remains radiocarbon dated to 11,280 to 10,170 uncalibrated years before present (13,630–11,705 cal yr BP—OxCal 4.2)."
22. Davis, "Solar-Aligned Pictographs at the Paleoindian Site of Painel do Pilão Along the Lower Amazon River at Monte Alegre, Brazil," 7.
23. Ibid.
24. Ibid., 14.
25. Ibid., 7–8.
26. Ibid., 8.
27. Ibid.
28. Ibid. It should be noted that since the latitude of Painel do Pilão is some 2 degrees south of the equator, Davis is technically in error to refer to the December solstice as the "winter solstice"—it is the summer solstice in the Southern Hemisphere.
29. Ibid., 10.
30. Ibid., 11.
31. Ibid., 16.
32. Ibid., 11.
33. For 2009, see Martti Pärssinen, Denise Schaan, and Alceu Ranzi, "Pre-Columbian Geometric Earthworks in the Upper Purús," *Antiquity* 83, no. 322 (December 1, 2009), 1094. For 2017, see Jennifer Watling et al., "Impact of Pre-Columbian 'Geoglyph' Builders on Amazonian Forests," *Proceedings of the National Academy of Sciences* 114, no. 8 (February 21, 2017), 1868. See also Pirjo Kristiina and Sanna Saunaluoma, "Visualization and Movement as Configurations of Human–Nonhuman Engagements: Precolonial Geometric Earthwork Landscapes of the Upper Purús, Bra-zil," *American Anthropologist* 119, no. 4 (August 23, 2017), 615.
34. Jonaas Gregorio de Souza and Denise Pahl Schaan, "Pre-Columbian Earth-Builders Settled Along the Entire Southern Rim of the Amazon," *Nature Communications,* March 27, 2018, 1.
35. Ibid., 3.
36. Ibid., 3–4.
37. Ibid., 6.
38. Ibid., 2.
39. Ibid.
40. The feats of cultural memory preservation and effective knowledge transmission over immense time periods that are manifested in the Amazonian geoglyphs—and that provide compelling evi-dence of the successful replication of geometrical and cosmographic "memes" on a millennial scale—were recognized in 2018 by Jennifer Watling, Francis Mayle, and Denise Schaan, who admit that they are "impressed at the timescale over which the knowledge, behaviours and ideol-ogy behind the geoglyphs were transmitted and propagated." See their paper "Historical Ecology, Human Niche Construction and Landscape in Pre-Columbian Amazonia: A Case Study of the Geoglyph Builders of Acre, Brazil," *Journal of Anthropology,* April 26, 2018, 134.
41. Denise P. Schaan, *Sacred Geographies of Ancient Amazonia* (Routledge, 2012), 170.
42. "Colonel Labre's Explorations in the Region Between the Beni and Madre de Dios Rivers and the

Purus," *Proceedings of the Royal Geographical Society and Monthly Record of Geography* 11, no. 8 (August 1889), 498.

17: THE VINE OF THE DEAD

1. Oxford dictionaries: https://en.oxforddictionaries.com/definition/celestial_pole.
2. John Francis Carson et al., "Environmental Impact of Geometric Earthwork Construction in the Pre-Columbian Amazon," *Proceedings of the National Academy of Sciences* 111, no. 29 (July 22, 2014), 1048. See also Martti Pärssinen, Denise Schaan, and Alceu Ranzi, "Pre-Columbian Geometric Earthworks in the Upper Purús," *Antiquity* 83, no. 322 (December 1, 2009), 1089. Also see Simon Romero, "Once Hidden by Forest, Carvings in Land Attest to Amazon's Lost World," *New York Times*, January 14, 2012, http://www.nytimes.com/2012/01/15/world/americas/land-carvings-at test-to-amazons-lost-world.html.
3. Denise Schaan et al., "New Radiometric Dates for Precolumbian (2000–700 BP) Earthworks in Western Amazonia, Brazil," *Journal of Field Archaeology* 37 (2012), 132–133. See also Jennifer Watling et al., "Impact of Pre-Columbian 'Geoglyph' Builders on Amazonian Forests," *Proceedings of the National Academy of Sciences* 114, no. 8 (February 21, 2017), 1868.
4. Cited in Romero, "Once Hidden by Forest, Carvings in Land Attest to Amazon's Lost World."
5. Pirjo Kristiina Virtanen and Sanna Saunaluoma, "Visualization and Movement as Configurations of Human–Nonhuman Engagements: Precolonial Geometric Earthwork Landscapes of the Upper Purus, Brazil," *American Anthropologist* 119, no. 4 (August 23, 2017), 622–623.
6. Ibid., 624.
7. Michael Ripinsky-Naxon, *The Nature of Shamanism: Substance and Function of a Religious Metaphor* (State University of New York Press, 1993), 69. See also Weston La Barre, *The Ghost Dance: The Origins of Religion* (George Allen and Unwin, 1970), 178.
8. Ibid., 74.
9. Graham Hancock, *Supernatural: Meetings with the Ancient Teachers of Mankind* (Century, 2005), from which several paragraphs in this chapter are extracted. The US edition was published by the Disinformation Company, New York, 2006.
10. Luis Eduardo Luna, "The Concept of Plants as Teachers," *Journal of Ethnopharmacology* 11 (1984), 135.
11. Luis Eduardo Luna, "Vegetalismo: Shamanism Among the Mestizo Population of the Peruvian Amazon," *Acta Universitatis Stockholmensis*, Stockholm Studies in Comparative Religion (Almqvist and Wiksell Publishers, 1986), 62. See also Glen H. Shepard Jr., "Psychoactive Plants and Ethnopsychiatric Medicines of the Matsigenka," *Journal of Psychoactive Drugs* 30, no. 4 (October–December 1998), 323ff: "Matsigenka consider hallucinogenic plants to be sentient beings with superhuman souls, described as 'owner,' 'master' or 'mother' of the plant."
12. Cited in Luna, "Vegetalismo," 62.
13. Graham Hancock, *Supernatural*, 44–45. Emphases added. The page numbers are those in the hardcover edition; the page numbers will be different in the paperback editions.
14. Ibid., 46.
15. Ibid., 50.
16. Ibid., 57.
17. Ibid., 45.
18. Though the names *ayahuasca* and *yagé* both refer to essentially the same potion made from similar plants, the approach varies greatly between ayahuasca and *yagé*. For example, *yagé* bark is usually pounded off, leaving only the woody core of the vine to be boiled; these brews contain less tannins and cause less vomiting than ayahuasca brews, which are usually prepared with the bark left on the vine. Ayahuasca bark is usually only slightly rasped and pounded before being boiled, leaving more tannins in the brew, causing a more powerful purgative effect in the recipient. The DMT element of *yagé* is not derived from *Psychotria viridis* (chacruna) but is derived from another vine, *Diplopterys cabrerana*, which contains both N,N-DMT and 5-MeO-DMT. Further information available in J. M. Weisberger, *Rainforest Medicine: Preserving Indigenous Science and Biodiversity in the Upper Amazon* (North Atlantic Books, 2013). And for more differences in the preparation and ceremonial practicing of *yagé* and ayahuasca, see this easily accessible article, "The Difference Between Ayahuasca and Yagé," Rainforest Medicine Gatherings: Preserving Indigenous Science and Biodiversity in the Upper Amazon, accessed July 30, 2018, https://rainforestmedicine.net/the-difference-between-ayahuasca-and-yage/.
19. G. Reichel-Dolmatoff, *The Shaman and the Jaguar: A Study of Narcotic Drugs Amongst the Tukano*

Indians of Colombia (Temple University Press, 1975), photographic plates between pp. 174 and 175, and 178 and 179.

20. Ibid., 167–173.
21. In this context the different patterns are accorded particular meaning by the Tukano. See Robert Layton in David S. Whitley, (ed.), *Handbook of Rock Art Research* (Altamira Press, 2001), 314.
22. See Benny Shanon, *The Antipodes of the Mind: Charting the Phenomenology of the Ayahuasca Experience* (Oxford University Press, 2002), 13; Jeremy Narby and Francis Huxley, *Shamans Through Time* (Thames and Hudson, 2001), 196, 267. See also A. Dawson, "Ayahuasca: The Shamanic Brew That Produces Out-of-Body Experiences," The Conversation (January 22, 2016), accessed July 23, 2018, https://theconversation.com/ayahuasca-the-shamanic-brew-that-produces-out-of-body -experiences-52836: "Ayahuasca literally translates from the Quechua language of the North Andes as 'soul vine' or 'vine of the dead' and has traditionally been consumed by indigenous communities such as the Aruák, Chocó, Jívaro, Pano, and Tukano across the upper reaches of the Amazon River system in Bolivia, Brazil, Colombia, Ecuador, and Peru."
23. Sanna Saunaluoma and Pirjo Kristiina Virtanen, "Variable Models for the Organization of Earthworking Communities in Upper Purus, Southwestern Amazonia: Archaeological and Ethnographic Perspectives," *Tipiti* 13 (2015), https://digitalcommons.trinity.edu/tipiti/vol13/iss1/2/.
24. Ibid.
25. Virtanen and Saunaluoma, "Visualization and Movement as Configurations of Human–Nonhuman Engagements," 617.
26. Ibid.
27. Ibid.
28. Ibid., 622.
29. G. Reichel-Dolmatoff, *Beyond the Milky Way: Hallucinatory Imagery of the Tukano Indians* (UCLA Latin America Center Publications, 1978), 1.
30. Ibid., 2.
31. Ibid., 1.
32. Ibid., 2.
33. Ibid.
34. Ibid., 3.
35. Ibid. See p. 5 for Reichel-Dolmatoff on the Tukano sacred trumpets. For detailed comparisons between Melanesia and the Amazon, see Appendix 1 herewith.
36. Reichel-Dolmatoff, *The Shaman and the Jaguar*, 98.
37. Reichel-Dolmatoff, *Beyond the Milky Way*, 13.
38. Reichel-Dolmatoff, *The Shaman and the Jaguar*, 85.
39. See the work of cognitive psychologist Benny Shanon, most notably, "Ayahuasca Visualization: A Structural Typology," in *Journal of Consciousness Studies* 9, no. 2 (February 2002), 24. Shanon creates a typology of the structural types or forms in which ayahuasca visions occur. He reports eighteen typological structures, in the order in which they arise during a session, the seventh of which is experience of "patterned geometric designs."
40. See Shanon, *The Antipodes of the Mind*, 386: "As I have made abundantly clear, this is a psychological book, not a philosophical one. . . . As described at the outset of this book, what impressed me greatly when I first partook of the brew were the similarities between the experiences I had with it and ones described in the anthropological literature. Some of the images that appeared in my visions were similar, at times identical, to ones reported by indigenous persons and by the first European explorers who encountered Ayahuasca. The extensive empirical research I have subsequently conducted corroborated these first impressions and led me to conclude that there are striking cross-personal commonalities in the contents of Ayahuasca visions, in their themes, and in the ideations that are associated with them."
41. This is the central theme of my 2005 book *Supernatural*.
42. Shanon, *The Antipodes of the Mind*, 132.

PART V

18: SUN

1. Sharon A. Brown, *Administrative History: Jefferson National Expansion Memorial National Historic Site*, chapter I: 1933-1935 "The Idea" (National Park Service, 1984). Available here: https://www.

webcitation.org/5wUnhhjCR?url=http://www.nps.gov/history/history/online_books/jeff/adhi1-1.htm.

2. William Iseminger, *Cahokia Mounds: America's First City* (History Press, 2010), 45–46, and Sally A. Kitt Chappell, *Cahokia: Mirror of the Cosmos* (University of Chicago Press, 2002), 113.
3. Iseminger, *Cahokia Mounds,* 46.
4. Ibid.
5. See for example Martin Byers, *The Real Mound Builders of North America: A Critical Realist Prehistory of the Eastern Woodlands, 200 BC–1450 AD* (Lexington Books, 2018), 21–29. Also see Sarah A. Baires, "White Settlers Buried the Truth About the Midwest's Mysterious Mound Cities" (Smithsonian, February 28, 2018), https://www.smithsonianmag.com/history/white-settlers-buried-truth-about-midwests-mysterious-mound-cities-180968246/.
6. Henry Brackenridge in 1811, cited in Timothy R. Pauketat, *Cahokia: Ancient America's Great City on the Mississippi* (Penguin Library of American History, 2010), 28.
7. The contrasting alternative to the "Moundbuilder Myth" arose among a set of scholars in the 1890s onward, most of whom were sponsored by the Bureau of American Ethnology and the Smithsonian Institution, who devoted their attention to surveying, mapping, and excavating earthwork sites. Squier and Davis's 1848 survey of Serpent Mound was in many ways the precursor to this movement. See Byers, *The Real Mound Builders of North America,* 22.
8. Pauketat, *Cahokia,* 28–29. See also Chappell, *Cahokia: Mirror of the Cosmos,* 89–91.
9. Pauketat, *Cahokia,* 15, 23.
10. Sparked by the publication of Ephraim G. Squier and Edwin H. Davis, *Ancient Monuments of the Mississippi Valley* (Smithsonian Institution, 1848). Reprinted and republished by the Smithsonian, with an introduction by David J. Meltzer, in 1998.
11. Iseminger, *Cahokia Mounds,* 42.
12. Ibid., 3.
13. Ibid., 40.
14. Sarah E. Bairres, "Cahokia's Rattlesnake Causeway," *Midcontinental Journal of Archaeology* 39, no. 2 (May 2014), 145.
15. William F. Romain, "Monks Mound as an Axis Mundi for the Cahokian World," *Illinois Archaeology* 29 (2017), 27.
16. Ibid., 30.
17. Ibid., 32.
18. Ibid.
19. Ibid., 34–36.
20. Ibid., 34.
21. The reader who wishes to pursue the matter further is directed to Romain, "Monks Mound as an Axis Mundi for the Cahokian World," 27–52.
22. Ibid., 40.
23. Pauketat, *Cahokia,* 2–4, 15.

19: MOON

1. Ray Hively and Robert Horne, "Hopewellian Geometry and Astronomy at High Bank," *Archaeoastronomy,* no. 7 (1984), S88.
2. Ohio Hopewell, http://anthropology.iresearchnet.com/ohio-hopewell/.
3. See, for example, Ephraim G. Squier and Edwin H. Davis, *Ancient Monuments of the Mississippi Valley* (Smithsonian Institution, 1848, reprinted and republished by the Smithsonian, with an introduction by David J. Meltzer, in 1998), 67–72.
4. Jonaas Gregorio de Souza and Denise Pahl Schaan, "Pre-Columbian Earth-Builders Settled Along the Entire Southern Rim of the Amazon," *Nature Communications* (March 27, 2018), 3–4.
5. Martti Pärssinen, Denise Schaan, and Alceu Ranzi, "Pre-Columbian Geometric Earthworks in the Upper Purús," *Antiquity* 83, no. 322 (December 1, 2009), 1087–1088.
6. Sanna Saunaluoma, Martti Pärssinen, and Denise Schaan, "Diversity of Pre-colonial Earthworks in the Brazilian State of Acre, Southwestern Amazonia," *Journal of Field Archaeology* (July 9, 2018), 7–8.
7. Ibid., 10–11.
8. Bradley T. Lepper, "The Newark Earthworks: A Monumental Engine for World Renewal," in Lindsay Jones and Richard G. Sheils (eds.), *The Newark Earthworks: Enduring Monuments, Contested Meanings* (University of Virginia Press, 2016), 41.

9. Ray Hively and Robert Horn, "Geometry and Astronomy in Prehistoric Ohio," *Archaeoastronomy,* no. 4 (1982), S4.

10. Bradley Lepper, "The Newark Earthworks," in Richard F. Townsend and Robert V. Sharp (eds.), *Hero, Hawk and Open Hand* (Art Institute of Chicago/Yale University Press, 2004), 75; Mark J. Lynott, *Hopewell Ceremonial Landscapes of Ohio* (Oxbow Books, 2014), 148.

11. Hively and Horn, "Geometry and Astronomy in Prehistoric Ohio," S4.

12. Ibid., S7–S8.

13. Lepper, "The Newark Earthworks: A Monumental Engine for World Renewal," 47.

14. Ibid., 75.

15. Ibid., 47.

16. Ohio History Connection, "Great Circle Earthworks," http://www.ohiohistorycentral.org/w/Great_Circle_Earthworks.

17. Lynott, *Hopewell Ceremonial Landscapes of Ohio,* 148–149.

18. Lepper, "The Newark Earthworks," 75.

19. T. Darvill et al., "Stonehenge Remodelled," *Antiquity* 86, no. 334 (2012), 1021–1040, esp. p. 1028: "Stonehenge first consisted of a circular bank and external ditch with an overall diameter of about 110m."

20. L. Falconer, "Interactive Virtual Archaeology: Constructing the Prehistoric Past at Avebury Henge," in the International Conference on Ubiquitous Computing and Communications and 2016 International Symposium on Cyberspace and Security (IUCC-CSS), December 2016, 153–158). See p. 155.

21. Lepper, "The Newark Earthworks: A Monumental Engine for World Renewal," 47–48.

22. Lepper, "The Newark Earthworks," 75.

23. Lepper, "The Newark Earthworks: A Monumental Engine for World Renewal," 48.

24. Ibid., and see also Ray Hively and Robert Horn, "The Newark Earthworks: A Grand Unification of Earth, Sky and Mind," in Lindsay Jones and Richard G. Sheils (eds.) *The Newark Earthworks: Enduring Monuments, Contested Meanings* (University of Virginia Press, 2016), 64.

25. William F. Romain, *Mysteries of the Hopewell: Astronomers, Geometers and Magicians of the Eastern Woodlands* (University of Akron Press, 2000), 63.

26. J. J. O'Connor and E. F. Roberson provide a concise history, beginning with the Egyptian Rhind papyrus that was scribed by Ahmes and was based on an original dating from 1850 BC or earlier. A square nearly equal in area to that of a circle is accomplished when the square is constructed on 8/9 of the circle's diameter. See J. J. O'Connor and E. F. Robertson, "Squaring the Circle" School of Mathematics and Statistics, University of St. Andrews, 1999, http://www-history.mcs.st-andrews.ac.uk/PrintHT/Squaring_the_circle.html.

27. Ray Hively and Robert Horn, "Geometry and Astronomy in Prehistoric Ohio," S8.

28. Ibid., S9.

29. Ibid.

30. Ibid.

31. Lepper, "The Newark Earthworks," 79. Emphasis added.

32. Lepper, "The Newark Earthworks: A Monumental Engine for World Renewal," 54–56.

33. Squier and Davis, *Ancient Monuments of the Mississippi Valley,* 50.

34. Ibid, Plate XVI. However, in Cyrus Thomas, *Report on the Mound Explorations of the Bureau of Ethnology* (Smithsonian Institution, 1894), p. 479, this figure is revised to 20.6 acres—about the same area as the circle.

35. Lepper, "The Newark Earthworks," 75; and Lynott, *Hopewell Ceremonial Landscapes of Ohio,* 148.

36. Discussed in chapter 17 of this book, and see Christopher Sean Davis, "Solar-Aligned Pictographs at the Paleoindian Site of Painel do Pilão Along the Lower Amazon River at Monte Alegre, Brazil," *PLoS One* (December 20, 2016).

37. Hively and Horn, "The Newark Earthworks: A Grand Unification of Earth, Sky and Mind," 63.

38. Ibid.

39. Ibid.

40. Ibid., 64.

41. Hively and Horn, "Geometry and Astronomy in Prehistoric Ohio."

42. Ibid., S11.

43. Ibid.

44. Ibid., S12.

45. Ibid.
46. Ibid.
47. Ibid.
48. Hively and Horn, "Hopewellian Geometry and Astronomy at High Bank," S94, S98.
49. Ibid., S95.
50. Ibid., S95–S96.
51. Ray Hively and Robert Horn, "A Statistical Study of Lunar Alignments at the Newark Earthworks," *Midcontinental Journal of Archaeology* 31 (Fall 2006), 306–307; and see the discussion in Lynott, *Hopewell Ceremonial Landscapes of Ohio,* 153.
52. Hively and Horn, "A Statistical Study of Lunar Alignments at the Newark Earthworks."
53. Hively and Horn's original observation to this effect in their paper "Geometry and Astronomy in Prehistoric Ohio," S11, has subsequently been confirmed by Christopher S. Turner in his "Ohio Hopewell Archaeoastronomy: A Meeting of Earth, Mind and Sky," *Time and Mind: The Journal of Archaeology, Consciousness and Culture* 4, no. 3 (November 2011), 308. Note, however that Hively and Horn did subsequently go on to identify solstice alignments at Newark, not in the earthworks themselves but between topographical features in surrounding hills in the midst of which the earthworks appear to have been deliberately situated. See Ray Hively and Robert Horn, "A New and Extended Case for Lunar (and Solar) Astronomy at the Newark Earthworks," *Midcontinental Journal of Archaeology* 38 (Spring 2013), in particular pp. 101–104.
54. Hively and Horn, "A New and Extended Case for Lunar (and Solar) Astronomy at the Newark Earthworks," 102.
55. Ibid.
56. Hively and Horn, "Hopewellian Geometry and Astronomy at High Bank," S94, S98.

20: THE POVERTY POINT TIME MACHINE

1. For example, Poverty Point.
2. For example, Emerald Mound and the Winterville Mounds.
3. For example, Moundville.
4. For example, the Pinson Mounds.
5. The prime example is, of course, Cahokia.
6. What's left of High Bank and Newark (much of the latter now in a private golf course and only open to the public 4 days a year), and also such sites as Mound City, Seip, the Great Miamisberg Mound, and Fort Ancient.
7. For more see Indian Country Today, "Florida's Incredible Indian Mounds" (Indian Country Today, October 13, 2011), https://newsmaven.io/indiancountrytoday/archive/florida-s-incredible-indian -mounds-H8O3ekXxpE2Buote33jInA/.
8. For more see Explore Georgia, "5 Native American Sites Not to Miss in Georgia" (November 2015), https://newsmaven.io/indiancountrytoday/archive/florida-s-incredible-indian-mounds-H8O3ek XxpE2Buote33jInA/ and "Etowah Indian Mounds State Historic Site," https://www.exploregeor gia.org/cartersville/general/historic-sites-trails-tours/etowah-indian-mounds-state-historic-site.
9. For more see Texas Historical Commission, "Caddo Mounds State Historic Site," http://www.thc. texas.gov/historic-sites/caddo-mounds-state-historic-site.
10. For more see Arkansas State Parks, "Toltec Mounds Archaeological State Park," https://www. arkansasstateparks.com/parks/toltec-mounds-archeological-state-park.
11. For more see Kentucky State Parks, "Wickliffe Mounds," https://parks.ky.gov/parks/historicsites/ wickliffe-mounds/.
12. For more see Indiana Museum, "Angel Mounds," https://www.indianamuseum.org/angel-mounds- state-historic-site.
13. See, for example, A. P. Wright, and E. R. Henry, *Early and Middle Woodland Landscapes of the Southeast* (University Press of Florida, 2013), 1: "The Early and Middle Woodland periods, respectively, to circa 1000–200 BC and 200 BC–AD 600–800." Note, however, that the dates vary from subregion to subregion and the authors' end date for the Middle Woodland period is fairly late compared to most cultural frameworks, the reasons for which are not of concern here. This is clear upon reflection of Late Woodland periodization by authors of the comprehensive compendium M. S. Nassaney and C. R. Cobb, *Stability, Transformation, and Variation: The Late Woodland Southeast* (1991), who ascribe a window of AD 600–900 to the Late Woodland Period.
14. Jenny Ellerbe and Diana M. Greenlee, *Poverty Point: Revealing the Forgotten City* (Louisiana State University Press, 2015), 60.

15. Ibid., 57.
16. Gary Everding, "Archaic Native Americans Built Massive Louisiana Mound in Less Than 90 Days, Research Confirms" (Washington University in St. Louis, January 28, 2013), https://source.wustl.edu/2013/01/archaic-native-americans-built-massive-louisiana-mound-in-less-than-90-days-re search-confirms/.
17. Mound B. See Ellerbe and Greenlee, *Poverty Point: Revealing the Forgotten City,* 28.
18. Ellerbe and Greenlee, *Poverty Point: Revealing the Forgotten City,* 57.
19. Ibid., 59.
20. Ibid., 57.
21. A. M. Byers, *The Real Mound Builders of North America: A Critical Realist Prehistory of the Eastern Woodlands, 200 BC–1450 AD* (Lexington Books, 2018), 22: Established nineteenth-century North American archaeologists believed that the earthworks were the result of an ancient Old World civilization "washing up" on the shores of North America. "The aggregate range of foreign sources postulated became quite broad, such as shipwrecked sailors from an ancient Mediterranean Phoenician colony, or wandering and lusting sets of Vikings, or one or other of the lost tribes of ancient Israel, or groups from ancient Irish and/or Scottish Celtic kingdoms, or even travelers from advanced civilisations from the lost civilisation of Atlantis, and so on," states Byers.
22. Anna C. Roosevelt et al., "Early Mounds and Monumental Art in Ancient Amazonia," in Richard L. Burger and Robert M. Rosenwig (eds.), *Early New World Monumentality* (University Press of Florida, 2012), 257.
23. Jon L. Gibson, "Before Their Time? Early Mounds in the Lower Mississippi Valley," *Southeastern Archaeology* 13, no. 2, Archaic Mounds in the Southeast (Winter 1994), 163.
24. Ibid.
25. Ibid.
26. A. L. Ortmann and T. R. Kidder, "Building Mound A at Poverty Point, Louisiana: Monumental Public Architecture, Ritual Practice, and Implications for Hunter-Gatherer Complexity," *Geoarchaeology* 28, no. 1 (2013), 66–86. And see Amélie A. Walker, "Earliest Mound Site," *Archaeology* 51, no. 1 (January/February 1998), https://archive.archaeology.org/9801/newsbriefs/mounds.html.
27. Joe W. Saunders et al., "A Mound Complex in Louisiana at 5400–5000 Years Before the Present," *Science* 277 (September 19, 1997), 1796.
28. Ellerbe and Greenlee, *Poverty Point: Revealing the Forgotten City,* 28, 110.
29. Ibid., 69.
30. Ibid., 111.
31. Robert C. Mainfort Jr. (ed.), *Archaeological Report No, 22: Middle Woodland Settlement and Ceremonialism in the Mid-South and Lower Mississippi Valley* (Mississippi Department of Archives and History, 1988), 12.
32. Ellerbe and Greenlee, *Poverty Point: Revealing the Forgotten City,* 42–44.
33. Reported in ibid., 42. Transcribed by Diana Greenlee from "Bringing the Past Alive," a seminar recorded in April 1989 at Louisiana State University.
34. Boston University, "Kenneth Bracher," https://www.bu.edu/astronomy/profile/kenneth-brecher/.
35. K. Brecher and W. G. Haag, "The Poverty Point Octagon: World's Largest Solstice Marker?" *Bulletin of the American Astronomical Society* 12, no. 4 (1980), 886.
36. Ibid.
37. As they themselves conceded 2 years later in Kenneth Brecher and William G. Haag, "Astronomical Alignments at Poverty Point," *American Antiquity* 48, no. 1 (January 1983), 161. See also Ellerbe and Greenlee, *Poverty Point: Revealing the Forgotten City,* 43.
38. Robert D. Purrington, "Supposed Solar Alignments at Poverty Point," *American Antiquity* 48, no. 1 (January 1983), 160.
39. Ibid., 161.
40. Brecher and Haag, "Astronomical Alignments at Poverty Point," 162.
41. Ibid.
42. Robert D. Purrington and Colby Allan Child Jr., "Poverty Point Revisited: Further Consideration of Astronomical Alignments," *Archaeoastronomy,* no. 13 (JHA, xx) (February 1, 1989), S49–S60.
43. Ibid., S54.
44. Ibid., S54–S55.
45. Ibid., S55.
46. Ellerbe and Greenlee, *Poverty Point: Revealing the Forgotten City,* 46.

47. Ibid., 50.
48. Ibid., 51.
49. William F. Romain and Norman L. Davis, "Astronomy and Geometry at Poverty Point," *Louisiana Archaeology*, no. 38 (2011), 49.
50. Ibid., 48.
51. Ibid.
52. Ibid.
53. Ibid.
54. Ibid., 46–47.
55. Ibid., 47.
56. Ibid., 49.
57. Joe Saunders et al., "An Assessment of the Antiquity of the Lower Jackson Mound," *Southeastern Archaeology* 20, no. 1 (2001), 75. See also Jon L. Gibson, "Navels of the Earth: Sedentism in Early Mound-Building Cultures in the Lower Mississippi Valley," *World Archaeology* 38, no. 2 (June 2006), 313.
58. John E. Clark, "Surrounding the Sacred: Geometry and Design of Early Mound Groups as Meaning and Function," in Jon L. Gibson and Philip Carr (eds.), *Signs of Power: The Rise of Cultural Complexity in the Southeast* (University of Alabama Press, 2010), Kindle locations 3795–3801.
59. Gibson, "Navels of the Earth," 315.
60. Ibid., 315–316.
61. Romain and Davis, "Astronomy and Geometry at Poverty Point," 47.
62. D. P. Mindell, *The Evolving World* (Harvard University Press, 2009), 224. How far Judaism dates back to and to what extent its roots extend into prehistory is, however, debatable and obviously depends on what elements of the faith one traces. Most agree, however, that it dates at least as far back as the establishment of the Iron Age Kingdom of Judah, c. tenth century BCE.
63. A predominant archaeological link between the Hindu Shiva cult and the Indus Valley civilization is, for example, the Pasupati Seal, displaying the horned "animal" manifestation of Shiva, which was carbon dated to 2500–2400 BC in the early twentieth century. See Earnest John Henry Mackay, *Further Excavations at Mohenjo-Daro: Being an official account of archaeological excavations at Mohenjo-Daro carried out by the Government of India between the years 1927 and 1931* (Delhi: Government of India, 1937–1938).

21: GLIMPSES BEHIND THE VEIL

1. Joe Saunders, "Early Mounds in the Lower Mississippi Valley," in Richard L. Burger and Robert M. Rosenwig (eds.), *Early New World Monumentality* (University Press of Florida, 2012), 26–27.
2. Ibid., 28.
3. Ibid.
4. Robert C. Mainfort Jr. (ed.), *Archaeological Report No 22: Middle Woodland Settlement and Ceremonialism in the Mid-South and Lower Mississippi Valley* (Mississippi Department of Archives and History, 1988), 9.
5. Joe W. Saunders et al., "A Mound Complex in Louisiana at 5400–5000 Years Before the Present," *Science* 277 (September 19, 1997), 1797; Saunders, "Early Mounds in the Lower Mississippi Valley," 36; Joe W. Saunders et al., "Watson Brake, a Middle Archaic Mound Complex in Northeast Louisiana," *American Antiquity* 70, no. 4 (October 2005), 665.
6. Kenneth E. Sassman and Michael J. Heckenberger, "Crossing the Symbolic Rubicon in the Southeast," in Jon L. Gibson and Philip Carr (eds.), *Signs of Power: The Rise of Cultural Complexity in the Southeast* (University of Alabama Press, 2010), Kindle location 4198.
7. Joe W. Saunders et al., "A Mound Complex in Louisiana at 5400–5000 Years Before the Present," 1798.
8. Saunders, "Early Mounds in the Lower Mississippi Valley," 39.
9. Joe Saunders and Thurman Allen, "Hedgepeth Mounds: An Archaic Mound Complex in North-Central Louisiana," *American Antiquity* 59, no. 3 (July 1994), 471.
10. *Cultural Resources Evaluation of the Northern Gulf of Mexico Continental Shelf, Vol I: Prehistoric Cultural Resources Potential*, Office of Archaeology and Historic Preservation, National Park Service, Washington DC, 1977, 243.
11. Saunders, "Early Mounds in the Lower Mississippi Valley," 39.
12. David G. Anderson, "Archaic Mounds and the Archaeology of Southeast Tribal Societies," in Jon

L. Gibson and Philip Carr (eds.), *Signs of Power: The Rise of Cultural Complexity in the Southeast* (University of Alabama Press, 2010), Kindle location 5180.

13. See, for example: Joe W. Saunders et al., "A Mound Complex in Louisiana at 5400–5000 Years Before the Present," *Science* 277 (September 19, 1997), 1796–1799; Joe W. Saunders, et al., "Watson Brake, a Middle Archaic Mound Complex in Northeast Louisiana," 631–668; Saunders, "Early Mounds in the Lower Mississippi Valley," 25–52, in particular 33 and 42.

14. Saunders, "Early Mounds in the Lower Mississippi Valley," 46.

15. Saunders et al., "A Mound Complex in Louisiana at 5400–5000 Years Before the Present."

16. Cited in Heather Pringle, "Oldest Mound Complex Found at Louisiana Site," *Science* (September 19, 1997), 1761–1762.

17. Ibid.

18. Saunders et al., "A Mound Complex in Louisiana at 5400–5000 Years Before the Present," 1797.

19. Norman L. Davis, "Solar Alignments at the Watson Brake Site," *Louisiana Archaeology*, no. 34 (2012), 97.

20. Saunders, "Early Mounds in the Lower Mississippi Valley," 35.

21. Sassman and Heckenberger, "Crossing the Symbolic Rubicon in the Southeast," Kindle location 4176.

22. Davis, "Solar Alignments at the Watson Brake Site," 97, supports the view that there are 12 mounds. Saunders, "Early Mounds in the Lower Mississippi Valley," 35, states that "the site is composed of 11 earthen mounds. . . . A probable (subject to verification) 12th mound lies outside the enclosure" immediately to the southeast.

23. Pringle, "Oldest Mound Complex Found at Louisiana Site."

24. Davis, "Solar Alignments at the Watson Brake Site," 97.

25. Saunders et al., "Watson Brake, a Middle Archaic Mound Complex in Northeast Louisiana," 631.

26. Saunders, "Early Mounds in the Lower Mississippi Valley," 37.

27. Ibid., 36–37.

28. Saunders et al., "Watson Brake, a Middle Archaic Mound Complex in Northeast Louisiana," 665.

29. Ibid.

30. Saunders, "Early Mounds in the Lower Mississippi Valley," 43.

31. Cited in Pringle, "Oldest Mound Complex Found at Louisiana Site."

32. The notion has good support from other knowledgeable archaeologists. See, for example, Saunders et al., "Watson Brake, a Middle Archaic Mound Complex in Northeast Louisiana," 662.

33. Sassman and Heckenberger, "Crossing the Symbolic Rubicon in the Southeast," Kindle location 4170.

34. For example, Insley Mounds.

35. Sassman and Heckenberger, "Crossing the Symbolic Rubicon in the Southeast," Kindle locations 4185–4191 and 4195–4205.

36. Davis, "Solar Alignments at the Watson Brake Site," 110.

37. Ibid.

38. Ibid., 97–115.

39. Notably William Romain, who wrote to the editor of *Louisiana Archaeology* to confirm that his own "findings for Watson Brake corroborate the central thesis of Norman L. Davis (as published in 2012 in *Louisiana Archaeology*) relative to the overall solstice alignment of the site." William F. Romain, letter to Dennis Jones, Editor, *Louisiana Archaeology*, in *Louisiana Archaeology*, no. 36, 2013 (2009), 3, https://www.laarchaeologicalsociety.org/product-page/number-36-2009-published-2013.

40. Davis, "Solar Alignments at the Watson Brake Site," 97.

41. Ibid., 104.

42. Ibid.

43. Ibid.

44. Ibid.

45. Ibid., 105.

46. Ibid., 105–106.

47. Ibid., 106–107.

48. Ibid., 110.

49. William F. Romain, letter to Dennis Jones, Editor, *Louisiana Archaeology*, in *Louisiana Archaeology*, no. 36, 2013 (2009), 3–4.

50. Davis, "Solar Alignments at the Watson Brake Site," 110.

51. Ibid.
52. Ibid.
53. Ibid., 113–114.
54. Ibid., 114.
55. Saunders, "Early Mounds in the Lower Mississippi Valley," 45–46.
56. Ibid.
57. Ellerbe and Greenlee, *Poverty Point: Revealing the Forgotten City,* 28.
58. Ohio History Connection, "Adena Culture," http://www.ohiohistorycentral.org/w/Adena_Cul ture.
59. See, for example, p. 1 of D. W. Dragoo, "Adena and the Eastern Burial Cult" in *Archaeology of Eastern North America* 4 (Winter 1976), 1–9: "Extensive research throughout the East in recent years has clearly shown Adena to be one of only several regional cultures present between 1000 BC and AD 200." This view has been maintained in the twenty-first century—see, for example, p. 453 of S. M. Rafferty, "Evidence of Early Tobacco in Northeastern North America?" *Journal of Archaeological Science* 33, no. 4 (2006), 453–458, which dates the Boucher Mound, Vermont: "The site has an extensive radiocarbon chronology, with dates ranging from 885 +-35 BC to as late as 49 BC uncalibrated, with a calibrated range indicating continuous use of the site through the majority of the first millennium BC, from as early as 1036 BC to as late as 49 BC. . . . The site features a rich and diverse assemblage of burial offerings, including numerous Adena-related artifacts."
60. Correspondence by my research assistant Holly Lasko with Bob Maslowski of the Council for West Virginia Archaeology on May 25, 2018, "Most Adena mounds I'm familiar with date between 400 and 200 BC." See B. Lepper, "How Old Is the Adena Mound?" Ohio History Connection Archaeology Blog (January 12, 2014), https://www.ohiohistory.org/learn/collections/archaeol ogy/archaeology-blog/2014/january-2014/how-old-is-the-adena-mound. This article is based on a paper published in the *Midcontinental Journal of Archaeology,* whose abstract states that Adena Mound (typesite) dating of 200 BC places it near the midpoint of radiocarbon-dated Adena culture sites. The reference for the paper is Bradley T. Lepper et al., "Radiocarbon Dates on Textile and Bark Samples from the Central Grave of the Adena Mound (33RO1), Chillicothe, Ohio," *Midcontinental Journal of Archaeology* (2014).
61. Edward W. Herrmann et al., "A New Multistage Construction Chronology for the Great Serpent Mound, USA," *Journal of Archaeological Science* 50 (October 2014), 121.
62. The oldest reliable Adena Mound date is arguably (by no means definitively) c. 400 BC and based on recent AMS dates from Cresap Mound. See William H. Tippins, Richard W. Lang, and Mark A. McConaghy, "New AMS Dates on the CRESAP Mound (46MR7)," *Pennsylvania Archaeologist* 86, no. 2 (2016), 2–20, Table 4, p. 17.
63. Jon L. Gibson, "Navels of the Earth: Sedentism in Early Mound-Building Cultures in the Lower Mississippi Valley," *World Archaeology* 38, no. 2 (June 2006), 316.
64. John E. Clark, "Surrounding the Sacred: Geometry and Design of Early Mound Groups as Meaning and Function," in Jon L. Gibson and Philip Carr (eds.), *Signs of Power: The Rise of Cultural Complexity in the Southeast* (University of Alabama Press, 2010), Kindle location 3741–3747.
65. Ibid., Kindle location 3770.

PART VI

22: QUIETUS?

1. Robert Bauval and Graham Hancock, *The Message of the Sphinx: A Quest for the Hidden Legacy of Mankind* (Crown, 1996), 79. *The Message of the Sphinx* was published in the United Kingdom by Heinemann as *Keeper of Genesis,* but with the same page numbering.
2. O. Neugebauer and Richard A. Parker, *Egyptian Astronomical Texts: 1. The Early Decans* (Brown University Press, 1960), 24–25 and 112ff. Jane Sellers, *The Death of Gods in Ancient Egypt: An Essay on Egyptian Religion and the Frame of Time* (Penguin Books, 1992), 39ff.
3. Robert Bauval (with Adrian Gilbert), *The Orion Mystery: Unlocking the Secrets of the Pyramids* (Heinemann, 1994).
4. Virginia Trimble, "Astronomical Investigations Concerning the So-called Air Shafts of Cheops's Pyramid," *Mitteilungen des Deutschen Archäologischen Instituts,* band 10 (1964), 183–187, and Alexander Badawy, "The Stellar Destiny of the Pharaoh and the So-called Air-Shafts in Cheops's Pyramid," *Mitteilungen des Deutschen Archäologischen Instituts,* band 10 (1964), 189–206.
5. Bauval, *The Orion Mystery,* 191.

6. Pyramid Texts, Lines 882–885 in R. O. Faulkner (ed. and trans.), *The Ancient Egyptian Pyramid Texts* (Oxford University Press, 1969), 154.
7. See, for example, the discussion by I. E. S. Edwards, *The Pyramids of Egypt* (Penguin, 1993), 285.
8. Information from site placard, Mound B, Moundville Archaeological Park, Alabama.
9. Information from Rattlesnake Disk exhibit placard, museum, Moundville Archaeological Park, Alabama.

23: THE PORTAL AND THE PATH
1. See, for example, Robert L. Hall, *An Archaeology of the Soul: North American Belief and Ritual* (University of Illinois Press, 1997), 21 and 162–163; George F. Lankford, "The 'Path of Souls,'" in Kent F. Reilly III and James F.Garber (eds.), *Ancient Objects and Sacred Realms: Interpretations of Mississippian Iconography* (University of Texas Press, 2007), 193ff; George Lankford, "World on a String," in Richard F. Townsend and Robert V. Sharp (eds.), *Hero, Hawk and Open Hand: American Indian Art of the Ancient Midwest and South* (Yale University Press, 2004), 212; and Ray A. Williamson and Claire R. Farrer (eds.), *Earth and Sky: Visions of the Cosmos in Native American Folklore* (University of New Mexico Press, 1992), 219–220.
2. See Andrew Collins and Gregory Little, *Path of Souls: The Native American Death Journey* (ATA Archetype Books, 2014), 7–9. Above Top Secret, "Southern Death Cult (Eye in the Hand)," (December 27, 2012), http://www.abovetopsecret.com/forum/thread912520/pg1 in conjunction with "The Mystery of Mayan and Egyptian Common Creation Myth," December 18, 2010, http://www.abovetopsecret.com/forum/thread909246/pg1.
3. Out of the tens of thousands of codices that existed before the conquest, only four have survived. See, for example, Michael D. Coe, *The Maya*, 4th ed. (Thames and Hudson, 1987), 161; and University of Arizona Library, "Mayan Codex Facsimiles," http://www.library.arizona.edu/exhibits/mexcodex/maya.htm.
4. Mark Seeman, "Hopewell Art in Hopewell Places," in Richard F. Townsend and Robert V. Sharp (eds.), *Hero, Hawk and Open Hand: American Indian Art of the Ancient Midwest and South* (Yale University Press, 2004), 57.
5. See, for example, Reilly and Garber, *Ancient Objects and Sacred Realms,* 112, 115, 118, 125, 193, 130, and so on.
6. Ibid., 5.
7. Lankford, "The 'Path of Souls,'" 175.
8. Ibid.
9. George Lankford, "The Great Serpent in Eastern North America," in Reilly and Garber, *Ancient Objects and Sacred Realms,* 134–135.
10. George Lankford, "Some Cosmological Motifs in the Southeastern Ceremonial Complex," in Reilly and Garber, *Ancient Objects and Sacred Realms,* 8.
11. Lankford, "The Great Serpent in Eastern North America," 134–135.
12. E. A. Wallis Budge, *The Book of the Dead* (Arkana, 1985), lxv.
13. Information from ibid, lxv–lxxi, and from Ian Shaw and Paul Nicholson, *British Museum Dictionary of Ancient Egypt* (British Museum Press, 1995), 47, 146.
14. Pyramid Texts, Lines 312–313 in R. O. Faulkner (ed. and trans.), *The Ancient Egyptian Pyramid Texts* (Oxford University Press, 1969), 68.
15. Ibid., 94, Line 474.
16. Ibid., 294, Lines 2057–2058.
17. E. A. Wallis Budge, *The Egyptian Heaven and Hell* (Martin Hopkinson, 1925) (3 volumes in one edition, page numbers reset to 1 with each volume), vol. 2, 196.
18. Cited in Ake Hultkrantz, *Conceptions of the Soul Amongst Native American Indians* (Ethnographical Museum of Stockholm, 1953), 70.
19. Ibid.
20. Budge, *The Book of the Dead,* 542.
21. Hultkrantz, *Conceptions of the Soul Amongst Native American Indians,* 116.
22. Ibid., 77.
23. Ibid.
24. Ibid., 79.
25. Ibid., 88.
26. Ibid., 112.
27. Ake Hultkrantz, *Shamanic Healing and Ritual Drama: Health and Medicine in Native American*

Religious Traditions (Crossroad, 1992), 32. See also Hultkrantz, *Conceptions of the Soul Amongst Native American Indians,* 26–27.

28. Lankford, "The 'Path of Souls,'" 175–176, 181.
29. F. Dunand and R. Lichtenberg, *Mummies and Death in Egypt* (Cornell University Press, 2006), x: "During the funeral, magical formulas were recited, and these and others were copied onto a Book of the Dead that lay in the tomb along with the deceased. A selection of figurines and ritual implements, along with a panoply of amulets and utilitarian objects from this life, accompanied the body. Once placed in the tomb, the individual would simultaneously move about in the realm where the dead were and also share in the course of the sun as it set and was reborn daily. The mobile 'soul,' the *ba,* soared up toward the daylight and then returned to animate its home base, the embalmed corpse in its coffin. The *ka,* the other 'soul' and the immaterial double of the material body, consumed the food and drink the survivors brought to the funerary chapel, at the same time perpetuating, by speaking it out loud, the name of the person, which they could read on a stela. This whole system—which implies a far more complex anthropological representation of a living, thinking being than our own—was believed to confer the potential capacities of a god on the deceased. The classical form of a sarcophagus—a mummy with the mask and the heavy wig that were proper to images of deities—served as the hieroglyphic symbol for the idea of superior dignity (the Egyptian word was *sah*)."
30. Pyramid Texts, Line 1109, in Faulkner, *The Ancient Egyptian Pyramid Texts,* 183.
31. Cited in Ake Hultkrantz, *The North American Indian Orpheus Tradition* (Ethnographical Museum of Stockholm, 1957), 121.
32. Lankford, "The 'Path of Souls,'" 181.
33. Cited in ibid.
34. Cited in Hultkrantz, *The North American Indian Orpheus Tradition,* 61.
35. Pyramid Texts, 138, Lines 747–748 in *The Ancient Egyptian Pyramid Texts.*
36. Budge, *The Egyptian Heaven and Hell,* vol. 3, 103–104.
37. Lankford, "The 'Path of Souls,'" 176.
38. Budge, *The Egyptian Heaven and Hell,* vol. 3, 104.
39. Lankford, "The 'Path of Souls,'" 176.
40. Pyramid Texts, in *The Ancient Egyptian Pyramid Texts,* 135, Line 723.
41. Ibid., 253, Line 1717.
42. Ibid., 259, Line 1763.
43. Ibid., 144, Lines 802–803.
44. Ibid., 236, Line 1561.
45. Ibid., 70, Line 326.
46. Ibid., 78, Line 379.
47. Lankford, "The 'Path of Souls,'" 176–177.
48. The Orion Nebula is one of the best-studied objects in the sky. See, for example, F. Palla and S. W. Stahler, "Star Formation in the Orion Nebula Cluster," *Astrophysical Journal* 525, no. 2 (1999), 772: "We study the record of star formation activity within the dense cluster associated with the Orion nebula. . . . This model assumes that stars are produced at a constant rate and distributed according to field-star initial mass function."
49. Lankford, "The 'Path of Souls,'" 193.
50. Ibid., 203–204.
51. Pyramid Texts, in *The Ancient Egyptian Pyramid Texts,* 166, Line 980.
52. Ibid., 156, Lines 890–891.
53. Ibid., 70, Line 324.
54. Ibid., 79, Line 392.
55. Ibid., 135, Line 727.
56. Ibid., 158, Line 907.
57. Ibid., 238, Line 1583.
58. Ibid., 249, Line 1680.
59. Ibid., 144, Line 799.
60. R. O. Faulkner, *The Book of the Dead* (British Museum Publications, 1972), 62, Spell 42.
61. Pyramid Texts, in *The Ancient Egyptian Pyramid Texts,* 253, Line 1720.
62. Susan Brind Morrow, *The Silver Eye: Unlocking the Pyramid Texts* (Head of Zeus, 2016), Kindle location 433.
63. *The Ancient Egyptian Pyramid Texts,* 144, Line 803.

64. Ibid., 253, Line 1717.
65. Ibid., 44, Line 151.
66. Ibid.
67. Lankford, "The 'Path of Souls,'" 177.
68. Budge, *The Egyptian Heaven and Hell*, vol. 3, 104.
69. George Lankford draws a specific parallel between the Native American traditions and the *Ancient Egyptian Book of the Dead* in George Lankford, *Reachable Stars: Patterns in the Ethnoastronomy of Eastern North America* (University of Alabama Press, 2007), 204. The same idea is proposed in F. Kent Reilly III, "The Great Serpent in the Lower Mississippi Valley," in *Visualizing the Sacred: Cosmic Visions, Regionalism and the Art of the Mississippi World* (University of Texas Press, 2011), 122–123.
70. Benny Shanon, *The Antipodes of the Mind: Charting the Phenomenology of the Ayahuasca Experience* (Oxford University Press, 2002), 132.
71. G. Reichel-Dolmatoff, *Beyond the Milky Way: Hallucinatory Imagery of the Tukano Indians* (UCLA Latin America Center Publications, 1978), 13.
72. Faulkner, *The Book of the Dead*, 90. Also see R. O. Faulkner, "The King and the Star-Religion in the Pyramid Texts," in *Journal of Near Eastern Studies* 25 (1966), 154n7. Virginia Lee Davis makes the link between the Milky Way and the "Winding Waterway" in *Archaeoastronomy* 9 (JHA xvi) (1985), 102. The archeoastronomer and Egyptologist Jane B. Sellers arrives at the same conclusion as V. L. Davis (J. B. Sellers, *The Death of Gods in Ancient Egypt* [Penguin Books, 1992], 97). For further discussion and additional sources, see also Bauval, *The Orion Mystery*, 119–121.
73. Budge, *The Egyptian Heaven and Hell*, vol. 3, 90.
74. Pyramid Texts, 258, Line 1760.
75. Ake Hultkrantz, *The Religions of the American Indians* (University of California Press, 1979) (originally published in 1967 as *De Amerikanska Indianernas Religioner*), 133.
76. Lankford, "The 'Path of Souls,'" 177.
77. Budge, *The Egyptian Heaven and Hell*, vol. 3, 89.
78. Ibid., 89–90.
79. Ibid., xii.
80. Sources for the foregoing all in ibid, notably 13–14, 59–60, 110–115, 136, 249–251, and 282–283 ("the Slaughterers of Apep").
81. Ibid., 109.
82. Ibid., 113.
83. Hultkrantz, *The North American Orpheus Tradition*, 97–98.
84. Lankford, "The Raptor on the Path," in *Visualizing the Sacred*, 243.
85. Alanson Skinner, *Observations on the Ethnology of the Sauk Indians* (Greenwood Press, first published 1923–25, reprinted by Greenwood Press 1970), 36.
86. See, for example, Hultkrantz, *The North American Indian Orpheus Tradition*, 54, 75; Lankford, 'The "Path of Souls,'" 178, 182–183, and Lankford, "The Raptor on the Path," 244–245.
87. Hultkrantz, *The North American Indian Orpheus Tradition*, 80; see also Lankford, "The 'Path of Souls,'" 178, 182–183, and Lankford, "The Raptor on the Path," 244–245.
88. Hultkrantz, *The North American Indian Orpheus Tradition*, 54. See also Lankford, "The 'Path of Souls,'" 178.
89. See discussion in Lankford, "The 'Path of Souls,'" 206–207, and likewise in Lankford, "The Great Serpent," 108–114.
90. Lankford, "The 'Path of Souls,'" 178.
91. Budge, *The Egyptian Heaven and Hell*, vol. 3, 37.
92. Ibid, vol. 1, opposite 102, Vignette "The Kingdom of Seker."
93. For example, see ibid., Vignette "The Kingdom of Seker," opposite 70, and 74. See also Faulkner, *The Book of the Dead*, 86—the Sa'Ta snake.
94. Lankford in *Ancient Objects and Sacred Realms*, 107ff and 174–175ff.
95. Cited in ibid, 112.
96. See discussion in Hultkrantz, *The Native American Orpheus Tradition*, 78–81.
97. Frances Eyman, "An Unusual Winnebago War Club and an American Water Monster," *Penn Museum Expedition* 5, (1963), no. 4: 33, https://www.penn.museum/sites/expedition/an-unusual-winnebago-war-club-and-an-american-water-monster/.
98. Lankford in *Ancient Objects and Sacred Realms*, 107–119.
99. Cited in ibid., 111.

100. Cited in ibid.
101. G. Elliot Smith, *The Evolution of the Dragon* (Manchester University Press, 1919), 94.
102. Lankford in *Ancient Objects and Sacred Realms,* 109–110.
103. Ibid., 111.
104. See, for example, the discussion in Graham Hancock, *Fingerprints of the Gods* (Crown, 1995), 423–424.
105. Reported in F. Kent Reilly III, "Visualising the Sacred in Native American Art of the Mississippian Period," in *Hero, Hawk and Open Hand,* 128.
106. R. O. Faulkner (trans. and ed.), *The Ancient Egyptian Coffin Texts* (Aris & Philips, 1973), vol. 1, 261.
107. Cited in James Mooney, *Myths of the Cherokee* (Government Printing Office, Washington DC, 1900, reprinted by Dover Publications 1995), 259.
108. Ibid.
109. Ibid.
110. Faulkner, *The Ancient Egyptian Coffin Texts,* vol. 1, 190, Line 326.
111. See, for example, F. F. Leek, "Further Studies Concerning Ancient Egyptian Bread," *Journal of Egyptian Archaeology* 59, no. 1 (1973), 199–204, esp. 199: "The two most common cereals to be found in all sites in Upper and in Lower Egypt were wheat and barley . . . *Triticum dicoccum*— emmer—was the most important variety of wheat grown." See also 201: "Two samples taken from the abdominal remains of mummified Thebes showed that emmer was the sole ingredient of bread eaten, and in another sample that it was mixed with another cereal. Since the remains came from Thebes, it suggests that emmer was commonly used in Upper Egypt."
112. Christopher Knight and Robert Lomas, *The Hiram Key: Pharaohs, Freemasons and the Discovery of the Secret Scrolls of Christ* (Arrow Books, 1997), 152: Knight and Lomas suggest that the ancient Egyptians considered Horus to be the "Morning Star" when Osiris says in 1000–1 of the Pyramid Texts:

> *The reed-floats of the sky are set in place for me, that I*
> *may cross by means of them to Re at the horizon. . . I*
> *will stand among them, for the moon is my brother, the*
> *Morning Star is my offspring.*

The authors go on to suggest that Pyramid Texts 357, 929, 935, and 1707 refer to the dead king's offspring—Horus—as being the morning star. On 153 they state, "In Egypt the new king, the Horus, is the morning star, arising (like the raised Freemason) from a temporary and figurative death." Also see Rolf Kraus, "Stellar and Solar Components in Ancient Egyptian Mythology and Royal Ideology," in Michael A. Rappenglecuk et al. eds., *Astronomy and Power: How Worlds Are Structured,* Proceedings of the SEAC 2010 Conference, BAR International Series 2794 (2016), 137–141.
113. James Brown, "On the Identity of the Birdman within Mississippian Period Art and Iconography," in Reilly and Garber, *Ancient Objects and Sacred Realms,* 71.
114. See E. A. Wallis Budge, *The Gods of the Egyptians* (originally published 1904, reprinted by Dover Publications, 1969), 284–287. Also see *The British Museum Dictionary of Ancient Egypt,* 88, 220.
115. Budge, *The Book of the Dead,* 538. See also Faulkner, *Book of the Dead,* 163.
116. Pyramid Texts, 191, Lines 1188–1189.
117. Hultkrantz, *The Religions of the American Indians,* 64.
118. See William F. Romain, *Shamans of the Lost World: A Cognitive Approach to the Prehistoric Religion of the Ohio Hopewell* (AltaMira Press, 2009), 48–51.
119. Pyramid Texts, Utterance 667A, 281, Line 1943.
120. Hultkrantz, *Conceptions of the Soul,* 97.
121. Ibid., 267.
122. Ibid., 432.
123. Veronica Ions, *Egyptian Mythology* (Newnes Books, 1986), 136.
124. For a fuller and more detailed account, see Graham Hancock and Santha Faiia, *Heaven's Mirror: Quest for the Lost Civilization* (Penguin, 1998), 68–75.
125. Alice C. Fletcher and Francis La Flesche, *The Omaha Tribe,* Twenty-Seventh Annual Report of the Bureau of American Ethnology (Smithsonian Institution, 1911), 590.
126. Joseph Epes Brown, *The Sacred Pipe* (University of Oklahoma Press, 1953, 1989), 29n13.
127. Hultkrantz, *The Religions of the American Indians,* 133–134.

128. Lankford in Reilly and Garber, *Ancient Objects and Sacred Realms*, 208.
129. Ibid., 210.
130. Ibid., 211.
131. Pyramid Texts, 93, Line 469.
132. Pyramid Texts, Utterance 697, 305, Line 2175.
133. Coffin Texts, vol. 1, 36, Line 185.
134. E. K. Holt et al. (eds.), *Concerning the Nations: Essays on the Oracles Against the Nations in Isaiah, Jeremiah and Ezekiel* (vol. 612) (Bloomsbury, 2015), 35. On the basis of Dead Sea Scrolls translations of Isaiah, Jeremiah, Judges, and Job, respectively, the authors understand the Hebrew phrases "City of the Sun" and "house of the sun" to be references to Heliopolis, or the Egyptian name *Iwnw*, "pillar town," which in Genesis 41:45 and Ezekiel 30:17 is referred to as *'ôn/'āwen*. Examples from the New American Standard of the bible here:

     He will also shatter the obelisks of Heliopolis, which is in the land of Egypt; and the temples of the gods of Egypt he will burn with fire. (Jeremiah 43:13)

     And Pharaoh called Joseph's name Zaphenath-paneah. And he gave him in marriage Asenath, the daughter of Potiphera priest of On. So Joseph went out over the land of Egypt. (Genesis 41:45)

     The young men of On and Pi-beseth
     Will fall by the sword,
     And the women will go into captivity (Ezekiel 30:17)
135. Ibid.
136. Budge, *The Egyptian Heaven and Hell*, vol. 3, 12.
137. Ibid., 3–4.
138. I. E. S. Edwards, *The Pyramids of Egypt* (Penguin, 1993), 286.
139. Reproduced in Von Del Chamberlain, *When Stars Come Down to Earth: Cosmology of the Skidi Pawnee Indians of North America* (Ballena Press/Centre for Archaeoastronomy, University of Maryland, 1982), 20.
140. Ibid., 24, 130.
141. P. Lacovara, *The World of Ancient Egypt: A Daily Life Encyclopedia* (2 volumes) (ABC-CLIO, 2016), 183. Anke Napp, "Priests of Ancient Egypt," http://www.ancient-egypt-priests.com/AE-Life-english.htm: "The high-ranking priests wore sashes, probably with gold ornaments similar to the ones the Pharaoh used, and a leopard skin. The leopard was considered a sacred animal, personification of the ancient sky-Goddess Mafdet. Perhaps the spots on the skin reminded the Ancient Egyptians of stars. Artificial leopard cloth had star-shaped items on it for the spots. A leopard skin was also seen as connected to the beliefs of regeneration and rebirth in the afterlife, and with Sun God Ra. This can be traced back to the pyramid texts of the Fifth Dynasty. So in particular the Sem-priests, who had to perform the rituals of inspiriting the mummy before the funeral, wore this special garment, but also the deceased person! It can be seen as some sort of christening robe. Apart of the sash, they do not wear any jewellery." Also see Anand Balaji, "Sem Priests of Ancient Egypt: Their Role and Impact in Funerary Contexts—Part 1" (Ancient Origins, May 6, 2018), https://www.ancient-origins.net/history/sem-priests-ancient-egypt-their-role-and-impact-funerary-contexts-part-0010007 and part 2 here: https://www.ancient-origins.net/history/sem-priests-ancient-egypt-service-king-and-country-part-ii-0010009.

     See also http://www.ancient-origins.net/history/sem-priests-ancient-egypt-their-role-and-impact-funerary-contexts-part-0010007 and http://www.ancient-origins.net/history/sem-priests-ancient-egypt- service-king-and-country-part-ii-0010009.
142. M. Verner, *Temple of the World: Sanctuaries, Cults, and Mysteries of Ancient Egypt* (American University in Cairo Press, 2013), 29; Anand Balaji, "Sem Priests of Ancient Egypt: Their Role and Impact in Funerary Contexts," parts 1 and 2.
143. *Cultural Resources Evaluation of the Northern Gulf of Mexico Continental Shelf, Vol I: Prehistoric Cultural Resources Potential*, Office of Archaeology and Historic Preservation, National Park Service, Washington, DC, 1977, 243.
144. See, for example, the discussion in Don W. Dragoo, "Mounds for the Dead: An Analysis of Adena Culture," *Annals of the Carnegie Museum* 37 (1963).
145. William F. Romain, *Mysteries of the Hopewell: Astronomers, Geometers and Magicians of the Eastern Woodlands*, 204.
146. Ibid., 204–205.

24: ASTRONOMY AND GEOMETRY IN THE AFTERLIFE

1. E. A. Wallis Budge, *From Fetish to God in Ancient Egypt* (Oxford University Press, 1934), 155.
2. W. B. Emery, *Archaic Egypt: Culture and Civilization in Egypt Five Thousand Years Ago* (Penguin Books, 1987), 31, 177.
3. E. A. Wallis Budge, *The Book of the Dead* (Arkana, 1985), 315.
4. Ibid., 266.
5. Ibid., 328.
6. E. A. Wallis Budge, *The Egyptian Heaven and Hell* (Martin Hopkinson, 1925) (3 volumes in one edition, page numbers reset to 1 with each volume), vol. 3, 43.
7. Ibid., vol. 1, 142–143.
8. Ibid., vol. 3, 152.
9. Ibid., 135.
10. Ibid., vol. 2, 142.
11. Ibid., vol. 3, 135.
12. R. O. Faulkner (ed. and trans.), *The Ancient Egyptian Coffin Texts* (Aris & Philips, 1973), vol. 2, 290.
13. Ibid., vol. 3, 104.
14. Budge, *The Book of the Dead*, clxxv.
15. Ibid., vol. 1, 89.
16. Ibid., 141.
17. Ibid., 161.
18. Ibid., 170ff.
19. Ibid., for example, see 123, 215, 240, 258 of vol. 1; and 13, 36 of vol. 2. The Duat was sometimes also known as Amentet, and references occur both to the "hidden circle of the Duat" and to the "hidden circle of Amentet," and also, coterminously, to the "secret circle of Amentet" and the "secret circle of the Duat."
20. Ibid., vol. 3, 89; and see Vignette in vol. 2, p. 303.
21. For further details of the specifically astronomical and stellar aspects of the ancient Egyptian religion, see Graham Hancock's *Keeper of Genesis/The Message of the Sphinx* and *Heaven's Mirror*.
22. Budge, *The Egyptian Heaven and Hell*, vol. 1, 22.
23. J. Gribbin and M. Gribbin, *From Here to Infinity: A Beginner's Guide to Astronomy* (Sterling, 2009), 40–41: "Both the Earth and the Moon are . . . orbiting around the balance point in the Earth-Moon system, its centre of mass . . . is like the balance point of a see-saw."
24. Budge, *The Book of the Dead*, 315.
25. Faulkner, *The Ancient Egyptian Coffin Texts*, vol. 3, 140–141, Spells 1060 to 1063.
26. Ibid., vol. 2, 212, Line 250.
27. R. O. Faulkner (ed. and trans.), *The Ancient Egyptian Pyramid Texts* (Oxford University Press, 1969), 290, Line 2016.
28. Ibid., 309, Line 2232.
29. Ibid., Line 2233.
30. Ibid., 159, Line 916.
31. Faulkner, *Book of the Dead*, 113, Spell 118.
32. Faulkner, *Pyramid Texts*, 289–290, Line 2011.
33. Budge, *The Egyptian Heaven and Hell*, vol. 1, 89.
34. Ibid., 93.
35. Faulkner, *Coffin Texts*, vol. 3, 133, Line 291.
36. Ibid., 168, Line 468.
37. Budge, *The Book of the Dead*, 318.
38. Faulkner, *Book of the Dead*, 184, Spell 183.
39. Budge, *The Egyptian Heaven and Hell*, vol. 2, 277–278.
40. Ibid., vol. 1, 258.
41. Ibid., 240.
42. Ibid., 258.
43. Ibid., 9.
44. Ibid., vol. 2, 38–39.
45. Ibid., 39.
46. As, for example, in "this secret Circle of the god Sokar, who is upon his sand"–ibid., 16.

47. George Lankford, "The Great Serpent in Eastern North America," in Kent F. Reilly III and James F. Garber (eds.), *Ancient Objects and Sacred Realms: Interpretations of Mississippian Iconography* (University of Texas Press, 2007), 107–135.
48. William Romain, "Adena-Hopewell Earthworks and the Milky Way Path of Souls," in Meghan E. Buchanan and B. Jacob Skousen (eds.), *Tracing the Relational: The Archaeology of Worlds, Spirits and Temporalities* (University of Utah Press, 2015), 54.
49. Ibid.
50. Ibid.
51. Budge, *The Book of the Dead*, 315.
52. Ibid.
53. Lankford, "The Great Serpent in Eastern North America," 107–135.
54. James Mooney, *Myths of the Cherokee* (Government Printing Office, Washington DC, 1900, reprinted by Dover Publications 1995), 297.
55. Ibid. And see discussion in Lankford, "The Great Serpent in Eastern North America," 114.
56. Budge, *The Book of the Dead*, 315.
57. Ibid., xxviii–xxix; Faulkner, *The Ancient Egyptian Pyramid Texts*, v.
58. In the case of Conly, for example. See chapter 22.
59. E. A. E. Reymond, *The Mythical Origin of the Egyptian Temple* (Manchester University Press, 1969), 8.
60. Ibid., 151: "The mythological situation which we have been analysing discloses a tradition which originated in another place."
61. Ibid., 55, 90, 105, 274.
62. Ibid., 55.
63. Ibid., 109, 113–114, 127.
64. For example, see 19: "The crew of the Falcon." See also 27, 177, 180, 181, 187, 202. There are repeated references throughout the Edfu texts to the crews of ships and to sailing. Thus, 180: "The Shebtiw sailed . . . ," and 187: "They were believed to have sailed to another part of the primeval world."
65. Ibid., 190.
66. Ibid., 274: "They journeyed through the unoccupied lands of the primeval age and founded other sacred domains."
67. Ibid., 122.
68. Ibid., 134.
69. Plato, *Timaeus and Critias* (Penguin Classics, 1977), 36.
70. Ibid.
71. G. Reichel-Dolmatoff, *Beyond the Milky Way: Hallucinatory Imagery of the Tukano Indians* (UCLA Latin America Center Publications, 1978), 2.
72. Ibid.
73. Reymond, *The Mythical Origin of the Egyptian Temple*, 274.
74. Ibid., 190.
75. Ibid., 8–10.
76. Ibid., 24: "the *Shebtiw* whose function is described as *din iht*, to name (= create) things." See also 180.
77. Ibid., 41.
78. Ibid., for example, 28, 66, 236.
79. See, for example, Robert L. Hall, *An Archaeology of the Soul: North American Indian Belief and Ritual* (University of Illinois Press, 1997), 163: "The use of the imagery of the belt of Orion as a protective device may have a history in North America extending back at least to 1000 BC, because in contexts that old in parts of the Northeastern United States, stone tablets and shell plaques have been found into which were drilled three holes, with one, apparently purposely, a little out of line with the rest, just as is one of the three stars of Orion's belt."

PART VII

25: ELOISE

1. Vance Haynes, in conversation with Richard Firestone, cited in Richard Firestone, Allen West, and Simon Warwick Smith, *The Cycle of Cosmic Catastrophes* (Bear, 2006), 37.

2. Bruce B. Huckell and C. Vance Haynes, "Palaeoecology as Viewed from Murray Springs, Arizona," in C. Vance Haynes and Bruce B. Huckell (eds.), *Murray Springs: A Clovis Site with Multiple Activity Areas in the San Pedro Valley, Arizona* (University of Arizona Press, 2007), 225.

3. Ibid.

4. See full discussion of the Younger Dryas in Graham Hancock, *Magicians of the Gods: The Forgotten Wisdom of Earth's Lost Civilization* (2015), part 2.

5. C. Vance Haynes, "Palaeoecology as Viewed from Murray Springs, Arizona," 225. The quotation continues as follows: "Many of them overlie terminal Pleistocene fauna remains, a few with Clovis artefacts. The . . . termination everywhere appears to have occurred . . . rapidly and at the same time . . . Could drought, deep freeze, and Clovis predation have occurred at all of these places at the same time? Probably not. With regard to the cause of the Pleistocene termination, something happened 13,000 years ago that we have not yet fully understood."

6. Vance Haynes, "Younger Dryas 'Black Mats' and the Rancholabrean Termination in North America," *Proceedings of the National Academy of Sciences* 105, no. 18 (May 6, 2008), 6520.

7. R. B. Firestone et al., "Evidence for an Extraterrestrial Impact 12,900 Years Ago That Contributed to Megafaunal Extinctions and the Younger Dryas Cooling," *Proceedings of the National Academy of Sciences* 104, no. 41 (October 9, 2007), 16016–16021.

8. Ibid. In subsequent papers the date of 12,900 years ago was revised downward by 100 years to around 12,800 years ago. See C. R. Kinzie et al., "Nanodiamond-Rich Layer Across Three Continents Consistent with Major Cosmic Impact at 12,800 cal BP," *Journal of Geology* 122, no. 5 (2014), 475–506.

9. See for example Julie Cohen, "Study Examines 13,000 Year-old Nanodiamonds From Multiple Locations Across Three Continents," (Phys Org, August 27, 2014), https://phys.org/news/2014-08-year-old-nanodiamonds-multiple-continents.html, and J. H. Wittke et al, "Nanodiamonds and Carbon Spherules from Tunguska, the K/T Boundary, and the Younger Dryas Boundary Layer," (the American Geophysical Union Fall Meeting, 2009), http://adsabs.harvard.edu/abs/2009AGUFMPP 31D1392W.

10. Michail I. Petaev et al., "Large Pt Anomaly in the Greenland Ice Cores Points to a Cataclysm at the Onset of Younger Dryas," *Proceedings of the National Academy of Sciences* 110, no. 32 (August 6, 2013), 12917–12920. See also Heather Pringle, "Did a Comet Wipe Out Prehistoric Americans?" *New Scientist* (May 22, 2007), http://www.newscientist.com/article/dn11909-did-a-comet-wipe-out-prehistoric-americans.html#.VJqZ88AgA; and Firestone et al., "Evidence for an Extraterrestrial Impact 12,900 Years Ago That Contributed to the Megafaunal Extinctions and the Younger Dryas Cooling," 16016.

11. James Kennett cited by Jim Barlow-Oregon in "Did Exploding Comet Leave Trail of Nanodiamonds?" *Futurity: Research News from Top Universities,* http://www.futurity.org/comet-nanodiamonds-climate-change-755662/. See also Kinzie et al., "Nanodiamond-Rich Layer Across Three Continents Consistent with Major Cosmic Impact at 12,800 cal BP," 476.

12. Richard Firestone quoted in Pringle, "Did a Comet Wipe Out Prehistoric Americans?"

13. Kinzie et al., "Nanodiamond-Rich Layer Across Three Continents Consistent with Major Cosmic Impact at 12,800 cal BP," 498–499.

14. Quoted in Julie Cohen, "Nanodiamonds Are Forever: A UCSB Professor's Research Examines 13,000-Year-Old Nanodiamonds from Multiple Locations Across Three Continents," *The Current,* UC Santa Barbara, August 28, 2014, http://www.news.ucsb.edu/2014/014368/nanodiamonds-are-forever.

15. Petaev et al., "Large Pt Anomaly in the Greenland Ice Cores Points to a Cataclysm at the Onset of Younger Dryas," 12918–12919.

16. Ibid., 12917.

17. W. M. Napier, "Palaeolithic Extinctions and the Taurid Complex," *Monthly Notices of the Royal Astronomical Society* 405, no. 3 (July 1, 2010), 1901–1906. See also Gerrit L. Verschuur, *Impact: The Threat of Comets and Asteroids* (Oxford University Press, 1996), 136.

18. Clube and Napier, *The Cosmic Winter,* 147.

19. W. M. Napier, "Comets, Catastrophes and Earth's History," *Journal of Cosmology* (November 6, 2009), 344–355

20. Ibid.

21. Clube and Napier, *The Cosmic Winter,* 153.

26: FIRE AND ICE
1. The Comet Research Group, https://cometresearchgroup.org/.
2. The Comet Research Group, "Comet Impact Scientists," https://cometresearchgroup.org/scientists-members/.
3. Christopher Moore et al., "Widespread Platinum Anomaly Documented at the Younger Dryas Onset in North American Sedimentary Sequences," *Scientific Reports* (March 9, 2017).
4. Ibid., 1.
5. Michail I. Petaev et al., "Large Pt Anomaly in the Greenland Ice Cores Points to a Cataclysm at the Onset of Younger Dryas, Proceedings of the National Academy of Sciences 110, no. 32 (August 6, 2013), 12917, 12918.
6. Moore et al., "Widespread Platinum Anomaly Documented at the Younger Dryas Onset in North American Sedimentary Sequences," 2–3.
7. Ibid., 3.
8. Ibid.
9. Ibid., 4–5.
10. Ibid., 7.
11. Ibid., Supplementary Information, 10–11. Platinum (Pt) is one of the platinum group of elements (PGE) that includes iridium (Ir), osmium (Os), ruthenium (Ru), and rhodium (Rh).
12. Ibid., 12–13.
13. Ibid., 13.
14. Ibid.
15. Ibid.
16. Wendy S. Wolbach et al., "Extraordinary Biomass-Burning Episode and Impact Winter Triggered by the Younger Dryas Cosmic Impact ~12,800 Years Ago," *Journal of Geology* 126, no. 2 (March 2018), 165–205.
17. Ibid. The full list of coauthors: Wendy S. Wolbach, Joanne P. Ballard, Paul A. Mayewski, Victor Adedeji, Ted E. Bunch, Richard B. Firestone, Timothy A. French, George A. Howard, Isabel Israde-Alcántara, John R. Johnson, David Kimbel, Charles R. Kinzie, Andrei Kurbatov, Gunther Kletetschka, Malcolm A. LeCompte, William C. Mahaney, Adrian L. Melott, Abigail Maiorana-Boutilier, Siddhartha Mitra, Christopher R. Moore, William M. Napier, Jennifer Parlier, Kenneth B. Tankersley, Brian C. Thomas, James H. Wittke, Allen West, and James P. Kennett.
18. Ibid., 165.
19. Ibid., 165, 167.
20. Ibid., 169.
21. Ibid., 170.
22. Ibid., 170–171.
23. Ibid.
24. Ibid., 171.
25. Ibid.
26. Ibid., 187, 189.
27. Ibid., 192.
28. Ibid.
29. Ibid., 192–193.
30. Ibid., 193.
31. Ibid., 194.
32. Josh Halliday and James Gant, "Andy Burnham Calls for More Support to Tackle Lancashire Wildfires" (*Guardian*, July 2, 2018), https://www.theguardian.com/uk-news/2018/jul/02/firefighters-need-support-to-tackle-lancashire-moorland-blaze-says-andy-burnham and Helen Pidd, "Firefighters From Seven Counties Fight Greater Manchester Moor Fires" (*Guardian*, July 1, 2018), https://www.theguardian.com/uk-news/2018/jul/01/firefighters-from-seven-counties-fight-greater-manchester-moor-fires.
33. Dale Kasler, "Northern California Wildfires Are Burning Much Earlier This Summer. Here's Why." (*Sacramento Bee*, July 2, 2018), https://www.sacbee.com/latest-news/article214198989.html.
34. CAL FIRE, "Incident Information," http://cdfdata.fire.ca.gov/incidents/incidents_stats?year=2017.
35. Matthew Rena, "Costs to Fight 2017 California Wildfires Shatter Records" (Courthouse News Service, January 8, 2018), https://www.courthousenews.com/costs-to-fight-2017-california-wildfires-shatters-records/.

36. Walbach et al., "Extraordinary Biomass-Burning Episode and Impact Winter Triggered by the Younger Dryas Cosmic Impact ~12,800 Years Ago," 165.

37. Matthew R. Francis, "When Carl Sagan Warned the World About Nuclear Winter," *Smithsonian Magazine*, November 15, 2017, https://www.smithsonianmag.com/science-nature/when-carl-sagan-warned-world-about-nuclear-winter-180967198/.

38. Cited in ibid.

39. R. B. Firestone et al., "Evidence for an Extraterrestrial Impact 12,900 Years Ago That Contributed to the Megafaunal Extinctions and the Younger Dryas Cooling," *Proceedings of the National Academy of Sciences* 104, no. 41 (October 9, 2007), 16020.

40. Probably just under 10,000 megatons. See Ashley Kirk, "How Many Nukes Are in the World and What Could They Destroy?" (*Telegraph*, October 11, 2017), https://www.telegraph.co.uk/news/0/many-nukes-world-could-destroy/. Note, however, that though this figure is based on statistics from the Arms Control Association, it is an estimate due to the secretive nature of governments' approach to weaponry.

41. Wolbach et al., "Extraordinary Biomass-Burning Episode and Impact Winter Triggered by the Younger Dryas Cosmic Impact ~12,800 Years Ago," 179.

42. Ibid., 200.

43. S. J. Fiedel, "The Mysterious Onset of the Younger Dryas," *Quaternary International* 242 (2011), 263.

44. David J. Leydet et al., "Opening of Glacial Lake Agassiz's Eastern Outlets by the Start of the Younger Dryas Cold Period," *Geology* (January 4, 2018).

45. Fiedel, "The Mysterious Onset of the Younger Dryas," 264.

46. Graham Hancock, *Magicians of the Gods: The Forgotten Wisdom of Earth's Lost Civilization* (2015), chapter 6, 121–122.

47. Wolbach et al., "Extraordinary Biomass-Burning Episode and Impact Winter Triggered by the Younger Dryas Cosmic Impact - 12,800 Years Ago," 179. Emphasis added.

48. Ibid., 179.

49. Ibid., 180.

50. Ibid., 175.

51. Ibid., 178.

52. Ibid., 179.

53. Ibid.

54. Ibid., 201.

55. Ibid., 179.

56. Ibid., 167.

57. Ibid., 168, 173, 177, 178, 188. See also Petaev et al., "Large Pt Anomaly in the Greenland Ice Cores Points to a Cataclysm at the Onset of Younger Dryas," 12917. And see W. M. Napier, "Palaeolithic Extinctions and the Taurid Complex," *Monthly Notices of the Royal Astronomical Society* 405, no. 3 (July 1, 2010), 1901–1906. The complete paper can be read online here: http://mnras.oxfordjournals.org/content/405/3/1901.full.pdf+html?sid=19fd6cae-61a0-45bd-827b-9f4eb877fd39, and downloaded as a pdf here: http://arxiv.org/pdf/1003.0744.pdf; and Victor Clube and Bill Napier, *The Cosmic Winter* (Wiley, 1990), 150–153. See also Gerrit L. Verschuur, *Impact: The Threat of Comets and Asteroids* (Oxford University Press, 1996), 136.

58. Firestone et al., "Evidence for an Extraterrestrial Impact 12,900 Years Ago That Contributed to Megafaunal Extinctions and the Younger Dryas Cooling," 16020.

59. Yingzhe Wu et al., "Origin and Provenance of Spherules and Magnetic Grains at the Younger Dryas Boundary," *Proceedings of the National Academy of Sciences* 110, no. 38 (September 5, 2013), e3564.

60. R. B. Firestone et al., "Analysis of the Younger Dryas Impact Layer," *Journal of Siberian Federal University. Engineering and Technologies* 1 (February 2010), 30, 47, 56.

61. Wolbach et al., "Extraordinary Biomass-Burning Episode and Impact Winter Triggered by the Younger Dryas Cosmic Impact -12,800 Years Ago," 195: "Peros et al.'s (2008) comprehensive analysis of North American pollen records indeed demonstrated that an abrupt, temporary decline in conifer forests (mostly Picea sp.) occurred widely across North America during the first 150 y of the YD climate episode. This loss was accompanied by a sudden expansion of Populus species (poplar, cottonwood, aspen) and sometimes Alnus (birch), which are opportunistic pioneers that often flourish following major forest disruptions such as wildfires. In turn, Populus species were replaced by conifers during the remainder of the YD. Thus, a large, pervasive, temporary change in

continental vegetation, as reflected in the North American pollen record, is consistent with a major biotic perturbation that would have resulted from widespread biomass burning at the YDB."

62. Ibid., 178.
63. Ibid., 198.
64. Firestone et al., "Analysis of the Younger Dryas Impact Layer," 57–58.
65. Ibid., 58.
66. Together with nineteen genera of North American birds. See James P. Kennett et al., "Potential Consequences of the YDB Cosmic Impact at 12.8 kya: Climate, Humans and Megafauna," in Albert C. Goodyear and Christopher R. Moore (eds.), *Early Human Life on the Southeastern Coastal Plain* (Florida Museum of Natural History, University of Florida Press, 2018), 184.
67. Wolbach et al., "Extraordinary Biomass-Burning Episode and Impact Winter Triggered by the Younger Dryas Cosmic Impact ~12,800 Years Ago," 195–196, 200–201.
68. Ibid., 200–201.
69. Kennett et al., "Potential Consequences of the YDB Cosmic Impact at 12.8 kya," 184–185.
70. Ibid., 186.
71. Ibid., 181–182.
72. Ibid., 182.
73. Ibid.
74. Terry L. Jones and Douglas J. Kennett, "A Land Impacted? The Younger Dryas Boundary Event in California," in Terry L. Jones and Jennifer E. Perry (eds.), *Contemporary Issues in California Archaeology* (Routledge, 2016), Kindle location 849.
75. David G. Anderson et al., "Multiple Lines of Evidence for Possible Human Population Decline/Settlement Reorganization During the Early Younger Dryas," *Quaternary International* 242 (2011), 578.

27: CAPE FEAR

1. Graham Hancock, *Magicians of the Gods: The Forgotten Wisdom of Earth's Lost Civilization* (2015), 86–108.
2. Since 2015, the number of papers that have been published that augment the case for a YD ET impact event has been quite staggering. Strongly supportive papers include:

W. M. Napier, "Giant Comets and Mass Extinctions of Life," *Monthly Notices of the Royal Astronomical Society* 448, no. 1 (2015), 27–36; A. V. Andronikov et al., "Geochemical Evidence of the Presence of Volcanic and Meteoritic Materials in Late Pleistocene Lake Sediments of Lithuania," *Quaternary International* 386 (2015), 18–29; R. Ellis, "The Carolina Bays, and the Destruction of North America," Ralph Ellis Research Center (2015); B. Napier et al., "Centaurs as a Hazard to Civilization," *Astronomy and Geophysics* 56, no. 6 (2015), 6–24; A. V. Andronikov et al., " Implications from Chemical, Structural and Mineralogical Studies of Magnetic Microspherules from Around the Lower Younger Dryas Boundary (New Mexico, USA)," *Geografiska Annaler: Series A, Physical Geography*, 98, no. 1 (2016), 39–59; J. L. Prado, C. Martinez-Mara, and M. T. Alberdi, "Megafauna Extinction in South America: A New Chronology for the Argentine Pampas," *Palaeogeography, Palaeoclimatology, Palaeoecology* 425 (2015), 41–44; A. V. Andronikov and I. E. Andronikova, "Sediments from Around the Lower Younger Dryas Boundary (SE Arizona, USA): Implications from LA-ICP-MS Multielement Analysis," *Geografiska Annaler: Series A, Physical Geography* 98, no. 3 (2016); A. Zamora, "A Model for the Geomorphology of the Carolina Bays," *Geomorphology* 282 (2017), 209–216; H. G. Burchard, "Younger Dryas Comet 12,900 BP," *Open Journal of Geology*, 7, no. 2 (2017), 193; M. B. Sweatman and D. Tsikritsis, "Decoding Göbekli Tepe with Archaeoastronomy: What Does the Fox Say?" *Mediterranean Archaeology and Archaeometry* 17, no. 1 (2017); P. Spurný et al., "Discovery of a New Branch of the Taurid Meteoroid Stream as a Real Source of Potentially Hazardous Bodies," *Astronomy and Astrophysics* 605 (2017), A68; H. Patton et al., "Deglaciation of the Eurasian Ice Sheet Complex," *Quaternary Science Reviews* 169 (August 1, 2017), 148–172; J. T. Hagstrum et al., "Impact-Related Microspherules in Late Pleistocene Alaskan and Yukon 'Muck' Deposits Signify Recurrent Episodes of Catastrophic Emplacement," *Scientific Reports* 7, no. 1 (2017), 16620; P. Roperch et al., "Surface Vitrification Caused by Natural Fires in Late Pleistocene Wetlands of the Atacama Desert," *Earth and Planetary Science Letters* 469 (2017), 15–26; W. C. Mahaney et al., "Evidence for Cosmic Airburst in the Western Alps Archived in Late Glacial Paleosols," *Quaternary International* 438 (2017), 68–80; I. Israde-Alcántara et al., "Five Younger Dryas Black Mats in Mexico and Their Stratigraphic and Paleoenvironmental Context," *Journal of Paleolimnology* 59, no. 1 (2018), 59–79; W. C. Mahaney et al., "Cosmic Airburst on Developing Allerød Substrates (Soils) in the Western Alps, Mt. Viso Area," *Studia Quaternaria* 35, no. 1 (2018), 3–23; W. C. Mahaney et al., "Did the Black-Mat Impact/Airburst Reach the Antarctic? Evidence from New Mountain Near the Taylor Glacier in the Dry Valley Mountains," *Journal of Geology* 126, no. 3 (2018), 285–305; A. V. Andronikov et al., "Geochemical Records of Paleocontamination in Late Pleistocene Lake Sediments in West Flanders (Belgium)," *Geografiska Annaler: Series A, Physical Geography* 100, no. 2 (2018), 204–220; H. P. Hu, J. L. Feng, and F. Chen, "Sedimentary Records of a Palaeo-Lake in the Middle Yarlung Tsangpo: Implications for Terrace Genesis and Outburst Flooding," *Quaternary Science Reviews* 192 (2018), 135–148; M. B. Sweatman and A. Coombs, "Decoding European Palaeolithic Art: Extremely Ancient Knowledge of Precession of the Equinoxes," *arXiv,* preprint arXiv:1806.00046 (2018).

3. Notably M. A. LeCompte et al., "An Independent Evaluation of Conflicting Microspherules Results from Different Investigations of the Younger Dryas Impact Hypothesis," *Proceedings of the National Academy of Sciences* 109, no. 44 (2018), e2960–e2969, doi:10.1073/pnas.1208603109; and Y. Wu et al., "Origin and Provenance of Spherules and Magnetic Grains at the Younger Dryas Boundary," *Proceedings of the National Academy of Sciences* 110, no. 38 (2013), e3557–e3566, doi:10.1073/pnas.1304059110.

4. See G. Hancock, *Magicians of the Gods,* chapters 4 and 5, 69–85.

5. Antonio Zamora has a multidisciplinary background in chemistry, computer science, and computational linguistics. Mr. Zamora was born in Mexico and came to the United States at an early age. He studied chemistry at the University of Texas (BS 1962), and computer and information science at Ohio State University (MS 1969). During his service in the U.S. Army from 1962 to 1965, Mr. Zamora studied medical technology at the Medical Field Service School (MFSS) in Fort Sam Houston and worked in hematology at Brooke Army Medical Center. Mr. Zamora worked for many years as an editor and researcher at Chemical Abstracts Service developing chemical information applications. He also worked as a senior programmer at IBM on spelling checkers and novel multilingual information retrieval tools. He holds thirteen patents. After his retirement from IBM, Mr. Zamora established Zamora Consulting, LLC, and worked as a consultant for the American Chemical Society, the National Library of Medicine, and the Department of Energy to support semantic enhancements for search engines. Mr. Zamora has been interested in astronomy since childhood when his father helped him build a refracting telescope. Since his retirement in 2011, Mr. Zamora completed massive open online courses in astronomy, geology, and paleobiology. He regularly attends the seminars of the Department of Terrestrial Magnetism at the Carnegie Institution of Washington.

6. Zamora, "A Model for the Geomorphology of the Carolina Bays," 209–216.

7. The Carolina Bays were first postulated to be of cosmic origin in 1933 when the Roosevelt administration took the first aerial photographs of the seemingly crater-dotted landscape to assist farmers during the Great Depression. For an example, consult G. Howard, "The Carolina Bays" (1997) on George Howard.net, http://www.georgehoward.net/cbays.htm, accessed August 21, 2018. See also William S. Powell, "The Carolina Bays" (Encyclopedia of North Carolina, 2006). Available here: https://www.ncpedia.org/carolina-bays.

8. For example, Richard Firestone, Allen West, and Simon Warwick-Smith, *The Cycle of Cosmic Catastrophes* (Bear, 2006).

9. See, for example, M. J. Brooks, B. E. Taylor, and A. H. Ivester, "Carolina Bays: Time Capsules of Culture and Climate Change," *Southeastern Archaeology* 29, no. 1 (2010), 146–163, esp. 148: "Based on 45 OSL dates, active shorelines and associated eolian deposition occurred during marine isotope stage (MIS) 2 to late MIS 3 (-12 to 50 ka), MIS 4 to very late MIS 5 (60–80 ka), and late MIS 6 (120–140 ka). . . . In addition to these age ranges, some OSL dates indicate that bays also were active during the Holocene and Sangamon Interglacials."

10. Zamora, "A Model for the Geomorphology of the Carolina Bays," 211ff.

11. Ibid., 209, 212.

12. ResearchGate, "Michael Davias," https://www.researchgate.net/profile/Michael_Davias.

13. ResearchGate, "Thomas H. S. Harris," https://www.researchgate.net/profile/Thomas_Harris8.

14. Michael E. Davias and Thomas H. S. Harris, "A Tale of Two Craters: Coriolis-Aware Trajectory Analysis Correlates Two Pleistocene Impact-Strewn Fields and Gives Michigan a Thumb," paper presented at the Geological Society of America, North-Central Section, 49th Annual Meeting, May 19–20, 2015.

15. Ibid.

16. R. B. Firestone et al., "Analysis of the Younger Dryas Impact Layer," *Journal of Siberian Federal University. Engineering and Technologies* 1 (February 2010), 57–58.
17. Davias and Harris, "A Tale of Two Craters."
18. Ibid.
19. Ibid.
20. Ibid.
21. Zamora, "A Model for the Geomorphology of the Carolina Bays," 215.
22. Email from Antonio Zamora to Graham Hancock, July 11, 2018.
23. Zamora, "A Model for the Geomorphology of the Carolina Bays," 212.
24. Ibid., 212, 214.
25. Ibid., 215.
26. Ibid.
27. Ibid.
28. Antonio Zamora, *Killer Comet: What the Carolina Bays Tell Us* (Zamora Consulting, third paperback edition, 2016), 71–75.
29. Firestone et al., "Analysis of the Younger Dryas Impact Layer," 57–58.
30. Graham Hancock Live in Arkansas (YouTube, 2018), https://www.youtube.com/watch?v=c-qIP1 lfok8&feature=share.
31. Firestone et al., "Analysis of the Younger Dryas Impact Layer," 30.
32. Donald F. Eschman and David M. Mickelson, "Correlation of Glacial Deposits of the Huron, Lake Michigan and Green Bay Lobes in Michigan and Wisconsin," *Quaternary Science Reviews* 5 (1986), 53–57.
33. Ibid., 56.

PART VIII

28: HUNTER-GATHERERS AND THE LOST CIVILIZATION

1. Email correspondence with Albert Goodyear, February 6, 2018.
2. William Mahaney et al., "Cosmic Airburst on Developing Allerød Substrates (Soils) in the Western Alps, Mt. Viso Area," *Studia Quaternaria* 35, no. 1 (2018), 3, 20–21.
3. W. C. Mahaney et al., "Did the Black-Mat Impact/Airburst Reach the Antarctic? Evidence from New Mountain Near the Taylor Glacier in the Dry Valley Mountains," *Journal of Geology* 126, no. 3 (May 2018), 285.
4. Wendy Wolbach et al., "Extraordinary Biomass-Burning Episode and Impact Winter Triggered by the Younger Dryas Cosmic Impact ~12,800 Years Ago," *Journal of Geology* 126, no. 2 (March 2018), 170.
5. Marc Barton, "Smallpox and the Conquest of Mexico" (Past Medical History, February 28, 2018), https://www.pastmedicalhistory.co.uk/smallpox-and-the-conquest-of-mexico/.
6. Thomas J. Williams et al., "Evidence of an Early Projectile Point Technology in North America at the Gault Site, Texas, USA," *Science Advances* (July 14, 2018), 1, http://advances.sciencemag.org/content/4/7/eaar5954.
7. Ibid., 2.
8. Ibid., 5.
9. Thomas et al., "Explaining the Origin of Fluting in North American Pleistocene Weaponry," 23, 24, 28. And see B. A. Storey et al., "Why Are Clovis Fluted Points More Resilient Than Non-Fluted Lanceolate Points? A Quantitative Assessment of Breakage Patterns Between Experimental Models," *Archaeometry* (July 2, 2018).
10. Personal correspondence with Al Goodyear, July 25, 2018. And see Lorena Becerra-Valdivia et al., "Reassessing the Chronology of the Archaeological Site of Anzick," *Proceedings of the National Academy of Sciences* (June 18, 2018), and Morten Rasmussen et al., "The Genome of a Late Pleistocene Human from a Clovis Burial Site in Western Montana," *Nature* 506 (February 13, 2014), 225.
11. Becerra-Valdivia et al., "Reassessing the Chronology of the Archaeological Site of Anzick," 3: "There is strong agreement between the Anzick-1 . . . date (12,905–12,695 cal B.P.) and all those obtained for the antler rods (12,990–12,840 cal B.P.). The results therefore suggest that Anzick-1 is temporally coeval with the antler rods, associated with the Clovis assemblage, and dates within the Clovis period."
12. Numbers on Clovis sites and points from Charles C. Mann, "The Clovis Point and the Discovery of America's First Culture," *Smithsonian Magazine,* November 2013, https://www.smithsonianmag.com/history/the-clovis-point-and-the-discovery-of-americas-first-culture-3825828/.

13. Becerra-Valdivia et al., "Reassessing the Chronology of the Archaeological Site of Anzick," 1. See also Rasmussen et al., "The Genome of a Late Pleistocene Human from a Clovis Burial Site in Western Montana," 225. The very fact that no other Clovis burials have ever been found means there's nothing to compare Anzick-1 with. To give an extreme example of the kinds of problems this raises, although we can make informed guesses, we cannot know for sure whether *every* deceased Clovis infant was buried in the same elaborate way with equally copious offerings of grave goods or whether Anzick-1 was an exceptional burial of an exceptional individual, perhaps from some exceptional lineage. Intuitively we feel it's more likely to be the latter than the former, but we can't prove it.

14. Personal correspondence with Al Goodyear, July 26, 2018. And see Thomas et al., "Explaining the Origin of Fluting in North American Pleistocene Weaponry," 23–24.

29: UNKNOWN UNKNOWNS

1. The reference is to this famously circuitous 2002 statement by former secretary of state Donald Rumsfeld concerning lack of evidence linking the government of Iraq with weapons of mass destruction: "Reports that say that something hasn't happened are always interesting to me, because as we know, there are known knowns; there are things we know we know. We also know there are known unknowns; that is to say we know there are some things we do not know. But there are also unknown unknowns—the ones we don't know we don't know. And if one looks throughout the history of our country and other free countries, it is the latter category that tend to be the difficult ones." Online here: http://archive.defense.gov/Transcripts/Transcript.aspx?TranscriptID=2636.

2. John Soennichesen, *Bretz's Flood: The Remarkable Story of a Rebel Geologist and the World's Greatest Flood* (Sasquatch Books, 2008), 131.

3. Graham Hancock, *Magicians of the Gods* (2015), part 2.

4. Henry T. Mullins and Edward T. Hinchley, "Erosion and Infill of New York Finger Lakes: Implications for Laurentide Ice Sheet Deglaciation," *Geology* 17, no. 7 (July 1989), 622–625.

5. "Smallpox and the Conquest of Mexico" (Past Medical History, February 28, 2018), https://www.pastmedicalhistory.co.uk/smallpox-and-the-conquest-of-mexico/.

6. Peter Tompkins, *Mysteries of the Mexican Pyramids* (Thames and Hudson, 1987), 21.

7. Friar Diego de Landa, *Yucatan Before and After the Conquest* (trans. with notes by William Gates) (Producción Editorial Dante, 1990), 9.

8. Ibid., 104.

9. Jose Fernandez, "A Stellar City: Utatlan and Orion," *Time and Astronomy at the Meeting of Two Worlds,* Proceedings of the International Symposium, April 27 to May 2, 1992, 72, 74. Cited in Graham Hancock and Santha Faiia, *Heaven's Mirror: Quest for the Lost Civilization* (Penguin, 1998), 35.

10. Jose Fernandez cited in David Friedel et al., *Maya Cosmos* (William Morrow, 1993), 103. Cited in Hancock and Faiia, *Heaven's Mirror,* 35.

11. Fernandez, "A Stellar City: Utatlan and Orion," 73. Cited in Hancock and Faiia, *Heaven's Mirror,* 35.

12. Hancock and Faiia, *Heaven's Mirror,* 23, 24. Regarding the Milky Way as the Mayan "Path of Souls," see Mary Miller and Karl Taube, *The Gods and Symbols of Ancient Mexico and the Maya* (Thames and Hudson, 1993), 114.

13. Hancock and Faiia, *Heaven's Mirror,* 22.

14. Ibid., 37.

15. Ibid., 35–37, 43–114.

16. Ibid.

17. Sylvanus Griswold Morley, *An Introduction to the Study of the Maya Hieroglyphs* (Dover, 1975), 32.

18. Ibid.

19. J. Eric S. Thompson, *The Rise and Fall of Maya Civilization* (Pimlico, 1993), 13–14.

20. The Dresden, Paris, Madrid, and Grolier codices. The latter, the Grolier codex, was long suspected to be a fraud but a 2016 study suggests it is genuine. See Erin Blakemore, "New Analysis Shows Disputed Maya "Grolier Codex" Is the Real Deal," *Smithsonian Magazine,* September 15, 2016, https://www.smithsonianmag.com/smart-news/maya-codex-once-thought-be-sketchy-real-thing-180960466/. Further confirmation came in August 2018 when Mexico's National Institute of History and Archaeology announced, after long deliberation, that the codex is genuine, that it dates between AD 1021 and 1154, and that it is therefore "the oldest-known pre-Hispanic document." See https://www.nbcnews.com/news/latino/experts-mexico-find-nearly-1-000-year-old-authentic-mayan-n905376.

21. See, in general, Father Pablo Joseph de Arriaga in L. Clark Keating (trans.), *The Extirpation of Idolatry in Peru* (University of Kentucky Press, 1968).

22. L. A. Clayton, E. C. Moore, and V. J. Knight (eds.), *The De Soto Chronicles,* vol. 1: *The Expedition of Hernando de Soto to North America in 1539–1543* (University of Alabama Press, 1995).

23. R. G. Robertson, *Rotting Face: Smallpox and the American Indian* (Caxton Press, 2001), 132.

24. Donald L. Fixico, "When Native Americans Were Slaughtered in the Name of 'Civilization,'" March 2, 2018, https://www.history.com/news/native-americans-genocide-united-states.

25. David E. Stannard, *American Holocaust: The Conquest of the New World* (Oxford University Press, 1992), 11.

26. US Indian Boarding School History, National Native American Boarding School Healing Coalition, https://boardingschoolhealing.org/education/us-indian-boarding-school-history/.

27. Cited in ibid.

28. Ephraim G. Squier and Edwin H. Davis, *Ancient Monuments of the Mississippi Valley* (Smithsonian Institution, Washington. DC, 1848, reprinted and republished by the Smithsonian, with an introduction by David J. Meltzer, in 1998), xxxix.

29. Jarrod Burks and Robert A. Cooke, "Beyond Squier and Davis: Rediscovering Ohio's Earthworks Using Geophysical Remote Sensing," *American Antiquity* 76 (October 2011), 680.

30. David J. Meltzer, introduction to Squier and Davis, *Ancient Monuments of the Mississippi Valley,* 37.

31. I put a similar question to David J. Meltzer (email exchange July 23 and 24, 2018), **GH:** I'm inclined to say in the relevant chapter of the book I'm just completing on ancient America that reliable figures simply don't exist for the whole Mississippi Valley and that no archaeologist or other researcher has ever attempted to estimate what has been lost across the whole region as a result of agricultural, industrial and other encroachments since the mid-19th century. Would that, in your opinion, be a true reflection of the state of knowledge on this issue, or would it be misleading? **DJM:** I think that is an accurate statement, though again not having expertise in the area I cannot be certain. I also think it important to add that one of the reasons why such an estimate might be impossible is that 200+ years ago there was no systematic count of these earthworks, so we have no idea what the denominator should be for the equation of "sites still extant / sites once present." Add to that the fact that the (un)systematic ballpark estimates of a Squier would not only have failed to capture all the small mounds and hamlets, many of those sites were probably plowed down without anyone (except the mule team doing the work) even noticing or recording.

32. Email exchange with David J. Meltzer, July 24 and 25, 2018.

33. Gregory L. Little, *The Illustrated Encyclopaedia of Native American Indian Mounds and Earthworks* (Eagle Wing Books, 2016), 3.

34. Sue Sturgis, "Wal-Mart's History of Destroying Sacred Sites," *Facing South,* September 3, 2009, https://www.facingsouth.org/2009/09/wal-marts-history-of-destroying-sacred-sites.html.

35. Sue Sturgis, "Alabama city destroying ancient Indian mound for Sam's Club," *Facing South,* August 4, 2009, online here: https://www.facingsouth.org/2009/08/alabama-city-destroying-ancient-indian-mound-for-sams-club.html

36. Ibid.

37. Terry L. Jones, "Archaeological Perspectives on the Extra-Terrestrial Impact Hypothesis, 12,900 BP: A View from Western North America," *Journal of Cosmology* 2 (November 10, 2009), 299–300.

38. Ibid. Emphasis added. And see D. Grayson and D. Meltzer, "Requiem for North American Overkill," *Journal of Archeological Science* 30 (2003), 585–593; S. Fiedel and G. Haynes, "A Premature Burial: Comments on Grayson and Meltzer's 'Requiem for Overkill,'" *Journal of Archeological Science* 31 (2004), 121–131; D. Grayson and D. Meltzer, "North American Overkill Continued? *Journal of Archeological Science* 31 (2004), 133–136.

39. Jones, "Archaeological Perspectives on the Extra-Terrestrial Impact Hypothesis, 12,900 BP," 299–300.

40. Ibid.

41. E. A. E. Reymond, *The Mythical Origin of the Egyptian Temple* (Manchester University Press, 1969), 122, 134.

42. Of most importance here are the Kiva structures of Native American origin myths and the remnants of them in the Americas today (i.e., the great kiva at Chaco Culture National Historical Park). For this consult G. A. David, *The Kivas of Heaven: Ancient Hopi Starlore,* (SCB Distributors, 2011), chapter 1.

30: THE KEY TO EARTH'S LOST CIVILIZATION

1. For a quick overview of the chronology of the most recent Ice Age, see Kim Ann Zimmerman, "Pleistocene Epoch: Facts About the Last Ice Age," *Live Science*, August 29, 2017, https://www. livescience.com/40311-pleistocene-epoch.html.

2. Thomas M. Cronin, *Principles of Climatology* (New York: Columbia University Press, 1999), 204.

3. The range of 140,000 to 120,000 years ago is approximate and Deméré himself (in personal correspondence) prefers 130,000 years ago down to about 115,000 years ago. There are nuances, as usual. For full details of recent discussions around the dating of the Eemian, see D. Dahl-Jensen et al., "Eemian Interglacial Reconstructed from a Greenland Folded Ice Core," *Nature* 493 (January 24, 2013), 489–494.

4. Frederick Soddy, *The Interpretation of Radium and the Structure of the Atom* (John Murray, 1920), 182.

5. Ibid.

6. Ibid., 182–183.

7. Allen Ginsberg, *The Yage Letters: Redux* (Penguin Modern Classics Kindle Edition, 2012), xiii. Later the name *Telepathine* would be applied more specifically to harmine, the most important active alkaloid in the ayahuasca vine.

8. Ibid.

9. By the traveler Rafael Zerda Bayón—see https://www.singingtotheplants.com/2007/12/the-telepa thy-meme/.

10. Benny Shanon, *The Antipodes of the Mind: Charting the Phenomenology of the Ayahuasca Experience* (Oxford University Press, 2002), 256–257.

11. W. Y. Evans-Wentz (ed.), *The Tibetan Book of the Dead* (Oxford University Press, 1960), xv.

12. Ake Hultkrantz, *The North American Indian Orpheus Tradition: A Contribution to Comparative Religion* (Ethnological Museum of Sweden, Stockholm, 1957).

13. A. H. Gayton, "The Orpheus Myth in North America," *Journal of American Folklore* 48, no. 189 (July–September 1935), 282: "The plot, using the term in its widest sense to include motivation, incidents and succession of incidents, has been maintained with remarkable consistency throughout its wide distribution and . . . is thoroughly integrated with cultural forms."

14. Hultkrantz, *The North American Indian Orpheus Tradition*.

15. Cited in ibid., 201.

16. Robert A. F. Thurman (trans.), *The Tibetan Book of the Dead* (Thorsons/HarperCollins, 1995), 80.

17. Ibid.

18. Ibid., for example, chapter 2: "The Tibetan Science of Death."

19. Thor Conway, "The Conjurer's Lodge: Celestial Narratives from Algonkian Shamans," in *Earth & Sky: Visions of the Cosmos in Native American Folklore*, Ray A. Williamson and Claire R. Farrer (eds.) (University of New Mexico Press, 1992), 243 and 246.

20. W. M. Napier, "Comets, Catastrophes and Earth's History," *Journal of Cosmology* 2 (2009), 344–355.

21. W. M. Napier, "Palaeolithic Extinctions and the Taurid Complex," *Monthly Notices of the Royal Astronomical Society* 405 (March 2010), 1901–1902 (for dimensions), and 1906 for entry into inner solar system.

22. Ibid., 1902, 1906. Comet fragmentation was witnessed in action in 1994 when Comet Shoemaker-Levy 9 broke up into twenty-one fragments, all of which then separately hit Jupiter.

23. Ibid., 1901.

24. Victor Clube and Bill Napier, *The Cosmic Winter* (Wiley, 1990), 153.

25. P. Spurný et al., "Discovery of a New Branch of the Taurid Meteoroid Stream as a Real Source of Potentially Hazardous Bodies," *Astronomy and Astrophysics* 605 (September 2017).

26. According to Professor Emilio Spedicato of the University of Bergamo, "Tentative orbital parameters which could lead to its observation are estimated. It is predicted that in the near future (around the year 2030) the earth will cross again that part of the torus that contains the fragments, an encounter that in the past has dramatically affected mankind." See G. Hancock, *Magicians of the Gods: The Forgotten Wisdom of Earth's Lost Civilization* (2015), chapter 19, and Emilio Spedicato, *Apollo Objects, Atlantis and Other Tales* (Università degli studi di Bergamo, 1997), 12–13.

27. Paul D. Kramer, Deputy Assistant Secretary of the Army to The Honourable Raul Grijalva, "Dakota Access Pipeline Notification," (February 7, 2017). Available here https://www.document cloud.org/documents/3456295-Dakota-Access-Pipeline-Notification-Grijalva.html.

28. ICT Staff, "Oil Flowing Through DAPL," (Indian Country Today, June 1, 2017), https://indian countrymedianetwork.com/news/environment/oil-flowing-dakota-access-dapl/.
29. Sam Levin, "Dakota Access Pipeline Has First Leak Before It's Fully Operational," (*Guardian*, May 10, 2017), https://www.theguardian.com/us-news/2017/may/10/dakota-access-pipeline-first-oil-leak.
30. See "Order Reconditions" (Civil Action No. 16-1534 (JEB) (and Consolidated Case Nos. 16-1769 and 16-267)) available via EarthJustice https://earthjustice.org/sites/default/files/files/Order-re-conditions.pdf and EarthJustice, "Citing Recent Keystone Spill, Federal Court Orders Additional Measures to Reduce Spill Risks From Dakota Access Pipeline" (December 4, 2017), https://earthjustice.org/news/press/2017/citing-recent-keystone-spill-federal-court-orders-addi tional-measures-to-reduce-spill-risks-from-dakota-access and EarthJustice, "The Standing Rock Sioux Tribe's Litigation on the Dakota Access Pipeline, 'Updates and Frequently Asked Questions,'" https://earthjustice.org/features/faq-standing-rock-litigation.
31. Associated Press, "Standing Rock Activist Accused of Firing at Police Gets Nearly Five Years in Prison" (*Guardian*, July 12, 2018).

APPENDIX 1

1. Thomas A. Gregor and Donald Tuzin (eds.), *Gender in Amazonia and Melanesia: An Exploration of the Comparative Method* (University of California Press, 2001), 1.
2. Key papers that constitute the Paleoamerican hypothesis are (in order of publication):
   C. L. Brace et al., "Old World Sources of the First New World Human Inhabitants: A Comparative Craniofacial View," *Proceedings of the National Academy of Sciences* 98, no. 17 (2001), 10017–10022; W. A. Neves and M. Hubbe, "Cranial Morphology of Early Americans from Lagoa Santa, Brazil: Implications for the Settlement of the New World." *Proceedings of the National Academy of Sciences* 102, no. 51 (2005), 18309–18314; R. González-José et al., "The Peopling of America: Craniofacial Shape Variation on a Continental Scale and Its Interpretation from an Interdisciplinary View," *American Journal of Physical Anthropology: The Official Publication of the American Association of Physical Anthropologists* 137, no. 2 (2008), 175–187; M. Hubbe, W. A. Neves, and K. Harvati, "Testing Evolutionary and Dispersion Scenarios for the Settlement of the New World," *PLoS One* 5, no. 6 (2010), e11105; D. L. Jenkins et al., "Clovis-Age Western Stemmed Projectile Points and Human Coprolites at the Paisley Caves," *Science* 337, no. 6091 (2012), 223–228; K. E. Graf, C. V. Ketron, and M. R. Waters (eds.), *Paleoamerican Odyssey* (Texas A&M University Press, 2014), 397–412; J. C. Chatters et al., "Late Pleistocene Human Skeleton and mtDNA Link Paleoamericans and Modern Native Americans," *Science* 344, no. 6185 (2014), 750–754.
3. Maanasa Raghavan et al., "Genomic Evidence for the Pleistocene and Recent Population History of Native Americans," *Science* 349.6250 (2015), aab3884.
4. Ibid.
5. S. Ivan Perez et al., "Discrepancy Between Canial and DNA Data of Early Americans: Implications for American Peopling," *PLoS One* (May 29, 2009), 1, http://journals.plos.org/plosone/article?id=10.1371/journal.pone.0005746.
6. Germán Manríquez et al., "Morphometric and mtDNA Analyses of Archaic Skeletal Remains from Southwestern South America," *Chungara: Revista de Antropología Chilena* 43, no. 2 (2011), 283.
7. Pontus Skoglund et al., "Genetic Evidence for Two Founding Populations of the Americas," *Nature* 525, no. 3 (September 2015), 107.
8. Ibid.
9. See, for example, Neves and Hubbe, "Cranial Morphology of Early Americans from Lagoa Santa, Brazil." Though not substantially in dispute, there are dissenting opinions. For a recent example, see Raghavan et al., "Genomic Evidence for the Pleistocene and Recent Population History of Native Americans," aab3884–7.
10. See Neves and Hubbe, "Cranial Morphology of Early Americans from Lagoa Santa, Brazil," 18309.
11. Ibid.
12. Ibid.
13. Ibid., 18313–18314.
14. Ibid., 18309.
15. Skoglund et al., "Genetic Evidence for Two Founding Populations of the Americas."

16. Raghavan et al., "Genomic Evidence for the Pleistocene and Recent Population History of Native Americans."

17. In an online discussion with Lev Michael, assistant professor in the Linguistics department at the University of California, Berkeley, and an expert on Amazonian languages who cites this comment by Dziebel in his "Evaluating the Linguistic Evidence for an Out of America Hypothesis," online here: https://anthroling.wordpress.com/2008/06/11/evaluating-the-linguistic-evidence-for-an-out-of-ameri ca-hypothesis/.

18. Austin Whittall, "Language Diversity and the Peopling of America," October 18, 2015, http:// patagoniamonsters.blogspot.co.uk/2015/10/language-diversity-and-peopling-of.html.

19. Ibid.

20. See "Papua New Guinea:" https://www.ethnologue.com/statistics/country.

21. Whittall, "Language Diversity and the Peopling of America."

22. Which he sources from Joanna Nichols, "Mobility and Ancient Society in Asia and the Americas," pp. 117–126, chapter titled "How America Was Colonised: Linguistic Evidence," https://link. springer.com/chapter/10.1007/978-3-319-15138-0_9.

23. Whittall, "Language Diversity and the Peopling of America."

24. Table from "Indigenous Languages of South America," http://aboutworldlanguages.com/indige nous-languages-of-south-america.

25. See A. I. Aikhenvald and A. Y. Aikhenvald, *Languages of the Amazon* (Oxford University Press, 2012), 1: "Lowland Amazonia boasts over 350 languages grouped into some fifteen language families, plus a fair number of isolates."

26. Ibid. "The linguistic diversity of the Amazon is remarkable in every respect. Its only rival is that of the New Guinea area."

27. Gregor and Tuzin, *Gender in Amazonia and Melanesia*, 1.

28. Ibid.

29. "Amazonia and Melanesia: Gender and Anthropological Comparison," details here: http://www. wennergren.org/history/amazonia-and-melanesia-gender-and-anthropological-comparison.

30. Gregor and Tuzin, *Gender in Amazonia and Melanesia*, 52–53.

31. Ibid., 302.

32. Ibid., 304.

33. Ibid., 147–149.

34. Ibid., 310.

35. Ibid., 38.

36. Ibid., 1, 309, 320–321.

37. Ibid., 315.

38. Ibid., 318.

39. Ibid., 310.

40. Ibid., 13–14: "Typically men's organisations are associated with meeting grounds, or men's houses, where men conduct secret initiations and feasts. The cults address similar spirit entities, conceal similar secret paraphernalia and sound-producing instruments and punish female intruders with gang rape or death. Taken together the pattern of spatial separation, initiations and punishment of female intruders constitutes a 'complex,' or adherence of traits, that is found widely throughout Melanesia, and in at least four major and distantly separated culture regions in lowland South America."

41. Ibid., 14.

42. Ibid., 330.

43. Ibid., 331–332.

44. Ibid., 1.

APPENDIX 2

1. Robert H. Fuson, *Legendary Islands of the Ocean Sea* 11 (Pineapple Press, Florida, 1995), in particular pp. 185–120. Fuson makes the case also that the island named Antilia, placed to the south of "Satanaze" on the Pizzagano Chart, is Taiwan. I review the whole matter in detail in *Underworld: The Mysterious Origins of Civilization* (2002), 626–639.

2. Graham Hancock, *Underworld*, 631.

3. Ibid., 22–23. All calculations of ancient sea levels in *Underworld* were the work of Dr. Glenn Milne, then of Durham University, a world expert in the subject.

4. Ibid., 500–502.

5. Graham Hancock, *Fingerprints of the Gods*, (Crown, 1995), 4–9.

6. Ibid., 3–25.
7. Ibid., 3–13.

APPENDIX 3

1. P. A. Colinvaux et al., "Amazonian and Neotropical Plant Communities on Glacial Time-Scales: The Failure of the Aridity and Refuge Hypotheses," *Quaternary Science Reviews* 19 (January 2000), 141.
2. Katherine J. Willis and Robert J. Whittaker, "The Refugial Debate," *Science* (February 25, 2000), 1406–1407.
3. P. A. Colinvaux and P. E. de Oliveira, "Amazon Plant Diversity and Climate Through the Cenozoic," *Palaeogeography, Palaeoclimatology, Palaeoecology* 166 (February 2001), 57, 60.
4. Thomas P. Kastner and Miguel A. Goni, "Constancy in the Vegetation of the Amazon Basin During the Late Pleistocene: Evidence from the Organic Matter Composition of Amazon Deep Sea Fan Sediments," *Geology* (April 2003), 291.
5. M. B. Bush et al., "Amazonian Paleoecological Histories: One Hill, Three Watersheds," *Palaeogeography, Palaeoclimatology, Palaeoecology* 214 (November 25, 2004), 359.
6. Carlos D'Apolito et al., "The Hill of Six Lakes Revisited: New Data and Re-Evaluation of a Key Pleistocene Amazon Site," *Quaternary Science Reviews* 76 (September 2013), 153–154.
7. Ibid.
8. John Francis Carson et al., "Environmental Impact of Geometric Earthwork Construction in Pre-Columbian Amazonia," *Proceedings of the National Academy of Sciences* 22 (July 2014), 10497.
9. D. Fontes, R. C. Cordeiro, et al., "Paleoenvironmental Dynamics in South Amazonia, Brazil, During the Last 35,000 Years Inferred from Pollen and Geochemical Records of Lago do Saci," *Quaternary Science Reviews* 173 (October 1, 2017), 177.
10. M. Goulding, R. B. Barthem, and R. Duenas, *The Smithsonian Atlas of the Amazon* (Smithsonian Books, 2003), 19. "Approximately 85 per cent of the South American rainforest . . . is found in the Amazon Basin."
11. All figures are taken from the World Bank, "Land Area (sq. km.)," https://data.worldbank.org/indicator/ag.lnd.totl.k2?name_desc=false, apart from Europe, taken from S. Adams, A. Ganeri, and A. Kay, *Geography of the World: The Essential Family Guide to Geography and Culture* (DK, 2006), 78.
12. Email from Graham Hancock to Professor Renato Cordeiro dated March 12, 2018.
13. Professor Cordeiro's kind reply (email of March 14, 2018) contained some technical terms that I feel I need to translate here before getting to the meat of what he said:
    • **Quaternary**—the reference is to our current era, roughly from 2.5 million years ago until the present.
    • **Edaphic characteristics**—the reference is to the role of factors such as water content, acidity, aeration, and the availability of nutrients, that is, factors inherent in the soil itself rather than consequent upon climate.
    • **Campinaranas**—these are neotropical ecoregions in the Brazilian Amazon.
    • **Caatingas**—another kind of ecoregion of the Brazilian Amazon, in this case characterized by desert vegetation.
    • **Pollinic**—the reference is to all matters relating to, containing, or derived from pollen.
    "In order to understand the vegetation fluctuations during the quaternary," Professor Cordeiro told me, "one must try to understand some of the current distribution of vegetation. Basically in the Amazon we have evergreen forests, deciduous forests, tree savanna, shrub savanna, open savanna and fields. In some regions vegetation is influenced by edaphic characteristics such as the *campinaranas* and *caatingas* of the Rio Negro where vast areas covered by quartz sands, with low nutrients and low water retention, limit the occurrence of vegetation with large biomass. Along the rivers are the gallery forests which, probably have been relatively well preserved during drier climatic periods. *Varzea* forests (floodplain forest) are still distributed along flood areas and inundated forests (regionally called *igapó*) that occur inside the river bed until 6 meters depth. This vegetation type mosaic produces variable amounts of pollens and therefore different responses in the sedimentary records as a function of the depositional environment (lakes near the Rios channel, e.g., Lago Saci, Lago La Gaiba; lakes far from the dynamics of rivers e.g. Carajás Lakes, Lagoa da Pata; marine deposits). As an example of this complexity of interpretations it is possible to mention that marine records have a pollinic signal very influenced by galleries forests and floodplain forests that would have been preserved during drier climatic periods. The Saci lake, because it is relatively close to the São Benedito II River, probably had a vegetation with higher biomass in relation to sites outside

of the river influence. Therefore, due to this complexity between the generation of the different types of pollens of different vegetation types in relation to the depositional environment, many interpretations do not accurately depict the regional vegetation physiognomy."

14. For example, see M. B. Bush et al., "Paleotemperature Estimates for the Lowland Americas between 30 Degrees South and 30 Degrees North at the Last Glacial Maximum," chapter 17 in *Interhemispheric Climate Linkages,* ed. Vera Markgraf (Academic Press, 2001), 303. See also Bush et al., "Amazonian Paleoecological Histories," 360.

INDEX

NOTE: The photo insert images are indexed as *p1, p2, p3*, etc.

Ab, 313
Above World, 240, 241, 243
Acre, 202, 212
Acuña, Cristóbal de, 145
Adena, 25, 26, 28, 29–30,
    263, 293, 344
ADEs. *See* Amazonian Dark
    Earths
Adovasio, James M., 56–57
Agassiz, Lake, *398,* 398–99
agriculture, 172–77, 255,
    432, 452, 455, 457, 467
Aju-Tasch (Bear Rock), 98
Aleutian Islanders, 124, 126,
    127, 128
Algonquian, 124, 128, 311,
    333
Allen, Thurman, 274
Alpha Cygni, 341
Altai, 84–97. *See also*
    Denisova Cave
Amazonia, 78, 137–49, 367
    agriculture in, 172–77,
    467
    Australasia and, 128,
    129–33, 150, 155, 434,
    437–38
    forests of, 168–72, 511–15
    in Ice Age, 150–51,
    155–56, 157, 515
    lost civilizations and, 467
    Melanesia and, 491–95
    Men's cults of, 227,
    497–501
    Native Americans in,
    119–22, 493–94
    Nazca Lines and, 182–86,
    183, 184, 186

Papua New Guinea and,
    124–25, 499
    plant medicines in,
    176–77
    shamans of, 220–30, *223,*
    325, 468, 476, 478
    smallpox in, 138, 145, 148,
    149
    terra preta in, 160–69, 467
*Amazonia: Man and Culture
    in a Counterfeit Paradise*
    (Meggers), 147–48, 180
Amazonian Dark Earths
    (ADEs), 160–69
Amazonian geoglyphs,
    178–250, *181, 187–91,*
    204, 205, 207–9, 230,
    232, 233–61, *234, 252,*
    468, *p2*
    ayahuasca and, 220–30,
    223
    Nazca Lines and, 182–86,
    183, 184, 186
    Stonehenge and, 196–97,
    199, 200, 216
American Holocaust
    (Stannard), 452–53
Amit, 340, *p3*
*Ancient Monuments of the
    Mississippi Valley* (Squier
    and Davis, E.), 253,
    455–56
Ancient Works, *252*
Anderson, David, 408
Anderson, Raymond, 5
Andros, *509,* 509–10, *510*
Angkor Wat, 18, 32–33, 36,
    179–80, 238, *p1*

Anker, Arthur, 186
Antarctica, 157, 393, 436,
    436, 507–9, *507–9*
Anthony, John, 364
antler tools, 77, 114, 116–17,
    439
Anzick-1, 114–20, 439
*The Archeological Atlas of
    Ohio* (Mills), 456–57
Arhuaco, 124, 128
Aroana, 213, 219
Asatryan, Papin, 96
astronomers, 343–45, *344*
astronomy, 346–69, 435. *See
    also specific topics*
Athabascans, 124, 127, 128
Atlantis, 365, *p3*
Australasia, 108, 110, *120,*
    120–28
    Amazonia and, 128,
    129–33, 150, 155, 434,
    437–38
    linguistic diversity in,
    495–97, *496*
    Native Americans and,
    126, 467, 492
autumn equinox
    at Angkor Wat, 18
    at Great Sphinx of Giza,
    20
    at Watson Brake, 288, *288*
Avebury, 11, 12, 197, *197,*
    200, *p2*
Aveni, Anthony F., 23
ayahuasca, 220–30, *223,*
    468
    death and, 228, 230, 325
    geometry and, *348,* 349

ayahuasca (*cont.*)
  Milky Way and, 227–28, 325
  as *Telepathine*, 476–77
azimuth, *22*
  at Monks Mound, 245
  at Poverty Point, 270, *275*
  at Saginaw Bay impact, 414
  at Serpent Mound, *21, 22,* 23
  of summer solstice, 32
  at Watson Brake, 286, 287, *287*
  at Woodhenge, 243
Azoury, Ricardo, *198*
Aztec library, burning of, 446

Ba, 312, *313, 337*
Baalbek, 474, *p4*
Badawy, Alexander, 305
Balboa, Vasco Nuñez de, 59
Balée, William, 165, 166, 218
Ballcourt Mound, at Poverty Point, 267, *267,* 272, *272, 274, 275*
Banana Bayou Mounds, 278
Barasana, 227, 499
Bardo (the Between), 481–82
Bauval, Robert, 303, 304–5, 357
Bear Rock (Aju-Tasch), 98
Belaude, Luisa, 224–25
Below World, 240, 241
bend-break technique, 74–75, 77
Bering land bridge, 4, 53–55, *54,* 122, 154–55, 397–98, 466–67
Beringian standstill model, for Siberia, 85–86, 123–24
the Between (Bardo), 481–82
Bimini, *509,* 509–10, *510*
biomass burning, in YD, 385, 391–97, 401, 402,

406, 437
Bird Mound, at Poverty Point, 264–67, *267, p3*
Birdman, 336, *337*
Black Earth (terra preta), 160–69, 467
Blackwater Draw, 51, 388, 389, 406
Bluefish Caves, 57–58, 71, 86
Bølling-Allerød interstadial, 69, 466–67, 471
Bonaldo, Alexandre B., 185–86
bone tools, 77, 106, *107,* 439
Bonnemère, Pascale, 499
Bonnichsen, Robson, 61–62
Book of Gates, 303, 353
Book of the Breaths of Life, 303
Book of What Is in the Duat, 314, *327,* 328–29, *329,* 350–51, 352–53
Book of What Is in the Netherworld, 303
bracelet, 102–7, *104, p1*
brain-smasher, 328, 330, 338–39
Brecher, Kenneth, 269
Brown, James, 336
Brown, Joseph Epes, 340–41
Budge, E. A. Wallis, 312, 318, 325, *327,* 328, 347, 353, 355
Builder Gods, 366
burins, 76–77
Burks, Jarrod, 455–57
Bush, M. B., 512

C-14. *See* carbon-dating
Cabral, Mariana Petry, 202–3, 205–6
Caddo, 124
Cahokia. *See* Monks Mound
Calado, Manoel, 205–6
California wildfires, 395
Callahan, Richard, 206
Cameron, Terry, 23, 44
Caney Mounds, 279, *279*
  equinox at, 291

summer solstice at, 291
Watson Brake and, 284–85, *285*
capsicum (chili peppers), 172
carbon-dating (C-14, radiocarbon dating)
  in Amazonia, 174
  at Anzick-1, 116
  at Caney Mounds, 279
  at Conly, 279
  at Fazenda Colorada, 193–94
  at Frenchman's Bend, 279
  in Mal'ta, 114
  at Monte Verde, 152
  at Painel do Pilão, 207
  of Poverty Point, 266
  at Rego Grande, 202
  of Severino Calazans and, 195
  at Watson Brake, 279
  for YD, 408, 469
Carlson, Randall, 298, 410–11
Carolina Bays, 411, 412–28, *413, 418*
Carvajal, Gaspar de, 139–47
Cashinahua, 498
cassava (manioc), 173–76
Caverna da Pedra Pintada, 156, 160, 206–7, *207*
Cerutti, Richard, 60–63, 66–67, *107,* 368, 470, *p1*
Champollion, Jean-François, 310
Channeled Scablands, 411, *444,* 444–45, 483
charcoal
  in ADEs, 164–65
  from Monte Sano, 279
  Murray Springs in, 406
  at Rego Grande, 202
  at Serpent Mound, 26, 28
  from YD, 393–94
Charles, Charles, 39
Cherokee, 37, 335, 362
chert, 73
Chickasaw, 311
chili peppers (capsicum), 172
Christianity, 360, 450, 478

Cinq-Mars, Jacques, 57–58, 86
Circle of Osiris, 353, *353*
circle-octagon, *247,* 248, 250, 253–54
cities
  in Amazonia, 137–49
  of gods, 355–56
City of the Sun *(Heliopolis),* 343
Clark, John, 274, 275, 294
Clement, Charles R., 172–73
climate change, 395–97, 461, 462. *See also* Younger Dryas
Clovis, 147, 374–79, 439–40, 459–60, *p1*
  Anzick-1 and, 116–18
  Bluefish Caves and, 57–58, 86
  extinction of, 408, 419, 432, 437, 461, 462
  land bridge and, 53–55, *54*
  lost civilizations and, 437–41
  Monte Verde and, 55–57, 124, 151–53
  at Murray Springs, 373, 374, 406, 437, *p4*
  Siberia and, 83–97
  South America and, 118, *120,* 133
  stone tools of, 51–52, *52,* 374, 437, 438–39
  Topper and, 72–78, 124
  YDB and, 461
Clube, Victor, 383–84
cocoa trees, 172
Coffin Texts, 303, 335, 343, 352, 354
Coles Creek culture, 263, 275–76
Colinvaux, P. A., 512
Collins, Andrew, 310
comet impact. *See also* Glacier Ice Impact Hypothesis; Younger Dryas Impact Hypothesis

consequences of, 485–86
materials from, 401–5
megafauna extinction from, 406–8
in North America, 376, 378–79, 416, 436–37, 443–45, 463–64
platinum from, 380–86
Comet Research Group (CRG), 387–91, 401, 410, 411, 412, 414, 421, 423, 426, 461
Comet Shoemaker-Levy 9, 381
comets
  Halley's, 27
  Taurid Meteor Stream and, *382,* 383–84, 431
Conceptions of the Soul Among North American Indians (Hultkrantz), 316
Condamine, Charles-Marie de la, 146
Conly, 279, *279*
consciousness powers, 475–77
Cooke, Robert, 455
Cooper, Alan, 109, 110
Coqueiral, 192, 248
Cordeiro, Renato, 513–15
Cordilleran ice sheet, 53, 118, 397, *398*
Cormack, Robert, 446
Cortés, Hernán, 445
The Cosmic Serpent: DNA and the Origins of Knowledge (Narby), 176
cotton, 174
Cree, 124, 128
Cretaceous-Paleogene Boundary, 378, 379
CRG. *See* Comet Research Group
Crook, A. R., 235, 236
cult of the dead, 344
Cycle of Cosmic Catastrophes (Firestone and West, A.), 427
Cygnus constellation, 341, *342*

Dakota Access Pipeline (DAPL), 487–89
Darenskikh, Elena, 96
Darwin, Charles, 35, 111
Darwin, Erasmus, 35
Daughter of the Sun, 225, 365
Davias, Michael E., 412, 413, *414, 415,* 415–16
Davis, Christopher Sean, 208, *208,* 210, 211
Davis, Edwin H., *2,* 9–11, 15–17, 21, 40, 251–52, *252,* 455–56
Davis, Norman L., 271–74, 286–91
Dawkins, Richard, 204, 302
De Oliveira, P. E., 512
de Soto, Hernando, 451
death (afterlife). *See also* soul; *specific texts and topics*
  astronomy after, 346–69
  ayahuasca and, 228, 230, 325
  Egypt and, 303–68
  geometry after, 346–69
  Mayans and, 447
  Milky Way and, 311
  Native Americans and, 317, 330–42, *331,* 358–69
  near-death experience, 297–302
  realm of, 302–5
  religion and, 479–84
debitage, at Topper, 73
Deméré, Tom, 47–50, 60–67, 79, 107, 368, 466–67, 470–71, *p1*
Demitroff, Mark, 410, 412, 422, 426, 427
Deneb, 341, *342*
Denisova Cave, 83–84, 86–97, *87,* 100–101, 131
  as Bear Rock, 98
  bracelet at, 102–7, *104, p1*
  DNA sequencing at, 99–101, 108

Denisova Cave (*cont.*)
megaliths at, 89–95, *93, 94*
Neanderthals at, 99, 109
needle at, 106, *107*
Denisovans, 69, 83–84
Australasia and, 108, 110, 131
characteristics of, 103
DNA sequencing of, 125
Neanderthals and, 102, 108, 121–22
Papua New Guinea and, 108
Timor Straits and, 125
Dennett, Daniel, 302
Derevianko, A. P., 102–3
Design Point 1 (DP1), for Poverty Point, 271–73, *272, 273*
Design Point 2 (DP2), for Poverty Point, 271–73, *272, 273*
Destruction of the World, in Dresden Codex, 448, *449*
Dillehay, Tom, 55–57, 151–53
dimethyltriptyamine (DMT), 220
DNA sequencing, 3
at Anzick-1, 115
for Australasia, 132–33, 150
at Denisova Cave, 99–101, 108
of Denisovans, 125
of MA-1, 115–16
of Native Americans, 83, 111–22
in Siberia, 83–97
dogs, 334–38
DP1. *See* Design Point 1
DP2. *See* Design Point 2
Draco constellation, 32–36, *33–35,* 360
Dragon/Serpent Megalith, 89, *93,* 93–94
Dresden Codex, 448–50, *449*

drills, 103, 153
drones, 6–7, *8,* 9, 15, 42–43
Dry Valley Mountains, 436
Duat Netherworld, 321, *321,* 323, 326–29, *327, 329,* 339, 355, *362,* 450
dwarfs, 337
Dziebel, German, 495

Eagle Mound, *250,* 250–51
Early Archaic, 292
Early Fort Ancient, 27
Early Mississippian, 5, 263
Early Primeval Age of the Gods, 364, 366, 462
Early Woodland, 30, 263, 266
East Gallery, of Denisova Cave, 100, 101, 102
Easter Island, moai of, 235
Eastern Woodlands, 240, 311
Eater of the Dead, 340, *p3*
Ecclesiastes, 255
ecliptic axis, *35,* 35–36
Edfu Building Texts, 364–65, 366, 462–63, 477, *p3*
Edwards, Donald L., *443*
Eemian, 62
Egypt, 277. *See also specific sites, texts, and topics*
astronomers in, 343–45, *344*
death and, 303–68
dogs and, 334–38
judgment and, 338–42, *p3*
lost civilizations and, 461
Mayans and, 447, 450
Orion constellation and, 313, 322–25, 359–60
solstice and, 353–54
soul in, 312–14, *313*
stars in, 321, *321*
Egyptian Book of the Dead, 43–44, 302–3, 315, 336, 354, 361–62, 450, 478, 481–82, *p3*
El Dorado, 138, 141
Ellis-Barrett, Louise,

328–29
Eloise (mammoth), 374–79, 437
Emerald Mound, 306
Emery, Walter, 347
equinoxes, 255
at Angkor Wat, *p1*
autumn, 18, 20, 288, *288*
at Caney Mounds, 291
at Frenchman's Bend, 291
at Monks Mound, *242, 243, p3*
at Painel do Pilão, 217
at Poverty Point, *272*
spring, 18, 20, 36, 288, *288*
Erlandson, Jon M., 48
European Fireball Network, 487
Eurydice, 480–81
Evans, Clifford, 201
Evans-Wentz, W. Y., 479–80, 481

Faiia, Santha, 6, 15, 31, 42–43, 59–60, 63, 64, 68, *93, 94,* 96, *183, 184,* 234, 297–300, 373–74, *423, p1, p3, p4*
Fairground Circle, *250,* 250–52
Faulkner, R. O., 324
Fazenda Atlantica, 188–90, *189, p2*
Fazenda Colorada, 188, *188,* 193–94, *230, p2*
Fazenda Inquiri II, *191,* 191–92, 248
Fazenda Parana, *187,* 187–88, 216, *p2*
Fenton Mounds, 458
Fernandez, Jose, 446–47
Fiedel, Stuart J., 117
Finger Lakes, *444, 445,* 483
Fingerprints of the Gods (Hancock), 48, 131, 303, 433, 465, 507
Firestone, Richard, 374, 376, 383–84, 414, 421, 427
Fisher, Daniel, 62

Fletcher, Alice C., 340
Fletcher, Robert, 23, 25–30, 44
flint-knapping, 77, 439
flood, 398–400, 402, 406, 443–44, 484
floods, 436–37
Fontes, Diana, 513–15
Ford, James, 268–70
forests, of Amazonia, 168–72, 511–15
Fort Ancient, 26–30, 37
Fowke, Gerard, 265
free-soul, 316, 318, 320, 325, 331, 338
Frenchman's Bend, 279, *279*, 284, 291
Fritz, Samuel, 146
Fullagar, Richard, 62
Fuson, Robert, 505–6

Garber, James, 311
Garrison, Thomas, 158
Gateway Arch, of St. Louis, 235
Gault Assemblage, 439
Gebhart-Sayer, Angelica, 221
Gender in Amazonia and Melanesia (Gregor and Tuzin), 499–501
genocide, 349, 445, 452–53
geoglyphs, 196–97, 246–61, 349. *See also* Amazonian geoglyphs
geometry, 179–80, 346–69
of Angkor Wat, 179–80
ayahuasca and, *348*, 349
of Monks Mound, 435
Ghost Dances, 489
ghost populations, 347, 367
Gibson, Jon L., 266, 275, 276, 281
gigantism, 218
Gillings, Mark, *198*
GISP2 Ice Core, 392
Gitché Manitou, 8
glacial erratics, 424, 444
Glacier Ice Impact Hypothesis, 412–28,

414, 419
Clovis extinction and, 419
Laurentide Ice Sheet and, 419, 420
megafauna extinction and, 419
in YD, 415, 419–20
Göbekli Tepe, 6, 131
gods. *See also specific examples*
cities of, 355–56
lost civilizations and, 434
Moon and, 347
Goeldi, Emílio, 201
gold, 141–42, 452
Goodyear, Albert "Al," 72–76, 408, 410, 432, 438, *pl*
Grand Plaza, *239*, 241
grave goods, 114, 117
Grayson, Donald, 48
Great Circle, *250*, 250–52
Great Hopewell Road, 254, 361
Great Horned Water Serpent, 331, 332, 362
Great Lowerworld Serpent, 361
Great Pyramid of Giza, 37, 167, 366
Amazonian geoglyphs and, 200
Banana Bayou Mounds and, 278
geometry of, 179–80, 325
megaliths of, 473–74
Monks Mound and, 238
Orion constellation and, *304*, 305, 319
relieving chambers of, 473–74
Severino Calazans and, 195, 196, 216, 238
Great Serpent with the Red Jewel in its Forehead, 331, 362
Great Sphinx of Giza, 366
autumn equinox at, 20
Leo constellation and, 361
spring equinox at, 20

Underwater Panther and, 334, *334*
Great Square, *251*
Greenland, 380, 381, 385, 392–93, 402, 437, 462
Greenlee, Diana, 265, 270–71
Gregor, Thomas A., 499–501
Griffin Megalith, at Denisova Cave, 89, *94*, 94–95
Guatemala, 158–59
Guidon, Niède, 154–55
Gulf Stream, 397–401, 436–37

Haag, William G., 268–70
Halley's Comet, 27
Hamilton, Ross, 6–7, 8, 11, 15, *29*, 31–32, 38–41, *41*, 360
Hancock, Graham, 33, *41*, 48, 131, 177, 303–5, 357, 364, 376, 386, *399*, 410, 411, 433, 444, 446, 447, 463, 465
on Glacier Ice Impact Theory, 423
near-death experience of, 297–302
Hand constellation, 320, *320*, 322, 324–25, *325*
Handelsman, Rebecca, 47–48, 49, 60, 63
Hansen, Michael G., 5, 6
haplogroup U, 116
Hardman, Clarke, *21*, 21–25, 43, 44
Hardman, Marjorie, *21*, 21–25, 43, 44
Harris, Thomas H. S., 412, 414–16, *415*
Hawkins, Gerald S., 185–86
Haynes, C. Vance, 53–55, 56, 147, 151, 374–77
Haynes, Gary, 48, 66
healing powers
of human consciousness, 475–76
of plant medicines, 176–77

Heaven's Mirror (Hancock), 33, 303, 446, 447, 463
Heckenberger, Michael, 148, 163–64, 284
Hedgepeth Mounds, 279, *279*
Heel Stone, at Stonehenge, 18, 19, *19*
Heliopolis (City of the Sun), 343
Helmsman, 226, 365
Heriarte, Mauricio de, 147
Herodotus, 310
Hidatsa, 311
High Bank Works, 246–61, *249, 259, 260*
Hill of Six Lakes, 513
Hinduism, 276, 478
Hively, Ray, 256–61, *258*
Holbrook, Jarita, 206
Holen, Steve, 62, 66–67
Holmes, W. H., 39–40
Holocene, 130, 156, 513
  Pleistocene-Holocene transition, 461, 494
Homeland of the Primeval Ones, 364, 368, *p3*
Homo erectus, 125
Homo sapiens, 102, 103, 108, 121
Hopewell, 248, 252–53, 263, 266, 267, 344–45, 450. *See also specific tribes and sites*
Hopewell, M. C., 248
Horn, Robert, 256–61, *258*
horses, 407
Horus, 336, *337,* 350, 352
Howard, Edgar B., 51
Howard, George, 410, 411
Hrdlička, Aleš, 50–51, 55
Huang, Shichun, 381
Hubbe, Mark, 493–94
Hultkrantz, Ake, 316, 330, 337, 338, 341, 480
human consciousness powers *(psi),* 475–77
hunter-gatherers, 124
  in Amazonia, 132, 142
  antler tools of, 439
  bone tools of, 439

in Ice Age, 78, 132
lost civilizations and, 364–65, 431–41
in Mesolithic, 116
Mound A by, 264, 266–67
Native Americans as, 476
in Papua New Guinea, 132
of South America, 464
stone tools of, 432–33, 438
in twenty-first century, 432
at Watson Brake, 282–93
in YD, 432

Ice Age, 78, 110, 131–32, 153, 442, 462, 465. *See also* Pleistocene
  Amazonia in, 150–51, 155–56, 157, 515
  coastal migration theory and, 86
  Denisova Cave and, 101
  Rego Grande in, 202
  sea levels and, 157, 465
Illustrated Encyclopedia of Native American Mounds and Earthworks, 458
Illych, Vladimir, 89–95
impact crater, at Serpent Mound, 4, *5*
impact winter, 395–97, 462
Inca, 450–51, 474, *p4*
The Interpretation of Radium (Soddy), 472–73
Ireland, 506–7
Iseminger, William, *p3*
Isis, 355
Islam, 478
island of megaliths, *509,* 509–10, *510*
Island of the Primeval Ones, 365–66

Jacó Sá, *198,* 199, 218, 223, *252, p2*
Jacobsen, Stein, 381
Japan, 505–6, *505–6*
Jefferson, George, 48
Jones, Terry, 460, 461
Judaism, 276

judgment, 338–42, *p3*

Ka, 312, 314
Kailasa Temple, 474, *p4*
Karitiana, 120, 493
karsts, 96–97
Kelp Highway migration model, 86
Kennett, James, 373–74, 376, 383–84, 407
Khaibit, 312, 314
khat, 312
Kheti, *362*
Khu, 312
Killer Comet (Zamora), 419–20
Kingdom of Sokar, 357
King's Chamber, 305, *p4*
Kinietz, Vernon, 315
Kootenay, 338
Kurgin, Sergey, 87–89

Labre, Antonio R. P., 212, 219
land bridge, 4, 53–55, *54,* 122, 154–55, 397–98, 466–67
Land of Sokar, 351, *352*
Land of the Dead, 359
Landa, Diego de, 446
Lankford, George, 311–12, 316, 321, 324–25, 326, 330, 341, *342,* 361, 362
Late Archaic, 292
Late Pleistocene, 133, 156, 491–92, 512
Late Pleistocene Extinction Event, 14, 374–75, 400
Late Woodland, 263
Laurentide Ice Sheet, 397, *398,* 416, 419, 420
LeCompte, Malcolm, 410, 412, 422, 424–25, 426, 427–28
Legendary Islands of the Ocean Sea (Fuson), 505
Leighton, Morris, 235–36
Leo constellation, 360, 361
Lepper, Bradley T., 25–30, 248, 254, 261–62

Levis, Carolina, 171
Library of Alexandria, 349,
    450, 507
Lidar (Light Detection and
    Ranging), *10*, 158, *240*,
    271, 275, *275*, 290, *290*
linguistic diversity, 495–97,
    496, 497
Little, Gregory, 310, 458
lost civilizations, 461, 464,
    465–89, 467
    Clovis and, 437–41
    hunter-gatherers and,
        364–65, 431–41
    of Ice Age, 442, 465
    shamans and, 483
Lower Jackson Mound,
    274–78, *275*, 293
Lowie, Robert, 497
LSU Mounds, 278
lunar standstill alignments,
    216, 256–61, *258–60*

MA-1, 114–16
Maat, 339–40, 353
Machiparo, 140, 144–45
Madurai Meenakshi Temple,
    179
Magicians of the Gods
    (Hancock), 364, 376,
    386, *399*, 410, 411, 444
Main Gallery, 100, 101
Mal'ta, 113–16
mammoth, 374–79, 406,
    437
Manchineri, 218, 223, 224
manioc (cassava), 173–76
Manitou, 8–9, 37, 42, *p1*
Massangana phase, 167
Master of Animals (Vai-
    mahase), 228
Master of the Beneath
    World, 331, 362
mastodons, 59–72, 368,
    470, *p1*
Maximum Extreme, of
    Moon, 256
Mayans, 158, 310, 446, 447,
    448–50, *449*, 450
Meadowcroft Rockshelter,

57, 71
medicine men, 485. *See also*
    shamans
Medina, José Toribio, 141
megafauna, 14, 54, 374–79,
    400, 406–8, 419, 460
megaliths
    of Amazonian geoglyphs,
        201–14, *204, 205,
        207–9*
    at Avebury, 197, *197, 198*
    at Denisova Cave, 89–95,
        93, 94
    of Great Pyramid of Giza,
        473–74
    island of, *509*, 509–10,
        510
    of North America, *p4*
    of Sacsayhuamán, 474
    at Serpent Mound, 38–41,
        41
Meggers, Betty, 146–48,
    180, 201–2
Melanesia, 227, 491–95,
    497–501. *See also*
    Australasia
meltglass, 377, 389, 406–7
Meltzer, David J., 48, 56,
    132–33, 455–56, 458
men's cults, 227, 497–501
Mercator world map, 508,
    508
meridian axis, of Serpent
    Mound, 11–12
Mesolithic, 116
Mesopotamia, 277, 347
Message of the Sphinx
    (Hancock and Bauval),
    303, 304, 357
Mexico, 445. *See also*
    Mayans
Middle Archaic, 280, 285,
    291, 292
Middle Woodland, 263, 266
Miles, Tom, 164, 165
Milky Way, 311, 335. *See
    also* Path of Souls
    ayahuasca and, 227–28,
        325
    Native Americans and,

326, 340–41
    Orion constellation and,
        310, 319, 347, 358, 447
Mills, William C., 456–57
Milner, George R., 457–58
Minimum Extreme, of
    Moon, 256
Mississippians, 311, 360,
    363, 461. *See also specific
    tribes and sites*
    Amazonian geoglyphs and,
        232, 233–61, *234, 252*
    cult of the dead of, 344
    Early, 5, 263
    Milky Way and, 358
    Orion constellation and,
        321, 358
mitochondrial DNA
    (mtDNA), 112, 492
moai, of Easter Island, 235
Mokhnataya, Mt., 89
monkeys, in Nazca Lines,
    184, 185
Monks Mound (Cahokia),
    234–45, *239, 240, 244*,
    263, 264, 435
    cult of the dead and, 344
    equinoxes at, *243, p3*
    Path of Souls and, 367
Monte Sano, 279, *279*, 344
Monte Verde, 55–57, 71,
    124, 151–53, *153*
Moon
    in Dresden Codex, 448
    gods and, 347
    High Bank Works/
        Newark Earthworks and,
        246–61
    lunar standstill
        alignments, 216,
        256–61, *258–60*
Mooney, James, 37
Moore, Chris, 410, 423,
    426, 427–28
Moorehead, Warren T.,
    235–36
Moreno-Mayar, J. Victor,
    132–33
Morley, Sylvanus Griswold,
    448

Morrow, Susan Brind, 323
Motley Mound, 265
Mound 1, at Watson Brake,
    286
Mound 2, at Watson Brake,
    286, 287, 288
Mound A
    at Caney Mounds, 284
    at Poverty Point, 264–67,
        267, p3
    at Watson Brake, 284,
        287, 289
Mound B
    at Caney Mounds, 284
    at Moundville, 306
    at Poverty Point, 264, 267,
        267, 272, 272
    at Watson Brake, 284,
        287, 289
Mound C
    at Caney Mounds, 284
    at Poverty Point, 267, 267,
        272, 272, 273, 273
    at Watson Brake, 282, 283
Mound D
    at Poverty Point, 267, 267,
        273, 273, 275–76
    at Watson Brake, 282,
        283, 287, 289
Mound E
    at Poverty Point, 267, 267,
        272, 272, 274, 275
    at Watson Brake, 282,
        283, 284, 287, 288, 289,
        293
Mound F
    at Caney Mounds, 284
    at Poverty Point, 267, 267
    at Watson Brake, 288
Mound G, at Watson Brake,
    288
Mound H, at Watson Brake,
    288
Mound I, at Watson Brake,
    282, 283, 284, 287
Mound J, at Watson Brake,
    282, 283, 284, 287, 288
Mound K, at Watson Brake,
    282, 283, 284
Mound L, at Watson Brake,

282, 282, 287
The Moundbuilders (Milner),
    457–58
Moundville, 306–9, 307
    cult of the dead and, 344
    geometry of, 435
    Orion constellation and,
        320, 320
    Path of Souls and, 362,
        367
    pottery from, 333, 341
Mountain of Sunrise, 354
mtDNA. See mitochondrial
    DNA
Mundurukú, 179, 498, 500
Murphy, Robert, 500
Murray Springs, 373, 374,
    406, 437, p4
Myers, Thomas P., 149

nanodiamonds, 377, 389,
    406–7
Napier, William, 380,
    383–84, 485–87
Narby, Jeremy, 176
National Native American
    Boarding School
    Healing Coalition,
    453–54
National Science Foundation
    (NSF), 56
Native Americans, 4, 53–55,
    54, 59–72, 83, 111–22,
    123–28, 314–16, 326,
    338–42, 476. See also
    specific sites, tribes, and
    topics
    in Amazonia, 119–22,
        493–94
    astronomers of, 343–45,
        344
    Australasia and, 126, 467,
        492
    Bering land bridge for, 4,
        53–55, 54, 122
    boarding schools for,
        453–54
    death and, 317, 330–42,
        331, 358–69
    DNA sequencing of, 83,

111–22
    dogs and, 334–38
    genocide of, 349, 452–53
    Hand constellation of,
        320, 320, 322, 324–25,
        325
    linguistic diversity of,
        495–96, 496
    Orion constellation and,
        309, 319–21
    protests of DAPL by,
        487–89
    shamans of, 240, 480
    stars of, 321, 321
    Turtle Island of, 368–69,
        463
Nazca Lines, 6, 182–86,
    183, 184, 186, p2
Neanderthals, 69
    at Denisova Cave, 99, 101,
        109
    Denisovans and, 108,
        121–22
    Homo sapiens and, 121
    as less-evolved human
        species, 102
    rock art by, 131
near-death experience,
    297–302
Nebraska Rainwater Basins,
    412–28, 413, 418
needle, 106, 107
Neolithic, 103, 105–8, 131,
    196–97, 471
Neves, Eduardo, 148,
    163–64, 167, 168, 206
Neves, Walter A., 493–94
New Guinea. See Papua
    New Guinea
New Mountain, 436
Newark Earthworks, 246–
    61, 247, 250, 251, 258
NGRIP Ice Core, 392, 437
Nimuendajú, Curt, 201
Noah's flood, 484
North America. See also
    specific locations and topics
    Amazonian geoglyphs
        and, 232, 233–61, 252
    comet impact in, 376,

378–79, 416, 436–37, 443–45, 463–64
Egypt and, 367–68
in Ice Age, 462
linguistic diversity in, *497*
lost civilizations in, 469–71, 483–84
megaliths of, *p4*
smallpox in, 451
The North American Indian Orpheus Tradition (Hultkrantz), 480
NSF. *See* National Science Foundation
nuclear power, 473

obliquity cycle, 23
Observatory Circle, 250, 253–54, *258,* 258–59
Observatory Circle Diameter (OCD), 253
Oceti Sakowin, 487–89
Oedipus complex, 500
Oglala, 311
Ojibwa, 124, 126, 128, 311, 315, 317, 330, 345
on comet impact, 485
Underwater Panther of, 332–34, *334*
Old Stone Age, 99
Olmec, 446
Omagua, 146
Omaha, 340
On, 343
Optically Stimulated Luminescence (OSL), 417–18
oral traditions, 453
Orellana, Francisco de, 137–49, 175
Orion constellation, *320,* 347, 358, 446, 447
Egypt and, 313, 322–25, 359–60
Great Pyramid of Giza and, *304,* 305, 319
Native Americans and, 309, 319–21
The Orion Mystery (Bauval), 305

Oronteus Finnaeus world map, 508, *508*
Orpheus, 480–81
Osiris, 322, 325, 339–40, 355, *p3*
OSL. *See* Optically Stimulated Luminescence
Otherworld, 228, *229, 230,* 325, 361, 480
ozone layer, 402

Paces, James, 62
PAHs. *See* polycyclic aromatic hydrocarbons
Painel do Pilão, 206–11, *207–9,* 217
Paleoamerican hypothesis, 491–95
Paleoindian Period, 460
Paleolithic, 99, 103. *See also* Upper Paleolithic
Papua New Guinea, 108, 124–25, 132, 394, 495–97, *496,* 498, 499
Amazonia and, 124–25, 499
linguistic diversity in, 495–97, *496*
Papyrus of Nebseni, 351, *351*
Pärssinen, Martti, 181–82, 187, *187, 188, 190,* 193, 195–96, 199, *230, p2*
Path of Souls, 326, 330, 332, 358–59, 361, 362, 367, 478
peanut, 174
Pedra Furada, 154–55
Pedra Pintada, 156, 206–7, *207*
Petaev, Michail, 381, 384–85
Petersen, James, 148
philosopher's stone, 472
Pickard, William, 25–30
Pickersgill, Barbara, 175
pictographs. *See* rock art
Pillar of Horus, 352
pineapples, 172, 173
Pinkerton map, 507, *507*

Piri Reis map, *509,* 509–10
Pitts, Mike, 19
Pizarro, Gonzalo, 137–39
Pizzagano Chart, 505–6, *505–6*
plant medicines, 176–77
platinum, 380–86, 423, 424
Plato, 365, *p3*
Pleistocene, 62, 123–28, 416, 419
Late, 133, 156, 491–92, 512
Rego Grande in, 202
Topper and, 75–76
Pleistocene Overkill theory, 460
Pleistocene-Holocene transition, 461, 494
pole star, 34–36, *35*
polycyclic aromatic hydrocarbons (PAHs), 406
Polynesian expansion, 125, 130
porcelain, in Amazonia, 140–41
Posth, Cosimo, 132–33
pottery, 26, 74, 161, 202, 333, 341
Poverty Point, *258,* 264–93, *267, 273, 275*
Adena culture and, 293
carbon-dating of, 266
equinox at, *272*
solstices at, 270
Pratt, Henry, 454
precession, 34–35
psi (human consciousness powers), 475–77
psychoanalysis, on men's cults, 500
Psychotria viridis, 220
Ptolemaeus Argentinae map, 506–7
Purepecha, 124
Purrington, Robert, 269–70
Pyramid of Quetzalcoatl, 238, 336–37, *p3*
Pyramid of the Sun, 238, *p3*
Pyramid Texts, 303, 305,

Pyramid Texts (*cont.*)
310, 314, 317–18, 322,
323, 326, 337–38,
341–42, 354–55

Quechua, 229
Quileute, 314–15
quinoa, in Amazonia, 174
quipus, 450

Ra (Sun God), 43–44, 350,
352–53, 354, 361–62,
450
radiocarbon dating. *See*
carbon-dating
Raghavan, Maanasa, 115,
123–28, 492, 494
Ramal do Capatará, *p2*
Ranzi, Alceu, 181–82, 187,
193, 195–96, 199
Rasmussen, Morten, 118
Rattlesnake Causeway, 238,
239
Rattlesnake Disk, 306–9,
307, p3
Realm of the Dead, 302–5,
322, 361
Reese-Taylor, Katheryn, 158
Rego Grande, 201–11, 204,
205, 206–11, 207–9,
209, p2
Reich, David, 119, 120–22,
123, 132–33, 155,
492–93
Reiche, Maria, 6, 183–84
Reichel-Dolmatoff, Gerardo,
226, 228, 365
Reilly, Kent, 311
religion, 276, 347, 478–84.
See also gods
Christianity, 360, 450, 478
remote viewing, 475–76
Ren, 312
Roberts, Frank H. H., 50
rock art (pictographs), 131,
207–8, 208, 210, 333,
365
Romain, William, 6, 11, 12,
240–41, 244, 252
on Hardmans, 22–25, 24

on Hopewell, 344–45, 361
on Poverty Point, 271–74,
276
on Serpent Mound
building date, 27–30
on Watson Brake, 290,
290, 291
Roman Catholic Church,
360, 450
Roosevelt, Anna Curtenius,
148, 156, 160, 168,
206–8
Rosetta Stone, 310
rubber trees, 172

sacred oval, at Watson
Brake, 281–83
Sacsayhuamán, 474, *p4*
Saginaw Bay impact,
413–25, 414, 415. *See
also* Glacier Ice Impact
Hypothesis
Sahu, 313, 322
Saint Croix River, 444, 445
Saldanha, Darcy de Moura,
202–3, 205–6
Salnikova, Irina, 100–101,
106
San bushmen, 78
Santa Elina rock shelter, 153,
153
Santa Isabel, 250
sarsens, 18–19
Sassman, Kenneth, 284
Satanaze, 505–6
Sauk, 330
Saunaluoma, Sanna, 189,
190, 191, 218, 223,
224–25
Saunders, Joe, 274, 278,
280–81, 282–93
Sawos, 498
Schaan, Denise, 181–82,
186, 187, 193, 195–96,
199, 211, 212
Schmidt, Klaus, 6
Scorpius constellation, 360,
361
sea levels, 4, 53, 56, 157,
462, 465, 483–84, 506

Seeman, Mark, 311
Sekhem, 312
Sekhet-Aaru, 356
Sekhet-Hetepet, 351, 351
The Selfish Gene (Dawkins),
204
Sem Priests, 344
Seminoles, 341
Sepik Wape, 498
Serpent Mound, 2, 4–44, 8,
10, 12, 29, 32, 41, 216,
255, 263, 361–62
Draco constellation and,
32–34, 33, 34, 360
impact crater at, 4–15, 5
Monks Mound and, 236
renovation of, 29–30, 37
as Solstice Ridge, 21,
21–25, 43
summer solstice at,
15–17, 16, 21, 21–25,
24, 31–32, 92, 189, 204,
204, 363
Watson Brake and, 281
Serpent Mound
Cryptoexplosion
Structure, 4, 5
Seth, 355
Sethite Mounds, 355
Seven Sages, 366
Severino Calazans, 194–95,
196, 200, 216, 238
sex chromosomes, 112,
115–16
shamans, 219–30, 240, 468,
478, 480, 483
ayahuasca and, 220–30,
223, 325, 468, 476–77
Shanon, Benny, 476–77
Shebtiw, 366
Sheriden Cave, 406–7
shilombish, 315
shilup, 315
Shipibo-Conibo, 221,
224–25, 348
Shunkov, M. V., 102–3, 107
Shurtz, Heinrich, 497
Siberia, 83–97, 113–16,
123. *See also* Bering land
bridge; Denisova Cave

Beringian standstill model for, 85–86, 123–24
Silva, Lailson Camelo da, 202
silver, 141–42
Sioux, 311, 332, 340–41
Skinner, Alanson, 330
Skoglund, Pontus, 115, 118, 119, 120–22, 123, 155, 492–93
Sky World, 312, 318, 319–20, 325, 326
slash-and-char, 164–65
smallpox, 138, 145, 148, 149, 451
Soddy, Frederick, 472–73, 475
Solstice Knob, 23
Solstice Ridge, 21, 21–25, 43
solstices, 217, 255, 353–54. See also summer solstice; winter solstice
soul. See also Path of Souls
    in Egypt, 312–14, 313
    free-soul, 316, 318, 320, 325, 331, 338
    of Native Americans, 314–16
    Tibetan Book of the Dead for, 481–82
South America, 120, 120–28, 153. See also Amazonia
    Antarctica and, 509
    Clovis and, 118, 120, 133
    comet impact and, 463–64
    linguistic diversity in, 497
The Specifications of the Mounds of the Early Primeval Age, 366
spiders, in Nazca Lines, 185–86, 186
spring equinox, 18, 20, 36, 288, 288
squash, 174
Squier, Ephraim, 2, 9–11, 15–17, 21, 40, 251, 252, 455–56

St. Louis, Gateway Arch of, 235
Standing Rock Sioux Reservation, 487–89
Stannard, David, 452–53
stars, 34–36, 35, 321, 321. See also specific constellations
Stepenov, Raisa, 89–95
Stone 16, 18–19, 19
Stone Age, 78, 99, 124–25, 131. See also Pleistocene
stone tools, 65–67, 77, 114, 432–33, 438
    of Clovis, 51–52, 52, 374, 437, 438–39
    at Denisova Cave, 100–101
    at Monte Verde, 151
    at Serpent Mound, 26
    at Topper, 72–78
Stonehenge, 11, 12, 18–19, 19, 40, 179–80, 204, 325
    Amazonian geoglyphs and, 196–97, 199, 200, 216
    Woodhenge and, 242
Stringer, Christopher, 109, 110
Stukeley, William, 197
Sumerians, 347
summer solstice, 32, 242, 243, 260, 261, 270
    at Caney Mounds, 291
    at Monks Mound, 242, 245
    at Serpent Mound, 15–17, 16, 21, 21–25, 24, 31–32, 92, 189, 204, 204, 363
    at Stonehenge, 18, 19, 19
    at Watson Brake, 285, 286–87, 287, 289, 290
Sun God (Ra), 43–44, 350, 352–53, 354, 361–62, 450
Sunda Shelf, 110, 442
Supernatural: Meetings with the Ancient Teachers of Mankind (Hancock), 177

Surui, 120, 124, 126, 128, 493

Taurid Meteor Stream, 382, 383–84, 431, 487
tcebai, 315
Tchau, 351
Teixeira expedition, to Amazonia, 145, 149
telekinesis, 475–76
Telepathine. See ayahuasca
telepathy, 475–76
Temple of Karnak, 17, 354
Tequinho, 190, 190, p2
terra preta (Black Earth), 160–69, 467
This World, 240, 312
Thomas, Cyrus, 251–52
Thompson, J. Eric S., 449–50
Thoth, 347
Thurman, Robert A. F., 482
Tiahuanaco, 179, p4
Tibetan Book of the Dead, 478, 479–83
Tikal, 179
Timor Straits, 86, 110, 125
Topper, 72–78, 124, 438, p1
Topper, David, 72, 73
transoceanic travel, 124–25, 130, 131, 155
Trilithon, 474, p4
Trimble, Virginia, 305
Tukano, 223, 223–27, 228, 229, 230, 365, 478
Tunguska, 383, 384
Tungus-Mongol, 219
Turtle Island, 368–69, 463
Tuzin, Donald, 499–501
Twin Mounds, 239
Two Bears, Cody, 488–89
230 Th/U radiometric dating, 62
Tyrannosaurus rex, 60

udjibbom, 315
udjitchog, 315
Uktena, 362
Underwater Panther, 332–34, 334, p3

Underworld, 6, 312, 480
Underworld (Hancock), 131, 433, 505
Upper Paleolithic, 113, 116, 130
  Denisova Cave in, 99, 102, 103, 105, 131
Upper Tapajos Basin, 211
Upper World, 6, 312
Ursua expedition, to Amazonia, 145

Vai-mahase (Master of Animals), 228
Vaupés, 499
Venus figures, in Mal'ta, 113, 114
Vialou, Denis, 153
Vine of the Dead/Vine of Souls. *See* ayahuasca
Virtanen, Pirjo Kristiina, 218, 223, 224–25
Viso, Mount, 435–36
Volkov, P. V., 103
Votrina, Olga, 88–89

Waldseemüller World Map, 503, *504*
Wallace's Line, 109, 110, 125
Walmart, 458
Watling, Jennifer, 196, 199
Watson Brake, 36, 278, 279, *279*, 280–94, *282, 288*, 293, 435
  Caney Mounds and, 284–85, *285*
  solstices at, 285, 286–87, *287, 289, 290*
Way of the Dead, *p4*
Wayuu, 124, 128
Webster, Hutton, 497
Wells, H. G., 466

Wenner-Gren Foundation, 498
West, Allen, 373–74, 376–78, 380–85, 387–91, 407, 410, 414, 427, *p4*
West, Nancy, 373–74
White Knife Shoshoni, 338
Whitehead, Neil, 148
Whittaker, Robert, 512
Whittall, Austin, 495–96
wildfires, 395
  biomass burning in YD, 385, 391–97, 401, 402, 406, 437
Wilkinson, David, 143–44, 145, 147–48, 149, 161, 168
Willerslev, Eske, 123–32, 155, 492, 494
Willis, Katherine, 512
Willoughby, Charles, 39
Wilson, Jeffrey, *10*
Winding Waterway, 326, 335, 342, 360
WinklerPrins, Antoinette, 164–66
winter solstice, 19, *19*, 204, *260*, 261, 270, 291
  at Fazenda Atlantica, *p2*
  at Great Sphinx of Giza, *p1*
  at Monks Mound, *242*, 245
  at Rego Grande, 204, *205*, 209, *209*
  at Temple of Karnak, 17, *p1*
  at Watson Brake, 285, 287, *287, 289, 290*
  at Woodhenge, *242*, 243
Winterville Mounds, 306
Wolbach, Wendy, 391, 399,

400–401, 406
Woodhenge, 238, *239*, 242, *242*, 243, 271, *p3*
Wright Square, *251*

Xavante, 120, 493
Xibalba, 447

yajé, 223
Yokut, Tachi, 317
Young, Bradley, 298
Younger Dryas (YD), 366, 374, 393–94, *400*, 424, 432, 462, 471
  biomass burning in, 385, 391–97, 401, 402, 406, 437
  carbon-dating for, 408, 469
  flood in, 398–400, 402, 406, 443–44
  Glacier Ice Impact Hypothesis in, 415, 419–20
  Gulf Stream and, 397–401
  Lake Agassiz and, *398*, 398–99
Younger Dryas Boundary (YDB), 374, 378, 379, 380, *385*, 400, 406, 436, *436*, 461, 462, 483–84
Younger Dryas Impact Hypothesis (YDIH), 376, 377, 381–82, 386, 410, 411, 427–28, 432, 461–64, 470, 486

Zamora, Antonio, 411–20, 422, 424–29, 437
Zindler, Alan, 381
Zumarraga, Juan de, 445–46